Botanica's
TREES &
SHRUBS

Botanica's
TREES & SHRUBS

Over 1,000 pages & over 2,000 plants listed

LAUREL GLEN

Laurel Glen Publishing
An imprint of the Advantage Publishers Group
5880 Oberlin Drive, San Diego, CA 92121–4794
www.laurelglenbooks.com

Library of Congress Cataloging-in-Publication Data

Botanica's complete trees & shrubs: over 1,000 pages and over
2,000 plants listed.
   p. cm
   ISBN 1-57145-649-X
   1. Ornamental trees. 2. Ornamental shrubs. I. Laurel Glen
Publishing. II. Title: Botanica's complete trees & shrubs. III. Title:
Complete trees & shrubs.

SB435.B63   1999
635.9'77~~dc21
                                  99-41602

4 5 6 7 8 08 07 06 05 04

Consultants: Geoff Bryant, Tony Rodd and Dr Gerlinde von Berg
Publisher: Gordon Cheers
Associate Publisher: Margaret Olds
Managing Editor: James Young
Editors: Anna Cheifetz, Clare Double, Loretta Barnard and
        Denise Imwold
Design: Stan Lamond
Cover Design: Bob Mitchell
Photolibrarian: Susan Page
Assembly: Joy Eckermann, Paula Kelly and James Young
Typesetting: Dee Rogers
Index: Glenda Browne
Production Manager: Linda Watchorn
Publishing Coordinator: Sarah Sherlock
Printed by Sing Cheong Printing Co. Ltd, Hong Kong
Film separation: Pica Colour Separation, Singapore

PHOTOGRAPHS, PRELIMINARY PAGES AND CHAPTER OPENINGS

Page 1:
Fuchsia 'Dark Eyes'

Pages 2–3:
Camellia japonica cultivar *(left)*, *Pieris formosa*
'Forest Flame' *(right)* and *Pachysandra terminalis*
(lower left)

Pages 4–5:
Populus species in snow

Pages 6–7:
Alchemilla mollis (yellow), *Picea abies* 'Reflexa'
(right) and *Acer palmatum* 'Dissectum
Atropurpurea' *(rear)*

Pages 8–9:
Quercus robur (background) and *Euphorbia
characias* subsp. *wulfenii (yellow)*

Pages 34–5:
Abies alba in snow

Pages 122–3:
Betula species

Pages 158–9:
Garden with *Crataegus laevigata (in flower)*,
Berberis ottawensis 'Superba' *(purple)* and *Taxus*
species *(clipped)*

Pages 306–7:
Dacrycarpus dacrydioides

Pages 332–3:
Eucalyptus regnans

Pages 374–5:
Fuchsia 'Waltzing Matilda'

Pages 424–455:
Hamamelis × *intermedia* shrouded in snow

Pages 456–7:
Juniperus species in Canyonlands National Park,
Utah, USA

Pages 490–1:
Luma apiculata (hedges) and *Ulmus glabrata*
'Camperdownenii' *(centre)*

Pages 530–1:
Nothofagus pumilio in frost

Pages 590–1:
Populus deltoides in snow

Pages 710–11:
Rhododendron 'Elizabeth'

Pages 838–9:
Serruria florida

Pages 884–5:
Ulmus procera

Pages 918–19:
Viburnum lantana

Contents

Introduction

Trees and shrubs are the framework of a garden. They are the quiet achievers that are always there and that define the character of the garden.

All but the smallest gardens need at least one or two trees, not only for their great beauty, but also for shade, shelter and privacy. Shrubs serve similar purposes and are often used to fill the spaces left under the trees. Because of their smaller size, they tend to be more colorful when in flower and their blooms are closer to eye level. And of course shrubs and trees are not just garden plants—they can be grown in containers in conservatories and greenhouses, or used as house plants.

That brings us to the difference between shrubs and trees. A botanist will tell you that a tree is a woody single-stemmed plant that grows over 10 ft (3 m) tall. But that doesn't take account of the many multi-trunked plants that are obviously trees; nor does it makes much sense to refer to a naturally multi-stemmed plant that grows to 30 ft (9 m) tall as a shrub.

In everyday horticulture and gardening the difference between a shrub and a tree really comes down to the height and shape and general 'feeling' of the plant rather than any set rules. Gardeners consider any multi-trunked plant less than 15–18 ft (5–6 m) tall a shrub and any plant over that, multi-trunked or not, a tree. Small trees are those obviously single-trunked plants under 18 ft (6 m) tall, such as many of the Japanese maples and dwarf fruit trees.

Prunus, Sato-zakura Group, 'Taihaku'
bringing springtime cheer to the garden

Right: Springtime in
a rhododendron
garden
Below: The same
garden in winter

Planning and plant selection

PLANNING THE GARDEN

Even if you want your garden to appear
as natural as possible, it still needs some
planning, especially when considering
the positioning of trees to screen out sunlight or prevent your being overlooked.

The plans don't need to be elaborate.
You may not even have to actually draw
a plan, but you do need to take the time
to stop and consider the implications of
your planting. Of course, a formal plan
may help, but often a little forethought
is all that is needed.

Trees, being by far the largest and
longest lived garden plants, should be
considered first. Trees not only beautify
a garden, they can modify its climate
and make your house more pleasant to
live in, by allowing in the sun in winter
and blocking it out in summer. Modern
houses incorporate large areas of glass
and are usually situated so the most important rooms face the sun. Provided

Above: A large informal hillside rock garden featuring many varieties of trees and shrubs

Left: A eucalypt seedling begins the perilous journey to treehood

the house is well insulated, this is ideal because it makes the best use of the limited winter sunlight, but in summer it can lead to stifling temperatures, even with air conditioning. Trees, especially deciduous trees, are nature's sunlight regulators. They are bare in winter, allowing in the sun, and in summer they are covered with shade-producing foliage. If need be, you can use shrubs to fill in the gaps under the trees.

Privacy is also important. Hedges may seem the obvious solution, but they require regular trimming, rob nutrients from the nearby soil and can make a small garden dark and damp. Most often, a few strategically placed large shrubs or small trees will be sufficient to shield you from prying eyes.

Trees with dense foliage can make a garden rather dark and gloomy. But there are many species that cast dappled, lacy shade, and the balance between these and the denser species is usually best, especially in hot climates, where year-round shade is desirable.

Consider the size of the garden too; choose trees that won't be too big for the available space. Remember, plant labels usually refer to the size of the tree at 10 years, which is not necessarily its maximum height or spread. Look around your neighborhood or visit your local botanic garden for a better appreciation of the ultimate size of your trees.

Because shrubs are usually much smaller than trees, garden size is not such a critical issue. However, keep in mind that shrubs are long-term plants. Unlike annuals and perennials it is not practical to plant for an immediate effect; you must consider how the plants will develop and what the garden will look like after a few years.

Most gardeners plant mixed shrubberies, often leaving room to add annuals and perennials for seasonal color. You may prefer, however, to devote parts of the garden to groups of similar plants, provided they can sustain interest over a long season. Roses and rhododendrons are among the most common choices. Roses generally do best on their own or in open beds with low-growing perennials, but rhododendrons and azaleas tend to look more at home as part of a larger woodland scene.

An alternative is to choose a theme—the Mediterranean look with lavender, oleander and silver-leafed shrubs, an alpine shrubbery, or a dry-country garden with predominantly South African and Australian plants.

Whatever you choose, take the time to plan the layout of your shrubs so that they blend well with the other elements of your garden and try to get it right first time. Granted, many shrubs will tolerate transplanting, but this should always be looked on as a last resort. Transplanting is always a shock and even the most obliging shrub will eventually suffer if moved with any regularity. It is not a matter of making a permanent commitment to a particular garden plan—there's always room for change—rather you are simply trying to minimize future work through careful planning.

Mixed roses around a
pergola

This *Ulmus* species loses its leaves in winter and allows warmth and sunlight to brighten the interior, while in summer it provides coolness and shade

CHOOSING SHRUBS AND TREES

A well-chosen selection of shrubs and trees combines all the features looked for in a good garden: interesting and attractive foliage, beautiful and unusual flowers, year-round interest and ease of maintenance. But it doesn't happen automatically. Be careful with your selection because the vast range that is available not only provides choice, it can also lead to complications that can trip up the unwary or the uninformed.

Ultimately the things that will most influence you are your personal likes and dislikes, the general nature of your garden and soil and the climatic conditions. All of these things must be considered before you even begin to weigh up which of the myriad of species and cultivars best suits your needs.

EVERGREEN OR DECIDUOUS?

Given the choice, most gardeners will opt for evergreens over deciduous plants. Experienced gardeners, however, know that deciduous trees have plenty to offer, not just in terms of their superiority as shade and compost providers, but as ornamental plants too.

Think of deciduous trees and the first thing that comes to mind is autumn foliage, those vivid tones of yellow, orange and red. However, don't underestimate the bright green of the new spring growth and the wide range of summer foliage color found among the deciduous trees. For example, the bright yellow of *Robinia pseudoacacia* 'Frisia', the deep blackish red of the copper beeches *(Fagus)* and the silvery gray of the weeping silver pear *(Pyrus salicifolia)*.

In recent years, urban gardeners have been rather dismissive of conifers, but they should not be overlooked either. Conifers offer a huge range of growth forms and foliage colors. Also, many change color with the seasons, like deciduous trees, but they retain their foliage. There are even a few deciduous conifers, such as the larches (*Larix*) and the dawn redwood (*Metasequoia glyptostroboides*), the autumn colors of which rival those of any broadleaf. Some conifers, like the ginkgo and the celery pines (*Phyllocladus*), don't really match our usual ideas of conifers at all.

FLOWERS AND FLOWERING SEASON

All broadleafed plants flower, although some trees are not particularly colorful; others may only bloom for a brief period. The flowering cherries (*Prunus*), dogwoods (*Cornus*) and the large magnolias are frequently planted for their flowers, but with other temperate climate trees, flowers are often a secondary consideration. Tropical and subtropical trees, on the other hand, often have very spectacular flowers over a long season.

Shrubs, of course, are far better known for their flowers. Everyone knows the camellias, rhododendrons and azaleas, but bear in mind that the flowers of most

shrub genera fall within a fairly narrowly defined color range. For example, there are hundreds of camellia hybrids, but almost all of them have flowers in various shades of white, pink or red. Even those genera that are available in a wide range of colors may lack one or two significant shades. However, there is a huge range of shrubs available, so it is definitely possible to find shrubs in just about any color.

Flower shape is enormously variable. There are the filamentous flowers of the bottlebrushes, the pea-like blooms of *Polygala* and the huge flowers of the tropical *Hibiscus*. Some have their blooms on weeping branches, others on strongly upright spikes. Flower color might often be the prime consideration when choosing a shrub, but don't forget

Camellia japonica cultivars provide a colorful display for the winter months

that the style of bloom may be just as important.

Although spring and summer are the predominant flowering seasons, there are shrubs and trees in flower every season of the year. Within the larger genera there is often a range of flowering seasons, so, for example, it is possible to have *Buddleia* in bloom for up to eight months just by planting a selection of different species and cultivars. Very early or very late flowers may be subject to weather damage, but they do extend the period of interest.

FRAGRANCE

When choosing fragrant shrubs consider where best to plant them in order to gain the maximum benefit. Some flowers are only scented in the evening and are therefore best planted near the house where they can be more readily appreciated; others are strongly scented and need to be in an open space to prevent them from becoming overpowering. The flowering season is all-important: witch hazel, for example, has a rather faint scent that would be lost in the mass of spring flowers, but because it flowers in winter, without competition, it is known and enjoyed for its fragrance.

Above: **The lush flowers of**
***Magnolia grandiflora* are**
attractive to bees
Left: ***Hydrangea***
***macrophylla* is an all-**
time favorite for a
consistent floral display

Above: Rainforest in the Watagan Mountains, NSW, Australia

Right: *Sequoiadendron giganteum* in snow, Sequoia National Park, California, USA

BARK

Bark is another often underestimated plant feature. The paper bark maple *(Acer griseum)*, silver birch *(Betula pendula)* and the eucalypts are known for their striking bark, but many other trees have bark that is just as attractive. Naturally, it is a feature that is more apparent on deciduous shrubs and trees.

LIFESPAN

Shrubs and trees are usually considered to be permanent plants, but they don't look the same indefinitely. Trees and some shrubs, such as rhododendrons and camellias, are seldom replaced until they die, but many shrubs are removed long before the end of their natural lifespan. That may be because the shrub has become too overgrown and untidy, or that the gardener is acknowledging a mistake, but often it is just because the novelty of that particular plant has worn off. Don't be concerned about admitting such things—after all it is your garden and part of the pleasure of gardening lies in making changes.

The Japanese take great care of their trees. This cherry (*Prunus* species) has been wrapped with insulation to protect it from the cold.

Cultivation

CLIMATE

Shrubs and trees vary enormously in their degree of hardiness; some will survive –40°F (–40°C) while others are totally intolerant of frost. The limits imposed by your climate cannot be ignored and may well have the greatest influence in your choice of plants. Frost is probably the biggest killer of plants, but do not underestimate the effects of wind, drought and coastal salt spray.

In the long run it is better to accommodate the climate than to constantly battle against it. However, gardeners are always tempted to grow plants that are on the extremes of climatic tolerance, and it is amazing what can be grown in the most unlikely places when shelter is provided. Covers made of light wooden stakes covered with hessian or frost cloth will provide some frost protection as will siting your more tender plants against sheltered walls and under overhanging eaves. Windbreak fences and hedges will protect against the worst excesses of the wind and should be considered essential in many coastal areas. Tender shrubs may be grown in containers and moved under cover for the winter.

EXPOSURE

Whether your garden receives sun, partial shade or shade, there are shrubs and trees to suit, and many will also tolerate a wide range of conditions. There are no hard and fast rules here, but generally plants that prefer shade, such as rhododendrons and fuchsias, will tolerate sunnier positions provided they are moist. However, plants that prefer full sun exposures, such as most of the Australian natives, tend to suffer and become leggy if they are too shaded. If in doubt, it is generally better to err on the bright side when deciding on a site.

SOIL CONDITIONS

All plants have a preferred range of soil conditions outside which they will not grow well. Some prefer dry stony soils, but most do better in moist, well-drained soil with plenty of additional compost or leaf mold to provide the all-important humus.

Most of the structural problems with soil can be corrected with time, but the

Right: *Hamamelis × intermedia* shrouded in snow

Below: *Pinus pinaster* thriving on the Italian Mediterranean coast

underlying pH (whether the soil is acid, alkaline or neutral) is usually very difficult to alter permanently. Most shrubs and trees prefer a neutral to slightly acid soil and you should avoid adding too much lime (which increases alkalinity) unless your soil is very acid. Neutral to moderately alkaline soils will benefit from mild acid fertilizers, but highly alkaline soil is often difficult to neutralize. Lime, in particular, is very soluble and tends to defeat most attempts at neutralization.

If you live in an area with limey soil, especially if it is due to the presence of limestone, you will have to accept a restricted plant choice. There are ways to work around this, such as using raised beds of specially built-up soil and by avoiding planting acid-soil plants in the lower parts of the garden where lime is likely to accumulate. It is usually better to stick to those plants that cope best in alkaline soil but it is still worth experimenting, as many plants will surprise you with their tolerance.

PLANTING

Having chosen a suitable site and plants for it, you must ensure that whatever you grow thrives. There's an old saying that's just as true today as it ever was— you shouldn't plant a five dollar tree in a one dollar hole. As with just about every aspect of gardening, the more time you put into preparation the better the results. When you've taken care and time to choose the right shrub or tree, why rush to plant it?

Dig over the soil to about 12 in (30 cm) below the depth of the new tree's root ball and to at least 12 in (30 cm) greater diameter than its current root spread. That will allow the tree to establish new roots quickly, which will help to boost its growth and to stabilize it.

A rose garden comes to life in spring

An orange tree (*Citrus*
species) with flowers and fruit

Dig in plenty of fine
compost to improve the soil
texture and increase its
moisture retention. If you
live in an area with a hard
clay subsoil use a crowbar
or a pick to break up the
clay or you may find that
your trees start to suffer
from poor drainage and im-
peded root development
once their roots strike the
subsoil.

The roots of a tree spread
far more widely and deeply
that those of a shrub. It's
not possible to incorporate
enough compost and fertilizer to keep a
tree happy for its entire life, so the best
you can do is give it a good start.

Having first moistened the soil, carefully remove the plant from its container. Don't force it out or you may
break off a large portion of the roots. If
the roots are spiralled around the root
ball, loosen them slightly, and then
adjust the plant in the planting hole
until it is at the same depth as it was in
the container. If the surface roots are
showing you may plant a little deeper
but take care that you don't bury the
union point of grafted or budded trees.

Hammer in a stout metal or wooden
stake, taking care not to damage the
roots. Tie the shrub or tree to the stake
with flexible ties that won't cut into the
bark. Remember to remove the stake

after a year or so, or it may eventually
rub against or cut into the bark.

After refilling, the ground around the
tree will need to be trodden down somewhat to firm up the plant, but don't
overdo it; it's better to firmly stake the
shrub or tree and keep the soil loose
than it is to compact down all that soil
you laboriously loosened up. In very dry
areas, or where the plant must fend for
itself, it is often a good idea to make a
small ridge of soil around the drip-line.
This ensures that any moisture dripping
from the foliage is channelled back to
the roots.

Remember that both sun and wind
can dry out a young plant. If the plant is
small, put three sticks around it and
drop a plastic shopping bag with the
bottom cut out over them. For a bigger

This huge *Pyrus* species loses its leaves in winter and the annuals and perennials beneath receive warmth and sunlight. In summer it will protect them from the harsh sun and heat.

tree, do the same with burlap stretched between three stakes. It need only be kept in place for six months or so.

Having planted the shrub or tree you may feel the need to add fertilizer, but it is usually best to allow an establishment period first. If you apply fertilizer before new growth begins, the plant may develop a too compact root system because there is no need for new roots to form and seek out soil nutrients. Making sure the plant is stable should be your first consideration—staking helps, but encouraging a quick root spread is the best way. When you apply fertilizer, put it just outside the drip-line and water it in well to encourage the roots to spread downwards and outwards.

Modern nurseries grow most plants in containers, which allows them to be planted at any time of the year. Large

deciduous trees are the exception—most are still lifted from the open ground, usually in winter when the trees are dormant. Ideally the nursery will pot the trees after lifting, but if you buy a bare rooted deciduous tree it must be planted right away. Once established in large containers, trees lifted from the open ground may be treated just like any other container-grown plants. They may be planted at any time, provided the soil is in a suitable condition to work and the weather is not exceptionally hot or cold.

Of course, you don't have to plant them; trees can be grown in containers permanently. However, a large tree in a large pot is very heavy and unwieldy, and will have considerable watering and feeding demands. Generally potted trees are treated as temporary plants that are transplanted to the garden when they become too large to be comfortably repotted.

After planting, spread mulch all over the bed to conserve water and keep weeds down. Weeds are great robbers of water and nutrients. Research has shown that a young tree growing in a patch of bare soil about 3 ft (1 m) wide needs only about a quarter of the water that it would if weeds were allowed to grow.

CONTAINER GROWING

Growing shrubs and trees in containers is easy. Select a suitable container, make sure it has adequate holes for drainage, fill it with a good commercial potting mix, and plant. Then water regularly— never let the plant dry out to the point of wilting; and fertilize regularly, as the constant watering will leach nutrients from the soil very rapidly. A slow release fertilizer is recommended.

The container should be big enough for the root system, so it needs to be quite large for an ordinary-sized shrub and even bigger for a tree; but even so the plant will eventually outgrow the container. There are two ways to deal with this—either plant into a bigger container, or remove it and prune the roots before putting it back with some fresh potting mix.

If you live in an apartment, remember that a tree in a tub or even a shrub in a container is heavy and you don't want to risk bringing the roof or balcony down, so seek the advice of a structural engineer first. Roofs and balconies are also apt to be windy places—remember that wind dries plants out very efficiently.

Citrus aurantium in Versailles planters in front of the Orangerie in the Bagatelle Gardens in Paris, France

Buxus sempervirens *(clipped hedges)* and *Olea europaea* subsp. *europaea* *(center and back)*

Maintenance

Maintenance is most important during the first two years after final planting. Established shrubs and trees can largely look after themselves. Trimming to shape, loosening ties and restaking, fertilizing and watering are all necessary to ensure that your trees get the best start.

Unless you intend to train a tree to a specific shape or style of growth, the pruning of young trees is generally just a matter of removing any damaged branches and those that are likely to head off at strange angles. Garden trees often look better if they're allowed to develop naturally. Just aim to maintain a clean trunk with good canopy development; there's no need to prune to a perfectly straight trunked forestry specimen.

If they have been planted in the right place, established trees rarely need pruning unless they have been damaged in

some way. If a large tree has to be trimmed, it's a job best left to a professional tree surgeon. Very few gardeners have the necessary ladders and climbing equipment to gain access to a large tree, let alone the experience to safely trim the tree once up it. Likewise, felling a tree, especially in a built-up area demands expertise.

Young trees are usually vigorous growers that are not greatly troubled by pests and diseases, but if problems do occur they can be treated in the same way a large shrub would be treated. However, large established trees are difficult to treat; they are often too tall to safely get to the top, and effective coverage with sprays is all but impossible with domestic gardening equipment. Controlling pests and diseases in large trees is usually an area for professionals, as they have the necessary equipment

equipment and skill. No tree is worth breaking your neck for. That said, most trees are worth the effort involved in trying to save them.

WATERING AND FEEDING

The first year or two after planting is the most important time for watering and feeding. The young plant is then getting its roots established and developing its branch structure. Provide care then, and you will be rewarded in the future with stronger, better shaped and more pest- and disease-resistant shrubs and trees.

Remove any weeds that appear and use mulch to control their development. The mulch also conserves moisture, reducing the amount of watering needed. Water when the weather is dry. Don't just sprinkle—wetting the soil surface alone does more harm than good because it encourages the development of roots close to the surface, where they suffer when the soil dries out again. The aim is to encourage the roots to go deep where the soil dries out more slowly. Not often but thoroughly is the rule.

Water retention varies with the soil type: sandy soils absorb water quickly, but don't hold it well and so dry out fast; clay soils absorb it slowly but hold it for longer. Water evaporates from the soil faster on hot days—and on windy ones—than it does in cooler weather. Watering in the heat of the day is wasteful, as much of your water will evaporate; the early morning or evening is preferable. Take care in adjusting your sprinklers so they don't deliver water faster than the soil can absorb it.

Mulching with compost or well-rotted manure fertilizes plants as well as stemming moisture loss; this can be boosted with a light dressing of something more concentrated as the regular growing season begins. Artificial fertilizer is fine, but it doesn't maintain the essential humus on which the continued health of the soil depends. For that, organic material is needed. Happily, trees and shrubs supply their own, by dropping their leaves. Leaving these to rot where they fall is one of the few times in life when laziness is rewarded!

Betula species showing new growth in spring

Established shrubs and trees benefit from feeding, but you need to get the fertilizer down deep where the roots are. Make a number of holes about 3 ft (1 m) apart across the entire spread of the roots. These should be about 2 in (5 cm) wide and at least 20 in (50 cm) deep. Divide the allowance of fertilizer by the number of holes and pour in the calculated amount, watering it in thoroughly.

PRUNING AND TRIMMING

There is a difference between pruning and trimming. Pruning is a training method—cutting a plant to make it grow in a desired direction or shape or encouraging the growth of a particular structure. Trimming is simply removing excess growth and reshaping an already existing structure.

Pruning promotes strong new growth, and helps produce a well-shaped healthy plant with a good crop of fruit or flowers. It also maintains ventilation, which reduces fungus problems, and allows light to penetrate to the center of the shrub or tree.

When shaping a plant you must have an understanding of the way it develops. Severe trimming and topping are damaging in most cases. Not only do they produce misshapen plants, they can also weaken them. Regularly repeated, severe trimming can lessen a plant's photosynthetic ability and deplete its stored reserves.

Heavy pruning can also produce branches that grow at acute angles. These are more easily damaged by wind or may eventually break under their own weight. Careful trimming and thinning, however, can strengthen a plant by removing weak branches and enabling it to channel its energies into stronger growth.

Consider the ultimate shape of the plant before you cut. Bearing in mind that any branch will tend to shoot from the bud immediately below a cut, it's clear that if the center is to remain open you must cut to buds facing away from the center of the plant. These are known as outward-facing buds. Some-

Saw off side branches leaving a slight stub; be sure to undercut first

Pruning paste is unnecessary unless the species is prone to disease

A good pair of secateurs is essential for pruning and trimming shrubs

This very formal garden in Villandry, France, although not to everyone's taste, shows just what can be achieved with careful pruning

known as outward-facing buds. Sometimes you may wish to leave a few inward-facing buds to fill in the center of an otherwise loose growing shrub.

Many times a plant is just too dense and twiggy to prune it with precision. In these cases an all over trimming and thinning will usually suffice. There's no point in attempting to cut to outward facing buds on something like a *Hebe* or a low bushy conifer.

THE PRACTICE OF PRUNING

The right time to prune depends on the type of plant and the severity of your winter climate. Hardy deciduous plants are usually best pruned in the winter. They are unlikely to be damaged by the cold and will be less likely to bleed (ooze sap) during winter. Spring-flowering plants should be pruned soon after flowering rather than in winter, which would remove the flower buds. Pruning frost-tender plants is best left until spring because cutting them in winter only exposes the vulnerable cut stems to more frost damage. Spring pruning will still allow for an entire season's growth before the next winter.

There's usually no reason why you shouldn't trim and thin in summer too.

Shaping during the growing season, when you can readily see the effects, is often easier than trying to envisage exactly how the growth will develop after winter pruning. But don't cut back in early spring when the sap is flowing quickly because the cuts can bleed excessively and refuse to heal properly.

How far to cut back is a question that always leads to confusion. You can find all sorts of theories about how hard to cut back and why, but it all comes down to the initial reasons for pruning: renewing vigor, maintaining health and shaping. As mentioned earlier, too severe a trimming may actually lead to reduced vigor and a poorly shaped plant.

Ensure that your secateurs (and saws or loppers too, if heavier equipment is needed) are sharp so that all the cuts are clean. Trim so that water runs away from the bud. When trimming side branches remember to first make an undercut on the lower side to avoid the bark tearing as the branch falls.

The exact method of cutting side branches is open to debate. The old school of thought was to cut as flush as possible to the main stem, then seal the wound with a pruning paste or paint. Recent research suggests that it may be better to leave a stub, or crown, and use pruning paste (preferably one with anti-bacterial agents) only on plants that are prone to infection, such as apples and pears. This appears to better replicate what happens when a tree naturally loses a branch, encourages a more rapid formation of callus tissue and therefore quicker healing.

The general methods for pruning shrubs and small trees are as follows:
- Completely remove any diseased, damaged or weak wood.
- Remove suckers and overly vigorous water-shoots.
- Locate the healthy main branches formed during last season's growth.
- Cut back to healthy outward-facing buds.
- Assess the results and adjust as necessary.

A pruning paint or paste can be used to seal the cuts but as mentioned above there are doubts about its long-term merits. It may prevent immediate fungal infection but could also slow down or prevent proper healing.

Because you may have disturbed fungal spores

Above left & left: **Lavatera** species, in winter and spring, showing the effect of good pruning. The tree is *Prunus*, Sato-zakura Group, 'Taihaku'.

Yew trees (*Taxus* species) on either side of a church porch in Stow-on-the-Wold, UK

that will find an easy entry to the plant by way of the freshly cut stems, always remove any fallen debris and spray with a fungicide after pruning.

TRANSPLANTING OR REMOVING TREES

Transplanting a mature tree is a big job and some trees never get over the inevitable damage to their roots. Magnolias, eucalypts and birches, for example, rarely survive transplanting. The best candidates for transplanting have densely fibrous root systems, like rhododendrons, or grow new roots vigorously if the old are cut, like willows, poplars, planes and palms.

Preparation for transplanting should begin about a year before, with pruning of the roots. This reduces the root ball to a manageable size and provokes the growth of a mass of fine new roots to nourish the tree in its new home and, incidentally, to bind the root ball together when it is lifted from the ground. Cut a circular trench about a third of the way out from the trunk to the outer branches and as deep as possible, using sharp spades and pruners if big roots are encountered. Then fill in with fine soil enriched with organic matter, watering as you fill.

At transplanting time (mid- to late winter in temperate areas, the start of the rainy season in the tropics) dig beneath the root ball, and sever roots that you couldn't get the first time. Lift and transport the tree by cradling it from below. If the tree is picked up by its trunk the roots will tear off, and the tender bark will be crushed.

Plant the transported tree at precisely the same depth as before. Orient it as before, so the same side will be in the sun. Do not loosen the soil from the roots. If the tree is a big one, the weight of the root ball may be enough to keep it steady once in place; but to be sure, give it three or four guy ropes.

It will be at least two or three years before you can remove the guys and allow the tree to look after itself. In the meantime, water regularly, and fertilize in spring.

Top 20 trees and shrubs for special purposes

FOR FRAGRANCE

Azara microphylla
Boronia megastigma
Bouvardia longiflora
Chimonanthus
  praecox
Citrus (many)
Daphne odora
Gardenia augusta
Hamamelis mollis
  and cultivars
Hymenosporum flavum
Lonicera fragrantissima
Michelia figo
Osmanthus delavayii
Philadelphus (many)
Pittosporum
  eugenioides
Plumeria rubra
Rhododendron nuttallii
Rhododendron
  'Fragrantissimum'
Rosa (many)
Syringa (many)
Viburnum (many)

FOR AUTUMN
FLOWERING

Abutilon × hybridum
  cultivars
Agonis flexuosa
Allamanda schottii
Aralia elata
Banksia ericifolia
Bauhinia × blakeana
Brugmansia
  suaveolens
Camellia sasanqua
  cultivars
Cunonia capensis
Erythrina crista-galli
Fuchsia (many)
Hoheria sexstylosa
Iochroma cyaneum
Luculia gratissima
Magnolia grandiflora
Mahonia lomariifolia
Nerium oleander
Protea neriifolia
Senna corymbosa
Tibouchina lepidota

FOR COLORFUL
AUTUMN FOLIAGE

Acer (many)
Berberis thunbergii
  and cultivars
Betula (many)
Cercidiphyllum
  japonicum
Cornus (many)
Cotinus coggygria
Enkianthus perulatus
Fraxinus (many)
Ginkgo biloba
Hamamelis (most)
Lagerstroemia indica
Liquidambar styraciflua
Liriodendron tulipifera
Metasequoia
  glyptostroboides
Nyssa sylvatica
Parrotia persica
Prunus (many)
Quercus (many)
Taxodium distichum
Viburnum (many)

FOR SHADY
SITUATIONS

Acer palmatum
  and cultivars
Arbutus unedo
Aucuba japonica
Camellia (many)
Corynocarpus
  laevigatus
Daphne odora
Fatsia japonica
Fuchsia (many)
Ilex aquifolium
  and cultivars
Kalmia latifolia
Mahonia lomariifolia
Nandina domestica
Osmanthus delavayi
Pieris (many)
Pseudopanax lessonii
Rhododendron (many)
Ruscus aculeatus
Sarcococca ruscifolia
Skimmia japonica
Viburnum davidii

FOR COASTAL
GARDENS

Acacia longifolia
Araucaria heterophylla
Argyranthemum
  frutescens cultivars
Brachyglottis greyii
  and cultivars
Cistus (many)
Coprosma repens
  and cultivars
Cordyline australis
Cupressus macrocarpa
  and cultivars
Dodonaea viscosa
Ficus rubignosa
Griselinia littoralis
Hebe speciosa and
  cultivars
Juniperus (many)
Melaleuca (many)
Metrosideros excelsus
Pittosporum crassifolium
Rhaphiolepis umbellata
Rosa rugosa and cultivars
Tamarix (many)
Westringia fruticosa

FOR FAST GROWTH

Acacia (many)
Callistemon citrinus
Casuarina
  cunninghamiana
Ceanothus papillosus
Choisya ternata
× Cupressocyparis
  leylandii and
  cultivars
Elaeagnus pungens
  and cultivars
Eriobotrya japonica
Escallonia rubra
Eucalyptus (many)
Grevillea robusta
Griselinia littoralis
Hoheria populnea
Paraserianthes
  lophantha
Paulownia tomentosa
Robinia pseudoacacia
Salix (many)
Sparmannia africana
Tibouchina
  urvilleana
Weigela florida

An olive tree (*Olea* species) surviving extreme conditions by the sea in Greece

HARDINESS ZONE MAPS

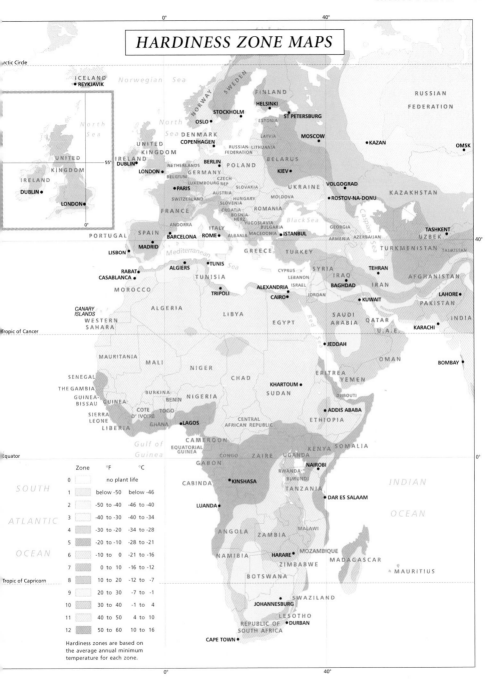

Zone	°F	°C
0	no plant life	
1	below -50	below -46
2	-50 to -40	-46 to -40
3	-40 to -30	-40 to -34
4	-30 to -20	-34 to -28
5	-20 to -10	-28 to -21
6	-10 to 0	-21 to -16
7	0 to 10	-16 to -12
8	10 to 20	-12 to -7
9	20 to 30	-7 to -1
10	30 to 40	-1 to 4
11	40 to 50	4 to 10
12	50 to 60	10 to 16

Hardiness zones are based on the average annual minimum temperature for each zone.

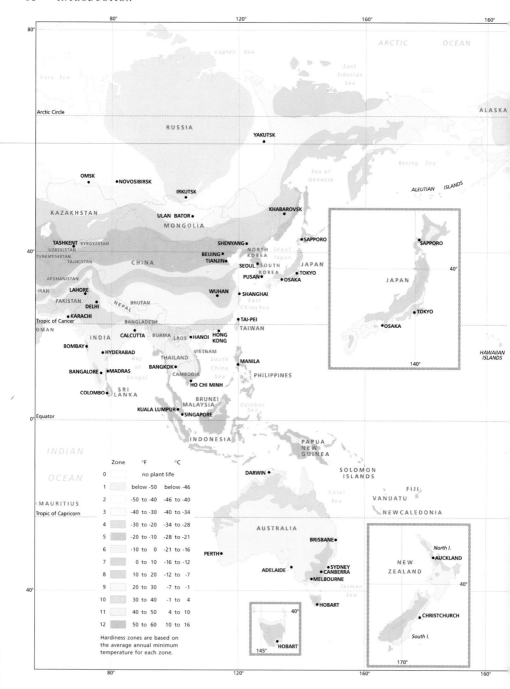

Zone	°F	°C
0	no plant life
1	below -50	below -46
2	-50 to -40	-46 to -40
3	-40 to -30	-40 to -34
4	-30 to -20	-34 to -28
5	-20 to -10	-28 to -21
6	-10 to 0	-21 to -16
7	0 to 10	-16 to -12
8	10 to 20	-12 to -7
9	20 to 30	-7 to -1
10	30 to 40	-1 to 4
11	40 to 50	4 to 10
12	50 to 60	10 to 16

Hardiness zones are based on
the average annual minimum
temperature for each zone.

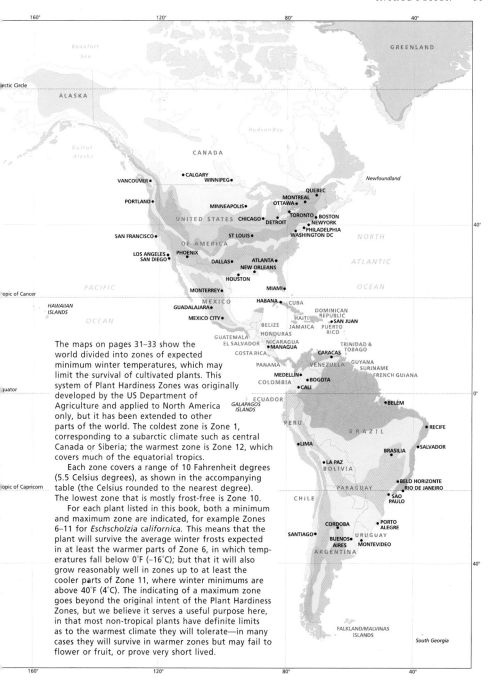

The maps on pages 31–33 show the world divided into zones of expected minimum winter temperatures, which may limit the survival of cultivated plants. This system of Plant Hardiness Zones was originally developed by the US Department of Agriculture and applied to North America only, but it has been extended to other parts of the world. The coldest zone is Zone 1, corresponding to a subarctic climate such as central Canada or Siberia; the warmest zone is Zone 12, which covers much of the equatorial tropics.

Each zone covers a range of 10 Fahrenheit degrees (5.5 Celsius degrees), as shown in the accompanying table (the Celsius rounded to the nearest degree). The lowest zone that is mostly frost-free is Zone 10.

For each plant listed in this book, both a minimum and maximum zone are indicated, for example Zones 6–11 for *Eschscholzia californica*. This means that the plant will survive the average winter frosts expected in at least the warmer parts of Zone 6, in which temperatures fall below 0°F (–16°C); but that it will also grow reasonably well in zones up to at least the cooler parts of Zone 11, where winter minimums are above 40°F (4°C). The indicating of a maximum zone goes beyond the original intent of the Plant Hardiness Zones, but we believe it serves a useful purpose here, in that most non-tropical plants have definite limits as to the warmest climate they will tolerate—in many cases they will survive in warmer zones but may fail to flower or fruit, or prove very short lived.

A

ABELIA

A genus of about 30 species of deciduous and evergreen shrubs from eastern Asia and Mexico, abelias are elegant and bear abundant small tubular or trumpet-shaped flowers throughout summer. They grow to about 6 ft (1.8 m) tall and have dark green foliage on arching canes.

CULTIVATION

Species vary from moderately frost hardy to somewhat tender. Frost-hardy species are trouble-free plants, capable of surviving harsh conditions. Abelias prefer sun or light shade, and need a well-drained soil with regular water in summer. They are easily propagated from cuttings and can withstand heavy pruning, making them good for low hedging.

Abelia floribunda *(below)*

This species has the largest and brightest flowers of the abelias, bearing clusters of bright rose carmine flowers, each 2 in (5 cm) long, along the arching branches in early summer. Only marginally frost hardy, in cold areas it prefers a warm sheltered spot, such as against a wall or fence. **ZONES 9–11.**

Abelia × grandiflora *(above)*

This hybrid between *Abelia chinensis* and *A. uniflora* grows to 6–8 ft (1.8–2.4 m) tall and wide. It has arching reddish brown canes and small, glossy dark green leaves. Small mauve and white flowers appear in early summer, usually with a second flush at summer's end. The dull pink calyces persist after the flowers fall, contrasting with the leaves which turn purplish bronze. The cultivar **'Francis Mason'** has yellow or yellow-edged leaves but it has a tendency to revert to plain green. **ZONES 7–10.**

Abelia × grandiflora 'Francis Mason' *(above)*

ABELIOPHYLLUM
WHITE FORSYTHIA

A

There is only one species in this genus: a rather open-growing deciduous shrub native to Korea. Named after the resemblance of its foliage to *Abelia*, it is really more closely related to *Forsythia*, *Fontanesia* and *Ligustrum*. It is a tough plant that is valued for its survivability and reliability more than any great beauty. Nevertheless, it puts on a good show of spring bloom with the bonus of mild fragrance.

CULTIVATION
At up to 6 ft (1.8 m) high and wide, white forsythia is a large shrub best suited to planting at the back of borders or among other deciduous shrubs of a similar size. Provided the drainage is adequate, it is not fussy about soil conditions and will grow in sun or partial shade. The only difficulty arises from its early flowering: the first flowers may be damaged by late frosts. Propagate by semi-ripe autumn cuttings or seed.

Abeliophyllum distichum (left)
White forsythia has narrow pointed leaves up to 3 in (7.5 cm) long. They appear after the first blooms have opened but before the spring display is entirely over. The flowers are white, flushed pink, and very like *Forsythia* in size and shape. They are borne in clusters along the fine twiggy stems of the previous season's growth—so don't prune this bush in winter. The flowers are sweetly scented and open from late winter, continuing well into spring. They are individually small but collectively make quite a show. There are also forms with darker pink flowers. ZONES 5–9.

ABIES

FIR

The true firs, sometimes known as silver firs to distinguish them from *Picea* (which have pendent, not upright, cones), comprise about 40 species of evergreen conifers. Among the most stately of all conifers, firs come from cool- to cold-climate mountain areas of the northern hemisphere. Most are from China and western North America, but a few species extend into the tropics on the high mountains of Central America and Southeast Asia. The short, stiff needles, which are distributed evenly along the twigs, usually have 2 longitudinal blue bands on their undersides.

CULTIVATION

Their narrow shape and often slow growth allow many species to fit comfortably into the larger suburban garden, but they will not tolerate urban pollution and prefer a moist climate without extremes of heat. Soils must have adequate depth, drainage and moisture retention. Propagation is from seed. Grafting is used for selected clones, including named cultivars. The only pruning or shaping needed is the removal of twin leading shoots as soon as they appear.

Abies alba *(below)*

EUROPEAN SILVER FIR

Originating in the mountains of central and southern Europe, this conifer can grow to 180 ft (55 m). It has glossy dark green needles with whitish undersides, arranged in 2 rows on the lateral branches. The bark is a dark grayish color and the cones are up to 6 in (15 cm) long, changing from green to reddish brown as they ripen. It is capable of fast growth but may be damaged by unseasonal frost and is liable to attack by aphids. ZONES 6–9.

Abies amabilis *(left)*

PACIFIC SILVER FIR, RED FIR

Native to the coastal mountains of northwestern USA, western Canada and southern Alaska, this species can grow to 260 ft (78 m) in the wild; in cultivation it seldom reaches 100 ft (30 m). Its glossy green leaves, deeply grooved above and banded bluish white beneath, give off a smell similar to orange peel when crushed. The cones, 4–6 in (10–15 cm) long, ripen from red to deep purple. ZONES 5–9.

Abies balsamea

BALSAM FIR

The 'balsam' in this fir's name is a clear, thin resin in its bark, once commercially important. The most widespread North American species, it extends from Canada (where it is a major source of paper pulp) south through the mountains of eastern USA as far as West Virginia. In cultivation, it is a short-lived slender tree, grown for its spicy fragrance, bluish green foliage and Christmas tree shape. Dwarf cultivars are most often seen in gardens with the most popular being **'Hudsonia'**, a compact miniature shrub up to 24 in (60 cm) high and **'Nana'**, a neat rounded shrub of similar size. ZONES 3–8.

A

Abies balsamea
'Hudsonia'
(right & above right)

Abies bracteata *(left)*
syn. *Abies venusta*
SANTA LUCIA FIR, BRISTLECONE FIR

Among the rarest *Abies* species in the wild, this fir comes from the higher parts of the Santa Lucia Mountains near the southern Californian coast. There it grows to 150 ft (45 m) tall. In cultivation it requires a mild climate, and may be short lived. It has a long-pointed crown, unusually long sharp needles, and egg-shaped cones covered in long appendages resembling the needles but narrower. ZONES 7–10.

A

Abies cephalonica *(left)*

GREEK FIR, CEPHALONIAN FIR

This fir belongs to a group of Mediterranean firs
with short, stiff, outward-pointing, prickly needles,
and occurs naturally in the mountains of Greece
and the Balkans. Widely grown, hardy and vigorous, it was introduced into Britain in the early
1800s, where native specimens have reached
heights equal to those in the wild, about 120 ft
(36 m). The brown cones are roughly cylindrical
and about 4 in (10 cm) long. ZONES 6–9.

Abies concolor

COLORADO FIR, WHITE FIR

This species grows wild in the Rocky Mountains
of western USA, where it reaches 150 ft (45 m);
a taller race, **Abies concolor** var. **lowiana** (Pacific
fir) is found closer to the coast in Oregon and
northern California. The needles, which are
bluish green on both sides and blunt tipped,
exude a lemon scent when bruised. Cones range
from deep dull purple to pale brown. A fine ornamental fir, it is also hardy and vigorous. Seedlings
vary in the blueness of their foliage. Some of the
best blue forms, propagated by grafting, are sold
under the name '**Glauca**'; even more striking is
the rare and slower-growing pale blue cultivar
'**Candicans**'. '**Compacta**' also has quite blue
foliage but is a dwarf cultivar, hardly exceeding
3 ft (1 m) in height. ZONES 5–9.

Abies concolor 'Glauca' *(left)*

Abies concolor var. *lowiana* *(below)*

A

Abies firma (right)
MOMI FIR, JAPANESE FIR

With foliage of a deep shiny green, the momi fir reaches 150 ft (45 m) tall in the mountains of southern Japan. It is densely branched with stiff, leathery needles, up to $1^1/_2$ in (35 mm) long, in 2 rows forming a wide V on twigs of the lower branches. The brown, egg-shaped cones are up to 4 in (10 cm) long. ZONES 6–9.

Abies grandis (above)
GIANT FIR, GRAND FIR, LOWLAND FIR

Among the world's tallest conifers, the giant fir reaches 300 ft (90 m) in forests on Vancouver Island, and its natural range extends south to Sonoma County in California. In cultivation it can grow 3 ft (1 m) a year in suitable climates, and is widely planted for its timber. It does best in deep, moist soils. The foliage resembles that of *Abies concolor* and when crushed smells like orange peel. The smallish cones ripen to dark brown. ZONES 6–9.

Abies homolepis (above)
NIKKO FIR

Native to central Japan, this species grows well in Europe and North America and is more tolerant of urban pollution than most firs. It can exceed 100 ft (30 m) in height, and is broadly conical when young. The crowded needles, up to $1^1/_2$ in (35 mm) long, are dark green with broad blue-white bands on the undersides and blunt tips. The bark on young trees and immature cones are purplish gray. The shrub-sized cultivar **'Prostrata'** lacks erect leading shoots and is propagated from cuttings. ZONES 5–9.

A

Abies koreana (above)

KOREAN FIR

In the wild known only from mountains in the far south of Korea, this fir has been grown in the West from the early 1900s. It is valued for its compact size, seldom exceeding 20–30 ft (6–9 m), and its early coning—it may produce its attractive small bluish cones when as little as 3 ft (1 m) high. The crowded needles are short and broad with notched tips and wide blue bands on the undersides. It is ideal for smaller gardens, or for a large rock garden. ZONES 5–9.

Abies lasiocarpa (above)

SUBALPINE FIR, ROCKY MOUNTAIN FIR

This species grows up to the tree line in the Rocky Mountains, from Arizona to southern Alaska. It may be a 100 ft (30 m) tall tree or a horizontal spreading shrub. The needles are crowded and overlapping, with bluish stripes on both surfaces. Cones are fat and dark purple. To the southeast of its range the typical species is replaced by **Abies lasiocarpa** var. **arizonica,** the corkbark fir, which has thick, corky, pale bark and blue-gray foliage. Selections of this variety valued as garden plants include '**Compacta**', silver-blue and slow growing but difficult to obtain as it is propagated by grafting, and '**Aurea**', which has yellowish foliage. ZONES 4–9.

Abies nordmanniana (left)

CAUCASIAN FIR, NORDMANN FIR

This handsome fir can grow to 200 ft (60 m) and is native to the mountains of the Caucasus. Its densely crowded needles are dark glossy green, with rounded and slightly notched tips and whitish bands on the undersides. When crushed they smell like orange peel. The long fat cones ripen to reddish brown. Vigorous and adaptable, with a narrow shape and a long straight leading shoot, it is widely grown as an ornamental. ZONES 4–9.

Abies numidica *(below)*
ALGERIAN FIR

In the wild this fir is known only from the Kabyle Ranges near Algiers, where it makes a broadly conical tree to 80 ft (24 m) tall. Its densely crowded needles, very flattened with broad blunt tips, are strongly banded with blue-white. Cones are long and narrow, ripening from deep green to dull brown. Very suitable for garden use, in cultivation it makes a cone of dense foliage. It needs adequate space to develop properly. ZONES 6–9.

Abies procera
syn. *Abies nobilis*
NOBLE FIR

A very tall conifer from the high-rainfall coastal region of northwestern USA, this species reaches over 250 ft (75 m). Smooth-barked and broadly conical when young, it develops a mast-like trunk and a high, pointed crown with foliage in horizontal tiers. The narrow, blunt-tipped needles vary from bluish green to strong silvery blue. Cones are large, fat and purplish brown. It adapts well to cultivation in a cool, moist climate and good, deep soil. It is susceptible to aphid attacks in warmer climates. Blue-foliaged 'Glauca' cultivars are usually grown. ZONES 4–9.

Abies pinsapo *(above)*
SPANISH FIR

A handsome column-shaped tree reaching 100 ft (30 m), often with multiple leaders and densely crowded branches, this fir adapts to a wide range of soils and climates. The very short, rigid needles are less flattened than in most firs, and have fine bluish white stripes on both surfaces. In spring small purple pollen cones appear on the lower branch tips. The seed cones, produced near the top of the tree, are brown when ripe. Seedlings are selected for bluish foliage, collectively referred to under the cultivar name '**Glauca**'. ZONES 5–9.

Abies procera 'Glauca' *(above)*

Abies pinsapo 'Glauca' *(center)*

ABUTILON
syn. *Corynabutilon*

CHINESE LANTERN, FLOWERING MAPLE

There are 100 or more species of mostly evergreen shrubs in this genus but only a few truly merit the name 'Chinese lantern'; that is only a few have pendent flowers on weak stalks comprising an inflated calyx above a bell of 5 overlapping petals. This flower type is adapted to pollination by hummingbirds. Most species have a wide open flower, like a small hibiscus, with petals most commonly yellow or orange. They are distributed widely through warmer countries, but most species are native to South America. A small group of species from the cooler parts of Chile has mauve flowers and deciduous foliage, and is sometimes placed in a separate genus, *Corynabutilon*.

CULTIVATION
They need well-drained soil and full sun or part-shade. In cooler climates they can be grown in containers in sheltered, sunny spots or in greenhouses. They need good watering, especially if in containers (in which they bloom best if root-bound). Propagate from cuttings in late summer. Flea-beetles, aphids and caterpillars can be problems in the garden.

Abutilon × *hybridum* 'Orange King'
(below right)

Abutilon × *hybridum* 'Kentish Belle' *(below)*

Abutilon ×
hybridum *(below left)*

CHINESE LANTERN

Abutilon × *hybridum* is a collective name for cultivars derived from hybridizing some South American species. The lantern-like flowers, borne from spring to autumn, can be yellow, orange, pink, white, mauve and scarlet. Named cultivars include **'Nabob'**; **'Golden Fleece'**, with rich golden yellow flowers; **'Kentish Belle'** with bright orange flowers; **'Orange King'**; **'Ruby Glow'**; **'Ashford Red'**; and **'Souvenir de Bonn'**, with variegated foliage and red-veined orange flowers. In warm climates they grow to 8 ft (2.4 m), some with a similar spread, and an open growth habit. Prune hard in early spring; tip prune to promote bushiness and flowering. These cultivars can be grown indoors in a cool but sunny room. ZONES 9–11.

Abutilon vitifolium 'Album'
(right)

Abutilon megapotamicum
'Variegatum' *(center left)*

Abutilon megapotamicum
(center right)
BRAZILIAN BELL-FLOWER

This species from southern Brazil and Uruguay comes in 2 growth forms: an almost prostrate shrub with branches that may self-layer, making it a good ground cover or rock-garden plant, and a vigorous shrub of up to 8 ft (2.4 m) with arching cane-like branches. Both have smallish, pendent, bell-shaped flowers with a deep red calyx and pale yellow petals. In cooler climates it is usually grown as a pot plant but in zone 8 it can be grown outdoors against a warm wall. Cultivars include **'Marianne'**, **'Thomsonii'**, **'Super'**, **'Wisley Red'**, and **'Variegatum'**. The latter has leaves heavily blotched yellow and a prostrate growth habit. ZONES 8–11.

Abutilon × suntense
(right)

This cool-climate hybrid will tolerate lower temperatures than *Abutilon vitifolium;* its other parent is *A. ochsenii* from the colder south of Chile. It reaches 12 ft (3.5 m) tall and about 8 ft (2.4 m) wide, has dark green leaves and profuse purple or mauve flowers from spring to early summer. The cultivar **'Jermyns'** has deep mauve flowers, fading with age. Moderately frost hardy, it requires shelter from strong winds. ZONES 8–9.

Abutilon vitifolium *(above right)*
syn. Corynabutilon vitifolium

This soft-wooded, short-lived, deciduous shrub from Chile grows to 10–12 ft (3–3.5 m). In summer it bears profuse clusters of mauve-purple to white flowers up to 3 in (8 cm) wide. It needs a cool moist climate and is one of the most cold hardy abutilons, but does best against a sheltered house wall or in a courtyard. Prune hard in early spring to prevent the shrub becoming straggly. Named cultivars include **'Veronica Tennant'** with fine, very pale lavender flowers; and **'Album'** with white flowers. ZONES 8–9.

ACACIA
WATTLE

A

This large genus contains over 1200 species of trees and shrubs from warm climates. Some are deciduous but most are evergreen. Over 700 are indigenous to Australia. They range from low-growing shrubs to tall trees and many have been introduced to other countries for economic and ornamental purposes. They are also common in tropical and subtropical Africa. Acacias have either bipinnate leaves or their leaves are replaced by flattened leaf stalks, known as phyllodes. The tiny flowers, ranging from deep golden yellow to cream or white, and crowded into globular heads or cylindrical spikes, are often fragrant and produce abundant, bee-attracting pollen. Fruit are either round or flattened pods.

CULTIVATION

The hard-coated seeds remain viable for up to 30 years. They should be treated by heating and soaking for germination in spring. Some need fire to germinate. In cultivation many species are fast-growing but short-lived (10–15 years). In their native regions they are often disfigured by insect or fungus attack. They do best in full sun and well-drained soil. Some will tolerate part-shade.

Acacia baileyana (above)
COOTAMUNDRA WATTLE, GOLDEN MIMOSA

A fast-growing, small, spreading tree to 20 ft (6 m), the Cootamundra wattle has a short trunk and arching branches, feathery blue-gray leaves, and fragrant golden yellow flower clusters in late winter. Widely used in warm-temperate gardens as a feature or shade tree, a specimen in full bloom can be a spectacular sight. Like most acacias, it tends to be short lived and prone to borer attack when declining. The cultivar '**Purpurea**' has purplish foliage, especially on the growing tips. ZONES 8–10.

Acacia cultriformis (left)
KNIFE-LEAF WATTLE, KNIFE ACACIA

This 6–12 ft (1.8–3.5 m) tall shrub from the cooler tablelands of New South Wales, Australia, has blue-gray phyllodes, up to 1 in (25 mm) long, and shaped like small paring-knife blades. These are stalkless, attached directly to the branches. The showy spring flowers are in profuse short sprays of round, fluffy yellow balls. It tolerates light frost and is happy in any sunny, well-drained position. ZONES 8–11.

Acacia decurrens *(right)*
GREEN WATTLE

This is an upright tree growing
to 50 ft (15 m) tall. With its
straight trunk, smooth brownish green bark, domed crown,
and fine, feathery, rich green
bipinnate leaves, it is one of the
fastest-growing and most attractive of the tall wattles. In late
winter it bears decorative,
fragrant, golden yellow flowers.
It prefers a warm-temperate
climate and deep, moist soil.
ZONES 9–10.

Acacia greggii *(right)*
CATCLAW ACACIA

A native of southwestern North
America, this deciduous shrub
reaches 6–8 ft (1.8–2.4 m) in
height and spread and can be
shaped into a small tree for patio gardens. Tiny, gray-green
leaves appear in mid-spring, followed by fuzzy yellow catkins in
late spring. The branches are
covered with thorns, making
the shrub useful for barrier
plantings. It loves heat and
is very drought tolerant once
established. ZONES 7–11.

Acacia iteaphylla *(right)*

Native to South Australia, this shrub has a weeping
habit. It grows to 15 ft (4.5 m) tall and has very narrow
gray-green phyllodes up to 4 in (10 cm) long. Pale yellow
fragrant flowers borne in autumn and winter are followed by attractive, long-lasting seed pods. It is moderately frost hardy and tolerates quite dry conditions. A
prostrate form is available. ZONES 8–10.

A

Acacia karroo
(right)

KARROO THORN

From South Africa, this
species has become
naturalized in parts of
southern Europe where
it was grown for orna-
ment and hedging. If
left unpruned it will
grow fairly fast into a
small or medium-sized
tree to 25 ft (8 m), but
it can be taller in the
wild. It has a stiff,
irregular growth habit,
and the branches are
armed with vicious
long spines in V-
shaped pairs. It bears
small bipinnate leaves
and a profusion of
deep yellow, sweetly
scented, ball-shaped
flowerheads in
summer. **ZONES 9–11.**

Acacia longifolia
(right)

SYDNEY GOLDEN WATTLE

Native to the eastern
Australian coast, this
shrub has a height and
spread of up to 15 ft
(5 m), a short trunk
and irregularly shaped
head. A semi-prostrate
form, **Acacia longifolia
var. sophorae**, may be
found on exposed
coastal dunes. It has
narrow, oblong, dark
green phyllodes and
long fingers of fragrant,
butter-yellow flowers
in late winter and early
spring. It is ideal for a
seaside hedge, wind-
break, or street plant-
ing. **ZONES 9–11.**

Acacia melanoxylon *(left)*

BLACKWOOD

Unlike most acacias, this tree from
the highland forests of mainland eastern Australia and Tasmania is long-
lived and moderately frost hardy. The
timber is highly valued for cabinet-
work. Growing to 90 ft (27 m), it has
dull, olive green phyllodes and bears
profuse balls of pale yellow flowers in
spring. In open sites, it has a spreading bushy crown and short thick
trunk. Fertile, moist soil and humid
climates suit it best, though it will
survive on poorer soils. It is unable to
survive through periods of drought.
ZONES 8–11.

Acacia neriifolia *(right)*

This abundantly flowering wattle occurs naturally in the dry woodlands of eastern Australia. A tall shrub or small tree to about 25 ft (8 m) with an erect, open growth habit, it has narrow, straight, grayish phyllodes and bears numerous sprays of bright golden yellow flowerheads in late spring and early summer. ZONES 9–11.

Acacia pendula
(right)

WEEPING MYALL, BOREE

Native to the plains of inland eastern Australia, this small, densely crowned tree, to 20 ft (6 m) tall, has vertically drooping branchlets like a weeping willow and makes a good shade or ornamental tree in semi-arid areas. It has narrow, lance-shaped, silvery gray phyllodes and bears yellow flowers in spring. It can survive harsh climates with low rainfall, but prefers heavy clay soils. ZONES 9–11.

Acacia podalyriifolia *(right)*

QUEENSLAND WATTLE, PEARL ACACIA, SILVER WATTLE

From the wooded hills of southeastern Queensland, this is a handsome large shrub of 20 ft (6 m) which spreads to about half that. It is fast growing but short lived. The silvery phyllodes are rounded and have a felty texture. Large sprays of fragrant golden flowers appear in winter and early spring. It prefers well-drained soil, full sun and a mild to warm climate. Young plants need staking. ZONES 9–11.

A

Acacia pravissima *(left)*

OVENS WATTLE

This evergreen, bushy shrub can grow to 20 ft (6 m) and spread to 15 ft (5 m) but is usually smaller. It has drooping branches and very distinctive small, triangular, olive green phyllodes. Small heads of golden yellow flowers appear in spring. The bronze buds and gold-tipped foliage are attractive throughout winter. There is a prostrate form. **ZONES 8–10.**

Acacia pycnantha *(left)*

GOLDEN WATTLE

A medium shrub or small tree up to about 20 ft (6 m) in height, this wattle is Australia's national floral emblem. In the wild it occurs mainly in Victoria and South Australia. It has a rounded crown with somewhat pendulous branches. Large, fragrant, golden, ball-shaped flowerheads are borne in spring. Although not long lived, it makes a fine garden specimen. It prefers sandy soils and needs shelter from heavy frost. Established trees tolerate quite dry conditions. **ZONES 9–11.**

Acacia verticillata *(right)*

PRICKLY MOSES

Indigenous to Tasmania and mainland southern Australia, this upright, bushy shrub grows to 10 ft (3 m) tall. It has needle-sharp phyllodes arranged in distinct whorls and bears creamy yellow flowers in spring and summer. Moderately frost hardy, it can be grown in southern England, especially in seaside gardens. **Acacia verticillata var. latifolia** is a name used for semi-prostrate forms that grow on exposed coastal cliffs and have broader, blunter phyllodes. **ZONES 8–10.**

ACALYPHA

A

This genus of evergreen shrubs and subshrubs consists of over 400 species from most warmer countries of the world; only a few are grown as ornamentals. Some of these are valued for the decorative, narrow spikes of crowded, feathery flowers borne by female plants (males are on different plants), while one species is grown only for its showy variegated foliage. The thin leaves usually have toothed margins.

CULTIVATION
They need a sunny to semi-shaded position, well-drained, light soil, plenty of water in summer and protection from wind. Plants are frost tender. Prune lightly to shape in late winter, then feed and water. Propagate from cuttings in summer. Watch for mealybug, red spider mite and white fly.

Acalypha hispida
(right)

CHENILLE PLANT, RED-HOT CAT-TAIL

Thought to be from Malaysia, this upright, soft-stemmed shrub has striking, tiny, bright red flowers that in summer hang in pendulous, tassel-like spikes on the females. Leaves are large, oval and bright green to reddish bronze. It grows to 6 ft (1.8 m) high and wide. Regular pruning will maintain a bushy shape. It does best in sheltered sites in full sun; in cool climates it needs a heated conservatory.
ZONES 11–12.

Acalypha wilkesiana

FIJIAN FIRE PLANT, COPPER LEAF

Originating in Fiji and nearby islands, this shrub grows to a height and spread of 10 ft (3 m). With erect stems branching from the base, it has large, serrated, oval leaves in a wide color range, some with contrasting margins. Inconspicuous tassel-like catkins of reddish bronze flowers appear in summer and autumn. It prefers a warm, sheltered position. Foliage colors are best in full sun. Cultivars include **'Macrophylla'** with large leaves, each differently variegated with bronze, copper, red, cream and yellow blotches; **'Godseffiana'** with narrow, drooping green leaves edged with cream; **'Macafeeana'** with deep bronze leaves splashed with coppery red; and **'Marginata'** with bronze-red leaves edged with cream or pale pink. **'Obovata'** has leaves tinged bronze, margined with pink. ZONES 10–11.

Acalypha wilkesiana 'Macrophylla' *(below)*

Acalypha wilkesiana 'Obovata' *(bottom)*

ACER

MAPLE

Maples are unrivaled for their autumn foliage coloring and variety of leaf shape and texture. They are also grown for shade and for timber. Many are compact enough for the average garden. The distinctive 2-winged fruit (samaras) are more noticeable than the flowers, which in most species are inconspicuous. Attractive bark is a feature of some maples—usually smooth and gray or greenish. Most species come from East Asia, particularly China (over 80 species), Japan (over 20) and the eastern Himalayas; 9 species are native to North America and a few to Europe, including *Acer heldreichii* subsp. *trautvetteri* (Greek maple). Most are deciduous but there are a few evergreen and semi-evergreen species from northern Turkey and the Caucasus.

CULTIVATION

Most maples prefer a cool, moist climate with ample rainfall in spring and summer. A planting position sheltered from strong winds suits them best. For best autumn color, grow them in a neutral to acid soil. Propagation is generally from seed for the species, by grafting for cultivars. Cuttings are difficult to root, but layering of low branches can be successful. Seed germination can be aided by overwintering in damp litter, or by refrigeration. Some species produce few fertile seeds, so it may be necessary to sow a large quantity to obtain enough seedlings.

Acer buergerianum
(below left)

TRIDENT MAPLE

Although tall in its native forests of eastern China, in cultivation this species usually makes a bushy-topped small tree with a thick, strong trunk. The bark is pale brown and dappled and the smallish leaves usually have 3 short lobes close together at the upper end (hence the common name). Autumn coloring is often two-toned, with scarlet patches on a green or yellowish background. It tolerates exposed positions and poor soils and is a traditional subject for bonsai. ZONES 6–10.

Acer buergerianum as a bonsai subject *(below)*

A

Acer campestre *(left)*
FIELD MAPLE, HEDGE MAPLE

A small to medium bushy-crowned tree, this European maple also occurs in western Asia and north Africa. In the UK it is also known as hedge maple, for its use in the traditional hedges that divide fields. It withstands heavy pruning and can be trimmed into dense, regular shapes. It has thick, furrowed corky bark; autumn brings golden yellow or slightly bronze tints to the foliage. It is easily grown from fresh seed. ZONES 4–9.

Acer cappadocicum 'Rubrum' *(left)*

Acer cappadocicum
COLISEUM MAPLE

This maple is found from southern Europe across temperate Asia to central China, with a number of geographic subspecies. Its smooth green leaves have regular, radiating triangular lobes, each lobe drawn out into a slender point. Fast growing, it can reach 100 ft (30 m) in the wild and is better suited to parks and streets rather than suburban gardens. Autumn color is a brilliant golden yellow. **'Rubrum'** has dark red new shoots, the young leaves expanding bright red before turning green. ZONES 5–9.

Acer cissifolium *(right)*
VINE-LEAF MAPLE, IVY-LEAFED MAPLE

Rarely reaching 30 ft (9 m) and with a broadly spreading crown, the vine-leaf maple is native to Japan. Unlike most maples, it has compound leaves consisting of a number of separate leaflets. Autumn color is yellow and orange or red. Although easily grown, it can be hard to obtain: male plants are rare so fertile seed is unavailable, and nurseries must propagate by the slower method of layering. ZONES 5–9.

A

Acer davidii *(right)*

FATHER DAVID'S MAPLE

This Chinese maple of open habit and flat-topped outline is named after its discoverer, French missionary-naturalist Armand David. The scope of this name has now been widened to include a number of subspecies, previously regarded as distinct species; David's original form is placed under **Acer davidii** subsp. *davidii*. A snakebark maple, it has bark striped silvery gray on an olive green background and leaves that are long pointed but mostly unlobed. The Dutch selection **'Serpentine'** has more strongly contrasting stripes on a deep purplish brown background. Autumn brings shades of yellow, orange and dull scarlet. In a cool, humid climate it grows rapidly to 20–25 ft (6–8 m). **A. d. subsp. *grosseri*** (syns *Acer grosseri, A. hersii*) differs in its shorter broader leaves with 2 short lateral lobes. This tree has an overall green coloring in summer, the bark striped paler gray-green; autumn tones are similar to subsp. *davidii*. Both subspecies are popular and are easily grown from fresh seed, but chance hybrids with other nearby snakebarks are likely. **'George Forrest'** is a broadly upright cultivar with mid- to dark green leaves. **ZONES 6–9.**

Acer × *freemanii*
'Autumn Blaze' *(right)*

Acer × *freemanii*

This hybrid between *Acer rubrum* (the red maple) and *A. saccharinum* (the silver maple) was raised by O. M. Freeman at the US National Arboretum in 1933, but has since frequently been found to occur spontaneously. Its foliage is intermediate between these species and it grows quite rapidly to 50 ft (15 m) or more, with erect branches and a rounded crown. A half-dozen cultivars of *A.* × *freemanii* have been named including the colorful **'Autumn Blaze'**. They are suitable specimens for street planting. They are normally propagated by layering. **ZONES 5–9.**

A

Acer griseum *(right & below)*
PAPERBARK MAPLE

Prized for its bark—chestnut brown with paler corky dots which it sheds each year in wide curling strips—this narrow-crowned tree grows to 30 ft (9 m) with a straightish trunk. In autumn its small, dark green leaves turn deep scarlet. In moist, sheltered conditions with good soil, growth can be rapid. No longer common in the wild in its native China, in cultivation it produces mostly infertile seed. **ZONES 5–9.**

Acer japonicum
(left)
FULL-MOON MAPLE

This maple's new growth is distinctive—very pale green with a coating of silky white hairs that disappear as the leaves mature into olive green tones. In autumn some leaves change early to orange or red, while others retain their summer colors into late autumn. Slow growing and of narrow, shrubby habit, it is intolerant of drying winds and likes a moist, sheltered position. It has long been cultivated in Japan. Its many cultivars include **'Aconitifolium'**, with ferny leaves that turn crimson in autumn, and **'Vitifolium'**, with leaves slightly more deeply lobed than the normal species and coloring more brilliant scarlet, orange or yellow. **ZONES 5–9.**

Acer japonicum 'Aconitifolium'
(below & below right)

Acer monspessulanum
(right)

MONTPELIER MAPLE, FRENCH MAPLE

Related to *Acer campestre* and occurring on stony hillsides around the Mediterranean, this bushy small tree, up to 30 ft (9 m) tall, has dark green, rather thick leaves 1¹/₂–2 in (3.5–5 cm) long with 3 blunt lobes. It is tolerant of dry conditions and its compact crown makes it well suited for streets and suburban lawns. It turns reddish in autumn. **ZONES 5–10.**

Acer negundo
(right & above right)

BOX-ELDER MAPLE, BOX ELDER

The only North American maple to have compound leaves (consisting of 3 to 7 leaflets), this species can reach 50 ft (15 m) with a thick trunk and upright branching habit, but is more often seen as a smaller tree with cane-like, bright green branches. It is fast growing and tolerates poor conditions but its branches break easily in high winds. In some areas it is regarded as a weed because of its free-seeding habits. Its several subspecies extend south into Mexico and Guatemala. Favorite cultivars include **'Elegans'**, **'Variegatum'** and **'Aureo-marginatum'**, with leaflets that are edged white or gold respectively; **'Aureo-variegatum'** has leaflets with broader, deeper yellow margins, retaining this coloring into autumn; the newer **'Flamingo'** is similar to 'Variegatum' but with leaves that are strongly flushed with pink on the new growth. The male clone **'Violaceum'** has purplish new shoots and twigs; the male flower tassels are also pale purple. None of these cultivars reach much more than half the size of the wild, green-leafed type. **ZONES 4–10.**

Acer negundo 'Violaceum'
(top right)

Acer negundo 'Variegatum'
(center left)

A

Acer palmatum *(below)*
JAPANESE MAPLE

The Japanese maple is the most widely grown maple in gardens. It is valued for its compact size, delicate ferny foliage, and brilliant autumn coloring—from rich gold to deepest blood red. In a garden it grows to 12–15 ft (3.5–4.5 m), branching low, with strong sinuous branches and a dense, rounded crown. Although more tolerant of warmer climates than most maples, it needs shade and shelter or leaves may shrivel. The more than 300 cultivars range from rock-garden miniatures to vigorous small trees, with a great variety of leaf shape, size and coloration. Nearly all need to be grafted to preserve their characteristics, so they are expensive. The most popular cultivar of tree size is **'Atropurpureum'**, dense and spreading, with dark purple spring foliage turning paler olive-purple in summer and deep scarlet tones in autumn; it usually comes true from seed. **'Sangokaku'** ('Senkaki') has coral red branches and twigs, which are displayed bare in winter; in autumn leaves have brilliant gold tones. **'Atrolineare'** has foliage color like 'Atropurpureum' but leaves

Acer palmatum 'Bloodgood' *(far left)*

Acer palmatum 'Dissectum' *(left)*

Acer palmatum 'Dissectum' in spring *(below far left)* **and in winter** *(below center)*

Acer palmatum 'Dissectum Atropurpureum' *(below)*

divided almost to the base into narrow lobes. In the **Dissectum Group**, the primary leaf lobes are deeply cut into a filigree pattern; their fine, drooping twigs grow down rather than upward, so they are grafted onto a standard. The height of the standard determines the height of the dome-shaped shrub. **'Dissectum'** is a small cultivar with leaves turning yellow tinged with orange in autumn. **'Dissectum Viridis'**, the original green cut-leaf maple, is slightly more sun-tolerant than **'Dissectum Atropurpureum'** ('Ornatum') which has purple leaves that are green in summer. Some other well-known cultivars include **'Bloodgood'**, **'Butterfly'**, **'Chitoseyama'**, **'Koreanum'**, **'Osakazuki'** and **'Shigitatsu Sawa'**. **'Red Pygmy'** is a vase-shaped cultivar with red leaves in spring, turning to gold in autumn. Some other popular forms include **'Linearilobum Rubrum'**, **'Trompenburg'**, **'Hessei'** and **'Lutescens'**. ZONES 5–10.

Acer palmatum 'Sangokaku' in spring *(top)* and in winter *(center right)*
Acer palmatum 'Lutescens' *(center left)*
Acer palmatum 'Ozakazuki' *(left)*
Acer palmatum 'Trompenburg' *(above)*

A

Acer pensylvanicum
(left)

STRIPED MAPLE, MOOSEWOOD

Erect, vigorous and with a single main trunk, the striped maple is native to eastern North America. The bark striping on younger limbs is the most richly colored of any of the snakebark maples—suffused with red as well as olive and white. Autumn color is a bright golden yellow. The popular cultivar **'Erythrocladum'** has striking red branches in winter. ZONES 5–9.

Acer pentaphyllum
(left)

A rare and distinctive maple, this species comes from a very limited area of central-western China. It has compound leaves, each consisting of 5 narrow leaflets arranged like fingers around a central stalk, a unique leaf type among maples. It grows to about 30 ft (9 m) eventually, with a spreading crown and pale gray bark. ZONES 6–9.

Acer platanoides
(right)

NORWAY MAPLE

This maple ranges from north of the Arctic Circle in Scandinavia across Europe, from France to the Urals, but is not found in the Mediterranean or the UK, though cultivated there for centuries. A large, round-headed tree, it thrives in a wide range of soils and situations, but not in warm climates. Yellow flowers appear before the leaves; autumn color is gold to reddish orange. Popular cultivars include **'Oregon Pride'**, **'Cleveland'**, **'Summershade'** and **'Drummondii'** which has variegated leaves. Cultivars with deep purplish foliage include **'Schwedleri'**, **'Faassen's Black'** and **'Crimson King'**. **'Columnare'**, with plain green leaves, has a narrow column shape. All except **'Oregon Pride'** are slow growing, and so suit smaller gardens. ZONES 4–9.

Acer platanoides 'Crimson King' *(right)*

Acer platanoides 'Drummondii' *(below)*

A

Acer pseudoplatanus
(above)

SYCAMORE MAPLE

This species, which occurs naturally from Portugal to the Caspian Sea and has been long established in England and North America, seeds so profusely that it is regarded a weed. Cultivated trees are 40–60 ft (12–18 m) tall and form a broad, dense, dark green crown. The thick, scaly bark is pale gray. Autumn color is not a feature. A useful park and street tree, it prefers a sheltered situation with deep moist soil, but tolerates more exposed sites. The cultivar **'Purpureum'** has

Acer pseudoplatanus **'Erythrocarpum'** *(right)*

Acer pseudoplatanus **'Brilliantissimum'** *(below right)*

leaves with deep plum undersides, the uppersides also slightly purplish. **'Erythrocarpum'** has red fruit in conspicuous clusters. The spring foliage of **'Brilliantissimum'** is pale creamy yellow flushed pink, changing in summer to whitish with green veining; it is slow growing and suits smaller gardens; **'Rubicundum'** has leaves flecked deep pink. **'Variegatum'** has cream markings. ZONES 4–10.

A

Acer rubrum (above)

RED MAPLE, SCARLET MAPLE

This large maple from eastern North America has brilliant deep red leaves in autumn, which contrast with the blue-white undersides. In the wild it grows to 100 ft (30 m) in forests on deep alluvial soil. As a planted tree it grows rapidly, with a straight trunk and narrow crown at first, but spreading broadly with age. Its timber is prized for furniture making. There are numerous popular cultivars including **'Bowhall'**, **'Red Sunset'**, **'Schlesingeri'**, the conical **'Scanlon'** and **'October Glory'**, which has glossy green foliage that turns a brilliant crimson in autumn. ZONES 4–9.

Acer rubrum 'October Glory' (left)

Acer rufinerve (left)

From the valleys of Japan, this snakebark maple forms an upright tree, reaching 20–30 ft (6–9 m). It has downy, bluish new growth and the bark of young branches is attractively striped. Autumn foliage is a deep dull crimson with orange tones. The thickish, 3-lobed leaves are 3–6 in (8–15 cm) long, with the central lobe the largest. ZONES 5–9.

A

Acer saccharinum *(left)*
syn. *Acer dasycarpum*
SILVER MAPLE

Ranging over eastern USA and Canada (except the arctic north), the silver maple grows large, branching low into several trunks with a broad crown of foliage. As an ornamental it is popular for its hardiness, rapid growth and rich golden autumn color. The cane-like branches are easily damaged by storms and heavy snow, but quickly grow back. American and European nurseries have developed many cultivars. **ZONES 4–9.**

Acer saccharum *(bottom right)*
SUGAR MAPLE

Commercially important for its sap (maple syrup) and durable timber, this maple ranges across eastern North America from Newfoundland and Manitoba in the north to Florida in the south, and west to Utah. In the south and west, regional sub-species occur, including *Acer saccharum* subspp. *floridanum, grandidentatum, leucoderme* and *nigrum*: all have been treated as distinct species by some botanists. Its leaf adorns the Canadian flag. Often slow growing in the first 10 years, in the garden it makes a low-branching, broad-crowned tree, 40–50 ft (12–15 m) high, though it will grow much taller in forests. Autumn color varies from tree to tree, with yellow, orange, scarlet and crimson all common. *A. s.* subsp. *grandidentatum* (bigtooth maple) is widely distributed in western North America. It has thicker leaves, and the bluish white undersides contrast with the deep green upper, and blunter, lobes. It has pale bark and makes a small, bushy-topped tree to 40 ft (12 m). Attractive cultivars include **'Globosum', 'Green Mountain', 'Legacy'** and **'Monumentale'**. **ZONES 4–9.**

Acer saccharum subsp. *nigrum*
(center)

Acer saccharum 'Globosum'
(far left)

Acer tataricum subsp. *ginnala* *(left)*

Acer tataricum *(top)*

TATARIAN MAPLE, AMUR MAPLE

This is the maple species with the widest east–west distribution, occurring wild from Austria eastward across Europe and temperate Asia all the way to Japan and far eastern Siberia. Tataria was the name used in the eighteenth century for central Asia and eastern Russia, where it is a common tree. The species is divided into 4 geographic subspecies of which the most commonly cultivated is *Acer tataricum* subsp. *ginnala* (syn. *Acer ginnala*) from northeastern China, Japan, Korea and eastern Siberia: a large shrub or small tree of 15–30 ft (4.5–9 m), it often branches from the base into several long cane-like stems; the leaves are long pointed and irregularly lobed, turning red in autumn and falling rapidly; red fruits are a feature during summer. A quick grower, it is fully frost hardy; 'Flame' is one of its cultivars. ZONES 4–9.

A

ACMENA

This small genus of handsome evergreen trees has species in the
rainforests of northern and eastern Australia, New Guinea and
the Malay Archipelago. Like the related *Syzygium*, it was formerly
included within the genus *Eugenia* (now restricted to mainly
American species). The trees have smooth-edged leaves arranged
in opposite pairs on the twigs. Sprays of small white flowers are
borne at the twig tips followed by pink, purple or white berries
with edible though spongy flesh which can be used for making
jam. Charming street and garden trees, they are grown successfully in other warm-climate countries. Seeds are readily germinated but must be fresh.

CULTIVATION
They prefer a near frost-free climate, fertile, moist soil and will
grow in sun or shade. Propagation is normally from seed, which
is extracted from the fleshy fruit straight away. These trees prefer
a humid, sheltered situation, at least when young.

Acmena smithii
(below left)
LILLYPILLY

Native to eastern
Australia from Queens-
land's Cape York
Peninsula to southern
Victoria, the lillypilly
varies from a low shrub
to a 70 ft (20 m) tree.
Leaves are rather short
and broad, narrowing
to a fine point. Sprays
of tiny white flowers
with prominent sta-
mens appear in early
summer followed by
white, pink or mauve
fruits in late summer.
A reliable garden plant,
it is usually seen as a
20–30 ft (6–9 m) com-
pact tree or grown as a
tall screening shrub or
hedge. It responds to
clipping and extra
water and fertilizer
with flushes of coppery
new growth. In more
humid areas, the
foliage is sometimes
marred by sooty mold
fungus. ZONES 9–11.

ADANSONIA

BAOBAB

These large trees have trunks that become hugely swollen with age into a bottle or flask shape. They amazed European explorers in Africa, Madagascar and northwestern Australia, the only areas where the 9 species are found growing wild (7 are endemic to Madagascar). They are usually deciduous in the tropical dry season. Leaves are divided into a number of leaflets radiating from the end of a common stalk. The large and attractive cream flowers, which open only at night, hang singly on pendulous stalks; they are adapted to pollination by nectar-feeding bats. The large oval fruits contain seeds embedded in a sour, edible pulp.

CULTIVATION

Propagate from seed or cuttings. Growth is slow until a good root system is established, but vigorous young trees with trunks beginning to swell make fine subjects for parks and streets. They are not too difficult to cultivate in the tropics or warmer subtropics and adapt well to wetter regions despite being from monsoonal climates with a long dry season.

Adansonia digitata
(below)

BAOBAB

The common name is thought to come from central Africa but this, the original baobab, is found in most of Africa, from dry sub-Saharan scrubland to the veld of northern Transvaal. Old trees can reach vast proportions, often branching near the ground into several hugely swollen trunks each of which may be 80 ft (24 m) or more high.
ZONES 11–12.

Adansonia gregorii (right)

AUSTRALIAN BAOBAB, BOTTLE TREE,
DEAD RAT TREE, BOAB

Confined in the wild to a small area of far northwestern Australia, this species is very closely related to the African baobab and young trees are hardly distinguishable. It does not generally grow quite as tall, but old trees reach an enormous girth. The unflattering name dead rat tree comes from the appearance of the gray seed pods.
ZONES 11–12.

A

ADENANDRA

This genus of 18 species of small-leaved evergreen shrubs from the Cape region of South Africa is related to *Coleonema* and *Agathosma*. Like the latter, the aromatic leaves of some of its species have been used there as a herbal tea in rural areas. Two species are grown as ornamentals, seemingly better known to gardeners outside their native South Africa. They are low, spreading shrubs producing very pretty, 5-petalled white or pink flowers whose size seems out of proportion to the small, narrow leaves.

CULTIVATION
They are best suited to rock gardens, where they should have a sunny position and gritty, well-drained soil; they can also be grown in pots or tubs. Water well in winter and spring but keep drier in summer. Propagate from seed or cuttings.

Adenandra
uniflora (below)
CHINA FLOWER

This twiggy shrub grows to 24 in (60 cm) tall and 3 ft (1 m) wide, with small, aromatic, deep green leaves on fine reddish stems. Although not fragrant, the flowers have great beauty—5-petalled, white and 1 in (25 mm) across, they have a porcelain-like appearance that gives the shrub its common name. ZONES 8–10.

A

ADENIUM

The name of this small genus of succulent shrubs and small trees is taken from their Arabic name *aden;* these plants may also have given their name to the port city of Aden on the Arabian Peninsula, from where they first became known to the West. They are deciduous in dry seasons, and some develop very fleshy, swollen trunks. Vivid, funnel-shaped flowers are borne from mid-winter through to spring (or in the tropical dry season). Up to a dozen species of *Adenium* have been recognized in the past, but now they are regarded as constituting a single variable species which includes 6 subspecies, ranging widely through tropical and subtropical Africa, from South Africa's Cape Province to the Red Sea, as well as southern Arabia.

CULTIVATION

Popular in tropical gardens, they prefer a position in full sun or part-shade and thrive best in climates with a well-marked dry season. Kept dwarfed and rootbound in a pot, they will often flower more profusely. As they are very prone to rotting, they require a gritty, well-drained soil. Propagate from seed or cuttings.

Adenium obesum
(right)
syns *Adenium multiflorum,*
A. coetanum
IMPALA LILY, DESERT ROSE

In the wild this species can make a small tree of 12 ft (3.5 m) or more with a swollen trunk and thick, crooked limbs; in cultivation it seldom exceeds about 5 ft (1.5 m), with a sparse branching habit. Whorls of lance-shaped to oval, glossy leaves are grouped at the branch tips, but when in flower in winter it is usually leafless. The very decorative, trumpet-shaped blooms are 1$^{1}/_{2}$–2 in (38–50 mm) long and vary considerably in color; most popular is a very pale pink or white with deep pinkish red margins. Cultivar names have been given to a number of the color forms, most of which appear to be derived from **Adenium obesum** subsp. *obesum,* which extends over the species' whole geographical range. Some of the other subspecies are more succulent, and are sometimes grown by succulent collectors.
ZONES 11–12.

A

AESCHYNANTHUS

Over 100 species of mostly epiphytic creepers and subshrubs in the African violet family make up this genus, found throughout the rainforests of Southeast Asia and the Malay Archipelago. Some have become popular as indoor plants, suited to hanging baskets and flowering freely for months on end. The stems are tough and wiry, sometimes clinging by roots. The fleshy, pointed leaves are arranged in opposite pairs and the flowers, clustered at the ends of branches, are trumpet-shaped but curved, often with the base enclosed in a conspicuous calyx.

CULTIVATION
Aeschynanthus grow happily outside in humid tropical and sub-tropical climates, preferring a position in part-shade and most at home in a hanging basket or established in the fork of a large tree. In cooler regions they adapt well to indoor use, but need strong light. Pot in a coarse indoor plant mix and water freely in the growing period. Propagate from cuttings.

Aeschynanthus speciosus (below)

A summer-flowering plant, native to Borneo, this species bears large clusters of tubular, 4 in (10 cm) long orange flowers with yellow throats. It has a trailing habit and reaches a height and spread of 12–24 in (30–60 cm). Stems are slender and arching and the dark green, lance-shaped leaves are carried in pairs or whorls with a terminal rosette surrounding each cluster of flowers. ZONES 11–12.

AESCULUS
HORSE-CHESTNUT, BUCKEYE

A

These deciduous trees and shrubs have a finger-like arrangement of leaflets and bear eye-catching spikes of cream to reddish flowers at the branch ends in spring or summer. The large, nut-like seeds, released from round capsules, resemble chestnuts but are bitter and inedible. At least half of the 20 or so species occur in North America, the remainder are scattered across temperate Asia and Europe.

Renowned as majestic park and avenue trees in European cities, in the wild they grow mainly on valley floors, where there is shelter, deep soil and good moisture.

CULTIVATION
Although most are frost hardy, they perform best in cool climates where seasons are sharply demarcated and summers are warm. They are propagated from seed or, in the case of selected clones and hybrids, by bud grafting.

Aesculus × *carnea*
(right)

RED HORSE-CHESTNUT

This hybrid tree, thought to have originated by chance in Germany in the early 1800s, grows to about 30 ft (9 m) and often comes true from seed. It gets the reddish pink of its flowers (borne in late spring) from one parent, *Aesculus pavia*; the other parent is *A. hippocastanum*. It adapts to warmer and drier climates than *A. hippocastanum*. The cultivar **'Briotii'** has larger spikes of brighter pink flowers.
ZONES 6–9.

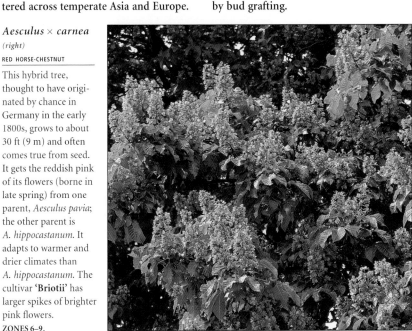

Aesculus × *carnea*
'Briotii' *(right)*

A

Aesculus flava
(right & below right)
syn. *Aesculus octandra*
YELLOW BUCKEYE, SWEET BUCKEYE

This ornamental tree is native to
fertile valleys in central-eastern
USA, and grows to 90 ft (27 m)
in the wild. Smallish creamy
yellow or occasionally pinkish
flowers appear in 6 in (15 cm)
panicles from late spring to
early summer, followed by fruits
each with 2 to 4 seeds. The dark
green leaves turn yellow before
falling. The bark is dark brown,
becoming furrowed with age.
ZONES 4–9.

Aesculus hippocastanum *(above & right)*
HORSE-CHESTNUT

This tree originated in the mountain valleys of the Greece–Albania
border region and is now widely planted in parks, avenues and large
gardens in Europe. It can reach 100 ft (30 m), though is usually
half that. Striking 'candles' of bloom are borne in spring and early
summer; individual flowers have crumpled white petals with a
yellow basal patch that ages to dull red. Fruit have a leathery case
covered with short prickles and in autumn release large seeds,
known as 'conkers' to British children. The dark green foliage turns
yellow-brown in autumn. **'Baumannii'** has longer-lasting double
flowers. **ZONES 6–9.**

A

Aesculus indica
(right)

INDIAN HORSE-CHESTNUT

This tree from the
northwest Himalayas,
tends to branch very
low and produces a
thick trunk and spread-
ing crown when grown
in an open site. In early
to mid-summer it
produces 12–15 in
(30–38 cm) spikes of
white flowers with
petals tinged yellow or
red. The shiny leaves
turn yellow in autumn;
the large fruit, brown-
ish and slightly rough,
lack prickles. It needs a
sheltered but sunny
position and moist soil.
ZONES 6–9.

Aesculus parviflora
(right, far right & below
right)

BOTTLEBRUSH BUCKEYE

This many-stemmed
shrub, native to the
southeastern USA,
reaches a height of
6–10 ft (1.8–3 m),
spreading into a broad
clump by new growths
from the roots. Leaves
have 5 large, strongly
veined leaflets which
are downy on the un-
dersides. In late sum-
mer it bears spikes of
spidery flowers with
small white petals and
long, pinkish stamens.
This species likes a hot
humid summer, deep,
moist soil and a shel-
tered site. ZONES 7–10.

A

Aesculus pavia *(left)*
RED BUCKEYE

From coastal plains and woodlands of eastern USA, this species forms a small tree to 20 ft (7 m) tall, or frequently a shrub to 10 ft (3 m) with dense, cane-like branches. It is valued for its deep crimson flowers, borne in upright spikes in early summer, and the reddish autumn tones of its smallish leaves, each with 5 leaflets. Although it is easily grown, it is rarely available from nurseries. The cultivar **'Atrosanguinea'** has darker crimson flowers. ZONES 7–10.

Aesculus turbinata
(left)
JAPANESE HORSE-CHESTNUT

This tree closely resembles the common horse-chestnut *(Aesculus hippocastanum)* in shape, but is slower growing and differs in its larger leaves, slightly smaller panicles of cream flowers that open a few weeks later, in early summer, and its fruit which lack spines or prickles. Its handsome foliage turns a fine orange in autumn. ZONES 6–9.

Agapetes incurvata
syn. *Agapetes rugosa*

AGAPETES
syn. *Pentapterygium*

These evergreen shrubs from the moist forests of southern Asia, mostly in the higher mountains, have leathery leaves and tubular flowers of a rather waxy texture. Most of the species grow as epiphytes in the forks of large trees, or frequently on cliffs or boulders. In some species, the stems arise from a curious woody tuber, which can get quite large with age.

This species is native to the Himalayan slopes in Nepal and northern India. It is a shrub, about 3 ft (1 m) tall, with long scrambling branches and strongly veined leaves 2–4 in (5–10 cm) long. From leaf axils near the branch tips it bears groups of pendent tubular flowers in summer, each about $^3/_4$ in (18 mm) long, pale flesh pink with much darker transverse bars. '**Scarlet Elf**' has flowers of a stronger red. ZONES 10–11.

CULTIVATION
They adapt to growing in the ground, but demand a well-drained, open-textured soil and need to be planted high, with the tuber or root bases exposed or covered only by coarse humus. They also benefit from shelter and humidity, but adapt readily enough to garden conditions.

Agapetes incurvata
'Scarlet Elf' *(right)*

Agapetes serpens
(below right)
syn. *Pentapterygium*
serpens

From Bhutan and Nepal in the eastern Himalayas, this shrub has low-arching branches that arise from a large woody tuber. It rarely exceeds 3 ft (1 m) tall, but may be twice that in width. The bristly brown stems bear rows of small glossy leaves and single rows of tubular, pale red flowers, each having 5 distinct angles and a pattern of V-shaped bars of darker red. ZONES 9–10.

A

AGATHIS

KAURI

This remarkable genus of large conifers consists of 20 or so species scattered through the southwest Pacific region from New Zealand to the Malay Peninsula. Nearly all are tall with massive, straight trunks and broad, leathery leaves quite unlike the needles of more familiar conifers. The cones are curious too— nearly spherical with a criss-cross pattern of scales. *Agathis* is Greek for 'ball of twine'. Kauri (or kaori) is their Polynesian name. Timber and resin are economic products derived from them.

CULTIVATION
The trees are marginally frost hardy and prefer full sun, deep moist soil and high humidity. They can be pruned to limit size or to maintain shape. Propagation is from seed.

Agathis australis
(left)
NEW ZEALAND KAURI

The largest of New Zealand's native trees, this occurs in the North Island's lowland forests, reaching 150 ft (45 m) with trunk diameters of 20 ft (6 m) and great spreading limbs. Slow growing in cultivation, it has a dense, narrowly pyramidal crown. The short, blunt, stiff leaves are mid-green, turning coppery brown in colder weather. Kauris prefer moderate temperatures. **ZONES 9–10.**

Agathis robusta
(above)
QUEENSLAND KAURI

Native to coastal Queensland, Australia, and Papua New Guinea, this tall tree up to 150 ft (45 m), has thick, deep green leaves about twice as large as those of the New Zealand kauri, and its growth is more vigorous. Young trees have straight trunks with short side branches. Its globular cones are the size of tennis balls. It prefers warm-temperate to tropical locations. **ZONES 9–12.**

AGONIS

A

This is a genus of about 10 species of warm-climate evergreen trees and shrubs indigenous to the southwest of Western Australia. They have narrow, thick-textured leaves, aromatic when crushed, and attractive small white flowers resembling those of tea-trees *(Leptospermum)*. They are valued for their toughness and freedom from pests and diseases. Some species are used for cut flowers.

CULTIVATION

They do best in full sun and sandy soil that is well drained but preferably enriched with organic matter for moisture retention. They are frost tender, but tolerate droughts when established. Propagation is from seed or cuttings. Plants sometimes self-propagate from seed.

Agonis flexuosa
(below right)

WILLOW-MYRTLE, PEPPERMINT TREE

Growing to about 30 ft (9 m) tall and wide, this tree has a brown-barked trunk with a diameter up to 3 ft (1 m), quite dispropor-tionate to its height. It has pendulous branches, rather like a small weeping willow. It is widely grown in parks and gardens of temperate Australia, including seaside loca-tions. **'Variegata'**, with cream and pink-striped leaves, lacks vigor but is a popular small tree. ZONES 9–10.

Agonis juniperina *(right)*

Reaching a height of 15–25 ft (4.5–8 m), this tree is more slender and upright than others of its genus. Its deep green leaves are small and rather prickly, crowded into clusters along the twigs. The small white flowers have brown centers and are borne through much of the year. This species has been grown for cut-flower production. ZONES 9–10.

A

AILANTHUS
TREE OF HEAVEN, SIRIS

This tree genus from eastern Asia and the Pacific region includes both winter-deciduous and dry-season-deciduous species, though only the former are generally cultivated. They are vigorous growers of medium size, with long pinnate leaves and branches terminating in large flower clusters. Male and female flowers are produced on separate trees and neither is very conspicuous, but those on female trees develop in summer into masses of winged, papery fruits that are very decorative. The winter-deciduous species are frost-hardy trees that adapt well to urban areas, even coming up from self-sown seed in the cracks of paving. They tolerate hard pruning, responding with vigorous new growths.

CULTIVATION
They do best in warm-temperate areas but will survive in most climates, preferring full sun or partial shade and deep, rich soil. Propagation is by means of seed in autumn and suckers or root cuttings from the female tree in winter.

Ailanthus altissima
(above)
syn. *Ailanthus*
glandulosa
TREE OF HEAVEN

Native to China, in some cities this tree is valued for its ability to withstand urban pollution, in other areas it is scorned as a weed. Planted on a large lawn it shows little inclination to sucker, growing to 50 ft (15 m), its dome-shaped crown scattered with bunches of pale reddish brown fruits in summer. The deep green, pinnate leaves, up to 3 ft (1 m) long on young trees, smell unpleasant if bruised. ZONES 6–10.

ALBERTA

Three species make up this genus of subtropical, evergreen trees, one from South Africa and two from Madagascar. They are noted for their handsome gardenia-like foliage and showy tubular flowers. A curious feature is the way 2 of the 5 sepals enlarge after flowering to form colored wing-like flaps on the woody fruit. The name honors the medieval scholar Albertus Magnus.

CULTIVATION

Frost tender, these plants are happiest in a warm coastal climate with ample rainfall and protection from salty winds. All 3 species prefer a fertile, well-drained but moist soil and need plenty of water during summer. Propagate from the autumn seed or by root cuttings.

Alberta magna

(right)

NATAL FLAME BUSH

From South Africa, this species grows to a tree of 30 ft (9 m) in the wild, but in gardens is generally only a shrub of 6–10 ft (1.8–3 m). The leathery leaves are shiny deep green, and from late autumn to summer it produces clusters of showy, upcurving scarlet flowers. These develop into small fruits, which are enclosed by pale red calyces. It is not frost hardy and needs a subtropical climate to perform well.
ZONES 10–11.

A

ALBIZIA

For the most part *Albizia* species are quick growing tropical trees and shrubs. They have feathery leaves and densely clustered small flowers with stamens far longer and more conspicuous than the petals. In the wild, they are often rather weedy small trees and frequently short lived, but can be shapely.

CULTIVATION
Springing up quickly from seed, *Albizia* species are easy to culti-vate, requiring summer warmth and moisture and a reasonably sheltered site.

Albizia julibrissin
(left)

SILK TREE

Ranging from Iran east to China, this decidu-ous tree is named for the long, silky stamens, creamy white to deep pink, the visible part of the flowerheads, borne in summer. Often less than 6 ft (1.8 m) tall, but flowering freely, in ideal conditions it be-comes a flat-crowned tree, 20–25 ft (6–8 m) tall, with luxuriant feathery foliage. The compressed seed pods are quite prominent. It likes a warm-temperate climate and thrives in large containers but seldom lives beyond 30 years. Exceptionally richly colored speci-mens are usually given the name **Albizia julibrissin** var. *rosea*. **ZONES 8–10.**

Albizia julibrissin var. *rosea* *(left)*

ALLAMANDA

A

A dozen or so species of twining climbers and shrubs belong to this tropical American genus. A few of them are widely planted in warm climates for their colorful trumpet flowers, which are mostly bright yellow. The glossy leaves are in whorls of 3 to 6 on the smooth stems, and will bleed milky sap if cut. The climbing species are among the most popular ornamentals in the tropics, ideal for growing over fences or against walls. They produce a succession of flowers for much of the year. In areas with cooler winters there may be some leaf fall.

CULTIVATION
In warm climates grow outdoors in a sunny, sheltered position in rich soil, watering freely in summer. In cool climates they require a large container in a hothouse or conservatory. Prune heavily in spring to maintain shape and encourage flowering. Propagate from cuttings and watch for mites which disfigure the leaves.

Allamanda schottii
(*right*)
syn. *Allamanda neriifolia*
SHRUBBY ALLAMANDA

The only true shrub in the genus, this upright evergreen grows to a height and spread of 6 ft (1.8 m) and has glossy green leaves. Its trumpet-shaped, golden yellow flowers, occasionally streaked with orange, are borne from summer into autumn. They are sometimes followed by large, shiny seed pods. It prefers a sheltered sunny position and should be pruned in spring to control its shape. It often benefits from having its stems tied to supports.
ZONES 11–12.

ALLOCASUARINA

A

SHE-OAK

The 60 species of this entirely Australian genus were until recently included in the genus *Casuarina*. Both genera are evergreen, with needle-like branchlets which serve the function of leaves; the true leaves are rings of tiny triangular scales at joints of the branchlets. Small male and female flower spikes, adapted for pollination by wind, are usually carried on separate plants. Only the males are noticeable, changing the branch tips to a rich brown when they appear in their countless thousands. With their attractive usually drooping foliage, she-oaks are grown for shade, windbreaks, timber and firewood.

CULTIVATION
Taller species grow fast and may live long; some survive very dry conditions. Propagate from seed in spring.

Allocasuarina decaisneana
(left & below left)
syn. *Casuarina decaisneana*

DESERT OAK

One of the most beautiful of all the she-oaks, this species grows in the most extreme environment—the low-rainfall red dunes of central Australia—where its deep roots tap reservoirs of subsoil moisture concealed beneath the sands. It grows to 50 ft (15 m), with a thick straight trunk, deeply furrowed corky bark, a dense crown of weeping gray-green branchlets and the largest seed 'cones' in the genus, making it a fine ornamental in hot, arid areas.
ZONES 9–11.

Allocasuarina littoralis
(right)
syn. *Casuarina littoralis*

BLACK SHE-OAK

Occurring along the east coast of Australia, this erect, evergreen tree grows to 30 ft (9 m) with an irregularly conical, pointed crown, though it is often smaller in exposed coastal sites. It has a short trunk with closely fissured gray-brown bark and very fine, dark green foliage. In winter, male flower spikes may tint male trees brown. The cylindrical 'cones' on female trees are narrow and often densely clustered. Fast growing and ornamental when young, it becomes sparse and unattractive after 15 to 20 years. It thrives in poor soils and tolerates sea spray. **ZONES 9–11.**

Allocasuarina torulosa *(above)*
syn. *Casuarina torulosa*

FOREST OAK, FOREST SHE-OAK

This graceful tree, with corky, deeply furrowed bark, grows fast to 40–50 ft (12–15 m) or more. The fine-textured, drooping branches and branchlets are green when young, turning a deep purple-bronze in winter. Occurring naturally in eastern Australia, it is useful for coastal planting on heavier soils, for ornament, or on farms for shade, shelter or fuel. Young trees can be lightly pruned to thicken growth. **ZONES 8–11.**

A

ALLOXYLON

The few species in this genus of evergreen rainforest trees are native to the warm east coast of Australia and to Papua New Guinea. Until recently they were included in the genus *Oreocallis*, now restricted to South American species, and earlier still in *Embothrium*. Not widely available in nurseries, they are worth seeking out for their magnificent heads of scarlet or crimson flowers.

CULTIVATION

While they can withstand very light frosts, they are really plants for tropical or subtropical gardens with regular summer rainfall. They do best on loamy or sandy, humus-rich soil and dislike root disturbance, so they should be planted while still small. Sudden and unexplainable death of sapling trees is a common problem, especially in areas that experience dry spells. Trees should be trained to a single trunk for the first 6 ft (1.8 m) or so. Propagate in spring from fresh seed.

Alloxylon flammeum (above)
syn. *Oreocallis* 'Wickhamii'
TREE WARATAH, SCARLET SILKY OAK

This species develops from a bushy, erect habit into a wide, irregular head of branches 30–50 ft (10–15 m) high. The variably lobed leaves are dark green and leathery. Terminal clusters of nectar-rich, orange-red flowers, which look like waratahs or spider chrysanthemums, are borne in profusion in late spring or early summer.
ZONES 9–11.

Alloxylon pinnatum (above)
syn. *Oreocallis pinnata*
DORRIGO WARATAH

Less well known than *Alloxylon flammeum* and more difficult to grow, this species makes a tree to 30–60 ft (9–18 m) in its natural rainforest, but in gardens it is usually an erect shrub of 12–20 ft (3.5–6 m). Shiny, dark green leaves are divided to the midrib into narrow lobes, appearing to be pinnate. Striking heads of crimson-pink flowers are borne at the branch tips in mid-summer.
ZONES 9–11.

ALNUS
ALDER

Upright trees related to the birches *(Betula)*, alders come mainly from cool to cold regions of the northern hemisphere. Though less attractive than the birches, they are very fast growing and their roots contain micro-organisms that can fix nitrogen from the air, adding to soil fertility. Light-loving trees, alders act as nurse trees for slower-growing conifers, but die after they are overtopped by them and shaded out. The egg-shaped female catkins hang in groups at the branch tips, becoming hard and woody in the seeding stage. The bark is brown or blackish and sometimes furrowed. Alders from cool-temperate regions are deciduous but produce little in the way of autumn color. A few species from subtropical mountain areas are evergreen or semi-evergreen.

CULTIVATION
Most alders require a cool-temperate climate, or at least one in which winters are distinctly cold. A common use is for wind-breaks. They do best in soil that is permanently moist; many alders will also grow in very infertile or polluted soils. When planted for ornament or shade, shape early to a single trunk and trim branches to above head height. Propagate from seed or hardwood cuttings.

Alnus firma (right)
JAPANESE ALDER

This beautiful alder from the mountains of Japan has narrow, sharply toothed and prettily textured leaves on gracefully arching branches. It may remain a large shrub to 10 ft (3 m) for many years, though it can ultimately reach 30 ft (9 m). It has attractive bark, with older squares of gray flaking off to reveal reddish new bark. The leaves often remain green late into autumn.
ZONES 5–9.

A

Alnus glutinosa
'Imperialis' *(above)*

Alnus rubra

(below right)

syn. *Alnus oregona*

RED ALDER

Ranging from Alaska to central California, this tree grows to 40–50 ft (12–15 m), usually branching into several trunks with pendulous lower branches. Bark is thin and pale gray. The large leaves have coarse marginal teeth and are dark green above with paler gray-green undersides often covered with orange down. Profuse yellow male catkins are borne at the branch tips in early spring. Reasonably frost hardy, it will soon outgrow a small garden. **ZONES 6–9.**

Alnus glutinosa

(below left)

BLACK ALDER, COMMON ALDER

In cold, bleak climates and on poor, boggy soils the common alder of Europe is sometimes the only tree apart from certain willows that will thrive. It can reach heights of 60 ft (18 m) in the wild but planted trees are seldom more than half that. The dark brown bark becomes deeply furrowed and checkered and the high crown of the tree is often irregular and open. The leaves of the cultivar **'Imperialis'** are dissected into narrow, pointed lobes. **ZONES 4–9.**

ALOYSIA

This genus consists of around 40 species of evergreen shrubs from North, Central and South America, grown for their attractive and strongly aromatic foliage. The branches are soft and cane-like with leaves arranged in opposite pairs or in whorls of 3. Tiny flowers are borne in panicles at the end of the branches.

CULTIVATION

They prefer a well-drained, loamy or light-textured soil and plenty of summer watering. Tolerant of only mild frosts, they do best in a sunny position in a warm, coastal environment. In cold areas, new specimens should be planted out each year. Remove dead wood in early summer, and prune well in late winter to maintain a bushy shape and encourage the flowers, which are borne on the current season's growth. Propagate by semi-hardwood cuttings in summer or soft-tip cuttings in spring.

Aloysia triphylla (above)
syn. *Lippia citriodora*
LEMON-SCENTED VERBENA

Grown for its heavily lemon-scented, crinkly, pale to mid-green leaves, this shrub has an open, rather straggling habit. It can reach a height and spread of 10 ft (3 m), and racemes of dainty, light lavender flowers appear through summer and autumn. It needs regular pruning to improve its shape. Oil of verbena is produced from the leaves. ZONES 8–11.

A

ALYOGYNE

These hibiscus-like shrubs from drier regions of southern and western Australia are fast-growing, erect, leggy plants about 6–10 ft (1.8–3 m) tall. Large, funnel-shaped flowers, borne singly near branch tips, are showy but delicate and short lived, usually lilac or mauve.

CULTIVATION

They will suit any frost-free warm climate and need full sun, shelter from strong winds and moderately fertile, well-drained soil. Regularly tip prune after flowering. Propagate from seed or cuttings in summer.

Alyogyne huegelii
(left & below left)
syn. *Hibiscus huegelii*
LILAC HIBISCUS

Native to Western Australia, this spreading, semi-deciduous shrub grows to 8 ft (2.4 m) high and wide. It bears lilac (sometimes pinkish) flowers, up to 6 in (15 cm) across, which open in succession from spring to late summer. The deeply lobed leaves are slightly hairy with irregularly serrated margins. Prune often for compact growth.
ZONES 10–11.

AMELANCHIER

A

SERVICEBERRY, SNOWY MESPILUS, JUNEBERRY

These shrubs and small trees, mostly native to cool regions of North America, belong to the pome-fruit group of trees and shrubs in the rose family, which includes apples, pears and quinces as well as many 'berry' shrubs. Most *Amelanchier* species are deciduous, with simple oval leaves and clusters of white flowers, frequently with long narrow petals. The small rounded fruit ripen to purple or black and are often sweet and edible. Some species make attractive, graceful trees, valued for the display of snowy white flowers in spring and for their autumn coloring.

CULTIVATION

They do best in moist, fertile soil in a grassy glade with the shelter of other trees but receiving ample sun. Propagation is normally from seed or by layering.

Amelanchier arborea (below right) syn. *Amelanchier canadensis* of gardens
DOWNY SERVICEBERRY

Occurring naturally in the eastern USA, this easily grown tree reaches about 20 ft (6 m) in gardens, usually with a narrowish crown and drooping lower branches. The finely toothed, pointed leaves are covered with white down as they emerge in spring. Profuse flowers, in short upright sprays, are followed in early summer by small fleshy fruit. In autumn the foliage turns red, orange or yellow. ZONES 4–9.

Amelanchier lamarckii (right)

The origin of this species has been the subject of speculation: in the past it has been much confused with *Amelanchier canadensis* and *A. laevis*. It makes a spreading shrub or small tree to 30 ft (9 m). The leaves are broad and deep green, with a coating of silky hairs when young. White flowers appear in spring in drooping clusters; small edible fruit ripen to black. ZONES 6–9.

A

ANACARDIUM

CASHEW

Although this genus includes 8 species of semi-deciduous small trees from tropical America, only *Anacardium occidentale*, the cashew, has been much cultivated. Both branches and foliage have a very awkward and untidy aspect, so it is rarely grown for its ornamental qualities. Stiff sprays of small pinkish flowers, which are fragrant at night, are followed by curious fruit, consisting of 2 parts. The 'cashew apple', actually a swollen, fleshy stalk, is colored, edible and up to 4 in (10 cm) long and 2 in (5 cm) in diameter. Sitting in its hollowed apex is the true fruit, curved like the nut, with an outer fleshy husk containing an extremely acrid, resinous sap. This can badly burn the skin and must be removed before the edible kernel can be used, requiring gloves to protect the skin. Most of the world's cashew crop comes from India, where the long, hot dry season suits its cultivation.

CULTIVATION
Fast growing when young, cashews grow in the tropics and the warmer subtropics. Propagate from fresh seed, planted directly into the ground.

Anacardium occidentale *(left)*

This species can grow to 25 ft (8 m), but usually reaches just half that height. It has a spreading, irregular crown and bears flowers early in the wet season, followed by the fruit. ZONES 11–12.

ANDROMEDA
BOG ROSEMARY

Only 2 species of low evergreen shrubs make up this genus from the colder parts of the northern hemisphere. They have tough short branches that root along the ground and small oblong leathery leaves. The small flowers, in short terminal sprays, are urn-shaped with a narrow mouth.

CULTIVATION
They are best grown in a shaded rockery, preferring moist yet well-drained, acid conditions. They will tolerate any frosts and prefer a cold climate. Propagate from seed or small tip cuttings.

Andromeda polifolia *(above)*

Growing to about 24 in (60 cm) high and wide, this species has narrow, deep green leaves, 1 in (25 mm) long, with pale undersides. The tiny white to pink flowers appear in sprays in spring. **'Compacta'** has a denser, more compact habit, with grayish leaves and pink flowers. ZONES 2–9.

A

ANGOPHORA
APPLE GUM

This genus is closely related to *Eucalyptus* and consists of 13 species of evergreen trees from eastern Australia, often found on sandstone-derived soils of low fertility. While *Angophora* has sharply ribbed fruit capsules and leaves in opposite pairs, *Eucalyptus* has mostly smooth capsules and adult leaves arranged alternately. *Angophora* species vary in size but can become 100 ft (30 m) trees. The bark of most species is rough and scaly. Where space is available, they make interesting subjects with their twisting branches. Flowers are creamy white, usually profuse.

CULTIVATION
They are easily grown in frost-free and near frost-free climates. Plant in light, well-drained soil, sheltered from strong winds. Propagate from seed.

Angophora costata

SYDNEY RED GUM, SMOOTH-BARKED APPLE

From Australia's east coast, this tree can reach 100 ft (30 m) with a sturdy trunk up to 4 ft (1.2 m) in diameter and a high, spreading crown of twisting branches. In spring it sheds its brownish pink bark to reveal salmon-pink bark. It is unpredictable in the speed and form of its growth. ZONES 9–11.

Angophora costata and *Xanthorrhoea* species *(left)*

Angophora costata and bush regeneration after fire *(below)*

ANISODONTEA

A

This genus of shrubby mallows from southern Africa have tough, wiry stems and small, irregularly lobed leaves. The small flowers, like miniature hibiscus, are carried on slender stalks from short lateral shoots near the tips of the branches. They have been recently rediscovered and popularized as free-blooming indoor plants, or in warm-temperate climates as garden shrubs. If grown indoors, they must receive some sun or very strong reflected light.

CULTIVATION

They need frequent watering in the warmer half of the year, little in the cooler seasons. Prune lightly after the flowers finish for a more compact plant and to encourage subsequent flowering. Propagation is normally from summer cuttings, which strike readily. Grow them in a cold frame.

Anisodontea
'African Queen'
(below)

This recent cultivar is compact in habit with foliage much like *Anisodontea capensis*, but with very profuse, slightly larger flowers of a soft, delicate pink. It is reported to have originated as a hybrid between A. × *hypomadarum* and A. *scabrosa*. ZONES 9–11.

Anisodontea capensis *(above)*
syn. *Malvastrum capensis*

This species will quickly grow to a shrub about 6 ft (1.8 m) high with long straggling branches and rather sparse foliage. Flowers, $^3/_4$ in (18 mm) in diameter, appear in successive flushes from spring through summer or almost the whole year in warmer climates; flesh pink with darker veining on opening, they age to very pale pink. ZONES 9–11.

Anisodontea × *hypomadarum* *(right)*

This evergreen, bushy shrub has an erect habit and can reach a height of 6 ft (1.8 m). Bowl-shaped, mid-pink flowers, up to $1^1/_2$ in (35 mm) across, with darker veins are borne from spring to autumn. Thought to be a hybrid, its true parentage is unknown. ZONES 9–11.

ANNONA

This genus of about 100 species of evergreen trees from the American tropics and subtropics includes some of the most delectably sweet tropical fruits, notably the cherimoya, custard apple and sweetsop. The trees have broad, oblong, strongly veined leaves and curiously shaped flowers. These often have a pungent fruity aroma, and emerge from the old wood on short stalks. The fruit consist of many fused segments and have tough green or brownish skin that may be covered in soft prickles or other protrusions. They contain many brown seeds embedded in a pulpy white flesh.

CULTIVATION
Happiest in most tropical and warmer subtropical areas, they prefer sheltered sunny positions and fertile, well-drained soils. They may flower and fruit through much of the year. Propagation is easy from freshly extracted seed, or by grafting for selected varieties.

Annona muricata
(below left)
SOURSOP

From northern South America, this tree grows to 15–20 ft (4.5–6 m), branching low with strongly ascending lateral growths. New growths have brownish silky hairs; older leaves are glossy bright green. The large green fruits are asymmetrically oval, covered in soft spines, and may be borne throughout the year. Despite the name, the fluffy white aromatic flesh is not very sour. ZONES 10–12.

Annona squamosa *(left)*
CUSTARD APPLE, SUGAR APPLE

There are many varieties of custard apple, a popular, semi-deciduous fruit tree that grows to 15 ft (5 m). Its flowers are pale green and pleasantly scented. The large fruit has a custard-like texture and is delicious when eaten fresh. Plant in a warm, sheltered position as the fruit yield may be damaged by low temperatures and the tree itself is frost tender. Propagate by grafting. ZONES 10–12.

ANOPTERUS

This genus consists of only 2 species of small evergreen tree or shrub: one confined to Tasmania, the other to subtropical hill forests of mainland Australia's east coast. Both are very ornamental, with long, spatula-shaped leaves, deep red or bronze on new growth-flushes, and heavy-textured white flowers in short terminal sprays. It is only the Tasmanian species that has been brought into cultivation to any significant extent.

CULTIVATION

They require a very sheltered position, moist, humus-rich soil and a cool humid climate, but are not very frost hardy. Plants grown from cuttings of mature wood often flower when only 12 in (30 cm) or so high.

Anopterus glandulosus (right)
TASMANIAN LAUREL

This shrub, normally 6–8 ft (1.8–2.4 m) tall, can grow to a tree of more than 20 ft (6 m) in moist Tasmanian forests. The glossy dark green leaves are very leathery, with blunt teeth. Pure white, cup-shaped flowers appear in spring in short sprays at the branch tips. ZONES 8–9.

A

APHELANDRA

This is a genus of around 170 species of subshrubs and shrubs, all native to tropical America. Their large, deeply veined, pointed leaves, usually deep green, sometimes with contrastingly colored veins, are arranged in opposite pairs on the stems. Dense terminal flower spikes have large, often brightly colored bracts from which protrude tubular orange, red or yellow flowers with a broad, 3-lobed lower lip. A handful of species have long been cultivated as decorative indoor and conservatory plants, valued for their foliage and flowers.

CULTIVATION

These tropical plants are very cold sensitive and liable to drop foliage if exposed to temperatures below 60°F (15°C), or to cool draughts for prolonged periods. In the tropics they can be planted outdoors in moist, humus-enriched, well-drained soil in part-shade; otherwise they require a position indoors in strong light, though not direct sun. Cut back stems after flowering. Propagate from seed or cuttings.

Aphelandra
squarrosa *(below left)*
ZEBRA PLANT

Widely grown as a house plant, this Brazilian species can grow to 6 ft (1.8 m) high in ideal conditions. It has green leaves up to 12 in (30 cm) long, with white or cream veins and midribs. The flower spike is around 8 in (20 cm) long, bright yellow and often tinted red or maroon. There are a number of cultivars, varying in leaf size and pattern, and in flower colors. 'Louisae' is the most commonly grown cultivar, with bright creamy white main veins and midribs. 'Dania' has yellow to orange-yellow flowers, which are rarely seen, and leaves with prominent white veins. ZONES 11–12.

Aphelandra squarrosa
'Dania' *(far left)*

Aphelandra squarrosa
'Louisae' *(left)*

Aralia chinensis
(right)

CHINESE ARALIA

As a young tree of up to about 10 ft (3 m), this species is usually single-stemmed with an irregular, umbrella-like crown. The dark green leaves, each about 4 ft (1.2 m) long, consist of large, oval leaflets with closely toothed margins. It flowers in early autumn, producing large panicles of creamy yellow umbels that droop over the foliage. With age it branches into smaller crowns, with smaller leaves and flower sprays, and may reach as much as 30 ft (9 m) in height. The leaves turn yellowish in autumn. ZONES 7–10.

Aralia elata 'Variegata'
(top right)

ARALIA

This genus of around 40 species of evergreen and deciduous shrubs, small trees and a few herbaceous perennials has a wide distribution in eastern and tropical Asia and the Americas. They have prickly stems, very handsome, large, compound leaves consisting of numerous leaflets, and large, terminal panicles of densely packed, small cream flowers. Young plants of these woody species often have a single, unbranched trunk with the leaves confined to the top, but as they age lateral branches develop and multiply to give a broad-headed small tree. Aralias can be eye-catching specimens when in full flower.

CULTIVATION

They need shelter from strong, drying winds and will tolerate full sun or part-shade beneath taller trees. While a moist, fertile soil suits them well, poorer soils are said to produce hardier, longer-lived specimens. Propagate from seed sown in autumn or suckers in spring.

Aralia elata *(right)*

JAPANESE ANGELICA TREE

Native to Japan and mainland northeast Asia, this highly ornamental, frost-hardy species can grow to a spreading tree of up to 30 ft (9 m), but is most commonly seen as a shrub with few branches. Large sprays of tiny white flowers are carried into early autumn, when the leaves have yellow and reddish tones. The leaflets of the cultivar 'Variegata' have whitish markings. ZONES 5–9.

ARAUCARIA

This remarkable, ancient genus of evergreen conifers is confined in the wild to South America, Australia, Norfolk Island, New Guinea and New Caledonia. Most are large trees with massive, straight trunks that continue to the apex of the tree, sharply distinct from the crowded, shorter, lateral branches. The leathery leaves are incurved and densely overlapping in some species, flatter and spreading in others. Male and female cones are borne on the same tree; the round, bristly seed cones develop right at the top of the trees.

CULTIVATION

Most are too large for gardens but may be used as park and street trees. They will grow in a range of soil types but prefer a deep, moist, well-drained soil and full sun. Growth may be quite fast when conditions suit them. Propagate from seed in spring.

Araucaria araucana (below)
syn. *Araucaria imbricata*
MONKEY PUZZLE

From South America, this tree enjoyed fad status in Britain in the 1840s. The remark that 'it would puzzle a monkey to climb it' gave rise to the common name monkey puzzle. It can grow 80 ft (24 m) tall and 4 ft (1.2 m) in trunk diameter. Young trees have a dome-like shape with interwoven branches; with age, the crown retreats to high above the ground, so that old trees resemble long-stemmed parasols. The glossy,

dark green leaves are rigid and fiercely prickly. Globular cones, 4–6 in (10–15 cm) long, are carried high on the crowns of mature trees. It needs a climate where the summers are cool and misty. ZONES 8–9.

Araucaria cunninghamii
(below)
HOOP PINE

Native to eastern Australian rainforests and found also in New Guinea, the hoop pine is moderately fast growing, reaching 100–120 ft (30–36 m) under

good conditions. Not very frost hardy, it is fairly resistant to dry conditions in winter once established, but prefers good summer rainfall. The tiny, pointed scale leaves curve inwards on the branchlets, but on juvenile growths they are longer and very prickly. The new bark is copper-hued; with age rougher, transverse ridges or 'hoops' develop. ZONES 9–12.

Araucaria heterophylla
(below)
syn. *Araucaria excelsa*
NORFOLK ISLAND PINE

This Norfolk Island native is widely planted in subtropical coastal regions. It is upright with a regular branching pattern, conical form and grows fast to 100 ft (30 m) or more. It is wind tolerant, retaining a quite vertical and symmetrical habit even in the face of incessant onshore gales, and can thrive in deep sand. It needs reliable water when young, but can tolerate dry spells once established. Shade tolerant when young, it can be long lasting in pots. ZONES 10–11.

ARBUTUS
STRAWBERRY TREE, MADRONE

A dozen or more species of evergreen tree belong to this genus, the majority from Mexico and the remainder found in the Mediterranean region and North America. Most are smallish trees with thick trunks and somewhat sinuous limbs; the bark often peels attractively. The thick-textured leaves are usually finely toothed and the flowers are small, white or pinkish bells in compact clusters at the branch ends. Some flowers develop into fleshy but hard, reddish yellow globular fruit, often with wrinkled surfaces, which take almost a year to ripen. This 'strawberry' fruit is edible but hardly palatable.

CULTIVATION
All *Arbutus* species prefer cool, humid climates, but tolerate dry conditions in summer; continental climates with extreme heat and cold do not suit them. They adapt equally to peaty, acid soils and limestone soil. Propagation is normally from seed, easily extracted from the fleshy fruit. Plant young: they dislike root disturbance.

Arbutus canariensis *(left)*

CANARY ISLAND STRAWBERRY TREE

From the Canary Islands, this species makes a neat, round-headed tree to 15 ft (4.5 m) high. In late summer and early autumn it produces pendulous clusters of small, light pink, lily-of-the-valley-like flowers, followed by quite large bunches of soft green fruit about ½ in (12 mm) in diameter, which ripen to red. The flaking, reddish brown bark is displayed throughout the year. **ZONES 8–10.**

A

Arbutus menziesii *(right)*

MADRONE

Native from California to British Columbia, the
madrone is the giant of the genus, reaching 100 ft
(30 m) in height and 6 ft (1.8 m) in trunk diameter. In the wild it grows mostly in humid areas
amongst tall conifers such as redwoods. It has
beautiful, smooth, orange-brown bark and
smooth-edged, glossy green leaves with whitish
undersides. Large clusters of pure white flowers
are followed by profuse small, orange-red fruit.
The American common name is a corruption of
madroño, the Spanish name for *Arbutus unedo*.
ZONES 7–9.

Arbutus unedo
(right)

ARBUTUS, STRAWBERRY TREE

Native to the western
Mediterranean and
Ireland, this bushy-
crowned, small tree can
attain 30 ft (9 m), though
10–15 ft (3–4.5 m) is
usual in gardens. The
bark is dark gray-
brown, rather fibrous
and scaly, and the
smaller branches and
twigs have a reddish
hue. In autumn the
white or pinkish flower
clusters, along with the
1 in (25 mm) orange
fruit from the previous
year, contrast with the
dark foliage. It is fairly
frost hardy and will tol-
erate neglect, but dis-
likes shade and damp
ground. **'Compacta'** is
a smaller cultivar.
ZONES 7–10.

ARCTOSTAPHYLOS

BEARBERRY, MANZANITA

Allied to *Arbutus*, this genus of around 50 species of evergreen shrubs or, rarely, small trees includes 2 species widely distributed through cool climates of the northern hemisphere; all others are native to western North America or Mexico. They are tough plants with very woody stems, smallish, leathery leaves and small clusters of white or pink, bell-shaped flowers. Some of the Californian species from the 'chaparral' evergreen scrub of the coastal ranges can survive the fires that periodically ravage the area. They mostly have very ornamental purple, red or orange bark that peels in thin shreds or flakes.

CULTIVATION

They need full sun or part-shade and moist but well-drained, fertile, lime-free soil. The seed, enclosed in a small fleshy fruit, is difficult to germinate, which explains why manzanitas are propagated from tip cuttings hardened off in winter; treatment with smoke may assist germination.

Arctostaphylos manzanita
(right)

COMMON MANZANITA

Native to California, the common manzanita (Spanish for 'little apple') reaches 8 ft (2.4 m) in height and spread or sometimes more. A slow-growing, stiff, woody shrub, it has thick, oval leaves coated in a whitish scurf when young; the striking, reddish brown bark is sometimes hidden by peeling strips of duller, older bark. Tight clusters of small, urn-shaped, deep pink flowers in early spring are followed by $\frac{1}{2}$ in (12 mm) red-brown berries. It tolerates long dry periods in summer. **'Dr Hurd'** is an upright, tree-like selection to 15 ft (4.5 m) with striking cinnamon-colored branches. ZONES 8–10.

Arctostaphylos uva-ursi
(right)

BEARBERRY, KINNIKINNICK

Found in the wild in the colder regions of the northern hemisphere, this species is best known as a completely prostrate shrub that can cascade over walls or embankments to form curtains of neat, dark green foliage. The leaves develop intense red tones in autumn and winter. In late spring it bears small clusters of dull pink, almost globular flowers, followed by green berries that ripen to red. It is readily propagated from cuttings. Cultivars include **'Massachusetts'**, **'Radiant'**, **'Wood's Red'** which is a dwarf cultivar, and **'Vancouver Jade'** which is an exceptionally vigorous and disease-resistant selection. **'Point Reyes'** is tolerant of coastal conditions. ZONES 4–9.

A

ARDISIA
MARLBERRY

This is a large genus consisting of over 250 species of evergreen trees and shrubs, widely distributed in tropical and subtropical regions of Asia and the Americas. The leathery leaves have mostly toothed, wavy margins. The smallish flowers are star-like, mostly white or pinkish, and the fruit are small, one-seeded berries (drupes), which are sometimes profuse and decorative.

CULTIVATION
When grown outdoors they are best suited to a moist, part-shaded position in well-drained, slightly acid soil that should have a high humus content. Some smaller-growing ardisias are well suited to pot culture for growing both indoors and in court-yards or patios, where they can be moved around to avoid sun and drying winds. Propagation is normally from cuttings, or by division in the case of rhizomatous species.

Ardisia crenata
(left)
syn. *Ardisia crenulata*
CORAL BERRY

Growing up to 6 ft (1.8 m) but more often seen at half that height or smaller, this shrub has a wide distribution in Southeast Asia extending to eastern China and southern Japan. Its leathery leaves have attractively wavy margins and are densely massed above a short, single trunk. Small, white flowers emerge in lateral sprays during the summer months and are followed by densely clustered, bright red berries that persist for a long period during the autumn and winter months. **'Alba'** has white berries; **'Variegata'** has new leaves with narrow red margins, which turn white as they mature. ZONES 8–11.

ARGYRANTHEMUM
MARGUERITE

Argyranthemum frutescens
(top row, left)
syn. *Chrysanthemum frutescens*

The true species, a 3 ft (1 m) tall, white-flowered shrub from the Canary Islands, is now rarely cultivated, and most of the commonly seen garden cultivars classified under this name may in fact be hybrids with other species. The numerous cultivars have a huge range of flower forms and sizes and range in color from white to deep pink and yellow. Some notable examples include 'Bridesmaid', 'California Gold', 'Harvest Gold', 'Jamaica Primrose', 'Little Rex', 'Margaret', 'Pink Lady', 'Rising Sun', 'Silver Leaf', 'Snow Man', 'Tauranga Star' and 'Weymouth Pink'. ZONES 8–11.

Argyranthemum maderense
(below right)

Although its name implies it comes from Madeira, this species is in fact endemic to the island of Lanzarote in the Canaries. It makes a weak shrub of up to 3 ft (1 m) with broad green leaves, less deeply lobed than in most other species. The large flower-heads are pale golden yellow. ZONES 9–11.

One of several horticulturally important genera now recognized in place of the once more broadly defined *Chrysanthemum*, this genus consists of 22 species of evergreen subshrubs from the Canary Islands and Madeira. They tend to be upright, rarely over 3 ft (1 m) tall, and bushy with deeply lobed or divided, bright green to blue-green leaves. From spring to autumn in cool climates, but mainly in winter–spring in warmer climates, the bushes are covered in 1–3 in (2.5–8 cm) wide daisies in white and a range of pink and yellow shades. Marguerites make good cut flowers and large numbers are sold potted by florists. In recent years there has been a renewed interest in breeding, resulting in many new cultivars.

CULTIVATION
Marguerites are very easy to cultivate in any light, well-drained soil in full sun. They grow particularly well near the sea and have naturalized in some coastal areas of the world. They should be cut back either in late winter or late summer to encourage fresh growth. Most species and cultivars tolerate light, irregular frosts only. Propagate from seed or cuttings.

Argyranthemum frutescens 'California Gold' *(above)*
A. frutescens 'Harvest Gold' *(top center)*
A. 'Rising Sun' *(top right)*
A. frutescens 'Weymouth Pink' *(center left)*

A

ARGYROCYTISUS
MOUNT ATLAS BROOM

This genus of only one species was previously included with many other brooms in the genus *Cytisus*. A large evergreen shrub or small tree from the Atlas and Rif Mountains of Morocco, it is distinctive for its dense foliage with leaves of 3 leaflets that are exceptionally large for a broom and coated in silky hairs, giving them a beautiful silvery sheen. Spikes of yellow pea-flowers terminate the branches; they are followed by flattened, hairy pods.

CULTIVATION

It prefers a sunny position and rather dry atmosphere. It is more frost tender than most European brooms and prefers a mild climate. It needs well-drained soil and is tolerant of a wide range of garden conditions. Propagate from seed or cuttings.

Argyrocytisus battandieri (below) syn. *Cytisus battandieri*

This shrub or small tree, 12 ft (3.5 m) high and wide, is mainly grown for the pineapple-shaped flowers, heavily scented with a pineapple perfume. ZONES 8–10.

ARONIA
CHOKEBERRY

A

A member of the pome-fruit group of the rose family, *Aronia* consists of only 3 deciduous shrub species from North America. All make fine garden shrubs of compact size with abundant displays of glossy red or black berries in late summer and autumn. They have oval leaves with finely toothed margins, and bear small umbels of flowers like miniature apple blossoms in spring.

CULTIVATION

Frost hardy and suited to most soils, they will grow well in part-shade but respond to full sun with more profuse fruit and brighter autumn foliage. Cut the oldest stems to the ground to encourage new growth. Propagate from seed or cuttings. The foliage is prone to disfigurement by the pear and cherry slug, the larva of a sawfly.

Aronia arbutifolia *(below right)*

RED CHOKEBERRY

Native to eastern North America, where it is a common understorey plant, this species grows to 6 ft (1.8 m) with many vertical stems forming spreading clumps. White flowers in spring are followed by bright red berries in autumn and early winter, popular with birds. Narrow, oval leaves turn bright red in autumn—this is best in **'Brilliant'** (sometimes listed as 'Brilliantissima'). ZONES 4–9.

Aronia melanocarpa *(right)*

BLACK CHOKEBERRY

Very similar in foliage and flowers to the red chokeberry *(Aronia arbutifolia)* and originating in the same region of the USA, the black chokeberry is a lower, more spreading shrub with more densely crowded stems. The leaves are less glossy and the berries, ripening a brilliantly glossy black, do not last long into autumn but drop soon after they ripen. **'Nero'** and **'Viking'** are both well-known cultivars. ZONES 5–9.

ARTEMISIA
WORMWOOD

This large genus of evergreen and deciduous perennials and shrubs from temperate regions of the northern hemisphere has many species from arid and semi-arid environments. They are grown for their decorative foliage, which is often aromatic, sometimes repellent to insects and may be coated with whitish hairs. Attractive in a flower border, the feathery foliage provides year-round interest. The small yellowish flowerheads are not showy.

CULTIVATION
Mostly quite frost hardy, they prefer an open, sunny situation with light, well-drained soil. Prune back lightly in spring to stimulate growth. Propagate from cuttings in summer or by division in spring. Transplant during winter.

Artemisia absinthium
'Lambrook Silver' *(left)*

Artemisia absinthium
COMMON WORMWOOD, ABSINTHE

Found widely in Europe and temperate Asia, common wormwood grows to 3 ft (1 m), though often rather lower, with much divided, dull gray foliage. It is a subshrub that spreads by rhizomes, the tangled, flopping stems also rooting as they spread. Inconspicuous, dull yellow flowerheads are borne in late summer. Trim after flowering to keep neat. **'Lambrook Silver'**, with its tidy habit is considered one of the better silver-leaved shrubs, and provides a restful contrast to brightly colored flowers in a herbaceous border. ZONES 4–10.

Artemisia vulgaris
'Variegata' *(top right)*

Artemisia ludoviciana
'Valerie Finnis' *(right)*

Artemisia ludoviciana
syn. *Artemisia purshiana*

WESTERN MUGWORT, WHITE SAGE

Native to western North America and Mexico, this rhizomatous species is grown for its lance-shaped, sometimes coarsely toothed leaves, which are densely white-felted beneath and gray- to white-haired above. Bell-shaped, grayish flowerheads are produced in summer. A spreading, invasive species, it reaches 4 ft (1.2 m) high and is very frost hardy. **'Valerie Finnis',** with its jagged leaf margins, together with **'Silver Queen'** are 2 of several popular cultivars. *Artemisia ludoviciana* var. *albula*, found naturally in California, has much smaller leaves. ZONES 4–10.

Artemisia 'Powis Castle' *(top left)*

This assumed hybrid between *Artemisia absinthium* and *A. arborescens* has finely dissected, silvery leaves and a gentle, 24–36 in (60–90 cm) mounding habit. Because it seldom flowers it remains more compact than other species; older plants benefit from a hard cutting back in early spring. It is useful in the garden for its distinctive foliage. In cold climates, grow indoors over winter for planting out in spring. ZONES 6–10.

Artemisia vulgaris
MUGWORT

The leaves of this well-known species are green with hardly a hint of the much sought-after silver gray and are less divided than those of other species, making it less popular with gardeners than other artemisias. **'Variegata'**, with its foliage marked with white specks, can make a useful addition to the garden in cooler areas. Mugwort was used to flavor beer before hops were used, and in ancient times was believed to have magical properties. ZONES 4–10.

A

ARTOCARPUS

Best known in the form of one of its many species, the breadfruit of Captain Bligh of the *Bounty* fame, *Artocarpus* is actually a very large tropical Asian genus of evergreen trees. It is closely related to *Ficus*, the fig genus, and in fact many of its species are hard to tell apart from figs when not in flower or fruit. The leaves, bark and twigs exude a milky sap when damaged, and the minute, greenish, female flowers are crowded onto short, fleshy spikes which after fertilization enlarge into aggregations of fleshy fruit, very large in the case of the species mentioned below.

CULTIVATION

Edible-fruited species are cultivated in the wet tropics, thriving best in deep, fertile, well-drained soil in sheltered positions. Propagation is from seed, or more commonly from root cuttings or aerial layers (marcotts), which perpetuate desirable clones.

Artocarpus altilis *(below left)*
syns *Artocarpus communis, A. incisa*
BREADFRUIT

Believed to be native to the Malay region and carried into the Pacific by colonizing Polynesians, this species has handsome foliage, with ascending branches bearing deeply incised, fresh green leaves up to 30 in (75 cm) long. Fast growing when young, it reaches 25 ft (8 m) in 10 years; old trees are not much taller but develop a rounded, bushy crown. The flower spikes are inconspicuous, the female ones developing into yellowish green globular fruit with starchy flesh that is eaten after baking or boiling. ZONE 12.

Artocarpus heterophyllus *(left)*
JACKFRUIT, JACA

This Southeast Asian species is easily confused with its close relative the chempedak *(Artocarpus integer);* both have similar gigantic, compound fruit and leathery, unlobed leaves, but the chempedak's fruit are sweeter. The jackfruit grows to 30 ft (9 m) tall with a single main trunk and dense, rounded crown of dark green leaves. The fruit may be up to 24 in (60 cm) long and weigh up to 40 lb (18 kg). Their outer surface is creamy brown with small conical protuberances, and the sticky yellow or pink flesh contains many large brown seeds which are edible, as is the sweet though malodorous flesh. ZONES 11–12.

ASCLEPIAS

A

MILKWEED

Found naturally in the Americas, this genus consists of over 100 species of perennials, subshrubs and (rarely) shrubs and includes both evergreen and deciduous plants. Most have narrow, pointed elliptical to lance-shaped leaves and all have milky white sap. The flowers are borne in stalked clusters arising from the upper leaf axils. They are small, with 5 reflexed petals below a waxy corona, a feature characteristic of the milkwood family. Elongated seed pods follow; the seeds have silky plumes and are dispersed on the breeze. Their sap is acrid and poisonous, and the butterfly larvae that feed on them are toxic to predators such as birds. A few species have become widespread weeds of warmer regions. Some African species with inflated, prickly pods are now placed in the genus *Physocarpus*.

CULTIVATION
They are easily grown in any well-drained soil in full sun. Hardiness varies considerably with the species. Some hardier North American species require a cool climate and will not survive in the dormant state where winters are too warm. Propagate from seed or semi-ripe cuttings.

Asclepias curassavica
(right & below right)

BLOOD FLOWER

This frost-tender annual or short-lived perennial evergreen subshrub is a South American native that has become something of a weed in tropical areas. It grows to around 3 ft (1 m) tall and wide and has narrow, lance-shaped leaves up to 6 in (15 cm) long. From late spring to autumn it produces umbels of bright orange-red flowers followed by spindle-shaped, 3 in (8 cm) long seed pods. ZONES 9–12.

A

ASIMINA
PAWPAW

Not to be confused with the tropical pawpaw or papaya (*Carica edulis*), this genus of some 7 or 8 species from North America is still related to a tropical fruit, but it is the custard apple (*Anona*), not the papaya. Despite its tropical origins, the genus is generally frost hardy, most species tolerating 5°F (−15°C) or lower. The flowers often appear rather dull at first, though their colors are interesting and the fruit that follows is edible and very tasty.

CULTIVATION
Most species are easily grown in any moist, well-drained soil in sun or partial shade. Prolonged drought is really the only threat to this native of river valleys and moist lowland areas. Pawpaw responds well to pruning and shaping and some can even be used for hedging, though this would undoubtedly lessen the crop of flowers and fruit.

Asimina triloba *(left & above)*

Found in central and eastern North America, this deciduous shrub or small tree can reach 30 ft (9 m) tall and is notable for both its flowers and fruit. The flowers, which open in spring, are a deep red-brown, about 2 in (5 cm) wide and pendulous. They are carried in clusters of 2–5 blooms and are followed in autumn by elongated fruits that are brown or black when ripe. The flesh of the fruit is sweet, aromatic and highly flavored. The foliage is also a feature: pointed, narrow, oval leaves are up to 10 in (25 cm) long. ZONES 5–10.

ASTARTEA

This Australian genus includes several species of needle-leaved, wiry-stemmed, evergreen heath-like shrubs. Although some are prostrate and spreading, they are generally upright bushes that in winter or spring produce small flowers in sprays along the stems, mainly at the tips. The leaves are tiny and sometimes rather sparse, though with good growing conditions astarteas can become quite densely foliaged.

CULTIVATION

A warm, well-drained, sunny position is best. Too much shade and the growth becomes lank and the flowers sparse. Occasional trimming and tip pinching will help to keep the bushes compact, but do not cut them back too severely or recovery may be slow and the branches could die back from the tips. Propagate by seed or from small, semi-ripe tip cuttings.

Astartea 'Winter Pink' *(above)*

This pink-flowered cultivar is a neat, compact bush that flowers from late winter or early spring until early summer. It grows to around 5 ft (1.5 m) tall but can be kept trimmed to 2^1/$_2$ ft (75 cm) if cut back immediately after flowering. Branches covered in sprays of tiny flowers can be cut and used in floral arrangements, where they last well. ZONES 9–11.

A

ATHEROSPERMA
BLACK SASSAFRAS, SOUTHERN SASSAFRAS

This single species genus occurs in the cool-temperate rainforests of Tasmania and southeastern mainland Australia, commonly in association with the better known *Nothofagus* (southern beeches). Aromatic, oily substances produced in the wood, bark and foliage include the compound safrole, which is also found in the original North American sassafras *(Sassafras albidum).* It is these oils with their distinctive smell that earned it the name 'sassafras'. Sassafras oil, although used in traditional folk medicine, is now regarded as dangerously poisonous.

CULTIVATION
Although rarely seen in cultivation, it is worth growing in a large collection for its symmetrical shape and scattered, small white flowers. It has been grown successfully in milder parts of the British Isles. A sheltered, humid location in deep, moist soil suits *Atherosperma moschatum* best. Propagate from seed or cuttings.

**Atherosperma
moschatum** *(left)*

This evergreen species, reaching almost 100 ft (30 m) in mountain gullies, appears conifer-like from a distance due to its fine grayish foliage and long-pointed crown. The musk-scented, narrow leaves in opposite pairs are dark green above and have a paler, furry coating beneath. Attractive white flowers are borne in spring. ZONES 8–9.

ATHROTAXIS

The island of Tasmania, Australia, with its cool-temperate rain-forests, is unusually rich in conifers, including the extremely handsome *Athrotaxis*. The genus shows some resemblance in foliage and cones to the Japanese *Cryptomeria* and American *Sequoiadendron*, but its 3 species are much slower growing and more compact in habit, though capable eventually of forming moderately large trees.

CULTIVATION

Athrotaxis species are not difficult to grow in a cool, moist climate. Do not expect them to reach tree size for at least 2 or 3 decades, but as dense, bushy saplings they are highly ornamental. Propagate from seed or cuttings.

Athrotaxis selaginoides (right)
KING BILLY PINE

The slow growth of the King Billy pine, a formerly important timber tree, is shown by the 30 or more annual growth rings per 1 in (25 mm) of diameter seen in some wood samples. It grows to 100 ft (30 m) with a trunk diameter of 8 ft (2.4 m), though half that height is more usual. Its leaves are incurved and sharply pointed, bright green on top with contrasting white-banded undersides. Small, orange-brown cones appear in spring. The soft reddish brown bark is very thick. ZONES 8–9.

ATRIPLEX
SALTBUSH

This is a genus of around 100 species of annuals, perennials, subshrubs and shrubs found throughout the temperate and sub-tropical zones, though most of the more ornamental or useful shrubby species come either from the western and central USA or from inland Australia. Most have a grayish white appearance due to a fine coating of scales or bladder-like surface cells. The leaves are variable and may be small and rounded or variously toothed and sometimes arrowhead shaped. The separate male and female flowers are usually small and insignificant; in some species the spongy fruit are a conspicuous feature. While scarcely spectacular, these plants are mainly grown for their interesting foliage and form. They are also fire resistant, can withstand varied conditions and are often useful in erosion control. Some are nutritious fodder plants, valued for their ability to thrive in saline soils.

CULTIVATION
Some species of this genus are natural coastal plants and thrive where they are exposed to salt spray that would kill lesser plants. Many others are from arid environments, and these thrive best in a dry atmosphere. They are easily grown in any soil, in full sun. Frost hardiness varies with the species, though most will tolerate moderate frosts. Propagate from seed or cuttings.

Atriplex cinerea
(left)
GRAY SALTBUSH

The gray saltbush is an attractive subshrub from sea coasts of southern Australia. It grows to 24–36 in (60–90 cm) in height and 6 ft (1.8 m) or more in spread, form-ing a loose mound. The narrowly tongue-shaped leaves are grayish and fleshy and the dull yellowish or reddish flowers are borne in short, dense, terminal spikes. ZONES 9–10.

AUCUBA
AUCUBA, SPOTTED LAUREL

This east Asian genus consists of 3 species of shrubs, valued for their tolerance of heavy shade and their large, often colorful, evergreen leaves. Clusters of large red berries appear in autumn but, with flowers of different sexes on different plants, it is only the females that fruit. The one species generally grown has given rise to many cultivars with variegated leaves in a range of patterns.

CULTIVATION
They are tough and resilient, tolerant of frost, neglect, pollution and heavy shading but responding to better treatment and stronger light with more luxuriant growth. The long-lasting but tender leaves should be protected from wind damage. Grow in any soil in full sun or part- or full shade, with filtered light for the variegated species. Propagate from seed or cuttings.

Aucuba japonica
'Variegata' *(right)*

Aucuba japonica
JAPANESE AUCUBA

Usually a shrub of 4–6 ft (1.2–1.8 m), this species will continue to spread by basal sprouting and self-layering of its weak, soft-wooded stems and, as it thickens up, the mass of stems will support one another, allowing it to reach 10 ft (3 m). The thick, soft, glossy leaves are up to 10 in (25 cm) long and very variably toothed. Sprays of small, reddish flowers in spring may be followed by drooping clusters of $^1/_2$ in (12 mm) long, red berries in early autumn. **'Variegata'** (female) has leaves densely spotted with yellow, and **'Crotonifolia'** (male) has leaves heavily splashed with yellow. ZONES 7–10.

A

AURINIA

This is a genus of 7 species of biennials and evergreen, subshrubby perennials, formerly included in *Alyssum*, found from central and southern Europe to the Ukraine and Turkey. They are mainly small, spreading, mound-forming plants. The leaves are initially in basal rosettes, mostly fairly narrow. They bear elongated sprays of tiny yellow or white flowers in spring and early summer.

CULTIVATION

Plant in light, gritty, well-drained soil in full sun. They are ideal for rockeries, rock crevices or dry-stone walls. Most species are very frost hardy and are propagated from seed or small tip cuttings; they will self-sow in suitable locations.

Aurinia saxatilis 'Citrina' *(left)*

Aurinia saxatilis
syn. *Alyssum saxatile*
BASKET OF GOLD, YELLOW ALYSSUM

This native to central and southeastern Europe is the only commonly grown species. It has hairy, gray-green leaves, forms rather loose mounds to 10 in (25 cm) high, and is smothered in bright yellow flowers in spring and early summer. It is very popular as a rockery or wall plant. There are a number of cultivars, including **'Argentea'** with very silvery leaves; **'Citrina'** with lemon yellow flowers; **'Gold Dust'**, up to 12 in (30 cm) mounds with deep golden yellow flowers; **'Sulphurea'** with glowing yellow flowers; and **'Tom Thumb'**, a 4 in (10 cm) high dwarf with small leaves. ZONES 4–9.

AUSTROCEDRUS
CHILEAN CEDAR

A

The only member of this temperate South American genus is a conifer of the *Thuja* type, with flattened sprays of branchlets that are themselves strongly flattened and with small, narrow cones consisting of weak, woody scales. In *Austrocedrus* the branchlets are quite fine and fern-like, attractively marked with bluish bands on the undersides. It is valued as a timber tree in its native Chile, where its fragrant, durable, easily worked, reddish wood is in demand for fine cabinet work.

CULTIVATION
It is a fairly frost-hardy conifer, able to survive in exposed positions but appreciating some shelter and deep, moist soil. Propagate from seed or cuttings.

Austrocedrus chilensis (right)

Native to the Andean slopes of Chile and Argentina at altitudes of 3,000–6,000 ft (900–1,800 m), this moderately fast-growing species can reach 80 ft (24 m). Young trees have a densely columnar habit but with age the crown lifts higher above a bare trunk and narrow cone of branches. The gray bark is finely scaled; some trees have more bluish foliage than others. ZONES 7–9.

A

AVERRHOA

These tropical fruit trees are close relatives of the humble *Oxalis* or wood sorrels, some species of which are detested weeds. Common to both are the flower structure of 5 overlapping pink or red petals and the 5-angled fruit, which in miniature in *Oxalis* split open to scatter tiny seeds rather than remaining fleshy as in *Averrhoa*. The genus consists of only 2 species, from Southeast Asia. These are small trees with densely twiggy crowns and short pinnate leaves, some of which yellow and drop in the dry season. The slightly fragrant flowers are borne in short lateral clusters on the old wood and the slow-ripening fruit hang in clusters from the branches.

CULTIVATION
The trees are easily grown in full sun in tropical and warmer subtropical, humid climates, making fine small shade trees. Propagation is from seed or more commonly by grafts or air-layers (marcotts) which preserve desirable clonal characteristics.

Averrhoa carambola (left)

CARAMBOLA, STAR FRUIT, FIVE-CORNER

In cultivation this upright species grows to about 20 ft (6 m) high. The leaflets of the compound leaves have the curious habit of folding together after being touched or at night. It flowers and fruits through much of the year, but with major flushes of flower in the middle of both the wet and dry seasons. The large, ornamental fruit ripen through pale yellow, when their flavor is pleasantly acid, to deep golden orange, when they become sweet and deliciously tangy, reminiscent of passionfruit. ZONES 11–12.

AVICENNIA

This mangrove genus of 6 species occurs on seashores and in estuaries throughout the tropics and elsewhere in the southern hemisphere, ranging as far south as New Zealand's North Island and the eastern shores of South Africa. They are small to medium-sized, spreading trees with smallish, glossy, thick-textured leaves in opposite pairs. The flowers are small in stalked clusters near the branch tips and the dry fruit each contain a single large seed that actually germinates on the tree, producing a thick taproot. After falling, the seeds may be carried away on receding tides, and if washed up elsewhere in the intertidal zone can rapidly take root. Another feature is the upward-growing aerial roots, stiff prongs that emerge from the mud to take in oxygen.

CULTIVATION
Mangroves are rarely if ever cultivated.

Avicennia marina (above & left)
GRAY MANGROVE

This species occurs in Asia, Africa and Australasia, with at least 3 regional sub-species. In temperate regions it forms pure stands in estuaries, but in the tropics is mixed with unrelated mangroves. The leaves are whitish underneath and the small, yellow-orange flowers appear in late summer (late dry to early wet season in the tropics). The hard wood is so dense that it sinks in water. ZONES 10–12.

A

AZADIRACHTA

Only 2 species belong to this genus of trees from India and South-east Asia. The genus is closely related to *Melia:* although similar in growth habit, *Azadirachta* is easily distinguished by its leaves being pinnate, not bipinnate as in *Melia*, with more regular ranks of leaflets which are curved in a sickle-like fashion. The leaves are deciduous in severe dry seasons but are evergreen in better-watered situations. Sprays of small white flowers at the branch tips are followed by profuse, ovoid yellow fruits. Only one species, *Azadirachta indica*, is cultivated. Although planted as a shade tree and for streets and parks, it is more commonly grown in plantations for use as a natural, safe and efficacious insecticide.

CULTIVATION

These plants have shallow roots, and need mulching or frequent watering in drier regions. They are susceptible to stem borers and termites. Propagate from seed, cuttings or suckers.

Azadirachta indica
(below left)
NEEM TREE, NIM

In its natural habitat the neem tree grows in dry coastal forests on deep sandy soils. In the wild it can reach 50 ft (15 m), but planted specimens are usually under 30 ft (10m) tall with a spreading or rounded crown. It flowers in the late dry season; the fruits appear shortly afterwards. In its native India, Burma and Sri Lanka, *Azadirachta indica* has long been renowned for its medicinal and insecticidal uses. Its potential value is being increasingly recognized in other countries, so that it is now one of the more commonly planted trees in tropical regions. Its foliage is valued for both fodder and green manure. The neem tree is also a useful source of firewood and yields a high quality timber.
ZONES 11–12.

AZARA

A

The 15 or so species of this temperate South American genus of shrubs and small trees include trees from Chilean subantarctic rainforests to drier slopes of the lower Andes. They have neat, glossy, evergreen foliage and massed, small, yellow flowers. A characteristic feature is the way each branch node has one small and one larger leaf. While they are quite attractive plants, azaras develop a certain 'legginess' with age.

CULTIVATION

Azaras prefer cool but mild and humid climates and grow best in sheltered sites in moist soil. In colder areas, they can be trained against walls to protect them from severe frosts. Propagate from cuttings in summer.

Azara lanceolata
(below far left)

This species from southern Chile is graceful in growth habit and foliage, making a slender shrub or small tree to 20 ft (6 m) with weak, drooping branches. The narrow, toothed, glossy dark green leaves, each accompanied by a smaller leaf make a distinctive pattern. In spring it produces short clusters of small, golden yellow flowers, consisting mainly of stamens, from the leaf axils. **ZONES 8–9.**

Azara serrata *(left)*

This small tree grows to 30 ft (9 m) in the wild, but in cultivation is usually a shrub of 10–15 ft (3–4.5 m), often with a twiggy habit and rather sparse foliage. The thick, glossy leaves have a broad, blunt apex and coarse teeth. Stalked clusters of fragrant, deep golden flowers appear in late spring or early summer. In cool climates it is easily grown in milder coastal areas. **ZONES 8–10.**

Azara microphylla
(left)

This fairly erect, small tree may reach 20 ft (6 m) in the garden, more in the wild in its native Chile and western Argentina. A vigorous grower with fine foliage, in late winter it produces many clusters of tiny, fragrant flowers half-hidden under the leaf sprays. The most adaptable member of the genus, but sometimes damaged by frost in southern England, **'Variegata'** has attractive cream variegations. **ZONES 7–9.**

B

BACCHARIS

This genus of approximately 350 species of perennials and shrubs in the *Compositae* (daisy) family is native to the Americas. Most are evergreen, densely foliaged, wiry-stemmed plants, many from drier regions or locations with saline soil or exposed to salt spray. The leaves, arranged alternately on the branches, are mostly tough and leathery, very variable in shape but usually toothed or lobed and often slightly resinous and sticky. The small, usually white or grayish flowerheads, borne in panicles at the ends of branches, lack the ray-like flowers of typical daisies. Most species have no ornamental value but some salt-resistant species are ideal plants for coastal gardens.

CULTIVATION
Any sunny location with reasonable soil will do. Some will toler- ate moderate to severe frosts but most are frost tender. Propagate from small tip cuttings or seed.

Baccharis pilularis
'Twin Peaks' *(left)*

Baccharis pilularis
DWARF COYOTE BUSH

A native of California and Oregon, this evergreen shrub grows to a height of 24–36 in (60–90 cm). It has small, oval, bright green leaves on spreading branches and tiny white flowers. It is adaptable to most soils in any sunny position and is resistant to frost and to very dry conditions. **'Twin Peaks'** is a selected compact form, under 30 in (75 cm) high and 10 ft (3 m) wide. It is valued as a hardy cover on dry slopes and for its fire-retardant qualities. ZONES 7–10.

BANKSIA

Named after the renowned English botanist Sir Joseph Banks, who discovered this genus at Botany Bay in 1770, *Banksia* consists of about 75 species of shrubs and small trees found widely in Australia, especially in the southwest. Habit and foliage vary, but all species have striking, dense, fuzzy spikes or heads of tightly packed, small flowers, followed by woody fruits that protrude from among the dead flowers. The leaves are generally long and narrow, often with toothed edges, and contain much woody tissue, so they remain stiff and springy even when dead. Banksias vary in their tolerance of garden conditions, but some are easily grown; the most decorative ones are now grown in plantations for the cut flower market. Some dwarf and prostrate ground cover forms are becoming popular as rock-garden plants. The flowers of all species are rich in nectar and attract birds.

CULTIVATION
Most species prefer well-drained, sandy soil with low levels of major nutrients, especially phosphates. They do best in full sun, and some are moderately frost hardy. Regular, light tip pruning maintains shape and foliage density. Propagate from seed, which is best extracted from the 'cones' with the aid of fire or a hot oven.

Banksia coccinea (right)
SCARLET BANKSIA

One of the most beautiful species and prized by the cut flower industry, the scarlet banksia from the far south of Western Australia has short, wide, erect cylinders of deep scarlet to orange flowers that open from downy gray buds from winter through to early summer. The very broad, stiff leaves are gray on the undersides. It has a rather stiff, narrow habit, growing usually to 6–12 ft (1.8–3.5 m) in height. Difficult to grow in gardens, it does not always flower readily and often succumbs to root-rot fungi in climates with wet summers. ZONES 9–10.

Banksia ericifolia *(right)*

HEATH BANKSIA

From the Australian temperate east coast and adjacent ranges, this is the smallest-leafed banksia and also one of the most vigorous growers. It is a freely branching shrub ranging in height from 6–12 ft (1.8–3.5 m) with glossy deep green foliage. It bears upright, bottlebrush-like spikes up to 10 in (25 cm) long in autumn and winter; their color varies from a washed-out orange to deep copper red. The heath banksia is one of the most easily cultivated banksias, surviving moderate frosts, salt spray on the coast, and adapting to richer soils. **'Port Wine'** has dull rose pink spikes, and the striking **'Burgundy'** has flowers of a deeper red than most. ZONES 8–11.

Banksia 'Giant Candles' *(left & far left)*

A hybrid between *Banksia ericifolia* and *B. spinulosa*, 'Giant Candles' grows to about 12 ft (3.5 m). It is a dense shrub with abundant bronze-yellow flower spikes, which may be as long as 15 in (38 cm), in autumn and winter. Tough and vigorous like its parents, it is a bushier shrub than either. ZONES 9–11.

Banksia integrifolia *(right)*

COAST BANKSIA

Of wide north–south distribution on the coast of eastern Australia, this salt-tolerant species forms at maturity a gnarled tree of up to 50 ft (15 m), with a trunk 18 in (45 cm) in diameter. Lime green flowers fading to dull yellow form cylindrical spikes about 4 in (10 cm) long from late summer to early winter. The distinctive silver-backed leaves, dull green above, are toothed only on young plants. In cultivation, this species makes remarkably rapid growth, especially in deep sandy soil. ZONES 9–11.

Banksia marginata *(right)*

SILVER BANKSIA

The most frost hardy of the banksias, this southeastern
Australian species varies in growth form depending on its
habitat. In lower regions with very poor soil it is commonly a dense, spreading shrub to about 6 ft (1.8 m),
while in mountain forests it is an upright, small tree as
much as 40 ft (12 m) high. The smallish dark green leaves
are toothed at the apex and silvery white beneath. Small
yellow-cream flower spikes appear from late summer to
early winter. Compact forms make attractive shrubs,
while taller forms are useful for screens and windbreaks.
It is also a suitable coastal plant as it is resistant to salt
damage. ZONES 8–11.

Banksia prionotes *(right)*

ACORN BANKSIA

From the dry temperate west coast of Australia, this fairly
fast-growing small tree has an open habit with long,
narrow, toothed leaves. It can grow to 20 ft (6 m) or
more, eventually forming a domed crown. Spectacular
orange-yellow flower spikes, up to 6 in (15 cm) long,
open from felty pure white buds in autumn and winter.
Producing outstanding cut flowers, it thrives in sandy, alkaline soil in areas with dry summers but does poorly
where summers are wet. ZONES 10–11.

Banksia serrata *(left)*

OLD MAN BANKSIA, SAW BANKSIA

This species is distinguished by its gnarled appearance; it has a short crooked trunk, thick, wrinkled,
fire-resistant bark, and leathery, saw-toothed leaves.
Large, greenish cream flower spikes appear from
summer through autumn. The common name old
man banksia derives from its bristly gray fruiting
spikes, which have protruding fruit like small noses
or chins. In its native southeastern Australia it grows
on coastal dunes as well as sandstone ranges, reaching
as much as 40 ft (12 m) in height; usually much
smaller in cultivation, it is long lived and moderately
frost hardy. ZONES 9–11.

B

BARLERIA

This is a large genus of 250 or more species of evergreen shrubs and subshrubs from the tropics of Asia, the Americas and Africa. The plants have simple leaves arranged in opposite pairs on the stems. The flowers are generally tubular and 2-lipped, emerging from between overlapping bracts on short spikes produced at the end of the branches or in the upper leaf axils. These soft-stemmed, quick-growing plants can be used in tropical and sub-tropical gardens for quick effect and as bedding plants; they can be grown in a conservatory in cooler climates.

CULTIVATION
Barlerias are nearly all frost tender. In cooler climates they may be grown as indoor plants, but require strong light. Outdoors in warm climates, they look attractive when grouped together in a shrub border. Tip prune to encourage bushiness. The plants require full sun and fertile, moist but well-drained soil. They are easily propagated from cuttings in summer.

Barleria cristata (above)
PHILIPPINE VIOLET

Despite its common name, this well-known tropical shrub is not native to the Philippines but to eastern India and Burma. It grows to around 3 ft (1 m) high and wide and is densely branched from ground level. For much of the year it produces small clusters of 2-lipped flowers from among bristly edged bracts in the upper leaf axils. Flowers vary from violet-blue to mauve, pink or white. It prefers a sheltered, humid position in part-shade. **ZONES 10–12.**

Bauera rubioides
(below)

RIVER ROSE

Occurring in the higher rainfall areas of south-eastern Australia, including Tasmania, this attractive species grows in moist, shady places, mostly on the banks of small streams. It grows to 3 ft (1 m) high with usually a greater spread; in some forms it is almost prostrate. The tiny, dark green leaves become reddish in winter, while the bowl-shaped, carmine pink to white flowers appear from late winter to mid-summer. **ZONES 8–10.**

BAUERA

Occurring naturally in eastern Australia and much admired as wildflowers, the 4 species of this genus of evergreen shrubs are grown in gardens mainly for their star-shaped, deep pink to white flowers. The genus was named by Sir Joseph Banks in honor of the botanical artists Ferdinand and Franz Bauer. The branches are thin and wiry, often scrambling among other shrubs. The small leaves appear as whorls of 6 at each node, though technically they are opposite pairs of compound leaves each with 3 leaflets. The flowers are borne from the leaf axils on very fine stalks.

CULTIVATION

Coming from mild, moist climates, they tolerate only light frosts and grow best in moist sandy or peaty soil in a sunny or part-shaded position. They appreciate soil kept cool by the shade of taller plants. Propagation is from cuttings in late summer. Light pruning after flowering produces a bushier plant and encourages abundant flowers.

Bauera sessiliflora *(right)*

GRAMPIANS BAUERA

This *Bauera* species from western Victoria is the most colorful in flower. In late spring and early summer, its branches are strung with tight clusters of bright rose-magenta flowers, ½ in (12 mm) in diameter. When supported by other shrubs it often scrambles to a height of 6 ft (1.8 m) or more, but can be kept trimmed if a neat bush is desired. Paler pink and white forms are also known. **ZONES 9–10.**

B

BAUHINIA

This is a variable genus of legumes, consisting of some 250 species of evergreen and dry-season-deciduous trees, shrubs and climbers, occurring in most tropical and subtropical regions of the world. Some botanists take a narrower view of the genus, splitting off about two-thirds of the species into other genera. All have characteristic 2-lobed leaves, but they are grown for their beautiful perfumed flowers whose similarity to orchids or butterflies is reflected in the common names of several species. The flattened brown seed pods that follow the blooms often persist on the branches for months. One of the more colorful species is *Bauhinia galpinii* (pride-of-de-Kaap, red bauhinia), a sprawling shrub with flowers ranging from rich apricot to brick red.

CULTIVATION

Bauhinias do best in warm climates and need protection from frost and cold winds. Full sun and fertile, light, well-drained soil suit them best. Pruning is not usually necessary, but vigorous growth may be thinned out after flowering. Propagate from seed in spring.

Bauhinia ×
blakeana *(below left)*
HONG KONG ORCHID TREE

Bauhinia × *blakeana* is a presumed hybrid between *B. variegata* and the rather similar *B. purpurea*. It was first found in China in 1908, and was later adopted as Hong Kong's floral emblem. It resembles the more widely grown *B. variegata* but makes a taller, more densely foliaged, evergreen tree with broader leaves. The slightly fragrant flowers, up to 6 in (15 cm) across on healthy specimens, are a purplish red with darker streaks on the inner petals, and are borne in late autumn and winter in shorter sprays than on *B. variegata*. It sets few seed pods. **ZONES 10–12.**

B

Bauhinia monandra *(right)*

This tropical species from the
West Indies and northern South
America makes a multi-
stemmed shrub or small tree
to 20 ft (6 m) high. It has
spreading branches and coarse
foliage, with large pale green
leaves. From the end of the dry
season to well into the wet it
produces a succession of flowers
at the branch ends; the large
petals open cream but age to
flesh pink with a dramatic red
splash on the upper petal. The
flowers are unusual in having
only one stamen. **ZONES 11–12.**

Bauhinia variegata *(right)*

ORCHID TREE, MOUNTAIN EBONY

This lovely small tree, native to
India, bears abundant large,
fragrant flowers in spring and
intermittently in summer. These
vary from near white to rose
pink, but always have a deeper
shade on the broader upper
petal. It grows 15–25 ft
(4.5–8 m) tall, larger in the
tropics, with a short trunk and
spreading branches. It is marginally frost hardy. In moist
tropical climates it is semi-
evergreen, but in cooler or drier
locations it is almost deciduous,
flowering on leafless branches.
After flowering the branches
usually become laden with
masses of large, flat seed pods,
which some gardeners find unsightly. **'Candida'** (syn. 'Alba'),
commonly known as white
mountain ebony, has fragrant
white flowers with lemon-green
markings. **ZONES 9–12.**

BERBERIS
BARBERRY

B

This is a large genus of well over 400 species of hardy evergreen and deciduous shrubs. They mostly branch below the ground into densely massed canes with weak to quite fierce spines where the leaves join the stems. The small to medium sized leaves are generally rather leathery and often have prickly marginal teeth. Clusters of small yellow, cream, orange or reddish flowers are followed by small fleshy fruits. Most species come from temperate East Asia, a few from Europe and several from Andean South America. North American species once placed in *Berberis* are now referred to *Mahonia*.

CULTIVATION
Barberries are easy to grow and thrive in most soil types. They withstand hard pruning and are useful for hedges. Full sun suits them best. Propagate from seed or cuttings. In some countries there are restrictions on growing barberries because some species harbor the overwintering phase of the wheat rust fungus.

Berberis julianae
trained as a hedge
(below)

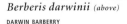
Berberis darwinii *(above)*
DARWIN BARBERRY

The showiest of several evergreen species from Chile and Argentina, all with small leaves and neat clusters of deep yellow to orange flowers, *Berberis darwinii* has dark green, glossy leaves with holly-like toothing and dense short sprays of bright golden yellow flowers in late winter and spring. These are followed by bluish berries. It grows 6 ft (1.8 m) or more high and wide with an irregular, open branching habit; branches are less spiny than most other species. ZONES 7–10.

Berberis julianae

This densely foliaged evergreen shrub from western China can grow to as much as 12 ft (3.5 m) tall and has strong, three-pronged, 1½ in (4 cm) long spines. Its large leaves, up to 4 in (10 cm) long, are dark green and finely serrated. In early summer it produces crowded clusters of ½ in (12 mm) wide yellow flowers that by autumn develop into small black berries with a bluish bloom. ZONES 5–10.

Berberis × stenophylla
(right)

This evergreen hybrid, a cross
between *Berberis darwinii* and a
related South American species
B. empetrifolia, has densely
crowded, woody stems and
arching branches. Growing to
8 ft (2.4 m) high and 10 ft (3 m)
wide, it has narrow, deep green
leaves, bluish beneath. A profusion of golden-yellow flowers
appear in spring, followed by
blue-purple berries. It makes a
good specimen shrub or can be
grown as a hedge. **'Corallina
Compacta'** is a dwarf clone only
12 in (30 cm) or so tall, with
yellowish leaves and coral fruit;
and **'Crawley Gem'** is tall and
free-flowering. ZONES 6–9.

Berberis × ottawensis 'Superba'
(right)

Berberis × ottawensis

Bred in Ottawa early this
century, this hybrid between
Berberis thunbergii and *B. vulgaris*, is best known in the form
of the clone **'Superba'** (syn.
'Purpurea'), which is similar
to and often confused with
B. thunbergii **'Atropurpurea'**
but is taller, around 6 ft (1.8 m),
and more vigorous, with new
growth bronze red rather than
dark purplish. Its red berries
appear in autumn. It is a popular and very hardy, deciduous
shrub with densely massed
stems. It is useful for hedging or
for contrast among green-leafed
shrubs. It is also prized by
flower arrangers. ZONES 3–10.

Berberis × stenophylla
'Corallina Compacta' *(right)*

Berberis thunbergii

THUNBERG BARBERRY, JAPANESE
BARBERRY

This species and its
cultivars are the most
widely planted
barberries. Native to
Japan, it is a low-
growing deciduous
shrub (almost evergreen
in warmer climates)
only 5 ft (1.5 m) in
height, with densely
massed stems and
small, neatly rounded
leaves. Its spines are
not particularly fierce.
The small, not very
decorative, bell-shaped
flowers that appear in
mid-spring are green-
ish yellow with dull
red stripes.
'Atropurpurea' has
deep purplish brown
foliage, turning
a metallic bronze
black in late autumn.
'Atropurpurea Nana'
(syns 'Crimson Pygmy',
'Little Favorite') is a
neat, bun-shaped
plant only 12–18 in
(30–45 cm) high, with
similar colored leaves
plus green tints.
'Keller's Surprise' is
compact and narrow,

Berberis thunbergii
'Atropurpurea Nana'
(above)

Berberis thunbergii
'Atropurpurea' *(right)*

with green or bronze
leaves splashed with
pink. **'Rose Glow'** has
rich purple leaves,
marked with pink, and
with green margins.
'Red Pillar' is an improved form of the
earlier cultivar **'Erecta'**

and has purple-red
foliage and a very
upright growth habit
to around 4–5 ft
(1.2–1.5 m) tall,
'Bagatelle' is compact
with purplish red foli-
age; **'Kobold'** is free-
fruiting. ZONES 4–10.

Berberis thunbergii
'Rose Glow' *(above)*

Berberis verruculosa *(above & above right)*
WARTY BARBERRY

This slow-growing, evergreen shrub from western China is normally about 5 ft (1.5 m) high with masses of strongly arching stems, their bark covered in small warty brown protuberances. The small, glossy leaves are crowded along the stems. Yellow flowers appear in late spring scattered singly among the leaves, followed by cylindrical purple-black berries with a blue bloom. ZONES 5–9.

Berberis wilsoniae *(above)*
WILSON BARBERRY

Deciduous, or almost evergreen in warmer climates, this Chinese species has small, narrow, toothless leaves with rounded tips and a densely bushy habit. It grows to 5 ft (1.5 m) but spreads into a broad mass of foliage, touching the ground. Rather inconspicuous yellow flowers from late spring to early summer are followed in autumn by abundant pink fruit which persist into winter; the fruits turn deeper red as the foliage takes on tints of yellow, orange and red. This highly ornamental species requires ample space. ZONES 5–10.

BERZELIA

This southern African genus of evergreen shrubs includes some 12 species, of which only one, *Berzelia lanuginosa*, is at all commonly grown. They are mostly upright bushes with fine branches clothed in quite soft needle-like leaves. The individual flowers are tiny but are borne in conspicuous button-shaped heads at the branch tips. *Berzelia* flowers last well when cut.

CULTIVATION

Plant in a warm sunny position in well-drained soil. A gritty or sandy soil with added humus is preferable to one that is clay based. Although berzelias can become rather open in habit, it is best not to trim them too heavily. A light trim after flowering or just cutting a few flowering stems for indoor decoration is enough. Propagate from seed or semi-ripe cuttings taken in autumn.

Berzelia lanuginosa *(above)*

This South African shrub can grow to over 6 ft (1.8 m) tall, but with light trimming it becomes a neat, densely foliaged 5 ft (1.5 m) bush. It has a strongly upright habit, rather like a young pine tree, with stems that are woody and brown when mature, wiry and reddish when young. Its fine needle-like leaves are only ¼ in (6 mm) long and are soft to the touch. Long-lasting white flower heads appear throughout the year, but are most numerous in spring. ZONES 9–11.

BETULA

BIRCH

Betula albosinensis
(below)

CHINESE RED BIRCH

The most beautiful feature of this western Chinese birch is its pale, coppery orange-red bark. A thin bloom of white powder coats the new bark, which is revealed as large, loose plates of the shiny older bark layer peel-off. It forms a medium-sized tree of 30–40 ft (9–12 m), often branching low, with jaggedly toothed leaves, up to 3 in (8 cm) long. A sheltered, sunny spot with moist soil suits it best. **ZONES 6–9.**

These deciduous trees extend to the far northern regions of the globe as well as growing on the lower-latitude mountains of the northern hemisphere. Birches are among the most admired of all trees as landscape subjects despite having fairly inconspicuous flowers and fruits. Their appeal lies in their sparkling white to pinkish brown trunks, combined with vivid green spring foliage and a delicate tracery of winter twigs. The short, broad, serrated leaves mostly turn gold in autumn before dropping. Their fast early growth, yet fairly modest final height make them ideal for use in gardens or streets. In the wild, birches often grow in dense stands rather than scattered among other trees.

CULTIVATION

To grow birches successfully, a climate cool enough for at least the occasional winter snowfall is needed. Birches are shallow-rooted and need water during dry periods. They grow best in full sun or dappled shade in deep, well-drained soil, but some adapt to poorer, shallower, even boggy soil. Propagation is normally from the small winged seeds, produced in vast numbers from the cylindrical female catkins.

Betula nana (above)

DWARF BIRCH

This birch is abundant over large areas above the Arctic Circle. A low shrub only 2–4 ft (0.6–1.2 m) high, it forms extensive thickets on the tundra, in bogs or on low hills. Further south it is restricted to high, bleak regions. The leaves are much smaller than in other birches and rather thick textured. It can make an interesting garden shrub, especially for damp, boggy areas, but will not thrive in mild climates. **ZONES 1–7.**

B

Betula nigra *(left)*

RIVER BIRCH

Widespread in warmer parts of eastern USA, this species' natural habitat is riverbanks. When mature it becomes broad crowned, forking 10–20 ft (3–6 m) above ground into several arching limbs. Older trunks have dark, furrowed bark at the base, but in young trees the bark is smooth and whitish. The luxuriant leaves are triangular, with irregularly toothed edges. Though most at home beside water, the river birch can reach 30 ft (9 m) in well-drained soil. **'Heritage'** has striking smooth bark in cream, salmon pink or pale brown, which peels off in large curling plates. ZONES 4–9.

Betula papyrifera
(bottom)

PAPER BIRCH, CANOE BIRCH

Famed for its tough papery bark, once used by Native Americans for their light but strong canoes, the paper birch is one of the most wide-ranging North American species and is extremely cold hardy. It reaches 60 ft (18 m) in cultivation, and has a sparse crown. Its chief ornamental value is in the bark, which is white or cream and peels off in thin, curling layers, exposing new bark of a pale orange-brown. **Betula papyrifera** var. **kenaica** is a smaller-growing tree from southern Alaska. It is up to 40 ft (12 m) with slightly smaller leaves and fissured bark at the base of older trees. ZONES 2–9.

Betula papyrifera var.
kenaica (above)

Betula pendula *(below)*

syns *Betula alba, B. verrucosa*

SILVER BIRCH, WHITE BIRCH

The silver birch is the most common birch in northern Europe and also one of the most elegant species. It has smooth gray-white bark and fine arching branchlets bearing small shimmering leaves. It is the most widely cultivated birch, ideal as a windbreak and generally trouble free in terms of pests and diseases. It reaches around 30–50 ft (9–15 m) in temperate climates but can reach 70–80 ft (21–24 m). Many cultivars have been named, including **'Purpurea'** with rich, dark purple leaves, **'Laciniata'** (commonly misidentified as 'Dalecarlica') with deeply incised leaves and weeping branches; **'Tristis'** with an erect trunk but weeping branchlets; and **'Youngii'** with growth like a weeping willow and no leading shoot, which requires grafting on a standard. ZONES 2–9.

B

Betula pendula 'Tristis' *(above)*

Betula pendula 'Youngii' *(right)*

B

Betula platyphylla *(right)*
JAPANESE WHITE BIRCH

Occurring widely through western and northern China, Japan, Korea, Mongolia and eastern Siberia, this species has several geographical varieties—the one common in the West is *Betula platyphylla* var. *japonica* (syn. *B. japonica*) from Japan and Siberia. In leaves and fruit this birch is similar to the silver birch, but it has dazzling pure white bark. A vigorous grower, it is a shapely tree of 40 ft (12 m) or more. **'Whitespire'** is a cultivar of very upright growth with clean white bark. ZONES 4–9.

Betula pubescens *(right)*
DOWNY BIRCH

Similar to the silver birch in geographic range, habitat and stature, this birch is less ornamental, usually with a more brownish cream bark (sometimes more whitish) and less pendulous branchlets. Its distinctive feature is the fine down on young twigs and its tolerance of more poorly drained soil. *Betula pubescens* subsp. *carpatica* is smaller with a more densely branched crown. ZONES 2–9.

Betula utilis
(right & above right)
HIMALAYAN BIRCH

From the middle altitudes of the Himalayas, this tree up to 60 ft (18 m) has pale, smooth, peeling bark and a broadly domed crown. The leaves, dark green with paler undersides and irregularly toothed, are up to 3 in (8 cm) long. Most widely grown is *Betula utilis* var. *jacquemontii* with dazzling white or cream bark that peels

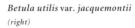

Betula utilis var. *jacquemontii* *(right)*

in horizontal bands. Several clones of this variety with outstanding bark qualities have been named as cultivars. There are also forms with darker orange-brown bark. *B. u.* var.

occidentalis normally has duller grayish white bark. **'Jermyns'** is a cultivar selected for the whiteness of its bark, uninterrupted by any darker markings or bands. ZONES 7–9.

BIXA
ANNATTO, LIPSTICK TREE

The one species in this tropical American genus is cultivated in warmer regions around the world as an ornamental and for the fat-soluble orange dye yielded by its abundant seeds. The dye (annatto) is used to color foodstuffs and fabrics. South American Indians used it as body paint. The plant is very distinctive with large heart-shaped, bronze-tinged leaves, erect clusters of small, pink, rose-like flowers and large almond-shaped fruit capsules covered in dense red bristles. It is illegal in some parts of the world.

CULTIVATION
This plant does well in warm, frost-free climates. In warm-temperate regions grow in a protected position. It may be trained into a small tree or kept as a bushy shrub. Propagation is best from cuttings.

Bixa orellana *(above & right)*

This colorful tree can sometimes reach 30 ft (9 m) but it is more commonly a spreading shrub of about 10 ft (3 m). The pink and white flowers, borne throughout summer, overlap with the clusters of bristly red fruit that persist on the branches long after they have released their seeds. **ZONES 10–12.**

B

BORONIA

Nearly all the 100 or so species of this genus of small- to medium-sized, compact evergreen shrubs are native to Australia, with 4 found in New Caledonia. They are noted for their aromatic foliage and for their attractive, 4-petalled flowers, which are mostly pink though a few plants have white, cream, brown or red. The genus is named in honor of the eighteenth-century Italian botanist, Francesco Borone. Many of the species flower prolifically in the wild but do not adapt well to garden cultivation and are often short lived.

CULTIVATION
These shrubs do best in sheltered positions in sun or part-shade in moist, well-drained acid soil. Many species will tolerate very light frosts. Tip prune after flowering to maintain shape. Propagate from semi-hardened tip cuttings.

Boronia 'Carousel'
(left)

This hybrid boronia grows to around 5 ft (1.5 m) tall and has an upright, open growth habit. Blooming over a long season from early spring, its pink flowers are pleasantly scented and redden as they age. A light trimming after flowering will keep the plant compact and bushy. ZONES 9–11.

Boronia heterophylla *(left)*
RED BORONIA, KALGAN BORONIA

This erect, compact shrub grows to 5 ft (1.5 m) tall and comes from the far south of Western Australia. Its dark green leaves are simple or occasionally pinnate. Masses of slightly aromatic rose-red, bell-shaped flowers are borne in late winter and early spring, and the petals persist on the developing fruit. A popular commercial cut flower in Australia, it prefers a cooler climate than some other boronias. Soil with added organic matter will ensure adequate moisture and a cool root run. ZONES 9–10.

Boronia megastigma
BROWN BORONIA

The sweet, heady perfume of this species' flowers is its main attraction, and their fragrance has been distilled for perfumery. The hanging, cup-shaped flowers, borne in late winter and spring, are brownish purple to yellow-green outside and yellow-green inside. Native to the far south of Western Australia, it grows to about 3 ft (1 m) and tolerates light frost; it is often difficult to grow and short lived. A number of varieties have been selected with different flower coloration, but they often lack the fragrance of the original species. **'Lutea'** has yellow flowers and yellow-green leaves; **'Harlequin'** is a brownish pink-and-white candy-striped variety. ZONES 9–10.

Boronia megastigma
'Harlequin' *(above right)*

Boronia molloyae *(right)*
syn. *Boronia elatior*
TALL BORONIA

Named after Georgiana Molloy, one of the few female plant collectors in nineteenth-century Australia, this species from the moist forests of southwestern Australia grows to 5 ft (1.5 m) tall, with very aromatic, finely divided foliage. The bell-like scarlet blooms never fully open and hang singly from the axils of the leaflets. They make excellent cut flowers, as the petals do not fade or fall easily. ZONES 9–11.

Boronia pinnata *(right)*
FEATHER-LEAFED BORONIA

One of the showiest boronias, this open, sometimes broadly spreading shrub from coastal New South Wales, Australia grows to 5 ft (1.5 m). It has feathery, fern-like, strongly scented dark green leaves with very narrow, somewhat irregular leaflets. Fragrant light pink or white flowers are borne abundantly in loose sprays in spring. **'Spring White'** has clear white flowers. ZONES 9–11.

B

BOUVARDIA

A genus of 30 or so species of soft-wooded evergreen shrubs and subshrubs, these frost-tender plants are found in Mexico, Central America and far southern USA. They are popular with florists and grown for their attractive, long-tubed, often fragrant flowers in a range of colors from white to red. The flowers are held in loose to dense clusters at the end of the stems; the soft, smallish leaves are in opposite pairs on the stems or in whorls of 3 or more.

CULTIVATION

These shrubs require a warm, sheltered position in part-shade, though in humid climates some can tolerate full sun. In cool climates they should be grown in a greenhouse or conservatory. The soil needs to be fertile and well drained. Water well and feed regularly during the growing period. Cut back stems by half after flowering to prevent plants becoming straggly. Propagate from cuttings. They are susceptible to attack by sap-sucking insects, such as white fly and mealybugs.

Bouvardia longiflora (above)
syn. *Bouvardia humboldtii*
SCENTED BOUVARDIA

A favorite with florists, this tender, weak-stemmed evergreen shrub grows to a height and spread of 3 ft (1 m) or more. Very brittle, it is easily damaged by strong winds. The strongly perfumed, snow white flowers are up to 3 in (8 cm) long and 1 in (25 mm) wide, borne in autumn and winter. ZONES 10–11.

Bouvardia ternifolia (left)
syn. *Bouvardia triphylla*

Although lacking scent, the striking red tubular flowers are an attractive feature of this species. Growing to 6 ft (1.8 m) wide, but usually half that height, it needs a well-drained soil in part-shade, shelter from frost and moist soil. Many cultivars exist, ranging in color from palest pink to deep red. ZONES 9–11.

BRACHYCHITON

This genus consists of around 30 species of warm-climate, evergreen or dry-season deciduous trees and shrubs, all Australian except one or two found in New Guinea. Some brachychitons feature spectacular bell-shaped flowers, the apparent petals actually being colored calyces, and in most species appearing just before the new leaves of summer. The leaves are diverse in shape but usually lobed, though lobing tends to disappear on adult trees. The fruits consist of 5-stalked, boat-shaped carpels, rather woody when mature. These split to release nut-like seeds that are edible but are surrounded by irritant hairs. Some species occur naturally in tropical and subtropical rainforests, others are found in semi-arid areas, where their leaves and bark may be used as fodder in dry seasons. Some of the arid-climate species have massive, swollen, water-storing trunks.

CULTIVATION

Noted for their drought-resistant qualities, brachychitons require light, well-drained, preferably acidic soil. They also prefer a sheltered position with protection from cold or salty winds and from frost when young. Several of the kurrajongs are widely planted in parks and streets. Propagate from fresh seed in spring or by grafting in the case of selected clones.

Brachychiton acerifolius
(below right)

FLAME KURRAJONG, ILLAWARRA FLAME TREE

The flame kurrajong, at its best one of the world's most spectacular flowering trees, is indigenous to the warm, wet, coastal slopes of eastern Australia. It can reach 40–50 ft (12–15 m) in cultivation, but is taller in its native rainforests. Profuse foamy sprays of bright scarlet flowers are borne in late spring or early summer on the leafless crown, or on individual branches which shed their leaves just prior to flowering. Flowering is erratic from year to year and seems best following a dry, mild winter. ZONES 9–12.

B

Brachychiton discolor *(above)*

LACEBARK KURRAJONG

A massive tree, to 80 ft (24 m) or more in its native rainforest, the lacebark kurrajong is smaller
in parks and gardens, but retains its distinctive
form. Its thick trunk has greenish bark and supports a dense canopy of large, maple-like leaves,
dark green above and silvery beneath. Clusters of
deep pink, velvety, bell-shaped flowers appear in
early summer, while the tree is briefly leafless.
ZONES 10–12.

Brachychiton populneus *(left)*
syns *Brachychiton diversifolius, Sterculia diversifolia*

KURRAJONG

Widely distributed on rocky hillsides, this bushy-headed
evergreen is grown chiefly for shade, or on farms for
fodder in times of scarcity. The deep olive green leaves are
variably lobed. Among the foliage in summer it produces
masses of greenish cream bell-shaped flowers, spotted inside with purple or yellow. It will tolerate limestone soils.
ZONES 8–11.

BRACHYGLOTTIS

This genus of about 30 species of low evergreen shrubs and small trees is mostly native to New Zealand, but one or two occur in Tasmania. Apart from their flowers, many are valued for their attractive foliage. Flowerheads are borne in small to rather large panicles at the branch tips, and may be white or golden yellow with conspicuous petals (actually ray florets), or small and greenish white with no ray florets.

CULTIVATION

These are rewarding garden plants in a suitable climate—they do best in cool but mild and rainy climates, in a sunny position with well-drained soil. The shrubby species respond to heavy pruning. Propagate from cuttings in late summer. Keep them in shape by cutting back.

B

Brachyglottis greyi *(above)*
syn. *Senecio greyi*

This many-branched evergreen shrub grows into a large mound, anything up to 6 ft (1.8 m) high and wider in spread. Its small, bright yellow, daisy-like flowers appear in summer and autumn and are less interesting than its hair-covered, leathery, green-gray leaves. This moderately frost-hardy species has long been grown in the UK. ZONES 7–9.

Brachyglottis repanda
syn. *Rangiora*

The rangiora is very different from most other *Brachyglottis* species, forming a striking small tree of rapid growth to about 20 ft (6 m). The saplings have straight, soft stems covered in opposite pairs of large, deep green, glossy leaves with wavy edges. In late winter to early spring each branch produces at its tip a large frothy panicle of thousands of small, greenish silver flowers. To maintain large leaf size cut back hard after flowering; this will, however, prevent it reaching its full height. '**Purpurea**' has leaves with deep purple uppersides. ZONES 9–11.

Brachyglottis 'Sunshine'
(above)

The commonest variety in a group known as the Dunedin hybrids, 'Sunshine' is though to be a *Brachyglottis compactus* × *B. laxifolius* hybrid. However, it is very similar in most respects to the plant known in gardens as *B. greyii*, except that its leaves

Brachyglottis repanda
'Purpurea' *(above)*

do not have wavy edges and it may bear slightly more flowers. It has silver-gray foliage with felted undersides, grows to around 6 ft (1.8 m) tall and is smothered in sprays of yellow daisies in summer. ZONES 7–10.

BROWALLIA
BUSH VIOLET

This is a genus of 6 species of bushy annuals and shrubby ever-green perennials, all native to tropical South America and the West Indies. They have a compact habit and dense foliage, with soft stems and simple, strongly veined, deep green leaves. The flowers, carried singly in the leaf axils, are like smaller versions of nicotianas (to which they are related) but with shorter tubes; they are usually in shades of blue, purple or white and can be quite profuse on well-grown plants.

CULTIVATION
In cool climates, browallias are grown as conservatory plants or treated as summer annuals. In frost-free climates they will grow well outdoors in moist, humus-rich, well-drained soil in a warm, part-shaded position sheltered from drying winds. Regular feed-ing with liquid fertilizer will keep the foliage lush and ensure steady flowering. Pinch back the stem tips to keep the plants bushy. Propagate from seed or tip cuttings.

Browallia speciosa
(left)

This shrubby perennial species grows to around 30 in (75 cm) tall and wide with leaves up to 4 in (10 cm) long. Its flowers, up to 2 in (5 cm) in diameter, are purple-blue to deep purple. The many cultivars have flowers in shades of blue and purple as well as white. **'Blue Troll'** is a dwarf cultivar, 12 in (30 cm) tall, with masses of blue flowers; **'White Troll'** is similar with white flowers. **'Marine Bells'** has deep indigo flowers; **'Sky Bells'** bears light blue flowers. ZONES 9–11.

Brugmansia ×
candida *(below right)*
syn. *Datura candida*

This rather untidy large shrub or small tree, 10–15 ft (3–4.5 m) high, branches low from a short trunk. Its long, oval, velvety leaves are confined to the branch tips. The pendulous white flowers, strongly scented at night, are up to 12 in (30 cm) long and have a widely flared mouth. They are borne mainly in summer and autumn, but also at other times. *Brugmansia* × *candida* is now believed to be a hybrid between *B. aurea* and *B. versicolor.* **'Plena'** has an extra frill of petals inside the main trumpet and **'Grand Marnier'** has flowers of soft apricot. ZONES 10–12.

BRUGMANSIA
syn. *Datura*
ANGEL'S TRUMPET

B

The large shrubs or small trees of this genus are grown for their very large, fragrant, pendent trumpet flowers. They are still often found under the name *Datura,* but the true daturas are short-lived, herbaceous plants with smaller, more upright flowers and capsular fruits that are usually prickly (brugmansias have fleshy, unarmed fruit that may be very long and narrow). Five or more species are currently attributed to *Brugmansia,* most originating in the Andes of northern South America, though even there they are usually associated with human habitation. They are evergreen or semi-evergreen and their leaves are large and soft, rather like tobacco leaves but smaller. All parts of the plant are narcotic and poisonous.

CULTIVATION

Frost tender to marginally frost hardy, these plants prefer a warm to hot climate, a sunny sheltered site and light, fertile, well-drained soil. Best grown as small trees, they can be shaped when young to obtain a single trunk or can be kept trimmed as dense, rounded shrubs. Water well during the growing season. Propagate from tip cuttings in spring or summer. Snails, whitefly and spider mite can cause problems.

Brugmansia × *candida*
'Grand Marnier' *(below)*

B

Brugmansia 'Charles Grimaldi' *(right)*

Named after a Californian landscape designer, this 6 ft (1.8 m)
tall hybrid cultivar ('Dr. Seuss'
× 'Frosty Pink') has very large,
pendulous, fragrant, pale
orange-yellow flowers, mainly
from mid-autumn to spring.
It has very large leaves and with
age will form quite a thicket of
stems. **ZONES 10–12.**

Brugmansia sanguinea *(right)*

syn. *Datura sanguinea*

RED ANGEL'S TRUMPET

This very distinctive
brugmansia has orange-red
flowers with yellow veins,
narrower across the mouth
than other species or hybrids.
Reported to grow at altitudes up
to 12,000 ft (3600 m) in its native Andes it is the most cold
hardy of the brugmansias and
can become a tree as much as
40 ft (12 m) high. It is normally
grown in gardens as a many-
stemmed shrub about
8 ft (2.4 m) high. Flower color
varies, some forms having paler
orange or yellow flowers.
ZONES 9–11.

Brugmansia suaveolens *(right)*

syn. *Datura suaveolens*

This many-branched, spreading evergreen shrub
or small tree reaches 4.15 ft (5 m) and has downy,
oval leaves up to 12 in (30 cm) long. The flowers
are narrower than in *Brugmansia × candida*, and
their tubes are heavily striped with green. They
are borne profusely at various times of the year.
Widely grown in tropical gardens, it is sometimes
seen pruned to a round-headed shrub. In cool
climates it does well in a moderately heated
greenhouse. **'Plena'** has semi-double blooms.
ZONES 10–12.

B

BRUNFELSIA

These evergreen shrubs or small trees from South and Central America bear delightfully fragrant flowers with a narrow tube that flares abruptly into 5 flat petals; these change color through successive days, with flowers of different ages sprinkling the bush. Most species are slow growing and bushy, with simple, rather leathery leaves. The plants may all contain poisonous alkaloids, particularly in their berry-like fruits, which have been known to poison dogs.

CULTIVATION

These plants need a frost-free site, in full sun or with afternoon shade, and fertile, well-drained soil with adequate water in summer or during dry spells. They do well in pots and are widely grown in greenhouses in Europe. Prune after flowering to promote bushiness. Propagate from tip cuttings. Mealybug and white fly may present problems.

Brunfelsia australis (below right) syns *Brunfelsia bonodora, B. latifolia*

YESTERDAY-TODAY-AND-TOMORROW

This attractive shrub grows to about 8 ft (2.4 m) tall and almost as wide, with a densely twiggy habit. Its slightly shiny leaves are purplish when young and in cool weather. At peak flowering, usually in mid-spring but sometimes in late winter or early summer, it bears masses of blossoms which open violet and fade to pale blue then white—all colors on the bush at the same time. It does well in coastal gardens as long as salt spray is not too heavy. **ZONES 9–12.**

Brunfelsia pauciflora (left) syns *Brunfelsia calycina, B. eximia*

BRAZIL RAINTREE

This small deciduous or semi-evergreen shrub is slower growing and less vigorous than *Brunfelsia australis*, growing to about 5 ft (1.5 m) tall and wide but rather open branched and with duller, dark green, leathery leaves. In bloom it is even more dramatic: large, abundant flowers open a rich purple and fade to mauve and white over successive days, throughout spring and early summer. **'Floribunda'** has smaller leaves and extremely abundant pale purple flowers. **ZONES 10–12.**

B

BUDDLEJA

Often spelt *Buddleia* (after seventeenth-century English botanist Adam Buddle), *Buddleja* is now ruled the correct form. This genus consists of shrubs and small, mostly short-lived trees, both evergreen and deciduous. Most of the cultivated species originate in China, but the genus also occurs in Africa, Madagascar, southern Asia and South America and includes many tropical and subtropical species. The leaves, usually in opposite pairs, are large, pointed and often crepe-textured. The small, tubular, spice-scented flowers are borne in dense spikes at the branch tips or sometimes in smaller clusters along the branches. They range in color through pinks, mauves, reddish purples, to oranges and yellows.

CULTIVATION
Buddlejas prefer full sun and good drainage, but thrive in any type of soil. Fairly hard pruning in early spring will control their straggly appearance. Propagate from cuttings in summer.

Buddleja alternifolia *(above)*

In full bloom in late spring and early summer, this tall deciduous shrub from northwestern China is transformed into a fountain of fragrant, mauve-pink blossom, the small individual flowers strung in clusters along its arching branches. It looks best trained to a single trunk so the branches can weep effectively from above, and should not be pruned back hard as it flowers on the previous summer's wood. ZONES 6–9.

Buddleja davidii

BUTTERFLY BUSH

The common buddleja of gardens, *Buddleja davidii* is native to central and western China. It is a deciduous or semi-evergreen shrub of about 12 ft (3.5 m) with gray-green foliage. In late summer and early autumn its arching canes bear at their tips long, narrow cones of densely packed flowers, mauve with an orange eye in the original form. These are attractive to butterflies, which feed on the scented nectar. Prune in late winter to encourage strong canes with larger flower spikes. Cultivars with flowers in larger spikes and richer tones include 'Cardinal', rich purple-pink; 'Black Knight', dark purple; 'Empire Blue', purple-blue with an orange eye; 'Royal Red', magenta; and 'White Bouquet', cream with an orange eye. 'Dubonnet' has large spikes of purple-pink flowers, and 'Pink Delight' has long narrow spikes of bright pink ones. The flowers of 'White Profusion' are white with golden yellow centers. ZONES 5–10.

Buddleja davidii 'Cardinal' *(top)*

Buddleja davidii 'Pink Delight' *(right)*

Buddleja davidii 'White Profusion' *(below right)*

Buddleja davidii 'Royal Red' *(below)*

Buddleja fallowiana

Grown for its richly fragrant blossoms, this deciduous shrub from China grows to 15 ft (4.5 m) and is moderately frost hardy. The stems are white and felty, and the leaves are dull green and gray-felted beneath. In summer, long panicles of very fragrant, pale lavender flowers with pale orange throats are borne on the current season's growth. **'Alba'** has creamy white flowers with an orange eye. **'Lochinch'** has very fragrant violet-blue blooms with an orange eye. **ZONES 8–9.**

Buddleja fallowiana 'Lochinch' *(above)*

Buddleja globosa *(left)*
ORANGE BALL TREE

Strikingly different from other buddlejas, this deciduous or semi-evergreen species from temperate Chile and Argentina bears deep golden orange balls of tiny flowers, like baubles, from the branch tips in late spring and summer. The strongly veined leaves are soft and covered in white felty hairs, as are the twigs and flower stalks. It is a tall shrub growing to 10–15 ft (3–4.5 m), making fast growth under suitably sheltered conditions, but inclined to be short lived. In cool but mild, moist climates it will thrive close to the sea. **ZONES 7–10.**

Buddleja × weyeriana

This name applies to hybrids between *Buddleja davidii* and *B. globosa*. In growth habit they resemble *B. davidii*, though taller and with longer canes, but the flower spikes are broken up into globular bunches of cream or orange-yellow flowers like the heads of *B. globosa*. **'Golden Glow'** has gold flowers, deep orange in the throat. **'Wattle Bird'** is a recent Australian hybrid with pale to rich yellow flowers in elongated spikes. **ZONES 7–10.**

Buddleja × weyeriana 'Wattle Bird' *(left)*

BUPLEURUM

Over 100 species belong to this genus of the carrot family,
including annuals, perennials and shrubs from Europe, Africa,
Asia and some cooler parts of North America. They differ from
most members of the family in their undivided, untoothed
leaves, mostly rather long and narrow but broader or even
almost circular in some species. The small greenish or yellowish
flowers are borne in rounded umbels, often with a circle or cup
of pointed bracts; the primary umbels are generally grouped into
compound umbels.

CULTIVATION

Some of the more shrubby evergreen species with leathery, salt-
resistant foliage are useful plants for seaside gardens. Plant in
a sunny position in light, well-drained soil. Propagate shrub
species from cuttings or by root division.

Bupleurum fruticosum *(above)*
SHRUBBY HARE'S-EAR

This southern European species is a spreading
evergreen shrub, 6–10 ft (1.8–3 m) tall, but only
3 ft (1 m) or less in exposed positions. Its leaves
are narrow and leathery with rounded tips, bluish
green, especially on the undersides, and up to
3 in (8 cm) long with prominent midribs. From
mid-summer it develops umbels of small, fleshy,
yellow flowers at the branch tips. ZONES 7–10.

BUXUS
BOX

B

Traditional evergreens of cool-climate gardens, boxes are grown for their small, neat, leathery leaves and dense, long-lived growth habit. The genus consists of around 30 species, only a few of which originate in Europe and temperate Asia; the majority are tropical and subtropical plants from Central America, the West Indies or southern Africa, most of them larger leafed and unknown in cultivation. The cultivated boxes are regarded as shrubs but can (except for some dwarf cultivars) grow into small trees with strong, contorted trunks and branches. Creamy yellow boxwood was once used for fine woodcut blocks for printing. The small clusters of small greenish yellow flowers are borne in profusion in the leaf axils in spring; they attract bees.

CULTIVATION
These tough plants have very simple requirements, thriving in most soils in sun or shade and adapting well to warmer climates. Boxes withstand regular close clipping, making them ideal for topiary, formal hedges and mazes. Pruning can be continued throughout the year. Propagate from cuttings.

Buxus balearica
(left)
BALEARIC BOXWOOD

From Spain, the Balearic Islands and northwestern Africa, this shrub or small tree, up to 30 ft (9 m) tall, can be distinguished from the more popular Japanese or European box by its larger, thicker leaves; these are mostly 1–1½ in (25–35 mm) long and more or less oblong or wedge-shaped. A vigorous grower, it has an erect narrow growth habit and gains height rather quickly, but can be used easily for hedging or topiary. It is less frost hardy than European box. ZONES 8–10.

Buxus microphylla *(above)* and as a clipped hedge *(right)*

Buxus microphylla var. *japonica* *(right)*

Buxus sempervirens 'Suffruticosa' *(far right)*

Buxus sempervirens as a clipped hedge *(below right)*

Buxus microphylla
JAPANESE BOX

This east Asian box, long grown in Japan but unknown in the wild, first came to Western gardens as a dwarf cultivar with distorted leaves. Later, wild forms were discovered in Japan, Korea and China and named as varieties: ***Buxus microphylla*** **var.** ***japonica*** (syn. *B. japonica*), *B. m.* **var.** *koreana* and *B. m.* **var.** *sinica* respectively. In leaf size and shape they are all quite similar to the European box but the leaves are slightly glossier and usually more rounded at the tip, with the broadest part just above the middle. A characteristic feature is the way the leaves turn a pale yellow-brown in frosty winters. In milder climates *B. m.* var. *japonica*, with slightly larger, rounder leaves, sometimes reaches 10 ft (3 m). ZONES 6–10.

Buxus sempervirens
EUROPEAN BOX, COMMON BOX

The common box can grow as tall as 30 ft (9 m) with a trunk 12 in (30 cm) thick, but as a garden shrub it is commonly only 3–6 ft (1–1.8 m) high. It is represented by a bewildering range of forms and cultivars, including the mound-forming **'Vardar Valley'**. The edging box, **'Suffruticosa'**, has a very dense, bushy habit and can be maintained as a dwarf hedge of 12 in (30 cm) tall or less. There are also many variegated clones, including **'Marginata'**, which has yellow-margined leaves, and **'Argenteovariegata'**, with white-edged leaves. ZONES 5–10.

C

CAESALPINIA

Caesalpinia is a diverse genus of legumes found in warmer regions of the world and includes 70 or so species of trees, shrubs and scrambling climbers, the latter often very thorny. Most are evergreen, some lose leaves in the tropical dry season. Some shrub species from the Americas have been distinguished in the past as the genus *Poinciana* (not to be confused with the 'poinciana' tree, now *Delonix*). *Caesalpinia* leaves are bipinnate, some very large with numerous leaflets; the flowers are in spikes from the upper leaf axils and may be quite showy, mostly in shades of red, yellow or cream, with separate petals and often conspicuous stamens. The seeds are in typical leguminous pods.

CULTIVATION

Most species appreciate a sheltered sunny spot and deep, sandy soil. The majority are frost tender; none will tolerate more than a few degrees of frost. Propagation is from seed, which may need abrading and hot-water soaking to aid germination.

Caesalpinia pulcherrima *(above)*
syn. *Poinciana pulcherrima*

PEACOCK FLOWER, BARBADOS PRIDE, RED BIRD
OF PARADISE

Mostly seen as a shrub of about 8 ft (2.4 m), this tropical American species can grow to 15–20 ft (4.5–6 m). Short lived and fast growing, it has an open, moderately spreading habit with coarse, prickly leaves and branches with a whitish waxy bloom, which terminate from spring to autumn in tall, upright sprays of vivid, scarlet and gold blossom. There is also a yellow-flowered form and a darker red one. **ZONES 11–12.**

Caesalpinia gilliesii *(above)*
syn. *Poinciana gilliesii*

DWARF POINCIANA, BIRD OF
PARADISE BUSH

This shrub or small tree, native to subtropical Argentina and Uruguay, seldom exceeds 10 ft (3 m) in cultivation and flowers when less than 3 ft (1 m) high. The fernlike leaves are divided into tiny leaflets, and short spikes of pale yellow flowers with very long crimson stamens appear in summer. Evergreen in warm, wet climates, elsewhere it is semi-deciduous or deciduous. **ZONES 9–11.**

CALCEOLARIA

LADIES' PURSE, SLIPPER FLOWER, POCKETBOOK FLOWER

Gardeners who know this genus only in the form of the gaudy 'slipper flowers' sold by florists may be surprised to learn that it contains upward of 300 species, ranging from tiny annuals to herbaceous perennials and even scrambling climbers and quite woody shrubs. All are native to the Americas, from Mexico southward to Tierra del Fuego, and all share the same curious flower structure, with a lower lip inflated like a rather bulbous slipper. Flower colors are mainly yellows and oranges, often with red or purple spots.

CULTIVATION

Calceolarias come from a wide range of natural habitats and vary greatly in cold hardiness. When grown outdoors they prefer a shady, cool site in moist, well-drained soil with added compost. Provide shelter from heavy winds as the flowers are easily damaged. Shrubby species may benefit from being pruned back by half in winter. Propagate from seed or softwood cuttings in summer or late spring.

Calceolaria integrifolia (right)

Native to Chile, this is a spreading shrub of rather loose and untidy habit though easily kept in shape by pruning, reaching a height of 6 ft (1.8 m). It has closely veined, slightly sticky leaves with an attractive, fine 'seersucker' texture, but is prone to insect damage. From late spring to early autumn a succession of bright yellow or bronzy yellow flowers appear in long-stalked clusters from the branch tips. It is the main parent of a group of hybrids, the Fruticohybrida Group. ZONES 8–10.

CALLIANDRA
POWDERPUFF TREE

The great majority of the 200 or so species of this large genus of evergreen shrubs and small trees are native to the Americas, mainly in the tropical regions, but a few are native to India, Africa or Madagascar. A small number are cultivated as ornamentals, valued for their showy flowerheads with numerous long stamens. The flowers are like those of the related acacias and mimosas but generally on a larger scale, usually in spherical or hemispherical heads. The leaves are always bipinnate but vary greatly in both number and in the size of the leaflets; in most species the leaves 'sleep' at night or in dull, stormy weather, the leaflets folding together.

CULTIVATION
Despite their often delicate appearance, many calliandras are tough, long-lived plants thriving in any well-drained, fertile soil in full sun. Cold hardiness varies between species, some tolerating a few degrees of frost as long as this is compensated for by hot summers. Water well in the summer growing season. Propagation is easiest from seed, but some produce few or no pods in cultivation and can be grown from cuttings.

Calliandra californica (left)
BAJA FAIRY DUSTER

A native of Baja California (a state of northwestern Mexico), this is a shrub of about 4 ft (1.2 m) in height of rather upright habit and open branched, the branches with paired prickles at the leaf bases. The leaves are small, with narrow gray-green leaflets only ¼ in (6 mm) long. The flowerheads are small and deep red to purplish. ZONES 10–12.

Calliandra haematocephala *(right)*
BLOOD-RED TASSEL-FLOWER, PINK OR RED POWDERPUFF

A native of tropical South America, this species produces large flowerheads around 3 in (8 cm) in diameter. The flowers appear almost year round but are most numerous in autumn and winter. It makes a large, broadly spreading shrub to a height of 12 ft (3.5 m) and an even greater spread with age. The leaves consist of rather few oblong leaflets about 2 in (5 cm) long, pink-flushed when first unfolding. It will grow and flower well in warm-temperate climates if sheltered from frost. ZONES 10–12.

Calliandra tweedii *(above)*
syn. *Inga pulcherrima*
RED TASSEL-FLOWER, TRINIDAD FLAME BUSH

Native to southern Brazil and Uruguay, this graceful shrub has a height and spread of 6–8 ft (1.8–2.4 m), with many tough stems arising from ground level. Its fern-like leaves consist of numerous tiny dark green leaflets, and striking scarlet pompon flowers appear among the foliage through spring, summer and early autumn. It prefers full sun, a light, well-drained soil and copious summer water. Prune after flowering to promote bushiness. ZONES 9–11.

C

CALLICARPA

BEAUTY BERRY

Deciduous and evergreen shrubs and small trees occurring in tropical regions around the world as well as more temperate regions of east Asia and North America, the 140 or so *Callicarpa* species can be untidy in growth but appealing in flower and especially in fruit. The branches are long and cane-like; the leaves, in opposite pairs, are usually downy on their undersides. In the popular deciduous species, sprays of small pink to purple summer flowers are followed in autumn by dense clusters of small shiny berries, white or mauve to purple, which may persist into winter on the bare branches. Fruiting branches are often cut for indoor decoration.

CULTIVATION

Only 3 or 4 species are commonly grown in cool climates but others from subtropical and tropical regions make good garden subjects. *Callicarpa* species do best in full sun and fertile soil. Cut back older branches in late winter to encourage strong flowering canes. Propagate from tip cuttings.

Callicarpa americana
(above)
AMERICAN BEAUTY BERRY

Not as commonly grown as it deserves, this deciduous species from southeastern and central USA makes a low, spreading shrub to 3–6 ft (1–1.8 m) in height. *Callicarpa americana* has broad, strongly veined leaves with downy undersides. The pink to violet-purple flowers are small but the brilliant mauve-magenta fruit are showy, in tight clusters like miniature bunches of grapes, and the fruit persist well into winter. ZONES 7–10.

Callicarpa bodinieri *(above)*
BODINIER BEAUTY BERRY

Very frost hardy and ornamental, this upright, deciduous bushy shrub from central China grows to about 6–10 ft (1.8–3 m)

Callicarpa bodinieri var. *giraldii* 'Profusion' *(above)*

tall and wide. It has dark green leaves with paler, downy undersides, small, dense sprays of lilac flowers and bluish mauve to purple fruit. *Callicarpa bodinieri* var. *giraldii* differs in its less downy leaves and flower stalks and is the form most commonly grown; it fruits more abundantly in gardens than typical *C. bodinieri* does. *C. b.* var. *g.* 'Profusion' bears an abundance of rich lavender fruit. ZONES 6–9.

CALLISTEMON
BOTTLEBRUSH

These evergreen Australian shrubs and small trees bear magnificent long-stamened, mostly red flowers in dense cylindrical spikes. The tips of the flower spikes continue to grow as leafy shoots, leaving long-lasting, woody seed capsules that eventually become half embedded in the thickening branch. Many species have a somewhat weeping habit and a few have striking papery bark, like that in the related genus *Melaleuca*. The flowers are nectar rich and attract birds, including small parrots (lorikeets) in their native regions. The 25 species hybridize freely and seed from mixed stands cannot be trusted to come true. In recent decades many hybrid cultivars have been named, most of uncertain parentage, with flowers in a variety of hues in the white, pink to red range.

CULTIVATION
The shrubby callistemons make a fine addition to the shrub border, where they attract birds. Larger species are popular as compact street and park trees for mild climates. In general, they are only marginally frost tolerant and prefer full sun and moist soil; some, however, will tolerate poor drainage. A light pruning after flowering will prevent seed capsules forming and help promote bushiness and flowering. Prune to make a single trunk on tree-like species. Propagate species from seed (preferably wild collected), cultivars and selected clones from tip cuttings.

Callistemon citrinus 'Burgundy'
(left)

C

Callistemon citrinus
'Splendens' *(left)*

Callistemon citrinus
'White Anzac'
(below left)

Callistemon citrinus

syn. *Callistemon lanceolatus*

SCARLET BOTTLEBRUSH, LEMON BOTTLEBRUSH

Widely distributed through coastal southeastern Australia, this stiff-leafed, bushy shrub was among the first bottlebrushes to be taken into cultivation. Its botanical epithet refers to a lemon scent in the crushed leaves, but this is barely detectable. A tough and vigorous plant, it usually grows quite rapidly to 10 ft (3 m) but may remain at much the same size for decades after, with a short basal trunk. The scarlet to crimson spikes are 4 in (10 cm) long and held erect, appearing in late spring and summer, often with an autumn flush as well. A variable species, it has a number of wild races as well as many cultivars, including **'Burgundy'**, with clustered, wine-colored brushes and leaves an attractive pinkish red when young; **'Mauve Mist'**, also with colored new leaves and abundant brushes that start mauve and age to a deeper magenta; **'Reeves Pink'**, a denser shrub with clear pink flowers; **'Splendens'** (syn. 'Endeavor'), an early cultivar making a compact bush bearing bright scarlet brushes over a long period; and **'White Anzac'** (syn. 'Albus'), with white flowers. **ZONES 8–11.**

Callistemon phoeniceus *(below)*

One of only two species from southwestern Australia, where it is widely distributed along streams and swampy depressions, *Callistemon phoeniceus* has thick, usually curved, gray-green leaves and can grow to 10 ft (3 m) high. Its flower spikes are deep scarlet tipped with golden pollen and are 4–6 in (10–15 cm) long. It is one of the most intensely colored bottlebrushes. **ZONES 9–11.**

Callistemon salignus *(right)*

WILLOW BOTTLEBRUSH, PINK TIPS, WHITE
BOTTLEBRUSH

This attractive small tree has a
wide natural distribution in
coastal eastern Australia, growing along swampy stream banks.
In the wild it may reach 60 ft
(18 m) but in gardens and
streets 15–30 ft (4.5–9 m) is
more usual. It is one of the few
species with papery, whitish
bark. The narrow, pointed, dark
green leaves are thinner than in
most other species, and on new
growth flushes are a striking
pinkish bronze color. The profuse flower spikes that appear in
spring and sparsely through
summer are normally pale
greenish yellow, though red-
flowered plants are now also
widely cultivated. ZONES 9–11.

Callistemon viminalis *(right)*

WEEPING BOTTLEBRUSH

From coastal lowland streams of Queensland and
northern New South Wales, this tree can reach up to
30 ft (9 m) in cultivation with a dense, domed
crown and pendulous branchlets. The flowers,
borne in profusion in spring with repeat flushes
through to autumn, have scarlet or crimson stamens.
Often planted as a street tree or used for screening,
this species is less frost hardy but more tolerant of
poor drainage than some others. It has many regional forms and is the parent of many cultivars,
some possibly of hybrid origin. '**Captain Cook**'
is a dwarf form to about 8 ft (2.4 m); the leaves are
smaller than in the species and pinkish while young,
becoming dark green. '**Hannah Ray**' grows to a
height and spread of 10 ft (3 m) and has lance-
shaped, gray-green leaves; the scarlet flowers grow
up to 4 in (10 cm) long and appear in early summer
and autumn. '**Harkness**' grows to 15 ft (4.5 m) on a
short trunk with a dense crown and has abundant
scarlet flower spikes up to 10 in (25 cm) long in
spring and early summer. ZONES 9–12.

Callistemon viminalis
'Hannah Ray' *(above)*

CALLITRIS
CYPRESS PINE

The true cypresses *(Cupressus)* of warmer parts of the northern hemisphere have their counterpart in Australia in the genus *Callitris*, strikingly similar in foliage and cones and showing a similar range of growth forms. Close examination shows that *Callitris* has its tiny scale leaves arranged in whorls of 3, as opposed to pairs in *Cupressus*. The globular, woody cones likewise have 3 large seed-bearing scales alternating with 3 smaller ones. There is a total of 19 species in the genus, of which 2 are endemic to New Caledonia and the remainder to Australia. Only a few have been regularly cultivated, having similar requirements to *Cupressus*.

CULTIVATION
Cypress pines make attractive lawn specimens, most effective in small groups, and are useful also for screens and hedges. Full sun and a well-drained, light textured soil suit them best. They tolerate light frosts only, and respond to summer watering. Most species can be kept clipped to a compact shape if desired. Propagation is from seed or cuttings.

Callitris columellaris
(below far left & center)

SAND CYPRESS PINE, BRIBIE ISLAND PINE

This species occurs wild mainly on old, wooded sand dunes of coastal southeast Queensland, where it makes a broad-headed tree of 70 ft (21 m) or more with dark, furrowed bark and very fine dark green foliage. In cultivation it is often strikingly different, making a dense column of slightly billowed form and retaining this shape even with age. ZONES 9–11.

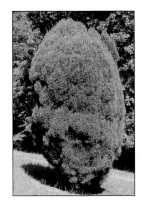

Callitris rhomboidea *(above right)*
PORT JACKSON PINE, OYSTER BAY PINE

Occurring widely in the rocky hills and ranges of southeastern Australia, including Tasmania, this species makes a small, columnar tree of up to about 30 ft (9 m), with gracefully drooping shoots at the apex of the crown. The fine foliage is mid-green, changing in cold winters to a deep purplish brown. The woody, angular cones form clusters on the branches within the foliage and persist for years without releasing their seed. *Callitris rhomboidea* will tolerate light shade, and can be trimmed as a hedge. ZONES 8–11.

CALLUNA

HEATHER, LING

The sole species of this genus, heather, is an evergreen shrub and is the dominant moorland plant of the colder parts of the UK and northern Europe; it is closely related to the heath genus *Erica*. White, pink, red or purple are the usual colors for the small bell-shaped flowers, borne in dense clusters. In winter the foliage turns brownish or dull purple. Mostly grown in gardens are the numerous cultivars, selected for dwarf or compact growth and for flower or foliage color.

CULTIVATION

It is an extremely frost-hardy plant, thriving in very exposed situations and often performing poorly under kinder conditions. The soil should be acidic, gritty, and of low fertility. After flowering cut back to keep bushes compact. In areas with warm, humid summers it is prone to root- and stem-rot. Propagation is usually from tip cuttings or rooted branches can be detached.

Calluna vulgaris 'Allegretto' *(above)*

Calluna vulgaris 'Dark Beauty' *(left)*

Calluna vulgaris

Common heather makes a spreading shrub 12–36 in (30–90 cm) high. The flowers of wild plants are pale pink to a strong purplish pink, occasionally white. Flowering time is variable: some races and cultivars flower through summer, others from mid-summer to early autumn. With over 400 cultivars available in the UK alone it is hard to decide which to mention, but the following are representative and will add interest and diversity to the garden. **'Allegretto'** is a low-growing compact form with cerise flowers. **'Allegro'** is medium sized with a neat habit and purple-red blooms. **'Anchy Ann'** has very long spikes of mauve flowers on 24 in (60 cm) bushes. **'Anthony Davis'** is a good variety for cutting with long sprays of single white flowers. **'Beoley Gold'** is 18 in (45 cm) tall with a spread of 24 in (60 cm) and has yellow-flushed foliage and single white flowers. **'County Wicklow'** is 10 in (25 cm) tall by 15 in (38 cm) and is a semi-prostrate shrub with double, pale pink flowers. **'Dark Beauty'** has rich, deep pinkish red flowers on small, compact plants. **'Darkness'** is 10 in

C

(25 cm) tall with a spread of 15 in (38 cm) and has crimson-purple single blooms. '**Elsie Purnell**' is a somewhat larger bush growing to 15 in (38 cm) and spreading to 30 in (75 cm) with gray-green foliage and long spikes of silvery pink double blooms that are good for cutting and/or drying. '**Fred J. Chapple**' forms neat, dense mounds dusted with white flowers. '**Gold Haze**' has a height and spread of 18 in (45 cm), pale golden foliage and white single flowers. '**H. E. Beale**' is quite a tall specimen to 30 in (75 cm) with grayish green foliage and long racemes of silvery pink double flowers held late in the season. '**Heidesinfonia**' is one of the best of the mauve-pink forms; flowers are produced abundantly on long spikes that are good for cutting. '**J. H. Hamilton**' is a dwarf plant to

6 in (15 cm) with a spread of 10 in (25 cm) and needs careful siting to prevent it being over-grown by larger varieties; it has double pink flowers. '**Joy Vanstone**' has light-colored foliage turning orange in winter and produces single pink flowers. '**Kinlochruel**' grows to 12 in (30 cm) tall with a spread of 15 in (38 cm) and has bright green foliage, turning bronze in the colder months, and double white flowers; it is very free flowering. '**Multicolor**' is 4 in (10 cm) tall with a 10 in (25 cm) spread and is a compact variety with interesting yellow-green foliage tinged orange and red with racemes of mauve blooms. '**Orange Queen**' is a very com-pact plant grown for its foliage, golden yellow in summer changing to deep burnt-orange in winter; it has single pink flowers. '**Robert Chapman**' is

12 in (30 cm) tall by twice this in width and is an excellent accent plant with golden yellow foliage in spring and summer turning to bronze shades during the colder months; it has laven-der flowers. '**Silver Queen**' is 15 in (38 cm) tall and spreads to 24 in (60 cm) with downy, silver-gray leaves offset by pale mauve single flowers. '**Velvet Dome**' is attractive in or out of bloom, forming tight buns of dense, deep green foliage. ZONES 4–9.

Calluna vulgaris 'Heidesinfonia' *(below left)*
Calluna vulgaris 'Multicolor' *(bottom left)*
Calluna vulgaris 'Orange Queen' *(below)*
Calluna vulgaris 'Robert Chapman' *(bottom center)*
Calluna vulgaris 'Velvet Dome' *(bottom right)*

CALOCEDRUS

Calocedrus means 'beautiful cedar' and its 3 species, from western USA, Taiwan, western China and adjacent Burma, are indeed beautiful trees, though only the American one is well known in gardens. The branchlets are arranged in strongly flattened sprays, each branchlet with small scale leaves that alternate between large (lateral) and small (facial) pairs. The cones have only 4 seed-bearing scales, and lying parallel in 2 opposite pairs, each scale has only 2 winged seeds.

CULTIVATION

These trees do best in cool, moist mountain areas in full sun or part-shade and in deep, moderately fertile soil, but may still grow well under poorer conditions as small, bushy but attractive trees. If liberally watered when young they will cope better with dry conditions when larger. Propagate from seed in spring or cuttings in late summer.

Calocedrus decurrens *(left)*
syn. *Libocedrus decurrens*
INCENSE CEDAR

Valued for its shapely, conical habit and attractive foliage, this fully frost hardy species grows slowly to 40–70 ft (12–21 m). The foliage is a glossy green and the cylindrical cones open with 3 splayed segments. **'Intricata'** is a compact dwarf cultivar; its twisted branches turn brown in winter. **ZONES 5–9.**

CALODENDRUM
CAPE CHESTNUT

This genus contains one beautiful evergreen tree species from South Africa, noted for its profusion of mauve-pink flowers covering the crown in late spring and early summer. It is widely cultivated as a street and park tree in the southern hemisphere and warmer parts of the USA. It needs protection from frost when young but once established will tolerate very light frosts. In cooler areas it may be deciduous or semi-deciduous.

CULTIVATION
Calodendrum prefers full sun and a light, moist, fertile soil with good drainage, and adequate water in dry periods. Young trees can be pruned to shape. Propagate from fresh seed sown in autumn; however, seedling trees may take up to 12 years to flower—grafted trees will flower sooner.

Calodendrum capense *(above)*

This shapely tree grows to 50 ft (15 m) tall, developing a wide-domed crown. The glossy, oval leaves, dark green above and paler underneath, are dotted with translucent oil glands. The pale pink to lilac flowers with prominent stamens appear in large terminal panicles, and are followed by woody, pustular seed pods that split into a star-like shape to release their large, nut-like but intensely bitter seeds. **ZONES 9–11.**

CALOTHAMNUS
NET BUSH, ONE-SIDED BOTTLEBRUSH

Some 40 species of evergreen shrubs make up this genus, which is endemic to Western Australia. They have narrow, almost needle-like, deep green leaves, 1–3 in (2.5–8 cm) long. In flower they somewhat resemble the related bottlebrushes *(Callistemon)*, except that the clusters of stamen filaments that make up each flower are fused for much of their length into a flat or concave portion, and flowers tend to be all on one side of the stem, usually the lower side, and open on older wood below the leafy branch tips. Most species of *Calothamnus* have red flowers that open in late winter and spring.

CULTIVATION
Plant in light, well-drained soil in full sun and protect from frost when young. All species tolerate poor soil and quite dry conditions. Although some may become rather woody, avoid pruning too heavily as the old wood is often reluctant to reshoot. They are propagated from seed or small, semi-ripe cuttings.

Calothamnus quadrifidus *(above)*
COMMON NET BUSH

Widely distributed in the southwest corner of Australia, this most commonly grown species is a heavily wooded, erect or spreading shrub 6–8 ft (1.8–2.4 m) in height and nearly as wide, with dark green or gray needle leaves up to 3 in (8 cm) long. The flowers are bright red tipped with yellow pollen, their fused filaments divided to the base into 4 strap-like portions (hence *quadrifidus*, meaning 4-parted). ZONES 8–11.

Calothamnus rupestris *(above)*
CLIFF NET BUSH

Rare in the wild near Perth, Western Australia, this very handsome species makes a medium-sized shrub of up to 10 ft (3 m) tall and nearly as wide. The slender, sharp-pointed needle leaves are slightly curved and only about 1 in (25 mm) long. In spring *Calothamnus rupestris* bears broad clusters of showy flowers; velvety hairs on the large gray-green calyx contrast with the reddish pink bundles of stamens, their fused portions quite broad. ZONES 9–11.

C

CALPURNIA

These small evergreen leguminous trees and shrubs are rather similar to the genus *Virgilia* so this genus was named after the second-rate Roman poet Calpurnius, who was an imitator of Virgil. The genus consists of 6 species, native to the wetter mountain areas of southern and eastern Africa, one found also in the mountains of southern India. They have pinnate leaves and pendulous clusters of yellow pea-flowers followed by flat, thin pods each holding a few seeds.

CULTIVATION
Preferring a sunny, sheltered position and reasonably fertile soil, these plants should be protected from frost when young and not allowed to dry out in summer, though they are more frost and drought tolerant at maturity. Propagate from seed sown in spring.

Calpurnia aurea *(above)*
NATAL LABURNUM, EAST AFRICAN LABURNUM

Native to southeastern Africa and southern India, this small tree usually reaches a height of 15–20 ft (4.5–6 m) with a light, open crown of foliage. The leaves consist of two rows of 1–1½ in (25–35 mm) long oval, grayish green leaflets that may be downy on the undersides. Clear yellow flowers appear through summer in pendulous sprays up to 10 in (25 cm) long on the new growths, even on young plants. ZONES 9–12.

CALYCANTHUS

ALLSPICE

Only 2 or 3 species make up this genus of deciduous, cool-climate shrubs from North America. The leaves, bark and wood all have a spicy aroma when they are cut or bruised. They are grown for their curiously colored flowers, which appear singly among the leaves in late spring or summer and resemble small magnolia flowers with narrow petals that are deep red-brown or dull reddish purple; the flowers make interesting indoor decorations.

C

CULTIVATION

Undemanding shrubs, they flower best in a sunny but sheltered position in fertile, humus-rich, moist soil. Propagation is usually by layering branches, or from the seeds which are contained in soft, fig-like fruits.

Calycanthus floridus *(right)*

CAROLINA ALLSPICE, SWEET SHRUB

A shrub from southeastern USA, this grows to about 6–9 ft (1.8–2.7 m) and has broad, glossy, pale green leaves with downy undersides. Its 2 in (5 cm) wide, early summer flowers consist of many petals that are dull brownish red, often with paler tips. ZONES 6–10.

Calycanthus occidentalis *(right)*

SPICE BUSH, CALIFORNIAN ALLSPICE

This species, from the ranges of northern California, makes a shrub of rather irregular growth up to 12 ft (3.5 m) tall. The leaves are larger than those of *Calycanthus floridus* and their undersides are not downy. The flowers are also larger, sometimes 3 in (8 cm) across, but with similar coloring to those of *C. floridus.* ZONES 7–10.

CALYTRIX
FRINGE MYRTLE

Calytrix consists of about 70 species of wiry-branched evergreen shrubs in the myrtle family, found scattered across the Australian continent though most are confined to the southwest. The small leaves, often very narrow, contain aromatic oils that give the crushed foliage a slightly pungent smell. The flowers are very distinctive, with an extremely fine tube flaring into 5 pointed petals; alternating with these are 5 thread-like sepals that persist on the small, dry fruits, elongating into fine bristles. The flowers are often massed and very showy, colored white or in shades of pink, red, purple or yellow.

CULTIVATION
Calytrix species require very well-drained, light-textured soil of low nutrient content. Full sun and a rather dry atmosphere suit most species. Propagate from seed or cuttings.

Calytrix tetragona
(left)

This is the most wide-ranging *Calytrix* species, occurring in most parts of Australia except the central deserts and the monsoonal north. It is also very variable—from 2 to 6 ft (0.6–1.8 m) high—and has many stems from the base and narrow, heath-like leaves of variable length. The starry, white to pink flowers are densely massed in heads at all the branch tips. The bristly fruit, deep purple-brown, can also make a fine display. ZONES 9–11.

CAMELLIA

Camellias are among the most popular of flowering shrubs and a profusion of beautiful garden varieties has been produced. Most of the many thousands of cultivars now listed are descended from *Camellia japonica*, introduced to Europe in the early eighteenth century from China. Two other species, *C. sasanqua* and *C. reticulata*, have also produced many cultivars. The genus of *Camellia*, however, has numerous additional species, most of which have never been cultivated. In the wild they are restricted to eastern Asia, ranging from Japan through southern and central China into Indochina, with a few outliers in the eastern Himalayas and the Malay Archipelago. Southern China accounts for the great majority of species, and discoveries by Chinese botanists in recent decades have tripled the number of known species, from under 100 in 1960 to almost 300 at the present time. All species are evergreen shrubs or small trees. The majority have small flowers of no great ornamental value, but there are nonetheless many beautiful species still awaiting introduction to gardens; some with appealing foliage or bark, rather than flowers, as their chief attraction. The flower color of camellias is always in the white-pink-red range, except for a small group of southern Chinese and Vietnamese species that have pale yellow to bronze-yellow flowers—their introduction to cultivation, which started in the 1970s, gave hope of introducing yellow into hybrid cultivars, but

success has so far been elusive. Hybridization between other species, however, has increased from a trickle in the 1930s (with the *C.* × *williamsii* hybrids) to an avalanche at the present time, and hybrid camellias (as opposed to straight japonicas, reticulatas or sasanquas) now account for a large proportion of new releases.

Apart from the ornamental species, there are camellias with economic importance of other kinds. Tea is the dried and cured young leaves of *C. sinensis*, now grown in many parts of the world in addition to its native southern China. Also from southern China is *C. oleifera*, grown there in plantations for the valuable oil pressed from its seeds, used in cooking and cosmetics; several other species are also grown for their oil.

CULTIVATION

Most camellias grow best in mild, humid climates and some species are very frost tender, but most of the cultivars are moderately frost hardy. They prefer well-drained, slightly acidic soil enriched with organic matter and generally grow best in part-shade, though some cultivars are quite sun tolerant. Good drainage is important to prevent phytophthora root rot, but they like to be kept moist. Many varieties are suited to pot culture and make handsome tub specimens. Pruning is largely unnecessary, but trim them after flowering or cut back harder if rejuvenation is required. Propagate from cuttings in late summer or winter, or by grafting.

Camellia cuspidata
'Spring Festival'
(far right)
Camellia hiemalis
'Somerset' *(bottom right)*

Camellia cuspidata

(right)

Native to western and central China, this attractive species has become fairly widely grown in the West and is the parent of a number of fine hybrids. It extends further north in the wild than most other camellias, and is valued for its cold hardiness. A shrub of up to 10 ft (3 m), it has smallish dark green leaves with long fine points, copper colored on new growths. The white flowers, up to 1½ in (35 mm) wide with broadly overlapping petals, are borne in profusion near the branch ends. **'Spring Festival'** has mid-pink flowers and narrow growth habit. **ZONES 7–10**.

Camellia × grijsii *(above)*

This 3–12 ft (1–3 m) tall shrub is a Chinese native with narrow, sharply toothed, 2–3 in (5–8 cm) long, elliptical leaves. The leaves are dark green above and lighter below, often with small wart-like protrusions on the undersides. In spring it bears small, simple, 5–6-petalled white flowers that are often sweetly scented. This species is among those cultivated for the production of camellia oil for cosmetics. **ZONES 8–10**.

Camellia hiemalis

The status of this camellia is problematic, and it has frequently been considered merely a cultivated form of *Camellia sasanqua* and indeed the cultivars associated with it are commonly listed as sasanquas. Long cultivated in Japan, it is known there as the 'cold camellia'. One school of botanical opinion now has it allied to

C. pitardii and *C. hongkongensis* and native to eastern China, another that it is more likely a hybrid between *C. sasanqua* and *C. japonica* that arose in Japan. It is a large shrub with thick, deep green leaves and white to pink 7-petalled flowers up to 2½ in (6 cm) across appearing mainly in winter. **'Shishigashira'** is the longest cultivated form, making a shrub with a dense, umbrella-shaped crown and smallish double reddish pink flowers; it is often grown in Japan as a neatly trimmed miniature. **'Showa-no-sakae'** has irregular double pale pink blooms with a musky fragrance; it has a vigorous spreading habit and can be used for ground cover or espaliered. **'Hiryu'**, an old favorite, is bushy and upright with bright to deep rosy red flowers. **'Somerset'** is a vigorous plant with lighter leaves than most and deep reddish pink, semi-double blooms. **ZONES 8–10**.

Camellia japonica

Wild plants of this best known camellia species are small, scraggy trees 20–30 ft (6–9 m) tall in their natural habitats in Japan, Korea and China, usually with red, somewhat funnel-shaped, 5-petalled flowers only 2–3 in (5–8 cm) across. In Japan the typical form, *Camellia japonica* subsp. *japonica*, is found in coastal scrubs of the south and is replaced in northwestern Honshu by the more cold-tolerant *C. j.* subsp. *rusticana,* known as the 'snow camellia'. Selection of desirable garden forms of *Camellia japonica* began at least 300 years ago in both China and Japan, the Chinese favoring double flowers and the Japanese singles. After its introduction to Europe in about 1745 an increasing number of these cultivars were imported, mostly renamed with Latin names such as **'Alba Plena'** and **'Anemoniflora'** on their arrival, and in the early nineteenth century many new cultivars were raised there. It was discovered that new flower types could be obtained by seedling selection and by watching for branch sports (vegetative mutations). By the late nineteenth–early twentieth century thousands of cultivars had arisen, not only in Europe but in California, Australia and New Zealand not to mention Japan, where new cultivars were actively being produced. Camellias fell from fashion to some degree during the period between World War I and World War II, but the 1950s saw them come back strongly and the majority of known cultivars date from this time and later. Even though hybrid camellias make up an increasing proportion of new listings,

cultivars of pure *C. japonica* origin remain as popular as ever. Camellia enthusiasts have devised classifications of the cultivars based on flower size and form: sizes run from **miniature** (under 2½ in [6 cm]) through **small, medium, medium-large** and **large** to **very large** (over 5 in [12 cm]); forms of flower are divided into **single, semi-double, anemone-form, informal double** or **peony-form, rose-form double** and **formal double**. By specifying their size class and form and describing their coloring, most cultivars can be pinned down at least to a small group. A subgroup of japonicas that deserve special mention are the **Higo camellias**, a collection of distinctively beautiful single cultivars from the southern Japanese island of Kyushu. *Camellia japonica* cultivars vary in flowering time from late autumn to early spring in mild climates, and from early to late spring in cooler climates. They will not survive outdoors where winter temperatures drop much below 15°F (–10°C). Among representative cultivars, some old favorites are **'Adolphe Audusson'** with large saucer-shaped semi-double dark red flowers sometimes with white markings and prominent yellow stamens; **'Guilio Nuccio'**, a very large semi-double with very broad, irregular coral red petals and prominent yellow stamens; **'Desire'**, a medium-large formal double with pale pink shading to darker pink or lilac on the outside; The best known miniature is **'Bokuhan'** (syn. 'Tinsie'), the tiny flowers having a ring of dark red petals surrounding a white bulb of petaloids; it is a very old Japanese cultivar. ZONES 5–10.

Camellia japonica cultivar *(right)*
Camellia japonica 'Aldolphe Audusson' *(below)*

C

Camellia japonica 'Betty
Sheffield Pink' *(above)*
Camellia japonica 'Bob Hope'
(above center)
Camellia japonica 'Bokuhan'
(above right)
Camellia japonica 'Bob's
Tinsie' *(right)*
Camellia japonica subsp.
rusticana 'Botan Yuki' *(below)*
Camellia japonica 'Colombo'
(below center)
Camellia japonica 'Debutante'
(below right)

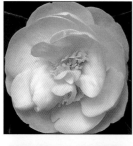

Camellia japonica 'Desire'
(above)

Camellia japonica 'Devonia'
(above)

Camellia japonica 'Dr Burnside'
(above)

C

Camellia japonica 'Elegans'
(top)

Camellia japonica 'Eximia'
(above)

Camellia japonica 'Flame'
(above right)

Camellia japonica 'Forest
Green' *(right)*

Camellia japonica 'Guilio
Nuccio' *(above)*

Camellia japonica 'Hagoromo'
(above)

Camellia japonica, Higo Group
cultivar *(above)*

C

Camellia japonica 'Higo-kyo-
nichiki' *(top left)*
Camellia japonica 'Kati'
(top center)
Camellia japonica 'Kick Off'
(top right)
Camellia japonica 'Komyo'
(above)
Camellia japonica 'Lady
Campbell' *(above center)*
Camellia japonica 'Lady
Vansittard White' *(above right)*
Camellia japonica 'Madame
Louis van Houtte' *(right)*

Camellia japonica 'Laurie Bray'
(above)

Camellia japonica 'Lavinia
Maggi' *(above)*

Camellia japonica 'MacCaskill'
(above)

C

Camellia japonica 'Masayoshi'
(above)

Camellia japonica 'Mrs Tingley'
(top center)

Camellia japonica 'Moshio'
(top right)

Camellia japonica 'Ohkan'
(right)

Camellia japonica 'Otome'
(below left)

Camellia japonica 'Rosedale's
Beauty' *(above)*

Camellia japonica
'Shishigashira' *(above)*

C

Camellia japonica 'Shiro-
Taoan' *(top left)*
Camellia japonica 'Snow Chan'
(top center)
Camellia japonica 'Tama No
Ura' *(above)*
Camellia japonica 'Tomorrow's
Dawn' *(above center)*

Camellia japonica 'Sylvia'
(top right)
Camellia japonica 'Ville de
Nantes' *(above)*
Camellia japonica 'White Nun'
(left)

Camellia oleifera *(right)*

OIL-SEED CAMELLIA, TEA OIL CAMELLIA

This camellia is widely grown in southern
China and parts of Indochina for its seed
oil, used as a cooking oil and in cosmetics.
Its wild origins are uncertain, but botanists
believe that *Camellia oleifera* and *C.
sasanqua* may have a common wild ancestor
as they are without doubt very closely allied.
As well as yielding oil, it makes a fine ornamental shrub or small tree and is one of the
more cold-hardy camellias. The white
flowers are up to 4 in (10 cm) across and
fragrant, opening from early autumn to
early winter. ZONES 7–10.

Camellia pitardii

An open-branched shrub or small tree to 20 ft (6 m), this species is native to southwestern and central China. Closely related to *Camellia reticulata* and blooming at the same time, it has smaller flowers and leaves than that species but is rather variable: the typical form has flowers 2 in (5 cm) or less in diameter with 5 or 6 rose pink to white petals; *C. pitardii* var. *yunnanica*, the most widely cultivated form, has slightly larger flowers in the same color range—a very pretty plant, it is increasingly being used as a parent of hybrid cultivars. **'Gay Pixie'** is an Australian-raised cultivar with incomplete double flowers, the orchid-pink petals striped darker pink; **'Snippet'** has a dwarf habit and its flowers have notched margins on the delicate, pale pink colored petals. ZONES 7–10.

Camellia pitardii 'Gay Pixie' *(below left)*
Camellia pitardii 'Snippet' *(below)*
Camellia reticulata cultivar *(bottom)*

Camellia reticulata

This species includes some of the largest flowered camellia cultivars, and many of these were culti-vated for centuries in southern China before one was brought to England in 1820. Not until much later a far smaller flowered plant was discovered growing wild in Yunnan and determined by bota-nists to be the wild ancestor of these early Chinese cultivars. Many additional cultivars have since been documented, mostly in Yunnan and often as temple trees up to 40 ft (12 m) tall and hundreds of years old—they are known as the **'Yunnan ca-mellias'**. *Camellia reticulata* makes a more up-right plant than *C. japonica,* with an open framework of sparser foliage and large, leathery leaves. They are late blooming for camellias, flowering from late winter to mid-spring. The wild form is sold as **'Wild Type'** and has rather irregularly cup-shaped single reddish pink flowers about 3 in (8 cm) wide. The original introduction from 1820, **'Captain Rawes'**, is still admired, with 6 in (15 cm) semi-double blooms of rich carmine-pink, the petals coarsely fluted. Newer

cultivars are more compact, for example the American **'Lila Naff'**, a single but with multiple broad petals of a most delicate pink, and **'William Hertrich'**, a very large semi-double with deep red petals. Many cultivars that are usually treated as reticulatas are in fact hybrids, with influence from other species. ZONES 8–10.

C

Camellia reticulata 'Blossom Time' *(top left)*
Camellia reticulata 'Curtain Call' *(top center)*
Camellia reticulata 'Ellie's Girl' *(top right)*
Camellia reticulata 'Inspiration' *(above left)*
Camellia reticulata 'Leonard Messel' *(above center)*
Camellia reticulata 'Lovely Lady' *(above right)*

Camellia reticulata 'Ted Craig' *(right)*

Camellia reticulata 'Mouchang' *(right)*
Camellia reticulata 'Royalty' *(far right)*

C

Camellia sasanqua 'Hiryu'
(top left)
Camellia sasanqua 'Paradise Belinda' *(top center)*
Camellia sasanqua 'Rubra' *(top right)*
Camellia sasanqua cultivar *(left)*
Camellia sasanqua 'Snow Flake' *(below left)*
Camellia sasanqua 'Setsugekka' *(below)*

Camellia sasanqua

Originating in southern Japan, this small-leafed species has given rise to many hundreds of cultivars. The most versatile camellias from the landscaping point of view, the sasanquas have greatly increased in popularity recently. They are densely leafed plants that can be grown as hedges and even as street trees, and some cultivars are suited to espaliering against a wall or fence. They have small, shiny, dark green leaves and small to medium-sized, delicately fragrant, mostly single or semi-double flowers in a variety of colors, profusely borne but individually short lived. Different cultivars extend the flowering season from early

autumn to mid-winter. Sasanquas are faster growing and more sun tolerant than most camellias, performing better in mild climates. Among superior cultivars are **'Jennifer Susan'** with clear pink semi-double flowers; **'Plantation Pink'**, an Australian-raised cultivar with larger single, saucer-shaped, soft pink

flowers, excellent for hedging; **'Paradise Belinda'**, semi-double with the outer stamens bearing small petal-like organs to give it an unusual effect; and **'Mine-no-yuki'** (syn. 'White Doves'), a creamy semi-double that can be espaliered. ZONES 9–11.

Camellia sinensis *(below right)*

TEA

All the world's tea comes from this species, grown mainly in plantations in the highlands of tropical Asia but also in southern China (its original home) and Japan, and more recently in other parts of the world where the climate is suitably mild and humid. Tender new shoots are plucked, fermented and dried in different ways to give black or green tea. It normally makes a shrub of 6–10 ft (1.8–3 m) tall with thin, serrated leaves and rather insignificant, white to cream flowers about 1 in (25 mm) across borne on recurved stalks from the leaf axils; when grown for tea the plants are kept trimmed to about chest height and flowers are rarely seen. *Camellia sinensis* var. *assamica* is the Assam tea now grown universally in India and Sri Lanka, with larger leaves and more vigorous growth. ZONES 9–11.

Camellia × vernalis

YULETIDE

This name covers a group of cultivars that are often included under the heading of sasanquas, but are now thought to have possibly originated as hybrids between *Camellia sasanqua* and *C. japonica*. They share many characteristics with *C. hiemalis* but what distinguishes them as a group is their late flowering, from mid-winter almost to mid-spring. **'Shibori-Egao'** is a virus-variegated form of **'Egao'** that has deep pink, semi-double flowers with a central column of yellow stamens. **'Yuletide'** is an American-raised cultivar of compact, bushy growth and scarlet flowers with prominent yellow stamens, blooming earlier than most of the group. ZONES 8–10.

Camellia × vernalis 'Yuletide' *(above)*
Camellia × vernalis 'Shibori-Egao' *(above left)*
Camellia sinensis var. *assamica* *(top left)*

Camellia × williamsii

Although hybrid camellias are dealt with separately under a general heading, this group is so well known it merits its own heading. All these hybrids are crosses between C. *japonica* and the western Chinese mountain species *C. saluenensis*, or seedlings of succeeding generations. The original C. × *williamsii* was raised in Britain in the 1930s and several cultivars became available in the 1940s, soon achieving popularity for their cold hardiness and profuse blooms in clear colors borne over a long winter and spring season. One of the earliest and best known is **'Donation'** with large orchid pink, semi-double flowers. **'Caerhays'** has medium-sized, semi-double, lilac-rose flowers on somewhat pendulous branches. **'E. G. Waterhouse'** is an Australian cultivar of erect habit with matt green foliage and formal double flowers of a rich fuchsia pink. **ZONES 7–10.**

C

Camellia × *williamsii* 'Ballet Queen' *(top)*
Camellia × *williamsii* 'Debbi' *(above)*
Camellia × *williamsii* 'E. G. Waterhouse' *(left)*
Camellia × *williamsii* 'Donation' *(below left)*
Camellia × *williamsii* 'Parkside' *(below)*

Camellia Hybrids

Few attempts were made to cross the different species of camellia in the nineteenth century, although hybrids in many other genera were being produced. There were some accidental camellia hybrids from China and Japan, but no successful deliberate cross was raised until the *Camellia × williamsii* hybrids were released around 1940. Hybrids slowly gained in popularity through the 1960s and 1970s and now make up a substantial proportion of new releases. The most widely used parents are *C. japonica, C. sasanqua* and *C. reticulata* but many others have also been used, including *C. saluenensis, C. pitardii, C. cuspidata, C. lutchuensis* and more recently some of the small-flowered species such as *C. tsaii*. In this way the diversity of foliage, flower and growth form is being extended. The addition of fragrance to camellia blooms is one direction breeders are taking. Some representative cultivars are **'Brian'** *(C. saluenensis × reticulata)*, which has rose pink pointed petals in a hose-in-hose arrangement up to 4 in (10 cm) across, with a vigorous, upright

habit; **'Cornish Snow'** *(C. cuspidata × saluenensis)* with profuse, delicate, small single white flowers sometimes flushed pink, a tall, open habit and very cold hardy;

'Scentuous' *(C. japonica* 'Tiffany' × *lutchuensis)* with semi-double white petals flushed pink on the reverse, the fragrance of *C. lutchuensis*, an open habit and bright green

leaves. **'Baby Bear'** *(C. rosiflora × tsaii)* is a small-flowered dwarf form with light pink blooms and a dense habit ideal for bonsai or rockery use. **ZONES 7–10.**

Camellia 'Barbara Clark' *(left)*
Camellia 'Betty Ridley' *(below)*

C

Camellia 'Lasca Beauty' *(above)*

Camellia 'Cornish Snow' *(top)*

Camellia 'Cornish Spring'
(above right)

Camellia 'Spring Festival'
(above)

Camellia 'Wirlinga Princess'
(above)

Camellia 'Rose Quart' *(above)*

Camellia 'Scentuous' *(above)*

Camellia 'Valentine Day' *(above)*

CAMPTOTHECA

The single deciduous tree species in this Chinese genus comes from the low-altitude valleys of Yunnan and Sichuan and is not regarded as frost hardy in cool-temperate countries. A fast-growing tree in its first 10 years, its main attraction is its foliage, the leaves being large, glossy and strongly ribbed; on new growth flushes they are pale pinkish bronze. In summer *Camptotheca* bears stalked, spherical heads of tiny white flowers close to the branch tips, followed in autumn by enlarged heads of curious yellow-green, sharply angled fruit which finally turn brown before falling.

CULTIVATION
In a moist, warm-temperate climate and deep, moist soil it makes a handsome tree. It is too weak to tolerate strong winds, which break branches and disfigure the foliage. Propagation is from seed.

Camptotheca acuminata *(above)*

This tree grows to a height of about 40 ft (12 m) with a straight, gray-barked trunk and spreading lateral branches. Growth subsequently slows and some trees go into early decline. Its expected life span is still uncertain. It is reported to be widely cultivated in parts of China. ZONES 10–11.

CANANGA

This genus consists of 2 fast-growing evergreen tree species from tropical Southeast Asia, the Pacific islands and the north of Australia. They are prized for their 6-petalled, wonderfully fragrant flowers borne in pendent clusters. A perfumery oil is distilled from the flowers.

CULTIVATION

Like their relatives the custard apple and soursop (see *Annona*), they are easily cultivated in a sheltered, shaded position in tropical and warmer subtropical areas. They prefer a moist, humus-rich soil. Propagation is from seed or cuttings.

Cananga odorata
(left)

YLANG YLANG

This handsome tropical tree reaching 80 ft (24 m) in the wild has pendulous, rather brittle branches and large, glossy green leaves. The flowers, with their long, twisted, drooping, greenish yellow petals and extraordinarily heavy perfume, appear mostly in autumn in thick clusters at the leaf axils, and are followed by small greenish fruit. The ylang ylang (its Malay name) is still cultivated in Hawaii for the perfume industry. **ZONES 11–12.**

C

CANTUA
SACRED FLOWER OF THE INCAS, MAGIC FLOWER

This small genus of 6 species of semi-evergreen shrubs from the Andes is characterized by pendulous, trumpet-shaped flowers on weak stalks. This is a feature of many unrelated flowers in the Americas that are pollinated by hummingbirds—with their amazing ability to hover they can obtain nectar from such flowers, which are inaccessible to other birds and insects. Only one species, *Cantua buxifolia,* is widely cultivated, valued for the elegance of its profuse flowers often in stark contrast with the bare, untidy stems and branches.

CULTIVATION
Cantuas require a mild climate without extremes of hot or cold, and a sunny open position; in colder areas they prefer a sheltered position against a warm wall. They do best in moist, well-drained, fertile soil. Improve shape by tying back stems and prune longer growths; but keep in mind that flowers are borne on the previous season's twigs. Propagate from seed or cuttings, which strike fairly readily.

Cantua buxifolia
(below)

This species grows to 6–10 ft (1.8–3 m) with erect stems and arching branches. The leaves are small, grayish green and rather fleshy. The flowers, borne in late spring, vary on different plants. In gardens a rose-purple shade is popular but pink, white and pink-and-white striped flowers are also seen. Sometimes the normal pink-flowering form also bears branches with yellow and white flowers and different foliage. ZONES 8–9.

CARAGANA
PEA SHRUB

About 80 species belong to this genus of pea-flowered deciduous shrubs and small trees from central and eastern Asia, of which several have been established in cultivation in Europe and North America. They are curious plants of a rather subdued attraction, with lemon yellow, orange or reddish flowers and small, pinnate leaves, in some species associated with weak spines. Slender, straw-colored pods appear in autumn after the flowers.

C

CULTIVATION
Although at their best in climates with cold winters and hot, dry summers, caraganas are adaptable in this respect with root systems not prone to rot diseases. Most are very frost hardy. They set plenty of seed in the pods, which ripen in mid-summer and provide an easy means of propagation.

Caragana arborescens 'Lorbergii' *(below)*

Caragana arborescens
SIBERIAN PEA TREE

This is the tallest species, attaining a height of 12–20 ft (3.5–6 m). A native of central Asia, Siberia and Mongolia, it has been cultivated in western Europe for almost 250 years and is valued for its frost hardiness and tolerance of poor conditions. The leaves are soft and spineless, consist-ing of 8 to 12 fresh green leaflets. Loose clusters of slender-stalked, pale yellow flowers hang among the leaves from late spring to early summer. Several cultivars have been named, including **'Lorbergii'** with long narrow leaves and small flowers; **'Pendula'** with weeping branches, which is usually grafted onto a standard; and **'Walker'**, a dwarf spreading plant used as a ground cover. ZONES 3–9.

CARISSA

This genus of 20 species of attractive evergreen, spiny shrubs occurs in eastern and southern Africa, Asia and Australia. Grown as
hedges and in containers in warm-climates, they are valued for
their masses of sweet-scented flowers, mostly snow white, and for
their neat appearance. All species bear edible fruits enjoyed by
both humans and birds. The glossy green leaves are thick and
tough; like the stems, they exude a milky sap when cut or broken.

CULTIVATION

They prefer warm summers and moderate rainfall, and require
full sun and well-drained soil. Plants in pots need moderate
water in the growing season, less in winter. Propagate from seed
when ripe in autumn or from cuttings in summer.

*Carissa
macrocarpa*
syn. *Carissa
grandiflora*
NATAL PLUM

Occurring naturally on
margins of evergreen
forest on the east coast
of southern Africa, this
dense shrub grows
quickly to a height of
10 ft (3 m) and a
spread of 15 ft (4.5 m).
The small, rounded
leaves have long, sharp
spines among them.
The white flowers ap-
pear from spring to
summer. The fruit that
follow are red, fleshy
and oval; they make a
delicious jelly. This
species tolerates salt-
laden winds.
'**Horizontalis**' is a
dense, trailing cultivar
with bright red fruit.
'**Emerald Carpet**'
grows to about 24 in
(60 cm). ZONES 9–11.

Carissa macrocarpa
'Horizontalis' *(left)*

CARMICHAELIA

Apart from a species endemic to Lord Howe Island, all 40 species of this genus are from New Zealand. Deciduous pea-flowered shrubs and small trees, they occur in a wide range of habitats. Their small leaves, consisting of 3 leaflets, are scarce or absent on the adult plants of most species, the flattened green branchlets taking over their photosynthetic function. The flowers, mostly quite small, from white to pinkish or purplish, are freely produced in small clusters along branchlets; they are often scented. Seeds are borne in small pods of unusual structure, the softer 'shell' shedding to expose the red or orange seed encircled by the persistent pod rim. Although rarely cultivated outside their native areas, many species have ornamental qualities.

CULTIVATION

Plant in sun or part-shade. They tolerate exposure and dry soil, but the taller species respond to shelter and better soil with denser foliage and more abundant flowers. Propagation is normally from seed, cuttings being difficult to strike.

Carmichaelia odorata *(below)*

SCENTED BROOM

This New Zealand shrub grows to 4–6 ft (1.2–1.8 m) and has spreading branches and massed, drooping branchlets that are very narrow. In late spring and summer it bears abundant sweetly scented white flowers with purple veins on short, erect spikes. ZONES 9–10.

CARPENTERIA
TREE ANEMONE, BUSH ANEMONE

Only one species from California belongs to this genus, an ever-green shrub with pure white flowers like those of *Philadelphus* but with 5 to 7 petals rather than 4, and a more conspicuous cluster of golden stamens. The leaves are narrow and soft, deep green above but paler and felty beneath, arranged in opposite pairs on the soft-wooded branches. It is a beautiful shrub when in full flower in late spring and early summer. Named for the American Professor Carpenter, it should not be confused with the palm genus *Carpentaria*.

CULTIVATION
Although requiring a fairly cool climate, this species only flowers well in regions with warm dry summers and needs ample sunshine, well-drained, gritty soil that must not dry out too much, and protection from strong winds. Propagation is usually from seed, as cuttings do not root easily.

Carpenteria californica (above)

In the wild this very attractive shrub is known only from a small area of central California, on dry mountain slopes. It can grow to 20 ft (6 m) tall but in gardens it is usually a sprawling shrub about 6–8 ft (1.8–2.4 m) tall that may need support and is best grown against a sunny wall. The flowers, solitary or in small groups, are normally 2–2½ in (5–6 cm) wide but may be up to 4 in (10 cm) wide with broadly overlapping petals. ZONES 7–9.

Carpinus betulus
(below right)

COMMON HORNBEAM, EUROPEAN HORNBEAM

Ranging from Asia Minor across Europe to eastern England, this species can grow to 80 ft (24 m) although 30 ft (9 m) is an average garden height. It has a broad, rounded crown and pale gray bark, fairly smooth and often fluted. The ovate leaves are ribbed and serrated, downy when young, and change from dark green in summer to yellow in autumn. Inconspicuous flowers in early spring are followed by clusters of pale yellow winged fruit. It likes cool, moist conditions. **'Columnaris'** is a compact grower to 30 ft (9 m) high and 20 ft (6 m) wide; **'Fastigiata'** (syn. 'Pyramidalis') develops into a taller, broadly conical tree. ZONES 6–9.

CARPINUS
HORNBEAM

The subtle beauty of hornbeams lies in their usually smoothly fluted trunks and limbs, their neatly veined, small, simple leaves that color attractively in autumn, and their bunches of dry, winged fruit hanging from the twigs. *Carpinus* is a small genus of catkin-bearing, deciduous trees scattered across cool-climate areas of the northern hemisphere. In foliage and fruits there is not a huge variation between the species, though overall size and growth habit are distinct for each. Most, and in particular the European *Carpinus betulus*, yield a timber that is exceptionally strong, hard and close grained; it is much used in the mechanism of pianos. Long lived and often slow growing, hornbeams are useful small to medium-sized trees for parks, streets and lawns.

CULTIVATION
These grow best in well-drained, moderately fertile soil in a sunny or part-shaded position. Propagation is normally from seed except for certain named clones, which must be grafted.

C

Carpinus betulus
'Columnaris' *(below)*

Carpinus japonica
(below left)

JAPANESE HORNBEAM

This species makes a medium-sized tree 30–40 ft (9–12 m) tall, forking rather low with broadly ascending branches. The smooth, dark gray bark often has lighter streaks and becomes scaly and furrowed with age. The leaves are larger than those of the common hornbeam, up to 4 in (10 cm) long and more closely veined, with edges more finely but sharply toothed and heart-shaped bases. The fruiting catkins are compact with broad, overlapping, jaggedly toothed bracts. ZONES 5–9.

C

CARPODETUS

About 10 species make up this genus of small evergreen trees, distantly related to *Escallonia*, 9 in the mountains of Papua New Guinea and one in New Zealand; the latter is the only one of interest to gardeners. It makes an attractive bushy shrub when young, with interesting foliage and small but profuse white flowers.

CULTIVATION

The New Zealand species fits into various situations in mild-climate gardens, and makes vigorous growth if planted in deep, fertile soil in a reasonably sheltered position. Propagate from seed or cuttings.

Carpodetus serratus *(above)*
PUTAPUTAWETA

This is a shapely small tree reaching heights of up to 30 ft (9 m) with grayish white bark and coarsely toothed, alternately arranged leaves that are often many lobed in the juvenile stages but rather leathery and elongated with a tapered base as the plant matures. White flowers are borne in panicles from late spring to early autumn and are followed by rounded, shiny black fruit.
ZONES 8–10.

Carya cordiformis
(below right)

BITTERNUT HICKORY

Widespread through much of eastern USA, this fast-growing tree grows to 80 ft (24 m) with spreading limbs and a rounded crown. The gray or pale brownish bark is smooth except on quite old trees, when it becomes shallowly furrowed. In winter its twigs are distinguished by striking yellow dormant buds. The rounded nuts are smallish and thin shelled, their kernels too bitter to eat. The timber is used in smoking hams and bacon. ZONES 4–9.

Carya illinoinensis
(below far right)

PECAN

This species produces one of the world's most popular edible nuts. From central USA, it occurs along broad river valleys and grows to 100 ft (30 m) tall with scaly gray bark. In cultivation, it grows quickly to become an open-crowned tree of about 30 ft (9 m) within 10 to 15 years. Although quite frost hardy, it needs long, hot summers to set fruit and for the wood to mature. The leaves are long, with many glossy green leaflets, and the elongated nuts occur in clusters. Many selections have been named, propagated by grafting. ZONES 6–11.

Carya ovata *(right)*

SHAGBARK HICKORY, SHELLBARK HICKORY

This species has a similar striking bark to that of *Carya laciniosa*. In its native valley forests in central-eastern USA it grows as a tall, slender tree to 80 ft (24 m) with a long, straight trunk and high, narrow crown,

CARYA
HICKORY

These medium to large, deciduous trees are valued for their strong wood and edible nuts. Some 20 species occur in North America and Asia. They have large, pinnate leaves that turn yellow, orange or rich gold in autumn. Male and female flowers appear on the same plant in late spring. The fruit are enclosed in a leathery husk that is neatly divided into 4 segments. *Carya illinoinensis* is the only commonly cultivated species.

CULTIVATION
Cold hardy and fast growing, hickory trees prefer sheltered, fertile sites with deep, moist soil in regions with cold winters and long, hot, humid summers. They should be grown from seed *in situ*, or planted out as very young seedlings.

but in the open it makes a much lower, broader column with foliage reaching almost to the ground. The leaves, of medium size with only 5 broad leaflets, turn a fine golden yellow in autumn. The smallish nuts are edible. ZONES 4–9.

CARYOPTERIS
BLUEBEARD

This is a genus of 6 species of deciduous, erect subshrubs or woody perennials in the verbena family, all native to eastern Asia. They have slender, cane-like stems with thin, toothed leaves arranged in opposite pairs, and bear small blue or purple flowers in dense stalked clusters in the leaf axils. Only 2 species have been grown much in gardens and even these are now largely replaced by the hybrid between them, represented by a number of cultivars.

CULTIVATION
These plants are often included in shrub borders where their grayish foliage and white or blue flowers blend well with plants of more robust color. They need to be placed in a full sun position, in well-drained, humus-rich soil. Cut well back in early spring to ensure a good framework for the new season's growth and consequent late summer to autumn flowering. Seed can be used for propagation, but in the case of the many cultivars it is necessary to take soft-tip or semi-ripe cuttings.

Caryopteris ×
clandonensis

HYBRID BLUEBEARD, BLUE-MIST
SHRUB

This subshrub, a cross between *Caryopteris incana* and *C. mongolica*, is prized for its masses of delicate, purple-blue flowers borne from late summer to autumn. It grows to a height and spread of 3 ft (1 m), and the oval leaves are gray-green and irregularly serrated. 'Ferndown' is a popular choice among the many cultivars, with dark violet-blue flowers, while 'Heavenly Blue' has blooms of deep blue. 'Kew Blue' has darker green leaves and dark blue flowers. ZONES 5–9.

Caryopteris ×
clandonensis
'Ferndown' *(left)*

Cassia fistula
(below right)

INDIAN LABURNUM, GOLDEN
SHOWER TREE, PUDDING PIPE
TREE, MONKEY-POD TREE

Native to tropical Asia, this widely cultivated species is a deciduous to semi-evergreen tree that can grow to around 60 ft (18 m) high though often only half that height or less in cultivation. It has pinnate leaves made up of 3 to 8 pairs of large leaflets. In summer it produces large, drooping clusters of fragrant, bright yellow flowers. It can be grown in a sheltered position in frost-free warmer temperate areas. **ZONES 10–12.**

Cassia javanica
(below right)

APPLE BLOSSOM TREE

This deciduous tree is native to Southeast Asia, where it may reach a height of 80 ft (24 m). Cultivated specimens are usually half that height, with a broad, flat-topped crown. *Cassia javanica* has long, pinnate leaves made up of very long, narrow leaflets covered in fine down when young. The showy flowers are carried in large clusters and range from pale pink to red. **ZONES 11–12.**

CASSIA

This genus, as now understood, consists of over 100 species of shrubs and trees from tropical and subtropical regions around the world. (Previously, *Cassia* was interpreted in a much broader sense, including a very large number of shrubs, small trees and herbaceous plants now separated as the genus *Senna*, listed later in this book.) Some are evergreen, some deciduous. Most have ferny, pinnate leaves and clusters of simple, bright golden yellow flowers with prominent stamens, often borne for a long period; these are followed by bean-like seed pods which are often very large.

CULTIVATION

Cassias grow in a wide range of conditions, but most prefer well-drained soil and a sunny position. Propagation is from pre-soaked seed in spring or from cuttings in summer.

C

CASSINIA

This is a genus of around 20 species of evergreen shrubs from
Australia and New Zealand closely related to *Helichrysum* and
with similar straw-like bracts surrounding the flowerheads, but
in *Cassinia* the heads are tiny and arranged in large, flat or elongated sprays, sometimes very tightly crowded. The twigs and
leaves are very aromatic, usually coated with a sticky resin that
gives off a strong musky smell most noticeable in hot weather.
The leaves are variable in shape and size but in many species are
small and heath-like. The color of the flowerheads, which are
borne abundantly in summer and autumn, varies from silvery
white to deep yellow. These are vigorous shrubs, often short lived
and of rather untidy habit.

CULTIVATION
Grow in full sun in fertile, well-drained, humus-rich soil. Heavy
pruning after flowering may improve shape, and some species
may have potential as commercial cut flowers. Propagate from
seed or cuttings.

Cassinia aculeata
(left)

From eastern Australia,
this shrub grows to
around 5 ft (1.5 m)
high with an erect,
open habit and deep
green, very narrow
leaves. Massed heads
of tiny, usually white
flowers, sometimes
pink or cream, open
during summer. In the
wild this makes an
open shrub but, with
light pruning after
flowering, a more com-
pact bush can be
achieved. ZONES 8–11.

CASSIOPE

Closely allied to the heathers, this genus of 12 species of dwarf evergreen shrubs is found in the arctic and alpine regions of the northern hemisphere, consequently it is only suited to gardens assured of moist, cool summers and moisture-retentive soil imitating the wild conditions. Cassiopes are low-growing plants, many stemmed from the base, with scale-like leaves and nodding, small, white or pink flowers. The name is taken from Greek mythology, Cassiope being the mother of Andromeda—her name was chosen for this genus because of its close relationship to the genus *Andromeda*. It should be pronounced with four syllables, like Penelope.

CULTIVATION
Cassiopes need to be grown in rather peaty soil to supply the required acidity and moisture, and although they enjoy an open position they need to be protected from the sun and from reflected heat if growing in containers or among rocks. Propagation is from cuttings in summer, while the mat-forming types can be increased from self-rooted stems.

Cassiope 'Edinburgh' *(above)*

This cultivar originated as a hybrid between *Cassiope fastigiata* and *C. lycopodioides*. It grows to about 12 in (30 cm) high with many stems from the base, in late spring bearing small white bells in rather tight clusters on short stalks. ZONES 4–8.

C

CASTANEA
CHESTNUT, CHINQUAPIN

These cool-climate deciduous trees, mostly from North America, all bear edible nuts enclosed in a prickly, burr-like husk. The leaves are elliptical with regularly toothed margins and a feather-like arrangement of veins. In spring or early summer, showy catkins of male flowers appear, and the less conspicuous female flowers on the same tree develop into the nuts. The larger species are highly valued for the fine timber they produce.

CULTIVATION
In a cool climate, chestnuts are easily grown in full sun or part-shade in deep, fertile soil. Hot, dry summers suit them well as long as ample soil moisture is available in winter and spring. All species are readily propagated from fresh seed; plant out seedlings early to avoid disturbing the tap root.

Castanea sativa
(left)

SWEET CHESTNUT, SPANISH CHESTNUT

This species comes from countries around the Mediterranean, Black and Caspian seas, but has been planted throughout Europe for its edible nuts since time immemorial. Young trees are vigorous and have a pyramidal crown, but the lower limbs become massive and spreading with age, and the bark deeply fissured. In autumn, the leaves turn from yellowish green to gold and russet. When planting for nuts, buy grafted named varieties from a source certified free of disease. ZONES 5–9.

CASTANOSPERMUM
QUEENSLAND BLACK BEAN, MORETON BAY CHESTNUT

This genus consists of a single species from the rainforests of northeastern Australia. Long valued for its beautiful chocolate brown timber, it grows slowly and has a stout trunk and a dense, domed crown. The leaves are pinnate with glossy dark green, oblong leaflets, sometimes semi-deciduous in late winter. In early summer it produces showy large orange and yellow pea-flowers in stiff panicles within the foliage canopy. These are followed in autumn by huge hanging pods, deep green ripening to brown, each containing 2 to 5 brown seeds which are 1½ in (35 mm) wide.

CULTIVATION
This tree needs a frost-free climate, well-drained, fertile soil enriched with organic matter and regular watering. Pruning is rarely necessary. Propagate from seed in spring.

Castanospermum australe (right)
This tree, widely planted in streets and for shade in parks and gardens on the east coast of Australia, commonly reaches a height of around 40 ft (12 m). The chestnut-like seeds are poisonous. **ZONES 10–12.**

CASUARINA

SHE-OAK, AUSTRALIAN PINE

Members of this genus of evergreen trees earned the name Australian pine from their conifer-like appearance. There are 6 species of wide distribution in Australia, and about as many again in islands to the north. Many other species once placed here are now classified under *Allocasuarina* or *Gymnostoma* (both genera are listed elsewhere in this book). Despite bearing only inconspicuous (male and female) flowers, casuarinas are graceful trees, fast growing, tolerant of strong winds and adaptable, often to very dry conditions. Casuarina wood makes excel-

lent firewood. They are grown as shade or amenity trees and are valued by some farmers for the shelter they provide for stock, while others maintain that they poison the ground; some nitrogen-fixing organisms do inhabit their roots and there is some evidence that compounds released from the fallen branchlets inhibit other plant growth.

CULTIVATION

Plant in full sun in fertile, moist, well-drained soil. Water well during the growing period, less so in winter. Propagate from seed in spring or cuttings in mid- to late summer. Pruning is rarely necessary.

Casuarina cunninghamiana (right)

RIVER OAK, RIVER SHE-OAK

The largest of the casuarinas, growing to 70–100 ft (21–30 m) tall, this species is much valued for its ability to stabilize riverbanks, its spreading roots helping to prevent erosion. Because of its rapid early growth with foliage persistent to ground level, it is useful as a fast windbreak. The tree requires adequate summer water; it will tolerate quite heavy frosts but growth will be slower and stunted in colder districts.
ZONES 8–12.

Casuarina equisetifolia
(above right)

BEACH SHE-OAK, HORSETAIL TREE

This tree of around 40–60 ft (12–18 m) tall, depending on soil and exposure, has a short trunk and long, weeping, silvery gray branchlets. It grows naturally on beaches and exposed coastal headlands, being very resistant to salt-laden winds and tolerant of poor, sandy soil. It is not at all frost hardy. Reputedly one of the best fuelwood trees in the world, beach she-oak is also

used for boatbuilding, house construction and furniture-making. It has the widest natural distribution of any casuarina, occurring on tropical seashores around most parts of the Pacific and Indian oceans.
ZONES 10–12.

CATALPA

CATALPA, INDIAN BEAN TREE

This genus consists of 11 species of fast-growing, deciduous trees from East Asia and North America. Catalpas have large, ovate leaves in opposite pairs, sprays of showy, bell-shaped flowers at the end of the branches, and extraordinarily long, thin fruits that open to release quantities of very light, winged seeds. They can be beautiful trees with a dense canopy of luxuriant foliage but may look scrappy if exposed to cold or dry winds or if soil is poor. Some species yield valuable timber.

CULTIVATION
Grow in moist, well-drained soil in a sunny but sheltered position. Propagate from seed in autumn or cuttings in late spring or summer, or by budding in late summer or grafting in winter.

Catalpa speciosa (above)

NORTHERN CATALPA, WESTERN CATALPA

This handsome, fast-growing tree reaches over 100 ft (30 m) in its home region, the central Mississippi basin between Arkansas and Indiana, where it grows in forests in rich, moist soil in valley bottoms and on lower slopes. It is sometimes planted for its timber. The leaves are larger than those of *Catalpa bignonioides* but the flowers, borne in mid-summer, are similar though individually slightly larger. Northern catalpa is usually regarded as less decorative overall than the southern species. ZONES 4–10.

Catalpa bignonioides (above)

SOUTHERN CATALPA

From Florida west to Mississippi in the USA, this species grows along riverbanks and around swamp edges. A reasonably compact tree of 25–50 ft (8–15 m) with a rounded, irregularly shaped crown it is cultivated as an ornamental tree for streets and parks. The heart-shaped leaves taper to a fine point and have downy undersides; they turn black before dropping in autumn. Sprays of 2 in (5 cm), white flowers with frilled edges and orange blotches and purple spots on their lower lips appear in summer. '**Aurea**' has lime-yellow leaves. ZONES 5–10.

C

CAVENDISHIA

The Andes of South America are the home of the 10 species that make up this genus, consisting of evergreen shrubs or small trees with bell-shaped or tubular flowers a bit like some *Erica* species but with broad, leathery leaves. Only one cavendishia has found its way into gardens in other parts of the world, and this has proved reasonably frost hardy and vigorous. Many are epiphytes, growing in cloud forests on mossy trees or sometimes on rocks.

CULTIVATION
All prefer filtered sun and peaty, humus-rich soil, a humid atmosphere and a climate without extremes of either heat or cold. Propagate from cuttings in summer or seed in spring or by layering in spring or autumn.

Cavendishia acuminata *(above)*
syn. *Cavendishia bracteata*

Native to Colombia and Ecuador, this is a shrub 3–6 ft (1–1.8 m) tall with somewhat scrambling, reddish brown branches, becoming pendulous at the tips. The new leaves are bronze-pink at the growing tips, hardening to glossy deep green. Clusters of tubular, waxy red to maroon flowers with paler yellowish tips burst from bud bracts from spring to late autumn. ZONES 9–10.

Ceanothus
arboreus

TREE CEANOTHUS, ISLAND
CEANOTHUS

One of the largest-
growing evergreen
species, *Ceanothus
arboreus* from islands
off the south Califor-
nian coast makes an
evergreen tree of up to
30 ft (9 m) but in gar-
dens it is normally only
half that, developing a
thick, low-branching
trunk. The leaves have
downy undersides and
are larger than in most
species and the flowers,
ranging from very pale
blue to deep blue, are
in loose clusters carried
just above the leaves in
spring and early sum-
mer. The plant makes
fast early growth in
suitable conditions.
'**Mist**' is one of the
palest forms with long
spikes of delicate gray-
blue blooms.
ZONES 8–10.

CEANOTHUS

CALIFORNIA LILAC

Brilliant displays of blue, violet, or occasionally pink or white
flowers are the chief attraction of most of the 50 or more species
of this genus of evergreen and deciduous shrubs (some reaching
small tree size), all of them North American but the vast majority
confined to the coast ranges of California. Some species that
grow on coastal cliffs develop dense, prostrate forms highly resistant to salt spray. The leaves are small to medium sized, blunt
tipped and usually toothed. The flowers, individually tiny with
thread-like stalks, are massed in dense clusters at the branch
ends; they appear in spring in most species.

CULTIVATION

As garden plants these shrubs can be outstandingly ornamental
but often short-lived, especially prone to sudden death in climates with warm, wet summers. They require full sun and prefer
shelter, particularly from strong winds, in well-drained soil.
Propagate from seed, often freely produced in small round capsules, or from cuttings.

Ceanothus arboreus
'Mist' *(right & below)*

C

Ceanothus 'Blue Cushion' *(left)*

This hybrid grows only about 3 ft (1 m) tall, but its arching branches spread to 8 ft (2.4 m) across. Unlike some other compact hybrids, it has an open appearance. Flowers, which are abundantly produced, are a soft pale lilac-blue. ZONES 8–10.

Ceanothus × *delilianus* 'Gloire de Versailles' *(left)*

Ceanothus × delilianus

This old French hybrid makes a sturdy, vigorous, deciduous shrub with mid-green leaves that are broad and oval. It originated as a cross between the New Jersey tea *(Ceanothus americanus)* of eastern USA and the tropical *C. coeruleus* from Mexico and Guatemala, which has sky blue flowers in very large sprays. It includes a number of fine cultivars, the best known being **'Gloire de Versailles'**, an 12 ft (3.5 m) shrub with erect, loose panicles of pale blue, scented flowers from mid-summer to early autumn. ZONES 7–9.

Ceanothus griseus *(left)*
CARMEL CEANOTHUS

A spreading, bushy shrub from the central Californian hills, this evergreen species grows to 8 ft (2.4 m) with rounded, dark green leaves, downy on the undersides. Starting in early spring, Carmel ceanothus produces abundant dense flower clusters of a pale violet-blue. *Ceanothus griseus* **var. *horizontalis*** is a name that covers various low-growing, densely spreading forms from coastal cliffs that make fine rock garden or ground cover plants for exposed sites; specific clones are grown under the names **'Yankee Point'** or **'Hurricane Point'**, referring to collection sites. ZONES 8–10.

Ceanothus impressus *(right)*
SANTA BARBARA CEANOTHUS

A free-flowering, small-leafed, evergreen species of dense, spreading habit, this is a first-class garden shrub under suitable conditions. The leaves are ½ in (12 mm) long or less, very thick and with the veins deeply impressed into the upper surface. In spring it produces a profuse display of small clusters of deep blue flowers. From 6–10 ft (1.8–3 m) in height, this coastal Californian species prefers tough, exposed conditions. '**Puget Blue**' features stunning blue flowers and is probably a hybrid with *C. papillosus*. ZONES 8–10.

Ceanothus papillosus *(right)*

This vigorous evergreen shrub or small tree is endemic to the coast ranges of central California. It grows to around 12 ft (3.5 m) high and has bright green, leathery leaves to about 1½ in (35 mm) long that densely clothe its strong branches. In spring the plant is covered in heads of deep blue flowers. It is tough and adaptable, doing well in coastal conditions and withstanding regular trimming. *Ceanothus papillosus* var. *roweanus* has narrower leaves and makes a lower, more spreading shrub up to 6 ft (1.8 m) tall. ZONES 8–10.

Ceanothus thyrsiflorus *(right)*
BLUE BLOSSOM CEANOTHUS

This is an evergreen shrub or small tree that grows to over 20 ft (6 m) in its native moist coastal forests of California, but the forms grown in gardens include some, for example *Ceanothus thyrsiflorus* var. *repens*, that are more compact shrubs of only 3–10 ft (1–3 m) with vigorous spreading branches. The shiny, oval, medium-sized leaves have 3 prominent longitudinal veins. In late spring and early summer the plant produces dense cylindrical clusters of lavender-blue to almost white flowers. '**Blue Mound**' is a low-growing hybrid of *C. thyrsiflorus* reaching 5 ft (1.5 m) in height and spreading to over 6 ft (1.8 m) wide, with medium blue flowers. '**Cascade**' on the other hand can grow to 25 ft (8 m) with broadly arching branches and pale blue flowers. ZONES 7–9.

CECROPIA
CECROPIA

These fast-growing trees with large, umbrella-like leaves are a striking feature of the Amazonian rainforest. They are soft wooded, with large, open crowns that often project above the surrounding trees. The thick branches are often hollow, containing a series of chambers that are inhabited by fierce ants which attack intruders on the tree, including both humans and leafcutter ants that feed on the foliage. Some Amazonian Indians made trumpet-like instruments from the hollow stems. The genus is widespread in tropical America, including some species of smaller size and less striking form.

CULTIVATION
These trees are easily enough cultivated in warm climates in sheltered, sunny positions and deep, moist soil, but the rampant saplings are weak and easily damaged. Propagation is from seed.

Cecropia palmata (above)
SNAKEWOOD TREE

This species from the West Indies and northeastern South America is particularly fast growing; the snakewood tree makes a tall, lanky tree of up to 50 ft (15 m) with few branches. The stems have a waxy blue coating and the leaves are about 24 in (60 cm) across, deeply segmented into 8 to 10 oblong lobes with rounded tips. The whole leaf is colored greenish white on the underside.
ZONES 11–12.

CEDRELA
CIGAR-BOX CEDAR

As formerly defined, the tropical tree genus *Cedrela* included many species from Asia, Australasia and the Americas, but it is now treated as a purely American genus, the Old World species removed to the separate genus *Toona*. Both genera have long, pinnate leaves and panicles of inconspicuous greenish flowers, and the soft, aromatic, reddish timber of both is very valuable and has been exploited in the past to the point of scarcity. *Cedrela* timber is used to make traditional West Indian cigar boxes.

CULTIVATION
These trees are easily grown in any sheltered spot in a warm, humid climate, preferring deep, moist soil. They make fast growth in the first decade or two, slowing down thereafter and making fine shade trees. Propagation is normally from fresh seed.

Cedrela mexicana
(left)

An evergreen forest tree of 100 ft (30 m) or more in its native Central and South America, this species when grown in the open takes on a broader form with a stout, straight central trunk and widely spreading limbs. The crown is rather open and coarsely branched, the pinnate leaves being up to 24 in (60 cm) long with fresh green leaflets. ZONES 10–12.

CEDRUS
CEDAR

This is a renowned genus of conifers belonging to the pine family; the 4 species are so similar that some botanists treat them as subspecies or varieties of a single species. All have needle-like leaves arranged in rosettes on the short but long-lasting lateral shoots, which arise from axils of the longer needles on stronger growths. The pollen cones, shaped like small bananas and up to 4 in (10 cm) long, release large clouds of pollen in early spring. The seed cones are broadly egg- or barrel-shaped, pale bluish or brownish; they eventually shatter to release seeds with broad papery wings. As cultivated trees the cedars are valued for the fine architectural effects of their branching, the texture and color of their foliage, and their vigorous growth.

CULTIVATION

In appropriate climatic conditions these conifers are long lived and trouble free, growing massive with age. They need full sun and well-drained, chalky soil. Propagation is normally from seed, though cuttings, layering and grafting are used for certain cultivars.

Cedrus atlantica
'Glauca' *(below)*

Cedrus atlantica
(below left & bottom far left)
syn. *Cedrus libani*
subsp. *atlantica*
ATLAS CEDAR

Native to the Atlas Mountains (*atlantica* is the adjectival form) of Morocco and Algeria, this tree in its younger stages has a neat, pyramidal shape with stiffly ascending branches, but with age it spreads into a broadly flat-topped tree with massive limbs up to 100 ft (30 m) or more high on good sites. The densely clustered needles are never more than 1 in (25 mm) long and vary from dark green to bluish, though it is mainly the bluish forms that are seen in gardens. This species prefers moderately cool climates. The collective cultivar name **'Glauca'** is used for selected seedling plants with bluish foliage. **'Glauca Pendula'** has long, completely pendulous branches and no leading shoot and is usually grafted onto a standard. ZONES 6–9.

Cedrus deodara 'Aurea'
(above right)

Cedrus deodara *(above)*
DEODAR, DEODAR CEDAR

The deodar (its Indian name) occurs in the western Himalayas, reaching over 200 ft (60 m) in the wild, but is now almost extinct over much of its former range. In cultivation it makes fast early growth. The long leading shoots nod over slightly, and smaller branches are quite pendulous. The foliage is a dark, slightly grayish green, with needles about 1½ in (35 mm) long on strong shoots. The deodar is at its best in milder, humid climates in deep soil, making luxuriant growth and reaching 30 ft (9 m) in about 10 years. The most popular cultivar is 'Aurea', with golden branch tips. ZONES 7–10.

Cedrus libani *(above)*
CEDAR OF LEBANON, LEBANON CEDAR

This magnificent tree has been all but wiped out in Lebanon, with only a few small groves surviving on Mount Lebanon; larger populations survive in Turkey. It was introduced to western Europe centuries ago, and trees in England are up to 120 ft (36 m) in height and 8 ft (2.4 m) in trunk diameter. As a young tree it has a narrow, erect habit but with age adopts a flat-topped shape with massive spreading limbs. The dark green needles are up to 1½ in (35 mm) long. It prefers a moist, cool climate. '**Aurea-Prostrata**' is a dwarf form with golden foliage; '**Nana**' is a very dwarf, slow-growing cultivar of semi-prostrate habit suited to rock gardens; '**Pendula**' is a weeping form, usually grafted onto a standard. *Cedrus libani* subsp. *stenocoma* is the geographical race from mountains of southwestern Turkey; it has a more narrowly conical or columnar growth habit. ZONES 6–9.

CEIBA
SILK COTTON TREE

This genus consists of 4 species of large, dry-season-deciduous trees with heavily buttressed spiny trunks, large palmate leaves and showy, 5-petalled flowers. The large football-shaped fruits split to release seeds embedded in kapok, a cottonwool-like fiber. They occur naturally in the tropics of Asia, the Americas and Africa and were once important as the main source of kapok, used for stuffing, insulation and flotation, still with some commercial uses though largely replaced by synthetics. The trees are widely used by local people as sources of fiber, fuel and timber.

CULTIVATION
These fast-growing trees can only be successfully cultivated in the wet tropics. They need regular rainfall, full sun, moist, well-drained soil and steady, warm temperatures. Propagate from seed or cuttings.

Ceiba pentandra *(above & above right)*
KAPOK

Reaching heights of over 200 ft (60 m) high, this African species is the tallest tree found in that continent. It also occurs wild in South America but in tropical Asia is considered introduced, hav-ing been planted for kapok production. Its trunk is spiny when young and the branches are held horizontally, giving the tree a distinctive pyrami-dal outline. Showy white, yellow or pale pink flowers, 6 in (15 cm) in diameter, are followed by 6 in (15 cm) long fruit. ZONE 12.

CELTIS
NETTLE TREE, HACKBERRY

This large genus of 70 species includes many evergreens, occurring mainly in the tropics, but the cool-climate, deciduous species from North America, Europe and Asia are the ones mostly cultivated. They are medium to fairly large trees with smooth or slightly rough bark. The leaves are smallish, oval and pointed at the tip, with few or many marginal teeth. Insignificant flowers, of different sexes and lacking petals, appear with the new leaves; fruits are small, hard drupes carried singly in the leaf axils. Birds eat the fruits and disperse the seeds, and some species self-seed and can become a nuisance. *Celtis* species are planted mainly as shade trees in streets and parks, where they make shapely, long-lived and trouble-free specimens.

CULTIVATION
In cooler climates, these fully frost-hardy trees like dry soil and full sun; in warmer areas they prefer rich, moist, well-drained soil and part-shade. Propagate from seed in autumn.

Celtis occidentalis (above)
AMERICAN HACKBERRY
This species comes from the east of the USA, the Mississippi Basin and eastern Canada. In its preferred habitat of forests in deep, rich, alluvial soils it can reach a very large size, but when planted in the open it makes a shapely, spreading tree of 40–60 ft (12–18 m). The bark, smooth on saplings, becomes rough as the tree matures. The pea-sized fruit ripen through red to dull purple. The foliage turns pale yellow in autumn; it can become a pest along riverbanks and channels in some countries. ZONES 3–10.

CEPHALOTAXUS
PLUM YEW

C

This is an interesting genus of conifers consisting of around 10 species of shrubs or small trees from eastern Asia, mostly with many stems sprouting from the base. The deep green, leathery leaves are rather like those of the true yews *(Taxus)*, though usually longer. The fleshy 'fruits' develop in stalked globular heads and are more like olives than plums, ripening reddish brown. Male pollen sacs are grouped in small, globular clusters on separate trees.

CULTIVATION
They are tough, resilient plants, but do best in cool, fairly humid climates and in sheltered positions. The occasional free-seeding specimen can cause minor problems by the quantity of 'fruit' dropping to rot on the ground. Propagate from seed, which may take 2 years to germinate, or from cuttings.

Cephalotaxus harringtonia 'Fastigiata' *(below)*

Cephalotaxus harringtonia
JAPANESE PLUM YEW

First known from Japan, this variable species also occurs in Korea and parts of China. The typical form is a spreading, bushy shrub 6–10 ft (1.8–3 m) tall with leaves up to 2½ in (6 cm) long. More commonly grown is *Cephalotaxus harringtonia* var. *drupacea*, a dome-like shrub to about 10 ft (3 m) with short blunt leaves in 2 erect rows. The most remarkable and attractive form is **'Fastigiata'**: very erect, it sends up a dense mass of long, straight stems from the base, with radiating whorls of recurving leaves. It forms a tight column 6 ft (1.8 m) or more high and 24–36 in (60–90 cm) across. **'Nana'** is a low-growing form, generally under 3 ft (1 m) high but spreading widely with almost prostrate branches, often self-layering. **'Prostrata'** forms a cushion of generally ascending branches to 24 in (60 cm) tall and spreads about 4 ft (1.2 m). ZONES 6–10.

CERATONIA
CAROB, ST JOHN'S BREAD

The single species in this genus comes from the eastern Mediter-ranean, where it forms a picturesque, round-headed tree of up to 40 ft (12 m). It is more commonly seen as a smaller tree or large shrub in cultivation and can be pruned hard to keep it in check. The bean-like pods, about 6 in (15 cm) long, commonly roasted and powdered as a chocolate substitute, can be picked in autumn when they are dark brown. They can also be eaten fresh and are used as stock fodder.

CULTIVATION
While it requires hot, dry summers to perform well, the carob will survive in warm, sheltered positions in cooler climates. Marginally frost hardy, it does best in full sun although it will tolerate light shade and is also tolerant of dry conditions; a moderately fertile, well-drained soil suits it best. Propagate from seed in autumn.

Ceratonia siliqua (above)

A long-lived evergreen tree, this species is used as a shade tree for streets, parks and large gardens, and as a farm shelter and fodder tree. It has glossy pinnate leaves and clustered spikes of small green-ish flowers in spring and autumn, which may be ill-smelling at close quarters. As some plants bear only male or female flowers, interplanting of both sexes may be needed for pod production. ZONES 9–11.

CERATOPETALUM

Members of this small Australian genus come from the moist
forests of the east coast; the 2 most important species are found
in New South Wales, where they are valued for their timber and
flowers. These evergreens bear flowers with small white petals
but with sepals that enlarge and turn red as the small, nut-like
fruits mature, appearing very flower-like and showy.

CULTIVATION

Ceratopetalums prefer a warm, almost frost-free climate and
free-draining soil in a sunny or part-shaded position, with protection from salty winds and plenty of water in spring and
summer. Propagation is from fresh seed or from cuttings.

Ceratopetalum
gummiferum *(left)*

NEW SOUTH WALES CHRISTMAS
BUSH

Occurring naturally in
coastal gullies and on
sheltered slopes in
mostly sandstone soils,
in the wild this species
makes an upright tree
to 30 ft (9 m) or more
in height. In gardens it
is often kept pruned as
a shrub or small tree of
about 12 ft (3.5 m),
and is grown for its
bright 'flowers' which
start white and become
pink or bright red in
early summer. The
shiny, soft green leaves
are each divided into
3 serrated leaflets. As
coloration is very vari-
able from seedling
stock, it is wise to buy
plants when in flower
or choose a clone such
as **'Albery's Red'**.
ZONES 9–11.

CERATOSTIGMA

This genus of 8 species of herbaceous perennials and small shrubs is primarily of Himalayan and East Asian origin, with one species endemic to the Horn of Africa. Most of the species grown in gardens are small deciduous shrubs and from spring to autumn they produce loose heads of blue flowers that indicate the genus's relationship with *Plumbago*. The small leaves are deep green, turning to bronze or crimson in autumn before dropping.

CULTIVATION
Ceratostigma species will grow in any moist, well-drained soil in sun or part-shade. Propagate from seed or semi-ripe cuttings, or by division. In cold climates they will reshoot from the roots even though the top growth may die back to ground level.

Ceratostigma willmottianum *(above)*
CHINESE PLUMBAGO

This 2–4 ft (0.6–1.2 m), deciduous shrub from western Sichuan, China, is prized for its small lilac-blue flowers that open from late summer to autumn. The leaves are deep green, roughly diamond-shaped and around 2 in (5 cm) long.
ZONES 6–10.

CERCIDIPHYLLUM
KATSURA TREE

Consisting of a single species of deciduous tree native to Japan and China, this genus is placed in a family of its own, allied to the magnolia family. The dull red flowers are rather insignificant, with different sexes on different trees. On female trees clusters of small greenish pod-like fruit follow the flowers. The katsura tree is valued chiefly for its foliage, which is reddish when first expanding in spring, then dark green, changing in autumn to various mixtures of yellow, pink, orange and red. *Katsura* is its Japanese name.

CULTIVATION

This tree prefers rich, moist but well-drained soil in a sunny or part-shaded position. It is fully frost hardy but the spring foliage is easily damaged by late frost, very dry conditions or drying winds. Propagate from seed or cuttings.

Cercidiphyllum japonicum 'Pendulum' *(left)*

In cultivation in the West *Cercidiphyllum japonicum* is known as a small, rather slender tree to about 40 ft (12 m) high, but in Japan and China it is the largest native deciduous tree—ancient specimens up to 130 ft (40 m) tall, with trunks over 15 ft (4.5 m) in diameter, are known. The trunk often forks at a narrow angle and the short branches spread horizontally in tiers. The heart-shaped leaves are mostly under 3 in (8 cm) wide, but larger in *C. j.* var. *magnificum;* the Chinese *C. j.* var. *sinense* has slightly different leaves and flowers. 'Pendulum' has a dome-shaped crown and pendulous branches. ZONES 6–9.

Cercidium
floridum
(below & below right)

PALO VERDE

The common name is Spanish for 'green stick' and describes the smooth bluish green bark and branches of this small tree. Native to the lower Colorado basin of southwestern USA and adjacent Mexico, *Cercidium floridum* matures into a broad-crowned small tree 25–30 ft (8–9 m) tall, with a short thick trunk and densely massed branches. In spring it is briefly transformed into a mass of golden yellow blossom. It is leafless for much of the time, unless regularly watered. ZONES 8–11.

CERCIDIUM

From the warmer and drier parts of the Americas, the legume genus *Cercidium* consists of small, wiry-branched trees that are commonly deciduous throughout dry periods, coming into leaf only after rain. The leaves are small and bipinnate, but for much of the time it is the wiry green branches that perform the function of photosynthesis. The fine-stalked flowers are yellow and cup-shaped, somewhat like *Cassia* flowers, and appear in profuse clusters all along the branches for a few weeks in spring. Some botanists suggest that all *Cercidium* species be transferred to *Parkinsonia*.

CULTIVATION

These trees can make fine ornamental and shade trees for very hot dry areas, though they do require a supply of deep subsoil moisture. Propagation is from seed, produced in small pods. They can become invasive, so excessive seedlings should be removed.

C

CERCIS

Cercis canadensis (below)

EASTERN REDBUD

JUDAS TREE, REDBUD

Native to eastern and central USA, this tree can reach 40 ft (12 m) in the wild and is strikingly beautiful in flower. In gardens it rarely exceeds 12 ft (3.5 m), branching close to the ground. The leaves are heart-shaped with a distinct point, and appear after the flowers. The buds are deep rose, and the paler rose flowers are profuse and showy; flowering may continue from spring into early summer. **'Forest Pansy'** has purple-colored leaves. In the southwestern part of its range the typical form is replaced by *Cercis canadensis* var. *texensis*, whose leaf undersides have a waxy bluish coating. ZONES 5–9.

This genus is made up of small, deciduous trees or shrubs from North America, Asia and southern Europe. Their profuse clusters of pea-like flowers, bright rose pink to crimson, line the bare branches in spring; even the neat, pointed buds, slightly deeper in color, make an elegant display, hence the American name redbud. The handsome, heart-shaped to almost circular leaves follow, along with flat seed pods up to 4 in (10 cm) long.

CULTIVATION

All 7 or 8 species are worth cultivating, though not all are easily obtained. They resent disturbance to their roots, especially transplanting. A sunny position suits them best and they thrive in hot, dry summer weather, as long as the soil moisture is adequate in winter and spring. They are easily propagated from seed, though growth is usually slow and it may take many years for them to become larger than shrub size.

Cercis canadensis 'Forest Pansy' *(left)*
Cercis siliquastrum 'Alba' *(below left)*

Cercis siliquastrum *(far right)*

JUDAS TREE, LOVE TREE

Native to regions close to the Mediterranean and Black Sea coasts, this tree seldom exceeds 25 ft (8 m) even after several decades. The leaves are slightly bluish green with rounded tips, and the late spring flowers, larger and deeper pinkish magenta than in other species, arise in clusters on previous years' growths. It is the most reliable ornamental species in regions

where winters are mild. Those forms having distinct flower coloration include the paler **'Alba'** and the deeper reddish **'Rubra'**. ZONES 7–9.

CESTRUM

This genus of the potato family is made up of almost 200 species of mostly evergreen shrubs native to Central and South America and the West Indies. The leaves are simple and smooth edged, often with a rank smell when bruised, and the smallish flowers are tubular or urn-shaped, gathered in clusters at the branch tips. The flowers vary in color from white to green, yellow, red and dull purplish, and some are night scented. Small round berries follow the flowers; these and other parts are poisonous.

CULTIVATION

Cestrums make rather straggly bushes but can be pruned hard to shape by removing older stems each year after flowering. In frost-free climates they grow easily in full sun and moderately fertile, well-drained soil with plentiful water in summer and regular fertilizing. In cooler climates they grow in a conservatory or against a wall for frost protection. Some species are free seeding and invasive. Propagate from soft tip cuttings.

**Cestrum
fasciculatum** *(right)*

Also from Mexico, this species is similar to *Cestrum elegans* with scarlet flowers but they are borne in denser, more pendent clusters and are slightly more urn-shaped with conspicuous velvety hairs. It is a slender, fast-growing shrub to 10 ft (3 m) with arching branches and hairy, long-pointed leaves. The flowers are borne in summer and occasionally throughout the year. ZONES 9–11.

Cestrum 'Newellii'
(right)

This is a popular cultivar of hybrid origin, possibly between *Cestrum elegans* and *C. fasciculatum*—it takes an expert eye, in fact, to distinguish between these and *C.* 'Newellii'. It reaches about 6 ft (1.8 m) high and produces clusters of crimson, unscented flowers through much of the year, followed by matching berries. Tougher than most cestrums, it is regarded as a weed in some mild areas. **ZONES 9–11.**

Cestrum nocturnum *(above)*

NIGHT-SCENTED JESSAMINE, LADY OF THE NIGHT

A rather untidy evergreen shrub to 12 ft (3.5 m) tall and almost as wide, this species has long, slender, arching branches springing densely from the base. Clusters of slender, pale green flowers appear in late summer and autumn, strongly and sweetly perfumed at night but scentless during the day. The green berries that follow turn a glossy china white in early winter. **ZONES 10–12.**

Cestrum parqui *(above)*
GREEN CESTRUM, WILLOW-LEAFED JESSAMINE

Native to Chile, this species is a rather non-descript shrub of up to about 10 ft (3 m) tall that suckers from the roots and has foliage with a rank, unpleasant smell. In warm climates it blooms throughout the year with yellow green, night-scented flowers in dense clusters, followed by small black fruit. In a mild, moist climate it self-seeds freely which, in combination with its tenacious root system, can make it a troublesome weed. **ZONES 9–11.**

Chaenomeles japonica
(below)
syn. *Chaenomeles maulei*
JAPANESE FLOWERING QUINCE

This low-growing species, native to Japan, is usually no more than 3 ft (1 m) high, making a dense mass of horizontally spreading, thorny branches. The flowers, appearing long after the plant has come into leaf, are about 1½ in (35 mm) across and usually orange-red but sometimes crimson. Produced from spring to summer, they are followed by small, round yellow fruit that have a pleasant scent. *Chaenomeles japonica* var. *alpina* is a dwarf form with semi-prostrate stems and small orange flowers. 'Sargentii' has large orange-red flowers. ZONES 4–9.

CHAENOMELES
FLOWERING QUINCE

Related to the edible quince *(Cydonia)* with similar large, hard fruits, these many-stemmed deciduous shrubs are valued for their display of red, pink or white flowers on a tangle of bare branches in early spring or even late winter. Originating in China, Japan and Korea, they are very frost hardy and adaptable. The tough, springy branches are often thorny on vigorous shoots; the leaves are simple and finely toothed. The flowers appear in stalkless clusters on the previous year's wood, followed in summer by yellow green fruits with waxy, strongly perfumed skins that make fine jams and jellies. The wild forms have been superseded by a large selection of cultivars.

CULTIVATION
They do best in a sunny spot in well-drained but not too rich soil and a dry atmosphere. Cut back hard each year. Propagate from cuttings.

C

C

Chaenomeles speciosa 'Nivalis' *(above left)*
Chaenomeles speciosa 'Moerloosii' *(above)*
Chaenomeles speciosa 'Apple Blossom' *(left)*

Chaenomeles speciosa

CHINESE FLOWERING QUINCE, JAPONICA

This species and its hybrids are the most commonly grown flowering quinces. Shrubs of 5–10 ft (1.5–3 m) high, they spread by basal suckers to form dense thickets of stems. Their leaves are larger than in *Chaenomeles japonica*, up to 4 in (10 cm) long and 1½ in (35 mm) wide, and the scarlet to deep red flowers, opening from late winter to mid-spring, are also larger. Modern cultivars vary in availability, but several older ones still widely grown include **'Apple Blossom'**, white, flushed pink; **'Nivalis'**, white; **'Moerloosii'**, white flushed and blotched pink and carmine; and **'Rubra Grandiflora'**, crimson. ZONES 6–10.

Chaenomeles × superba

(left)

This is a hybrid between *Chaenomeles japonica* and *C. speciosa* with a height about midway between that of the two parents. It has given rise to a number of first-class cultivars like **'Knap Hill Scarlet'** with bright orange-scarlet flowers; **'Crimson and Gold'** with deep crimson petals and gold anthers; **'Nicoline'** which has a rather sprawling habit and scarlet flowers; **'Pink Lady'** with large, bright rose pink flowers; and **'Rowallane'** with blood crimson flowers. ZONES 6–10.

CHAMAECYPARIS
FALSE CYPRESS

In the nineteenth century botanists classified these conifers as *Cupressus* (true cypresses), and indeed the differences are slight—*Chamaecyparis* has its tiny branchlets more flattened with the scale-like leaves of two types, and the cones are smaller and release their seed earlier. Nearly all the 8 *Chamaecyparis* species occur in cooler, moister, more northerly regions in North America and eastern Asia, while true cypresses mostly occur further south and in drier regions. Several species have many cultivars, which feature colored foliage (usually gold, bluish or bronze); narrow, fastigiate, columnar or dwarf habit; bizarre foliage traits; or needle-like juvenile foliage.

CULTIVATION
These frost-hardy trees grow well in a cool, moist climate; they respond with fast growth to deep, rich, well-drained soil and a sheltered position. Cultivars are easily propagated from cuttings, the typical tree forms from seed.

Chamaecyparis funebris *(right)*
syn. *Cupressus funebris*

CHINESE WEEPING CYPRESS, MOURNING CYPRESS

This attractive species is widespread at lower altitudes in central China. It reaches a height of 30–50 ft (9–15 m) and is of broadly co-lumnar habit, with a straight central trunk and ascending branches drooping at the tips, the small branchlets arranged in very elongated, pendu-lous, loosely flattened sprays. The foliage is a bright green. Globular green cones appear in profusion in summer. **'Aurea'** has foliage of a slightly paler yellowish green. ZONES 9–11.

C

Chamaecyparis lawsoniana
'Argentea Compacta' *(above)*
Chamaecyparis lawsoniana
'Alumii' *(far left)*
Chamaecyparis lawsoniana
'Golden Wonder' *(left)*

Chamaecyparis lawsoniana *(top left)*

PORT ORFORD CEDAR, LAWSON CYPRESS

From the humid coastal forests of northwestern USA, this is the most widely planted member of the genus in its typical form, as well as having given rise to a larger number of cultivars than any other conifer species. Planted trees are up to 120 ft (36 m) tall with trunks up to 4 ft (1.2 m) in diameter, narrowly conical with pendulous side branches producing rippling curtains of bluish green to deep green foliage. Over 180 cultivars are currently available and many more have been named. '**Alumii**', of erect, conical habit with very bluish, dense foliage, grows to 10–15 ft (3–4.5 m) or more. '**Argentea Compacta**' is a dwarf shrub with green foliage variegated with cream. '**Aurea Densa**' has golden yellow foliage. '**Croftway**' has gray foliage fading to dark green. '**Ellwoodii**' is a dense, conical shrub with blue-tinged foliage. '**Erecta**' is plain green with very erect, narrow sprays of foliage tightly crowded together; it can reaches 30 ft (9 m) with age. '**Erecta Aurea**' grows upright and has bright yellow foliage. '**Fletcheri**' has gray-blue foliage in smaller, less regular sprays and is semi-juvenile, the leaves somewhat needle-like. '**Fraseri**' has gray-green foliage. While not a very spectacular color, it is an excellent shade for offsetting brighter conifers or for use as a subtly toned hedge. '**Green Globe**' is a dense dwarf cultivar to 18 in (45 cm) with fine, dark green foliage. '**Lane**' makes a narrower column with lemony yellow foliage in late spring and summer changing to bronze-gold in winter. '**Lemon Queen**' has pale yellow foliage and '**Golden Wonder**' is very similar. '**Lutea**' makes a narrow column or cone

C

Hedge of *(from left)* Chamae-
cyparis lawsoniana 'Fraseri',
'Lutea' and 'Alumii', and *Taxus
baccata (above)*
Chamaecyparis lawsoniana
'Erecta' *(above right)*
Chamaecyparis lawsoniana
'Green Globe' *(right)*
Chamaecyparis lawsoniana
'Lane' *(far right)*

and has golden yellow foliage.
'Pembury Blue' bears pendent
sprays of silvery blue foliage.
'Stewartii', a golden cultivar,
rapidly reaches 15–25 ft
(4.5–8 m), with a broad base
and crowded nodding sprays of
rich buttery foliage; it is often
used in landscaping for a gold
effect on a large scale. **'Wisselii'**
grows to 80 ft (24 m) and is a
narrowly conical tree with
bluish green foliage. **'Winston
Churchill'** is a popular recent
cultivar; it has a pronounced
conical growth habit and golden
yellow foliage. ZONES 6–10.

Chamaecyparis lawsoniana
'Pembury Blue' *(above)*
Chamaecyparis lawsoniana
'Winston Churchill' *(right)*

C

Chamaecyparis nootkatensis
'Pendula' *(left)*
Chamaecyparis obtusa
'Crippsii' *(bottom left)*
Chamaecyparis obtusa 'Kosteri'
(below)
Chamaecyparis obtusa
'Minima' *(bottom right)*

Chamaecyparis nootkatensis *(above left)*

NOOTKA CYPRESS, ALASKA CEDAR

From western North America, this cypress ranges much further north than *Chamaecyparis lawsoniana*, up through the west coast of Canada right into Alaska. A large forest tree, it is conical in shape, growing to about 100 ft (30 m) in height and 25 ft (8 m) in spread; the small blue-green cones have a recurved, pointed flap at the center of each scale. *C. nootkatensis* is an attractive tree and thrives under more adverse conditions of soil and climate. **'Pendula'** has vertically hanging sprays of foliage and an open crown in maturity. ZONES 4–9.

Chamaecyparis obtusa

HINOKI CYPRESS, HINOKI FALSE CYPRESS

The normal, tall form of this fine tree from Japan, with richly textured, deep green foliage, is seldom seen in gardens; the species is usually represented by its dwarf or colored cultivars. One of Japan's most valued timber trees, it reaches 120 ft (36 m) in the wild with a trunk to 4 ft (1.2 m) in diameter and thick, red-brown bark. In cultivation it grows 60 ft (18 m) high, broadly columnar with dense,

C

Chamaecyparis obtusa 'Nana Gracilis' *(left)*

Chamaecyparis pisifera 'Filifera Aurea' *(below)*

Chamaecyparis pisifera

SAWARA CYPRESS, SAWARA FALSE CYPRESS

This vigorous Japanese species grows to 150 ft (45 m) in the wild. A broad, conical tree, the lower sides of the branchlets are strongly marked bluish white and the tiny scale leaves on juvenile growth are quite prickly. The cultivars fall into 4 groups: the **Squarrosa Group**, the **Plumosa Group** (the largest group), the **Filifera Group** and the **Nana Group**. **'Squarrosa'** itself is a broadly pyramidal, small tree to 65 ft (20 m) with pale bluish gray juvenile foliage that turns dull purple in winter. **'Squarrosa Intermedia'** is a dwarf cultivar. **'Boulevard'** is narrowly conical, to 10 ft (3 m), with foliage of a bright steel blue mixed with green. The Plumosa Group includes **'Plumosa'**, a conical or columnar tree to 20 ft (6 m) with mid-green foliage, the leaves shorter and less prickly than 'Squarrosa'; **'Plumosa Aurea'** with yellow-green foliage; and **'Plumosa Compressa'**, a dwarf cultivar to 18 in (45 cm) with yellowish green foliage. Of the Filifera Group, the best known are: **'Filifera'**, with slender shoots and dark green leaves, seldom grown now; **'Filifera Aurea'**, a broadly pyramidal shrub of up to 10 ft (3 m); its bright gold and green foliage has flattened fans of branchlets mixed with elongated 'rat's tail' branchlets that arch gracefully. **'Nana'** is a hemispherical shrub with crowded, tiny sprays of foliage; it can take 10 years or more to reach 12 in (30 cm). ZONES 5–10.

spreading branches that touch the ground. **'Crippsii'** makes a broad, golden pyramid with a vigorous leading shoot and is usually about 10–15 ft (3–4.5 m) tall. **'Tetragona'** and **'Tetragona Aurea'** are of similar height but narrower and more irregularly branched, their scale leaves in 4 equal ranks and branchlets tightly crowded; the former is a deep, slightly bluish green, the latter green and gold. Of the dwarf cultivars, the smallest under 12 in (30 cm) in height, the best known are **'Flabelliformis'**, with pale green leaves to 6 in (15 cm); **'Kosteri'** with apple-green foliage; **'Minima'**, under 4 in (10 cm) after 20 years and with mid-green foliage; **'Nana'**, a spreading tree to 3 ft (1 m) in height with dull, dark green foliage; **'Nana Gracilis'** and its many variants, little bun-shaped plants normally 12–24 in (30–60 cm) high with crowded fans of tiny branchlets producing a richly textured effect; **'Nana Aurea'**, which has golden tips to the fans and more of a bronze tone in winter; **'Spiralis'**, an erect, stiff tree; **'Tempelhof'**, which grows to 8 ft (2.4 m) and has greenish yellow foliage that turns bronze in winter; and **'Verdon'** with yellow-green young growth. ZONES 5–10.

C

Chamaecyparis pisifera
'Plumosa' *(above far left)*

Chamaecyparis pisifera
'Plumosa Aurea' *(above center)*

Chamaecyparis pisifera
'Boulevard' *(above)*

Chamaecyparis thyoides
(below right)

ATLANTIC WHITE CEDAR, SOUTHERN
WHITE CEDAR

From eastern North America,
this very frost-hardy tree
reaches about 60 ft (18 m) in
the wild, less in cultivation. It is
narrowly columnar when
young. The dull gray-green
branchlets are grouped into very
small fans crowded irregularly
on the branches and do not
produce the rippled foliage
effect of most other species.
'Andelyensis' is a conical form
with bluish green leaves.
'Ericoides' makes a broad pyramid 6–8 ft (1.8–2.4 m) high; its
soft, persistent, juvenile foliage
is bronze-green in spring and
summer, changing to deep plum
tones in winter. **'Red Star'** is a
compact tree to 6 ft (1.8 m)
with soft, feathery, silvery green
foliage turning rich purple in
winter. ZONES 4–9.

Chamaecyparis pisifera
'Squarrosa' *(left)*

Chamaecyparis thyoides
'Red Star' *(above)*

CHAMAECYTISUS

A broom genus consisting of about 30 species of deciduous and evergreen shrubs from the Mediterranean region and the Canary Islands, *Chamaecytisus* is closely related to *Cytisus* and its species were formerly included in the latter genus. They range from dwarf to quite tall shrubs but all have leaves consisting of 3 leaflets and produce clusters of white, yellow, pink or purple pea-flowers. Some are attractive rock garden subjects, while at least one taller species is grown as a fodder and green manure plant.

CULTIVATION
The smaller species should be grown in full sun in very well-drained soil, preferably in a raised position such as a rock garden. They seldom survive transplanting. The taller species are less fussy and will grow in most soils, fertile or infertile, and in a range of situations. Propagate from seed or cuttings.

Chamaecytisus purpureus *(above)*
syn. *Cytisus purpureus*
PURPLE BROOM

Native to southeastern Europe this is a low-growing deciduous shrub reaching a height of about 18 in (45 cm), with a broadly spreading habit. Showy lilac-purple flowers ¾ in (18 mm) in length are produced in late spring and early summer, in clusters of 1 to 3 at each leaf-axil. Flowering in the next season is promoted by cutting back as soon as flowering has finished. ZONES 6–9.

CHAMELAUCIUM

This genus of 20 species of evergreen shrubs of the myrtle family is endemic to Western Australia. As well-known Australian commercial cut flowers, they are also grown in other countries. The narrow, almost needle-like leaves contain slightly aromatic oils; flowers are slender-stalked with 5 rounded, white or pink to purple petals around a central cup containing nectar. They are beautiful flowers, long-lasting when cut, but the shrubs have a reputation for being difficult to grow since they do not tolerate cold winters, wet summers or high humidity.

CULTIVATION
Try them in full sun and slightly alkaline, gravelly soil with perfect drainage and prune fairly hard after flowering. They may be short-lived. Avoid root disturbance. Propagate from cuttings in summer.

Chamelaucium uncinatum
(left & below left)
GERALDTON WAXFLOWER

The common name refers to the town of Geraldton, north of Perth, where this species is most abundant. It is a commonly grown species and the chief parent of most recently bred cultivars. A brittle, spreading shrub of up to 10 ft (3 m) tall and wide, it has fine needle-like foliage and large, airy sprays of waxy white, mauve or pink flowers borne profusely in late winter and through spring. New cultivars appear regularly but all seem prone to root-rot in wet soil. ZONES 10–11.

CHILOPSIS
DESERT WILLOW, DESERT CATALPA

Consisting of a single species that occurs wild in dry streambeds of inland southwestern USA and northern Mexico, *Chilopsis* belongs to the bignonia family and has the showy trumpet-shaped flowers typical of that family. Despite the common name it is quite unrelated to willows, though the leaves do resemble those of many willows, narrow and drawn out into a long point. The flowers are borne in short spikes at the branch ends, opening in succession. It is a lank, untidy shrub, worth growing only for its attractive flowers.

CULTIVATION
It does best in a hot, dry climate with cool, crisp nights. The soil should be open and well-drained but with deep subsoil moisture available. Propagation is from seed or cuttings.

Chilopsis linearis
(right)

The desert willow can make a tree of 30 ft (9 m) or more, but in gardens is usually a shrub of 10–15 ft (3–4.5 m) with an open habit of growth, the slender branches arching and twisted at odd angles. The sparse leaves are pale green, sometimes as much as 12 in (30 cm) long, and the 2 in (5 cm) flowers, borne through late spring and summer, can be white, pale pink or a deep cerise-pink, paler in the throat. **ZONES 7–10.**

C

CHIMONANTHUS
WINTERSWEET

This small genus of 6 species of deciduous shrubs from China belongs to a primitive flowering-plant family allied to the magnolia family; one species is popular in gardens for its deliciously scented flowers produced from early to mid-winter. The leaves are simple and thin textured, clustered at the ends of the stiff branches. Smallish flowers are clustered just below branch tips; they are multi-petalled and cup-shaped, with a translucent waxy texture, and are followed by leathery-skinned fruit of a strange shape, like little bags stuffed with balls, which turn out to be the large seeds.

CULTIVATION
Quite frost hardy, it will grow in most positions. In cold climates position against a warm wall to protect the flowers. Immediately after flowering thin out weaker stems and, if desired, shorten larger stems. Propagate from seed or layer multiple stems by mounding with soil.

Chimonanthus praecox (left)
syn. *Chimonanthus fragrans*

The wintersweet makes a thicket of stiff, angular stems 10–15 ft (3–4.5 m) high and wide, with harsh-textured, mid-green leaves. The flowers appear in abundance on bare winter branches or, in milder climates, among the last leaves of autumn; the petals are pale yellow to off-white with a dull pink or red basal zone showing on the inside. The fruits are yellowish brown when ripe. **'Luteus'** has late blooming, buttercup-yellow flowers. ZONES 6–10.

CHIONANTHUS
FRINGE TREE

Belonging to the olive family, the genus *Chionanthus* used to contain only 2 species of deciduous tree, one from temperate North America and one from China, but botanists have now transferred to it many tropical evergreens from the genus *Linociera*. The deciduous species, though, are of most interest to gardeners. In late spring the crowns of these small trees are sprinkled with clusters of delicate white flowers—each slender-stalked flower has 4 narrow, diverging white petals. A good specimen in full flower is very beautiful. The smooth-margined leaves are in opposite pairs; the summer fruits are like small olives.

CULTIVATION
These cool-climate trees are easily grown but may be slow and can take 10 years to flower. A sunny but sheltered position with good soil and drainage suits them best. Propagate from seed in autumn.

Chionanthus retusus
(below right)
CHINESE FRINGE TREE

Native to China and Taiwan, this tree can reach 30 ft (9 m), developing a broad, umbrella-like crown with age. The shiny leaves vary in shape and size on the one tree. The flowers, with petals about 1 in (25 mm) long, are borne in profuse, upright clusters that stand above the foliage in late spring or early summer. This seems to be the more climatically adaptable species, flowering well in cool, warm and even subtropical regions. ZONES 6–10.

Chionanthus virginicus
(below right)
AMERICAN FRINGE TREE

The individual flowers of this species are similar to those of *Chionanthus retusus*, but the leaves are larger and less shiny and the longer, drooping flower sprays appear among the foliage rather than standing above it. In its native forests of southeastern USA it grows in rich, moist soil close to streams, occasionally 30 ft (9 m) tall but often only a shrub. Away from its native regions it can be a shy bloomer, performing better in continental climates of central Europe than in the UK and not doing so well in climates warmer than that. ZONES 5–9.

CHOISYA

This genus of 8 species of evergreen shrubs belongs to the same family as citrus, from Mexico and the far south of the USA. One species is widely cultivated for ornament in warm-temperate climates. Their leaves are compound with 3 to 7 leaflets radiating from the stalk apex; from the leaf axils arise clusters of fragrant star-shaped white flowers, resembling orange-blossoms. The crushed or bruised leaves are also aromatic.

CULTIVATION

They are excellent hedging plants as well as being attractive additions to shrub borders, growing best in full sun or part shade and a slightly acid, humus-rich, well-drained soil. Protect from strong winds, fertilize in spring and trim lightly after flowering to keep foliage dense and ground-hugging. Propagate from tip cuttings in autumn.

Choisya 'Aztec Pearl' *(below left)*

This is a recently developed hybrid between *Choisya arizonica* and *C. ternata*, the first produced in this genus. It is an elegant shrub growing to 6 ft (1.8 m) or more, with aromatic leaves divided into 3 to 5 narrow, channelled leaflets. Flowers are similar to those of *C. ternata* but slightly larger, pink-flushed in the bud and opening white—it commonly produces 2 flushes of bloom, in early and late summer. ZONES 8–11.

Choisya ternata
(below left)

MEXICAN ORANGE BLOSSOM

One of the most frost hardy evergreens to come from the highlands of Mexico, this popular species makes a compact, rounded bush to 6 ft (1.8 m) or more. Its attractive leaves consist of 3 glossy deep green leaflets. Tight clusters of small white, fragrant flowers appear among the leaves in spring, and sometimes again in late summer. **'Sundance'** has golden yellow foliage when young, maturing to yellow-green. ZONES 7–11.

Choisya ternata 'Sundance' *(above)*

CHORISIA

This genus is made up of 5 species of deciduous South American trees with distinctively spiny, somewhat swollen trunks, the bark otherwise smooth and greenish. They belong to the kapok or silk-cotton family of tropical trees, with digitately compound leaves, hibiscus-like flowers, and large capsular fruit with silky fibers packed around the seeds. The showy flowers are borne on branches that may be leafless. In a recent botanical study *Chorisia* is treated as a synonym of *Ceiba*.

CULTIVATION

At least one species has gradually gained popularity in recent years, as a striking flowering tree for sunny, warm-temperate climates such as that of southern California. In more tropical climates they prefer those with a pronounced dry season. They do best in full sun and fertile, light, well-drained soil, with regular water in summer. Poorer or drier soils restrict the trees' size. Propagate from freshly collected seed or by grafting of selected clones.

Chorisia speciosa (below)
syn. *Ceiba speciosa*
FLOSS-SILK TREE

Growing rapidly to 50 ft (15 m) or more with a spreading crown, this subtropical South American species is the one most commonly seen and is grown for its striking large flowers profusely scattered over the crown on bare or leafy branches from late summer to early winter. The saucer-sized flowers range from rose pink through salmon shades to burgundy, with gold or white throats. Flowers vary greatly from one seedling plant to another, also the density and persistence of spines on the trunk. ZONES 9–11.

CHORIZEMA
FLAME PEA

A genus of 18 species of evergreen pea-flowered subshrubs, all
but one endemic to southwestern Australia the single exception
occurring in coastal eastern Australia. The name comes from the
Greek *choros*, 'dance', and *zema*, 'drink', because the French
botanist-explorer Labillardière and his exhausted party danced
for joy when they found water and this plant in the same location. The cultivated species are very floriferous, often with a
combination of hot colors in each flower, hence the common
name. Leaves are simple, the margins prickly toothed in some
species.

CULTIVATION
These plants are marginally frost hardy and need full sun or very
light shade and a well-drained, light soil. They should be kept
well mulched in summer to prevent the roots from drying out.
Propagate from seed sown in spring or cuttings in summer.

Chorizema
cordatum *(left)*
HEART-LEAFED FLAME PEA

This gaudy native of
southwestern Australia
bears sprays of yellow
to orange-red pea-
flowers with a pink to
dark red central blotch,
in spring. A thin-
branched, scrambling
shrub, it has heart-
shaped, mid-green leaves
with small prickly
marginal teeth. It pre-
fers shady conditions
and grows to a height
of 3–5 ft (1–1.5 m).
Some botanists now
treat *Chorizema*
cordatum as a synonym
of *C. ilicifolium*.
ZONES 9–11.

CHRYSANTHEMOIDES

This southern African genus of evergreen shrubs contains only 2 species, of which one is widely cultivated and naturalized in other parts of the world. Somewhat short-lived and soft-wooded, they have leathery, toothed leaves. The yellow flowerheads are like small daisies and the fruitlets that follow are fleshy and juicy—these are attractive to birds, which effectively disperse the seed.

CULTIVATION

Easily grown from seed or cuttings, they may be useful as summer bedding or tub plants in cool climates, but demand full sun. They have become pests in some areas, forming dense, impenetrable stands, and should be grown only in areas where they will not choke out native vegetation.

Chrysanthemoides monilifera (right)

BUSH-TICK BERRY, BITOU BUSH, BONESEED

This fast-growing shrub has 2 subspecies, rather different in growth habit and ecology. *Chrysanthemoides monilifera* subsp. *monilifera* is an erect, bushy shrub of 4–6 ft (1.2–1.8 m) with dull green, thin-textured, coarsely toothed leaves and grows mainly away from the seashore. **C. m.** subsp. *rotundata*, the coastal race, is usually 5–10 ft (1.5–3 m) tall and as much as 20 ft (6 m) across, forming a broad, dense mound of bright green foliage. The glossy leaves are rounded and barely toothed, with cobweb-like hairs on the undersides and young shoots. It can grow very quickly on dunes and seeds itself freely. Both subspecies can flower for most of the year. ZONES 9–11.

C

CINNAMOMUM

This genus of the laurel family consists of around 250 species of evergreen trees from tropical and subtropical Asia and Australasia with smooth, strongly veined leaves. Highly aromatic compounds are present in the leaves, twigs and bark of all species. The flowers are small and white or cream in delicate sprays and are followed by small fleshy berries containing a single seed. The bark of *Cinnamomum zeylanicum* yields the spice cinnamon; *C. cassia* provides the spice cassia used in drinks and sweets. *C. camphora* is a source of commercial camphor and used in China to make storage chests.

CULTIVATION

Most species require tropical or subtropical conditions, with fairly high rainfall; only *C. camphora* is adaptable to warm-temperate climates. They do best in full sun or dappled shade in deep, free-draining soil with plentiful water in summer. Propagate from seed in autumn.

Cinnamomum camphora (left)

CAMPHOR LAUREL, CAMPHOR TREE

Native to China, Taiwan and southern Japan, this fast-growing tree is known to reach 120 ft (36 m) in height with a rounded crown spreading to 50 ft (15 m) wide, but half this height is more usual in gardens. The short, solid trunk has scaly gray bark. The leaves, pinkish when young, turn pale green and finally deep green as they age. Widely grown as a shade tree in parks and gardens and as a street tree, it self-seeds freely and can become invasive in subtropical climates—in parts of east-coastal Australia it has become a serious pest. ZONES 9–11.

CISTUS
ROCKROSE

These evergreen shrubs from around the Mediterranean and the Canary Islands are valued for their attractive, saucer-shaped flowers, which have crinkled petals in shades of pink, purple or white and a central boss of golden stamens, like a single rose. Although short-lived, most bloom over a long season, some for almost the whole year, and they do very well in shrub borders, on banks or in pots; some examples include **'Peggy Sammons'**, **'Santa Cruz'**, **'Snow Mound'** and **'Warley Rose'**. Some species exude an aromatic resin which the ancient Greeks and Romans called *labdanum* and used for incense and perfume, as well as medicinally.

CULTIVATION
These shrubs are easily cultivated provided they are given a warm, sunny position and very well-drained, even rather dry soil; they like being among large rocks or other rubble where their roots can seek out deep moisture. If necessary they can be tip pruned to promote bushiness, or main branches shortened by about a third after flowering. Most species are moderately frost hardy; all are resistant to very dry conditions. They will thrive in countries with cool- to warm-temperate climates, but not in subtropical regions with hot, humid summers. Propagation is normally from cuttings, although seed is readily germinated.

Cistus 'Snow Mound'
(left)

C

Cistus albidus *(left)*
WHITE-LEAFED ROCKROSE

This attractive species, with felty, gray-green foliage and large, lilac-pink flowers with a small yellow blotch at the base of each petal, is very sensitive to excess moisture. From the far southwest of Europe and northwest Africa, it grows to 4 ft (1.2 m) high and 8 ft (2.4 m) wide with foliage right down to the ground, concealing thick, twisted branches. The flowers appear mainly in spring. ZONES 7–9.

Cistus ladanifer
CRIMSON-SPOT ROCKROSE

The most upright and slender species, *Cistus ladanifer* grows to around 5–6 ft (1.5–1.8 m) tall but quickly becomes sparse and leggy and does not take well to pruning. The whole plant, apart from the flower petals, is coated with a shiny resin that in the heat of the day becomes semi-liquid and very aromatic. Its leaves are narrow and dark green and the flowers, among the largest in the genus at 3–4 in (8–10 cm) across, have pure white petals each with a reddish chocolate basal blotch; they appear from mid-spring to early summer. The cultivar **'Albiflorus'** has pure white petals. ZONES 8–10.

Cistus ladanifer 'Albiflorus'
(right)

Cistus laurifolius *(left)*

The laurel-leafed cistus from southwestern Europe and Morocco is not one of the largest in flower—the blooms are only about 2½ in (6 cm) wide—but it is a very beautiful, free-flowering plant. It has pure white flowers that are in gleaming contrast all through the summer against the leathery deep green leaves. Capable of growing to 6 ft (1.8 m) high, it has the best reputation for cold hardiness of any *Cistus*. ZONES 7–9.

C

Cistus × lusitanicus *(above)*

This hybrid between *Cistus ladanifer* and *C. hirsutus* makes a densely foliaged shrub about 24 in (60 cm) high. It has narrow, dark green leaves and white flowers 2½ in (6 cm) across with a prominent crimson blotch at the base of each petal. **'Decumbens'** is a low, spreading form with flowers that have darker crimson blotches. ZONES 8–9.

Cistus × purpureus 'Brilliancy' *(above)*

Cistus × purpureus *(above right)*
ORCHID ROCKROSE

This hybrid between *Cistus ladanifer* and *C. creticus* has deep pink flowers with prominent, dark reddish chocolate blotches on the petals. It is frost hardy and free flowering. Several clones have been named including **'Brilliancy'**, with clear pink petals, and **'Betty Taudevin'**, a deeper reddish pink. ZONES 7–9.

Cistus × pulverulentus 'Sunset' *(above)*

Cistus × pulverulentus

A compact, spreading shrub, this hybrid between *Cistus albidus* and *C. crispus* bears small rose pink flowers in summer. The leaves are gray-green and about 1½ in (4 cm) long. It grows to a height of 24 in (60 cm). **'Sunset'**, a superior cultivar has abundant colorful flowers 2½ in (6 cm) in diameter. ZONES 8–10.

Cistus salviifolius *(above)*
SAGELEAF ROCKROSE

This species has deeply veined leaves that are thinner than most other cistus, and smaller, slender-stalked flowers. It makes a rounded shrub, about 24–36 in (60–90 cm) high, reaching 6 ft (1.8 m) wide, with thin, densely massed twigs. The neat disc-like flowers, pure white except for a small, orange-yellow basal blotch on each petal, are scattered profusely from late winter to early summer. It can be cut back harder than other species. **'Prostratus'** is a dwarf form. ZONES 8–10.

C

CITRUS

The number of original wild species in this genus of evergreen small trees, originally native in the Southeast Asian region, is very uncertain as many of the cultivated forms are probably of ancient hybrid origin following their domestication, which took place mainly in China and India. While largely cultivated for their fruit, citrus plants have the bonus of looking attractive in the garden, with glossy evergreen leaves and fragrant flowers. Most species are frost tender to some degree but a few tolerate very light frosts; the lemon is the most cold resistant, especially when grafted onto the related *Poncirus trifoliata* rootstock, and the lime is the least cold resistant, doing best in subtropical locations. All citrus can also be grown in pots, as long as the containers are large and the citrus are grown on dwarfing rootstocks.

CULTIVATION

Very well-drained, friable, slightly acid, loam soil is best. They need full sun, regular watering and protection from wind, especially during the summer months. Citrus also need regular feeding, including large amounts of nitrogen and potassium for good fruiting. Prune only to remove dead, diseased and crossing wood. Subject to a range of virus diseases, they can be invaded by many pests including scale, leaf miner, bronze orange bug, spined citrus bug and fruit fly. They are rarely propagated by home gardeners as this is done by grafting, a specialist task.

Citrus aurantifolia
(below)
LIME

Best in tropical and subtropical climates, the lime is stronger in acidity and flavor than the lemon. It is an erect tree, to 15–20 ft (4.5–6 m) tall, with spiny, irregular branches, making it less ornamental than other citrus plants. The Tahitian lime, the most popular variety, bears fruit all year round. The Mexican lime has smaller fruit with high acidity and a stronger flavor, and is also a thornier tree. ZONES 10–12.

Citrus aurantium *(right)*

SOUR ORANGE, SEVILLE ORANGE

These marginally frost-hardy small trees are grown as ornamental shrubs or for their fruit, which are used to make marmalade and jelly. The heavy-fruiting **'Seville'** is the premium marmalade orange. **'Chinotto'** is excellent in containers or borders, with small, dark green leaves and a compact habit. The dwarf **'Bouquet de Fleurs'** is a more fragrant, ornamental shrub. Watch for melanose (dark brown spots on the wood and fruit) and citrus scab. **ZONES 9–11.**

Citrus limon

LEMON

The lemon tree does best in warm Mediterranean climates with mild winters. It grows to around 20 ft (6 m) and is prone to collar rot, so plant it with the graft union well above the soil and keep mulch away from the stem. **'Eureka'** is probably the most commonly grown cultivar, producing fruit and flowers all year round. It is an attractive, almost thornless tree, the best variety for temperate locations and coastal gardens. The smaller and hardier **'Meyer'** bears smaller fruit and is a suitable cultivar for growing in pots. **'Lisbon'** is popular with commercial growers since it is reliable and heavy fruiting; it is good for hot areas but is thorny. **ZONES 9–11.**

Citrus limon 'Meyer'
(right)

Citrus × paradisi *(right)*

GRAPEFRUIT

Easily grown in mild areas, the grapefruit can make a dense, rounded tree to 20–30 ft (6–9 m) or more. Its large, golden-skinned fruits are well known and widely appreciated. Popular frost-hardy cultivars include **'Marsh'**, **'Morrison's Seedless'** and **'Golden Special'**. The seedless and **'Ruby'** cultivars are more tender, preferring a frost-free climate. All are usually grown from cuttings or grafts. **ZONES 10–12.**

C

Citrus sinensis *(right)*

ORANGE

Attractive trees to 25 ft (8 m) or more tall with a rounded head, oranges can be grown in most non-tropical climates. They have glossy foliage and sweet-scented white flowers, and will tolerate very light frosts. **'Valencia'** is perhaps the most frost hardy of all oranges, and produces fruit in spring and summer that is most commonly juiced but can also be eaten fresh. **'Joppa'** is a good variety for tropical gardens. **'Ruby Blood'** has oblong fruit with a reddish color to its rind, flesh and juice; it is the best known and best tasting of the 'blood oranges'. Navel oranges are mutated forms with a 'navel' at the fruit apex, and no seeds: **'Washington Navel'**, which fruits through winter, has very large and sweet, bright orange fruit and is best suited to slightly cooler areas. New varieties available to commercial growers may be found by gardeners at specialist nurseries. ZONES 9–11.

Citrus × tangelo *(right)*

TANGELO

This evergreen tree grows 20–30 ft (6–9 m) high and 10 ft (3 m) wide. It is derived from a cross between the tangerine *(Citrus reticulata)* and the grapefruit *(C. paradisi)*. The tangelo is renowned for its juice and as a superb dessert fruit with a tart, yet sweet flavor. Plant in a warm site sheltered from frost. ZONES 9–11.

CLADRASTIS
YELLOWWOOD

This genus of 5 species of deciduous small leguminous trees occurs wild in eastern USA, Japan and China. The pinnate leaves have rather few leaflets and the pendulous sprays of small to medium-sized, fragrant white or pinkish pea-flowers that appear in summer are slightly reminiscent of *Wisteria* flowers. The flowers are followed by flattened pods, each containing a row of small, hard seeds. They are elegant trees, valued for their late flowering and, in the case of the American species, for their autumn foliage.

CULTIVATION
Fully frost hardy, they prefer full sun and fertile, well-drained soil. They also need protection from strong winds as the wood is brittle. Propagate from seed in autumn or from cuttings in winter.

Cladrastis lutea
(right)
syn. *Cladrastis kentukea*
AMERICAN YELLOWWOOD

The natural range of this species is from North Carolina to Alabama and Missouri, in rich soils on hill slopes or along ravines near streams. There it grows to 60 ft (18 m) with a trunk diameter to 3 ft (1 m), forking not far above the ground with steeply angled limbs. In cultivation it rarely exceeds 30 ft (9 m). The leaves consist of 5 to 9 broad, veined leaflets that are rich green in summer turning yellow in autumn. White flowers appear in early summer. Some trees flower only every second year. ZONES 6–10.

C

CLERODENDRUM

This genus of over 400 species ranges through the world's tropics and warmer climates. It contains trees, shrubs, climbers and herbaceous plants, both deciduous and evergreen, some with very showy flowers. The features that unite them are leaves in opposite pairs; tubular flowers, usually flared or bowl-shaped at the mouth with 4 long stamens and a style protruding well beyond the tube; and fruit, a shiny berry sitting at the center of the calyx that usually becomes larger and thicker after flowering.

CULTIVATION

They vary greatly in their cold hardiness, though only a few species from China and Japan are suited to cool climates. They all appreciate a sunny position, though sheltered from strong wind and the hottest summer sun, and deep, moist, fertile soil. Propagate from cuttings, which strike readily under heat. Many species sucker quickly from the roots.

Clerodendrum bungei *(above)*
syn. *Clerodendrum foetidum*
GLORY FLOWER

This suckering shrub from China and the Himalayas has many vertical stems topped in summer with wonderfully fragrant heads of rose pink flowers. The leaves are large and coarse, and have an unpleasant smell if crushed or bruised. The stems will reach 6 ft (1.8 m) unless cut to the ground each spring; new growths will then flower on 3 ft (1 m) stems. It will spread rapidly if not contained or controlled. ZONES 7–10.

C

Clerodendrum trichotomum *(above)*

HARLEQUIN GLORY BOWER

Native to Japan and China, this is one of the most frost hardy species. It makes an elegant deciduous tree to 15–20 ft (4.5–6 m) in height, of erect growth and sparse branching habit, drooping lower branches and thin, downy leaves. In late summer it produces at the branch tips gracefully drooping panicles of slightly upturned, sweet-scented white flowers, that age to pale mauve with large, dull pinkish calyces that are sharply ribbed. The small blue fruit, cupped in enlarged red calyces, can make quite a display. ZONES 7–10.

Clerodendrum ugandense *(above)*

BLUE BUTTERFLY BUSH

Requiring a frost-free climate, this species from East Africa will take rather cooler conditions than most tropical clerodendrums. It is a rangy and open evergreen shrub to 10 ft (3 m) with a spread of 6 ft (1.8 m). Through summer and autumn its slightly arching branches bear terminal sprays of butterfly-shaped flowers in two shades of clear blue. It can be pruned back continually to keep the long branches in check. ZONES 10–11.

CLETHRA

A scattering of deciduous tree and shrub species across North America and eastern Asia, plus a larger number of evergreens in warmer climates, principally Southeast Asia, and one outlying species on the island of Madeira make up the 30 species in this genus. The frost-hardy deciduous species mostly behave as spreading shrubs in cultivation, producing a thicket of stems concealed by dense foliage. The leaves are thin textured with closely toothed margins. In summer and autumn small, white flowers are borne in delicate loose sprays, followed by numerous, tiny seed capsules.

CULTIVATION
Clethras prefer sheltered, moist half-shaded spots and peaty, acid, moist but well-drained soil. Propagate from seed, cuttings or layers.

Clethra arborea (above)
LILY-OF-THE-VALLEY TREE

This species from Madeira requires milder conditions than others of the genus. An attractive densely leafed shrub or small tree 20–25 ft (6–8 m) tall, it has glossy leaves and long panicles of lily-of-the-valley-like flowers. Prune occasionally for shaping. ZONES 9–10.

Clethra barbinervis (above)
JAPANESE CLETHRA

This species from mountain woodlands of Japan can make a 30 ft (9 m) tree in the wild with peeling orange-brown bark. In gardens it usually makes a shrub of less than 10 ft (3 m) with crowded stems that tend to lean outward and strongly veined leaves with a fuzz of very short hairs on the veins. The attractive flowers appear in short panicles at the branch tips. ZONES 6–9.

CLIANTHUS

Until recently this genus was regarded as including 2 species, one from Australia and one from New Zealand. The Australian species is the famous Sturt's desert pea, a prostrate hairy annual with spectacular red and black flowers; but recently it has been moved to the large Darling-pea genus *Swainsona*. This leaves only the rather different New Zealand species in *Clianthus*. This is an evergreen shrub or scrambling climber with pinnate leaves; it bears elongated pea-flowers in stalked clusters on short side branches.

CULTIVATION

Easily grown in mild climates, *Clianthus* is moderately frost tolerant. Often rather short-lived, it is inclined to become woody and occasional cutting back helps to rejuvenate it. It is prone to attack by leaf miners. Propagation is from seed or from semi-ripe cuttings.

Clianthus puniceus
(right)

KAKA BEAK, PARROT BEAK

The kaka is a New Zealand parrot and the long-pointed flowers of this shrub are reminiscent of its sharp beak. This species is now rare in the wild but is widely cultivated. In gardens it often grows into a shrub of about 5 ft (1.5 m) but is capable of climbing to 20 ft (6 m) if supported by other vegetation or a wall. The flowers, borne in spring and early summer, are normally red, but pink forms and white forms such as **'Alba'** are also available. **'Kaka King'** flowers heavily with lush foliage. **'Roseus'** has pinkish red flowers.
ZONES 8–10.

Clianthus puniceus
'Roseus' *(left)*

CLUSIA

This is a very large genus of tropical American evergreen trees
and shrubs, little known outside the Americas except as curiosi-
ties in botanical garden greenhouses but very diverse in their
native rainforests. Many start life as epiphytes on other trees but
soon put down a curtain of aerial roots to the ground, which may
ultimately fuse together into a self-supporting trunk. The leaves
of *Clusia* species may be quite large and are generally smooth
and fleshy or leathery. The flowers, borne singly or in short
sprays at the branch tips, are often large and showy, with male
flowers more conspicuous than female ones though both appear
on the same tree. They are cup or bowl shaped, often with 6 or
more overlapping petals, and a dense, doughnut-shaped ring of
stamens in the center; in females this is replaced by a broad,
domed ovary with shiny stigmas fused to its surface.

CULTIVATION
Some species are vigorous trees tolerant of exposed coastal conditions, and these adapt well to street or park planting in tropical
cities. All species prefer rich, moist but well-drained soil in a
sheltered position. Propagation is from cuttings under heat, or
by air-layering.

Clusia rosea (left)
syn. *Clusia major*
COPEY, BALSAM APPLE

From the Caribbean re-
gion, this is one of the
most widely planted
species. It makes a tree
of about 30 ft (9 m) tall
with a broadly spread-
ing crown of irregular
shape and rather dense
foliage, often forked
into several trunks
from ground level and
sending down aerial
roots, like some figs.
The thick, olive-green
leaves are paddle-
shaped with broad,
rounded tips. Pale
pinkish flowers 2–3 in
(5–8 cm) in diameter
dot the crown in sum-
mer and early autumn.
ZONES 11–12.

CODIAEUM

This genus consists of about 15 species of evergreen shrubs and small trees native to southern Asia, the Malay region and Pacific Islands. One species, *Codiaeum variegatum*, has given rise to a large number of cultivars with highly colored and sometimes bizarrely shaped leaves. These are popular garden plants in tropical regions, and house or greenhouse plants in temperate climates. Where they can be grown outdoors, the larger-growing cultivars make good hedges. The small yellow flowers and tiny seed pods are quite insignificant—the plants are grown strictly for their magnificent foliage.

CULTIVATION

They will not withstand prolonged cold or dry conditions and prefer moist, humus-rich soil in sun or dappled shade. As indoor plants they are grown in a rich but freely draining potting mix, and watered and fed freely during the summer growing season. Propagate from tip cuttings or by air-layering.

Codiaeum variegatum

CROTON, GARDEN CROTON

This species occurs throughout the geographical range of the genus, making a small tree with plain green leaves in the wild. The cultivated forms are more shrubby and show enormous variation of leaf color and pattern with shades of green, red, yellow, orange and purple, sometimes on the one plant. Some cultivars can grow to 8 ft (2.4 m) or more tall, with leaves to 12 in (30 cm) long; they must be propagated vegetatively, usually by cuttings, to maintain their foliage color. **'America'** has green, red, orange and yellow leaves, the variegation following the veins and margins; **'Petra'** is similar to 'America' but has more clearly defined margins; **'Imperiale'** has yellow leaves with pink margins and green midribs; **'Interruptum'** has yellow, recurved leaves with green margins and red midribs; **'Mrs Iceton'** (syn. 'Appleleaf') has elliptic leaves, metallic purple at the edges, yellow to rose in the center. ZONES 11–12.

Codiaeum variegatum **'Petra'** *(above)*

COFFEA
COFFEE

This genus of some 40 species of shrubs and small trees is native mainly to tropical Africa, with a few in Asia. Best known is *Coffea arabica*, the original source of coffee and still the most prized species. Most have tiered branches and deep green, smooth-edged leaves arranged in opposite pairs. Attractive white flowers are clustered in the leaf-axils, followed by small, fleshy, 2-seeded fruits that turn red as they ripen.

CULTIVATION
The preferred growing environment is humus-rich soil with light shade and steady mild temperatures. Propagation is from seed or semi-ripe cuttings. As would be expected of tropical plants, most are frost-tender. They adapt well to being grown as house plants. Propagation is from seed, which must be fresh but germinates very rapidly.

Coffea arabica (left)
ARABIAN COFFEE

Originating in mountain rainforests of Ethiopia, this is the coffee of commerce. It is a very attractive evergreen shrub for frost-free gardens or for large containers. It can grow to 15 ft (4.5 m) high. Small, fragrant white flowers are clustered along the branches behind the leaves and are followed by the dark red fruits; each contains 2 'beans' which are extracted, dried and roasted to make coffee.
ZONES 10–12.

Coleonema album
(below)

WHITE DIOSMA, WHITE BREATH OF HEAVEN

Often misnamed *Diosma ericoides*, this species has white flowers from mid-winter to mid-spring. It grows to about 5 ft (1.5 m) high and wide. The deep green, individual leaves are somewhat broader than those of the more popular *C. pulchellum*. ZONES 9–10.

COLEONEMA

These small, evergreen shrubs from South Africa are often wrongly called diosmas, but *Diosma* is a different genus, rarely cultivated. There are 8 species, mostly restricted in the wild to western Cape Province. They have short, needle-like leaves on fine, wiry twigs and tiny, starry flowers in winter and spring, occasionally repeating through summer. The foliage is aromatic, smelling a little like ants.

CULTIVATION

They withstand regular trimming to shape, usually done immediately after flowering. Plant in light but moist, well-drained soil in full sun. Occasional applications of very dilute iron sulphate solution will keep it looking healthy. Propagate from cuttings.

C

Coleonema pulchellum
(below far left)
syn. *Coleonema pulchrum* of gardens

CONFETTI BUSH, PINK BREATH OF HEAVEN

This, the most widely grown species, is a 5 ft (1.5 m) high shrub with fine heathy foliage and profuse pink starry flowers in winter and spring. Long misidentified in gardens as *Coleonema pulchrum*, several forms are cultivated with paler or deeper pink flowers. **'Compactum'** is a more compact form; **'Sunset Gold'** is a very popular cultivar with bright yellow foliage and light pink flowers. Also more compact, it usually grows as a low, flat-topped bush no more than 18 in (45 cm) high. ZONES 9–10.

Coleonema pulchellum 'Sunset Gold' *(left)*

C

COLQUHOUNIA

This genus consists of 3 species of evergreen or semi-evergreen shrubs or subshrubs in the mint family and comes from the Himalayas and Southeast Asia. The aromatic leaves are finely toothed and borne in opposite pairs on the square stems. The tubular, 2-lipped flowers are carried on terminal spikes. Pronunciation of the name might present problems to non-Scots— the surname of botanical collector Sir Robert Colquhoun, after whom the genus is named, was pronounced 'co-hoon', if present-day Scottish usage is a guide.

CULTIVATION
They need a sheltered position and well-drained soil in full sun. They may be cut down by frost in cold areas. Propagation is from cuttings in summer.

Colquhounia coccinea (left)

This very handsome though rather sprawling shrub from the Himalayas, has large, felty, aromatic leaves and terminal clusters of pale pink to reddish orange flowers that are yellowish inside. It grows to 10 ft (3 m) high and wide.
ZONES 8–10.

COLUMNEA

With over 150 species of shrubs, subshrubs and climbers from tropical America, this is one of the largest genera of the African violet and gloxinia family, as well as being one of the most important in terms of ornamental indoor plants. Coming from regions of high rainfall and humidity, many grow as epiphytes, with long trailing stems and rather fleshy leaves. The beautiful and unusual flowers, mostly in colors of red, orange and yellow, have a long tube and often a hooded or helmet-shaped upper lip; they are adapted to pollination by hummingbirds, which hover under the flower and brush pollen from anthers beneath the hood onto their heads while sipping nectar from the tube.

CULTIVATION
Some species demand constant high humidity, but many can grow outdoors in warm climates in a suitably sheltered spot in filtered light; in cooler climates they need the protection of a greenhouse or conservatory. Hanging baskets are ideal for most columneas, whether they are of the type with quite pendulous stems or more erect, scrambling plants. Grow in an open, fibrous compost, including, for example, sphagnum moss, peat and charcoal. Water freely in summer, reducing water as the weather cools. Propagate from cuttings.

Columnea gloriosa
GOLDFISH PLANT

Similar to its relative the lipstick plant (*Aeschynanthus*), this Central American native has semi-erect hairy stems and fleshy, convex leaves up to 1½ in (38 mm) long clothed in velvety hairs. Over a long period from spring to autumn it produces an abundance of brilliant scarlet and yellow flowers over 3 in (8 cm) long, from the leaf axils. **'Purpurea'** is a cultivar with purple leaves. ZONES 11–12.

Columnea gloriosa
'Purpurea' *(right)*

COMBRETUM

Members of this large genus occur across tropical and subtropical Africa, Asia and the Americas and include shrubs and small to medium-sized trees, as well as some climbers. While many are evergreen, some South African species are deciduous, the foliage coloring well in autumn. The flowers appear in spikes, and in many species have inconspicuous petals but prominent, colorful stamens. The attractive, 4-winged fruit that follow persist on the branches until dispersed by the wind.

CULTIVATION
Combretums are adapted to summer-rainfall tropical and subtropical climates and will grow in most soils provided drainage is good. A position in full sun suits them best. They are easy to propagate from fresh seed or from cuttings.

Combretum erythrophyllum
(left & below left)
RIVER BUSHWILLOW

Of wide distribution in southeastern Africa, this species is a deciduous small, spreading tree to 30 ft (9 m) or more tall, often branching at ground level into several stout trunks with smooth yellow-brown bark. New growths are pale green, maturing mid-green, and the foliage turns yellowish then deep red in autumn. Inconspicuous clusters of small greenish yellow flowers appear in winter and spring, followed in summer by masses of straw colored hop-like fruit that may be cut for dried decorations. It makes fast growth and the seeds germinate readily. ZONES 9–11.

Coprosma 'Kiwi Silver' *(below right)*

'Kiwi Silver' is a low, mound-forming plant to 12 in (30 cm) high and 3 ft (1 m) across. It bears elliptic, glossy mid-green leaves with pale yellow margins. ZONES 9–11.

Coprosma lucida
(below far right)
KARAMU

A very different New Zealand species, *Coprosma lucida* makes a large, open shrub or small tree to as much as 20 ft (6 m) tall, with broad glossy leaves up to 6 in (15 cm) long, broadest near the tips. Male flowers are yellow-green in dense clusters in the leaf axils, while female plants bear ½ in (12 mm) long orange-red fruits. ZONES 8–10.

Coprosma repens
(right)
syn. *Coprosma baueri* of gardens

TAUPATA, MIRROR BUSH, LOOKING-GLASS PLANT

Native to New Zealand seashores, this species withstands coastal winds. Usually shaped to a dense mound 3–6 ft (1–1.8 m) high, it will occasionally grow taller if left unpruned. It has brilliantly glossy, leathery, deep green leaves. Insignificant flowers are followed on female

COPROSMA

Most of the 90 species of evergreen shrubs and small trees in this genus are native to New Zealand, though there are also a number in southeastern Australia and islands of the South Pacific. Several species are valued for their great tolerance of salt-laden winds and are commonly grown as coastal hedging and shelter planting. Leaves vary greatly in size and shape but are always borne in opposite pairs and are rather leathery and usually glossy; in some species the bruised foliage is unpleasant smelling. Flowers are inconspicuous, mostly greenish, reduced to bunches of stamens and long stigmas respectively in the male and female flowers which are always on separate plants. The small berry-like fruits, though, can be quite showy, in colors of red, white, blue or purple.

CULTIVATION
Best in full sun and in light, well-drained soil, they are fast growing and easily maintained. Pruning maintains foliage production. Propagate from seed in spring and semi-ripe cuttings in late summer.

plants by small, orange-red fruit in late summer and autumn. The leaves of **'Gold Splash'** are predominantly golden yellow; **'Marble Queen'** is a variegated form with paler green and cream leaves, often

producing pure cream growths; **'Picturata'** has a central yellow blotch surrounded by dark glossy green; and **'Pink Splendour'** is a variegated form with pink-flushed leaves. ZONES 9–11.

Coprosma repens 'Gold Splash' *(above)*

C

CORDIA

This genus is made up of around 300 species of evergreen and deciduous shrubs and trees from most tropical and subtropical regions of the world. Some are used as timber trees, others hollowed out for canoes, and the leaves of a few species are used to make dyes. Most have large, smooth, oval leaves and small to moderately large, trumpet-shaped flowers that stand out against the dark foliage. The fruit is typical of the genus.

CULTIVATION
They need steady, warm temperatures and moist, well-drained soil. Propagate from seed or semi-ripe cuttings.

Cordia sebestena
(left)

GEIGER TREE, SCARLET CORDIA

This evergreen shrub or small tree is native to the West Indies, Florida and Venezuela and is widely cultivated for ornament in the tropics. It grows to 25 ft (8 m) high and has 8 in (20 cm) long, oval leaves. It produces tight clusters of bright orange-red flowers through much of the year, followed by 1 in (25 mm) oval, white, edible fruit. ZONES 10–12.

Cordia wallichii *(left)*
A native of tropical Asia, this is a large shrub to small spreading tree, 12 to 20 ft (3.5 to 6 m) high. The leaves are broad and dark green. Flowers, borne in dense panicles in the upper leaf axils, measure rather less than 1 in (2.5 cm) across. It makes a bushy shrub that could be used as a screen or shelter plant in subtropical to tropical gardens. ZONES 10–12.

CORDYLINE

CABBAGE TREE, TI

Most species of this genus of 15 or so species of somewhat palm-like evergreen shrubs and small trees are tropical or subtropical, but a few are moderately frost hardy. Cordylines resemble dracaenas in habit and foliage, but differ in the flowers which are small and starry, borne in large panicles, and in the red, black or whitish fruits. Their underground rhizome, which sometimes emerges through the drainage apertures of a pot, appears to be food storage.

CULTIVATION
Cordylines do well in rich, well-drained soil. Narrower-leafed New Zealand species are the most sun hardy, and *Cordyline australis* tolerates salt spray near the ocean; the species with broader, thinner leaves prefer a sheltered position in part shade, though will tolerate full sun if humidity is high. Most can be kept in pots or tubs for many years as indoor or patio plants. They are easily propagated from seed or stem cuttings.

Cordyline australis 'Albertii' *(far right)*

Cordyline australis
(right)
syn. *Dracaena australis*

NEW ZEALAND CABBAGE TREE, TI KOUKA

This striking New Zealand native is moderately frost hardy, occurring in some of that country's southernmost areas. The seedlings, with very narrow, elegantly arching leaves, are sold as indoor plants and last for years in this juvenile state; planted outdoors they begin to form a trunk and the brownish green leaves can be almost 3 ft (1 m) long and 2 in (5 cm) wide. The first large panicle of small white sweet-scented flowers, opening in summer, terminates the stem at a height of 6–8 ft (1.8–2.4 m); the stem then branches into several leaf rosettes, each in time flowering and branching again. It is the largest species, frequently reaching over 20 ft (6 m) tall with a stout trunk. **'Purpurea'** with bronze purplish leaves is popular. **'Albertii'**, a variegated cultivar with leaves striped cream, more pinkish on new growths, is less vigorous. **ZONES 8–11.**

C

Cordyline banksii *(left)*
TI NGAHERE

Also from New Zealand, this compact tree resembles *Cordyline australis* but has slightly broader, softer leaves, up to 3 in (8 cm) wide. It is usually a large shrub of about 10 ft (3 m) with a similar spread. The small, fragrant white flowers in long drooping panicles appear in late spring and summer. It does best in a protected position with regular water in the warm months. **ZONES 9–11.**

Cordyline fruticosa cultivar *(left)*

Cordyline fruticosa
syn. *Cordyline terminalis*
TI NGAHERE

This well known species probably originated somewhere in the vicinity of Papua New Guinea but was long ago spread through the Pacific by Melanesians and Polynesians, who valued its starchy rhizomes as food. It grows to at least 10 ft (3 m) high, forming a strong, branched trunk, but is more often seen as a 3–6 ft (1–1.8 m) shrub in gardens or as a house plant. The thin, lance-shaped leaves are up to 30 in (75 cm) long and 6 in (15 cm) wide, clustered at the top of the stem. The 12 in (30 cm) panicles of small, scented, white to dull mauve flowers, borne in summer, may be followed by crowded red berries. The many colored and variegated foliage forms are favorite landscaping plants in the tropics; they vary also in leaf size and shape. **'Imperialis'** has dark green leaves streaked pink and crimson. **ZONES 10–12.**

CORIARIA

A small genus of about 30 species of subshrubs, shrubs and small trees, *Coriaria* has a puzzling, patchy distribution around the world—New Zealand and South America account for most species, but others occur in Mexico, East Asia, the Mediterranean and Papua New Guinea. They have angled branchlets and usually a neat 2-rowed arrangement of the oval leaves. Flowers are inconspicuous, in short to long lateral spikes, but the tiny petals enlarge greatly after flowering, becoming thick, fleshy and colored enclosing the very small true fruits. The 'fruits' are poisonous and hallucinogenic, and have been used as an insecticide. Some species yield useful dyes.

CULTIVATION
They are easily grown in any normal garden soil, though appreciating some shelter. Most cultivated species will tolerate light to moderate frosts and even if damaged by frost will shoot again from the base if soil has not frozen. Propagate from seed, cuttings or by root division.

Coriaria japonica *(above)*
From Japan, this species is a low subshrub with arching stems that makes a good ground cover. It has conspicuous red fruit and the leaves color well in autumn. **ZONES 8–10.**

CORNUS
CORNEL, DOGWOOD

About 45 species of shrubs, trees and even 1 or 2 herbaceous perennials make up this genus, widely distributed in temperate regions of the northern hemisphere. They include deciduous and evergreen species, all with simple, smooth-edged leaves that characteristically have prominent, inward-curving veins. The flowers are small, mostly greenish, yellowish or dull purplish: few are decorative, but in one group of species they are arranged in dense heads surrounded by large white, pink or yellow bracts that can be showy. Another shrubby group has stems and twigs that are often bright red or yellow, giving a decorative effect especially when leafless in winter. One such species is the common European dogwood, *Cornus sanguinea*. The fleshy fruits are also ornamental.

CULTIVATION
The various species all do best in sun or very light shade. Most appreciate a rich, fertile, well-drained soil, though some of the multi-stemmed shrub species will grow well in boggy ground. Many are quite frost hardy but *Cornus capitata* will tolerate only light frosts. The species with decorative red stems can be cut back annually almost to ground level to encourage new growths, which have the best color. Propagate from seed or rooted layers struck in a moist sand-peat mixture.

Cornus alba *(below)*
RED-BARKED DOGWOOD, TATARIAN DOGWOOD

Shiny red branches and twigs, brightest in winter or late autumn, are the feature of this northeast Asian deciduous shrub. It makes a dense thicket of slender stems 6–10 ft (1.8–3 m) high and often twice that in spread, with lower branches suckering or taking root on the ground. In late spring and summer it bears small clusters of creamy yellow flowers, followed by pea-sized white or blue-tinted fruit. It thrives in damp ground and is effective by lakes and streams. Cultivars include 'Elegantissima', with gray-green leaves partly white on their margins; '**Sibirica**', with bright red leaves and stems; and '**Spaethii**', with brilliantly gold-variegated leaves. ZONES 4–9.

Cornus alba 'Elegantissima' *(left)*

Cornus capitata *(right)*
syns *Benthamia fragifera, Dendrobenthamia capitata*

HIMALAYAN STRAWBERRY TREE, EVERGREEN DOGWOOD,
BENTHAM'S CORNUS

From the Himalayas and China, this evergreen dogwood makes a rounded, low-branched tree of 30 ft (9 m) after many years, with dense grayish green foliage. In late spring and early summer its canopy is decked with massed flowerheads, each with 4 large bracts of a beautiful soft lemon yellow. In autumn it has large, juicy (but tasteless), scarlet compound fruit. ZONES 8–10.

Cornus controversa *(right)*
TABLE DOGWOOD, GIANT DOGWOOD

Native to China, Korea and Japan, this handsome deciduous species makes a tree to about 40 ft (12 m) with age, with a straight trunk and horizontal tiers of foliage. The glossy, strongly veined leaves are arranged alternately on the reddish twigs, a feature shared by *Cornus alternifolia* only. In bloom it is one of the showiest of the species lacking large bracts, with white flowers in flat clusters about 4 in (10 cm) across borne in early summer. The fruit are shiny black, and autumn foliage is red to purplish. **'Variegata'** has leaves with creamy white margins. ZONES 6–9.

Cornus florida *(bottom right)*
FLOWERING DOGWOOD

Popular for its beauty and reliability, this species reaches 20 ft (6 m) or more tall with a single, somewhat crooked trunk, and in mid-spring bears an abundance of flowerheads, each with 4 large white or rose pink bracts. In late summer the scattered red fruit make a fine showing, and in autumn the foliage is scarlet and deep purple with a whitish bloom on the leaf undersides. *Cornus florida* prefers a warm summer and may not flower well in cool-summer climates. **'Rubra'** has dark rose bracts that are paler at the base. **'Apple Blossom'** has pale pink flower bracts. ZONES 5–9.

Cornus controversa 'Variegata'
(left)
Cornus florida 'Rubra'
(below)

C

Cornus kousa
(right & below right)

JAPANESE FLOWERING DOGWOOD, KOUSA

Occurring wild in Japan, China
and Korea, *Cornus kousa* can
reach 20 ft (6 m) or more at maturity with dense, deep green
foliage and tiered lower branches.
In early summer when the
leaves have fully expanded, the
flowerheads with large, pure
white bracts appear, each bract
tapering to an acute point. The
small compound fruit are dull
red. As popular in gardens as
the typical Japanese race is **C. k.
var. *chinensis***, with slightly
larger 'flowers' and more vigorous growth. **ZONES 6–9.**

Cornus kousa var. *chinensis*
(above)

Cornus mas *(right)*

CORNELIAN CHERRY

When it flowers in late winter or early spring on the
leafless branches, this tree species looks unlike most
other dogwoods. The flowers are tiny and golden
yellow, grouped in small clusters without decorative
bracts, but so profuse on the small twigs as well as on
thicker branches, that they make a fine display. Stiff
and rather narrow at first, with maturity it becomes a
spreading tree of 25 ft (8 m) or so. Edible fruit ripen
bright red in late summer. Native to central and
southeastern Europe, *Cornus mas* provides much-
needed winter color for streets, parks and gardens.
'Variegata' has white-margined leaves. **ZONES 6–9.**

Cornus nuttallii

(right, below right & below far right)

PACIFIC DOGWOOD

In the wild, in the Pacific Northwest of North America, this is a slender tree to 50 ft (15 m), but in gardens is often only a tall shrub. The flower-heads are 4–5 in (10–12 cm) across with 4 to 7 pure white bracts, ageing pinkish, and the small cluster of flowers at their center is dull purple. Flowering occurs from mid-spring to early summer. The autumn foliage is yellow and red. This beautiful but short-lived tree is somewhat frost tender, but thrives in a cool, rainy climate in a part-shaded position. **ZONES 7–9.**

Cornus stolonifera 'Kelsey Gold'

(below)

Cornus stolonifera

(above center)

syn. *Cornus sericea*

RED-OSIER DOGWOOD

This shrubby species is similar to *Cornus alba* but native to eastern North America and has a tendency to spread faster into large clumps. The winter stems are bright red, as are the fruit, while the flowers are white. Both species make excellent winter accent plants against white snow or dark evergreens. **'Flaviramea'** has yellow winter stems; **'Kelsey Gold'** has bright

Cornus stolonifera 'Flaviramea'

(above)

yellowish green leaves; **'Silver and Gold'** has variegated leaves with yellow winter stems. **ZONES 2–10.**

COROKIA

This genus consists of 3 species of evergreen shrubs from New Zealand grown largely for their unusual angular, interlacing branch pattern. Attractive star-shaped, small yellow flowers are followed by colorful berries. Reasonably frost hardy, they suit mild coastal climates and can tolerate wind.

CULTIVATION

They should be planted in full sun or light shade and need moderately fertile, well-drained soil. A trim after flowering will maintain shape and leaf growth. They are propagated from softwood cuttings in summer.

Corokia buddlejoides *(above)*

This densely foliaged shrub grows to about 10 ft (3 m) high and wide. It has long, narrow, leaves that are quite glossy when young. The flowers appear in spring and early summer and are followed by small red to black berries. A tough, adaptable bush that withstands regular trimming and is ideal for hedging, it also tolerates salt spray and is a very effective coastal plant. ZONES 8–10.

Corokia* × *virgata *(above)*

Originating in the wild as spontaneous crosses between *Corokia buddlejoides* and *C. cotoneaster*, this hybrid is variable but its botanical characters are generally intermediate between the 2 parents. It bears its flowers in spring and early summer, followed by bright orange, egg-shaped berries. The glossy green leaves have a downy undersurface. It grows to a height and spread of 10 ft (3 m) and adapts to most soils and conditions, doing best in full sun. Cultivars include: **'Red Wonder'**, with bright red berries; **'Yellow Wonder'**, with golden berries; and **'Bronze Lady'**, so-called for its leaf color in maturity. ZONES 8–10.

C

Coronilla emerus
(below right)

SCORPION SENNA, FALSE SENNA

Of wide natural distribution in Europe, this low, somewhat sprawling deciduous shrub has bright yellow flowers borne in small groups from the leaf axils in spring. They are followed by slender seed pods that are articulated, like a scorpion's tail. The leaves are small with few, rounded, bright green leaflets. Normally less than 3 ft (1 m) high it will sometimes reach twice this height. ZONES 6–9.

Coronilla valentina (bottom)
syn. *Coronilla glauca*

This bushy, often short-lived evergreen shrub is a native of the Mediterranean region. If grown in a sunny spot in well-drained soil it will thrive and bear pretty heads of yellow, fragrant flowers in late winter and early spring and again in late summer. The leaves are dark green and have up to 13 leaflets. It grows to a height and spread a little over 5 ft (1.5 m). **Coronilla valentina subsp. *glauca*** has blue-green leaves with 5 to 7 leaflets. The epithet *valentina* means 'of Valencia' (Spain). ZONES 9–10.

CORONILLA
CROWN VETCH

A legume genus of 20 or so species of annuals, perennials and low, wiry shrubs, native to Europe, western Asia and northern Africa. They have pinnate leaves with small, thin or somewhat fleshy leaflets, and stalked umbels of small pea-flowers a little like some clover or medic flowers. Certain perennial and shrub species are grown as ornamentals, valued for their profuse flowers blooming over a long season, though not especially showy. *Coronilla* is Latin for 'little crown', referring to the neat circular umbels of some species.

CULTIVATION

They need full sun, moderately fertile, well-drained soil and protection from cold winds. Cut leggy plants back to the base in spring. Propagate from seed, cuttings, or division of rootstock.

C

CORREA
AUSTRALIAN FUCHSIA

This small Australian genus allied to *Boronia* consists of 11 species of evergreen shrubs, mostly of irregular habit, some semi-prostrate. They have smallish leaves arranged on the stems in opposite pairs, mostly felted with hairs on the underside. The flowers, mostly borne singly in leaf axils, are bell-shaped or tubular with a thin felt of hairs on the outside and protruding stamens. They attract nectar-feeding birds.

CULTIVATION
They adapt to most mild, non-tropical climates and do best in sun or part-shade in moderately fertile, free-draining but moist soil. Some species are short lived, and plants should be replaced every 3–5 years. Tip prune to promote densely leafed bushes. Propagate from cuttings.

Correa backhousiana
(below left)

From coasts of Tasmania, this species resembles *Correa alba* in foliage and growth habit, making a densely spreading shrub about 4 ft (1.2 m) high. The thick, rounded leaves are about 1 in (25 mm) in length, with felty undersides. The solitary or clustered flowers are tubular, 1 in (25 mm) long, cream to pale green in color, and produced through winter. It adapts to most soils and can tolerate salt spray as well as wet ground for short periods. ZONES 8–10.

Correa 'Dusky Bells' *(left)*

Of uncertain origin but possibly a hybrid between *Correa pulchella* and *C. reflexa*, this spreading, dense shrub takes its name from the delightful dusky deep pink, narrowly bell-shaped flowers that appear from autumn to spring. It grows to 24 in (60 cm) with a spread of 3 ft (1 m). ZONES 9–10.

Correa pulchella
(right)

SALMON CORREA

This species from coastal South Australia occurs on better soils in sheltered places along stream banks. It is a semi-prostrate to erect, densely leafy shrub up to 3 ft (1 m). From autumn to spring it bears a profusion of attractive 1 in (25 mm) long bells in shades of pink, salmon or orange. **ZONES 9–10.**

C

Correa reflexa 'Fat Fred' *(left)*

Correa reflexa *(left)*

COMMON CORREA, AUSTRALIAN FUCHSIA

This is the most widely distributed species of *Correa*, ranging from southern Queensland to Tasmania and South Australia, and from coastal dunes to semi-arid hills of the interior. Its habit can be prostrate or upright, from 12 in (30 cm) to more than 4 ft (1.2 m) in height. Leaves are in widely spaced pairs, rather harsh-textured and scattered with small rusty hair tufts, as are the outsides of the nodding or pendent flowers; these are tubular to bell-shaped, $1–1\frac{1}{2}$ in (25–38 mm) long with the 4 petal tips gently reflexed. The color is variable, most commonly deep red with pale green tips, but pink and cream flowered forms are also found. **'Fat Fred'** is a cultivar with exceptionally wide, swollen, pink flowers with green tips; **'Salmon'** has slender salmon-pink flowers. **ZONES 9–10.**

CORYLOPSIS
WINTER HAZEL

These deciduous shrubs from China and Japan produce short, usually pendulous spikes of fragrant, 5-petalled, pale yellow or greenish flowers on the bare branches before the blunt-toothed leaves appear in late spring. The fruits, ripening in summer among the leaves, are small, woody capsules each containing 2 black seeds. The subtle appeal of these shrubs lies mostly in the repetitive pattern of flower spikes on the bare branches.

CULTIVATION
They are best suited to a woodland setting in a reasonably moist, cool climate, providing a foil for bolder shrubs such as rhododendrons. The soil should be fertile, moist but well-drained and acid. Propagation is normally from seed.

Corylopsis glabrescens (left)
FRAGRANT WINTER HAZEL

Native to Japan where it grows in the mountains, this species makes a broadly spreading shrub of 15 ft (4.5 m) tall, sometimes more. The small flowers are lemon yellow with rather narrow petals and appear in mid-spring. **ZONES 6–9.**

Corylopsis spicata (left)
SPIKE WINTER HAZEL

This species from Japan was the first one known in the West. It is low growing, seldom exceeding 6 ft (1.8 m) and often less, and broadly spreading. The narrow, pale greenish yellow, spring flowers have red anthers, the short spikes bursting from particularly large, pale green bracts which persist on the spikes. The arrangement of flowers is more informal than that of some other species. **ZONES 6–9.**

CORYLUS

HAZEL, FILBERT

C

The 10 or more deciduous trees and large shrubs in this genus are best known for their edible nuts. The commonly grown species have massed stems that spring from ground level, but some others have a well developed trunk. The branches are tough and supple, and bear broad, toothed leaves that are somewhat heart-shaped and strongly veined. Male and female flowers grow on the same plant; the males in slender catkins that appear before the leaves expand; and the females are inconspicuous. The latter develop into the distinctive nuts, each enclosed in a fringed green husk and ripening in summer.

CULTIVATION

Provide ample space, full sun or part-shade and fertile, moist but well-drained, chalky soil. Propagate by detaching suckers, or by fresh nuts. For fruit set, there is a cold requirement of about 1000 hours below 45°F (7°C). Cool, moist summers also assist nut production.

Corylus avellana
(below)

COMMON HAZEL, COBNUT,
EUROPEAN FILBERT

This species occurs throughout Europe, western Asia and northern Africa. It typically makes a broad mass of stems about 12–15 ft (3.5–4.5 m) high. In winter, the bare twigs are draped with catkins, which make quite a display. The nuts are half enclosed in a fringed tube. In autumn the leaves turn pale yellow. '**Contorta**' is a bizarre cultivar with branches that wander and wriggle in all directions; when leafless they are cut for sale by florists. '**Wunder von Bollweiler**' is a popular European cultivar. ZONES 4–9.

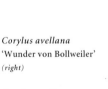

Corylus avellana
'Wunder von Bollweiler'
(right)

Corylus avellana
'Contorta' *(below right)*

C

Corylus maxima *(left)*

FILBERT

The filbert, a native of southern Europe, is similar in most respects to the hazel but is more inclined to become tree-like and has sticky hairs on the young twigs. The most obvious difference, though, is the much longer tubular husk completely enclosing each nut, which is also more elongated. As an ornamental it is best known by the cultivar **'Purpurea'**, which has deep, dark purple, spring foliage, softening to a dull greenish purple in summer. **ZONES 4–9.**

Corylus maxima 'Purpurea' *(below)*

CORYMBIA

The 113 species of trees from Australia and Papua New Guinea that make up this newly recognized genus are still treated as 'eucalypts' in the broad sense. Mainly tropical, they comprise mostly the 'bloodwood' group of eucalypts with soft, crumbly or corky bark and cream, pink or red flowers carried in showy clusters at tips of branches—the spectacular red-flowering gum of Western Australia, *Corymbia ficifolia,* is a typical example. But just to confuse the issue, some 'bloodwoods' (in the botanical sense) have smooth bark, for example the well-known lemon-scented gum *(C. citriodora).* Then there is another group of species known as the 'paper-fruited bloodwoods' which produce their smaller flowers and fruits usually in the space of one tropical wet season: these are little known in cultivation but one *(C. aparrerinja)* is the well-known 'ghost gum' of Central Australia.

CULTIVATION
The species vary in their requirements and ease of cultivation. Many come from tropical regions with a short wet season and long dry season, and these rarely adapt well to more temperate climates. A number have proved more adaptable, though, and are popular in cultivation. They prefer full sun, and thrive in most soils, from heavy clay to light sand. All are drought tolerant once established. They are easily propagated from seed and should be planted in their permanent positions when not more than 24 in (60 cm) high.

Corymbia aparrerinja (right)
syn. *Eucalyptus papuana*
GHOST GUM

Found near watercourses over much of northern inland Australia and around Port Moresby in Papua New Guinea, the ghost gum is a broad-crowned, single-trunked tree to 50 ft (15 m) high with an open, domed canopy of light green, lanceolate leaves. Its common name comes from the white, smooth, chalky bark. Small clusters of white flowers are produced in summer, followed by urn-shaped fruit. Well-drained soil and a warm, frost-free climate suit it best; it is tolerant of quite dry conditions.
ZONES 10–12.

C

Corymbia calophylla *(left)*
syn. *Eucalyptus calophylla*

MARRI

From the south of Western Australia, this tree can grow to 200 ft (60 m) tall, though 40–80 ft (12–24 m) is more common. The thick, straight trunk has rough, grayish brown bark, often stained with red sap. Large cream or rarely pink flowers are borne in summer and autumn, followed by 1 in (25 mm), goblet-shaped seed capsules. It hybridizes readily with *Corymbia ficifolia*, the hybrids usually being pink. ZONES 9–11.

Corymbia citriodora
(right & far right)
syn. *Eucalyptus citriodora*

LEMON-SCENTED GUM

This fast-growing adaptable tree from the open forests and dry slopes of tropical northeastern Australia is widely grown in more temperate areas. Tall and straight trunked, to 100 ft (30 m), it has smooth, sometimes dimpled bark in subtle shades of white, gray or pale pink that is shed during the summer months. The foliage is held aloft on an open crown; when crushed, the long, narrow leaves have a lemony scent. The winter flowers are creamy white. ZONES 9–12.

Corymbia ficifolia
(right)
syn. *Eucalyptus ficifolia*

SCARLET-FLOWERING GUM, RED-FLOWERING GUM

This most spectacular eucalypt bears large terminal clusters of scarlet to orange flowers in late spring or summer, followed by large, urn-shaped fruit. (Forms with crimson or pink flowers are suspected of being hybrids of *E. calophylla*.) It grows to about 30 ft (9 m) with rough bark and a spreading crown of lance-shaped foliage. It per-

forms best in a winter-rainfall climate. ZONES 9–10.

Corymbia maculata
(above right)
syn. *Eucalyptus maculata*

SPOTTED GUM

This 100 ft (30 m), straight-trunked tree of broadly columnar or conical form occurs over much of temperate east-coastal Australia. Thick, mottled, gray-green bark sheds in patches to

create a patchwork of gray, green, pink and ochre. The pointed adult leaves are up to 8 in (20 cm) long. The large white flowers appear in winter, followed by small, urn-shaped seed capsules. Spotted gum yields a valuable, close-grained timber. ZONES 9–11.

CORYNOCARPUS

This small genus of evergreen trees and shrubs consists of only 6 species, occurring in eastern Australia, New Zealand, New Caledonia, Papua New Guinea and Vanuatu. It has no close relatives. The leaves are simple, smooth-edged and leathery, spirally arranged on the stems. Terminal panicles of small 5-petalled flowers are followed by plum-like fruit. Only the New Zealand species is cultivated, admired for its foliage and fruit; grown by the Maori for food, the kernels were ground and baked.

CULTIVATION
Useful trees for shelter and screening, they adapt to seashore conditions with salt spray. Frost tender, they need full sun or part-shade and moisture-retentive, well-drained soil. Water regularly while in flower. Propagate from seed or cuttings.

Corynocarpus laevigata (above)
KARAKA, NEW ZEALAND LAUREL

This New Zealand evergreen normally makes a 20–30 ft (6–9 m) tree with a dense, rounded crown. The broad leathery leaves are lustrous green and up to 8 in (20 cm) long. Clusters of small yellow-green flowers are followed in autumn or winter by orange-yellow fruit ¾–1½ in (18–38 mm) long, each containing a large, highly poisonous seed—only after careful treatment was it safe to eat by the Maori. A cultivar with variegated foliage is **'Albus Variegatus'** with irregular creamy margins. ZONES 9–11.

C

COTINUS
SMOKE BUSH, SMOKE TREE

Only 3 species make up this genus of deciduous shrubs or small trees: one is from temperate Eurasia, one from eastern North America, and one confined to southwestern China. They have simple, oval, untoothed leaves. A striking feature is the inflorescences, much-branched with delicate, thread-like dull purplish branchlets, only a few of which carry the small flowers; they produce a curiously ornamental effect like fine puffs of smoke scattered over the foliage. Both flowers and fruits are tiny and inconspicuous. The foliage is another attraction, coloring deeply in autumn, and in some cultivars the spring foliage offers good color. In earlier times a commercial yellow dye was extracted from the wood of these trees.

CULTIVATION

Smoke bushes are easily grown, adapting to a range of temperate climates but most at home where summers are moderately warm and dry. Soil that is too moist or fertile discourages free flowering. Propagate from softwood cuttings in summer or seed in autumn.

Cotinus coggygria covered in ice *(below)*

Cotinus coggygria
syn. *Rhus cotinus*
VENETIAN SUMAC, SMOKE TREE
Of wide distribution from southern Europe to central China, this bushy shrub is usually 10–15 ft (3–4 m) in height and spread, and has oval, long-stalked leaves. The inflorescences appear in early summer and are pale pinkish bronze, ageing to a duller purple-gray. Some of the flowers produce small, dry, flattened fruit in late summer. Autumn foliage has strong orange and bronze tones. **'Purpureus'** is widely grown—it has rich, purplish spring foliage becoming greener in summer and glowing orange and purple in autumn; **'Royal Purple'** is very similar but spring and summer the foliage is deeper purple; the leaves of **'Velvet Cloak'** are purple and turn dark reddish purple in autumn. ZONES 6–10.

Cotinus coggygria 'Royal Purple' *(above)*

C

Cotinus coggygria
'Velvet Cloak' *(left)*

Cotinus obovatus *(above)*
syns *Cotinus americanus, Rhus cotinoides*
AMERICAN SMOKE TREE

From southeastern USA, this species can make a
small tree of up to 30 ft (9 m), though may remain a tall shrub. The leaves are larger than those
of *Cotinus coggygria* and bronze pink when young,
turning mid-green in summer and finally orange-
scarlet to purple in autumn. The inflorescences
are also larger but sparser, and male and female
flowers are on different trees. **ZONES 5–10.**

COTONEASTER

This temperate Eurasian genus of shrubs (rarely small trees) includes both deciduous and evergreen species and is one of the small-fruited genera of the pome-fruit group of the rose family, that includes *Pyracantha, Crataegus* and *Amelanchier*. The name dates from Roman times, and means something like 'useless quince'. The lower-growing species are popular for rockeries, embankments and foundation plantings. They are mostly very frost hardy, often of dense, spreading habit, and provide a good display of red berries. Some species make good hedges and espaliers.

CULTIVATION
The evergreen species especially provide fine displays of berries, even in warmer temperate climates. All do best in full sun in moderately fertile, well-drained soil. They are prone to the bacterial disease fireblight. Propagate from seed or cuttings.

Cotoneaster dammeri
'Coral Beauty' *(left)*

Cotoneaster dammeri
BEARBERRY COTONEASTER

Most distinctive of the fully prostrate cotoneasters, this central Chinese evergreen species has relatively large, round-tipped leaves with the veins deeply impressed into their dark green upper surfaces; the scattered starry white flowers appear through summer and are followed by solitary red fruit that last well into winter, when the leaves turn bronze. The varietal name *radicans* is often added, but there is confusion as to which form of the species it belongs; all cultivated forms have very similar qualities. **'Coral Beauty'** has profuse, bright orange fruit. ZONES 5–10.

Cotoneaster franchetii *(above)*
This attractive evergreen from western China grows to about 10 ft (3 m) tall, with long, cane-like branches. The smallish, pointed leaves have curved veins strongly impressed into the glossy upper surface and woolly undersides. In early summer it bears small clusters of pink-tinged white flowers, followed by tight groups of salmon pink to pale orange berries which last into winter. A reliable shrub, it adapts to most garden conditions, in both warm and cool climates. ZONES 6–10.

Cotoneaster horizontalis *(right)*

ROCK COTONEASTER

Popular in cooler areas where its fine foliage takes on bronze purple, orange and reddish autumn hues, this semi-prostrate shrub has horizontal, flattened sprays of branches building up in stiff tiers with age to 3 ft (1 m) high and up to 8 ft (2.4 m) wide. The small flesh pink summer flowers are followed by much showier, deep red fruit. Native to mountain areas of western China, it is deciduous in cool climates but only semi-deciduous in warmer climates. The named forms include **'Variegatus'** with leaves edged with white; *Cotoneaster horizontalis* **var. *perpusillus*** is a more compact, dwarf plant with tiny leaves. ZONES 5–10.

C

Cotoneaster 'Hybridus Pendulus' *(right)*

This semi-deciduous hybrid is a shrub of high or-namental value, with weak, pendulous branches and rather narrow leaves, enlivened from late summer onward by loose bunches of bright red berries. Planted on its own roots, it mounds up eventually to about 3 ft (1 m) tall, and the branches can trail effectively over walls or rocks. Alternatively, grafted onto a standard of one of the taller species, it can make an attractive weep-ing specimen with curtains of foliage. ZONES 6–9.

Cotoneaster lacteus *(right)*

syn. *Cotoneaster parneyi*

ROCKSPRAY COTONEASTER

This evergreen Chinese shrub is similar to *Cotoneaster glaucophyllus* but has a more persist-ent coating of wool on its leaf undersides, and more conspicuous veining on the upper. The white flowers appear early in summer, followed by large bunches of orange-red fruits that persist through winter. It adapts well to warmer climates. ZONES 7–11.

C

Cotoneaster microphyllus
(below)

This compact, densely twiggy species from the Himalayas has small, thick, glossy evergreen leaves and plump crimson to purplish red fruit from late summer to winter. Its growth

habit varies from completely prostrate to upright or mound-like, 3–4 ft (1–1.2 m) in height; mature plants have a framework of tough, woody branches. Vigorous and very frost hardy, it needs a fairly exposed location in full sun. For a formal look, and to display its fruit more effectively, it can be clipped into dense mounds. **Cotoneaster microphyllus var. cochleatus** (syn. *Cotoneaster cochleatus*) is almost prostrate, with profuse fruit. **C. m. var. thymifolius** is a stiffly upright shrub to 24 in (60 cm) with a finely twiggy habit and narrow, wedge-shaped leaves. **ZONES 5–10.**

Cotoneaster salicifolius
(above)

WILLOWLEAF COTONEASTER

This attractive evergreen species from western China features narrow leaves with a network of veins deeply impressed into their convex, glossy upper surfaces. The profuse large bunches of bright red berries last long into winter, when the leaves may also take on bronze and yellow tones. It is variable in habit; some forms are low and spreading, others reach 10–15 ft (3–4.5 m) with long, arching growths. It takes well to trimming and makes a fine hedge plant. **'Herbstfeuer' ('Autumn Fire')** is low and spreading and bears abundant orange-red fruit. **ZONES 6–10.**

Cotoneaster salicifolius covered in ice *(above)*

Cotoneaster splendens *(left)*

An attractive small-leafed but very vigorous deciduous shrub from northwestern China, this species was initially introduced to Sweden in the 1930s by the Swedish collector Harry Smith and was only popularized elsewhere in the West much more recently. It is a medium-sized shrub growing to 5–10 ft (1.5–3 m) with arching shoots, grayish green, glossy leaves that turn red in autumn, solitary pinkish flowers in summer and reddish orange fruit up to almost ½ in (12 mm) long. **ZONES 5–9.**

COUROUPITA

Three species of trees from northern South America make up this genus. They have large, elliptical leaves, usually clustered at the branch tips. The flowers are large and complex in structure, usually 6-petalled, and sometimes smell like garlic. They are followed by spectacular large, spherical fruit.

CULTIVATION

These are plants for tropical or warm subtropical areas and will not tolerate frost or prolonged cold. They prefer to grow in deep, moist, humus-rich soil in full sun but in a sheltered position. Propagation is normally from seed.

Couroupita guianensis
(above right & right)
CANNONBALL TREE

This species is an upright, evergreen tree capable of growing to 100 ft (30 m) high, though 30–40 ft (9–12 m) is a more usual size. Pendulous flowering branches emerge directly from the trunk, right down to the ground, and all year produce 3 in (8 cm) diameter, brilliant red and orange fragrant flowers with hundreds of stamens arranged in 2 groups, one in the flower's center and the other on a lower petal. Showy as the flowers are, the fruit are the main feature—they are brown spheres up to 10 in (25 cm) across filled with a smelly, soft red pulp, and one tree may bear hundreds of them. They look like small cannonballs and burst explosively on falling from the tree. ZONES 11–12.

CRATAEGUS
HAWTHORN, MAY

Native to cool-climate areas of Europe, Asia and eastern North America, *Crataegus* belongs to the pome-fruit group of the rose family and the resemblance of the fruits to miniature apples can easily be seen and tasted. Most of the 200 species have long, sharp thorns on the summer growths; the leaves are either toothed or lobed, and the white or rarely pink flowers are clustered in flat to rounded umbels in late spring or summer. They are followed in autumn by a display of fruits mostly in shades of red, often also with attractive foliage colors.

CULTIVATION
Hawthorns are robust, frost-hardy, deciduous trees, most of them compact enough even for quite small gardens. They are sun-lovers and not very fussy about soil type or drainage. Some species sucker from the base, but suckers can be removed to produce a tree form. Some hawthorns are prone to fireblight, controlled only by prompt removal and burning of affected branches. Foliage may also be disfigured by the 'pear and cherry slug' (larva of a sawfly); spray severe attacks with an insecticide. Propagate from cold-stratified seed, or by grafting of named clones. In winter they are easily transplanted.

Crataegus diffusa *(above)*

A species from northeastern USA, this makes a tree of up to 30 ft (10 m), the branches armed with long spines. Leaves are pale green and shallowly lobed. Umbels of smallish white flowers in late spring or early summer are followed by red fruit about ⅜ in (9 mm) in diameter. ZONES 4–9.

Crataegus flava *(above)*
YELLOW HAW, SUMMER HAW

This species is believed native to eastern USA, but is not now found in the wild. It is a tree with smallish, smooth, toothed or shallowly lobed leaves, fairly large white flowers borne in early summer, and greenish yellow fruit about ⅝ in (15 mm) in diameter. It is not one of the more ornamental hawthorns. ZONES 4–9.

C

Crataegus laevigata *(above)*
syn. *Crataegus oxyacantha*

MIDLAND HAWTHORN, MAY,
ENGLISH HAWTHORN

This small tree reaches 25 ft
(8 m) or more in height and
spread. Native to Europe and
North Africa, it is easily confused with the English may
(Crataegus monogyna). It has
mid- to dark green, glossy leaves
with shallow, rounded lobes and
produces few thorns. Abundant
white flowers open in late
spring. Cultivar **'Paul's Scarlet'**

Crataegus laevigata 'Paul's
Scarlet' *(above)*
Crataegus laevigata 'Punicea
Flore Pleno' *(above right & right)*

has bright crimson, double
flowers in late spring; **'Punicea'**
has deep pink single flowers
with white centers; **'Punicea
Flore Pleno'** is similar but with
double flowers. **ZONES 4–9.**

Crataegus lavallei in
winter *(right)* and in
summer *(far right)*

*Crataegus ×
lavallei*
syn. *Crataegus ×
carrierei*

LAVALLE HAWTHORN, CARRIERE
HAWTHORN

This hybrid originated
in France in about 1880,
the result of a cross
between *Crataegus crus-
galli* and *C. pubescens*.
A densely branched,
almost thornless tree
of 15–20 ft (4.5–6 m),
the broad, irregularly
toothed leaves are
darker glossy green

than most hawthorns
and are semi-evergreen
in warmer climates.
The white flowers with
red stamens open in
loose clusters in early
summer, then large
yellow fruit ripen to
orange-red. Its autumn
foliage tones intensify
after the first hard
frost. **ZONES 6–10.**

C

Crataegus monogyna *(left)*
HAWTHORN, MAY

Native to Europe, this small tree is most commonly
cultivated as a hedgerow, but when growing wild it can
reach 30 ft (9 m). The leaves have 5 to 7 jagged lobes,
and turn yellow-brown in autumn. The fragrant single
white flowers open in late spring, mid-May in England
though according to the old calendar they opened
around May Day (May 1). The small dark red fruit that
follow hang onto the twigs into winter. *Crataegus
laevigata* is very similar but *C. monogyna* is easily
distinguished by its single style and fruit stone.
C. monogyna subsp. *azarella* has leaves with very
downy undersides. ZONES 4–9.

Crataegus phaenopyrum *(left)*
syn. *Crataegus cordata*
WASHINGTON THORN

This elegant though very thorny tree from southeastern
USA reaches 20–30 ft (6–9 m). Round-headed and
densely branched, with long, sharp thorns, the leaves
have 3 to 5 sharply toothed lobes, and are glossy green.
Fragrant white flowers in mid-summer are followed in
autumn by profuse clusters of small, shiny orange-red
berries. ZONES 4–10.

Crataegus punctata *(left)*
THICKET HAWTHORN

This species from eastern USA makes an attractive tree,
growing to about 30 ft (9 m) with a stout trunk and
crown of horizontally spreading branches. It has broad
dark green leaves with toothed or slightly lobed margins and downy on the undersides. In early summer it
produces clusters of white blossom up to 4 in (10 cm)
wide. The fruit are large, slightly pear-shaped, dull
crimson with paler dots. It is one of the most ornamental of the North American species. '**Aurea**' has yellow
fruit. ZONES 5–9.

Crataegus viridus 'Winter King' *(above)*

Crataegus viridis
GREEN HAWTHORN

Making a small tree of up to about 30 ft (9 m), this
species from southeastern USA has fairly broad, glossy
dark green leaves that are toothed or lobed in the upper
half; in late spring–early summer it bears white flowers
in small and rather sparse clusters, followed by smallish
red fruit. '**Winter King**' is a superior cultivar with silvery bark, a vase-like form with relatively few thorns,
good red autumn color and bright red fruit that last
well into winter. ZONES 4–9.

CROWEA

Four species of attractive small shrubs make up this temperate Australian genus. They are compact evergreens with narrow, mid-green leaves and masses of smallish, 5-petalled, usually pink flowers. These are borne most heavily in late spring, but plants are seldom without bloom.

CULTIVATION
They are easily grown in light but moist, well-drained soil in full sun or very light shade; a light trim after flowering helps to keep them neat. The dwarf cultivars make attractive rockery plants. Croweas are usually propagated from small cuttings.

Crowea exalata (left)

This species from southeastern Australia is usually about 24 in (60 cm) high, with a bushy habit. Its leaves smell slightly of aniseed when crushed. Its deep pink flowers are about ¾ in (18 mm) in diameter. **'Bindelong Compact'** is a recent cultivar notable for its dwarf, bushy growth— to about 18 in (45 cm)—and lavish display of flowers. **ZONES 8–10.**

Crowea exalata
'Bindelong Compact'
(right)

C

CRYPTOMERIA

JAPANESE CEDAR, SUGI

One species is accepted in this conifer genus from China and Japan, though there are many variations. Often fast-growing, the branches and branchlets of this evergreen are clothed in short, leathery needle leaves that are densely overlapping and curve inward slightly. Male (pollen) and female (seed) cones are on the same tree, the former in profuse clusters and releasing clouds of pollen in spring, the latter in sparser groups behind the branch tips. Its handsome shape and uniformity of growth make it highly suitable for windbreaks, hedges and avenues. In Japan it is grown for its timber, but is also venerated in historic groves.

CULTIVATION

Very frost hardy, it prefers full sun or part-shade and deep, fertile, moist but well-drained soil. It likes plenty of water. Propagation is from seed, or from cuttings for the cultivars.

Cryptomeria japonica var. *sinensis* *(below left)*
Cryptomeria japonica 'Globosa Nana' *(left)*
Cryptomeria japonica 'Elegans' *(below)*

Cryptomeria japonica *(top left)*

This species can grow 20–25 ft (6–8 m) in 10 years; old trees in Japan are up to 150 ft (45 m) high, with massive trunks. The thick, brown bark has straight, vertical furrows. Growth habit is conical with a long, pointed leader. The Japanese race has thicker branchlets and stiffer habit than the Chinese one, *Cryptomeria japonica* var. *sinensis*. There are at least 50 cultivars, most dwarf but not all. Best known of the taller ones is 'Elegans', which makes a solid column of foliage to 30 ft (9 m) high and 8 ft (2.4 m) across; needles are long and soft; in winter the tree turns a striking dull bronze or plum color. 'Elegans Nana' is similar but a dwarf form. 'Araucarioides', with a bizarre tangle of long rat's tail branches, reaches 10 ft (3 m) and makes an interesting foliage contrast in a mixed conifer planting. 'Globosa Nana', the most popular lower-growing cultivar, makes a dense, intricately branching ball, soft to the touch; new growth is pale green in spring and summer. While listed as a dwarf, in good soil it may grow to 10 ft (3 m) across in only 15 years. 'Bandai-Sugi' makes a globose plant that becomes irregular in shape, to 6 ft (1.8 m); the foliage is thick and turns dull bronze in winter. 'Jindai-Sugi' is a slow-growing bush, irregularly shaped with a flattish top; foliage is bright green and dense. Tiny 'Vilmoriniana', growing 12 in (30 cm), is suitable for rockeries. ZONES 7–10.

CUNONIA

One species in this small genus of evergreen trees and shrubs comes from South Africa, while most of the remaining 14 come from New Caledonia. They are evergreen, damp-loving trees with thick, leathery leaves and star-shaped, 5-petalled flowers. The genus is related to the Australian genus *Ceratopetalum*.

C

CULTIVATION

Fairly frost tender, they do best in full sun in well-drained, fertile soil, but will grow in sandy or gravelly soil if given sufficient moisture. Prune to establish a single leader if a tree form is desired. Propagate from seed or cuttings.

Cunonia capensis
(right)

SPOON BUSH, RED ALDER

This species occurs wild in southern coastal districts of South Africa. It is quite fast growing and will become a rounded tree to 50 ft (15 m) with a single trunk where conditions suit it, or a bushy shrub in lesser conditions. It has attractive, shiny leaves that are divided into pairs of lance-shaped, serrated leaflets, dark green with a reddish tinge. From the tip of each branch projects a pair of large reddish stipules, closely pressed together and shaped like a spoon, hence the common name. Tiny, creamy white flowers with long stamens are borne in autumn, densely crowded on long spikes. ZONES 9–10.

C

CUPHEA

From Central and South America, this genus consists of over 250 species of annuals, evergreen perennials, sub-shrubs and shrubs. They are mostly rather low growing with weak stems and smallish, simple leaves. The flowers have a long tubular calyx and small circular red, pink, yellow or white petals, the latter sometimes hardly visible. Most are frost tender but as they are fast growing they can be treated as annuals. The many species vary quite considerably. They bloom almost throughout the year.

CULTIVATION
They prefer moist, well-drained soil in sun or very light shade. Propagation is usually from small tip cuttings, though seed is easily raised.

Cuphea hyssopifolia *(below)*
FALSE HEATHER

A small shrub from Mexico and Guatemala, this species is popu-lar worldwide as a pot plant for window ledges and balconies. It grows to about 2 ft (0.6 m) high, has a mound-like form and small dark green oblong leaves. The small flowers appear in the axils of the new shoots from late spring to winter; they have only a short tube and prominent pink to reddish purple petals. It is short lived but self-seeds very readily and may become a pest, especially in warm areas. ZONES 10–12.

Cuphea micropetala *(right)*
This Mexican species is like a larger version of *Cuphea ignea*. The leaves are up to 2½ in (6 cm) long, bright green and elliptical with a prominent midrib. The 1½–2 in (3.5–5 cm) tubular flowers occur in rows at the branch tips and are orange-red with golden yellow tones, tipped with greenish yellow. Tougher than most, this species will withstand occa-sional light frosts. Although

in the wild *C. micropetala* occurs on streamsides, it grows well in normal garden soils. ZONES 9–11.

Cuphea ignea *(left)*
syn. *Cuphea platycentra*
CIGAR FLOWER, CIGARETTE PLANT

This species from Mexico and the West Indies gets its common names from the flowers, which are small, orange and tubular. Each has a white tip with a touch of black, suggesting the ash at the tip of a cigar or ciga-rette. The leaves are small, ellip-tical and bright green. A bushy subshrub, it grows to about 24 in (60 cm) high; occasional trimming keeps it compact. ZONES 10–12.

× CUPRESSOCYPARIS

The '×' in front of the name indicates that this is a bigeneric hybrid, that is, a hybrid between 2 different genera, in this case *Cupressus* and *Chamaecyparis*. Although the name applies to any hybrid between these genera (including later generations and backcrosses), it is best known in the form of the one which first appeared in England in 1888 as a chance hybrid between the frost-hardy *Chamaecyparis nootkatensis* and the less hardy *Cupressus macrocarpa*. Two additional hybrids have since been raised, their *Cupressus* parents being *C. glabra* and *C. lusitanica* respectively.

CULTIVATION
These conifers combine rapid growth with reasonable frost-hardiness, and adapt well to poorly drained soil but not to arid climates. They are widely planted for fast-growing hedges as they respond well to frequent trimming. However, if they are left untrimmed they rapidly grow to tree size. Propagate from cuttings, which strike readily under nursery conditions. Although seed is fertile, the resulting seedlings might vary.

× *Cupressocyparis leylandii*
'Haggerston Gray' *(above)*

× *Cupressocyparis leylandii* *(right)*
LEYLAND CYPRESS

Representing the original cross between *Chamaecyparis nootkatensis* and *Cupressus macrocarpa*, this name encompasses a number of seedling clones, some of which have been named as cultivars. When used without specifying a cultivar name it usually refers to '**Haggerston Gray**' or '**Leighton Green**', which both make very vigorous, upright trees with a long, open leading shoot and slightly irregular outline; foliage is deep green or slightly grayish. In good soil it will reach 30 ft (9 m) in 10 years and double that in 30 years, ultimately growing to 100 ft (30 m) or more. '**Naylor's Blue**' has more strongly bluish green foliage and is more columnar in habit. **ZONES 5–10.**

CUPRESSUS
CYPRESS

This conifer genus has been cultivated since classical times but species are seldom planted where winters are severe due to limited cold tolerance. Most of the 20 or so species occur wild in western USA, Mexico and Guatemala. As well as the wild forms the cypresses include many cultivars. These handsome ornamentals come in many foliage hues; they range from tall to dwarf, from columnar to weeping or high-crowned and spreading. Dense foliage and rapid growth makes them useful screens and windbreaks.

CULTIVATION
Some species are very tolerant of dry conditions, others need a moister climate. Soil and sunlight requirements vary; generally they prefer full sun, well-drained soil and protection from cold winds. They are easy to propagate from seed, and cultivars are almost as easily raised from cuttings. Some cypress species suffer from cypress canker, which disfigures trees and finally kills them.

Cupressus arizonica (below left)
ARIZONA CYPRESS, ROUGH-BARKED ARIZONA CYPRESS

Originating in Arizona, USA, and sometimes confused with *Cupressus glabra*, this pyramidal species grows to 50 ft (15 m). Its mature foliage is gray-green and does not display the white spots of the smooth Arizona cypress. It has short-stalked, large, round cones, up to 1 in (25 mm) across, and a brown, stringy and furrowed bark. It is grown both as a specimen tree and as a hedge. ZONES 7–10.

Cupressus cashmeriana (right)
KASHMIR CYPRESS

Despite its name, this species is not native to Kashmir but to Bhutan. It should by rights be called 'Bhutan cypress', except that *Cupressus torulosa* has a prior claim to this common name. This beautiful cypress has long, weeping sprays of blue-green, aromatic foliage, but is difficult to grow. In a suitable warm, moist climate it grows fast at first, attaining 20–30 ft (6–9 m) in 15 years, but is easily damaged by wind and may die in hot or dry spells. Some fine specimens grow in cooler mountain areas of the wet tropics, and it does well in wetter hill areas of the Mediterranean, the western USA, eastern Australia and New Zealand. ZONES 9–11.

Cupressus lusitanica *(right)*

CEDAR OF GOA, MEXICAN CYPRESS

This cypress is native to the mountains of western Mexico but was long ago introduced to Portugal (*Lusitania* in Latin), where it is now common in parts. In warm climates it is a vigorous grower, but also tolerates cold and dry conditions. It makes a bushy, broad-crowned tree with dense, grayish green foliage that has an attractive loose, foamy texture. *Cupressus lusitanica* **var**. ***benthamii*** has greener, more drooping foliage with branchlets in small, flat sprays. Both this and the typical form grow to 30 ft (9 m) or more in about 15 years. **ZONES 8–11.**

C

Cupressus macrocarpa
(above)

MONTEREY CYPRESS

Endemic to a very short stretch of the central Californian coast near Monterey, this grows into one of the largest of all cypresses, reaching 120 ft (36 m) tall with a trunk diameter of 8 ft (2.4 m). When planted in a grove it forms a tall, straight trunk, but in the open in good soil it branches low with massive, spreading limbs, producing a broad, dense crown of deep green with a rather spiky outline. Close up, the foliage is rather coarse, and it has a slightly sour smell when bruised. The cones are large and wrinkled. It grows best in cool but mild climates with winter rainfall and takes only 10 years or so to form a dense 30–40 ft

(9–12 m) tree. It is one of the most popular farm hedging trees in New Zealand. Golden cultivars include **'Brunniana'**, somewhat columnar, the foliage ageing almost green; the vigorous **'Aurea'**, with long, golden spikes of foliage spreading almost horizontally; and **'Aurea Saligna'** with remarkable weeping, gold-tipped branchlets and

Cupressus macrocarpa
'Greenstead Magnificent' *(above)*

Cupressus macrocarpa 'Aurea'
(left)

elongated scale leaves. A lower-growing cultivar to 4 ft (1.2 m) is **'Greenstead Magnificent'**, which spreads to form a flat-topped, dense mat of pale gray-green foliage, drooping around the edges; as the plant ages it becomes raised above the ground on a short trunk. The small conical **'Goldcrest'** has golden foliage. **ZONES 7–10.**

C

Cupressus sempervirens
FUNEREAL CYPRESS, ITALIAN CYPRESS, MEDITERRANEAN CYPRESS

This species, familiar in Italy, France and Spain, came from the eastern Mediterranean. It has fine dark grayish green foliage with very tiny scale leaves in slightly flattened sprays, and large, slightly elongated, pale brown cones. In its growth habit the Mediterranean cypress exhibits a curious phenomenon: the form usually cultivated, known as **'Stricta'**, is narrowly columnar, but a proportion of its seedlings grow into trees with side branches at a wide angle to the trunk; this form is often known as **'Horizontalis'**. More tolerant of dry conditions and slower growing than most cypresses, it makes quite vigorous growth under good conditions in a warm climate. The 'Stricta' form can reach 15–20 ft (4.5–6 m) in 10 years, often as a slim column at this stage, but old trees of 30–40 ft (9–12 m) are usually much broader. It takes well to topiary. **'Swane's Golden'**, an Australian cultivar with foliage flecked golden yellow with deeper gold tips, is slower growing than 'Stricta' but can still reach 20 ft (6 m) or more. It is rather frost tender. **'Gracilis'** is a narrowly columnar cultivar raised in New Zealand, slow growing and maturing at about 15 ft (4.5 m) with a width of about 3 ft (1 m). It has bright green foliage. ZONES 8–10.

Cupressus sempervirens 'Stricta' *(above)*

Cupressus sempervirens 'Swane's Golden' *(above)*

Cupressus torulosa *(left)*
BHUTAN CYPRESS, HIMALAYAN CYPRESS

This tall conifer reaches 150 ft (45 m) in its native Himalayas, though in cultivation 50–80 ft (15–24 m) is more usual. An elegant tree with a long-pointed crown broader at the base, it is valued for its fast growth and fragrant timber. Its small branchlets are slender and slightly curved, consisting of tiny deep green scale leaves that are blunt tipped. The small cones are purple when young but ripen shiny brown, and the brown fibrous bark peels into strips. It grows best in mild, very moist climates. ZONES 8–10.

CUSSONIA
SOUTH AFRICAN CABBAGE TREE

The 20 species of small evergreen trees of this South African genus, related to *Schefflera*, have unbranched trunks in their younger stages. As these long-lived trees mature, they become multi-branched. They are topped by a thick mass of large, compound leaves; the leaflets radiate from a central point and are usually lobed or further divided into leaflets. Densely clustered spikes of small, greenish flowers stand well above the canopy; they are followed by the succulent fruits which are dull red to black.

CULTIVATION
Although frost tender, they will grow in cooler areas in a sheltered, sunny location. They can be grown in containers provided they have adequate water in the growing season. Propagation is from fresh seed.

Cussonia spicata
(right)

SPIKED CABBAGE TREE,
KIEPERSOL

This is the only species to be widely cultivated and its juvenile form is well known as an indoor plant. Usually single trunked, to 20 ft (6 m) high, its 8 in (20 cm) diameter leaves, carried on long, thick stalks, divide into 5 to 9 leaflets. The flowers are borne in spring and summer. Although often defoliated by heavy frosts, it can reshoot provided it is not repeatedly frozen. ZONES 8–11.

CYDONIA
QUINCE

These small deciduous trees are quite unusual and ornamental. Native to temperate Asia, they belong to the pome-fruit group of the rose family. They are small, crooked, very woody trees with smooth bark and simple, oval leaves, downy at least on the underside and clustered on short spur-shoots (as in apples) except on the long summer growths. The flowers are solitary at the ends of the spur shoots, and have downy calyces and pink petals. The large fruits have waxy or almost greasy skins that are pleasantly aromatic.

CULTIVATION

Quinces only thrive in cooler-temperate climates, although the Chinese species tolerates warmer, more frost-free areas than the common quince. They require moist, deep soil and a sunny position. Propagation is from seed, which is easily obtained from over-ripe fruit, or by grafting for named varieties.

Cydonia oblonga
(left)
COMMON QUINCE

A spreading, bushy tree of 12–15 ft (3.5–4.5 m), this species forks low down on its trunk into crooked limbs. The leaves are moderately large and deep green above but downy on the undersides and on young twigs. The very attractive flowers, about 2 in (5 cm) in diameter and usually a clear pale pink, appear in late spring. The fruit, edible when cooked, ripen to pale or deep yellow and are up to 6 in (15 cm) long with hard flesh. ZONES 6–9.

CYPHOMANDRA

This genus of about 30 species of evergreen shrubs, climbers and small trees from tropical America is closely related to *Solanum*. They have thin, usually hairy leaves, 5-petalled pink to purple flowers in branched sprays in the leaf axils, and berry-like fruits of varying size, which are edible in some species. *Cyphomandra betacea* is grown for its fruit.

CULTIVATION

The tamarillo is best suited to subtropical or frost-free, warm-temperate climates. Train against a wire fence or stake to protect from wind, as it is inclined to be top-heavy. It is a shallow-rooted plant that prefers moist but not wet soil. Prune lightly after fruiting and pinch out growing tips at 3 ft (1 m) high to encourage branching. Propagate from cuttings, and plan to replace it after 5 years or so because it is short lived.

Cyphomandra betacea (above)

TAMARILLO, TREE TOMATO

This large shrub from South America grows to about 10 ft (3 m) tall with a tree-like form and a wide crown. It bears large green leaves and small sprays of pinkish flowers in the branch forks over much of the year. A succession of egg-shaped fruits follow, which are about 2–3 in (5–8 cm) long with shiny dark red skin (yellow-orange in some varieties). Tamarillos can be used for jam or the pulp can be eaten as a dessert. ZONES 9–11.

CYRILLA
AMERICAN LEATHERWOOD, SWAMP CYRILLA

This genus consists of only one species of small tree or often only a shrub that includes both deciduous and evergreen races. This fact is partly explained by its very wide climatic range, from Virginia in eastern USA south through Florida and the West Indies, and into South America as far as Brazil. The plants usually grown in gardens are the northern, deciduous forms. They are tall shrubs with spatula-shaped leaves, producing many long, tapering racemes of tiny, white, fragrant flowers from just below the new leaves.

CULTIVATION
In the wild, cyrilla forms dense thickets along the margins of swamps, while in gardens it is an undemanding shrub worth growing for the elegance of its flowers. It does best in a sunny but sheltered spot in fertile, humus-rich, moist but well-drained soil. Propagation is normally from seed.

Cyrilla racemiflora (above)

This shrub often only grows to about 5 ft (1.5 m) high, but under good conditions can reach 20 ft (6 m) or more with a central woody stem and open branching habit, the lateral branches wiry and tending to curve upward. The rather sparse leaves are glossy green and turn dull red one by one before falling in late autumn. The white flower spikes start opening in early summer and may continue almost to autumn. The flowers are followed by tiny, dry fruit. ZONES 6–11.

CYTISUS
BROOM

Cytisus × praecox
WARMINSTER BROOM, MOONLIGHT BROOM

This hybrid between the tall *Cytisus multiflorus* and the lower-growing *C. purgans* includes several popular cultivars, all making free-flowering shrubs of 3–4 ft (1–1.2 m), with massed, slender branchlets arising from ground level and spreading gracefully. The original hybrid has cream and yellow flowers, with a heavy fragrance, borne in mid- to late spring. More recent cultivars include **'Allgold'**, with cascading sprays of soft, golden yellow blossom, and **'Goldspear'**, a lower and broader shrub with deeper gold flowers. ZONES 5–9.

Cytisus × praecox 'Allgold'
(below)

The brooms are a diverse group of usually yellow-flowered, leguminous shrubs and subshrubs from Europe and the Mediterranean region which include a number of genera—the most important are *Cytisus* and *Genista*. *Cytisus* alone is a large and variable genus, in habit ranging from tall and erect to prostrate. Some of the 30 species have well-developed leaves, either simple and narrow or composed of 3 leaflets, while others are almost leafless with photosynthesis performed by the green, angled branchlets. All have pea-flowers in small, profuse clusters along new growth.

CULTIVATION
Generally easy garden subjects, they flower well under most conditions except deep shade, tolerating both dry and boggy soils, fertile or quite infertile. Some smaller species demand warm dry positions in a rock garden in pockets of well-drained soil. They are easily propagated from seed, cuttings or, in the case of some named cultivars, by grafting.

Cytisus scoparius
(bottom left)
COMMON BROOM, SCOTCH BROOM

Widely distributed in central and western Europe including the UK, this is one of the taller and most vigorous species of *Cytisus*, reaching 6–8 ft (1.8–2.4 m) in height and making a great show of golden yellow blossoms in late spring and early summer. The black seeds ripen in mid-summer, scattering their seed with a sharp, cracking sound in hot, dry weather. In cooler areas of some southern hemisphere countries it has become a troublesome weed. **'Pendulus'** is a rare cultivar with pendulous branches. ZONES 5–9.

Cytisus scoparius 'Pendulus'
(left)

D

DABOECIA
ST DABEOC'S HEATH, IRISH HEATH

Only 2 species make up this genus of small-leafed, evergreen shrubs native to areas of western Europe and the Azores Islands. Low and spreading, they are commonly grouped with the heaths and heathers *(Erica* and *Calluna)* as suitable for heather gardens, rock gardens and retaining walls. Conspicuous white to purple urn-shaped flowers, which contract to a small mouth, are borne on nodding stalks along bare stems that stand above the foliage. The petal tube falls after flowering, unlike that of many heaths and heathers.

CULTIVATION
Frost hardy to marginally frost hardy, they require permanently moist, acidic soil in a sunny position. Trim after flowering. Named varieties normally require propagation from cuttings, but they do produce fertile seed which may breed true to type.

Daboecia cantabrica
'Alba' *(left)*

Daboecia cantabrica *(left)*

Dispersed along the Atlantic coasts of France and Ireland, this species grows to 24 in (60 cm) high and has narrow, lance-shaped, dark green leaves with white hairs beneath. The rose-purple flowers, borne throughout summer and autumn, are about ½ in (12 mm) long. **'Alba'** has pointed dark green leaves and white flowers; **'Atropurpurea'** has deep rosy purple flowers; **'Bicolor'** has white, purple and some striped flowers; **'Creeping White'** has white flowers and a low creeping habit. **ZONES 7–9.**

DACRYCARPUS

This genus of conifers, once included in *Podocarpus* and related to *Dacrydium,* is a mixture of both and shows their affinity. It consists of about 9 species from moist areas of Malaysia, the Philippines, New Caledonia, Fiji and New Zealand. Many are large forest trees which have at times been important timber trees. Most species are frost tender.

CULTIVATION
Although rarely available, species could make attractive trees for damp to wet sites in frost-free environments. Propagate from seed or from cuttings.

Dacrycarpus dacrydioides *(above)*
syn. *Podocarpus dacrydioides*
KAHIKATEA, NEW ZEALAND WHITE PINE

In the wild, this New Zealand native reaches 150 ft (45 m) with a trunk diameter of up to 5 ft (1.5 m), but in cultivation it is likely to be smaller. Its habit is upright and conical and its foliage is fine and cypress-like with an overall bronze color when mature. The gray bark scales off in flakes. Old specimens may have a buttressed trunk.
ZONES 8–10.

DACRYDIUM

Of the original 15 species of *Dacrydium*, some are now reclassified as *Lagarostrobos* or *Halocarpus*. All come from the South Pacific but a few range as far as mainland Southeast Asia. These beautiful conifers all have graceful branchlets clothed in overlapping fine needle leaves. The small pollen cones are borne on male trees, and female trees produce solitary, large seeds each surrounded by fleshy scales.

CULTIVATION

Dacrydium species do not adapt well to cultivation; they require moderately cool climates without severe frosts or high summer temperatures, and adequate rainfall and humidity. Even then, growth is rather slow. Propagate from seed or cuttings.

Dacrydium
cupressinum *(left)*
RIMU, NEW ZEALAND RED PINE

In the wild, the rimu is one of New Zealand's tallest natives, but in cultivation it rarely reaches 30 ft (9 m). In winter it turns a deep reddish brown. Adult trees have shorter, fleshier needles and are more closely branched than juvenile ones. Female trees bear small bluish seeds, each sunk in a bright red fleshy cup. ZONES 8–9.

DAIS

This small genus consists of 2 species of evergreen or semi-deciduous trees and shrubs from southern and eastern Africa and Madagascar. One species is grown in warm climates for its showy pompon-shaped clusters of flowers. The branches have thin, very tough bark and the leaves are simple and oval. The silky-haired, tubular flowers have 5 spreading lobes and are borne in dense heads.

CULTIVATION

Frost tender, they need full sun, moderate shelter, light, fertile, free-draining soil and adequate summer water. Propagate from seed in spring or cuttings in summer.

Dais cotinifolia *(above)*
POMPON BUSH, POMPON TREE

Native to Africa, this bushy, rounded shrub or small tree grows to about 12 ft (3.5 m). It has reddish bark and oval, blue-green leaves up to 3 in (7 cm) in length. In late spring it bears fragrant flower clusters of tubular pink blooms. It is evergreen in warm areas and deciduous in cool climates. ZONES 9–11.

DANÄE

This genus consists of only one species of evergreen clump-forming perennial from western Asia. It is grown for its elegant arching stems and its attractive foliage and fruit.

CULTIVATION

Frost hardy, it grows in a humus-rich, moist but well-drained soil in sun or shade. Old or damaged stems can be cut back to ground level if necessary in spring. Propagate from seed or by division.

Danäe racemosa *(above)*

ALEXANDRIAN LAUREL

This native of Turkey and Iran makes an elegant evergreen plant to 3 ft (1 m) high and across. Its tiny greenish white flowers are produced in summer and followed by red berries that can persist well into winter. Whole branches can be cut and last well in a vase. **ZONES 7–10.**

DAPHNE

DAPHNE

Daphne bholua
(below)

This species from the eastern Himalayas can be evergreen or deciduous depending on the form selected. It usually grows into an upright shrub up to 12 ft (3.5 m) tall and 5 ft (1.5 m) wide. It has clusters of highly scented soft pink flowers in late winter. Selected forms include 'Gurkha', which is deciduous, and 'Jacqueline Postill', which is evergreen. ZONES 6–9.

Indigenous to Europe, North Africa and temperate Asia, this genus includes 50 or so deciduous and evergreen shrubs. They have simple, leathery leaves and small, highly fragrant flowers clustered at the shoot tips or leaf axils. Although the flower parts are not differentiated into true petals and sepals, for the sake of simplicity here they are called 'petals', of which there are always 4, characteristically pointed, recurving and rather fleshy. In the wild many daphnes occur on mountains in stony ground, often on limestone.

D

CULTIVATION

They prefer cool, well-aerated, gritty, humus-rich soil; intolerant of root disturbance, they are best planted out while small. The taller species are better adapted to sheltered woodlands, the smaller ones to rock gardens. Propagate from cuttings or layers. Fresh seed usually germinates readily but many species fail to fruit.

Daphne bholua
'Ghurka' *(above right)*

Daphne bholua
'Jacqueline Postill'
(right)

D

Daphne × *burkwoodii* 'Somerset' *(above)*

Daphne × *burkwoodii* *(above left)*

This popular hybrid *(Daphne cneorum* ×
D. caucasica) was raised early in the twentieth
century by the Burkwood brothers, well-known
English nurserymen. It is a low, rounded semi-
evergreen shrub up to 3 ft (1 m) tall. Its pale pink
flowers, darker in bud, appear in mid- to late
spring, sometimes through summer. The most
easily grown deciduous daphne, it flowers best in
full sun. **'Somerset'** is slightly more vigorous and
has deep pink flowers with pale pink lobes.
ZONES 5–9.

Daphne cneorum *(above)*
GARLAND FLOWER, ROSE DAPHNE

This low-growing, to 16 in (40 cm), evergreen
shrub from southern Europe has a loose, semi-
prostrate habit, with trailing main shoots and
dense lateral branches. It has small dark green
leaves and bears fragrant rose pink flowers in
mid-spring. It is a sun-loving plant but requires
moist, well-drained soil. ZONES 4–9.

Daphne mezereum *(left & above)*
MEZEREON, FEBRUARY DAPHNE

This slow-growing, short-lived, deciduous shrub
grows to 5 ft (1.5 m) tall, and has long narrow
leaves and purplish pink to purplish red, fragrant
flowers clustering along bare twigs in early spring.
Below the leaves, poisonous red fruit ripen in late
summer. It needs moisture and shelter. ZONES 5–9.

Daphne odora *(right)*

WINTER DAPHNE

A Chinese evergreen shrub long
cultivated in Japan, *Daphne odora* is
too frost tender for many cooler
regions of the northern hemisphere, but it thrives in temperate
southern regions. It is a spreading,
twiggy shrub to 4 ft (1.2 m), with
dark green leaves. From late autumn to mid-spring its rose purple
buds open to almost pure white,
waxy flowers. **'Alba'** is wholly
white; **'Aureo-marginata'** has yellow-edged leaves and flowers
marked with reddish purple.
ZONES 8–10.

D

Daphne pontica *(right)*

This evergreen shrub to 5 ft (1.5 m) comes from
southeastern Europe, Turkey and the Caucasus. It
is similar to *Daphne laureola* in many respects,
preferring semi-shade and having greenish night-
scented flowers in spring. Its berries are dark burgundy at first, turning black. ZONES 5–9.

Daphne retusa
(right)

This species may be a
form of *Daphne
tangutica*; authorities
vary in their opinions.
It makes a compact
shrub to 30 in (75 cm)
high with fragrant pale
pink flowers in spring
and glossy rich green
foliage. ZONES 6–9.

DAVIDIA
DOVE TREE, HANDKERCHIEF TREE

Native to western China, this genus contains just one species, though some varieties occur. In China, it can reach over 60 ft (18 m), with a rounded crown, and in full flower it is one of the most striking of all deciduous trees outside the tropics. 'Like huge butterflies hovering' is how plant explorer E. H. Wilson described the long-stalked flowerheads, each nestled between 2 large, drooping white or cream bracts. The surface of the large, soft, toothed leaves is deeply creased by veins.

CULTIVATION
The tree is frost hardy, but the bracts need protecting from wind. It needs rich, porous soil and full sun or part-shade. Propagate from the whole fruit, which may take up to 3 years to germinate. Cold treatment assists germination.

Davidia involucrata *(above)*

This conical tree has broad leaves up to 6 in (15 cm) long, and small, deep set, brownish red flowers surrounded by 2 white bracts of unequal lengths. The greenish brown, pendent, ridged fruit are up to 2 in (5 cm) across. The more common cultivated form is **Davidia involucrata var. vilmoriniana,** which has paler and less downy leaf undersides. ZONES 7–9.

DELONIX

Ten species make up this genus of tropical deciduous, semi-evergreen or evergreen trees from Africa, Madagascar, Arabia and India. The 5-petalled flowers appear in terminal racemes, and the elegant leaves are bipinnate and fern-like. The fruits, typical of the legume group, are large, flattened, woody, bean-like pods. Frost tender, they do well as shade trees in warmer areas.

CULTIVATION
Plant in full sun in fertile, moist but well-drained soil and provide shelter from strong winds. Prune only when young to establish a single trunk. The vigorous roots can damage paths and foundations. Seedlings vary considerably in flower shape, color and size, and may take 10 or more years to flower. Propagate from seed or cuttings.

Delonix regia *(above & right)*

POINCIANA, ROYAL POINCIANA, FLAMBOYANT TREE, FLEUR-DE-PARADIS, FLAME OF THE FOREST

This native of Madagascar grows only about 40 ft (12 m) tall, but its canopy may be wider than its height. The long, feathery leaves have lighter green undersides. Clusters of brilliant red or orange flowers, with one white petal marked with yellow and red, appear in late spring, followed by dark brown pods up to 12 in (30 cm) long. ZONES 11–12.

DENDROMECON
TREE POPPY, BUSH POPPY

Native to southwestern USA and Mexico, this is a genus of two
species of evergreen shrubs in the poppy family. They are much-
branched, woody plants with simple, leathery leaves. The profuse
golden flowers, borne singly and 4-petalled, are very like Californian poppies *(Eschscholtzia)* but larger.

CULTIVATION
A frost-tender plant, the tree poppy requires a sunny, well-
drained site and hot dry summers. In cool climates, grow in
a cool greenhouse using a good potting mix. Ensure it receives
direct sunlight and good air circulation. Propagate from seed or
cuttings.

Dendromecon rigida *(above)*

This lovely evergreen shrub can grow to 10 ft
(3 m) or more tall. It has leathery gray-green
leaves to 4 in (10 cm) long and masses of golden
yellow poppy-like flowers throughout the warmer
months. These are about 3 in (8 cm) across and
are lightly fragrant. **Dendromecon rigida subsp.**
harfordii (syn. *D. harfordii*) can grow to a small
tree, with a rounded crown to 20 ft (6 m) high.
ZONES 8–10.

DESFONTAINEA

This genus consists of one species, an evergreen shrub from the Andes of western South America, long cultivated for its interesting foliage and showy flowers. It is a stiff-branched shrub, branching basally, with the leaves arranged in opposite pairs. The flowers, borne singly in the upper leaf axils, are roughly trumpet-shaped, with a gradually broadening tube and cupped, overlapping petals; they point downward and are presumably adapted to pollination by hummingbirds.

CULTIVATION

Moderately frost hardy, it requires mild, rainy conditions for best results. Plant in moist, peaty, acidic soil and in shade in drier regions. Propagate from cuttings in summer.

Desfontainea spinosa (above)

This dense, bushy shrub usually grows up to 5 ft (1.5 m) tall, but sometimes reaches twice this height and spreads widely. The shiny dark leaves resemble those of English holly *(Ilex aquifolium)*. The flowers vary from pale yellowish orange to bright orange-scarlet with pale tips and appear from mid-summer to late autumn. ZONES 8–9.

DEUTZIA

These summer-flowering, deciduous shrubs from East Asia and the Himalayas are closely related to *Philadelphus* but they bear their smaller, white or pink flowers in more crowded sprays, with 5, rather than 4, pointed petals. Like *Philadelphus*, the plants have long, straight, cane-like stems. The leaves occur in opposite pairs and are mostly finely toothed. There are many frost-hardy species and fine hybrids available, especially those bred by the Lémoine nursery at Nancy, France, from 1890 to 1940.

CULTIVATION

Deutzias prefer a sheltered position, moist fertile soil and some sun during the day. Avoid pruning the previous year's short lateral shoots; thin out canes and shorten some of the thickest old stems after flowering. Propagate from seed or cuttings in late spring.

Deutzia × elegantissima
(above)
ELEGANT DEUTZIA

Including some of the finest and largest-flowered pinks among its clones, this hybrid of *Deutzia purpurascens* and *D. sieboldiana* reaches 4–6 ft (1.2–1.8 m) with purplish red twigs and flower stalks. The Lémoine nursery released the 2 original cultivars: **'Elegantissima'**, near-white inside and rose pink outside; and **'Fasciculata'**, with a slightly deeper rose flush. The Irish hybrid **'Rosealind'** has deeper flesh pink flowers. ZONES 5–9.

Deutzia crenata
var. *nakaiana*
'Nikko' *(below left)*
syn. *Deutzia gracilis*
'Nikko'

One of the smallest deutzias, it makes a low spreading mound often rooting as it spreads. It is a good rock garden plant or ground cover in a shrub border, growing to about 24 in (60 cm) tall and as much as 4 ft (1.2 m) wide. The starry white flowers are produced in summer in spikes and the pale green foliage often turns burgundy before shedding. ZONES 5–9.

Deutzia purpurascens *(left)*

A graceful species from Yunnan discovered by the famous missionary-botanist Abbé Delavay, this slender arching shrub to 5 ft (1.5 m) tall has flowers that are white inside and purple on the outside. This species has been used extensively in hybridization. ZONES 5–9.

Deutzia × rosea
(right)

One of the earliest Lémoine crosses between *Deutzia gracilis* and *D. purpurascens*, it reaches a height and spread of 30 in (75 cm) and has the low, spreading habit of the former species with the pink coloration of the latter. The original clone has flowers of the palest pink, in shorter, broader sprays than in *D. gracilis*. **'Carminea'** has larger panicles of pink flowers with a stronger carmine pink on the back. ZONES 5–9.

Deutzia × rosea
'Carminea' *(above)*

Deutzia scabra *(center right)*

This, the longest established and most robust, cold-hardy species in Western gardens, has thick canes to about 10 ft (3 m), and long, dull green, rough-textured leaves. Large panicles of white, bell-shaped flowers terminate upper branches from mid-spring to early summer. **'Flore Pleno'** has double flowers, striped dull pink on the outside; **'Candidissima'** is a pure white double; **'Pride of Rochester'**, another double, has larger flowers faintly tinted mauve outside. ZONES 5–10.

Deutzia scabra 'Pride of Rochester' *(right)*

DIOSPYROS
PERSIMMON, EBONY

This genus consists of several hundred species of mostly ever-green trees from the tropics and subtropics, as well as several deciduous species in temperate Asia and America. *Diospyros ebenum* from Sri Lanka provides the now rare timber ebony. Some species bear edible fruit, notably the black sapote *(D. digyna)* and the Japanese and American persimmons. All have strong branches, smooth-edged leaves, and flowers with rolled-back petals and a leaf-like calyx that enlarges as the pulpy fruit develops; the fruits of most species are edible. For good crops, grow plants of both sexes.

CULTIVATION
Fully frost hardy to frost tender, these trees prefer well-drained, moist soil, with ample water in the growing season and, being brittle, need shelter from strong wind. Propagate from seed.

Diospyros kaki *(below left)*
CHINESE PERSIMMON, KAKI

This native of China that has been cultivated in Japan for centuries, is a deciduous tree, which grows to about 20 ft (6 m) tall with spreading branches. Its dark green, oval leaves turn yellow to deep orange in autumn. It has small cream flow-ers, which are followed by orange or yellow fruit about 3 in (8 cm) across. The fruit have delicious sweet flesh when ripe. There are many cultivars. **ZONES 8–10.**

Diospyros virginiana *(left)*
AMERICAN PERSIMMON, POSSUM WOOD

This spreading tree can reach over 100 ft (30 m) in its native eastern USA, in alluvial river valley forests, but in cultivation it usually reaches 20–30 ft (6–9 m). It has cream flowers and sweet edible fruit, 1½ in (35 mm) across, ripening to orange or purple-red. The timber (white ebony) is valued for its durability. **ZONES 5–9.**

DIPELTA

Only 4 species from China make up this genus of deciduous
shrubs, and only one is well established in Western gardens—but
even that is uncommon. They are related to and resemble
Weigela and *Kolkwitzia*, with richly marked, bell-shaped flowers
in large clusters. The fruits are partly concealed by two rounded
bracts enlarging at their base after the flowers are shed.

D

CULTIVATION
They are frost hardy, and prefer a sunny position with moist, fertile, well-drained soil and shelter from strong winds. Propagate
from seed or cuttings.

Dipelta floribunda
(left)

From the lower moun-
tains of China, this
shrub grows to about
10 ft (3 m), with woody
stems and pale peeling
bark. It bears broad,
soft leaves and large,
drooping clusters of
pale pink, fragrant
flowers, 1½ in (35 mm)
long; these are deeper
pink on the outside of
the tube and have
orange-yellow mark-
ings in the throat.
ZONES 6–9.

D

DISANTHUS

Just a single species of deciduous, ornamental shrub belongs to this Japanese genus in the witch-hazel family. Its leaves are almost circular with pronounced bluish undersides; the flowers, appearing in autumn as the leaves color, are small, with straplike purplish red petals, borne in pairs along the old wood. Even in summer the strongly veined leaves are bronze tinted but by early autumn they turn a deep metallic bronze purple and finally fade to red or orange before falling.

CULTIVATION
Although fairly frost hardy, *Disanthus* requires sheltered conditions and deep, moist, friable soil. The seeds, produced in small capsules, can be used for propagation, but cuttings or ground layering are more effective.

Disanthus cercidifolius (left)

This slow-growing, spreading shrub eventually reaches 10 ft (3 m) or more. It has stiff, wiry branches, usually with a number of stems diverging from the base. The flowers, ½ in (12 mm) across, are slightly fragrant. ZONES 8–10.

DODONAEA
HOPBUSH

This is an almost entirely Australian genus of about 60 species of evergreen trees and woody shrubs. Its common name refers to the abundant, winged, capsular, hop-like fruits once used for brewing beer by early European settlers. In many species, male and female flowers appear on separate plants. The flowers are small and insignificant, but the fruits are large on some species.

CULTIVATION
Hopbushes grow in full sun or part-shade and prefer moderately fertile, light, free-draining soil. They are frost tender, but some will withstand drought and coastal salty winds. Lightly prune in early spring. Propagate from seed in spring or cuttings in summer.

Dodonaea boroniifolia *(right)*
FERN-LEAF HOPBUSH, HAIRY HOPBUSH

A bushy shrub to 5 ft (1.5 m), this species has dark green, fern-like leaves with sticky leaflets. The insignificant flowers are followed in summer by attractive 4-winged red fruit capsules. This species will tolerate extended dry periods. ZONES 9–11.

Dodonaea viscosa

This variable species grows throughout Australia and New Zealand, as well as in the tropical regions of America, Africa and Asia. It has elliptic to linear, slightly sticky, light green leaves with wavy margins. The showy yellowish 3-winged capsules, produced in terminal clusters, turn brown, pink or purple at maturity. Dense and fast growing, prune to an upright shrub, 10 ft (3 m) or more tall; it is useful for screening and hedging. 'Purpurea', a popular bronze-leafed cultivar from New Zealand, has purplish red fruit capsules. ZONES 9–12.

Dodonaea viscosa 'Purpurea' *(right)*

DOMBEYA
WEDDING FLOWER

This genus of about 200 species of evergreen, deciduous or semi-deciduous shrubs and small trees is from Africa and Madagascar; only a few species from the eastern summer-rainfall regions of southern Africa are widely cultivated. The leaves are mostly circular, heart-shaped or maple-like in outline, and have a scurf of downy hairs at least on the underside. The flowers are pretty, cup-shaped with overlapping white, pink or red petals, in small to large clusters all over the crown; these petals persist while the small capsular fruits ripen and turn brown.

CULTIVATION
Dombeyas thrive in most warm-temperate and subtropical climates with good summer moisture; some species are moderately frost hardy. Grow in moist but well-drained, fertile soil in sun or part-shade. Propagate from seed in spring or cuttings in summer.

Dombeya ×
cayeuxii (left)

Of uncertain origin, this shrub or small tree possibly has *Dombeya burgessiae* as one parent; it is of similar growth habit but the leaf lobes have longer points. Profuse, pale pink flowers are borne on large, hemispherical heads at all branch tips from summer to autumn. ZONES 10–12.

Dombeya tiliacea (left)
syn. *Dombeya natalensis*
NATAL WEDDING FLOWER

This evergreen with slim, blackish, multiple trunks comes from Natal in eastern South Africa. It is a bushy-crowned tree of 20–25 ft (6–8 m). From autumn to early spring it bears small pendulous clusters of pure white flowers. Some leaves may turn red in autumn. ZONES 9–11.

DOVYALIS

This genus of about 22 species of trees and shrubs is largely restricted to Africa, with a few species in Madagascar and Sri
Lanka. Most are spiny, particularly on coppice shoots and young
growth. The leaves are simple and alternately arranged. The
small flowers are greenish or yellowish in clusters along the
branches. Male and female trees are separate. The globular fruits
are edible, mostly pale yellow when ripe. *Dovyalis* species are occasionally grown for their fruits, used in pickles and preserves.
Heavily pruned, they make a formidable spiny hedge.

CULTIVATION
Frost tender, the plants are suitable for subtropical climates.
Plant in fertile, humus-rich, well-drained soil in full sun. If they
are grown for fruit it is usual to bud females onto seedling
stocks, with one or two male trees nearby to pollinate. Propagate
from seed or by layering.

Dovyalis caffra
(right)
KEI APPLE

From southern Africa,
this evergreen shrub or
small tree grows to
about 20 ft (6 m) in
height and width. Of
upright habit, it has
thorny stems and
small, shiny, oval
leaves, usually at the
base of the spines. The
tiny, yellowish flowers
are followed by
rounded yellow fruit
that are edible but
acidic. ZONES 9–11.

Dovyalis hebecarpa *(right)*
CEYLON GOOSEBERRY

This bushy, small tree grows vigorously, reaching about 20 ft (6 m) in
height. The velvety leaves have an undulating surface, and red stalks and
veins. The green flowers appear in summer and autumn in leaf axils followed
by velvety fruit about 1 in (25 mm) in
diameter, which ripen from yellowish
green to dull purple. The fruit are not
highly palatable, but this species has
been crossed with *Dovyalis abyssinica* to
give a better-tasting hybrid. ZONES 10–12.

D

DRACAENA
syn. *Pleomele*

This genus of some 40 species of evergreen trees and shrubs, many originating from equatorial Africa and Asia, is grown for foliage, often as greenhouse or indoor plants. Those grown indoors are sometimes confused with species of *Cordyline* and are often termed 'false palms' because of their cane-like stems and crowns of sword-like leaves.

CULTIVATION

Outdoors, dracaenas need warm-temperate to subtropical conditions, full sun or part-shade and well-drained soil. Cut back to almost soil level in spring. Propagate from seed or by air-layering in spring or from stem cuttings in summer. Watch out for mealybugs.

Dracaena draco
(left)

DRAGON'S-BLOOD TREE, DRAGON TREE

This slow-growing tree from the Canary Islands is long lived. It may reach 30 ft (9 m) high with a trunk to 3 ft (1 m) in diameter and a crown of rosettes of stiff, lance-shaped, blue-green leaves to 24 in (60 cm) long and nearly 2 in (5 cm) wide. It bears insignificant flowers followed by orange berries in summer. **ZONES 10–11.**

Dracaena fragrans

CORN PLANT

A many-branched tree-like dracaena to 50 ft (16 m) tall, this African species (found from Sierra Leone to Malawi) is grown for its lush heads of highly scented yellow flowers. The leaves are very narrow, 3 ft (1 m) long and usually hang loosely. The flowers are carried on large, erect or overarching inflorescences. There are several variegated cultivars, of which **'Massangeana'** (leaves yellow and cream in the center) is the most popular. The ***Dracaena deremensis* cultivars,** such as **'Lemon and Lime'** and **'Yellow Stripe'** are similar but the leaves are usually not as long. **ZONES 11–12.**

D

Dracaena marginata
'Tricolor' *(below)*

Dracaena marginata *(above)*

A slow-growing tree or shrub from Madagascar, this species reaches 15–20 ft (4.5–6 m) in warm climates. Its narrow, sword-like leaves have red margins. The cultivar '**Tricolor**' with a cream stripe and red edge is commonly grown as a house plant. This species tolerates some shade and quite low winter temperatures but not frost. ZONES 10–12.

Dracaena reflexa 'Song of India' *(right)*

Dracaena reflexa

SONG OF INDIA

A shrub or small tree up to 15 ft (4.5 m) tall, this native of Madagascar and Mauritius has relatively short, 8 in (20 cm) leaves that are densely packed on the stems. The foliage is so evenly colored as to look artificial, which often prompts touching to see it the tree is plastic or real. The flowers are green outside with white interiors. While also used as a common name for the species, '**Song of India**' is now a recognized name for a particularly graceful white-variegated foliage cultivar. ZONES 11–12.

Dracaena fragrans
cultivar *(opposite page left)*

DRACOPHYLLUM
GRASS TREE, NEI NEI

A widely variable genus of some 50 or so species and shrubs and small trees, most of which are native to the subalpine and alpine areas of New Zealand. The remainder occur in nearby Pacific areas, including Australia, New Caledonia and Lord Howe Island. The species range from prostrate mat-forming shrubs to trees reminiscent of *Dracaena* and *Cordyline*. The species tend to be variable and frequently naturally hybridize, making identification difficult. Allied to *Epacris* most bear sprays of small heath-like and fine, narrow foliage, though some have long strappy leaves.

CULTIVATION
Because of their fine, heath-like roots, most species resent drying out. However, they don't like being waterlogged either and must have good drainage. A gritty soil with added compost or leaf mold for humus and moisture retention is ideal. Propagation is usually by seed as cutting can take a considerable time to strike roots.

Dracophyllum traversii *(left)*
MOUNTAIN NEI NEI, PINEAPPLE TREE

A prominent feature in the wetter high altitude bush areas of New Zealand's South Island, this is the largest and most spectacular species in the genus. It looks very like a large *Dracaena* with gray-green to bronze foliage, a tropical appearance quite out of character with its alpine environment. It grows to as much as 30 ft (9 m) tall with narrow leaves to 2 ft (60 cm) long. In summer, large panicles of cream flowers develop among the foliage clusters. Mountain nei nei is difficult to cultivate, demanding constant soil moisture, a damp atmosphere and steady cool temperatures.
ZONES 7–9.

DURIO

There are 20 or more species in this genus of tall evergreen trees, native to tropical Southeast Asia. They have elliptical, dull green, scaly leaves and produce their usually creamy white, heavily scented flowers on the old wood and often bloom twice a year. Some flowers develop into large, prickly fruits that fall and split open when ripe to reveal a strong-smelling, edible pulp.

D

CULTIVATION
As tropical plants, they are not happy in areas where the temperature falls much below 65°F (18°C). They prefer moist, humus-rich soil with full sun or dappled shade. Plants may be propagated from seed but the best fruiting cultivars are grafted or budded.

Durio zibethinus *(above)*
DURIAN

The durian, notorious for its putrid smell, is widely cultivated as a fruit tree in Asia. The tree grows to 120 ft (36 m) in the wild. The leaves are 8 in (20 cm) long, dark green above and paler on the undersides. The greenish white or pink flowers, in clusters of 3 to 30, grow directly on the trunk and branches. The large, spiny, green to yellow fruits are up to 15 in (38 cm) long.
ZONE 12.

E

ECHIUM

Indigenous to the Mediterranean, Canary Islands and Madeira in western Europe, the 40 or so species of annuals, perennials and shrubs in this genus are grown for their spectacular bright blue, purple or"eènk flowers that appear in late spring and summer. The hairy leaves form rosettes at the bases of the flowering stems. They look best in mixed borders. Ingestion of the plants can cause stomach upsets.

CULTIVATION

Very frost hardy to frost tender, *Echium* species require a dry cli-mate, full sun and a light to medium, well-drained soil. They be-come unwieldy in soil that is too rich or damp. Prune gently after flowering to keep them compact. Coastal planting is ideal. Propa-gate from seed or cuttings in spring or summer. In mild climates they self-seed readily.

Echium candicans
(left)
syn. *Echium fastuosum*

PRIDE OF MADEIRA, TOWER OF JEWELS

This soft-wooded shrub from Madeira has fuzzy gray-green leaves, broadly sword-shaped and clustered in large rosettes at the branch ends. In spring and summer, 24 in (60 cm) spires of sapphire-blue to violet-blue flowers with reddish pink stamens are produced, each only about ½ in (12 mm) wide but borne in hundreds together. Sprawling in habit, it grows to about 6 ft (1.8 m) tall but spreads wider. ***Echium thyrsiflorum*** is quite similar to *E. candicans* but has taller, straighter spikes of pale lavender flowers; it is a less showy species and the spikes look untidy as they mature. **ZONES 9–10.**

EDGEWORTHIA
PAPER BUSH

This genus comprises 3 deciduous shrub species related to *Daphne* and native to China and the Himalayas. Only the Chinese species is widely cultivated, famous for its traditional use in Japan as a source of high-quality paper; it is also an ornamental shrub of some distinction. Tight heads of small tubular flowers cluster on the ends of the bare branches in spring; the outside of each flower is concealed by a layer of silky white hairs, the yellow, orange or red color only appearing on the inner faces at the tip.

CULTIVATION
They are moderately hardy but easily damaged by late frosts. They prefer a sheltered, sunny spot in well-drained soil. Pruning is not normally necessary. Propagation is usually from cuttings.

Edgeworthia chrysantha (above)
syn. *Edgeworthia papyrifera*

From central China, this low-branching, single-stemmed shrub may grow to about 6 ft (1.8 m) high and wide, but is usually seen at 3–5 ft (1–1.5 m). The red-brown twigs are extraordinarily tough and flexible and the soft, pale green leaves are inclined to wilt and shed in hot weather. The tips of the flowers, borne in mid-spring, are normally golden yellow, contrasting prettily with the pure white silky tubes. Red-flowered forms are also grown, including '**Red Robin**' and '**Red Dragon**'. ZONES 7–9.

E

ELAEAGNUS

This genus of about 45 species of deciduous and evergreen shrubs, small trees and scrambling climbers comes from Europe, Asia and North America, with one species extending to Australia. All have alternate, entire leaves which, together with the young stems, flower buds and fruits, glisten with tiny silvery or rusty brown scales. Small flowers, clustered in leaf axils, are tubular at the base with 4 spreading petals. The fruits, pale fleshy drupes, are edible in some species.

CULTIVATION

Frost hardy and generally vigorous and trouble free, they thrive in most soils and positions. The evergreen species will tolerate shade. Most species can be cut back heavily if a bushy shape is desired. Propagate from seed for deciduous species and from cuttings for the evergreens.

Elaeagnus pungens *(above)*
SILVERBERRY, THORNY ELAEAGNUS

The most common species of the genus, this frost-hardy, evergreen bush or scrambling climber has long, prickly, horizontal branches and glossy, oval leaves which are dark green above and silvery beneath. It is excellent for hedges, growing to a height and width of 10–15 ft (3–4.5 m). In autumn it bears fragrant, tiny, bell-shaped, cream flowers. **'Variegata'** has narrow, irregular, cream-margined leaves; and **'Maculata'** has leaves with a central splash of gold. ZONES 7–10.

Elaeagnus
angustifolia
(below left)
OLEASTER, RUSSIAN OLIVE

This deciduous species extends from southern Europe to China. A large shrub or small tree, it grows to 30 ft (9 m) high, the new branches and the undersides of the narrow leaves coated in silvery scales. In late spring and early summer clusters of small, perfumed, pale yellow flowers appear, followed in late summer by edible yellowish fruit, also coated in silvery scales. It makes a striking ornamental but needs warm, dry summers to bring out its silvery foliage. ZONES 7–9.

Elaeagnus pungens
'Variegata' *(left)*

ENKIANTHUS

Enkianthus campanulatus
(below right)

REDVEIN ENKIANTHUS

From Japan and southern China, this is the most popular species, reaching 8–12 ft (2.4–3.5 m) high, of narrow, open habit and rather slow growing. Abundant flowers, cream but heavily striped and tipped dull crimson, appear in spring. In autumn the leaves turn to shades of gold, scarlet and dull purple. *Enkianthus campanulatus* var. *palibinii* has more reddish flowers.
ZONES 6–9.

About 10 species of deciduous shrubs from East Asia make up this genus, valued for their small, bell-shaped flowers, densely clustered and prettily marked in most species, and fine autumn foliage colors. Growth is rather open and the smallish leaves are clustered at the end of each season's growth, producing a layered effect. The stalked, pendulous flowers are produced in numerous short sprays.

CULTIVATION

Very frost hardy, they like similar conditions to many rhododendrons and azaleas: moist woodland with humus-rich but not too fertile, acid soil. They will not thrive in heavy shade. Avoid pruning to a rounded shape as the flowers will not be so well displayed. Propagate from seed or cuttings in summer.

Enkianthus perulatus
(below right)

WHITE ENKIANTHUS

From Japan, this is rather distinctive among *Enkianthus* species in its lower, bushier habit and more sparsely scattered urn-shaped flowers that are pure white or greenish white, without markings and contracted at the mouth. They are borne on nodding stalks in early spring. This species likes a very cool, sheltered position and has brilliant red autumn foliage color.
ZONES 6–9.

EPHEDRA
JOINT-FIR, MORMON-TEA

Ephedra is a genus of around 40 species of gymnosperms from southern Europe, North Africa, temperate Asia and the Americas. They show no close relationship with other major plant groups and are presumed to be an evolutionary dead end. These near-leafless shrubs form a mass of slim, dull green, jointed stems—such as those of *Ephedra californica*—and are tolerant of dry conditions. Tiny scale-like leaves are present for a brief period after rain. They do not produce true flowers but have separate male and female, yellow, flower-like cones (strobili) that are usually followed by berry-like fruits. This genus is best known for its association with ephedrine, used as an allergy and asthma treatment, a stimulant and a metabolic accelerator. Some herbal extracts of ephedrine are known as Ma Huang or Mormon tea.

CULTIVATION
Very frost hardy to marginally frost hardy, they demand a light, stony or sandy soil with good drainage and full sun. No pests or diseases are known. Propagate from seed.

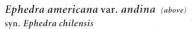

Ephedra americana var. *andina* *(above)*
syn. *Ephedra chilensis*

This variety is native to the Andes mountain range, from Ecuador to Patagonia, and is usually a sprawling shrub to 8 ft (2.4 m), although it is sometimes a small tree to 12 ft (3.5 m) high. The young shoots are green and finely ridged. The leaves when present are small, no more than ¼ in (6 mm). Its berries are vivid red to orange and up to ½ in (12 mm) long. **ZONES 6–9.**

Ephedra gerardiana *(above)*

This species, native to China and the Himalayas, can be a tiny creeping shrub as low as 2 in (5 cm) in height, although it can be found up to 24 in (60 cm) high with a spread of up to 10 ft (3 m). The fruit are red and to ¼ in (6 mm) long. **ZONES 7–10.**

ERICA
HEATH

This large genus is made up of more than 800 species of small-leafed, free-flowering, evergreen shrubs. The vast majority are native to South Africa, but a relatively small number of species occur in Europe and elsewhere in Africa. In Europe, several *Erica* species plus the closely related *Calluna* (heather) dominate moorland vegetation. The Cape heaths from South Africa, often with long, tubular flowers, are fine garden plants in mild-winter climates where summer humidity is low. The European species bear smaller, bell-shaped flowers in a more limited white to deep pink color range but are frost hardy and are very popular garden plants.

E

CULTIVATION
Most heaths like full sun, well-drained, neutral to acid soil and dislike lime and animal manure. Prune after flowering to keep plants bushy and compact. Propagate from seed or from cuttings in late summer.

Erica arborea
TREE HEATH, BRUYÈRE

The largest of the heaths, this frost-hardy species also has the widest distribution, from the Canary Islands and Portugal right across to Iran and south through the high mountains of Arabia, Ethiopia and equatorial Africa, where it forms mist-shrouded forests of trees 20 ft (6 m) high with stout trunks. It has contorted woody stems, finely fibrous bark and dark green needle-like leaves. It bears masses of small white flowers in spring. 'Alpina' is less than 6 ft (1.8 m) high, has bright green foliage and white flowers in dense cylindrical racemes. ZONES 8–10.

Erica species *(right)*

Erica arborea 'Alpina' *(below)*

Erica australis *(left)*

SPANISH HEATH, SOUTHERN
HEATH

This marginally frost-
hardy, erect shrub to
6 ft (1.8 m) tall and
about 3 ft (1 m) wide is
native to the western
Iberian Peninsula and
Morocco. It produces
tiny tubular to bell-
shaped flowers of a
bright magenta-pink in
spring and summer. A
number of selections
have been named, in
colors from white to
deep pink. The foliage
is very fine and dark
green. **ZONES 9–10.**

Erica bauera 'Alba'
(left)

Erica bauera

BRIDAL HEATH

More cold hardy than some other South African
species, the bridal heath also has the most beautiful flowers of all. The waxy tubes are china white
to soft rose pink, 1½ in (35 mm) long and nar-
rowed toward the mouth, opening progressively
along the erect branches from spring to autumn.
It makes a small, slender shrub only about 3 ft
(1 m) high and appreciates a sheltered position.
'Alba' has pure white flowers.
ZONES 9–10.

Erica carnea
syn. *Erica herbacea*
WINTER HEATH, SNOW HEATH

From the mountains of central and southern
Europe, this frost-hardy species and its numerous
cultivars are among the few heaths that will thrive
in chalk soils. It forms a low, spreading subshrub
usually less than 12 in (30 cm) high with densely
crowded branches. Through most of winter and
into early spring it produces a fine display of
small, urn-shaped, purple-pink flowers with protruding darker stamens. This is an ideal ground
cover between taller shrubs or beneath deciduous
trees, or in rock gardens. Well-known cultivars
include **'December Red'** with purplish pink
flowers and **'March Seedling'**, which flowers until
late spring. Others are **'Myretoun Ruby'**, with
very dark green leaves against bright rose pink
flowers; **'Ruby Glow'** with deep rose red flowers;
'Springwood Pink' with a vigorous trailing habit
and rose pink flowers; and **'Springwood White'**
with a spreading habit, vigorous growth and
white flowers. ZONES 5–9.

Erica carnea 'March Seedling' *(above)*
Erica carnea 'Myretoun Ruby' in snow *(top)*
Erica carnea 'Springwood White' *(above right)*

Erica cerinthoides *(right)*
SCARLET HEATH, FIRE HEATH

This South African species is one of the showiest
of all ericas, with bright orange-scarlet flowers
about $1\frac{1}{2}$ in (35 mm) long, clustered at the ends
of long, straight or slightly arching branches
through winter and spring. There are also forms
with white, pink and crimson flowers. It is no
more than 3 ft (1 m) high and wide. ZONES 9–10.

Erica cinerea
BELL HEATHER, TWISTED HEATH

Native throughout western Europe including the
British Isles, this heather is one of the prettiest of
the frost-hardy heaths. Its small, crowded, rose
pink bells are produced over a long season from
early summer to early autumn. Low and spreading, the stiff ends of the twisted branches ascend
to 12–18 in (30–45 cm). Bell heather dislikes hot
summer weather, which scorches its foliage and
may kill the plant. The many named cultivars vary
chiefly in flower color from white to rich rose
purple; some also have golden or coppery foliage.
'**Kerry Cherry**' has deep pink flowers, '**Crimson
King**' is crimson; '**Golden Drop**' has summer foliage gold with coppery tints, turning red in winter. ZONES 5–9.

Erica × darleyensis 'Darley
Dale' *(above)*

Erica × darleyensis
'Silberschmelze' *(center right)*

Erica × darleyensis *(above left)*
DARLEY DALE HEATH

Erica × darleyensis is a hybrid of the two frost-hardy species *Erica
erigena* and *E. carnea* and has proved to be a valuable garden plant.
It forms a dense, bushy shrub to 24 in (60 cm) high with dark green
foliage, and from late autumn through spring is covered in
crowded, short spikes of cylindrical, pale rose flowers with protruding, darker stamens. It tolerates chalk soils. The original clone is
now known as '**Darley Dale**' but others, with flowers ranging from
white to deep pink, are listed: '**Dunwood Splendour**' spreads widely
and produces a spectacular display of mauve-pink flowers; '**Epe**' is
relatively low growing with white flowers tinged pink; '**George
Rendall**' is a compact grower with purplish pink flowers throughout winter; '**Jack H. Brummage**' has golden to red-tinted winter
foliage and purplish pink flowers; and '**White Perfection**' has bright
green foliage and pure white flowers. '**Silberschmelze**' has silver-
white flowers and dark green leaves, tinged red in summer.
ZONES 6–9.

Erica cinerea 'Crimson
King' *(opposite page left)*

Erica erigena
syns *Erica hibernica,*
E. mediterranea

IRISH HEATH, MEDITERRANEAN
HEATH

This western European
species has deep green
foliage and massed,
urn-shaped, bright
pink flowers in winter
and spring. It grows to
6 ft (1.8 m) high and
3 ft (1 m) wide.
Cultivars include '**Alba
Compacta**', a compact,
white-flowered form;
'**Ewan Jones**', a vigorous grower with
mauve-pink flowers set
against dark green
leaves; '**Hibernica**'
with shell-pink flowers;
'**Hibernica Alba**', a
spectacular white-
flowered form growing
about 3 ft (1 m) tall.
'**Irish Dusk**' with rose-
pink flowers and gray-
green leaves; '**Mrs
Parris Lavender**' an
upright form to 18 in
(45 cm) tall with
mauve flowers; '**Mrs
Parris White**', an
albino form of the
previous cultivar;
'**Silver Bells**' with
white, scented flowers;
'**Superba**' with pale
pink, perfumed
flowers; and '**W. T.
Rackliff**', a compact
grower with white
flowers. ZONES 7–9.

Erica erigena 'Alba
Compacta' *(right)*

Erica erigena
'Hibernica' *(below)*

Erica erigena 'W. T.
Rackliff' *(bottom)*

E

Erica linnaeoides (right)

This South African species grows to no more than 3 ft (1 m) tall and is noteworthy for its delicate color. Like all its tribe, it flowers in early spring and makes a fine pot plant. Give it a light trim when the flowers are finished to keep it compact. ZONES 9–10.

Erica lusitanica (left)

PORTUGUESE HEATH, SPANISH HEATH

From Portugal, Spain and France, this erect shrub, seldom more than 6 ft (1.8 m) high, has extremely fine, delicate, mid-green foliage. Through winter it bears densely massed, small, tubular flowers, white flushed pale pink, the pink soon disappearing. This species is lime tolerant but not very frost hardy. It has become naturalized in the USA, Australia and New Zealand. ZONES 8–10.

Erica mackaiana

syns Erica crawfordii, E. mackaii, E. mackayana

MACKAY'S HEATH

This neat little shrub from Spain and Ireland grows to about 18 in (45 cm) tall and 30 in (75 cm) wide. Its branches are hairy while young and its dark green leaves are arranged in whorls of four. The flowers are usually pink and produced in terminal clusters from summer to early autumn, although many different colors have been selected and named. 'Galicia' grows less than 8 in (20 cm) tall and has mauve-pink flowers that open from orange buds; 'Maura' is a small form to 6 in (15 cm) tall with gray-green foliage and semi-double purple flowers; 'Shining Light' grows to 10 in (25 cm) tall by 24 in (60 cm) wide and has pure white flowers. ZONES 6–9.

Erica mackaiana
'Galicia' (above)

Erica melanthera (right)

This species from South Africa has small, bell-shaped flowers reminiscent of the European ericas. It is a bushy shrub 3 ft (1 m) high and wide, with bright green foliage that from late autumn disappears beneath the pinkish purple flowers. This species is widely grown as a cut flower. **ZONES 9–10.**

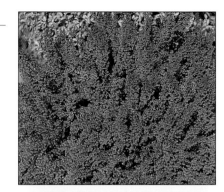

Erica regia (right)

ELIM HEATH

This shrub from southern parts of South Africa's Cape Province is widely cultivated. It grows to about 6 ft (1.8 m) high and 3 ft (1 m) wide, is wind resistant and tolerates some frost. The flowers, which appear mainly in spring, are shiny and white with red or red and purple tips; about 1 in (25 mm) long, they hang down in whorls from the stem tips. **ZONES 9–10.**

Erica sessiliflora (right)

GREEN-FLOWERED HEATH

Among the hardier of the South African ericas, the green-flowered heath reaches around 4 ft (1.2m) tall, sometimes more, and has rather stiff branches. Like most ericas, it has narrow needle-like leaves, though they are slightly broader than most. What really sets this species apart is its flowers, which are a soft pale green, tubular, up to 1¹/₄ in (30 mm) long and borne in spikes near the stem tips. It flowers from autumn to spring and has occasional blooms throughout the year. **ZONES 9–11.**

E

Erica × stuartii 'Irish Lemon' (left)

Erica × stuartii is a cross between Erica mackaiana and E. tetralix. This small, upright shrub to 18 in (45 cm) tall with gray-green foliage bears pink flowers through summer and autumn. 'Irish Lemon' produces brilliant yellow spring growth which greens later. The urn-shaped flowers are mauve and are borne from late spring well into summer. ZONES 6–9.

Erica vagans (above)
CORNISH HEATH

This vigorous, spreading, European species, 30 in (75 cm) high and wide, has deep green foliage and rounded, bell-shaped, pink, mauve or white flowers in clusters in summer and autumn. 'St Keverne' has clear pink flowers in profusion. ZONES 5–9.

Erica vagans
'St Keverne' (above)

Erica × veitchii
'Exeter' (left)

Erica × veitchii
VEITCH'S HEATH

This hybrid between Erica arborea and E. lusitanica is a marginally frost-hardy shrub to 6 ft (1.8 m) tall. It has small white, lightly scented, cylindrical flowers from late winter into spring. 'Exeter' bears profuse, fragrant flowers in spring; 'Pink Joy' is soft pink. ZONES 8–9.

ERIOBOTRYA

This genus, which belongs to the rose family, includes 30 species
of evergreen shrubs and trees. Only the loquat, *Eriobotrya
japonica*, is commonly grown. Widely distributed through eastern Asia, from the eastern Himalayas to Japan, they include trees
growing to 30 ft (9 m). All types bear leathery, deeply veined
leaves with silvery or felty undersides. The creamy white, scented
flowers are held in loose sprays at the tips of the branches during
autumn, and are followed by edible, decorative fruits.

E

CULTIVATION
Easily grown, they are marginally frost hardy and will tolerate
dry as well as coastal conditions. Grow in a fertile, well-drained
soil in a sunny position. Propagate from seed or cuttings in
early summer.

Eriobotrya japonica *(above)*
LOQUAT

Native to China and Japan, the loquat can grow
to 20–30 ft (6–9 m) tall. It forms a shapely conical
tree, but in gardens it can be kept considerably
more compact if pruned after the golden yellow
fruit have been harvested. The large, deep green
leaves are pale and felty underneath. *Eriobotrya
japonica* blooms in late autumn and the fruit,
which set in winter, ripen in spring. It is very susceptible to fruit fly, and birds can also damage the
crop. This is a plant for temperate areas where
ample moisture is available as the fruit mature.
ZONES 8–10.

ERIOGONUM
WILD BUCKWHEAT, UMBRELLA PLANT

This is a large genus of the polygonum family, of some 150 species native to North America, mainly the western side. They may be annuals, perennials or small shrubs often with silvery or white leaves. The long-lasting flowers are small but are produced in clusters surrounded by attractive toothed or lobed bracts. Most come from mountain habitats or alkaline desert areas.

E

CULTIVATION
Due to the wide distribution of the genus their frost tolerance varies, but all like a sunny, well-drained site. If kept dry in winter they will stand more cold than if damp. Cut back immediately after flowering unless seed is required. Propagate from seed in spring or autumn or by careful division in spring or early summer.

Eriogonum arborescens (left)
SANTA CRUZ ISLAND BUCK-WHEAT

This loosely branched, shrubby species from coastal California grows to about 5 ft (1.5 m). The leaves are usually crowded to the tips of the stems and are white downy beneath. Its flowers are produced from early summer to autumn; they are usually pink to rose in terminal clusters to 6 in (15 cm) across. This species makes a good cut flower. ZONES 9–10.

Eriogonum umbellatum (left)
SULFUR BUCKWHEAT

This woody-based subshrub from the Rocky Mountains in British Columbia is grown for its attractive heads of tiny, bright yellow flowers borne in summer and turning copper with age. It is a useful rock garden plant, growing to a height of 12 in (30 cm) and a spread of 24 in (60 cm). It has a prostrate to upright form and the dense green leaves have white, downy undersides. In cooler, wetter areas some shelter is required. *Erigonum umbellatum* var. *subalpinum* has creamy yellow flowers that turn dull mauve with age. ZONES 6–9.

ERYSIMUM
syn. *Cheiranthus*

WALLFLOWER

These 80 species of annuals and perennials range in the wild
from Europe to central Asia, with a smaller number in North
America. Some form woody bases and become leggy after a few
years, at which time they are best replaced with younger specimens. A number are fine winter- to spring-flowering plants,
while some flower all winter or all year in very mild regions. The
older types are sweetly scented, while the newer cultivars have no
fragrance but bloom well over a long season. Botanists have now
placed all species of *Cheiranthus* into this genus.

CULTIVATION
Mostly frost hardy, they do best in well-drained, fertile soil in an
open, sunny position. Cut back perennials after flowering so only
a few leaves remain on each stem. Propagate from seed in spring
or cuttings in summer.

Erysimum bicolor
(left)

This is an evergreen
shrubby species to 3 ft
(1 m) tall from Ma-
deira and the Canary
Islands. The flower
spikes are produced at
the tips of the stems
and consist of beauti-
fully fragrant white to
pale yellow flowers that
turn pale lilac as they
age. ZONES 9–10.

E

Erysimum 'Bowles' Mauve' *(left)*
syn. Erysimum 'E. A. Bowles'

This shrubby evergreen flowers almost continuously in mild climates. The deep rosy purple flowers on elongating stems are nicely set off against the glaucous foliage. Plants develop into mounds 3 ft (1 m) tall and 4 ft (1.2 m) wide. Prune back lightly when flowering slows to encourage another flush of blooms. Flowering ceases in very hot weather, but will continue through winter in spite of occasional light frosts. ZONES 6–11.

Erysimum 'Harpur Crewe' *(left)*
syn. *Erysimum × kewensis* 'Harpur Crewe'

This lovely hybrid between *Erysimum cheiri* and *E. bicolor* has sweetly scented, double yellow flowers. It grows to 12 in (30 cm) high. It has been known since the seventeenth century. ZONES 8–10.

ERYTHRINA
CORAL TREE

The 108 species of deciduous and semi-evergreen trees and shrubs in this genus occur wild in tropical and subtropical regions around the world, though with most species in the Americas and Africa. Belonging to the bean tribe of the legumes, they are grown as ornamentals for their vividly hued flowers. Their trunks and branches are protected by short, sharp prickles; many species have weak branches that tend to fall in storms. The leaves are compound with 3 broad, often diamond-shaped leaflets. Bean-like flowers in scarlet, crimson or orange are borne in racemes towards the ends of the branches at varying times of the year (some species in mid-winter), followed by narrow seed pods that dry and brown as they ripen.

CULTIVATION
Most species are not frost hardy, but some are happy enough in exposed coastal locations. They all enjoy full sun and well-drained soil. Spider mites may be a problem. Propagation is from seed in spring or cuttings in summer.

Erythrina caffra *(left)*
syns *Erythrina constantiana,*
E. insignis
SOUTH AFRICAN CORAL TREE, KAFFIRBOOM

This semi-evergreen tree with a broad, open crown quickly reaches about 30–60 ft (9–18 m) and is often grown as a shade tree in its native South Africa. The compound leaves, 6 in (15 cm) wide, have 3 broad leaflets. From late spring to early summer clusters of pale orange to orange-red flowers are borne on almost bare branches (sometimes quite thorny). The cultivar 'Flavescens' has pale cream flowers and is equally attractive. ZONES 9–11.

E

Erythrina crista-galli *(right)*
COMMON CORAL TREE, COCK'S COMB

This species from South America is the best known coral tree in temperate climates, where it is treated almost as an herbaceous plant, being cut back almost to the ground in autumn after flowering, transferred to a large pot and over-wintered under glass. It is also grown permanently in the greenhouse and again pruned severely in late autumn. It grows about 6 ft (1.8 m) tall under these conditions. In subtropical climates it grows into a gnarled, wide-crowned tree 15–30 ft (4.5–9 m) tall and bears its scarlet or coral-red flowers in spring and summer. ZONES 8–11.

Erythrina fusca *(right)*

Found in many tropical areas, this deciduous tree grows to 80 ft (24 m) tall with a crooked trunk. Its pinnate leaves are 8 in (20 cm) long. The flowers are rich scarlet with creamy green wings and keel. They are followed by slim pods which are up to 12 in (30 cm) long. ZONES 10–12.

Erythrina × sykesii *(below)*
syn. **Erythrina indica** of Australian gardens

This large deciduous tree can reach 50 ft (15 m) tall and almost as wide, with a short main trunk and ascending branches, often prickly. Although with maturity it can form a very large crown, the canopy is not overly dense. In late winter and early spring it is covered with clusters of rich red flowers. The handsome, heart-shaped leaves follow. ZONES 9–11.

Erythrina humeana *(above)*
DWARF ERYTHRINA, NATAL CORAL TREE

This deciduous species from South Africa is a sturdy, erect shrub reaching 12 ft (3.5 m). In summer to early autumn it bears long, upright sprays of nodding tubular flowers of rich scarlet splashed with yellow and green. This species will tolerate light frosts and prefers reasonably fertile soil. ZONES 9–11.

ESCALLONIA

There are about 60 species of these mostly evergreen shrubs and occasionally small trees (for example, *Escallonia myrtilloides*) from temperate South America, mainly from Chile where they may grow in hillside scrubs or on exposed coasts. The smallish, toothed leaves are usually shiny and slightly succulent. The flowers, crowded into dense panicles, have separate white or pink petals that in many species are pressed together to form a tube but with the tips recurving. The fruits are small globular capsules shedding fine seed. A number of attractive cultivars were raised by the Slieve Donard nursery in Ireland, including 'Donard Beauty', an evergreen shrub to 5 ft (1.5 m) high with an arching habit, small oval, glossy leaves and deep pink flowers from early to mid-summer; 'Donard Star' has a neat compact habit to 6 ft (2 m) and large, deep rose flowers; and 'Pride of Donard' to 5 ft (1.5 m) tall with small, oval, glossy leaves and profuse rose-red flowers in summer. Other popular named hybrids include 'Lou Allen' and 'Newport Dwarf'.

CULTIVATION
Most of the species and cultivars are frost hardy or moderately frost hardy and many are capable of sprouting profusely from the base after being cut back by frost. Grow in full sun in well-drained soil. Valuable as seaside hedging plants, they suffer salt damage only in the most exposed positions. Propagate from cuttings.

Escallonia 'Donard Star' *(left)*

Escallonia × exoniensis *(right)*

This hybrid between the two Chilean species *Escallonia rosea* and *E. rubra* originated last century in England. A vigorous shrub, it grows to 15 ft (4.5 m) in suitable climatic conditions. It has a rather open, branching habit, becoming very woody at the base, and bears loose sprays of very pale pink flowers at the branch ends from late spring through to autumn. Lopping back the branches will produce denser growth if desired. **'Frades'** produces carmine blooms in 3 in (8 cm) panicles. ZONES 8–10.

Escallonia rubra *(above)*

This Chilean species has flowers of a deeper color and firmer texture than any other species, and is the dominant parent of most hybrid escallonias. Always shrubby and multi-stemmed, it varies greatly in the wild in stature as well as in leaves and flowers. Several forms have been introduced to gardens. Some shrubs are delicate and small, with small leaves and arching sprays of flowers with narrow red tubes and pale pink, recurved tips. *Escallonia rubra* **var**. *macrantha* is a vigorous, large shrub up to 10 ft (3 m) tall with succulent, glossy leaves and tight clusters of white to pink and sometimes crimson flowers; **'Crimson Spire'** is an erect variety ideal for hedges. ZONES 8–10.

EUCALYPTUS
EUCALYPT, GUM TREE

Australia is the original home of all but a few of over 700 species that
make up this genus of evergreen trees of the myrtle family. Beyond
Australia, a handful of species are native to southern New Guinea and
southeastern Indonesia, and one *(Eucalyptus deglupta)* is known only
from northern New Guinea and the southern Philippines. But eucalypts
are possibly the world's most widely planted trees, especially in drier
subtropical and tropical regions, for example in Africa, the Middle
East, India and South America. They are renowned for their fast
height growth and ability to thrive on poor or degraded land, providing shelter, timber and fuel—even stands of 5-year-old saplings yield
dead leaves, bark and twigs for fuel in places where other fuels are
scarce. Against these benefits are set the increasing complaints, notably in India, that widespread plantings of eucalypts create environments hostile to other plants and animals of importance in traditional
rural culture.

Eucalypts are unusual trees, with leaves that tend to hang vertically
so foliage provides only partial shade; the leaves contain aromatic oil
in small translucent cavities, eucalyptus oil being an important prod-
uct of certain species. The nectar-rich flowers are abundant, mostly
white, but yellow, pink or red in a minority of species, with the
massed stamens the most conspicuous part. Petals and sepals are
fused into a cap-like structure (operculum) that is shed as the
stamens unfold; fruits are woody capsules, mostly quite small. The
bark of many eucalypts is smooth and shed annually, and the new and
old bark can make a colorful contrast while this is happening. Other
groups of eucalypts have persistent bark of varying texture, examples
being the stringybark and ironbark groups.

A recent development in the botanical study of eucalypts is the
splitting off of 113 species, mainly 'bloodwoods', into the new genus
Corymbia. Only a few cultivated species are affected.

CULTIVATION
There are species to suit most climates except those where winter temperatures fall below about 10°F (−12°C), but the great majority of
species will tolerate only the lightest frosts. Drought hardiness also
varies greatly, some species requiring fairly moist conditions. With
rare exceptions eucalypts are grown from seed, which germinates freely.
They should be planted out into the ground when no more than 18 in
(45 cm) high, ensuring that roots have not coiled in the container at
any stage. They seldom survive transplanting, and are not long-lived
as container plants. They prefer full sun at all stages of growth.

E

Eucalyptus camaldulensis
(below & right)

RIVER RED GUM

The river red gum can grow up to 150 ft (45 m) tall with a generous spread and trunk to 12 ft (3.5 m) in diameter. It is valued for its impressive appearance. Occurring along watercourses over much of inland Australia, it is an invaluable shade and shelter tree able to cope with extended dry periods or waterlogging. It is widely cultivated in warm-climate areas of Africa and Asia. **ZONES 9–12.**

Eucalyptus dalrympleana
(right)

MOUNTAIN GUM

This species comes from the mountains of southeastern Australia. It can grow 70 ft (21 m) or more tall and has creamy white bark blotched with yellow, pink and olive green (even red in cold climates). Its white flowers are produced in summer and it has narrow, gray-green adult foliage and broader blue-green juvenile leaves. **ZONES 8–9.**

E

Eucalyptus erythrocorys
(right)

ILLYARRIE, RED-CAP GUM

This Western Australian spreading shrub or small tree has thin stems rising from a swollen woody base below ground level. The red flower cap provides an interesting contrast to the yellow flowers, which appear in early summer. Growing usually to about 25 ft (8 m), it is suited to warm climates without summer humidity, requiring good drainage. Prune to prevent top-heaviness. **ZONES 9–11.**

Eucalyptus globulus *(below right)*

TASMANIAN BLUE GUM

The first eucalypt to be introduced to Europe and North America, this large tree can grow to over 200 ft (60 m), with a trunk to 6 ft (1.8 m) in diameter. The bluish bark is shed in long strips. Juvenile leaves are silvery blue and rectangular, while the adult form is deep green and sickle shaped, to 18 in (45 cm) long. Occurring naturally in coastal areas of Tasmania and far southern Victoria, it prefers moist conditions. **'Compacta'** reaches only 30 ft (9 m) and retains its silvery blue juvenile foliage for some years. **ZONES 8–10.**

Eucalyptus leucoxylon *(right)*

YELLOW GUM, SOUTH AUSTRALIAN BLUE GUM, WHITE IRONBARK

A tree from high rainfall regions of South Australia, this shapely eucalypt grows to 100 ft (30 m) with an open canopy. Its distinctive bark is fissured at the base but smooth and dappled with yellowish white and blue-gray spots above. The leaves are grayish or bluish green and taper to a point. The large, 1½ in (35 mm) wide flowers, which may be cream or dark pink, are borne in small clusters. Crimson-flowering plants may be sold as *Eucalyptus leucoxylon* 'Rosea'.
ZONES 9–11.

Eucalyptus nicholii *(below)*

NARROW-LEAFED BLACK PEPPERMINT, WILLOW LEAF PEPPERMINT

This fibrous-barked species from the highlands of northeastern New South Wales makes an excellent shade or street tree. Its white flowers can only be appreciated when the tree is small. The fine, sickle-shaped, blue-green leaves are held aloft on a high crown. Withstanding mild frosts and strong winds, it grows to 40–50 ft (12–15 m).
ZONES 8–11.

E

Eucalyptus pauciflora (right)
syn. *Eucalyptus coriacea*

SNOW GUM

This 30–60 ft (9–18 m) tree is found in southeastern Australia, commonly growing in frost-prone
highland valleys. It tends to have a rather twisted
trunk, with reddish brown or gray bark peeling in
irregular strips to reveal white and beige underbark. Small cream flowers are borne in spring and
summer. Alpine snow gum, **Eucalyptus
pauciflora** subsp. **niphophila** (syn. *E. niphophila*),
occurs at altitudes over 5,000 ft (1,500 m) where
snow lies through most of winter; it is smaller and
lower branching. **ZONES 7–9.**

Eucalyptus pauciflora
subsp. *niphophila*
(right)

Eucalyptus regnans
(below right)

MOUNTAIN ASH

This magnificent spe-
cies which reigns over
the mountain forests of
far southeastern Aus-
tralia and Tasmania is
the tallest hardwood tree
in the world, specimens
of over 320 ft (96 m)
tall being known. It has
a long, straight trunk
and relatively small,
open crown, the bark
being almost white and
shed annually in long
ribbons. The white
flowers are small and
rarely noticed. Despite
the great beauty of
mountain ash forests
and the value of its
timber, it is seldom
cultivated. **ZONES 9–11.**

E

Eucalyptus rubida *(left)*

CANDLEBARK

Found in cooler regions of southeastern Australia, this is an open-crowned tree that is usually 40–80 ft (12–24 m) tall. It has narrow leaves to 6 in (15 cm) long and grayish brown old bark which may turn deep pink or red in winter before revealing the cream new bark. Small cream flowers open from late summer. ZONES 8–9.

Eucalyptus salmonophloia *(left)*

SALMON GUM

From inland Western Australia, this handsome eucalypt is mostly 30–40 ft (9–12 m) tall with a long, sinuous, smooth trunk topped by a dense, umbrella-shaped crown. The new bark is an attractive salmon pink, turning gray as it ages before being shed. The mature leaves are shiny, green and tapering, and the small, white flowers appear in spring and summer. It can be grown in areas of very low rainfall and can withstand some frost. ZONES 9–11.

Eucalyptus sideroxylon *(left)*

RED IRONBARK, MUGGA, PINK IRONBARK

This species from temperate eastern Australia is allied to *Eucalyptus leucoxylon* but its bark is black, deeply furrowed and never shed. The bluish to dull green leaves are diamond-shaped to slightly sickle-shaped. The showy, pale pink to near-crimson flowers, about 1 in (25 mm) across, are followed by small, goblet-shaped seed capsules. Forms with deeper pink flowers are selected for cultivation. ZONES 9–11.

Eucalyptus torquata *(right)*
CORAL GUM

This small Western Australian tree grows to 20 ft (6 m) with a fairly narrow, upright habit. Its blue-green, sickle-shaped leaves are 4 in (10 cm) long, and the rough brown bark flakes rather than peels. Orange-red, lantern-shaped buds, 1 in (25 mm) long, open to a mass of creamy orange and yellow or pink and yellow stamens, followed by large seed capsules. It can withstand dry conditions but does better with regular moisture. **ZONES 9–11.**

Eucalyptus viminalis *(right)*
MANNA GUM, RIBBON GUM, WHITE GUM

This species has a wide distribution in the cooler hill country of southeastern Australia. It has smooth, whitish bark except for some roughish bark at the base of the trunk. The upper limbs shed bark in long ribbons, hence the common name ribbon gum. It is a favored food tree of the koala and can grow to 180 ft (55 m) tall. Small white flowers are produced in summer. It makes a fine shade tree but the fallen bark can be messy. **ZONES 9–10.**

E

EUCRYPHIA

This small genus of about 6 species is made up of evergreen or semi-deciduous trees from the southern hemisphere. All species have pure white flowers of singular beauty, rather like small single roses with 4 petals and a 'boss' of red-tipped stamens. There are 2 species indigenous to Chile and 4 indigenous to Australia. Eucryphias have been grown in the British Isles for more than a century, especially in mild, moist, Atlantic coastal districts where the climate suits them well. Several garden hybrids are more vigorous and floriferous than the species.

CULTIVATION
Frost hardy, they require a humid microclimate and constant soil moisture combined with good drainage. Good flowering demands that the tree crown be in the sun but the roots shaded. Propagate from seed or cuttings in summer.

Eucryphia cordifolia (left)
ULMO

Growing to a medium to large tree in the wettest coastal rainforests of southern Chile, this tree was called ulmo (meaning elm) by the Spanish settlers. The simple, oblong, wavy edged, shiny dark green leaves are gray beneath. White flowers 2 in (5 cm) across are borne singly in late summer. In cultivation this evergreen species has proved more tender than the others and, while its foliage is interesting with reddish new growths, it is not very free flowering. In very mild, wet climates it grows tall and slender, up to 20–25 ft (6–8 m) in under 10 years. ZONES 9–11.

Eucryphia × *intermedia*
'Rostrevor' *(above)*

Eucryphia lucida
'Leatherwood Cream'
(right)

Eucryphia × intermedia

This hybrid between the Chilean *Eucryphia glutinosa* and the Tasmanian *E. lucida* first appeared as a chance seedling at Rostrevor in Ireland; several clones are available but '**Rostrevor**' is the most widely planted. It makes an upright tree of slender habit, reaching 30 ft (9 m) in time, and under good conditions makes a profuse show of flowers in late summer. **ZONES 8–9.**

Eucryphia lucida
TASMANIAN LEATHERWOOD

From Tasmanian rainforests, this slender evergreen tree can reach 100 ft (30 m) in the wild and has been felled for its close-grained, pinkish timber, but it is best known for the aromatic honey that the introduced honeybee makes from its abundant, fragrant, early summer flowers. It has sticky buds and small, shiny simple leaves. In cultivation it is rather slow growing, seldom exceeding 20 ft (6 m). '**Pink Cloud**' is a pink-flowered cultivar recently introduced; '**Leatherwood Cream**' has leaves irregularly margined with cream. **ZONES 8–9.**

E

Eucryphia moorei
(left)

PINKWOOD

From the far southeast of mainland Australia, this species grows in sheltered gullies in the coastal ranges. It reaches 25 ft (8 m) in height and has pinnate leaves, each leaf consisting of about 5 to 7 neat, oblong leaflets with white undersides. The shoots and leaves are less sticky and shiny than on other eucryphias. The flowers are about 1½ in (35 mm) wide, borne among the ferny foliage from mid-summer to early autumn. Pinkwood is very ornamental and sometimes grows vigorously in cultivation. **ZONES 9–10.**

Eucryphia × nymansensis *(left)*

This name covers all hybrids between the 2 Chilean species *Eucryphia glutinosa* and *E. cordifolia* and arose first at Nymans, Sussex, in 1914. A small, compact tree of narrow habit, in time it may exceed 30 ft (9 m). The leaves vary in shape and size and can be simple or composed of 3 leaflets. It flowers in late summer, and in a sunny spot the tree may be covered in white blossoms. Several clones have been raised but the most popular in Britain is still one of the original seedling clones now known as **'Nymansay'** (from its initial tag 'Nymans A'). **ZONES 8–9.**

EUONYMUS
SPINDLE TREE

This genus of about 175 species consists of both deciduous and evergreen trees, shrubs and creepers from the northern hemisphere, centered mainly in East Asia including the Himalayas. All have simple leaves in opposite pairs, usually with toothed margins. Flowers are inconspicuous, greenish or yellowish, in small groups along the lower parts of the current year's growth. While deciduous plants, such as 'Red Chief', have rich autumn foliage, it is the capsular fruits that provide the main interest, splitting open in autumn to reveal bright yellow, red or orange seeds. Birds, attracted to the oily outer layer, distribute the seeds.

Euonymus alatus
(bottom)

WINGED SPINDLE, WINGED EUONYMUS

From Japan, China and Korea, this decorative, spreading, much-branched, deciduous shrub grows to about 6–8 ft (1.8–2.4 m) tall, the small branches distinctive for the broad 'wings' of corky tissue attached to either side of the green twig. In late spring it bears small, green flowers in inconspicuous sprays and by autumn the small, purplish, 4-lobed capsules split to reveal orange-red seeds. At the same time the leaves turn vivid deep red, sometimes showing paler scarlet tones before falling. *Euonymus alatus* var. *apterus* has equally good autumn color but has a more lax habit and rarely produces the corky wings of bark; **'Compactus'** grows to around 6 ft (1.8 m) tall. **ZONES 5–9.**

CULTIVATION
Mostly frost hardy, they grow best in a sheltered position with ample sun and fertile, well-drained soil. Propagate from seed or cuttings.

Euonymus alatus
'Compactus' *(above)*

Euonymus europaeus *(right)*
EUROPEAN SPINDLE TREE

This deciduous shrub or small tree is usually single stemmed at the base and occasionally reaches 20 ft (6 m). It is native to Europe, including the UK, and can be found growing in woodlands and often on limestone or chalk soils. The wood of this and the few other European species was once used to make spindles, used in spinning wool. It has inconspicuous flowers followed in autumn by pink or red fruit that split open to reveal the large orange seeds. At the same time the leaves turn to shades of yellow and scarlet. **'Aldenhamensis'** is a form selected for the larger size and brilliant pink coloring of its fruits; **'Red Cascade'** is often pendulous with the weight of its large red, orange-seeded berries. ZONES 6–9.

Euonymus fortunei
syn. *Euonymus radicans*

WINTERCREEPER EUONYMUS

This creeping shrub spreads or climbs by aerial roots like ivy and can climb a brick or stone wall as high as 20 ft (6 m). As a ground cover it has an indefinite spread, but it is mostly more compact forms that are grown in gardens. From early to mid-summer it bears greenish white flowers on the branching, non-clinging adult stems. **'Emerald Gaiety'** is a small, compact cultivar with dark green leaves margined with white and often pink tinged in winter; it grows to 3 ft (1 m) tall and 5 ft (1.5 m) wide. **'Emerald 'n' Gold'** is a very bushy, small form with broad gold edges to its rich green leaves often tinged pink in winter; it grows to about 12 in (30 cm) tall and 3 ft (1 m) wide. **'Silver Queen'** has broad white margins to its leaves which are pink tinged in winter; it is a bushy shrub up to 6 ft (1.8 m) tall and wider than its height. **'Variegatus'** (syn. 'Gracilis') is a climbing or trailing form with larger leaves with white margins, often pink tinted. ZONES 5–9.

Euonymous fortunei 'Emerald 'n' Gold' *(below)*

E

Euonymus fortunei   Euonymous fortunei
'Emerald Gaiety' *(above)*   'Silver Queen'
(above right)

Euonymus japonicus *(right)*

JAPANESE SPINDLE TREE

Generally known in gardens by its variegated
cultivars, this spreading, evergreen shrub from
Japan has shiny, dark green leaves in its typical
state, reaching 10–12 ft (3–3.5 m). Pale greenish
flowers appear in early summer, and the autumn
foliage may be enlivened by scattered pinkish capsules opening to reveal orange seeds. The variegated cultivars are all lower and denser:
'Albomarginatus' has white-margined leaves.
'Aureomarginatus' has oval, yellow-margined
leaves and small, star-shaped, green flowers in
summer; it makes a good hedge. '**Microphyllus
Variegatus**' is a small, dense shrub to 3 ft
(1 m) tall with small,
crowded leaves with
white margins. **'Ovatus
Aureus'** has broad,
irregular margins of
bright yellow. All forms
can withstand seashore
conditions. ZONES 8–10.

Euonymus japonicus
'Ovatus Aureus' *(right)*

EUPATORIUM

This genus contains about 40 species of perennials and subshrubs, mainly from the Americas but a few from Asia and Europe. Only a few are cultivated for their large terminal panicles of small flowerheads, which come in white or shades of purple, mauve or pink.

CULTIVATION

Mostly quite frost hardy, they need full sun or part-shade and moist but well-drained soil. The shrubs should be pruned lightly in spring or after flowering. Propagate from seed in spring, from cuttings in summer or by division in early spring or autumn.

Eupatorium megalophyllum *(below left)*
syn. *Bartlettina megalophylla*
MIST FLOWER

A native of Mexico, this species grows to a height of 5 ft (1.5 m) and spreads—branching at the ground—to 6 ft (1.8 m). In spring it bears dramatic, wide heads of lilac flowers. The very large leaves, up to 10 in (25 cm) long and 8 in (20 cm) wide, are dark green and velvety on the upper surface and paler on the underside. Immature stems are covered in fine purple hairs. This species will not survive even the mildest of frosts. **Eupatorium sordidum** is a similar species but with smaller leaves and flowerheads. ZONES 10–11.

Eupatorium purpureum *(left)*
JOE PYE WEED

This robust perennial grows to a height of 5–8 ft (1.5–2.4 m) with a spread of about 4 ft (1.2 m) or more. It provides a bold accent for the autumn garden, with 12 in (30 cm) long leaves and large heads of tiny, purplish flowers. Native to eastern and central North America, it is usually found where there is plenty of water as it needs lots of moisture for full growth. ZONES 4–9.

Euphorbia
mellifera *(below)*

HONEY SPURGE

This handsome ever-green shrub usually grows little more than 6 ft (1.8 m) tall and as wide in cultivation. It has soft green leaves up to 8 in (20 cm) long with a conspicuous, whitish midrib. The honey-scented spring flowers consist of rounded heads of bronze-green bracts surrounding the tiny green flowers. Although not very frost hardy, in favorable positions in a sunny, sheltered garden it will make an impressive feature plant. It is native to Madeira and is quite rare in the wild. ZONES 8–10.

EUPHORBIA

MILKWEED, SPURGE

The genus is very large, with close to 2000 species, among them numerous succulent species that at first sight look remarkably like cacti. There is a great variety of forms, which suggests that the genus should be divided, but the flowers of all species are almost identical. They are very much reduced, consisting of only a stigma and a stamen, always green, and usually carried in small clusters. Many species have showy bracts, these are the most widely cultivated; examples include *Euphorbia cognata* and *E.* 'Excalibur'. Mainly tropical and subtropical, the genus also includes many temperate species. All euphorbias have milky sap which is corrosive to sensitive areas of the skin; some can cause temporary blindness if sap contacts the eyes.

CULTIVATION
Plant species of *Euphorbia* in sun or part-shade in moist, well-drained soil. Cold tolerance varies greatly depending on the species; the more highly succulent species are generally frost tender. Propagate from cuttings in spring or summer, allowing succulent species to dry and callus before placing in barely damp sand, by division in early spring or autumn or from seed in autumn or spring.

E

E

Euphorbia milii *(left)*
syn. *Euphorbia splendens*
CROWN OF THORNS

This slow-growing, ferociously thorny, semi-succulent shrub with bright green leaves is native to
Madagascar. Deciduous in cooler areas, it tolerates dry conditions and grows to a height of about
3 ft (1 m). It is excellent in frost-free rock gardens
or sunny courtyards, and is often used as a low
hedge in coastal areas. Throughout the year,
especially during spring, it carries tiny yellowish
flowers among pink-red bracts, which are borne
in showy flat sprays. *Euphorbia milii* var.
splendens is a semi-prostrate variety with oblong
leaves. ZONES 10–12.

Euphorbia pulcherrima
(left)
POINSETTIA, MEXICAN FLAME TREE

Potted poinsettias are a familiar
Christmas decoration all over
the northern hemisphere, but
this native of Mexico is only a
garden plant in frost-free climates. It makes a rather open
shrub up to 12 ft (3.5 m) tall,
usually dropping its leaves as
flowering commences. The
broad bracts, which give each
flower cluster the appearance of
a single, huge flower, last many
weeks. There are many named
cultivars, which extend the color
range from the original blood
red to pink and cream. It thrives
best in subtropical regions and
likes fertile soil and sunshine.
The leaves are large but not
especially attractive. Cultivars of
the normal tall-growing poinsettia include **'Henrietta Ecke'** with
additional smaller red bracts.
Most cultivars now sold for indoor use are semi-dwarf:
'Annette Hegg' is red, while
'Rosea' (pink) and **'Lemon
Drop'** (pale yellow) are similar
except for color. ZONES 10–12.

EURYOPS

Part of the large daisy family, this genus consists of around 100 species of annuals, perennials and evergreen shrubs, most of which come from southern Africa. They are grown for their colorful yellow to orange flowerheads which are held above fern-like foliage.

CULTIVATION

Frost hardiness varies between species. Generally, a well-drained soil and a position in full sun are the main requirements of these attractive plants, otherwise the shrubs tend to grow leggy and the flowers are not as plentiful. They respond to light pruning after the flowers have faded but do not respond well to root distur-bance. Propagate from seed in spring or cuttings in summer.

E

Euryops pectinatus *(below right)*

GRAY-LEAFED EURYOPS

This widely cultivated, frost-tender shrub from the southwestern Cape region of South Africa, grows well in most temperate con-ditions. From winter to spring it bears bright yellow daisies up to 2 in (5 cm) across, for which the finely cut, gray-green leaves are an attractive foil. It is a single-stemmed, bushy shrub growing up to 4 ft (1.2 m), and can be lightly pruned to main-tain a rounded shape. It likes to be kept moist during dry weather. **ZONES 9–11.**

Euryops virgineus *(right)*

RIVER RESIN BUSH

A species easily distinguished by its small, bright green leaves and upright habit, this 4 ft (1.2 m) high shrub has stiff branches densely clothed in fine foliage. Flowering throughout the year, it blooms most heavily in late winter and spring, when it produces masses of small daisies at the branch tips. It is very much at home in seaside gardens. **ZONES 9–10.**

EUSCAPHIS

This genus contains just a single species. It is a small, deciduous tree with short, weak branches and attractive foliage, flowers and fruit. While none of these features is outstanding on its own, they combine to make an appealing, undemanding tree.

CULTIVATION

Any well-drained soil in sun or dappled shade will do. Propagation is from seed, which may require two periods of stratification, or from cuttings taken in early summer.

E

Euscaphis japonica *(above)*

Endemic to China and Japan, this species grows to 30 ft (9 m) high. It has 10 in (25 cm) long pinnate leaves made up of 7 to 11 leaflets, each 2–4 in (5–10 cm) long. In spring it produces small yellow flowers in long panicles that develop into attractive hollow red fruit. When the leaves fall, the white-striped, purple bark is an interesting and unusual feature. **ZONES 6–10.**

EXOCHORDA
PEARL BUSH

**Exochorda ×
macrantha**
(below right)

This hybrid was raised
in France around 1900
by crossing *Exochorda
racemosa* with the cen-
tral Asian *E. korolkowii.*
Sometimes reaching
10 ft (3 m) tall, in mid-
to late spring it pro-
duces elongated clus-
ters of pure white
flowers, each about
1½ in (35 mm) across,
from every branch tip.
'The Bride' is one of
the loveliest varieties of
pearl bush. It makes a
weeping shrub up to
6 ft (1.8 m) or so tall
and about as much in
width. 'The Bride' pro-
duces masses of large
white flowers on arch-
ing stems in spring.
ZONES 6–9.

There are 4 species of deciduous shrubs in this genus from central Asia and northern China. They have weak, pithy branches
and thin-textured, paddle-shaped leaves. In spring the branch
ends are clustered with 5-petalled, white flowers of delicate, informal beauty. The fruits are capsules with wing-like segments,
splitting apart when ripe to release flattened seeds.

CULTIVATION
Species of *Exochorda* are quite frost hardy but they prefer climates with sharply defined seasons and dry summers for the best
display of flowers. A sheltered position in full sun and well-
drained soil are desirable. Prune older stems back to their bases
after flowering for vigorous new growth and abundant flowers.
Propagate from seed in autumn or from cuttings.

*Exochorda ×
macrantha* 'The Bride'
(above right)

Exochorda racemosa *(right)*

From northern China this species, long established in western gardens, makes a lovely display
when well grown. It grows to about 10 ft (3 m)
high with arching branches and has narrow, pale
green leaves to 3 in (8 cm) long. The flowers are
borne in late spring, with loose, slender sprays
appearing from the branch tips, each flower being
1½ in (35 mm) wide with narrow petals.
ZONES 6–9.

FG

FAGUS
BEECH

Although these long-lived, deciduous trees, to 130 ft (40 m), are scattered across Europe, the UK, Asia and North America, most of the 10 species are confined to China and Japan. They are absent from far northern forests as well as lowland Mediterranean-type forests. Most species have a rounded crown of delicate foliage that turns golden brown in autumn and smooth, gray bark. They bear brown-scaled, pointed winter buds and prominently veined, ovate to elliptic leaves. In spring new leaves are briefly accompanied by small, individual clusters of male and female flowers. In early autumn, small shaggy fruit capsules split open to release angular, oil-rich seeds (beech nuts) that are a major food source for wildlife. Their valuable timber is close-grained and readily worked; it is used for flooring, furniture and making kitchen utensils.

CULTIVATION
Frost hardy, beeches require well-drained, reasonably fertile soil and some shelter from strong wind; they do best in areas with long, warm summers. Purple-leafed forms prefer full sun and yellow-leafed forms a little shade. Propagate from fresh seed; cultivars must be grafted. They are prone to attack by aphids and powdery mildew.

Fagus orientalis *(left)*
ORIENTAL BEECH

This species once formed extensive forests in Greece, Turkey, northern Iran and the Caucasus, replacing *Fagus sylvatica* at low altitudes. It resembles that species except that it has noticeably longer leaves that turn brownish yellow in autumn and larger nuts. In a suitably warm climate it can grow vigorously to 70 ft (21 m) in height and 50 ft (15 m) in spread. **ZONES 5–10.**

Fagus sylvatica (right)
COMMON BEECH, EUROPEAN BEECH

Although regarded as an 'English' native, this species ranges across Europe and western Asia. Growing to about 80 ft (24 m), it bears drooping balls of yellowish male flowers and greenish clusters of female flowers in spring. Cultivars selected for their habit, intricately cut leaves and colorful foliage, include **'Aspleniifolia'**; **'Dawyck'** with a narrow columnar habit to 50 ft (15 m) and dark purple foliage; **'Pendula'** with branches that droop from a mushroom-shaped crown; *Fagus sylvatica* **f.** *purpurea* (syn. 'Atropunicea'), a round-headed copper beech with purple-green leaves that turn copper and; **'Riversii'**, the purple beech, with very dark purple leaves; **'Rohanii'** with brownish purple deeply cut leaves; **'Rotundifolia'** with strong upright growth and small rounded leaves; **'Tricolor'** (syn. 'Roseomarginata'), a smaller tree with purplish leaves edged and striped pink and cream; and **'Zlatia'** with yellow young foliage turning green. ZONES 5–9.

F

Fagus sylvatica f. *purpurea* (above)

FALLUGIA
APACHE PLUME

This genus contains just one species, a small deciduous shrub
from arid regions of southwestern North America. It is grown for
its attractive foliage and flowers and as a source of oilseed.

CULTIVATION
It is moderately frost hardy, but not in areas with wet winters.
Grow in full sun in a sharply drained soil with shelter from cold
winds and severe frosts. Propagate from seed or cuttings.

F

Fallugia paradoxa *(above)*

This shrub reaches 8 ft (2.4 m) high with slender
branches and shedding white bark. The finely cut
dark green leaves are downy underneath. Single
creamy white flowers, borne on slender stalks in
summer, are followed by leathery nutlets, each
with a purplish, feathery plume. **ZONES 7–10.**

× FATSHEDERA
TREE IVY

The one species of this hybrid genus, combining *Fatsia* and *Hedera*, is an evergreen erect or scrambling shrub grown mainly for its foliage and often used as a conservatory or house plant in cool climates. It grows to 6 ft (1.8 m) or more high with palmately 5- or 7-lobed lustrous dark green leaves. Rounded heads of small greenish white flowers are borne in terminal panicles in autumn.

CULTIVATION
Grow this frost-hardy plant in fertile, well-drained soil in full sun or part-shade. It will withstand coastal exposure and can be grown in seaside gardens. Propagate from cuttings in summer.

F

× *Fatshedera lizei* (above)

This is a spreading open shrub with glossy lobed leaves to 10 in (25 cm) across. It is used extensively as ground cover, or it can be trained against a wall or tree trunk. **'Variegata'** has leaves with a narrow, creamy white edge. For bushy growth, regularly pinch back when the plant is young.
ZONES 7–11.

FATSIA

The 2 or 3 species of evergreen shrubs or small trees that make up this genus come from Japan, Korea and Taiwan. They are closely related to ivy *(Hedera)*, a relationship evident in the flowers and fruit as well as in leaf texture. *Fatsia*, however, have thick, erect stems, small branches and deeply lobed leaves larger than those of ivy. Rounded heads of creamy white flowers occur in large panicles and are followed by small black berries. Their affinity with *Hedera* is demonstrated by the hybrid × *Fatshedera lizei.*

CULTIVATION
They tolerate cold better than most other evergreens with leaves of this size, yet adapt to warm climates if shaded and moist. In mild areas grow in well-drained, humus-rich soil in sun or light shade. In very cold regions they are usually grown as indoor plants. Propagate from seed in autumn or spring, or from cuttings in summer.

Fatsia japonica (above)
syns *Aralia japonica, A. sieboldii*
JAPANESE ARALIA, JAPANESE FATSIA

This handsome shrub or small tree reaches a height of 5–12 ft (1.5–3.5 m). The lustrous, palmately lobed leaves are 12 in (30 cm) or more across. The flowers appear in autumn. Though tough, this frost-hardy species needs to be protected from fierce summer sun, making it suitable for a position beneath trees or in a courtyard. **'Variegata'** has leaves with creamy white margins. ZONES 8–11.

F

FEIJOA
PINEAPPLE GUAVA

Named after Brazilian botanist de Silva Feijo, this genus of 2 species from subtropical Brazil and Argentina consists of evergreen shrubs that reach about 15 ft (4.5 m) tall with a similar spread; they are grown for their showy, edible flowers and guava-like fruits. The fruits appear only after a hot summer and may be damaged by autumn frosts. The oval, glossy green leaves have a silvery underside. Some botanists prefer to classify this genus as *Acca*.

CULTIVATION
Feijoas prefer a warm, frost-free climate, but can grow in areas with very mild frosts in a sheltered, sunny spot. In colder climates they are best grown in a greenhouse. Plant in well-drained, humus-rich soil and ample water while the fruits mature. They are easily propagated from seed but cultivars produce better fruits. Fruit fly is a problem in some areas.

F

Feijoa sellowana
(right)
syn. *Acca sellowiana*
PINEAPPLE GUAVA, FEIJOA

This species, with pruning, can be formed into a single-trunked small tree or it can be clipped as a hedge. The flowers, carried on the new season's growth, have red petals that are white underneath and almost overshadowed by prominent, dark red stamens. The elongated fruit have a tangy flavor and are eaten raw or made into jam. ZONES 9–11.

FELICIA
BLUE DAISY

This genus, which ranges from southern Africa to Arabia, consists of 80 species of annuals, perennials and evergreen subshrubs. Named after Herr Felix, mayor of Regensburg on the Danube in the 1800s, they are sprawling plants with aromatic foliage. In mild climates, they flower on and off almost all year. The daisy-like, usually blue flowerheads with yellow disc florets are borne in masses.

F

CULTIVATION
They are fully frost hardy to frost tender and require full sun and well-drained, humus-rich, gravelly soil. They do not tolerate wet conditions. Deadheading prolongs the flowering season. Prune straggly shoots regularly. Propagate from cuttings taken in late summer or autumn or from seed in spring.

Felicia aethiopica
(left)

This bushy evergreen to 24 in (60 cm) high has small, smooth, obovate leaves to 1 in (25 mm) long. It bears solitary blue flowerheads to 1½ in (35 mm) across on glandular stalks in summer. ZONES 9–11.

Felicia echinata *(left)*

Felicia echinata is a rounded bushy subshrub to 24 in (60 cm) high, with small, recurved sometimes toothed leaves which taper to sharp points. Lilac to white flowerheads are borne in groups of up to 6 in summer. ZONES 9–11.

FICUS
FIG

This genus consists of about 800 species of evergreen and deciduous trees, shrubs and climbers from tropical and subtropical
areas of the world. It includes the common fig, *Ficus carica,*
which bears edible fruit, but most species are grown for their
ornamental foliage and for shade. The tiny flowers are enclosed
in the fruits which develop in the leaf axils and are borne all year.

CULTIVATION
Some grow to great heights in gardens and most have vigorous,
invasive root systems. Marginally frost hardy to frost tender,
many make good pot plants when young. Figs prefer full sun to
part-shade, humus-rich, moist but well-drained soil and shelter
from cold winds. Water potted figs sparingly. Propagate from
seed, cuttings, or aerial layering.

F

Ficus benghalensis
(below right)
BANYAN, INDIAN BANYAN

From southern Asia,
the banyan is outstand-
ing for its aerial roots,
which descend from
branches to the ground
and eventually form
secondary trunks. An
old tree, which only
may be 70 ft (21 m)
high, can spread to
shelter an entire village.
It has pale gray bark,
large glossy mid-green
leaves, bronze when
young, and round red
figs borne in pairs.
ZONES 11–12.

Ficus benjamina *(right)*
WEEPING FIG, WEEPING CHINESE BANYAN

A tropical Asian evergreen tree, the weeping fig
can reach 50 ft (15 m) in height and a much
greater spread, sometimes supported by aerial
roots. It has shiny, pointed, oval leaves, insignificant fruit and an invasive root system. This species and its cultivars are used extensively as potted
house plants. **'Exotica'** has twisted leaf tips;
'Variegata' has rich green leaves splashed with
white. ZONES 10–12.

F

Ficus carica (left)
COMMON FIG

The edible fig, with its distinctive 3-lobed leaves, is indigenous to Turkey and western Asia and has been cultivated for millennia. A small deciduous tree, it reaches 30 ft (9 m) and needs a sunny site in a warm climate with dry summers, as rain can split the ripening fruit. There are many named cultivars. **'Black Mission'** is the well-known black fig grown in California; the fruit is of excellent quality and in warm regions it bears 2 crops per year. **'Brown Turkey'** is a productive, vigorous tree with large, purplish brown fruit with pink flesh and a rich flavor. **'Genoa'** bears greenish yellow fruit with a rich flavor and amber flesh. **ZONES 8–11.**

Ficus dammaropsis
(right)
DINNERPLATE FIG

From the mountains of New Guinea, this small tree grows to 30 ft (9 m). Unlike many *Ficus* species it is single-trunked, forming neither buttresses nor aerial roots. The large rough leaves, up to 24 in (60 cm) long, with deeply corrugated surface, are deep green above and paler beneath, sometimes with red veins. The large figs ripen to a deep purple and are clothed in overlapping scales. **ZONES 10–12.**

Ficus elastica 'Decora' *(above)*
Ficus elastica 'Doescheri' *(right)*

Ficus elastica

INDIA RUBBER TREE, RUBBER PLANT

From tropical Asia, this tree can reach
100 ft (30 m) tall and forms massive
aerial roots and high buttresses with
age. An aggressive root system means
sites must be chosen with care. Outside
the tropics it is usually seen as a potted
plant. Its rosy new leaves make an
attractive contrast to deep green mature
leaves. Cultivars include **'Decora'** with
bronze new leaves, and **'Doescheri'**
with variegated gray-green and creamy
white leaves with light pink midribs.
ZONES 10–12.

Ficus lyrata *(right)*
syn. *Ficus pandurata*

BANJO FIG, FIDDLELEAF FIG

This spreading, evergreen tree from
tropical Africa grows to 100 ft (30 m)
but is often seen as a house plant. It
features broad, violin-shaped leaves:
bright glossy green, heavily veined, and
up to 15 in (38 cm) long. Figs are long
and green. **ZONES 10–12.**

F

Ficus macrophylla *(left)*

MORETON BAY FIG, AUSTRALIAN BANYAN

This large, spreading evergreen tree occurs in coastal rainforests of eastern Australia. It grows to 130 ft (39 m) tall with a spread nearly as great and a but-tressed trunk. It bears large, leathery, dark green leaves, rust-toned under-neath, and abundant figs ripening red-dish brown. **ZONES 10–12.**

Ficus microcarpa

syn. *Ficus retusa*

CHINESE BANYAN, INDIAN LAUREL FIG

When mature, this large evergreen tree reaches 100 ft (30 m) and can form dense curtains of aerial roots. The small, pointed oval leaves are held on as-cending branches, the tips of which have a weeping habit. A native of Australia, **Ficus microcarpa var. hillii** is used for multiple plaited plantings or as a single standard either in a container or in a garden. The Indian laurel fig, **F. m. var. nitida,** has dense, up-right branches. **ZONES 9–12.**

Ficus microcarpa var. *nitida (left)*

Ficus religiosa
(right)

BO TREE, PEEPUL, SACRED FIG

Indigenous to India and Southeast Asia, this species resembles the banyan although not as tall. It has an open crown and poplar-like leaves with long thread-like tips and bears small purple figs. It is believed that Buddha was meditating beneath a bo tree when he received enlightenment. Many trees have been propagated from the tree at Anaradhapura, Sri Lanka, recorded as having been planted in 288 BC. **ZONES 11–12.**

Ficus rubiginosa 'Variegata' *(right)*

Ficus rubiginosa

RUSTY LEAF FIG, PORT JACKSON FIG

This salt-resistant evergreen, native to Australia, grows 30–50 ft (9–15 m) tall and almost as wide. The main trunk is buttressed and sometimes aerial roots are produced. The foliage is shiny deep green on top, downy and rust-colored underneath. Pairs of globular yellow fruit mature in autumn. **'Variegata'** has prominent golden markings on the leaves. **ZONES 10–11.**

F

FORSYTHIA

Since their introduction to Western gardens from China and Japan in the nineteenth century, the 7 species of forsythia have been popular shrubs valued for their brilliant yellow or gold blossoms in mid-spring. They make excellent cut flowers. Deciduous or sometimes semi-evergreen and of medium stature, they have soft-wooded stems branching from near the ground. The rather narrow, bluntly toothed leaves appear after the 4-petalled flowers, which are paired or clustered at the twig nodes.

CULTIVATION

Fully frost hardy, they are not fussy about soil type but fertilizer and compost encourage growth. They prefer a sunny position, but climate is crucial: they seldom flower in warm climates, requiring winter temperatures well below freezing point. Prune only to remove older branches. Propagate from cuttings in early summer.

Forsythia ×
intermedia 'Arnold
Giant' *(below)*

Forsythia ×
intermedia
(below left)
BORDER FORSYTHIA

An arching or spreading deciduous shrub with dark green, lance-shaped leaves, this species grows 8–10 ft (2.4–3 m) tall and slightly wider. A hybrid between *Forsythia suspensa* and *F. viridissima*, it was first recorded in Germany in about 1885. Some fine cultivars include 'Lynwood' and 'Spectabilis'. In 1939 Karl Sax at the Arnold Arboretum in Massachusetts created the first artificial tetraploid, 'Arnold Giant', and subsequently bred 'Beatrix Farrand' and 'Karl Sax', all carrying large, brilliant gold flowers. ZONES 5–9.

Forsythia suspensa
(below left)
WEEPING FORSYTHIA

Indigenous to China, this deciduous species was cultivated for centuries in Japan before being taken to Europe. It makes a shrub of 8–10 ft (2.4–3 m), or taller if supported, with dense, slender, arching branches. From early to mid-spring the branches carry profuse golden flowers with narrow petals. ZONES 4–9.

FORTUNELLA
KUMQUAT, CUMQUAT

The renowned Scottish plant collector Robert Fortune (1812–80) introduced the kumquat to the conservatories of the UK, where it has flourished ever since. The genus comprises 5 evergreen shrubs or small trees, most of which have a small spine at the junction of leaf and branch. Originally they were included in the *Citrus* genus, to which they are closely related. They make compact, small shrubs bearing fragrant white flowers in spring and small, edible orange fruits from summer to autumn. They make perfect container plants for small gardens or sunny patios.

F

CULTIVATION

Frost tender, kumquats require an open position in full sun and fertile, moist but well-drained soil. Apply fertilizer in spring and water during the growing season, especially when the fruits are forming. In frost-prone areas grow in containers and overwinter in a greenhouse. Propagate species from seed or cuttings and varieties by budding onto rootstock in autumn or spring.

Fortunella japonica (above)
KUMQUAT, ROUND KUMQUAT, MARUMI CUMQUAT

Reaching 8–12 ft (2.4–3.5 m), or smaller when container-grown, this species from China bears decorative, small, golden orange fruit. They persist for a considerable time, but are best picked as they ripen to maintain the tree's vigorous growth.
ZONES 9–11.

FOTHERGILLA

From southeastern USA, this genus consists of 2 species of deciduous shrubs grown for their spring flowers and autumn foliage color. The fragrant, petal-less flowers are in upright, conical,
brush-like spikes with conspicuous creamy white stamens. They
appear before the foliage, which is roughly diamond-shaped,
heavily ribbed and hazel-like. The leaves start out bright green,
mature to deep green and develop intense yellow, orange and red
autumn tones.

F

CULTIVATION
Frost hardy, they do best in humus-rich, moist but well-drained,
acidic soil in sun or light shade and can be trimmed to shape
after flowering if necessary. Propagate from seed or cuttings or
by layering.

*Fothergilla
gardenii (left)*
WITCH ALDER, DWARF
FOTHERGILLA

A small bushy shrub
24–36 in (60–90 cm)
high from coastal plain
areas of eastern USA,
this species thrives in a
cool climate with
moist, well-drained
soil. It produces fra-
grant white flowers
1½ in (35 mm) long in
early spring, and the
2–3 in (5–8 cm) long
leaves that follow de-
velop brilliant autumn
colors. **ZONES 5–10.**

Fothergilla major (left)
syn. *Fothergilla monticola*
MOUNTAIN WITCH HAZEL, ALABAMA FOTHERGILLA

This shrub thrives in cool, shady mountain areas.
The best known of the genus, it grows to 6–10 ft
(1.8–3 m) tall and nearly as wide. Fragrant, white,
puffball flowers appear in spring and again in
autumn. The dark green leaves, slightly blue
beneath, turn vibrant yellows, oranges and reds in
autumn. **ZONES 5–9.**

Franklinia
alatamaha (below)

The name is taken from the Altamaha River in Georgia, where this species was first discovered. It makes a small, spreading tree of about 15–20 ft (4.5–6 m), often several trunked. The glossy, bright green leaves turn scarlet in autumn, while the 3 in (8 cm) wide fragrant flowers open in late summer and early autumn. ZONES 7–10.

FRANKLINIA
FRANKLIN TREE

Named for Benjamin Franklin and consisting of a single species, this genus became extinct in the wild shortly after its discovery in about 1765 in Georgia, USA, due to the rapid spread of white settlement and clearing of the forests. It is a small deciduous tree with large white flowers with crinkled, overlapping petals and a central bunch of golden stamens similar to those of the closely related *Camellia*. The fruit, large woody capsules, have 5 compartments and split to release 2 flattened seeds.

F

CULTIVATION

Frost hardy, it prefers humus-rich, moist but well-drained soil and a sheltered, warm position in full sun. Growth is slow. Climates with long, hot, humid summers produce the best flowering. Propagate from fresh ripe seed.

FRAXINUS
ASH

This genus of 65 mainly deciduous, fast-growing tree species ranges throughout the northern hemisphere except for the coldest regions and lowland tropics. Unlike other woody members of the olive family (Oleaceae) it has pinnate leaves consisting of several leaflets, small insignificant flowers that in most species lack petals, and single-seeded, winged fruits called samaras. One group, the 'flowering ashes', typified by *Fraxinus ornus*, produces showier flowers with small petals in large terminal panicles at the tips of branches. Some large species are valued for their tough, pale timber.

CULTIVATION
Ashes are mostly quite frost hardy and can survive exposed or arid conditions, but thrive in shelter with fertile, moist but well-drained soil. Widely planted as street and park trees, they are seldom affected by pests or diseases. Propagate from seed in autumn; for cultivars, graft onto seedling stock of the same species.

Fraxinus americana
'Autumn Purple' *(left)*

Fraxinus americana
WHITE ASH

The most valued ash in North America, this species occurs naturally through eastern USA and in southeastern Canada. In the wild it reaches about 80 ft (24 m) with a long straight bole and furrowed gray-brown bark and a somewhat domed canopy. The pinnate leaves have 7 to 9 large, dark green leaflets with silvery undersides. The inconspicuous flowers appear before the leaves. Autumn color is most commonly a fine yellow. A number of forms are available including *Fraxinus americana* var. *juglandifolia,* which has a slender, columnar habit, and **'Autumn Purple'** with leaves that turn reddish purple in autumn. ZONES 4–10.

F

Fraxinus angustifolia
syn. *Fraxinus oxycarpa*

NARROW-LEAFED ASH

This species is related to *Fraxinus excelsior*, with similar foliage, flowers and fruit but darker bark and leaves in whorls of 3 to 4, not in pairs. It can grow in semi-arid climates and has a broadly columnar to rounded crown. **F. a. subsp.** *oxycarpa* (the desert ash), has leaves with up to 7 leaflets, hairy under the midribs. '**Raywood**', apparently a clone of subspecies *oxycarpa*, is known as the claret ash for its wine-colored autumn foliage. ZONES 6–10.

Fraxinus angustifolia subsp. *oxycarpa* *(above left)*
Fraxinus angustifolia 'Raywood' *(above)*

Fraxinus excelsior *(above)*
EUROPEAN ASH, COMMON ASH

One of Europe's largest deciduous trees, this species can reach 140 ft (42 m); in the open it is usually 50–60 ft (15–18 m), with a broad crown. It bears dark green leaves with 9 to 11 narrow, toothed leaflets that turn yellow in autumn. Velvety, blackish flower buds are noticeable in winter. '**Aurea**' and the more vigorous '**Jaspidea**' have pale yellowish green summer foliage that deepens in autumn; the twigs turn yellow in winter. '**Pendula**', the weeping ash, has branches often weeping to the ground. ZONES 4–10.

Fraxinus excelsior 'Aurea' *(left)*

F

Fraxinus ornus *(above)*
FLOWERING ASH, MANNA ASH

From southern Europe and Asia Minor, the
widely cultivated flowering ash makes a round-
topped tree of 30–50 ft (9–15 m) with a short,
fluted trunk and smooth gray bark. The leaves
have 5 to 9 oval leaflets, dull green with downy
undersides. In late spring it bears foamy panicles
of white blossoms all over the crown, and then
small, narrow fruit. **ZONES 6–10.**

Fraxinus pennsylvanica *(left)*
RED ASH, GREEN ASH

Similar to *Fraxinus americana*, this tree is also a
fast-growing native of North America but is not as
large; it reaches 70 ft (21 m) in height with a similar spread. Its green leaves are divided into 5 to 9
leaflets and are sometimes hairy, resembling
stalks. This species prefers a moist soil. **'Summit'**
has an upright, cylindrical habit with leaves turning yellow in autumn; *F. pennsylvanica* var.
subintegerrima has long, narrow, sword-shaped
leaves. **ZONES 4–10.**

FREMONTODENDRON
syn. *Fremontia*

FLANNEL BUSH

This unusual small genus consists of 2 species of evergreen or semi-evergreen shrubs or small trees from the far southwestern USA and Mexico. The young stems have a felty coating of hairs, as do the lobed leaves on their pale undersides. The large bowl-shaped flowers consist of 5 petal-like, large golden sepals. They are named after Major-General John Charles Fremont (1813–90), an American explorer and distinguished amateur botanist.

F

CULTIVATION
Frost hardy, these plants are not difficult to grow in a sheltered, sunny position with neutral to alkaline, well-drained soil, but they tend to be short lived. Plant out in spring when the danger of frost has passed. They do not perform well in climates with hot, wet summers. Propagate from seed in spring or cuttings in summer.

Fremontodendron californicum *(above)*

This is the best known and hardiest species, ranging along California's Sierra Nevada foothills and coast ranges. It can reach 30 ft (9 m), but is usually a sparse, crooked shrub 20 ft (6 m) tall with dark brown bark. It produces a succession of 2 in (5 cm) wide golden flowers from mid- to late spring. *Fremontodendron californicum* subsp. *decumbens* has a dwarf habit and orange-yellow flowers. ZONES 8–10.

Fremontodendron 'San Gabriel' *(above)*

This spreading, rounded evergreen shrub has rounded 3- or 5-lobed dark green leaves. In summer it produces saucer-shaped bright yellow flowers with long, slender-pointed lobes. ZONES 8–10.

FUCHSIA

This genus consists of about 100 species and thousands of hybrids and cultivars developed for their pendulous flowers, which come in a fascinating variety of forms (though usually with a long or short perianth tube, spreading sepals and 4 broad petals) and a wonderful range of colors in shades of red, white, pink and purple. They are deciduous or evergreen trees, shrubs or perennials treated almost as herbaceous plants. The genus is confined to South and Central America except for 4 species in New Zealand and one in Tahiti. Most of the larger-flowered American species inhabit areas of very high rainfall, sometimes growing as epiphytes or on boulders in moss forests: they are pollinated by hummingbirds. Habit varies from upright shrubs to spreading bushes. Trailing lax varieties are ideal for hanging baskets or are trained as weeping standards. Strong upright types may be trained as compact bushes, standards or espaliers.

CULTIVATION
Moderately frost hardy to frost tender, these plants require moist but well-drained, fertile soil in sun or partial shade and shelter from hot winds and afternoon sun. In most cases, pinching back at an early age and then pruning after flowering will improve shape and flower yield. Propagate from seed or cuttings, and check for white fly, spider mite, rust and gray mold.

Fuchsia arborescens (left)
syn. *Fuchsia arborea*
LILAC FUCHSIA, TREE FUCHSIA

This large erect evergreen shrub from Mexico and Central America grows to about 18 ft (5.5 m) with narrow, elliptic deep green leaves offset by small rose-purple tubular flowers in erect clusters from late spring to early autumn. Marginally frost hardy, it tolerates a warmer climate than most other species but needs a humid, protected position. ZONES 9–11.

Fuchsia denticulata *(left)*

From Peru and Bolivia, this species grows to 8 ft (2.4 m) high and has large leaves up to 6 in (15 cm) long. The long-tubed flowers have bright red petals and sepals that fade to cream and green at the tips. ZONES 9–11.

F

Fuchsia boliviana *(above)*

Native to the forested foothills of the Peruvian Andes, this frost-tender shrub or small tree grows to 12 ft (3.5 m) high. It has soft, gray-green leaves, sometimes with reddish veins, and pendent clusters of long-tubed scarlet flowers. *Fuchsia boliviana* var. *alba* has flowers with white tubes and sepals with scarlet markings at the base. ZONES 10–11.

Fuchsia magellanica 'Versicolor' *(below)*

Fuchsia magellanica *(below)*

LADIES' EARDROPS, HARDY FUCHSIA

From Chile and Argentina, this vigorous erect shrub grows up to 10 ft (3 m) tall. It has lance-shaped to ovate leaves usually held in whorls of three. The pendulous red tubular flowers with red sepals and purple petals are produced over a long period in summer and autumn; black fruit follow. Prune it back to maintain its shape. 'Alba' can grow to a considerable size and bears white flowers. 'Thompsonii' has scarlet tubes and sepals and pale purplish petals; although the flowers are smaller than type, they are more profuse. 'Versicolor' (syn. 'Tricolor') has gray-green leaves that are flushed red when immature and irregularly white-splotched margins when mature; the flowers are small and deep red. ZONES 7–10.

F

Fuchsia paniculata *(above)*

Native to southern Mexico and Panama, this unusual species has foliage resembling that of *Fuchsia magellanica* but its pink flowers are very small and are massed in large panicles. It bears rounded, deep purplish red berries that are often more conspicuous than the flowers. ZONES 9–11.

Fuchsia triphylla 'Billy Green' *(right)*

Fuchsia triphylla *(left)*
HONEYSUCKLE FUCHSIA

From the West Indies, this evergreen shrub grows to a height of 30 in (75 cm) and has pairs or whorls of lance-shaped leaves with a purple undersurface. The orange-scarlet flowers have a slender tapered tube and small petals. They are borne in dense terminal clusters. The leaf color is most intense if the plant is grown in light shade. The honeysuckle fuchsia grows best in a frost-free climate. Many cultivars are available. 'Billy Green' is an example. ZONES 10–11.

FUCHSIA HYBRIDS
syn. *Fuchsia* × *hybrida*

Fuchsia 'Beacon Rosa' *(below)*

This upright, compact shrub with dark green foliage with wavy edges bears single flowers with rose-red tubes and sepals and pink petals with red veins. ZONES 8–11.

This useful gardener's name covers the thousands of modern large-flowered hybrid cultivars derived mainly from *Fuchsia magellanica* and *F. fulgens.* Those derived from *F. triphylla* have slender, long-tubed, single flowers and the leaves usually have a purplish undersurface. All cultivars may be grown in pots, hanging baskets or planted in the garden. Those of upright habit may be trained as standards, while trailing cultivars look very attractive in hanging baskets and window boxes. Frost hardiness varies sligthy between cultivars, as the hardiness zones indicate.

Fuchsia 'Bicentennial' *(above right)*

Of lax habit, this shrub grows to 18 in (45 cm) high and 24 in (60 cm) wide. The double flowers have white tubes, orange sepals and magenta corollas. ZONES 9–11.

Fuchsia 'Cara Mia' *(right)*

Free-flowering, this vigorous, trailing shrub has semi-double, medium-sized flowers composed of pale pink tubes, reflexed sepals and deep crimson petals. They are produced generously along the branches, making this a superb pot plant or basket specimen. ZONES 9–11.

F

Fuchsia 'Dark Eyes' *(left)*

This bushy, upright shrub which grows to 24 in (60 cm) high bears medium-sized double flowers with deep red tubes and sepals and deep violet-blue petals. ZONES 9–11.

Fuchsia 'Display' *(above)*

A strong, upright, branching shrub which grows to 30 in (75 cm) high, 'Display' bears medium-sized, single saucer-shaped flowers in shades of pink. ZONES 9–11.

Fuchsia 'Garden News' *(left)*

A free-flowering upright shrub to 24 in (60 cm) high, this hybrid bears double pink flowers with pale pink tubes and sepals. ZONES 8–11.

Fuchsia 'Gartenmeister Bonstedt' *(above)*

A vigorous hybrid of *Fuchsia triphylla*, this is a spreading shrub with red-tinted bronze leaves. The flowers are long-tubed and bright red overall. ZONES 10–11.

Fuchsia 'Hidcote Beauty' *(above)*

This upright shrub grows to a height and spread of up to 24 in (60 cm). The single flowers have creamy white tubes and sepals and pinky salmon petals. It is marginally frost hardy. ZONES 9–11.

Fuchsia 'La Campanella' *(right)*

This trailing shrub to 12 in (30 cm) high and 18 in (45 cm) wide bears small, semi-double flowers with white tubes and sepals and purple petals. *Fuchsia* 'La Campanella' is free-flowering and makes an excellent hanging basket subject. ZONES 9–11.

Fuchsia 'Lord Byron' *(above)*

This free-flowering upright bushy shrub has mid-green serrated leaves. The single flowers to 3 in (8 cm) long have short, thin cerise tubes, scarlet sepals and very dark purple petals with red veining that shade to a paler purple at the base. The petals are expanded to an open saucer shape. ZONES 8–11.

Fuchsia 'Marinka' *(left)*

A trailing shrub to 12 in (30 cm) high with a spread of up to 24 in (60 cm), this hybrid bears abundant, single, red flowers with petals of a deeper red. It makes an excellent pot plant or an attractive hanging basket specimen. ZONES 8–11.

Fuchsia 'Mrs Popple' *(right)*

A vigorous bushy shrub which grows to a height and spread of about 3 ft (1 m), this hybrid has single flowers with scarlet tubes and sepals and purple petals with a deep pink center. This fuchsia is more frost hardy than most. ZONES 8–11.

F

Fuchsia 'Orange Drops' *(left)*

This bushy upright or semi-trailing shrub is probably one of the best orange-flowering fuchsias. The single flowers have light orange tubes and sepals and darker rich orange petals. The flowers tend to hang in clusters. ZONES 9–11.

Fuchsia 'Royal Velvet' *(left)*

A vigorous upright shrub to 30 in (75 cm) high, this plant has large double flowers with waxy red tubes and red reflexed sepals and deep purple petals. This is an excellent variety for training as a standard. ZONES 9–11.

Fuchsia 'Swingtime' *(left)*

This vigorous shrub has medium to large double flowers with red tubes and sepals and creamy white, red-veined petals. With its spreading habit, it is considered one of the best choices for a hanging basket or window box. It grows to 24 in (60 cm) in height. ZONES 9–11.

Fuchsia 'Tom Thumb' *(above)*

This small upright bushy shrub to 12 in (30 cm) high bears profuse small, single flowers with pinkish red tubes and sepals and pinkish purple petals veined red. This free-flowering plant makes an excellent miniature standard. ZONES 8–11.

Fuchsia 'Thalia' *(above)*

An upright bushy shrub to 3 ft (1 m) tall, this hybrid has velvety dark green leaves with purplish undersides and bears masses of small, orange-red flowers with very long tubes. ZONES 10–11.

Fuchsia 'Waltzing Matilda' *(above)*

This trailing shrub has dark green leaves with finely toothed edges. The medium-sized double blooms are pale pink with faint deep pink veins. The wavy sepals are green tipped. ZONES 9–11.

Fuchsia 'White Spider' *(above)*

This vigorous, upright, branching shrub bears abundant single pale pink flowers with pink tubes and some pink veining. It is good for training as a standard. ZONES 9–11.

GARDENIA

Evergreen shrubs or small trees with glossy deep green leaves and extremely fragrant white or cream flowers, gardenias are popular in warm-climate gardens worldwide. The genus includes some 200 species, most from tropical Asia or southern Africa.

CULTIVATION

They need well-drained, neutral to acid soil and prefer light shade. Generous water in the warmer months and a regular dressing of compost and fertilizer ensures good flowering and keeps foliage a deep glossy green. Frost tender and lovers of humidity, they are best grown in heated greenhouses in cooler climates. They are easily propagated from cuttings in summer.

Gardenia augusta (above)
syns *Gardenia florida, G. grandiflora, G. jasminoides*
COMMON GARDENIA, CAPE JASMINE

This is the best known species, an evergreen, glossy-leafed shrub from southern China, though long supposed native to the Cape of Good Hope, hence the common name. It is commonly seen in gardens and flower shops in one of its double-flowered cultivars, all with white, strongly perfumed flowers changing to pale yellow as they age. The best known is **'Florida'**, a 3 ft (1 m) shrub with flowers to 3 in (8 cm) wide; **'Magnifica'** is larger in all its parts though less generous with flowers; **'Radicans'** is almost prostrate, with small flowers and leaves. Flowers appear over a long season from late spring. **ZONES 10–11.**

G

Gardenia thunbergia
(above left & left)

STARRY GARDENIA

From the humid forests of southern Africa, this erect shrub grows to 10 ft (3 m) or more high and almost as wide with stiff, erect branches. The large fragrant white flowers are held singly towards the branch tips in early summer. Being surface rooted, *Gardenia thunbergia* appreciates regular fertilizing, ample water and a yearly mulch of compost. ZONES 9–11.

GARRYA

The only genus in its family, *Garrya* comprises some 13 species of evergreen shrubs and small trees from western USA, Mexico and the West Indies. They are cultivated for their handsome leaves and pendent catkins, which are longer and more attractive on male plants. The most important species in gardens is the silk-tassel bush, *Garrya elliptica.*

CULTIVATION

They require a mild-temperate climate with shelter from freezing winds. Grow in rich, well-drained soil in full sun or part-shade. Slow growing, they need little pruning and dislike being transplanted. Propagate from cuttings in summer.

G

Garrya elliptica
(left)

SILK-TASSEL BUSH

This dense, bushy shrub from California and Oregon grows to 8–25 ft (2.4–8 m) high and wide. It can be trained in espalier form. The leaves are broadly oval, dark green, leathery and wavy edged. Curtains of tassel-like, cream and dull pink catkins are borne from midwinter to early spring on male plants (which are the only ones normally cultivated). The cultivar '**James Roof**' has silvery catkins with golden anthers. **ZONES 8–9.**

GAULTHERIA
syns × *Gaulnettya, Pernettya*

Named after Dr Gaultier, an eighteenth-century physician, this genus of 170 or so species of evergreen shrubs are widely distributed in moist temperate regions of the world, also in higher mountain areas of the tropics. They have attractive glossy leaves which may be aromatic when crushed. The flowers are pink or white and are usually bell- or urn-shaped. The fruits, though capsules, are berry-like and aromatic.

CULTIVATION
Marginally to very frost hardy, they prefer well-drained, humus-rich, acid soil, and a sheltered position in part-shade. Propagate from seed in autumn or cuttings in summer or by division of suckers in autumn or spring.

G

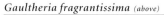

Gaultheria fragrantissima (above)
From the mountains of southern Asia, this large, dense shrub or small tree reaches 10 ft (3 m). The leathery, elliptical leaves, 4 in (10 cm) long, smell strongly of oil of wintergreen when crushed. In maturity the green adult leaves develop a brown underside. In spring fragrant, bell-shaped flowers, white or pale pink, appear on last season's growth. The rounded fruit ripen mid- or pale blue. ZONES 8–10.

Gaultheria mucronata (above)
syn. *Pernettya mucronata*
PRICKLY HEATH

This thicket-forming, suckering shrub from Chile and Argentina grows to 5 ft (1.5 m) high and wide and has deep green, glossy leaves ½ in (12 mm) long with sharp tips. It bears clusters of small, white, pendulous flowers and small, fleshy, pinkish purple fruit. There are separate male and female plants. Cultivars include '**Bell's Seedling**' with deep dusky pink berries; '**Mother of Pearl**' with pale pink berries; '**Mulberry Wine**' with purple berries; and '**White Pearl**' with white berries. '**Wintertime**' has pure white berries. ZONES 7–9.

Gaultheria shallon
(left)

SHALLON

From northwestern North America, this suckering shrub grows to 4–10 ft (1.2–3 m) high and wide. In spring it produces terminal panicles of small, pinkish white, lily-of-the-valley flowers. These are followed by ½ in (12 mm) fleshy, purple fruit. **ZONES 5–9.**

Gaultheria × wisleyensis *(left)*
syn. × *Gaulnettya wisleyensis*

These vigorous hybrids, bred in England from *Gaultheria shallon* and *G. mucronata*, though variable are usually dense and less than 6 ft (1.8 m) high. They have small leathery leaves, white flowers and large bunches of dark red berries that persist until late winter. Several named cultivars are available. **ZONES 7–9.**

GENISTA
syns *Chamaespartium, Teline*

BROOM

From Europe and the Mediterranean to western Asia, this legume genus consists of about 90 species of deciduous and evergreen shrubs, grown for their profuse, fragrant, pea-like flowers. Many of the species have very reduced leaves, sometimes bearing their flowers on leafless green branches. In ancient times their flowers were used to make dyes.

CULTIVATION
Many are only marginally frost hardy; they prefer a temperate climate and some are good seaside plants. Full sun and a not-too-rich, well-drained soil suit them best. The frost-tender species can be grown in a well-ventilated greenhouse. They resent being transplanted. Prune to encourage a compact, bushy shape. Propagate from seed in spring or cuttings in summer.

G

Genista hispanica
(below right)

SPANISH GORSE

From southwestern Europe, this dwarf deciduous shrub is ideal for rockeries and dry, sunny banks. It has few leaves and many spines. It grows 30 in (75 cm) tall and 5 ft (1.5 m) wide, forming a neat dome covered in spring and early summer with dense clusters of tiny, golden yellow flowers. ZONES 6–10.

Genista lydia *(right)*

This mound-forming, deciduous shrub from the Balkans reaches 24–36 in (60–90 cm) tall and wide; it has arching branches and bluish green leaves. Bright yellow pea-like flowers are borne in abundance in early summer. Fully frost hardy, this is an excellent plant for rockeries, banks and for trailing over walls. ZONES 7–9.

Genista pilosa 'Vancouver Gold' *(below)*

Genista pilosa

This deciduous, prostrate to erect European species grows to 16 in (40 cm) high and twice as wide. Fully frost hardy, it bears small, narrow, lance-shaped, dark green leaves with a silky undersurface and profuse small yellow pea-flowers in early summer. **'Vancouver Gold'** has a domed habit to 18 in (45 cm) high and golden yellow flowers. **ZONES 5–9.**

Genista sagittalis *(above)*
syn. *Chamaespartium sagittale*

This prostrate shrub from Europe reaches 6–12 in (15–30 cm) high with a spread of up to 3 ft (1 m). It has very distinctive, broadly winged stems, sparsely scattered dark green oval leaves and dense terminal clusters of deep yellow pea-flowers in early summer. **ZONES 4–9.**

Genista × spachiana *(above)*
syns *Cytisus fragrans, C. racemosus, Genista fragrans*

This dense, evergreen broom is a hybrid between *Genista canariensis* and *G. stenopetala*. Although frost tender, it tolerates dry, windy conditions and infertile soils, growing quickly to about 6 ft (1.8 m). The dark green leaves are shiny above and pale and silky beneath. A profusion of fragrant yellow pea-flowers appear in long spikes in winter and spring; **'Nana'** is similar but has a smaller growth habit. Both are widely sold as a flowering pot plant. **ZONES 9–11.**

Genista × spachiana 'Nana' *(above)*

Genista tinctoria *(right)*

DYER'S BROOM, WOADWAXEN

Used as a medicinal herb and as a source of yellow dye, this tough, deciduous, green-stemmed 3 ft (1 m) shrub ranges from Europe to Siberia. It has 1 in (25 mm) long leaves with fine hairs beneath. Golden yellow, pea-flowers appear in summer after other brooms have finished flowering. **'Flore Pleno'** (syn. 'Plena') is a dwarf cultivar, 12 in (30 cm) high, with double flowers. **'Royal Gold'** has golden yellow flowers arranged in conical panicles to 3 in (8 cm) long. **ZONES 3–9.**

Genista 'Yellow Imp' *(right)*

'Yellow Imp' is one of a group of beautiful hybrid brooms. It is a sprawling shrub 5–6 ft (1.5–1.8 m) tall that flowers in late spring. The flowers can be pure yellow, or variously flushed and tinted with maroon or cream. **ZONES 8–10.**

GINKGO
GINKGO, MAIDENHAIR TREE

The Ginkgoales, seed-bearing plants more primitive than the conifers and more ancient, first appeared in the Permian Period (about 300 million years ago) and flourished through the Jurassic and Cretaceous Periods. About 100 million years ago they began to die out, leaving the maidenhair tree a sole survivor—and then only in China. It is now unknown in a wild state, and probably would no longer exist if ancient trees had not been preserved in temple grounds and young ones planted there. The common name 'maidenhair' refers to the leaf shape and vein pattern, resembling some of the maidenhair fern *(Adiantum)* species. Male trees bear small spikes of pollen sacs, females solitary naked seeds ('fruits') with an oily flesh around the large kernel.

CULTIVATION
A tree of temperate climates, it resists pollution and seems to have outlived any pests it may have once had. It does, however, need shelter from strong winds and does best in deep, fertile soil. City authorities prefer to grow male trees, as females drop smelly fruit; in China female trees are preferred as the seeds are edible and nutritious. Fruit do not appear before the tree is at least 20 years old, however. Propagate from seed or autumn cuttings.

Ginkgo biloba
(below)

The ginkgo grows at least 80 ft (24 m) tall, upright when young and eventually spreading to 30 ft (9 m) or more. Deciduous, the 4 in (10 cm) long, matt green, fan-shaped leaves turn golden yellow in autumn. A fleshy, plum-like orange-brown fruit with an edible kernel appears in late summer and autumn if male and female trees are grown together. **'Fastigiata'** is a slender, erect cultivar that reaches 30 ft (9 m). **'Princeton Sentry'** has a narrow, upright habit and is male. ZONES 3–10.

Ginkgo biloba
'Fastigiata' *(below)*

Gleditsia triacanthos

HONEY LOCUST

Native to eastern and central USA and reaching 100 ft (30 m), this species has an open, vase-shaped canopy and a thorny trunk. Fern-like, shiny, green bipinnate leaves with small leaflets turn deep yellow in autumn. Twisted black pods, up to 18 in (45 cm) long and 1½ in (35 mm) wide, hang from the branches in autumn and winter. ***Gleditsia triacanthos* f. *inermis*** is thornless as are most modern cultivars. **'Imperial'** has rounded leaves and few seed pods; **'Shademaster'** is fast growing and broadly conical with bright green leaves; **'Skyline'** has dark green leaves that turn yellow in autumn; **'Stevens'** is wide spreading with bright green leaves turning yellow in autumn; and **'Sunburst'** has bright yellow young leaves that turn pale green in summer. ZONES 3–10.

Gleditsia triacanthos 'Skyline' *(above right)*

Gleditsia triacanthos 'Shademaster' *(above far right)*

Gleditsia triacanthos 'Sunburst' *(right)*

GLEDITSIA
LOCUST

Occurring in temperate and subtropical regions of North and South America as well as Africa and Asia, this genus of about 14 species of deciduous, broadly spreading, usually thorny trees is grown for attractive foliage, ease of cultivation and for shade. They have pinnate or bipinnate leaves, inconspicuous flowers and large, often twisted, hanging seed pods that are filled with a sweetish, edible pulp. The locust referred to in the Bible is the related *Ceratonia siliqua*, but in North America 'locust' has been used for both *Gleditsia* and *Robinia*, the latter not closely related.

G

CULTIVATION

Gleditsias grow best in full sun in rich, moist soil and tolerate poor drainage. They are fast growing and mostly frost hardy, although young plants may need protection from frost. Prune young trees to promote a single, straight trunk; thorns on the lower trunk can be removed. Propagate selected forms by budding in spring or summer and species from seed in autumn.

GORDONIA

This genus of about 70 species of evergreen trees and shrubs allied to *Camellia*, is native to Southeast Asia, except for one North American species. Their handsome, white-petalled, camellia-like flowers and glossy, dark green leaves make them popular ornamental plants for warm climates.

CULTIVATION

They do best in sun or dappled shade in friable, slightly acidic soil—they enjoy conditions similar to those preferred by camellias. Mulch, feed and water regularly. Tip pruning during the first few years of growth will improve their slightly open habit. Propagate from seed in autumn or spring, or from cuttings in late summer.

G

Gordonia axillaris
(left)

Though it may become a tree up to 25 ft (8 m) tall and wide, this beautiful evergreen from China with dappled orange-brown bark grows slowly, and is usually seen as a tall shrub. The dark green, glossy leaves to 6 in (15 cm) long turn scarlet before they fall, a few at a time, throughout the year. The white flowers are about 4 in (10 cm) wide with broad, crumpled petals and golden stamens. ZONES 9–11.

GOSSYPIUM

This genus contains 40 species of annuals, subshrubs or shrubs found in warm-temperate and tropical regions worldwide. Best known are the 4 to 5 species grown as commercial crop plants (cotton). The flowers resemble those of *Hibiscus* (to which it is closely related) and may be cream, yellow or rose colored, sometimes with a dark spot at the base. They are followed by globular pods which split open to release their oily seeds, embedded in cotton fibers. Apart from the cotton-yielding species, several others are grown as ornamental plants, mostly the Australian species with pink or mauve flowers. These are best suited to fairly hot, semi-arid climates.

CULTIVATION

Frost tender, they need moist but well-drained soil, long, hot summers and a sheltered position in full sun. Propagate from seed or cuttings.

G

Gossypium sturtianum *(above)*

STURT'S DESERT ROSE

This species, the floral emblem of the Northern Territory, Australia, is an evergreen shrub that grows over 6 ft (1.8 m) high and wide. It has oval, gray-green leaves and beautiful large mauve flowers with overlapping petals that are darker at the base. It is a useful ornamental plant for hot, arid regions, surviving with minimal irrigation, but adapts well enough also to higher-rainfall areas and tolerates light frosts. ZONES 9–11.

GREVILLEA

Some 250 species of evergreen shrubs and trees in the protea family make up this genus. Variable in habit, foliage and flowers, most grevilleas are native to Australia with a few from New Caledonia and Papua New Guinea. The small flowers are mostly densely crowded into heads or spikes, their most conspicuous feature being the long styles which are at first bent over like a hairpin and then straighten out. Many are adaptable and easy to grow, with a long flowering period, and are popular with nectar-seeking birds. The leaves are commonly deeply divided and may be very decorative in their own right, the foliage of some species being grown for cutting. In the last several decades hundreds of hybrid grevillea cultivars have been bred, nearly all in Australia, and many are extremely floriferous. Some of the most beautiful species are low growing or prostrate; these may be planted in a rock garden, as ground cover or in pots.

CULTIVATION

Moderately frost hardy to frost tender, grevilleas do best in well-drained, slightly dry, neutral to acid soil in full sun. Strong roots develop early and it is important not to disturb these when planting out. Pruning of shrubby species and cultivars is recommended immediately after flowering to promote healthy new growth and a compact habit. They are generally pest free although scale insects and leaf spot may pose a problem. Propagate from seed in spring, from cuttings in late summer, or by grafting for some of the species most prone to root-rot.

Grevillea banksii (left)
BANKS'S GREVILLEA

Named after Sir Joseph Banks, this subtropical Australian east coast species is a variable shrub or small open-branched tree growing 8–30 ft (2.4–9 m) tall, though some forms from coastal headlands are almost prostrate. The gray-green leaves are deeply divided; the branches terminate in large, cylindrical, cream, red or rich pink flowerheads, which appear profusely in spring and summer. It adapts well to coastal climates in mid-temperate zones. **ZONES 9–11.**

Grevillea baueri *(right)*
BAUER'S GREVILLEA

This small shrub to 3 ft (1 m) high has closely packed, light green oblong leaves to 1 in (25 mm) long, often bronze on new growths. Deep pink and cream flowers are carried in tight globular heads on short branches in winter and spring. It is moderately frost hardy and may be lightly trimmed to form a neat small hedge. **ZONES 8–10.**

G

Grevillea 'Bonnie Prince Charlie' *(right)*

This free-flowering cultivar is a small compact shrub to 3 ft (1 m) high with a similar spread. The dark green oblong leaves to 2 in (5 cm) long have whitish undersides. Pendent, spidery clusters of red and yellow flowers are produced from late winter to mid-summer. It is marginally frost hardy and is well suited to growing in a container. **ZONES 9–10.**

Grevillea 'Canberra Gem' *(above)*
syn. *Grevillea juniperina* 'Pink Pearl'

This dense, bushy shrub grows to 8 ft (2.4 m) with a similar spread, its erect stems crowded in a hedge-like form. It has narrow, pointed, dark green leaves and is irregularly scattered with small clusters of bright pink and red flowers from winter to late summer. A hybrid between *Grevillea juniperina* and *G. rosmarinifolia*, it is moderately frost hardy and responds well to hard pruning. It can be grown as a hedge, though not very long-lived. **ZONES 7–10.**

Grevillea 'Clearview David' *(above)*

This free-flowering hybrid cultivar is an erect bushy shrub to about 10 ft (3 m) high and across. It has crowded, needle-like, deep green leaves with silky undersides. Abundant deep red, pendent, spider-type flowerheads are borne along the branches in winter and spring. Marginally frost hardy, it responds well to regular pruning and is suitable as a hedging plant. **ZONES 8–10.**

Grevillea 'Honey Gem' *(left)*

This hybrid cultivar grows to 12 ft (3.5 m) or more tall and 6 ft (1.8 m) or more wide. It carries large orange toothbrush-like flower-spikes for most of the year with the main flush in early spring. The finely divided, dark green leaves up to 12 in (30 cm) long have silvery undersides. Frost tender, it is best suited to warm-temperate and tropical climates. ZONES 10–12.

Grevillea juniperina *(right)*
PRICKLY SPIDER FLOWER

This semi-prostrate to upright rounded shrub to 6 ft (1.8 m) or more high from temperate eastern Australia has bright green, crowded, needle-like leaves. Profuse scarlet to orange or pale yellow, spider-like flowerheads appear from late winter to early summer. This is one of the most variable grevilleas and many forms and cultivars are grown. Most are moderately frost hardy and long lived. **Grevillea juniperina f. *sulphurea*** (sometimes sold as **'Aurea'**) has an upright habit to 4 ft (1.2 m) high and pale yellow flowers. **'Molonglo'** is a semi-prostrate cultivar to 30 in (75 cm) high with a spread of 6 ft (1.8 m) or more across; it produces abundant apricot flowers and is a popular ground cover for large areas. **'Pink Lady'** is a low-spreading shrub to 24 in (60 cm) high and 10 ft (3 m) across; it has pale pink flowers that are not always borne freely. ZONES 8–10.

Grevillea lanigera
WOOLLY GREVILLEA

This species from mountains of southeastern Australia has narrow, grayish, furry leaves and red and cream flower clusters from late winter to spring. It varies in size—some forms are prostrate and others grow to about 3 ft (1 m) tall and wide. This is one of the most frost-hardy species, but it does resent summer humidity. **'Mt Tamboritha'** is a popular, small, prostrate form with soft gray-green foliage and reddish pink and cream flowers. ZONES 7–9.

Grevillea lanigera 'Mt Tamboritha' *(below)*

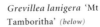

G

Grevillea robusta *(above)*

SILKY OAK

From subtropical rainforests of the Australian east coast, this tree grows to 100 ft (30 m) and has long been valued for its beautiful timber, used for furniture making. The fern-like leaves with silvery undersides are partly shed just before branches are almost hidden by the masses of long, golden yellow blooms which appear in late spring. Moderately frost hardy once established, it tolerates fairly dry conditions—in fact it will hardly succeed without a warm, dry summer. **ZONES 8–11.**

Grevillea 'Robyn Gordon' *(above)*

This free-flowering offspring of *Grevillea banksii* and *G. bipinnatifida* is widely regarded as the best hybrid grevillea. It makes a rather dense bush a little more than 3 ft (1 m) tall and 6 ft (1.8 m) wide. The olive green leaves, russet when young and sometimes turning gray, are much divided and, though stiff and prickly, look fern-like. The cylindrical, soft red flowerheads appear almost all year, peaking in spring and autumn. It is marginally frost hardy. Its foliage may provoke allergic reactions in some people. **ZONES 9–11.**

Grevillea rosmarinifolia *(above)*

ROSEMARY GREVILLEA, SPIDER FLOWER

This dense, spreading shrub to 6 ft (1.8 m) tall from cooler parts of southeastern Australia has bright green, needle-like leaves mostly under 1 in (25 mm) long. The pendent, red spider-like flowerheads are produced mainly from early winter to late spring. Moderately frost hardy, it takes well to being clipped to shape as a hedge. **'Jenkinsii'** is a decorative cultivar that is a little less prickly than its parent. **ZONES 8–10.**

Grevillea victoriae *(above)*

ROYAL GREVILLEA

This variable species from the mountains of southeastern Australia makes an upright, spreading shrub to 6 ft (1.8 m) high and 10 ft (3 m) across. It has ovate gray-green leaves to 6 in (15 cm) long with silvery undersides. Pendent clusters of rusty red, spider-type flowerheads appear in spring and again in late summer and autumn. Occurring at elevations of up to 6000 ft (1800 m), it is one of the most frost-hardy grevilleas. **ZONES 7–9.**

GREYIA

This South African genus encompasses 3 species of evergreen or semi-deciduous shrubs or small trees grown for their attractive, bottlebrush-like clusters of bell-shaped flowers with protruding stamens, and their colorful autumn foliage. The genus is named in honor of Sir George Grey, governor of the Cape in the nineteenth century. Only one species, *Greyia sutherlandii,* is generally cultivated, although *G. radlkoferi* is also occasionally cultivated.

CULTIVATION
Marginally frost hardy, they are best suited to warm, dry climates and need full sun and fertile, well-drained soil. Lightly prune after flowering to keep them compact. Water generously during the growing season, less while the shrub is dormant in winter. Propagate from seed in spring or from cuttings in summer.

Greyia sutherlandii (above)
NATAL BOTTLEBRUSH

This dome-shaped, rather gaunt, woody evergreen shrub from the drier hills of South Africa grows to 10 ft (3 m) or more high. Its almost circular shallowly toothed leaves turn red in autumn, but it is mainly grown for its brilliant orange-red flowers. Appearing in late winter and early spring, the dense spikes of many small flowers with protruding stamens are borne at the ends of the bare branches. ZONES 9–11.

GRISELINIA

This genus is made up of 6 species of evergreen shrubs and trees from New Zealand, Chile and Brazil, of which only the 2 New Zealand species are commonly cultivated. They are grown for their foliage and bushy habit, the pale greenish flowers being tiny and inconspicuous. The flowers are followed by black berries on female plants only.

CULTIVATION
They are only moderately frost hardy and require a temperate climate, well-drained soil and sunshine. They are resistant to salt and are suitable for coastal areas. With a little trimming the shrubs make good hedges. Propagate from summer cuttings or seed.

G

Griselinia littoralis
(right)
KAPUKA

Growing 20–40 ft (6–12 m) tall, this spreading tree or shrub from New Zealand has dense, bright green foliage and yellow-green flowers. It withstands salt-laden winds and dry conditions and, although frost hardy, appreciates the protection of a wall in colder areas. If used as a hedge, the plants are best trimmed in summer. The leaves of **'Dixon's Cream'** are splashed creamy white, while **'Variegata'** has blotched white variegations.
ZONES 8–10.

G

Griselinia lucida
'Variegata' *(above)*

Griselinia lucida *(above)*

PUKA

This fast-growing species from New Zealand is
somewhat more erect and open branching than
Griselinia littoralis. It grows to 20 ft (6 m) high,
with larger, more glossy and darker green leaves.
The leaves of the frost-tender **'Variegata'** are
marked creamy yellow. ZONES 8–10.

GYMNOCLADUS

Distinctive for their enormous, handsome bipinnate leaves, the
4 deciduous trees of this genus, allied to *Gleditsia*, come from
North America and East Asia. Small, greenish white flowers appear
only in prolonged warm weather. The seeds and pods of different
species have been used for soap and as a coffee substitute. Only
female trees bear fruits.

CULTIVATION
Cool-climate plants, they require full sun and deep, well-drained,
fertile soil. Propagate from seed in autumn.

G

Gymnocladus dioica (right)
KENTUCKY COFFEE TREE

From moist woodland
areas of the eastern
USA, this slow-growing
tree reaches 70 ft (21 m)
tall and 50 ft (15 m)
wide. The large com-
pound leaves, up to 3 ft
(1 m) long, are pinkish
bronze when young.
The small, star-shaped
white flowers are
fragrant and are borne
in early summer fol-
lowed, on the female
plants, by pendent red-
dish brown pods to
10 in (25 cm) long.
The seeds were once
roasted and ground for
a coffee-like beverage.
ZONES 4–10.

H

HAKEA

This genus consists of 130 species of evergreen shrubs and small trees from Australia. They are closely allied to the grevilleas and, like them, are well-regarded garden plants in their home country, though the most easily grown species are not necessarily the most spectacular. They are also popular in California but are less valued in South Africa where several species have become weeds. There is great variety in the foliage, from needle-like to broad, though the leaves are always stiff and leathery. The flowers are borne in small clusters, and the bracts are woody follicles, sometimes quite large. The bushier species are suitable for informal hedges, those with prickly leaves being impenetrable.

H

CULTIVATION
Fast growing but not always long lived, they prefer mild-winter climates, sunshine and well-drained soil and dislike phosphorus-rich fertilizers. Some tend to do poorly in summer-rainfall climates, especially the Western Australian species. Propagation is usually from seed; outstanding forms can be perpetuated from summer cuttings. Watch for root-rot in moist soil.

Hakea laurina
(above)
PINCUSHION BUSH, SEA URCHIN

This shrub or small tree from Western Australia grows to 20 ft (6 m) tall and 10 ft (3 m) wide. The long, narrow leaves are gray-green and leathery. During winter and spring it bears fragrant, ball-shaped, crimson flowerheads with long creamy styles protruding like pins from a pincushion. Useful for hedges and screens, this hakea must have perfect drainage. If grown too fast it becomes top heavy and may be toppled by strong winds. ZONES 9–11.

Hakea microcarpa
(right)

NEEDLE BUSH

The most cold-hardy
hakea, this open,
rounded shrub from
the mountains of
southeastern Australia
grows to 6 ft (1.8 m) in
height and spread. The
green leaves are vari-
able, but are usually
needle-shaped with
sharp points. The
small, creamy white
flowers appear from
late winter to summer;
they have a honey-like
fragrance. **ZONES 8–10.**

H

Hakea victoria *(above)*

ROYAL HAKEA

This upright, 10 ft (3 m) tall shrub has spectacular foliage. The leathery leaves have a similar
shape to scallop shells and display striking variegation in shades of yellow or orange on a gray-
green background, those on the long-flowering
branches being the brightest. The flowers are pale
pink and inconspicuous. It is difficult to propagate and grow, needing a dry climate with little
frost, sandy (or at least very well-drained) soil
and abundant sunshine. **ZONES 9–11.**

HALESIA
SILVERBELL, SNOWDROP TREE

The 5 species of this genus of deciduous trees and shrubs are found in eastern USA and in China in rich, moist woodlands and beside streams. They are grown mainly for their attractive bell-shaped flowers, opening in clusters as the leaves unfold, and the unusual winged fruit capsules that follow.

CULTIVATION
Cool-climate plants, they prefer a sheltered position in part- to full sun and grow best in well-drained, moist, neutral to acid soil. Propagation is from seed in autumn or from softwood cuttings in summer. Halesias have little trouble with pests and diseases.

H

Halesia carolina (above)
syn. *Halesia tetraptera*
CAROLINA SILVERBELL

This ornamental, spreading tree grows 25–40 ft (8–12 m) high and somewhat wider. It flowers profusely, even when young, producing masses of drooping, bell-shaped white or pink-flushed flowers in mid- to late spring. The flowers are followed by 4-winged green fruit that ripen to pale brown. The mid-green leaves are downy when they first appear and turn yellow in autumn.
ZONES 3–9.

HALIMIUM
SUN ROSE

This useful genus is very similar to the popular *Cistus* and *Helianthemum* and some species have even been included in these other genera. It comes from the Mediterranean region and includes about 14 species. They are herbaceous perennials or dwarf shrubs with small, narrow leaves and 5-petalled, white or yellow flowers with a reddish, purple or brown blotch at the base of the petals.

CULTIVATION
They prefer full sun and a moderately fertile, well-drained soil and are frost hardy. Water sparingly and prune regularly to maintain their shape and encourage flowering. Propagation is from cuttings.

H

Halimium lasianthum *(above)*
syn. *Halimium formosum*

This low-spreading evergreen is a native of Spain and Portugal. It has gray-green foliage and in spring and summer bears rich yellow flowers, each petal marked with a central crimson blotch. Although frost hardy, it needs shelter in colder areas. Like *Cistus*, it is admirably suited to coastal gardens. It grows to a height of 3 ft (1 m) and can spread to 5 ft (1.5 m). ZONES 8–9.

HAMAMELIS
WITCH HAZEL

This genus contains 5 species of deciduous shrubs or small trees from East Asia and North America. They are prized for their fragrant flowers, borne on bare stems through winter, and for their foliage, which turns yellow with red and orange tints in autumn. The fruits are small capsules containing 2 black seeds.

CULTIVATION

Hamamelis are good shrubs for cool-climate gardens, preferring an open, sunny position (although they will tolerate semi-shade) in fertile, moist but well-drained, loamy, acid soil. Propagate selected forms by grafting in winter, from heeled cuttings in summer or by budding in late summer. Species can be raised from seed, but germination may take a full year. Check for coral spot and honey fungus.

Hamamelis ×
intermedia (below left)

The name covers a group of cultivars derived from *Hamamelis japonica* and *H. mollis*, deciduous shrubs with oval leaves 3–6 in (8–15 cm) long that color well in autumn. Fragrant flowers appear on bare twigs in winter, their color varying from light yellow to deep orange depending on the cultivar. 'Arnold Promise' has bright yellow flowers; 'Diane' has fragrant, spidery, deep red flowers in late winter and large leaves that turn red and yellow in autumn; 'Jelena' is bright orange; and 'Ruby Glow' (syn. *H. japonica* 'Rubra Superba') has coppery red flowers and rich foliage colors in autumn. ZONES 4–9.

Hamamelis ×
intermedia 'Diane'
(below far left)

Hamamelis ×
intermedia 'Ruby Glow' (below)

Hamamelis japonica *(right)*

JAPANESE WITCH HAZEL

This open, upright shrub grows to a height of 10–15 ft (3–4.5 m) and about as wide. Its perfumed yellow flowers with twisted petals are carried in clusters on the bare branches from mid- to late winter. Flowering branches are often cut for indoor decoration. The oval, mid-green leaves appear in spring and turn yellow before dropping in autumn. **ZONES 4–9.**

H

Hamamelis mollis *(right)*

CHINESE WITCH HAZEL

This upright, open shrub has extremely fragrant, golden-yellow flowers, borne on bare branches from mid-winter to early spring. It grows to a height and spread of 10–15 ft (3–4.5 m) and the large, thick leaves are mid-green above and downy beneath; they turn deep golden yellow in autumn. **'Coombe Wood'** has slightly larger flowers; **'Pallida'** has dense clusters of large, sweetly scented sulfur-yellow flowers and yellow leaves in autumn. **ZONES 4–9.**

Hamamelis virginiana *(right)*

VIRGINIAN WITCH HAZEL, COMMON WITCH HAZEL

This species has an open, upright habit and grows to a height and spread of 12–20 ft (3.5–6 m) but can be readily adapted to tree-like form by training to a single trunk in early years. Small, fragrant, curled and twisted yellow flowers appear in autumn as the leaves fall. The dark green, broadly oval leaves turn a bright buttercup yellow in autumn. **ZONES 7–9.**

HEBE
VERONICA

The large genus *Veronica* used to be interpreted more broadly to include all these shrubby hebe species (native to New Zealand and nearby islands, with a couple in Chile). With over 100 species of evergreen shrubs, the hebes include many first-rate garden plants. They have neat, attractive leaves and often showy flower-spikes, which arise in the axils of the leaves, as in *Hebe* 'Wiri Joy', 'Autumn Beauty' and 'Pamela Joy'. There are 2 main groups: the broad-leafed hebes, fast-growing shrubs with pleasing foliage and abundant spikes of small flowers, ranging from white through pink to violet and blue over a long summer to autumn season; and the whipcord hebes with small leaves that give them the appearance of dwarf conifers, and white or pale mauve flowers.

CULTIVATION
Most hebes are best suited to temperate to warm climates. In warm climates they grow equally well in sun or shade; in cooler climates sun is preferred. They like moist but well-drained soil and the broad-leafed types benefit from a post-flowering trim. Many mountain whipcord hebes are tricky to grow at low altitudes. Propagate from cuttings in summer.

Hebe albicans *(left)*

This distinctive, frost-hardy species has $\frac{1}{2}$ in (12 mm) blue-gray leaves that are coated with a fine grayish, grape-like bloom. The leaves are tightly packed on the stems. This very neat plant grows to about 18 in (45 cm) high and wide, and rarely needs trimming. The flowers, which appear in early summer, are white with purple anthers and are carried in short spikes. **'Boulder Lake'** is a low, spreading cultivar. ZONES 8–10.

H

Hebe 'Alicia Amherst'
(left)

syn. *Hebe veitchii*

This robust, frost-hardy shrub, with a height and spread of 4 ft (1.2 m) has mid- to dark green leaves about 4 in (10 cm) long. From late summer to autumn racemes of violet-purple flowers appear. **ZONES 9–10.**

Hebe cupressoides
(center left)

This unusual, densely branched whipcord hebe comes from the South Island of New Zealand and may grow 3–6 ft (1–1.8 m) tall with a spread of up to 10 ft (3 m). It has tiny, $\frac{3}{4}$ in (18 mm), glaucous, cypress-like leaves and in summer bears small, pale lilac flowers that fade to white. It is resistant to both frost and dry conditions. **'Boughton Dome'** is a dwarf form with a more rounded appearance and a less glaucous tinge to the leaves. **ZONES 8–10.**

Hebe diosmifolia
(below right)

This densely foliaged, twiggy shrub grows 2–4 ft (0.6–1.2 m) high and 3–5 ft (1–1.5 m) wide. The dark green leaves are about $\frac{1}{2}$ in (12 mm) long. The branches tend to lie flat, creating a tiered effect. The pale mauve flowers, occurring from spring to autumn, are carried in short spikes near the branch tips. This usually compact species requires little trimming, but is short lived and best replaced after about 10 years. **ZONES 8–10.**

Hebe × franciscana 'Blue Gem' (left)
syn. Hebe latifolia

From summer to early winter, this spreading evergreen bears dense spikes of small, violet-pink flowers and has oblong, densely arranged, mid-green leaves. Frost hardy, it grows to a height of about 24 in (60 cm) with a spread of about 3 ft (1 m). ZONES 8–10.

Hebe 'Hagley Park' (center left)
syn. Hebe 'Lady Hagley'

This cultivar makes a small, low-growing shrublet with elliptic to ovate leaves that have a prominent midrib and seam outlined in black. The dainty flowers are pastel pink and appear in open, airy clusters. ZONES 8–10.

Hebe 'Hartii' (below)

This is a prostrate, spreading shrub to 4 in (10 cm) in height with a spread of up to 3 ft (1 m). It has ½ in (12 mm) lanceolate, glossy green leaves, tinged purple. It bears many pale, mauve flowers in summer. ZONES 8–10.

Hebe 'La Séduisante' (left)
syn. Hebe speciosa 'Ruddigore', H. s. 'Violacea'

This is a low, frost-hardy shrub 3–6 ft (1–1.8 m) in height with thick, narrow, glossy green, 3–4 in (8–10 cm) leaves. It bears 4 in (10 cm) spikes of violet-purple flowers in summer and intermittently through to late autumn. ZONES 8–10.

Hebe ochracea 'James Stirling' *(right)*

Hebe × lindsayi *(above)*

This hybrid is a 2 ft (60 cm) high and wide rounded bush with small, leathery oval leaves. From late spring it is smothered in spikes of small rose-pink flowers. It is a tough, easy-care bush that responds well to trimming after flowering and which can even be grown as a low hedge. A white-flowered form, **'Alba'**, is also available. **ZONES 9–11.**

Hebe 'Pamela Joy'
(right)

This rounded shrub presents its vibrant violet-purple flowers in compact spikes at the ends of the branches. The leaves are elliptic and mid-green. **ZONES 8–10.**

Hebe ochracea

A frost-hardy whipcord species with olive green to golden brown stems, *Hebe ochracea* is most commonly represented by **'James Stirling'**, a particularly bright golden cultivar. The shrub grows to about 18 in (45 cm) high and 3 ft (1 m) wide. The inflorescences of about 10 white flowers are rarely seen in cultivation. Do not prune this species unless absolutely necessary as it may lead to dieback. **ZONES 6–10.**

Hebe pinguifolia *(right)*

This variable and adaptable small shrub from the drier mountain districts of the South Island of New Zealand can grow to 3 ft (1 m) high and wide. The pale blue-green leaves are margined with red, and the white flowers are borne in small dense terminal spikes. It can tolerate a wide range of growing conditions and is frost hardy. **'Pagei'** is a low, spreading form with small, blue-gray leaves and many small white flowers in spring. It is an ideal rock garden plant. **ZONES 6–10.**

Hebe speciosa *(left)*
SHOWY HEBE

This evergreen, compact shrub grows 2–5 ft (0.6–1.5 m) high, and spreads to 4 ft (1.2 m) wide in a broad, bun shape. It has oval, glossy foliage and bears a profusion of reddish purple flowers in terminal clusters from early summer to late autumn. This species is more prone to wilt than other hebes. Many attractive cultivars exist, including **'Variegata'** with creamy white leaf margins; all tolerate some frost. **ZONES 9–10.**

H

Hebe 'Wiri Joy' *(left)*

This showy, large-flowered hybrid grows into a rounded shrub densely clothed with glossy oblong leaves. Purple-pink flowers appear in summer. **ZONES 8–10.**

Hebe 'Wiri Mist'
(left)

This low shrub grows to 18 in (45 cm) and can spread to 3 ft (1 m). It has thick, green leaves margined with yellow and is covered with white flowers towards the end of spring. **ZONES 8–10.**

HELIANTHEMUM
ROCK ROSE, SUN ROSE

Helianthemum means flower of sunshine, an appropriate name for flowers that only open in bright sunlight. Allied to *Cistus,* the genus contains over 100 species found on rocky and scrubby ground in temperate zones around the world. Sun roses are sturdy, short-lived, evergreen or semi-evergreen shrubs or subshrubs. Their bushy foliage ranges in color from silver to mid-green. There are many garden forms, mostly of low, spreading habit. Wild plants have flowers resembling 1 in (25 mm) wide wild roses, but garden forms can be anything from white through yellow and salmon-pink to red and orange, and some varieties have double flowers.

CULTIVATION
Plant in full sun in freely draining, coarse soil with a little peat or compost added during dry periods. As the flowers fade, they should be cut back lightly to encourage a second flush of bloom in autumn. Propagate from seed or cuttings.

H

Helianthemum 'Fire King' *(above)*

This cultivar is similar to *Helianthemum* 'Fire Dragon' but its flowers are a brighter orange. This plant forms low, spreading mounds of gray-green leaves. ZONES 6–10.

HELICHRYSUM
EVERLASTING, PAPER DAISY, STRAWFLOWER

As understood until recently, this was a genus of around 500 species of annuals, perennials and shrubs, their highest concentration being in southern Africa followed by Australia, with smaller numbers in the Mediterranean, west and central Asia, and New Zealand. Belonging to the daisy family, they all have flowerheads with no ray florets or 'petals' but instead papery, mostly whitish bracts that are long-lasting when dried, hence the common names. But study by botanists has shown this to be an unnatural group, and they have been busy carving off both large and small groups of species and renaming them as distinct genera. This study is ongoing, and many species still in *Helichrysum* will eventually be reclassified, particularly among the South African species. The 'true' helichrysums include the Mediterranean and Asian species and an uncertain number from southern Africa; some well-known Australasian species have been reclassified under genera such as *Bracteantha, Ozothamnus* and *Chrysocephalum.*

CULTIVATION
Most species will tolerate only light frosts and are best suited to mild climates with low summer humidity, but a few are more frost hardy. They require gritty, well-drained soil that is not too fertile and a warm, sunny position. Propagate from seed, cuttings, or rhizome divisions.

Helichrysum petiolare *(below left)* syn. *Helichrysum petiolatum* of gardens
LICORICE PLANT

This South African evergreen is an excellent foliage plant; its gray, heart-shaped leaves and its stems are covered with cobweb-like white hairs. It is a sprawling subshrub forming dense mounds 24 in (60 cm) or more high and 6 ft (1.8 m) or more wide, with new stems springing from a network of rhizomes. It is well adapted to sun or shade and to dry conditions. The flowers, only occasionally produced, are not showy. **'Limelight'** has pale chartreuse foliage, and **'Variegatum'** has a creamy variegation. Both of these cultivars do better in shade and are superb summer container plants in cold climates. ZONES 9–10.

Helichrysum splendidum *(above)*
syns *Helichrysum alveolatum, H. trilineatum*

This dense evergreen shrub occurs in the mountains of Africa from Ethiopia to the Cape. It grows to 5 ft (1.5 m) high and wide. It has crowded narrow leaves clothed in cobweb-like white hairs. Profuse small heads of golden-yellow flowers are borne from summer through autumn. Frost hardy, it should be kept compact with regular pruning. ZONES 7–10.

HETEROMELES
CALIFORNIA HOLLY, CHRISTMAS BERRY, TOYON

This genus consists of one species, an evergreen tall shrub or small tree that was formerly included in *Photinia*. Indigenous to the drier regions of California, it is often planted as an informal screen, and can be clipped to form a tall hedge. It grows to 30 ft (9 m). When young it can be pruned to maintain a single trunk if a tree form is desired. A member of the rose family, its name comes from the Greek words for 'different' and 'apple tree'.

CULTIVATION
Heteromeles arbutifolia needs full sun or part-shade and moderately fertile, well-drained soil. It is frost hardy, although in colder regions it needs protection. Propagate from cuttings in summer or seed in autumn.

Heteromeles arbutifolia *(above)*
syn. *Photinia arbutifolia*

This shrub or tree has thick, leathery, glossy dark green leaves with quite sharply toothed margins. The flattened heads of flowers appear in summer. They are followed by bright red berries that persist, as they are not eaten by birds, until winter in its native habitat. ZONES 9–11.

HIBISCUS

While the genus name conjures up the innumerable cultivars of *Hibiscus rosa-sinensis*, the genus of around 220 species is quite diverse, including hot-climate evergreen shrubs and small trees and also a few deciduous, temperate-zone shrubs and some annuals and perennials. The leaves are mostly toothed or lobed and the flowers, borne singly or in terminal spikes, are of characteristic shape with a funnel of 5 overlapping petals and a central column of fused stamens.

CULTIVATION

Easy to grow, the shrubby species thrive in sun and slightly acid, well-drained soil. Water regularly and feed during the flowering period. Trim after flowering to maintain shape. Propagate from seed or cuttings or by division, depending on the species. Check for aphids, mealybugs and white fly. The *H. rosa-sinensis* cultivars make greenhouse subjects in frosty climates, and compact-growing cultivars are gaining popularity as house plants.

H

Hibiscus arnottianus (above)

This shrub of variable size, up to 20 ft (6 m), has long, arching branches covered with mid-green leaves and lightly scented, white single flowers with 5 petals surrounding a central red column. It is a warm-climate shrub suited to full sun; it can stand neglect, but responds well to regular watering and feeding. **'Wilder's White'** is a free-flowering cultivar now regarded as belonging to this species rather than to *Hibiscus rosa-sinensis*. ZONES 9–11.

Hibiscus coccineus (above)

This tall shrubby perennial species from the marshes of Georgia and Florida in the USA has distinctively shaped petals, each petal narrowing at the base to a slender basal stalk. The elegant flowers, up to 8 in (20 cm) wide, also have the long column of stamens typical of many hibiscus, which dusts the head and back of birds with pollen. ZONES 7–11.

Hibiscus mutabilis *(left)*

CONFEDERATE ROSE, COTTON ROSE

A multi-branched shrub or small deciduous tree with a low-branching habit, the cotton rose comes from China and grows to about 12 ft (3.5 m) tall and almost as wide. The large flowers open white and age from pale pink to deep pink; they appear in autumn and are held among the felty, multi-lobed leaves. **'Plenus'**, with its double flowers, is the most commonly grown cultivar. ZONES 8–10.

Hibiscus rosa-sinensis *(above left)*

CHINESE HIBISCUS, RED HIBISCUS, SHOEFLOWER

The name shoeflower is Jamaican, from the un-romantic use of crushed flowers to polish black shoes. The species itself is of ancient hybrid origin from the Indian Ocean region and is a glossy leafed evergreen shrub, sometimes as much as 15 ft (4.5 m) high and wide, with blood red flowers borne just about all year. It is less often seen than its numerous garden cultivars, some pure bred and others, like the enormous bloom-ing **Hawaiian Hybrids**, carrying the genes of other species. These plants grow 3–10 ft (1–3 m) high, and the flowers can be 5-petalled singles, semi-double or fully double, the colors ranging from white through pinks to red; the Hawaiian Hybrids offer yellow, coral and orange, often with 2 or 3 shades in each flower. The flowers range upwards in size from about 5 in (12 cm): some of the Hawaiian hybrids are as large as dinner plates. Each flower only lasts a day, opening in the morn-ing and withering by evening, but they appear in long succession as long as the weather is warm.

Hibiscus rosa-sinensis, Hawaiian Hybrid cultivars *(above center & above right)*

Hibiscus rosa-sinensis 'Surfrider' *(below)*

All the *Hibiscus rosa-sinensis* cultivars like a frost-free climate. They include **'Surfrider'** with single flowers that are deep orange with a red center; **'Fiesta'** with dark apricot flowers with red and white centers; **'Covakanic'** with flowers in beauti-ful varying tones of orange and apricot; as well as **'Apple Blossom'**, **'Cooperi'**, **'Madonna'** and **'Sabrina'**. ZONES 10–12.

H

Hibiscus schizopetalus (right)

From tropical Africa, this evergreen shrub grows
to 12 ft (3.5 m) with rounded, toothed, deep
green leaves and long-stemmed, pendulous, scarlet flowers; their petals are recurved and much
cut, and the staminal column hangs as though on
a silken thread. Pruning is not necessary as its
natural, somewhat slender, drooping habit is part
of this plant's charm. This species is closely allied
to *Hibiscus rosa-sinensis* and has interbred with it.
ZONES 10–11.

Hibiscus syriacus

BLUE HIBISCUS, ROSE OF SHARON

This upright, deciduous shrub (evergreen in
warmer climates) from temperate Asia is the most
frost hardy of the genus. It flowers freely in summer in varying shades of white, pink, soft red,
mauve and violet blue. The single, semi-double
and double flowers are bell-shaped and are borne
in the axils of the leaves. It has small, hairless
leaves and grows to 12 ft (3.5 m) tall with a spread
of 3–6 ft (1–1.8 m). Prune to shape in the first 2
years of growth, trimming lightly thereafter to
maintain compact form. Popular cultivars include
'Ardens' with large, mauve flowers with crimson
centers; 'Blue Bird' with single, violet blue flowers
with red centers; 'Diana' with broad, pure white
flowers; and 'Woodbridge' with 2-toned pink
blooms at least 4 in (10 cm) across. ZONES 5–10.

Hibiscus syriacus 'Diana' (right)
Hibiscus syriacus cultivar (below left)
Hibiscus syriacus 'Blue Bird' (below center)
Hibiscus syriacus 'Woodbridge' (below right)

HIPPOPHAË

These 3 species of thorny, deciduous shrubs and trees are valued for their toughness and their showy autumn berries. Both male and female plants must be grown together to obtain the fruit. Inconspicuous flowers appear in spring. Indigenous to cold-climate regions of Asia and northern Europe, they are found along the coast or river banks and in sandy woodlands. They are wind and salt resistant and make excellent hedges for coastal areas.

CULTIVATION
Species of *Hippophaë* grow best in full sun and tolerate dry or very sandy soil. Propagation is from seed in autumn or from cuttings in summer.

Hippophaë rhamnoides (left)
SEA BUCKTHORN

Growing to a height and spread of about 20 ft (6 m) with a bushy, arching habit, this shrub or small tree has very narrow, gray-green leaves with paler undersides. Insignificant, yellowish flowers appear in clusters in spring, before the leaves. The bright orange berries are borne in dense clusters on the shoots of female plants and usually persist through winter.
ZONES 2–9.

HOHERIA

This genus consists of 5 species of evergreen and deciduous small trees native to the forests of New Zealand. Of slender, upright habit, they are grown for their showy clusters of faintly perfumed white flowers which appear in summer and autumn. Plants can be anywhere between 20–50 ft (6–15 m) high and flowering is usually followed by the appearance of fruit capsules.

CULTIVATION
Happiest in warm-temperate climates with high summer rainfall, these species grow in sun or semi-shade in fertile, well-drained soil. Prune straggly plants by about one-third in winter; all plants benefit from a light annual pruning of the outer branches to maintain a tidy shape and abundant foliage. Propagate from seed in autumn or from cuttings in summer.

H

Hoheria lyallii *(above)*
syn. *Plagianthus lyallii*
LACEBARK

This deciduous tree from New Zealand can grow to 20 ft (6 m) tall. It has thick, fibrous bark, which gives it its common name. The toothed, oblong leaves are gray-green with a felty white underside; they are up to 4 in (10 cm) long. Fragrant white flowers appear in late summer and are followed by leathery, capsular fruit. The lacebark prefers a sunny position and soil rich in humus; it tolerates alkaline soil. ZONES 7–10.

H

Hoheria populnea *(left)*

HOUHERE, NEW ZEALAND LACEBARK

This fast-growing evergreen tree forms a
slender dome about 20 ft (6 m) high.
Glistening white, 5-petalled flowers with
golden yellow stamens are borne in profuse clusters on young shoots in late
summer and early autumn; winged fruit
capsules follow. The glossy, toothed
leaves resemble those of a poplar. Mature trees have distinctive, often flaky,
pale brown and white bark. **ZONES 9–11.**

Hoheria sexstylosa *(left)*

RIBBONWOOD

Narrowly conical in habit, this evergreen
tree grows to 20 ft (6 m) tall; it has an
erect trunk and main branches with
drooping branchlets. The leaves are
bright green and oval, with sharply
toothed margins. Small clusters of
sweetly fragrant star-shaped white flowers
are borne abundantly in late summer
and autumn, followed by small, brown,
winged fruit capsules. When young the
plant is bushy and has more deeply
toothed leaves. **ZONES 7–10.**

HOVENIA

This genus consists of 2 species of deciduous trees from Asia, only one of which is widely grown. They have small fragrant yellow flowers and small, spherical, capsular fruits held in branched stalks which become thick and fleshy. The leaves are toothed and oval to heart-shaped.

CULTIVATION
Graceful trees for temperate-climate gardens, they prefer full sun and well-drained, reasonably fertile soil. Protect from dry winds. Propagate from fresh seed in autumn or from cuttings in summer. Where wood is not fully ripened, check for coral spot.

H

Hovenia dulcis (left)
JAPANESE RAISIN TREE

Indigenous to China and Japan, this tree grows to 50 ft (15 m). Its large, heart-shaped leaves produce brilliant autumn hues. The summer flowers are inconspicuous and lightly fragrant and are borne in clusters on thick stalks. As the small capsular fruit ripen, the stalks become fleshy and are also edible; they have a sweet taste like raisins. **ZONES 8–10.**

HYDRANGEA

These deciduous or evergreen shrubs, climbers and sometimes
small trees occur over a wide area of temperate Asia and North
and South America. Most species have large oval leaves with serrated edges; some develop good autumn foliage color. The flower
clusters contain tiny fertile blooms and showy sterile ones with
4 petal-like sepals. Although most species produce panicles of
flowers with few sterile flowers, many cultivated forms have heads
composed almost entirely of sterile flowers and are called by
gardeners mobcaps, mopheads or hortensias (for *Hydrangea
macrophylla* cultivars only). Intermediate forms with a ring of
sterile flowers surrounding fertile flowers are called lacecaps.
Flower color may vary with the acidity or alkalinity of the soil:
blue blooms in acid soil, pink or red in alkaline; white cultivars do
not change. In some but not all cultivars the old flowers gradually
fade to shades of green and pink, regardless of soil type.

CULTIVATION
Except in cool, moist climates, hydrangeas need shade or part-
shade or both leaves and flowers will scorch; while soil should be
constantly moist and rich in humus, it should be well drained.
They are best pruned immediately after flowering by cutting out
all stems that have just flowered and leaving the others alone.
Propagate from cuttings or seed. Check regularly for powdery mildew, leaf spot, honey fungus and aphids, scale insects and spider
mites.

Hydrangea arborescens
'Grandiflora' *(left)*

Hydrangea arborescens
SNOWHILL HYDRANGEA, SMOOTH HYDRANGEA

This frost-hardy, shade-loving shrub from eastern
USA grows 6–8 ft (1.8–2.4 m) tall, usually with a
greater spread. It forms a lax mound of many
suckering stems which are clothed in big, simple,
serrated leaves up to 6 in (15 cm) long. Hemispherical heads of many small white flowers are
produced in late spring and summer; these turn
green as they age. **'Grandiflora'** is commonly sold
but **'Annabelle'** is an improved variety with bigger blooms that are produced about 2 weeks later.
ZONES 6–9.

Hydrangea aspera
(right)

This species occurs naturally over much of southern and eastern Asia, showing much variation in the wild. In cultivation it grows to around 10 ft (3 m) high and wide. Its serrated-edged leaves vary from narrow to oval, and are 3–10 in (8–25 cm) long. The large flowerheads that occur in summer are lacecap style with pale, sterile flowers and tiny, purplish blue, fertile flowers. The flower color varies little with soil type. The **Villosa Group** bear broad heads of blue or purple flowers in the center of the shrubs and larger white flowers towards the periphery. Deciduous and upright, they grow to a height and spread of 10 ft (3 m) and are very frost hardy. ZONES 7–10.

Hydrangea heteromalla

Growing to a height of around 10 ft (3 m), this deciduous shrub from western China and Tibet produces many stems from ground level to form a loose, rounded shrub. The leaves are broadly lanceolate or narrowly ovate, pointy and toothed along their edges. The summer flowers are of the lacecap variety with a cluster of tiny fertile flowers surrounded by bigger, more showy infertile, white or pink blooms. The cultivar **'Bretschneideri'** is shrubbier than the species and has narrower leaves, peeling, reddish brown bark and flatter flower sprays. ZONES 6–9.

Hydrangea heteromalla 'Bretschneideri' (above)

H

Hydrangea macrophylla 'Altona' *(above)*
Hydrangea macrophylla 'Libelle' *(top right)*
Hydrangea macrophylla 'Geoffrey Chadbund'
(left)

Hydrangea macrophylla *(top left)*

BIGLEAF HYDRANGEA, GARDEN HYDRANGEA

This species in its typical wild form comes from Japan and is rather rare in cultivation. The name also covers a large race of garden varieties derived from it, though in fact many of these may have originated as hybrids between *Hydrangea macrophylla* and *H. aspera*. The major group known as 'hortensias' (once *H. hortensia)* have flowerheads of the 'mophead' type, with densely massed sterile florets. A smaller group are the 'lacecaps'; examples are **'Blue Sky'** and **'Blue Wave'.** There are many named cultivars, ranging in growth from less than 3 ft (1 m) tall and wide

to twice that size; 5 ft (1.5 m) is the average. As a rule, the deeper the color the smaller the plant. **'Geoffrey Chadbund'** is a lacecap form with rich, bright red flowers; **'Libelle'** (also a lacecap) has extra large, pure white infertile flowers that give the head a crowded, full look; **'Altona'** is a hortensia form with flowers that vary from deep pink to purplish blue; **'Générale Vicomtesse de Vibraye'** (also a hortensia) bears large flowerheads in pink or pale blue. **'Lilacina'** (lacecap) has pink flowers that may be tinged purple; **'Shower'** (lacecap) produces elegant heads of clear, hot pink; **'Sir Joseph Banks'** (hortensia) is pink flowered; **'Sunset'** (lacecap) is a big, vigorous shrub, which often grows to over 5 ft (1.5 m) across and produces many heads of rich pinkish scarlet blooms; **'Taube'** is similar to 'Sunset' but does not grow quite as large and has softer pink blooms; and **Veitchii'** (lacecap) bears flowers that open white but turn soft pink as they age. ZONES 6–10.

Hydrangea macrophylla 'Veitchii' *(above)*
Hydrangea macrophylla 'Taube' *(top)*

Hydrangea paniculata *(center right)*
PANICLE HYDRANGEA

This large deciduous shrub from China and Japan
grows to 15 ft (4.5 m) or more, with a broad,
dome-shaped crown the same in width. It has
large, oval, dark green leaves and in mid-summer
bears small cream, fertile flowers and larger flat,
creamy white, sterile flowers that turn rose purple
as they age. Prune back hard in late winter or
spring for larger flowerheads. **'Grandiflora'** is the
form most commonly grown. **'Tardiva'** does not
flower until autumn. ZONES 5–9.

Hydrangea paniculata
'Grandiflora' *(above)*

H

H

Hydrangea quercifolia *(above)*

OAK-LEAF HYDRANGEA

Native to the USA, this deciduous shrub grows to
a height of 6–8 ft (1.8–2.4 m), spreading by
stolons to 12 ft (3.5 m) or more. Deeply lobed,
dark green leaves turn orange-scarlet in autumn.
The flowers, borne from mid-summer to mid-
autumn, are a mixture of small, fertile and sterile
flowers. The white, sterile flowers fade to pink
and violet. It performs best in dappled shade.
ZONES 5–9.

Hydrangea serrata
'Bluebird' *(below)*

Hydrangea serrata

This species, a lacecap
style hydrangea, is very
closely allied to
Hydrangea macrophylla
and sometimes in-
cluded there as a sub-
species. It forms a
rounded shrub up to
5 ft (1.5 m) tall with a
similar spread. The
leaves are more nar-
rowly ovate than
H. macrophylla and are
prominently toothed.
'Bluebird' is typical of
the species with wide,
flattish flowerheads
over most of summer.
ZONES 6–10.

HYMENOSPORUM
AUSTRALIAN FRANGIPANI, SWEETSHADE

This genus consists of a single species of evergreen tree originating in the subtropical rainforests of east coast Australia and New Guinea. It has showy tubular flowers and oval to oblong, glossy leaves. The name comes from the Greek *hymen*, a membrane, and *sporos*, a seed, referring to the winged seeds.

CULTIVATION
A relatively fast-growing tree, it adapts to most soil types but prefers moist, humus-rich soil where it is less likely to be checked by long dry spells. It flowers best in a sheltered position in full sun, but will tolerate some shade. Propagation is easy from seed or from cuttings.

Hymenosporum flavum *(above)*

Growing to 30 ft (9 m), taller in the wild, this tree has a straight, smooth trunk and open, columnar shape, with widely spaced horizontal branches and dark green glossy leaves clustered towards the ends. In spring it bears clusters of very fragrant cream flowers that age over several days to deep golden yellow. They are followed by flattish seed pods with small, winged seeds. ZONES 9–11.

HYPERICUM
ST JOHN'S WORT

This is a large and varied genus of 400 species of annuals, perennials, shrubs and a few small trees, some evergreen but mostly deciduous, grown for their showy flowers in shades of yellow which have a central mass of prominent golden stamens. They are found throughout the world in a broad range of habitats. Species range in size from tiny perennials for rockeries to plants over 10 ft (3 m) tall.

CULTIVATION
Mostly cool-climate plants, they prefer full sun but will tolerate some shade. They do best in fertile, well-drained soil, with plentiful water in late spring and summer. Remove seed capsules after flowering and prune in winter to maintain a rounded shape. Cultivars are propagated from cuttings in summer, and species from seed in autumn or from cuttings in summer. Some species are susceptible to rust.

Hypericum beanii
'Gold Cup' *(below left)*

Hypericum beanii

A vigorous, evergreen shrub from western China, this variable species may grow to 6 ft (1.8 m) tall with dense, arching branches. The mid-green leaves are usually elliptical and paler beneath. Large, star-shaped, golden yellow flowers with showy stamens appear in summer. This species is often used for bank retention. **'Gold Cup'** (syn. *Hypericum* × *cyathiflorum* 'Gold Cup') grows to 5 ft (1.5 m) tall and produces 2 in (5 cm) wide, cup-shaped, golden yellow flowers in summer. **ZONES 7–10.**

Hypericum frondosum *(above)*
GOLDEN ST JOHN'S WORT

A rounded deciduous shrub from the southeastern States of the USA, golden St John's wort grows up to 4 ft (1.2 m) tall with a similar spread. The many stems are upright and densely clothed with curving, oblong leaves that are a blue-green color with a powdery bloom. In summer clusters of showy, bright yellow flowers are produced. The cultivar **'Sunburst'** is an improvement on the species and worth seeking out. **ZONES 5–10.**

Hypericum 'Hidcote' *(right)*

This dense bushy shrub reaches 4 ft (1.2 m) in
height and has a spread of 5 ft (1.5 m). It bears
large, cup-shaped, 2½ in (6 cm) golden-yellow
flowers from mid-summer to early autumn and
has lance-shaped, dark green leaves. ZONES 7–10.

Hypericum monogynum *(center right)*
syn. *Hypericum chinense*

This long-flowering, semi-evergreen shrub is
from China, Japan and Taiwan. It grows to 5 ft
(1.5 m) tall and 18 in (45 cm) wide. There is also a
low-growing form. The thick, rounded, leathery
leaves are mid-green on their upper surface, paler
beneath. Lemon or golden-yellow, star-shaped
summer flowers, 2½ in (6 cm) across, crowd
towards the outer parts of the plant; they are followed by capsular fruit. ZONES 9–10.

Hypericum × moserianum

GOLD FLOWER

This species bears star-shaped, bright yellow
flowers. '**Tricolor**', with its green, cream and pink
leaves, is one of the most desirable variegated
shrubs; it grows 24–36 in (60–90 cm) tall and
rather wider, bearing modest bowl-shaped flowers
from summer to autumn. ZONES 7–10.

Hypericum × moserianum 'Tricolor' *(right)*

Hypericum 'Rowallane' *(below)*

This semi-evergreen, arching shrub bears large,
bowl-shaped, deep golden-yellow flowers from
mid-summer to autumn. The oval leaves are a
rich green. It reaches a height and spread of 5 ft
(1.5 m). ZONES 8–10.

H

I J K

IBERIS

This genus consists of around 50 species of annuals, perennials and evergreen subshrubs, which are mainly from southern Europe, northern Africa and western Asia. Highly regarded as decorative plants they are excellent for rock gardens, bedding and borders. The showy flowers are borne in either flattish heads in colors of white, red and purple, or in erect racemes of pure white.

CULTIVATION
Fully to marginally frost hardy, they require a warm, sunny position and a well-drained, light soil, preferably with added lime or dolomite. Propagation is from seed in spring or autumn (they may self-sow, but are unlikely to become invasive) or from cuttings in summer.

Iberis gibraltarica *(above)*
GIBRALTAR CANDYTUFT

This species, a sprawling, shrubby perennial from Gibraltar and southern Spain grows to 12 in (30 cm) in height. It has narrow, dark green leaves and produces clusters of pink- or red-tinged white flowers in summer. Although normally frost hardy, it is susceptible to damage when frost is combined with wet winter conditions. ZONES 7–11.

IDESIA
WONDER TREE, LIGIRI

This genus consists of one species of deciduous tree. Indigenous to central and western China, Korea, Japan and neighboring islands, it is grown for its striking foliage and fruit, and makes a handsome shade tree. To obtain the fruit, both male and female plants are needed.

CULTIVATION
Grow in sun or part-shade. Moderately fertile, moist but well-drained neutral to acid soil and a cool to warm-temperate climate are best. Prune when young to establish a single main trunk and a shapely crown. Propagate from seed in autumn or cuttings in summer.

Idesia polycarpa
(right)

This fast-growing, shapely tree grows to a height of 40 ft (12 m), with a broad crown spreading to 20 ft (6 m). It has large heart-shaped, red-stalked dark green leaves; fragrant, greenish flowers are borne in spring and summer. *Idesia polycarpa* is frost hardy, particularly after long, hot summers which promote well-ripened wood. Female plants produce large hanging clusters of pea-sized berries that turn deep red in autumn. ZONES 6–10.

ILEX
HOLLY

The 400 or so evergreen and deciduous trees and shrubs that make up this large genus come mostly from temperate regions of the northern hemisphere. They are grown for their foliage and clusters of small glossy berries. Hollies make excellent hedges, border plants, tub plants or screens for privacy. Male and female plants must be grown together to obtain the red, yellow or black berries in summer, autumn or winter. Clusters of small, greenish white flowers precede them.

CULTIVATION
Hollies grow well in deep, friable, well-drained soils with a high organic content. They are fully to marginally frost hardy. An open, sunny position is best in cool climates. Water in hot, dry summers. Hollies do not like transplanting. Prune carefully in spring to check vigorous growth. Propagate from seed or cuttings. Check for signs of holly aphid and holly leaf miner.

Ilex × *altaclerensis*
(above)

HIGHCLERE HOLLY

This group of evergreen hybrid hollies, reaching a height of about 50 ft (15 m), has larger, variable leaves and larger flowers and berries than the English holly (*Ilex aquifolium*). Its many cultivars include **'Belgica Aurea'** (syn. 'Silver Sentinel'), an upright female with few-spined leaves that have gray-green centers and irregular yellow margins; **'Camelliifolia'**, a

Ilex altaclarensis
'Lawsoniana' *(above)*

female with purple-tinged shoots, leaf stems and petal bases, larger berries and long leaves with only a few spines; **'Golden King'**, a frost-hardy female, with smooth-edged, deep green leaves with yellow margins, which makes an excellent hedge (requires pollination with a male cultivar such as **'Silver Queen'**, a cultivar of *I. aquifolium*, to bear its red berries); **'Hendersonii'**, a compact female with long-lasting red berries and dull green foliage; **'Hodginsii'**, a robust male clone with dark purple twigs and glossy, very deep green foliage; **'Lawsoniana'** a sport of 'Hendersonii', which has good crops of red berries and sparsely spined leaves with irregular light green and gold centers; and **'Wilsonii'**, a moderately frost-hardy female growing to 20 ft (6 m) with a spread of 12 ft (3.5 m), broad, spiny, dark green leaves and masses of large scarlet fruits which make it good for hedging. Able to resist pollution and harsh coastal conditions, this is a useful plant for industrial and maritime areas. ZONES 6–10.

Ilex aquifolium (right)
ENGLISH HOLLY

Native to Europe, North Africa and western Asia, this evergreen is a popular Christmas decoration in the northern hemisphere with its glossy, spiny-edged dark green leaves and bright red winter berries. It reaches 40 ft (12 m) with a spread of about 15 ft (4.5 m) or more and has an erect, branching habit. Commonly grown cultivars include **'Amber'**, which has lovely yellow fruit and almost thornless leaves; **'Angustifolia'**, which has green or purple twigs and lanceolate dark green foliage with a neat pyramidal shape; **'Aurea Marginata'**, a small, bushy, silver holly with yellow margins on its spiny foliage and red berries on the female form; **'Ferox'**, the hedgehog holly, a male with more compact growth to 20 ft (6 m) and leaves with spines over their entire surface; **'Ferox Argentea'**, a male with purple twigs and small, cream-edged dark green leaves; **'Golden Milkboy'**, with variegated golden leaves; **'Golden Queen'**, a dense male clone with spiny, dark green leaves with pale green and gray shading and substantial yellow margins; **'Handsworth New Silver'**, a free-fruiting clone whose leaves have a creamy white margin while its twigs are purple; **'J. C. van Tol'**, which grows to 15 ft (4.5 m) with dark green, almost spineless leaves and crimson berries; **'Madame Briot'**, a female clone with large, strongly spined, glossy green leaves, broadly edged in gold, and scarlet berries; **'Pyramidalis'**, a good fruit-bearing female clone with a conical habit when young, broadening with age; **'Pyramidalis Fructu Luteo'**, much the same as the previous clone, but with yellow fruit; **'Silver Milkmaid'**, with scarlet fruit and green-edged golden leaves that are prone to revert to green and must be cut out if they do so; and **'Silver Queen'**, with leaves that are pink when young, maturing to a very dark green in the middle with creamy white margins and gray-green in between. **'Ovata Aurea'** has purple stems and leaves with gold margins. ZONES 6–10.

Ilex aquifolium 'Amber' *(center)*

Ilex aquifolium 'Ferox Argentea' *(right)*

Ilex aquifolium 'Golden Queen' *(top)*

Ilex aquifolium 'Pyramidalis'
(above left)

Ilex aquifolium 'Silver Milkmaid'
(above right)

Ilex aquifolium 'Silver Queen' *(left)*

Ilex × aquipernyi

This hybrid between *Ilex aquifolium* and *I. pernyi* is a conical, evergreen small tree. It grows to 20 ft (6 m), with a spread of 12 ft (3.5 m). It has glossy, dark green spiny leaves and bears red fruit. **'Meschick'** colors a pinkish bronze. **ZONES 6–10.**

Ilex × aquipernyi
'Meschick' *(right)*

Ilex cornuta *(left)*
CHINESE HOLLY

Self-fertile and well suited to mild-winter climates, this fully frost-hardy, dense, rounded shrub from China grows to 12 ft (3.5 m) with a spread of 15 ft (4.5 m). The thick glossy leaves are almost rectangular, with spiny points; the berries, while not as profuse as on English holly, are larger and borne throughout summer. **ZONES 6–10.**

Ilex crenata *(left)*
JAPANESE HOLLY

From Japan, this frost-hardy, compact, evergreen shrub has stiff branches, small scalloped leaves, dull white flowers and glossy black berries. Often used for hedges and topiary, it can grow to 15 ft (4.5 m) with a spread of 10 ft (3 m), but is usually smaller. Cultivars include **'Convexa'**, with almost spineless, glossy black-green leaves and purplish stems; **'Golden Gem'**, a compact but rarely flowering shrub, with soft yellow foliage; **'Green Lustre'**, a compact male shrub with very dark green leaves and no fruit; **'Helleri'**, a female clone of spreading habit that can reach 5 ft (1.5 m) in height and spread, with sparsely spined leaves and black fruit; and **'Schwoebel's Compact'**, a low-spreading dwarf form to 3 ft (1 m) tall. Variegated or pale-leafed forms do best in full sun; green-leafed forms do well in partial shade. **'Microphylla'** has narrow leaves and an upright growth habit. It can develop into a small tree to 10 ft (3 m) tall. **ZONES 6–10.**

Ilex crenata 'Convexa' *(left)*

Ilex crenata 'Golden Gem' *(above)*

Ilex crenata 'Microphylla' *(left)*

Ilex glabra 'Compacta' *(bottom left)*

Ilex glabra

INKBERRY

An evergreen from eastern North America, this erect shrub reaches 10 ft (3 m) tall and has narrow, deep green leaves; glossy black fruit follow the inconspicuous white flowers. Cultivars include **'Compacta'** and **'Nordic'**, both ideal for hedging; and **'Ivory Queen'**, a white-berried form. It can be propagated from seed, but germination is slow; cuttings, taken in late summer, are faster and more reliable. The species is surface rooting and easily damaged by digging around its base. ZONES 3–9.

Ilex × meserveae
'Blue Angel' *(right)*

Ilex × meserveae
'Blue Prince' *(below)*

Ilex × meserveae
MESERVE HYBRID HOLLY

This group of hybrids was derived from *Ilex aquifolium* and *I. rugosa*. It is noted for the bluish green foliage, purple stems, red berries and frost hardiness of its members. Most have a dense, pyramidal shape and make attractive, strong-growing hedges. The cultivars **'Blue Girl'**, **'Blue Boy'** and **'Blue Angel'** are the most commonly available. Others include **'Blue Prince'**, a male plant of spreading habit which grows to 10 ft (3 m) in height and spread, and has glossy bright green leaves; and **'Blue Princess'**, with extra glossy foliage and very abundant red berries on a shrub up to 10 ft (3 m) tall. ZONES 5–9.

Ilex opaca *(above)*
AMERICAN HOLLY

The best known American species, this evergreen tree grows to a height and spread of about 30 ft (9 m); it has an erect habit and produces red berries in winter. The leaves are dull green above and yellowish underneath, with spiny or smooth edges. It prefers a sunny position and acid soil, and does not do well near the sea. ZONES 5–10.

Ilex pernyi (above)
PERNY'S HOLLY

From central and western China, this densely branched evergreen tree was named after the French missionary Paul Perny. It grows to a height of 30 ft (9 m), with distinctive, diamond-shaped, triangular-spined leaves and oval red berries. The flowers are yellowish. This species is very frost hardy, but does not tolerate dry conditions; water well in summer. ZONES 5–10.

Ilex verticillata (left)
WINTERBERRY, BLACK ALDER, CORAL BERRY

From eastern USA, this deciduous shrub grows 6–10 ft (1.8–3 m) high and has a spread of 4–10 ft (1.2–3 m). The toothed leaves are purple-tinged in spring and turn yellow in autumn. The bright red berries stay on the bare branches for a long period, persisting until spring. This shrub tolerates wet conditions. Cultivars include '**Cacapon**', a female which produces abundant berries when grown with a male; '**Nana**' (syn. 'Red Sprite'), a dwarf female which reaches 4 ft (1.2 m) tall and has a spread of 5 ft (1.5 m); and '**Winter Red**', an extra vigorous female with a height and spread of 10 ft (3 m) and good crops of bright red berries when grown with a male plant. ZONES 3–9.

ILLICIUM

This interesting genus originates from the temperate to sub-tropical regions of East Asia and the Americas. It contains about 40 frost-hardy evergreen shrubs and small trees, grown for their handsome foliage and fragrant flowers. The flowers are not unlike magnolias, to which the genus is related closely enough to have been included, at one time, in the family Magnoliaceae. The blooms are followed by distinctive woody fruit shaped like 8-pointed stars, each lobe containing a seed. The largest species, *Illicium verum*, is the source of star anise, a spice much used in Chinese cooking. The name *Illicium* itself comes from a Latin word meaning 'alluring', and the plants have an especially allur-ing fragrance.

CULTIVATION

Moderately to marginally frost hardy, they grow best in part-shade or shade. They prefer moist, sandy, lime-free soil with added leafmould. Propagate from cuttings in summer or by layering in autumn.

Illicium anisatum
(left)
syn. *Illicium religiosum*

FALSE ANISE, JAPANESE ANISE TREE

Notable for its aromatic bark, which was used for incense in Japan and China, this moderately frost-hardy species grows slowly to a height and spread of 20 ft (6 m) and has a conical form. The daphne-like leaves are aromatic and glossy dark green, and the fragrant greenish yellow, many-petalled flowers are borne in mid-spring. The fruit are poisonous if eaten in quantity so do not use in cooking. *Illicium anisatum* prefers a sheltered position. ZONES 8–11.

INDIGOFERA

More than 700 species of annuals, perennials, shrubs and small trees make up this large leguminous genus. Mostly from tropical and subtropical regions, species are found in both hemispheres. Cultivated species are generally subshrubs or small, deciduous, woody plants with smallish pinnate leaves and panicles of pea-like flowers, usually in summer.

CULTIVATION

Frost-tender to moderately frost hardy, they prefer light, moist, well-drained soil in sun or part-shade. Propagate from seed in autumn or cuttings or basal suckers in summer.

Indigofera australis *(right)*

AUSTRALIAN INDIGO

Native to Australia, this elegant, spreading shrub grows to a height and spread of 6 ft (1.8 m); it has blue-gray leaves divided into leaflets and is moderately frost hardy. It bears small, mauve-pink flowers in long heads from winter to summer, followed by brown pods. **ZONES 9–11.**

Indigofera decora 'Alba' *(below)*

Indigofera decora

syn. *Indigofera incarnata*

This bushy deciduous shrub from China and Japan grows to 24 in (60 cm) and spreads to 3 ft (1 m); wider in mild climates. Moderately frost hardy, stems may die back to ground level, but the plant usually shoots again from the rootstock. The glossy, dark green, pinnate leaves, up to 10 in (25 cm) long, are composed of 7 to 13 oval leaflets. Long wisteria-like spikes of mauve-pink pea-shaped flowers appear through the warmer months. The cultivar **'Alba'** is a white-flowering form. **ZONES 7–11.**

IOCHROMA

Members of the nightshade family, these brittle-wooded, tropical and subtropical, evergreen shrubs from Central and South America are suited to warm, humid climates. Usually erect, with softwooded, arching branches, clusters of long tubular blue, purple, red or white flowers appear through summer and autumn. They are suitable for the garden, the greenhouse or as potted plants.

CULTIVATION

These frost-tender plants need full sun to part-shade and fertile, well-drained soil. In the garden, a sheltered position is best for protection from wind. Young plants can be pruned lightly to make them bushy, and flowered stems should be cut back heavily in early spring. Propagate from cuttings or seed. Potted plants should be watered well in summer. They may be prone to attack from white fly and spider mites.

Iochroma cyaneum (right)
syns *Iochroma tubulosum, I. lanceolatum*
VIOLET TUBEFLOWER

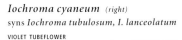

This fast-growing, semi-erect shrub grows to 10 ft (3 m) high with a spread of 5 ft (1.5 m). *Iochroma cyaneum* brings a deep purple accent to the warm-climate garden; it can be grown in a greenhouse in cooler areas. It has gray-green felty leaves; deep purple-blue flowers are borne in large pendent clusters through summer and autumn. Prune to shape in early spring. **ZONES 9–11.**

Iochroma grandiflorum (right)

Indigenous to Ecuador, this shrub or small tree grows 10–20 ft (3–6 m) high and 6–12 ft (1.8–3.5 m) wide. Its soft, deep green, pointed oval leaves are up to 8 in (20 cm) long and are slightly downy when young. The flowers, borne in late summer and autumn, are long, pendent, bright purple tubes with widely flared mouths. Pulpy, purplish green, berry-like fruit follow. **ZONES 9–12.**

ISOPLEXIS

This is a small genus of 3 species of soft-wooded evergreen
subshrubs, native to Madeira and the Canary Islands, which
are related to foxgloves *(Digitalis)*. They are under pressure in
their native habitat, as is much of the world's island flora. They
are showy plants suitable for shrub borders in virtually frost-free
climates.

CULTIVATION

Although marginally frost hardy to frost tender, these are reasonably undemanding plants. They prefer a well-drained soil and
must be adequately watered in summer. Plant in sun or part-
shade and regularly remove any spent flower spikes. Propagation
is usually from seed in spring, although cuttings taken in summer will also give good results.

Isoplexis canariensis *(left)*

This is the showiest
species in the genus
and comes from
Tenerife in the Canary
Islands. Frost-tender, it
is an erect shrub which
grows to 5 ft (1.5 m)
tall and with a similar
spread as it matures.
The leaves are long and
narrow, and almost
leathery and slightly
felty in texture. Its
spikes of flared tubular
flowers are produced
mainly in summer in
shades of orange-
yellow through rusty
orange to yellow-
brown. ZONES 9–11.

ISOPOGON
DRUMSTICKS

This genus of some 30 species of evergreen shrubs from Australia is admired for its attractive light green foliage, which is hard and prickly, though frequently dissected and ferny in appearance. It is also valued for its globular heads of fragrant white, cream or pink flowers borne in spring or summer. Plants of quiet charm, they are somewhat overshadowed by their more spectacular relatives, the grevilleas and banksias. The flowers are followed by woody, knob-like fruiting heads resembling small pine cones or drumsticks—hence the common name. These may persist on the bare, straight stems after both flowers and leaves have died.

CULTIVATION
Marginally frost hardy, they need a sunny spot and well-drained soil, and a dry-summer climate. Water freely in dry periods. Propagate from ripe seed in winter or from cuttings in late summer and autumn.

Isopogon anemonifolius *(left)*
DRUMSTICKS

From eastern Australia, this upright bushy species grows to a height and spread of 6 ft (1.8 m); low-growing, prostrate forms are also seen. In spring it bears prominent, cone-shaped, creamy yellow flowerheads, followed by cones. Marginally to moderately frost hardy, it needs watering generously in dry periods. ZONES 9–11.

Isopogon dawsonii *(right)*

Native to the Blue Mountains of New South Wales, this attractive species is found on sandstone slopes and cliffs. It is an open tall shrub that reaches 10 ft (3 m) in height and has divided leaves with flattened segments. Its pale yellow, pink-tinged flowers are followed by silver-gray fruiting cones. ZONES 9–11.

ITEA

Of the 10 species of evergreen and deciduous shrubs and trees in this genus, most are from tropical and temperate Asia but one species is native to North America. They are grown for their showy, fragrant autumn flowers. They are frost hardy, although in some colder areas they need the protection of a wall. These are useful plants for specimens or for growing in a shrubbery. The botanical name *Itea* comes from the Greek, meaning 'willow', to which some species bear a slight resemblance.

CULTIVATION

They will thrive in anything but very dry soil and prefer a part-shaded position, but will tolerate full sun. Propagate from cuttings in summer and plant out in autumn or spring.

Itea ilicifolia (above)

HOLLY SWEETSPIRE

This handsome, bushy, evergreen shrub from western China grows to a height and spread of 10 ft (3 m). The leaves, borne on arching branches, resemble those of holly, only narrower. In late summer to early autumn, it bears long racemes of small, greenish or cream flowers. It does best in moist, deep, rich soil, preferring partial shade. ZONES 7–10.

Itea virginica (above)

SWEETSPIRE, VIRGINIA WILLOW

The best known member of the genus, this deciduous North American shrub of upright, slender form grows 3–5 ft (1–1.5 m) tall and in summer bears fragrant, creamy white flowers in semi-erect panicles. Its finely toothed, deciduous, bright green leaves do not fall until early winter, when they sometimes turn red. It is suitable for mass planting, particularly in wet, low places and is more frost hardy than *Itea ilicifolia*. ZONES 5–9.

JACARANDA

This genus consists of about 50 species of medium to large deciduous and evergreen trees from Brazil and other parts of tropical and subtropical South America. All species have fern-like, bipinnate leaves and white, purple or mauve-blue, bell-shaped flowers. The best known species, the mauve-blue *Jacaranda mimosifolia*, is one of the most widely planted and ad-mired of all warm-climate flowering trees. It yields a richly figured timber, but the tree is so valued as an ornamental it is rarely cut; the timber, Brazil rosewood, is usually from *J. filicifolia*, a larger, less decorative species with white flowers.

CULTIVATION
Marginally frost hardy, they grow in fertile, well-drained soil and full sun. Young plants need protection from frost. Potted specimens should be watered freely when in full growth, less so at other times. Propagate from seed in spring or from cuttings in summer.

J

Jacaranda mimosifolia (above)
syns *Jacaranda acutifolia, J. ovalifolia*
JACARANDA

From the high plains of Brazil, Paraguay and Argentina, this fast-growing, deciduous tree can reach 50 ft (15 m) in height with a spread of up to 40 ft (12 m). It has a broad, rounded crown. The vivid green, fern-like foliage is bipinnate, with 12 or more leaflets. Depending on climate, the leaves may be shed in winter or early spring before ter-minal clusters of mauve-blue to lilac trumpet-shaped blossoms appear. Flat, leathery seed pods follow the blooms. Pruning is not desirable; if branches are removed, they are replaced by verti-cal shoots which spoil the shape of the tree. The trees are shallow rooted, which can pose problems for underplanting. ZONES 9–11.

JASMINUM
JASMINE

The name jasmine is synonymous with sweet fragrance, although among this large genus of some 200 deciduous, semi-evergreen and evergreen shrubs and vines, mostly from Asia and Africa, there are many that offer nothing to the nose. The leaves are usually compound and the flowers white, yellow or more rarely reddish pink. Most of the species cultivated for their fragrance are climbing plants.

CULTIVATION
Some are frost hardy, although most thrive best in subtropical to tropical areas. Plant in full sun in fertile, moist but well-drained soil. Prune as required after flowering. Propagate from cuttings in summer.

Jasminum humile
'Revolutum' *(below)*

Jasminum humile *(above)*
ITALIAN YELLOW JASMINE

This large evergreen, bushy shrub can exceed 12 ft (3.5 m) in height and spread. A moderately frost-hardy species, it has bright green leaves. Its bright yellow, occasionally scented flowers are produced from early spring to late autumn and can be ½ in (12 mm) or more across. Although commonly called Italian yellow jasmine, it actually comes from the Middle East, Burma and China— another case of a deceptive common name. The cultivar **'Revolutum'** has larger leaves and fragrant flowers up to 1 in (25 mm) across.
ZONES 8–11.

Jasminum mesnyi (right)
syn. *Jasminum primulinum*

YELLOW JASMINE, PRIMROSE JASMINE

This marginally frost-hardy evergreen shrub from western
China grows to 6–10 ft (1.8–3 m) in height and spread. Its
long, arching canes eventually form a wide, fountain shape.
The deep green leaves are made up of 3 leaflets, and bright
yellow, scented blooms appear during late winter and early
spring. Remove old canes to thin, crowded plants. ZONES 8–10.

Jasminum nudiflorum (above left & above)
WINTER JASMINE

This green-stemmed, spreading shrub or lax climber from
northern China is deciduous but has great appeal in winter
when it flowers. Its leaves, in groups of three, are simple elongated oval structures. Its flowers—solitary, bright yellow and
unscented—are fairly plain, but, appearing when the plant is
devoid of foliage, they really stand out. Winter jasmine is easily
grown and quite hardy, though the flowers may be damaged by
repeated heavy frosts. ZONES 6–10.

Jasminum officinale (left)
COMMON JASMINE, POET'S JASMINE, JESSAMINE

Introduced to Europe from China in the sixteenth century, this
deciduous or semi-evergreen shrubby climber can be maintained as a neat 3–5 ft (1–1.5 m) shrub or allowed to ramble.
The dark green leaves have 7 to 9 leaflets; clusters of deep pink
buds followed by very fragrant, starry white flowers occur
through summer and autumn. This frost-hardy species likes full
sun, well-drained, fertile soil and ample water in warmer
months. It is an excellent container plant for a sunny terrace.
The essential oil of this species is used in perfume and as a food
flavoring, such as in maraschino cherries. Pink-flowered and
variegated-foliage forms are also available. ZONES 6–10.

JUGLANS
WALNUT

This genus, consisting of 15 species of deciduous trees, is distributed from the Mediterranean region and the Middle East to East Asia and North and South America. They are grown for their handsome form and elegant, aromatic foliage. All species bear edible nuts—usually produced within 12 years—and several yield fine timber used in furniture making. Greenish yellow male catkins and inconspicuous female flowers appear on the same tree in spring before the large pinnate leaves. They are followed by the hard-shelled nuts. The fallen leaves are said to be toxic to other plants (so do not put them on the compost heap). The name *Juglans* is derived from the Latin *Jovis glans*, meaning 'Jupiter's acorn'. These are excellent ornamental trees for parks and large gardens.

CULTIVATION
Cool-climate trees, they prefer a sunny position. Although quite frost hardy, young plants and the new spring growth are susceptible to frost damage. Deep rich alluvial soil of a light, loamy texture suits them best, and they need regular water. Propagate from freshly collected seed in autumn.

J

Juglans regia *(left)*
COMMON WALNUT, PERSIAN WALNUT, ENGLISH WALNUT

From southeastern Europe and temperate Asia, this slow-growing tree reaches 50 ft (15 m) tall with a spread of 30 ft (9 m). It has a sturdy trunk, a broad, leafy canopy and smooth, pale gray bark. The leaves are purplish bronze when young, and yellow-green catkins appear from late spring to early summer. They are followed by the edible nut, enclosed in a green husk that withers and falls. The timber is valued for furniture making. Cultivars include **'Wilson's Wonder'**, which fruits younger than most at about 7 years old. ZONES 4–10.

JUNIPERUS
JUNIPER

Slow growing and long lived, the 50 or so species of evergreen shrubs and trees in this conifer genus occur throughout the northern hemisphere. Juvenile foliage is needle-like, but at maturity many species develop shorter scale-like leaves, closely pressed to the stems and exuding a pungent smell when crushed. Both types of foliage are found on adult trees of some species. Male and female cones usually occur on separate plants. The bluish black or reddish seed cones have fleshy, fused scales; known as berries, some of which are used to flavor gin. The fragrant, pinkish, cedar-like timber is soft but durable. Various species of juniper are used medicinally.

CULTIVATION
Easily cultivated in a cool climate, they prefer a sunny position and any well-drained soil. Prune to maintain shape or restrict size, but do not make visible cuts as old, leafless wood rarely sprouts. Propagate from cuttings in winter, layers if low-growing, or from seed; cultivars can be propagated by grafting.

Juniperus chinensis
CHINESE JUNIPER

Native to the Himalayas, China, Mongolia and Japan, this frost-hardy species usually matures to a conical tree up to 50 ft (15 m) in height with a spread of 6–10 ft (1.8–3 m). Sometimes, however, it forms a low-spreading shrub. Both adult and juvenile foliage may be found on adult trees. The berries are fleshy and glaucous white. **'Aurea'** grows to at least 35 ft (11 m) tall, with a conical habit and soft, golden foliage; **'Blaauw'** is somewhat spreading when young, but becomes an upright 5 ft (1.5 m) shrub; **'Kaizuka'** is a small tree to 20 ft (6 m), with twisted spear-like branches; **'Obelisk'** is an attractive plant of upright form that can reach 10 ft (3 m) tall and has bluish green juvenile foliage; **'Pyramidalis'** grows to 15 ft (4.5 m) tall, with dense, blue-green leaves and a columnar habit; and **'Variegata'** grows to 20 ft (6 m) tall, glaucous with white markings.
ZONES 4–9.

Juniperus chinensis
'Kaizuka' *(above)*

Juniperus chinensis
'Aurea' *(above left)*

Juniperus communis
'Depressa Aurea' *(left)*

Juniperus communis
'Hibernica' *(green
column at rear)*
surrounded by *Erica
erigena* 'W. T. Rackliff'
(below)

J

*Juniperus
communis* *(above)*

COMMON JUNIPER

Ranging widely
through northern
Europe, North America
and western Asia, this
is either an upright tree
growing to 20 ft (6 m)
or a sprawling shrub
with a height and
spread of 10–15 ft
(3–4.5 m). It has
brownish red bark and
grayish green leaves.

Fleshy, greenish berries
take 2 to 3 years to
ripen to black and are
used for flavoring gin.
Hardiness varies
according to subspecies
or cultivar. Popular
cultivars are **'Com-
pressa'**, a dwarf, erect
form suitable for the
rock garden, growing
to 30 in (75 cm) tall
and 6 in (15 cm) wide
with silvery blue nee-
dles; **'Depressa Aurea'**,

a dwarf form 24 in
(60 cm) tall and 6 ft
(1.8 m) wide with
bronze-gold foliage;
'Hibernica', growing
10–15 ft (3–4.5 m) tall
and 2–4 ft (0.6–1.2 m)
wide, forming a dense
column of dull, blue-
green foliage when
young but becoming

broader and conical
with age; and **'Horni-
brookii'**, an excellent
prostrate shrub with
gray-green foliage that
rarely exceeds 10 in
(25 cm) in height,
but will spread to
more than 4 ft (1.2 m)
wide. ZONES 2–9.

Juniperus
horizontalis *(above)*

This cold-climate pros-
trate shrub from north-
ern North America is
fast spreading and
tough. Its branches
form a mat of blue-
green or gray leaves up
to 18 in (45 cm) thick.
Cultivars include '**Bar
Harbor**' with grayish
green foliage, turning
mauve in winter; '**Blue
Chip**' with blue-green
foliage; '**Douglasii**',
with glaucous gray-
green leaves, turning
plum purple in winter;
'**Glauca**', a prostrate
form that exceeds 6 ft
(1.8 m) in spread with
a height of only 2 in
(5 cm) or so, with blue-

gray foliage often
tinged purple in win-
ter; '**Plumosa**', which
has an ascending habit
unlike other forms of
this species and spreads
to about 10 ft (3 m)
wide and 24 in (60 cm)

tall in a star-shaped
pattern, with blue-gray
foliage turning rich
purple in winter; and
'**Wiltonii**', blue, with
trailing branches.
ZONES 4–10.

Juniperus horizontalis
'Wiltonii' *(above)*

Juniperus × *media* 'Plumosa Aurea' *(above)*
Juniperus × *media* 'Pfitzeriana' *(top)*

Juniperus × media

This group of cultivars, mainly derived from *Juniperus chinensis* and valued in cool to cold climates for their foliage, are all spreading shrubs, 1 or 2 being semi-prostrate. Their mainly scale-like, gray-green leaves have an unpleasant smell when crushed; the berries are white or blue-black. **'Blaauw'** grows to a height and spread of 6 ft (1.8 m) with blue-green foliage; **'Gold Coast'**, possibly the finest golden form of this group, makes a neat, spreading ground-cover shrub to 3 ft (1 m) tall and wide; **'Dandelight'**, to 24 in (60 cm) with a 6 ft (1.8 m) spread, has golden yellow new growth ageing to yellow-green; **'Old Gold'**, a sport of 'Pfitzeriana Aurea', is a neat plant ideal for large rock gardens or as a tall ground cover, reaching 30 in (75 cm) tall with a spread of 5 ft (1.5 m) and attractive golden foliage; **'Pfitzeriana'**, by far the best known cultivar, grows to 10 ft (3 m) tall with a spread of 10–15 ft (3–4.5 m), a broadly pyramidal habit and wide-spreading branches with weeping tips and gray-green leaves; **'Pfitzeriana Aurea'**, only for those with plenty of space, is a hardy juniper with spray-like branches that reach up to 3 ft (1 m) in height with a spread of more than 10 ft (3 m); **'Plumosa Aurea'** reaches a height of 3 ft (1 m) and spread of 6 ft (1.8 m) with arched, weeping tips to the branches and green-gold foliage turning bronze in winter; and **'Plumosa Aurea-Variegata'** will grow to 12 in (30 cm) tall with a spread of more than 3 ft (1 m) and has gray foliage with sprays of creamy yellow foliage splashed throughout. ZONES 4–10.

Juniperus recurva

COFFIN JUNIPER, HIMALAYAN JUNIPER

Native to Burma, southwest China and the Himalayas, this tree grows to 50 ft (15 m) tall and 15 ft (4.5 m) wide. It has spreading, pendulous branches and needle-like, aromatic, gray- or blue-green incurved leaves. The reddish brown bark peels in vertical strips; its glossy berries are dark purple. Its aromatic wood was used in China to make coffins. *Juniperus recurva* **var.** *coxii* has smaller leaves. ZONES 7–11.

Juniperus recurva var. *coxii* *(above)*

Juniperus rigida *(right)*

NEEDLE JUNIPER

From Japan and Korea, this cool-climate tree grows to 20 ft (6 m) in height, although it often forms a shrub when grown in gardens. It has pendulous branches and needle-like leaves with a band of white on the upper surface. The fruit ripens through brown to blue-black. ZONES 4–9.

Juniperus sabina *(right)*

SAVIN JUNIPER

This spreading shrub from cold-climate Europe
and Asia reaches 12 ft (3.5 m) high and 10–15 ft
(3–4.5 m) wide. It has flaking, reddish brown
bark and deep green, mainly scale-like leaves; the
berries are blue-black. It does well in limestone
soil. **'Tamariscifolia'** makes a broad mound
to 3 ft (1 m) with a spread of 5–10 ft (1.5–3 m).
ZONES 3–9.

Juniperus squamata
'Blue Star' *(right)*

Juniperus squamata

HOLLYWOOD JUNIPER

This species ranges in height from 1–20 ft (0.3–6 m)
with a spread of 3–15 ft (1–4.5 m) depending on
the variety. Needle-like green or blue-green leaves
clothe densely crowded branchlets and the bark is
flaky and reddish brown; the berries are fleshy
and black. **'Blue Carpet'** is another blue-needled
juniper which makes a mat of foliage about 10 in
(25 cm) deep with a spread of up to 3 ft (1 m).
'Blue Star', a dense, rounded shrub with blue foliage, grows to 18 in (45 cm) tall and 24 in (60 cm)
wide. **'Holger'** is a lovely shrub with a spreading,
star-shaped habit; it grows up to 24 in (60 cm) tall
and 6 ft (1.8 m) wide. Its steely blue needles are
attractively ornamented in spring by golden tips.
'Meyeri' has steely blue foliage with a rich silver
sheen and reaches a height and spread of 15 ft
(4.5 m). **ZONES 4–10.**

Juniperus virginiana *(right)*

EASTERN RED CEDAR, PENCIL CEDAR

From North America, this is the tallest of the junipers commonly grown in gardens, reaching 50–60 ft (15–18 m) in
height. It has a conical or broadly columnar habit and both
scale- and needle-like, gray-green leaves. The berries are fleshy,
small, glaucous and brownish violet. The wood is used in making lead pencils, hence the common name. **'Glauca'**, a columnar form with blue-green foliage, grows to 25 ft (8 m) tall with
a spread of 8 ft (2.4 m); **'Hetzii'** has layers of gray-green foliage
and reaches 10–12 ft (3–3.5 m) high and wide; **'Sulphur Spray'**
(syn. *Juniperus chinensis* 'Sulphur Spray') is a popular sport of
'Hetzii' with soft yellow-green new growth ageing to gray-
green. **ZONES 2–9.**

Juniperus virginiana
'Glauca' *(right)*

JUSTICIA
syns *Adhatoda, Beloperone, Drejerella, Jacobinia, Libonia*

This genus of about 420 species of shrubs and evergreen perennials is found in subtropical and tropical areas of the world, especially in the Americas. Widely grown in most warm areas, and
in greenhouses in cooler climates, the leaves are simple and arranged in opposite pairs; the tubular flowers, in shades of cream,
yellow, pink, orange or red, are mostly held in upright terminal
spikes or clusters.

CULTIVATION
Frost tender, they prefer well-drained soils in full sun or bright
filtered light. They require shelter from wind as many have brittle stems. Plants can be kept neat and bushy by pinching out
growing tips. They are easily propagated from cuttings of non-
flowering shoots taken in spring.

J

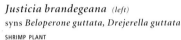

Justicia brandegeana (left)
syns *Beloperone guttata, Drejerella guttata*
SHRIMP PLANT

The curved spikes of salmon to rose pink or pale
yellow bracts surrounding the white flowers of
this attractive, evergreen shrub resemble shrimps.
Growing to 3 ft (1 m) with a spread of 24 in
(60 cm) or more, it flowers mainly in summer. It
can survive temperatures as low as 25°F (−4°C) by
behaving like a perennial when the tops are frozen
back. A weak, sprawling plant, it needs regular
pruning. ZONES 9–11.

Justicia carnea (left)
syns *Jacobinia carnea, J. pohliana*
BRAZILIAN PLUME

This handsome shrub bears dense, erect spikes of
white, pink or rose purple flowers from summer
to autumn. Frost tender, it grows to 5 ft (1.5 m)
with a spread of 30 in (75 cm), and has pointed,
veined, deep green leaves. Potted plants need to
be watered freely in full growth, less so at other
times. Prune hard in early spring to encourage
branching. Watch for caterpillars and snails.
ZONES 10–12.

Kalmia angustifolia
(below right)

SHEEP LAUREL, HOBBLE BUSH, LAMBKILL

This open, twiggy shrub growing to 3 ft (1 m) tall and 4 ft (1.2 m) wide can be kept in a neat, compact shape suitable for shrubberies, rockeries or containers if trimmed after flowering. The leaves are 1–2 in (2.5–5 cm) long, and bright green to bluish green. The flowerheads, usually bright reddish pink, appear in late spring and early summer. In its native USA, it acquired its common names because sheep were often caught in the low, sprawling branches. Propagate by layering. *Kalmia angustifolia* f. *rubra* has deeper, almost red flowers. ZONES 2–9.

Kalmia latifolia
'Ostbo Red' *(bottom)*

KALMIA

From North America, this genus contains some very beautiful spring-flowering evergreen shrubs, although the 6 species in the genus are poisonous. English writer and critic John Ruskin waxed eloquent about *Kalmia latifolia*, describing its flowers as little bowls 'of beaten silver, the petals struck by the stamens instead of with a hammer'. However, they are not silver but a very delicate pale pink. The 2 common species are quite different in their general appearance, but both bloom in late spring and early summer and bear heads of pink flowers opening from buds that look as if they were made by a cake decorator. The flowers of *K. angustifolia* are far smaller than those of *K. latifolia*.

CULTIVATION

They prefer a cool, moist climate, lime-free, humus-rich, well-drained soil and a position in part-shade. They are among the hardiest of broad-leafed evergreens. Propagate from seed in autumn or cuttings in summer, or by layering.

K

Kalmia latifolia *(above far right)*
MOUNTAIN LAUREL, CALICO BUSH

While its leathery, evergreen leaves are quite attractive (and are the reason for the common name 'laurel'), this shrub is grown mainly for its flowers which appear in late spring to early summer. Clusters of distinctive, bright pink buds open to heads of small, pale pink flowers with stamens arranged like umbrella ribs. Mountain laurel can grow to 12 ft (3.5 m), but is more commonly 5 ft (1.5 m) in height and spread. '**Ostbo Red**' is a cultivar with deeper pink flowers that open from red buds; '**Carousel**' has purple-striped white flowers; and '**Elf**' is a pink-flowered dwarf form. ZONES 3–9.

KERRIA
JAPANESE ROSE

This genus from China and Japan contains one species, a deciduous shrub with many upright 6 ft (1.8 m), deep green stems
emerging directly from the ground. The leaves are 1 in (25 mm)
long, bright green and roughly diamond-shaped with finely
serrated edges. The true species has simple, bright golden yellow
flowers up to 2 in (5 cm) across.

CULTIVATION
A very tough, fully frost-hardy, adaptable plant, it does well in
moist, well-drained soil in dappled shade. Trim lightly after
flowering to thin out the older canes. Propagate from basal suckers or cuttings in summer or by division in autumn.

Kerria japonica 'Pleniflora'
(above & left)

Kerria japonica

The bright golden blossoms of this shrub, which appear
in spring on lateral shoots along its branches, make
delightful cut flowers; the small leaves that follow only
sparsely clothe the arching branches. Although *Kerria
japonica* is single-flowered, the double form **'Pleniflora'**
is more common in gardens and was introduced to
European gardens nearly 50 years before the wild
species was discovered. **ZONES 5–10.**

KIGELIA

This African genus consists of a single species of tropical and subtropical trees. The bell-shaped flowers borne in long pendent racemes, mostly orange or red, are adapted for pollination by bats. The large, woody, sausage-shaped fruit enclose a woody, fibrous pulp with many large seeds.

CULTIVATION
These frost-tender trees require a warm climate, full sun, well-drained soil and plenty of water, and do best in areas of high humidity. Propagate from seed or cuttings in spring.

K

Kigelia africana
(right)
syn. *Kigelia pinnata*
SAUSAGE TREE

This evergreen tree grows to about 40 ft (12 m) and has a wide crown of spreading branches. The leaves are about 12 in (30 cm) long. The flowers, borne in panicles up to 6 ft (1.8 m) long in early summer, open at night and are crinkled and rich dark red inside, but duller outside. They have an unpleasant smell which attracts the bats that pollinate them. The light brown fruit, up to 18 in (45 cm) long and weighing up to 4 kg (8 lb), are not edible. It grows vigorously in fertile, well-drained soil with adequate water.
ZONES 10–12.

KINGIA
SKIRTED GRASS-TREE

This genus of a single species is from higher rainfall areas in southwestern Australia. Distantly allied to the grass-trees *(Xanthorrhoea)*, it is very slow growing: the tallest plants have been estimated to be up to 1,000 years old.

CULTIVATION

Rarely cultivated, this species thrives in sandy loam with good drainage and is happiest in full sun or light shade. Young plants can be grown in pots, but larger plants resent transplanting. Propagation is from seed, which may take up to 6 months to germinate.

Kingia australis *(above)*

This plant eventually reaches 20 ft (6 m) in height, with a cylindrical, distinctively textured trunk packed with remnant leaf bases and topped by a dome-shaped tuft of smooth, needle-like leaves up to 24 in (60 cm) long. The dead leaves persist for some time, hanging down like a skirt around the trunk. Creamy white flowers are clustered in ball-shaped heads on upright stems which appear in a ring among the upper leaves.
ZONES 9–11.

KOELREUTERIA

Grown for their foliage, flowers and decorative fruit, this small genus of 3 species of deciduous trees is from dry valley woodlands in East Asia. They are useful small trees and bear pyramid-shaped panicles of long, bowl-shaped flowers followed by inflated fruit capsules.

CULTIVATION

Moderately frost hardy, they thrive in full sun in fertile, well-aerated soil with free drainage. They can withstand hot, dry summers, but seaside conditions do not suit them. Propagate from root cuttings in late winter or from seed in autumn. Prune in the early years to establish a single trunk.

Koelreuteria bipinnata *(right)*
PRIDE OF CHINA, CHINESE FLAME TREE

From central and western China, this shapely tree grows 30–50 ft (9–15 m) tall with a single trunk and broadly conical crown. The bipinnate leaves are a clear yellow-green, turning deep golden in autumn. Bright yellow flowers, blotched scarlet at the base, are borne during summer. The fruit are like miniature Chinese lanterns, green at first then turning bright pink in autumn and paper-brown in winter. ZONES 8–11.

K

Koelreuteria paniculata *(right)*
GOLDEN RAIN TREE, VARNISH TREE

From China and Korea, this slow-growing, wide-spreading tree can reach 30–50 ft (9–15 m), but is often smaller in gardens. It has a convex crown and a single or divided main trunk. The bark is furrowed and the branches droop at the ends. The mid-green leaflets turn deep golden yellow to orange in autumn. Large clusters of clear yellow flowers are borne in summer, followed by papery, bladder-like, pinkish brown pods. It does well in alkaline soil.

'**September**' (syn. 'September Gold') is similar to the species, but flowers late in the season. ZONES 4–10.

KOLKWITZIA
BEAUTY BUSH

This genus consists of a single species of deciduous shrub from China, much admired in temperate and cool-climate gardens for its lavish spring display. However, as its foliage is undistinguished during summer, it should be placed where other plants can attract the eye.

CULTIVATION

Fully frost hardy, *Kolkwitzia amabilis* grows in any well-drained soil and does well in sun or light shade. It can become very untidy if old wood is not removed from time to time; avoid winter pruning as this will simply cut away the flowering wood. Propagation is from cuttings in summer.

Kolkwitzia amabilis *(above)*

This bushy shrub develops into a mass of upright, cane-like stems to 12 ft (3.5 m) high. The leaves are in opposite pairs, oval, 1½ in (35 mm) long and deep green. The pale pink, trumpet-shaped flowers, which open in spring, form profuse clusters at the ends of the side branches. They are followed by small fruit covered with bristles. 'Pink Cloud' has clear pink flowers and is slightly larger than the type. ZONES 4–9.

KUNZEA

This Australasian genus of the myrtle family is made up of 30 species of small evergreen shrubs with small heath-like leaves that are pungently aromatic when crushed. Their individual flowers consist mainly of fluffy bunches of stamens, but in spring these cover the bushes and are usually pale colored—white, pink or lilac—although *Kunzea baxteri* has bright crimson flowers.

CULTIVATION
These plants are best grown *en masse* to make an impact. They tend to be short lived and straggly, but this can be overcome by a post-flowering trim. Moderately frost hardy to frost tender, they do best in mild climates, moist but well-drained soils and light shade. Old bushes are easily replaced from late-summer cuttings; they can also be propagated from seed in spring.

Kunzea ericoides *(right)*
syn. *Leptospermum ericoides*
KANUKA

Found over much of New Zealand and southeastern Australia, *Kunzea ericoides* is a wiry-stemmed large shrub or small tree with tiny, narrow, bronze-green leaves. It is often treated as a near weed, but is a valuable pioneer and nurse plant in forest regeneration. Its tiny cream flowers are an important food source for nectar-feeding geckoes and are also favored by apiarists for the rich honey that bees produce from the nectar.
ZONES 8–11.

Kunzea parvifolia *(left)*
VIOLET KUNZEA

This spreading shrub from cooler hill areas of southeastern Australia grows to about 5 ft (1.5 m) tall with a spread of 10 ft (3 m). Often fairly open, it can be kept compact by regular clipping, making it useful as a hedge. The tiny, heath-like leaves are hairy when young, and in late spring and early summer the shrub bears masses of showy, violet balls of blossoms towards the ends of the branches. **ZONES 8–10.**

K

LABURNUM
GOLDEN CHAIN TREE

Two species of deciduous small trees from Europe and western Asia make up this genus of legumes, allied to *Cytisus* and other brooms. They have compound leaves with 3 leaflets that are larger and thinner than other members of the broom tribe. The bright yellow pea-flowers borne in profuse pendulous sprays are also relatively large and are followed by brown seed pods. All parts of the tree are very poisonous; handle with gloves.

CULTIVATION

Cool-climate plants, they prefer full sun, some humidity and tolerate any moderately fertile soil with free drainage—they do not like being waterlogged. Prune competing leaders in the early years to establish a tree-like form. Owners of large gardens can create 'laburnum arches' of 2 rows of trees tied down over a trellis, so that the flower sprays hang below like wisterias. Watch for leaf miner insects; protect young trees from snails. Propagate species from seed in autumn, cultivars by budding in summer.

L

Laburnum anagyroides *(left)*
COMMON LABURNUM, GOLDEN CHAIN TREE, GOLDEN RAIN

From the mountain regions of central and southern Europe, this small, spreading tree grows to a height and spread of 25 ft (8 m). The gray-green leaves are downy on the undersides. The densely clustered flowers are borne in 6–10 in (15–25 cm) long pendulous racemes in late spring and early summer. Blooms are followed by hairy brown pods containing black seeds. The cultivar **'Aureum'** has pale yellowish green foliage. ZONES 3–9.

Laburnum × watereri
VOSS LABURNUM, WATERER LABURNUM

Now the most commonly grown laburnum, this hybrid between *Laburnum anagyroides* and *L. alpinum* makes a tree of similar size to the parent species. It has dark green leaflets and in late spring and early summer it produces dense racemes, up to 18 in (45 cm) long, of fragrant rich yellow flowers. **'Vossii'** produces rich, buttercup yellow flowers in racemes 24 in (60 cm) long. ZONES 3–9.

Laburnum × watereri
'Vossii' *(right)*

LAGERSTROEMIA
CRAPE (OR CREPE) MYRTLE

From southern and eastern Asia and ranging as far as northern
Australia, this is a genus of around 50 species of evergreen and
deciduous small to large trees, a few grown in warm and hot
climates for their showy flowers. Their most distinctive feature is
the crinkly margin and slender basal stalk of each of the 5 petals
that make up a flower; the flowers in turn are massed into large,
dense panicles at the branch tips. The 'crape' (alternatively
crepe) in the name arose from the similarity of the flowers' texture to the once popular fabric crape; 'myrtle' alludes to their
close links with the large myrtle family. They make fine garden
plants and are easily grown. Some species have attractive smooth,
green, brown or reddish bark. The timber of some species is
highly prized for shipbuilding.

CULTIVATION
These plants thrive in full sun in well-drained, humus-rich soil.
Shelter from strong summer winds, which destroy the delicate
flowers. Propagate from cuttings in summer or from seed in
spring. Watch for powdery mildew.

L

Lagerstroemia indica (right)
CRAPE (OR CREPE) MYRTLE, PRIDE OF INDIA

This deciduous tree grows to about 25 ft (8 m) tall
with an open, spreading, rounded head and smooth
beige bark streaked red-brown. In mid- to late
summer it bears large clusters of frilly pink to deep
red flowers. In cool areas, the small oval leaves
turn gold in autumn. Flowerheads are largest on
strong growth, encouraged by pruning the main
branches in winter; if not pruned, the tree develops an attractive, open shape, with massed
smaller heads. The original form of this species is
now almost forgotten in cultivation, replaced by
an array of cultivars (including some of dwarf
habit). **'Petite Snow'**, of dwarf habit, has white
flowers; **'Ruby Lace'** has frilly, deep red blooms.
Some cultivars, such as **'Eavesii'** with its broad,
open habit and pale mauve flowers and **'Helio-
trope Beauty'** with pale lilac-pink flowers, are believed to be of hybrid origin: *Lagerstroemia indica*
× *L. speciosa* hybrids re-crossed with *L. indica*.
Some modern American cultivars are hybrids between *L. indica* and *L. fauriei*, including **'Natchez'**
with creamy flowers; **'Seminole'** with pink flowers;
and **'Tuscarora'** with crimson flowers. ZONES 6–11.

L

Lagerstroemia speciosa *(above)*
syn. *Lagerstroemia flos-reginae*
QUEEN'S FLOWER, QUEEN CRAPE MYRTLE

This deciduous species from the jungles of India, Sri Lanka and Burma reaches 80 ft (24 m) in the wild, with a single trunk and a spreading broad head. It has long, leathery leaves that turn coppery red in autumn. Showy panicles of large, rose pink to purple flowers are borne from summer through to autumn. The bark is shed in irregular patches, giving the smooth gray trunk a yellowish, mottled appearance. **ZONES 11–12.**

LANTANA

This genus of the verbena family consists of around 150 species of evergreen shrubs and many-stemmed perennials, native to warmer parts of the Americas with a few from southern Africa. Several species are notorious weeds of tropical and subtropical regions, most notably *Lantana camara*. The plants have rough, slightly prickly stems with oval leaves in opposite pairs, their surfaces harsh and closely veined. Very small, trumpet-shaped flowers in compact button-like heads open progressively from the center of each head, their color changing in the older flowers towards the perimeter. Tiny fruits like blackberry drupelets may follow. Several species and their cultivars are useful greenhouse or conservatory plants in cool climates, where they may also be treated as summer bedding plants; in warm-climate gardens they can be grown as outdoor shrubs or ground covers.

CULTIVATION
These plants prefer fertile, well-drained soil and full sun. Plants in containers should be top-dressed annually in spring and watered well when in full growth, less at other times. Tip prune young growth to promote a bushy habit and propagate from cuttings in summer or from seed in spring. They are generally not affected by pests, but check then regularly for white fly and spider mite.

L

Lantana camara
'Radiation' *(below)*

Lantana camara
'Chelsea Gem' *(left)*

L

Lantana camara

COMMON LANTANA, SHRUB VERBENA

This is the Dr Jekyll and Mr Hyde of the plant world, reviled in warmer, wetter parts of the world for its rampant invasion of forests and pastures and poisoning of cattle, but valued as an ornamental in cooler or drier regions. Much of this split personality is explained by its great variability, causing botanists to doubt whether it is in fact a single species. At least 25 weedy strains have been identified in Australia, only a few of which were introduced as ornamentals; many of the ornamental cultivars show no signs of becoming weedy. The weedy forms produce long scrambling canes and can mound up to 20 ft (6 m) even without trees to climb over; the garden forms are mostly rounded or spreading shrubs 2–6 ft (0.6–1.8 m) high. The tiny flowers typically open cream, yellow or yellow-red and age to pink, red, orange or white, the heads appearing in a long succession from spring to autumn. There are many cultivars ranging in color from the golden orange and red of **'Radiation'** and the yellow of **'Drap d'Or'** to the white blooms of **'Snowflake'**. **'Chelsea Gem'** is one of the oldest cultivars, an excellent compact shrub with profuse orange and red flowerheads; it makes an attractive standard. ZONES 9–12.

LARIX
LARCH

From cool mountainous regions of the northern hemisphere, these deciduous, fast-growing conifers have a handsome, graceful form and fresh green spring foliage as well as strong, durable timber; the bark is sometimes used for tanning and dyeing. Mainly conical in shape, they lose their leaves in autumn, bursting into leaf in early spring. With the new foliage appear both drooping yellow male (pollen) cones and upright red female cones, which mature over the following summer to short, erect seed cones with thin scales; these persist on the tree after shedding their seeds. Up to 15 species of *Larix* have been recognized, but recent studies have merged some of these, reducing the number to as few as 9 species.

CULTIVATION
Cold- to cool-climate plants, they do best in well-drained, light or gravelly soil; most resent waterlogged soil. Propagation is from seed. Check regularly for larch canker or blister and infestation by larch chermes (a type of aphid).

Larix decidua *(left & above)*
EUROPEAN LARCH

From the mountains of central and southern Europe, this tree reaches a height of 100 ft (30 m); it has a conical crown when young, spreading with maturity. The branches are widely spaced and the branchlets have a graceful, weeping habit. The soft, bright green, needle-like leaves turn yellow in autumn before dropping. The mature seed cones are egg-shaped, brown and upright. The gray bark becomes red-brown, fissured and scaly with age. ZONES 2–9.

L

Larix kaempferi *(above)*
syn. *Larix leptolepis*
JAPANESE LARCH

This fast-growing Japanese species is widely used
for ornamental landscaping and is grown in plantations in the UK. Broadly conical, it grows to
100 ft (30 m) high with a spread of 20 ft (6 m). Its
soft needle-like leaves are gray- to blue-green;
mature cones are brown and almost globular, their
broad scales spreading at the tips to give a rosebud appearance. The scaly bark is reddish brown,
or orange-red on older branches. ZONES 4–9.

LAURUS

This genus consists of 2 species of ever-green shrubs and trees from the Mediter-ranean region, Canary Islands and the Azores. The common laurel *(Laurus nobilis)* has been grown as an ornamental since ancient times and has always had great symbolic significance. Among other uses, its dark green leaves have been used in funeral and remembrance wreaths, though the glossy leaves of the unrelated cherry laurel *(Prunus laurocerasus)* are now generally substituted. The highly aromatic leaves are also dried and used as a culinary herb (an essential ingredient in bouquet garni). Both species are useful evergreen screen plants and tub speci-mens, and are often used for topiary.

CULTIVATION

Cool- to warm-climate plants, they are moderately frost hardy and do best in sheltered positions in sun or part-shade in fertile, well-drained soil. They are tolerant of coastal conditions. Propagation is from seed in autumn or from cuttings in summer.

Laurus azorica *(above)*
syn. *Laurus canariensis*

AZORES BAY, CANARY ISLAND BAY

Similar to *Laurus nobilis*, this species is a large tree up to 70 ft (21 m) high. Its flowers are a mass of yellow filaments ½ in (12 mm) long and carried in clusters of 5 to 9 blooms; they are followed by small black berries. The leaves, which are ever-green, are elliptical and up to 6 in (15 cm) long. ZONES 8–11.

Laurus nobilis *(above)*

SWEET BAY, BAY TREE, BAY LAUREL, LAUREL

A broadly conical tree, this species grows up to 40 ft (12 m) high and 30 ft (9 m) wide, but is gen-erally smaller in cultivation. Its glossy, dark green leaves are smooth and leathery and in classical times were used to make the victor's 'crown of laurels'. It produces small, star-shaped, fragrant yellowish flowers in late spring to early summer, followed by small, round, green berries that ripen to dark purplish black in autumn. This tree is suited to clipping and shaping. **'Aurea'** is a yellow-leafed form and **'Saratoga'** is best suited to training as a single-trunked tree. ZONES 7–10.

LAVANDULA
LAVENDER

These fragrant, evergreen, aromatic shrubs, of which there are around 25 species, are valued for their attractive lacy, fragrant, usually grayish foliage. Most species grow 24–36 in (60–90 cm) high and a similar width. The small mauve-purple or bluish purple flowers emerge from between bracts in erect, short spikes held on stalks above the foliage. The flowers mostly appear in spring. Oil glands at the bases of the flowers produce the pungent oil of lavender, which is ob-tained commercially by distillation from *Lavandula angustifolia* and *L. stoechas.*

CULTIVATION

These plants prefer full sun and fertile, well-drained soil; they will thrive in both acid and alkaline soils. The woodier species, such as *L. dentata,* are excellent as low hedges, and a light trim after bloom-ing keeps them neat. Hardiness varies with the species, although most are moderately frost hardy if the growth is well ripened by warm autumn weather. Propagate from seed or cuttings in summer.

Lavandula angustifolia
syns *Lavandula officinalis, L. spica, L. vera*
LAVENDER

This dense, bushy subshrub grows to about 3 ft (1 m) tall though usually lower, with narrow, furry gray leaves. It is grown mainly for the long-stemmed heads of purple, scented flowers that appear in summer and through the warm months; these are easily dried for lavender sachets, pot-pourri and the like. It makes an attractive low hedge and can be trimmed after flowering. There are a number of selected cultivars, of which 'Munstead' and the dwarf 'Hidcote' are outstand-ing. 'Alba' grows to 24 in (60 cm) with a 3 ft

Lavandula angustifolia 'Alba' *(above)*

Lavandula angustifolia 'Munstead' *(top right)*

Lavandula angustifolia 'Hidcote' *(above left)*

(1 m) spread; it has yellowish gray bark on its woody stems, pale gray-green foliage and white flowers in whorls. 'Jean Davis' grows to 15–18 in (38–45 cm) and has attractive blue-green foliage and tall pinkish white flowers. ZONES 6–10.

Lavandula dentata *(right)*

Densely packed, soft spikes of mauve-blue flowers remain on this shrub from autumn through to late spring in warm climates. A native of the western Mediterranean and Atlantic islands, its gray-green aromatic leaves are fern-like with blunt teeth or lobes. It grows to a height and spread of 3–4 ft (1–1.2 m). A marginally frost-hardy species, resistant to dry conditions and adaptable to most soils, it is often used as an edging plant to soften the harsh lines of paving. **ZONES 8–10.**

Lavandula × intermedia

ENGLISH LAVENDER, LAVANDIN

These naturally occurring and cultivated hybrids between *Lavandula angustifolia* and *L. latifolia* show considerable variation in plant size and flower form. Few exceed 3 ft (1 m) tall but they are otherwise something of a catch-all group. **'Provence'** has green foliage and small-bracted spikes of mauve-pink flowers. **ZONES 6–10.**

Lavandula × intermedia 'Provence' *(right)*

Lavandula stoechas *(right)*

SPANISH LAVENDER, FRENCH LAVENDER

Native to the western Mediterranean, this marginally frost-hardy species and some of its varied forms are the most striking of all lavenders when in flower. A small neat shrub, 20–30 in (50–75 cm) high, it has pine-scented, narrow silvery green leaves with inward-curling edges. In late spring and summer it is covered with spikes of deep purple flowers. Several bracts at the apex of each spike are elongated into pinkish purple 'rabbit ears' of varying size. **'Merle'** is a compact bush with long-eared, magenta-purple flowerheads. **'Marshwood'** is a particularly heavy flowering, long-blooming cultivar. *Lavandula stoechas* subsp. *lusitanica* has very narrow leaves and dark purple flowers with paler 'rabbit ear' bracts. *L. s.* subsp. *pedunculata* (syn. *L. pedunculata*), from Spain, North Africa and the Balkans, grows 18–24 in (45–60 cm) tall, with flower stalks reaching 2–3 in (5–8 cm). It has light green foliage and the tiny flowers are purplish, with terminal bracts of mauve pink. *L. s.* subsp. *luisieri*, which is a native of Portugal, is an upright bush with green rather than silver-gray foliage and large purple flower spikes. **ZONES 7–10.**

Lavandula stoechas 'Marshwood' *(above)*

L

LAVATERA

Closely related to the mallows and hollyhocks, this genus of 25 species of annuals, biennials, perennials and softwooded shrubs has a scattered, patchy distribution around temperate regions of the world, mostly in Mediterranean or similar climates. Some favor seashores. A few species are cultivated for their colorful mallow flowers, generally produced over a long season. These plants are upright in habit with simple to palmately lobed leaves, often downy to the touch. The shrubs and perennials in this genus are not very long-lived.

CULTIVATION
Moderately to very frost-hardy, these plants prefer a sunny site in any well-drained soil. Prune after a flush of blooms to encourage branching and more flowers. Propagate annuals, biennials and perennials in spring or early autumn from seed sown *in situ* (cuttings do not strike well), and shrubs from cuttings in early spring or summer.

Lavatera thuringiaca
(left)

This shrubby perennial from central and south-eastern Europe produces a glorious display of rose-pink, hollyhock-like flowers all summer on a sturdy bush up to 5 ft (1.5 m) tall. Softly mid-green leaves are an attractive foil for the flowers. Use at the back of a border or as a colorful hedge. Several cultivars with distinct flower colors are available. '**Barnsley**' bears sprays of pale pink flowers with deep pink centers throughout summer. It is very frost hardy. ZONES 6–10.

Lavatera thuringiaca 'Barnsley' *(below left & below)*

LEDUM

The 4 species in this genus are bushy evergreen shrubs resembling small versions of their close relatives the rhododendrons,
They are found widely in the cooler northern temperate regions
and into subarctic territories. They vary in height from 1–6 ft
(0.3–1.8 m) depending on the harshness of the environment in
which they are grown. In spring and summer the bushes are
covered in small, 5-petalled white flowers with protruding stamens.

CULTIVATION
Treat *Ledum* in the same way as cool-climate rhododendrons:
plant in cool, humus-rich, moist but well-drained soil in shade or
morning sun. They are among the most frost hardy of broad-leafed
evergreen plants. Propagate from seed or cuttings or by layering.

Ledum groenlandicum *(above)*
LABRADOR TEA

One of the few shrubs to survive the rigorous
climate of Greenland, this species is also found in
northern North America. It grows 3 ft (1 m) high
and 4 ft (1.2 m) wide. The wiry branches are covered in red-brown hair, as are the undersides of
the 1–2½ in (2.5–6 cm) long leaves. Clusters of
flowers open at the branch tips from late spring.
The leaves and stems are used in folk medicine as
inhalants or insect repellents. ZONES 2–8.

LEONOTIS

This genus of the mint family consists of around 30 species of annuals, perennials, subshrubs and shrubs, native to tropical and southern Africa except for one species that extends to tropical Asia and America. Only one species is widely grown as an ornamental, with showy 2-lipped flowers that are densely hairy on the outside (said to resemble lion's fur). The leaves are arranged in opposite pairs on square stems.

CULTIVATION
Plant in full sun in rich, well-drained soil. Do not over-water. The plants can be pruned back quite heavily in early spring. Propagate from seed in spring or from softwood cuttings in early summer.

L

Leonotis leonurus
(left)

LION'S EAR, WILD DAGGA,
LION'S TAIL

This semi-evergreen, shrubby perennial from South Africa is popular in all countries with warm-temperate or subtropical climates. A striking plant growing to 6 ft (1.8 m), its tall straight stems bear whorls of tawny orange, furry, tubular flowers in late summer and autumn. The leaves are lance-shaped and aromatic. This plant is fairly resistant to dry conditions and thrives in coastal situations. '**Harrismith White**' is a white-flowered cultivar.
ZONES 9–11.

LEPTOSPERMUM
TEA TREE

This genus of evergreen shrubs or small trees in the myrtle family is unrelated to tea *(Camellia sinensis);* the name 'tea tree' arose when Captain Cook and his crew used the aromatic leaves to make a 'tea' on their landfalls in both Australia and New Zealand, believing it would protect them from scurvy. The genus consists of 80-odd species, the great majority Australian but 1 or 2 from New Zealand and a handful scattered through the mountains of the Malay Archipelago and Peninsula. They are mainly upright growers with small, sometimes prickly leaves, and bear 5-petalled, white or pale pink flowers along the branches in spring or summer. These are followed by small capsules that release fine, elongated seeds—*Leptospermum* means 'slender seed'. Tea trees are widely planted in their native countries, also in California, for their rapid growth, pretty flowers and graceful habit. A few of the most frost-hardy species can be grown outdoors in the UK. Many cultivars have been named, mostly derived from the red-flowered New Zealand forms of *L. scoparium,* some with double flowers in shades from white to red.

CULTIVATION
They prefer a mild-winter climate, full sun and well-drained soil; some tolerate poor soils, dry conditions, or ocean spray. In cool climates they can be grown as conservatory plants or placed outdoors in tubs in summer. Prune lightly, if at all. Propagate from seed or cuttings in summer.

Leptospermum laevigatum *(right)*
COAST TEA TREE, AUSTRALIAN TEA TREE

Growing naturally among sand dunes along much of the east coast of Australia, this tall, bushy shrub or small tree bears attractive white flowers in profusion in spring and early summer. The small leaves are rounded at the tips and grayish green. It grows to about 20 ft (6 m) tall with a similar spread, and its shaggy-bark becomes gnarled and twisted with age. In South Africa it has become a much-hated weed. ZONES 9–11.

Leptospermum macrocarpum *(right)*
syn. *Leptospermum lanigerum* var.
macrocarpum

This shrub is known only from a small area of the Blue Mountains near Sydney, Australia. Mostly 2–6 ft (0.6–1.8 m) high and becoming very woody, it adapts to a range of soils and climates. The broad leaves are purplish green, and the flowers have an unusually large greenish yellow central receptacle, up to $\frac{3}{4}$ in (18 mm) across that glistens with nectar; it is out of proportion to the circular, usually flesh pink petals. The woody capsules are correspondingly large. It withstands pruning and can make a bonsai specimen. ZONES 8–11.

Leptospermum petersonii (left)
syn. *Leptospermum citratum*
LEMON-SCENTED TEA TREE

From the subtropical east coast of Australia, this frost-tender shrub or small tree grows to a height of 25 ft (7.5 m) with an open branching habit and rather pendulous branchlets, giving it a willow-like appearance. The narrow leaves have a characteristic lemon scent when crushed; new foliage is bronze red. A vigorous grower, it bears pendent sprays of small white flowers in spring and early summer. **'White Swan'** grows to 20 ft (6 m) tall; it responds well to pruning and is covered with a mass of white flowers. ZONES 9–11.

Leptospermum scoparium (above)
MANUKA, NEW ZEALAND TEA TREE

This species occurs throughout New Zealand and in the far southeast of Australia (mainly Tasmania). It is an adaptable plant, growing to 10 ft (3 m) tall, with mainly erect growth, small, broadly needle-like leaves and sweetly scented, white or pale pink flowers. The numerous cultivars have been selected or bred mainly in New Zealand, though in California the famous rose and camellia breeder Walter Lammerts created a number in the 1950s. Cultivars include

'Abundance' with salmon-pink double flowers in winter; **'Gaiety Girl'** with dark-centerd deep pink flowers; **'Keatleyi'** with pale pink flowers; **'Kiwi'**, a dwarf form with crimson flowers; **'Pink Cascade'** with horizontal branches and pink flowers; **'Pink Pixie'** with pink blooms; **'Ray Williams'** with dark-centerd white flowers striped with pink; **'Red Damask'** with double crimson blooms; **'Ruby Glow'** with dark foliage and double, dark red blooms over winter and spring; and **'Helene Strybing'**, which is especially popular in the USA. ZONES 8–10.

*Leptospermum
scoparium* 'Kiwi'
(above)

*Leptospermum
scoparium* 'Ruby Glow'
(above right)

*Leptospermum
scoparium* 'Pink
Cascade' *(right)*

*Leptospermum
scoparium* 'Red Damask'
as topiary *(right)*

LESCHENAULTIA
syn. *Lechenaultia*

This genus of 26 species of small evergreen shrubs, subshrubs and perennials, is from Australia; most species, including the most attractive ones, come from southwestern Australia where they grow in very poor sandy soil. Weak-stemmed plants, often with a suckering habit, they have small, flat or needle-shaped leaves. The flowers have 5 radiating petals, each with a smooth central portion, broad crinkled margins and broadly notched tips; some are brilliantly colored, in shades of blue, yellow, orange or red.

CULTIVATION

These are not the easiest plants to grow but they are worth trying in areas with mild winters, low summer humidity and well-drained, sandy soil. Plant in full sun or part-shade and provide moderate water. Potted specimens should be moderately watered during growth, less at other times. Propagate from seed in spring or from cuttings in summer.

Leschenaultia biloba *(left)*

BLUE LESCHENAULTIA, FLOOR OF THE SKY

With flowers among the most brilliant blues of any plant, this native of Western Australia's Perth region is an erect or straggling shrub, growing to a height and spread of 24 in (60 cm). It has small, soft, grayish green leaves and from late winter to late spring bears terminal groups of flowers that vary from pale to deep blue, sometimes with a central splash of white or sometimes all white. It needs a dry, sunny position and usually proves short lived in cultivation. It is easily grown from cuttings, so young plants can be held in reserve. Cut back over-long stems after blooming. ZONES 10–11.

Leschenaultia formosa *(left)*

RED LESCHENAULTIA

Common on poor soils in the far south of Western Australia, this suckering subshrub makes a low mound seldom more than 12 in (30 cm) high and sometimes with a much wider spread. The gray-green leaves are tiny and crowded and the showy scarlet, orange or yellow flowers appear from late winter to early summer, sometimes so profuse as to almost hide the foliage. It needs warm, dry summer conditions and a very free-draining, gritty soil. ZONES 9–11.

LEUCADENDRON

Closely allied to the proteas, this South African genus consists of 84 species of shrubs and small trees, the great majority of them native to western Cape Province. They are popular garden plants where soil and climate allow, and are grown commercially for cut flowers. The leaves are simple and leathery, varying greatly in shape and size and sometimes clothed in silvery hairs. The small flowers, are borne in dense globular or conical heads at the ends of the branches, but the heads are usually surrounded by a flower-like collar of bracts that also vary greatly in size and color. Male and female flowerheads are borne on separate plants. A number of hybrid cultivars have appeared in recent years, some bred for the cut flower industry.

CULTIVATION
Frost tender to marginally frost-hardy, leucodendrons do best in full sun and perfectly drained, sandy or gritty soil with added humus, preferably with low levels of phosphorus and nitrogen. Potted specimens should be well watered in periods of growth, less at other times. Propagate from seed or cuttings.

Leucadendron argenteum (right)
SILVER TREE

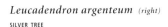

One of South Africa's rarest and most beautiful trees, the silver tree survives in the wild only on some slopes of Table Mountain. It grows 20–30 ft (6–9 m) tall, unbranched when young but later forming a narrow crown of erect branches, all covered in large, pointed gray leaves clothed in long silky hairs that give a silver cast to the whole tree. The bracts around the rather insignificant flowerheads, borne in winter and early spring, are hardly different from the normal leaves. Silver tree can only be raised from seed and makes fast growth, but is often very short lived in cultivation; it does not tolerate any root disturbance. ZONES 9–11.

Leucadendron eucalyptifolium (left)

This vigorous species is common in the wild in the coastal ranges of Cape Province, growing in deep, sandy soils. It makes an erect shrub up to 15 ft (4.5 m) tall with a single trunk at the base and a dense, bushy crown. Despite the name, the narrow leaves are no more eucalyptus-like than those of many other members of the protea family. A profusion of small flowerheads with long, narrow, bright yellow bracts surrounding the yellow-cream knob of flowers is produced in winter and spring. This easily grown species is becoming important in the cut flower trade. ZONES 9–10.

Leucadendron laureolum (left)

Confined to the Cape Town region, this is one of the most widely grown species in many parts of the world and has given rise to a number of cultivars. Growing to 6 ft (1.8 m) high, this bushy shrub has leathery oblong leaves and flowerheads with bracts cupped at the base, the color typically grading from soft yellow in the center to pale green outside; some forms have deeper gold bracts. It is a moisture-loving plant. ZONES 9–11.

Leucadendron 'Safari Sunset' (left)

A hybrid between Leucadendron salignum and L. laureolum, 'Safari Sunset' was developed in New Zealand, where it is much grown for use as a cut flower. A vigorous erect shrub, it grows rapidly to about 5 ft (1.5 m) with a densely branched, bushy habit. The deep green, oblong leaves are flushed with red, and the stems and bracts are a deep wine red in autumn to winter, at the height of the flowering season; these turn pale to golden yellow as the season progresses. Full sun is needed for maximum color. ZONES 9–11.

Leucadendron salignum (left)

Rather similar to Leucadendron laureolum and just as widely grown, this species has a much wider natural distribution in Cape Province and differs in its often red-tinged foliage, reddish buds, and bracts with reddish tips, though plain yellow-and-green forms are also known, as well as forms with rich red bracts. The bracts spread widely, especially on male plants; female flowers have a strong yeasty smell. It usually grows only 3 ft (1 m) tall and has many erect, branching stems. This species does poorly in humid-summer climates. ZONES 9–11.

Leucadendron 'Silvan Red' *(right)*

'Silvan Red' is a vigorous hybrid of the same parentage as 'Safari Sunset'. It is similar in style and coloring, but has more slender branches and narrower floral bracts. ZONES 9–11.

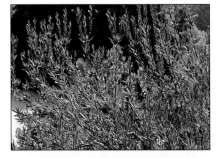

Leucadendron strobilinum 'Waterlily' *(center)*

Leucadendron strobilinum

Known only from the Cape Peninsula near Cape Town, this very attractive species is endangered in the wild. It is a shrub growing to more than 6 ft (1.8 m) with broad, incurved leaves. The conspicuous spring flowerheads have very broad, creamy yellow bracts that overlap and form a smooth cup around each fat, globular flowerhead. **'Waterlily'** is a selected female form with large bracts that pass through several color changes: initially bright green, they become cream at the center, then light yellow, and finally red-edged; the flowerhead itself is reddish brown. ZONES 9–11.

Leucadendron tinctum *(right)*

TOLBOS

Common in the hills and mountains of southwest Cape Province, this species grows to 4 ft (1.2 m) tall and to much the same width, and both male and female flowerheads are beautiful. The female cones are dark red, the males yellow, and both are enclosed by broad, red-suffused yellow bracts. It is a popular garden specimen in South Africa due to its beauty and its tolerance of wind and some frost. ZONES 9–11.

LEUCOPHYTA
CUSHION BUSH

This genus of the daisy family consists of a single species of ever-green subshrub, native to the southern seashores of Australia and formerly included in the genus *Calocephalus*. It is an intricately branched, mound-like plant with small scale-like leaves; all parts of the plant are clothed in silvery hairs that reflect light strongly, including the small knob-like flowerheads, though these give glimpses of cream florets. *Leucophyta brownii* is one of the plants most highly resistant to ocean spray, growing on the most ex-posed headlands and dunes. It also adapts well to garden con-ditions in mild climates, but shelter results in looser growth.

CULTIVATION
It prefers light, open soils of moderate fertility and must have sun. Once established the plants seldom need watering; they are not very long lived, often rotting at the base after a few years. Propagate from cuttings in summer.

Leucophyta brownii *(above)*
syn. *Calocephalus brownii*

This spreading shrub has a dense, rounded habit, growing at the most to 3 ft (1 m) high, but some-times wider, and making a silvery mound with its intricate, silvery gray branches. It flowers in sum-mer with creamy white, rounded knobs, which appear silver when in bud. The form from West-ern Australia has longer, slightly recurving leaves and is even more silvery. ZONES 9–11.

LEUCOSPERMUM
PINCUSHION

Leucospermum cordifolium
(below)
syn. *Leucospermum nutans*
NODDING PINCUSHION

Growing 3–6 ft (1–1.8 m) tall with a spread of about 3 ft (1 m), this species has a well-branched habit with sturdy, flowering branches bearing gray-green, very broad leaves and terminal flowerheads. These distinctive, dome-shaped blooms in yellow, orange and red tones are held over a long period through summer. 'Flame Spike' has deep orange-red flowerheads. '**Red Sunset**', a hybrid with *Leucospermum lineare*, bears red and gold flowers in spring. ZONES 9–11.

This genus might be confused with *Leucadendron*, another genus of protea allies from South Africa, but a quick look will show that their flowerheads are quite different in structure. It consists of about 50 species of woody evergreen shrubs, all but a very few native to western Cape Province with only about 4 from the summer-rainfall eastern regions, one of them extending just into Zimbabwe. Unlike proteas and leucadendrons they do not have showy bracts surrounding their terminal flowerheads, the flowers themselves being the showy part. Borne in tight clusters, they have long projecting styles giving the whole inflorescence the appearance of a pincushion. Long lasting and often brilliantly colored, they are favorite cut flowers. The leaves are usually stiff and leathery and often toothed around the tip. They are much grown in Australia and New Zealand, in the highlands of Hawaii from where they are exported to flower shops in the USA, and in Israel for the European market. Florists usually sell them as 'proteas' rather than accustom their buyers to the long Greek name, which means 'white seed' from the shining seed vessels.

CULTIVATION
They are mostly compact, attractive bushes full of flowers, which should be cut to encourage more. They need well-drained, slightly acidic soil and sunshine in a warm-temperate climate with low summer humidity. Propagate from seed or cuttings.

L

Leucospermum cordifolium 'Flame Spike' *(above)*

Leucospermum grandiflorum (left)

Found in the hills and mountains of southeastern Cape Province, this 5 ft (1.5 m) tall species is noted for its unusual flowerheads. They open from mid-winter to early summer and have relatively few styles. The styles, which are yellow, point almost directly upwards and are tipped with red pollen receptacles. ZONES 9–11.

Leucospermum reflexum (bottom)
ROCKET PINCUSHION

This species makes an erect shrub up to 10 ft (3 m) tall with a spread of 6 ft (1.8 m). The small, silvery leaves are clasped to the stems in a compact manner, and terminal crimson, yellow-tipped, spiky, reflexed flowers are borne profusely through spring and summer. *Leucospermum reflexum* var. *luteum* grows to over 12 ft (3.5 m) tall and has light, gray-green foliage and clear light yellow flowers. 'Chittick Red' is one of several New Zealand-raised Chittick cultivars. It has deep orange-red flowers. ZONES 9–10.

Leucospermum reflexum var. *luteum* (above left)

Leucospermum reflexum 'Chittick Red' (above right)

Leucospermum tottum *(above)*
syn. *Leucospermum gueinzii*

FIREWHEEL PINCUSHION

This dense shrub, to 5 ft (1.5 m) high and wide, has long, narrow, gray-green, oblong leaves covered with fine, short hairs. The dome-shaped flowerheads, 3–4 in (8–10 cm) wide, open in spring and summer, and are pinkish red with numerous cream styles radiating from the central boss. '**Scarlet Ribbon**' is a cross between *Leucospermum tottum* and *L. glabrum* with bright pink flowers and yellow styles. '**Golden Star**', a cross between *L. tottum* and *L. cordifolium*, has light yellow flowers on long slender stems. **ZONES 9–11.**

Leucospermum tottum
'Scarlet Ribbon' *(right)*

LEUCOTHOË

This genus, containing about 50 species of deciduous and ever-green shrubs allied to *Pieris*, is widely distributed in cool- to warm-climate regions from southern USA to the mountains of South America, with a few in East Asia. The plants have simple, alternate leaves and produce white or pink flowers in short axil-lary or terminal spikes. The fruits are small capsules containing many seeds.

CULTIVATION
These shrubs prefer moist, acidic, well-drained soil and a shel-tered position in sun or part-shade. Propagation is from seed, cuttings or from the suckering root sections of the plant, or by division.

Leucothoë davisiae *(left)*
SIERRA LAUREL

An evergreen shrub from the USA, this species will grow 3 ft (1 m) tall with a spread of 5 ft (1.5 m). In summer, it has 6 in (15 cm) long clus-ters of white, bell-shaped flowers and needs regu-lar water during the growing season. ZONES 5–10.

Leucothoë fontanesiana *(left)*
syn. *Leucothoë catesbaei*
PEARL FLOWER, DROOPING LEUCOTHOE

Indigenous to the southeastern states of the USA, this evergreen shrub grows 3–5 ft (1–1.5 m) tall. The arching stems bear leathery, long-pointed dark green leaves and pendulous spikes of small bell-shaped white or pinkish flowers through spring. **'Rainbow'** (or 'Golden Rainbow'), is a very popular cultivar, with cream and pink-mottled green leaves. ZONES 6–10.

LIGUSTRUM
PRIVET

This genus of about 50 species of shrubs and trees from temperate Asia, Europe and North Africa offers more than just the ability to grow in almost any soil or position and tolerance of regular clipping; some species are rather decorative. They range from shrubs to small trees, some evergreen, others deciduous; all grow very rapidly and bear abundant sprays of small white flowers in summer, almost always scented, though sometimes unpleasantly. The flowers are followed by black berries, which can look very striking against the gold-splashed leaves of the variegated cultivars. Birds feast on these and can easily overpopulate the whole district with privet seedlings. In the USA, Australia and New Zealand several species have become detested weeds in native woodland.

CULTIVATION
Grow in sun or part-shade in moist, well-drained soil. The roots are very greedy, and usually make growing anything else within their reach frustrating. Privets grow all too easily from seed in autumn or spring or by division; selected varieties need to be propagated from cuttings. They may be damaged by aphids, scale insects and leaf miner.

L

Ligustrum japonicum
'Rotundifolium'
(above left & right)

Ligustrum japonicum
JAPANESE PRIVET

This bushy, evergreen shrub from Asia has a dense habit and reaches 10 ft (3 m) tall with a spread of 8 ft (2.4 m). It has oval, glossy, dark green leaves and bears large conical panicles of flowers from mid-summer to early autumn, followed by blue-black berries. It can be used as a hedge plant. **'Rotundifolium'** is dense and slow growing, with thick, rounded leaves. ZONES 7–11.

Ligustrum lucidum *(right)*
GLOSSY PRIVET, WAXLEAF PRIVET

This upright evergreen shrub from China, Japan and
Korea reaches a height of 30 ft (9 m) and a spread of 25 ft
(8 m). It has large, pointed, glossy dark green leaves and
bears large panicles of small creamy white flowers in late
summer and early autumn. It has been declared a weed in
some areas of warm, wet climate. The leaves of **'Tricolor'**
are variegated with yellow, pink when young. **'Excelsum
Superbum'** is a vigorous cultivar with flecked deep yellow
leaves and small, cream-edged, tubular white flowers.
Although the blue-black fruit are poisonous, they are
used medicinally in China; it is claimed they prevent bone
marrow loss in chemotherapy patients and are a potential
treatment for AIDS, respiratory infections, Parkinson's
disease and hepatitis. **ZONES 7–11.**

Ligustrum lucidum
'Tricolor' *(left)*

Ligustrum vulgare *(above)*
EUROPEAN PRIVET, COMMON PRIVET

This bushy shrub from Europe, North
Africa and temperate Asia is deciduous or
semi-evergreen and reaches a height and
spread of 10 ft (3 m). It has dark green,
pointed, oval leaves and bears panicles of
small, strongly perfumed white flowers
from early to mid-summer, followed by
black berries. There are several cultivars
with variegated leaves. If using as a hedge,
prune back hard for the first few years of
growth then trim regularly. **ZONES 4–10.**

Ligustrum obtusifolium *(above)*

This deciduous Japanese shrub reaches 10 ft (3 m) in
height. It has graceful mid-green foliage and white
flowers in summer. ***Ligustrum obtusifolium* var.
*regelianum*** is frost hardy and has a horizontal branching pattern, growing 5–6 ft (1.5–1.8 m) tall. Its leaves
may turn purplish in spring and autumn, and the white
flowers are followed by black berries that last into winter. **ZONES 3–10.**

Liquidambar orientalis *(top)*

ORIENTAL SWEET GUM

This broadly conical tree from southwestern Turkey reaches 20 ft (6 m) tall with a spread of 12 ft (3.5 m). Slow growing, it bears bluntly lobed, smooth, matt green leaves that turn orange with purplish tones in autumn. Small yellow-green flowers appear along with the new leaf growth, followed by clusters of small, brown, rounded fruit. Thick, orange-brown liquid storax is obtained from the bark of this species. ZONES 8–11.

Liquidambar styraciflua *(below)*

SWEET GUM

This widely grown deciduous tree is native to eastern USA and Mexico and reaches a height of 80 ft (24 m) and spread of 40 ft (12 m). Young branches and twigs often have distinctive ridges of corky bark and its wood, known commercially as satin

LIQUIDAMBAR

This genus contains 4 species of deciduous trees from Turkey, East Asia, North America and Mexico belonging to the witch-hazel family. They are grown for their shapely form, handsome foliage and superb autumn colors. The leaves are deeply lobed, resembling a typical maple leaf. Some species produce a resinous gum known as liquid storax that is used to scent soap, as an expectorant in cough remedies and to treat some skin diseases.

CULTIVATION

They are temperate-climate plants, requiring sun or part-shade and fertile, deep, loamy soil with adequate water during spring and summer. They will not thrive in shallow, sandy soil. The trees are best allowed to develop their lower branches to ground level. Propagate by budding in spring or from seed in autumn.

walnut, is used for furniture-making. Its glossy dark green leaves color orange to red and purple in autumn. Globular heads of small yellow-green flowers appear in spring, followed by spiky, ball-like fruit clusters. Cultivars valued for their rich autumn coloring include **'Moraine'**; **'Burgundy'**: deep purple-red; **'Festival'**: pink through

yellow; **'Palo Alto'**: orange-red; **'Rotundiloba'**, an odd form bearing leaves with very rounded lobes;

'Variegata': streaked yellow; and **'Worplesdon'**: purple through orange-yellow. ZONES 5–11.

Liquidambar styraciflua 'Worplesdon' *(below right)*

LIRIODENDRON
TULIP TREE

Some botanists recognize only *Liriodendron tulipifera* in this genus. Most, however, accept *L. chinense* as another species, not just as a variety. Their 4-lobed leaves are distinctive: they look as though someone has cut their ends off with scissors. The flowers are also striking, in pale green with orange at the bases and numerous stamens. They do not, in fact, look much like tulips, but are more like their cousins the magnolias. Both are handsome trees, with straight boles and symmetrical crowns, but are too big and fast growing for any but the largest of gardens.

CULTIVATION
They prefer a temperate climate, sun or part-shade and deep, fertile, well-drained, slightly acid soil. Propagate from seed or by grafting. They are difficult to transplant.

Liriodendron tulipifera
(below right)

From eastern USA, this is an outstanding tree for cool climates, reaching 100 ft (30 m) or more with a spread of about 50 ft (15 m). A vigorous grower with a broadly conical habit, it bears green, lobed leaves that turn rich golden yellow in autumn. Its summer-blooming flowers are followed by conical brown fruit. The pale timber, called 'yellow poplar', is not very hard or durable but being fairly light and strong is much used in furniture-making. **'Aureomarginatum'** has green leaves heavily edged with yellow; **'Fastigiatum'** is about half the size, with an erect, columnar form. ZONES 4–10.

Liriodendron chinense *(below left)*
CHINESE TULIP TREE

From China, this deciduous tree is smaller and denser than *Liriodendron tulipifera*, reaching a height of 80 ft (24 m) and a spread of 40 ft (12 m). Fast growing with a broadly columnar habit, it has dark green, lobed leaves that turn yellow in autumn. The leaf undersides are gray-blue and covered with minute hairs. Flowers are borne singly on the ends of shoots in mid-summer, followed by conical, pale brown clusters of fruit that fall apart when ripe. ZONES 8–10.

Liriodendron tulipifera 'Aureomarginatum' *(above)*

LITCHI
LYCHEE

This genus consists of just one evergreen tree from southern China and Southeast Asia, which is grown throughout the subtropics for its foliage and delicious fruit. The lychee is grown commercially by the air layering or grafting of superior varieties.

CULTIVATION
It requires full sun and shelter from wind and cold, although it can withstand an occasional light frost. Deep, moist soil is best, with regular water. Propagate from seed in summer or by budding in spring. Trees raised from seed start to bear fruit after about 5 years.

L

Litchi chinensis
(right)
LYCHEE

A graceful, slim-trunked tree, the lychee reaches a height of 30 ft (9 m) and a spread of 10–15 ft (3–4.5 m). Bright green pinnate leaves, gold or pink when young, form a low-spreading crown. Clusters of small, greenish yellow, petalless flowers are borne in abundance in spring, followed by the bright red, edible fruit that contain a sweet, whitish pulp and a brown seed. The pulp is reminiscent in texture and flavor to grapes.
ZONES 10–11.

LOBELIA

This genus of 370 species of annuals, perennials and shrubs is widely distributed in temperate regions, particularly the Americas and Africa. Growth habits vary from low bedding plants to tall herbaceous perennials or shrubs. They are all grown for their ornamental flowers and neat foliage and make excellent edging, flower box, hanging basket and rock-garden specimens. Some are suitable for wild gardens or for growing beside water.

CULTIVATION
These frost-hardy to somewhat frost-tender plants are best grown in well-drained, moist, light loam enriched with animal manure or compost. Most will thrive in sun or part-shade but resent wet conditions in winter. Prune after the first flush of flowers to encourage repeat flowering, and fertilize weekly with a liquid manure in this season. Propagate from seed in spring or by division in spring or autumn. Transplant from late autumn until early spring.

Lobelia laxiflora *(above)*
TORCH LOBELIA

This clump-forming evergreen subshrub from Mexico and Guatemala grows to more than 3 ft (1 m) high and 24 in (60 cm) wide. Its arching leafy canes have axillary clusters of slender-stalked, tubular, red and yellow flowers. Marginally frost hardy, it blooms year round in warm climates; in cooler areas it is grown in conservatories. An annual trim will control legginess. ZONES 9–11.

Lobelia gibberoa *(above)*

This spectacular giant lobelia from the mountains of Africa can reach 30 ft (9 m) in height. It is rarely seen away from its homelands as it is not very amenable to cultivation. ZONES 9–10.

LOMATIA

From both sides of the South Pacific in eastern Australia and Chile, these 12 species of evergreen shrubs and trees are members of the protea family. They have leathery leaves, which vary from toothed to deeply and finely dissected, and grevillea-like flowers, which have distinctive spidery, twisted petals and styles that uncurl from the buds. The fruits are pod-like, somewhat woody follicles.

CULTIVATION

Mostly plants for cool but mild, humid climates, they require sun or part-shade and sandy, acidic, well-drained soil, preferably rich in organic matter. Some are moderately frost hardy but will need shelter from cold winds. Propagate from cuttings or seed in summer.

Lomatia ferruginea (right)
RUST BUSH

Native to southern Chile and Argentina, this tall shrub or small tree grows to 30 ft (9 m) tall, often with erect branches from the base. The new growths are covered with a brown, felt-like down; the fern-like, divided leaves consist of many olive-green leaflets. The flowers, which appear in late winter and spring, are produced in dense, branched spikes from the leaf axils; each flower has a red base, grading to yellow-green at the petal tips. **ZONES 8–10.**

Lomatia silaifolia
(right)
CRINKLE BUSH

From coastal areas of southeastern Australia, this several-stemmed shrub grows from a woody root-mass to about 5 ft (1.5 m) tall and has 8 in (20 cm), deeply dissected leaves that are silky when young. It produces showy, long terminal panicles of white flowers in summer. **ZONES 9–11.**

LONICERA
HONEYSUCKLE, WOODBINE

This diverse genus, found widely in the northern hemisphere, consists of around 180 species of shrubs and woody twining climbers, both evergreen and deciduous. They have leaves in opposite pairs and mostly smooth-edged, and 2-lipped flowers with a short to long tube, usually sweetly scented and yielding nectar to visiting bees or birds. Many honeysuckle species and their hybrids are valued garden plants as they are hardy, long lived and disease free, but often become straggly unless pruned annually. The shrub species are excellent for borders.

CULTIVATION
They are plants of temperate climates, easily grown in sun or light shade and not fussy about soil. They benefit from regular pruning to keep them from becoming hopeless tangles. Propagate from seed in autumn or spring or from cuttings in summer or late autumn. Watch for aphids.

Lonicera fragrantissima (above)
WINTER HONEYSUCKLE

From China, this bushy, deciduous or semi-evergreen shrub reaches a height of 6–8 ft (1.8–2.4 m) and a spread of 10 ft (3 m). The most fragrant of the shrubby species, winter honeysuckle bears short creamy white flowers in pairs, in some forms stained with rose carmine, in winter and early spring. The berries are dark red. New, dark green oval leaves appear shortly after the flowers and except in the coldest climates, will remain on the plant throughout winter. ZONES 4–10.

Lonicera nitida *(right)*

BOX HONEYSUCKLE

This evergreen shrub is possibly the smallest-leafed honeysuckle, forming a dense bush with masses of fine twigs bearing tightly packed, ½ in (12 mm) long, leathery, dark green glossy leaves. Gold and variegated foliage forms, such as **'Aurea'**, are available. The small, creamy white, spring flowers are not showy and the purple fruit are rarely seen in cultivation, so it is best regarded as a foliage plant. It withstands heavy trimming and is often used for hedging. **'Baggesen's Gold'** has tiny, bright yellow leaves, insignificant yellowish green flowers and mauve fruit. ZONES 6–10.

Lonicera nitida
'Baggesen's Gold' *(right)*

Lonicera × purpusii *(above)*

This deciduous or semi-evergreen hybrid bears small clusters of fragrant, creamy white, short-tubed flowers with yellow anthers in winter and early spring. The berries are bright red. It is a dense, bushy shrub with a height and spread of up to 6 ft (1.8 m). The oval leaves are dark to mid-green. It is frost hardy. ZONES 6–10.

Lonicera tatarica *(above)*

TATARIAN HONEYSUCKLE

This deciduous, bushy, medium-sized shrub ranges from the Caucasus region to central Asia. It grows to a height of 12 ft (3.5 m) and spreads to 10 ft (3 m). In late spring and early summer the dark green foliage is covered with trumpet-shaped flowers in shades from white to deep pink; blooms are followed by red berries. **'Arnold Red'** has darker green leaves and red flowers. ZONES 2–9.

LOPHOMYRTUS

This genus of 2 species of evergreen shrubs or small trees from New Zealand has been included in the genus *Myrtus* by many botanists. They are grown for their decorative foliage, which can be colorful and attractively aromatic, and for their small white flowers and dark red berries.

CULTIVATION

Moderately frost hardy, they prefer full sun, well-drained, fertile soil and ample water in the warmer months. Tip pruning in spring will keep them compact. Propagate in summer from seed or cuttings for the species, and from cuttings for the cultivars.

Lophomyrtus bullata 'Variegatum' *(left)*

Lophomyrtus bullata
syn. *Myrtus bullata*
RAMARAMA

This species grows to 25 ft (8 m) high and is characterized by its 1–2 in (2.5–5 cm) long, puckered (bullate), oval leaves. The foliage varies in color depending on where the plant is grown: in shade it is deep green, in sun it develops purple and red tones. Small cream flowers open in summer, followed by reddish purple berries. **'Variegatum'** has cream-edged leaves. ZONES 9–10.

Lophomyrtus obcordata *(center)*

This erect, bushy shrub grows to about 6 ft (1.8 m) high, its many twiggy branches holding small, notched leaves. Young foliage turns bronze purple during the winter months; small, white, summer flowers are followed by red berries that ripen to black. ZONES 8–10.

Lophomyrtus × ralphii

The many naturally occurring hybrids between the 2 species of this genus all take the name *Lophomyrtus × ralphii*. Selected clones grown in New Zealand include the widely seen **'Purpurea'**, which reaches about 6 ft (1.8 m) high, with puckered or crinkly leaves of a deep purple bronze throughout the year; **'Lilliput'**, a dwarf, compact shrub with tiny red and green leaves; **'Pixie'** with leaves that are pinkish red; and **'Variegata'** with rounded, deep green leaves with cream variegations. These forms are propagated from cuttings, best taken in early autumn as the new season's growth hardens. ZONES 8–10.

Lophomyrtus × ralphii
'Lilliput' *(left)*
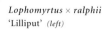

Lophostemon confertus
(below & below right)
syn. *Tristania conferta*
BRUSH BOX, BRISBANE BOX

Tall and massive in its natural habitat, the brush box grows to over 100 ft (30 m) and is native to coastal Queensland and New South Wales. Usually a dome-headed tree in an open position, it has mid-green foliage, smooth pinkish tan bark that peels in summer to reveal greenish cream new bark and profuse flowers hidden among the leaves. **'Variegata'** has cream central markings on the leaves, while **'Perth Gold'** has yellow coloration towards the leaf margins. ZONES 10–12.

LOPHOSTEMON

The 6 species of evergreen trees in this genus are related to *Metrosideros* and *Tristania* and occur mainly in tropical Australia and subtropical eastern Australia, also in southern New Guinea. Only the most southerly species, *Lophostemon confertus*, is widely grown, and it is also the tallest and most handsome. They have simple, leathery leaves grouped in pseudowhorls (like rhododendron leaves) on the branchlets, and white to cream flowers with 5 delicately fringed petals. The flowers are followed by woody seed capsules, very like those of *Eucalyptus*. In warm climates *L. confertus* is widely planted as a street or shade tree, and also for timber.

CULTIVATION
Frost-tender, they require a humid climate with ample summer rainfall. Plant in full sun or part-shade in fertile, well-drained, neutral to acid soil. Propagate from seed in spring or from cuttings in summer.

L

LUCULIA

This is a genus of 5 species of deciduous and evergreen shrubs and small trees from the Himalayas. They are much admired by gardeners for their attractive large, pointed leaves and clusters of scented pink or white flowers, but they have a reputation for being difficult to grow.

CULTIVATION

They need a humid, warm-temperate climate free from both severe frosts and dry conditions, and also acidic soil and perfect drainage to prevent root-rot. If the plants grow straggly—as they often do—they can be pruned gently after flowering. In cooler climates they succeed in mildly warmed greenhouses, altering their natural flowering season from earliest spring to summer. Propagation is from seed or summer cuttings.

Luculia gratissima
(left)

Reaching 20 ft (6 m) in height in its native eastern Himalayas, this semi-evergreen or evergreen shrub is normally no more than 8 ft (2.4 m) tall in gardens. It is grown in mild climates for its large, viburnum-like heads of fragrant pink flowers, up to 8 in (20 cm) across, which appear from mid-autumn to early winter. The leaves are bronze green, soft and up to 10 in (25 cm) long. **ZONES 10–11.**

Luculia intermedia
(left)

This beautiful evergreen shrub from China and the Himalayas reaches 12 ft (3.5 m) in height. It has perfumed pale pink flowers. **ZONES 9–11.**

LUMA

This genus consists of 4 species of evergreen shrubs and trees from Argentina and Chile, closely related to *Myrtus* in which genus they were formerly included. They have small, leathery, pointed, oval, deep green leaves and a dense, bushy growth habit. The small, creamy white, starry flowers are borne from mid-summer. The attractive bark of most species is a year-round feature; it is a reddish brown and flakes off to reveal white to pink new bark.

CULTIVATION

Although generally shrubby, old specimens can eventually grow to tree size but they can be kept as shrubs with trimming. Some species are suitable for hedging. They prefer moist, well-drained soil in sun or light shade. Propagate from seed or cuttings in late summer.

Luma apiculata
(right)
syns *Myrtus luma,*
Eugenia apiculata

An upright, bushy shrub or small tree, this species grows to around 50 ft (15 m) tall in the wild but can be kept to 10 ft (3 m) high with regular trimming and may be used for hedging. The small leaves are aromatic and the flaking bark is cinnamon brown with white wood underneath. The flowers have conspicuous stamens and smother the bush from mid-summer to mid-autumn. The fruit are dark purple berries.
ZONES 9–11.

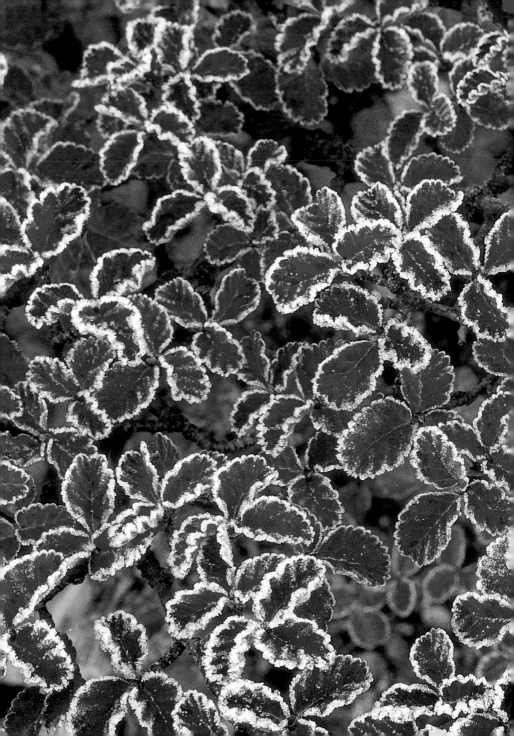

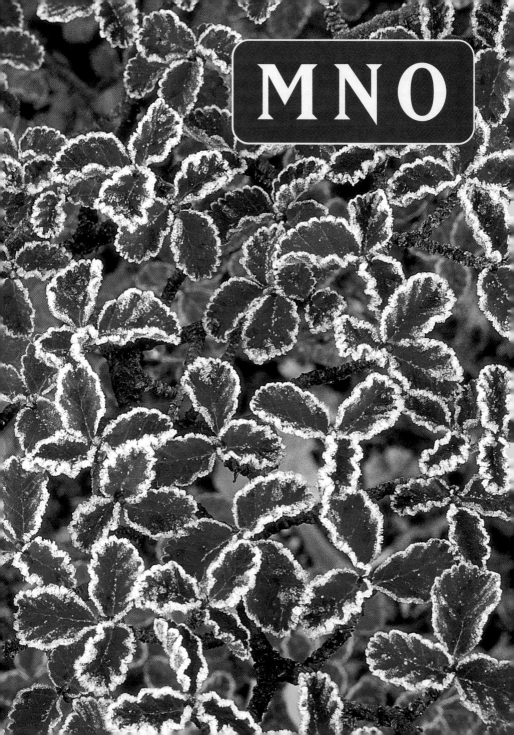

MNO

MACADAMIA

Consisting of 11 species, this relatively small genus from Australia, Sulawesi in Indonesia and New Caledonia is made up of small to medium evergreen rainforest trees. Their leathery, narrow leaves, usually in whorls of 3 or 4 on the twigs, have smooth or toothed edges. They bear small flowers, crowded on cylindrical spikes, and nuts that take up to 9 months to mature.

CULTIVATION

These frost-tender trees require sun, plenty of water and fertile, moist but well-drained soil. They flower and fruit year-round in the tropics and in summer in temperate climates, with the nuts ripening in late summer, usually 5 years after planting. The best crops come from selected cultivars commonly grafted onto seedlings. Propagate from ripe seed in autumn.

M

Macadamia tetraphylla (left)

ROUGH SHELL MACADAMIA NUT, BOPPLE NUT

Growing to about 40 ft (12 m) in height with a bushy habit when given room, this handsome tree has pink or white flowers on long, pendulous spikes. Its toothed, dark green leaves may be prickly. The young branchlets are pinkish red before darkening with age. ZONES 10–11.

Mackaya bella
(right)

FOREST BELL BUSH

This shrub is erect when young but develops a more spreading habit with maturity and eventually reaches 8 ft (2.4 m) in height. From spring to autumn, spikes of 5-petalled, funnel-shaped, pink flowers with dark veins are borne; it will flower into winter in warm climates. The leaves are glossy, deep green and oval shaped.
ZONES 10–11.

M

MACKAYA

A member of the acanthus family, this genus consists of a single species of evergreen shrub. Native along stream banks in forests of southern Africa, it has lustrous, deep green leaves. The short racemes of pale lilac, trumpet-shaped flowers with 5 large flared lobes with deep purple veining add to its attractive appearance.

CULTIVATION
To flower profusely, this frost-tender plant needs a semi-shaded position in a warm-climate garden or a sheltered microclimate and moist, well-drained, fertile soil. Propagate from cuttings in spring or summer, or seed in spring.

MAGNOLIA

This large, varied genus of 100 or more species of deciduous and evergreen trees and shrubs from East Asia and the Americas was named after French botanist Pierre Magnol. Magnolia leaves are usually oval and smooth edged. The flowers are generally large, fragrant and solitary, come in white, yellow, pink or purple, and vary in shape from almost flat and saucer-like to a narrow goblet shape. The fruits are cone-like or roughly cylindrical.

CULTIVATION

Magnolias require deep, fertile, well-drained soil. Some species require alkaline soil while others prefer a mildly acid, humus-rich soil. The roots are fragile so the plants do not transplant readily. They thrive in sun or part-shade but need protection from strong or salty winds. The flower buds are frost sensitive. Propagate from cuttings in summer or seed in autumn, or by grafting in winter.

Magnolia acuminata (above)
CUCUMBER TREE

This most stately of American deciduous magnolias reaches 90 ft (27 m) in the wild and develops a wide pyramid shape. The 10 in (25 cm) long, mid- to dark green leaves have downy undersides. The cup-shaped, slightly fragrant, greenish yellow flowers with erect petals appear singly in early summer; the green cucumber-shaped fruit ripen to red. ZONES 4–9.

Magnolia campbellii

This deciduous Himalayan species grows 80 ft (24 m)tall with a 40 ft (12 m) wide crown. Slightly fragrant flowers appear on leafless branches from late winter to mid-spring. Plants raised from seed take 20 or more years to flower. 'Alba' has pure white flowers; 'Charles Raffill' is white and rose purple; 'Lanarth' is a deeper rose purple; and *Magnolia campbellii* subsp. *mollicomata* flowers at an earlier age. ZONES 7–10.

Magnolia campbellii 'Charles Raffill' *(left)*

Magnolia campbellii
in winter *(above)*

Magnolia campbellii
'Lanarth' *(below)*

Magnolia campbellii
in summer *(above)*

Magnolia campbellii
(below)

M

Magnolia grandiflora (right)

SOUTHERN MAGNOLIA,
BULL BAY

One of few cultivated evergreen magnolias, this southern USA species forms a dense 60–80 ft (18–24 m) dome of deep green leathery leaves, rust-colored underneath. Cup-shaped white or cream blooms 10 in (25 cm) across appear during late summer, followed by reddish brown cones. It usually prefers warm, moist conditions, but many cultivars (including the Freeman hybrids with *Magnolia virginiana*) are hardier; others, such as **'Exmouth'**, have a more conical habit and fragrant flowers from an early age. **'Edith Bogue'** is renowned for its cold tolerance. Narrow semi-dwarf **'Little Gem'**, with smaller flowers, reaches up to 12 ft (3.5 m) tall or so in 15 years. **'Russett'** has a compact upright habit with beige suede-like leaf under-sides and compara-tively large flowers to 12 in (30 cm) across. ZONES 6–11.

Magnolia liliiflora
(left)
syn. *Magnolia quinquepeta*
LILY MAGNOLIA

A deciduous, bushy shrub, this Chinese species reaches 10 ft (3 m) tall and 15 ft (4.5 m) wide. The mid- to dark green leaves, downy on the under-sides, taper to a point. Fragrant, narrow, purplish pink flowers, whitish inside, are borne among the leaves from mid-spring to mid-summer. **'Nigra'** has large, dark wine purple flowers that are pale purple inside. *Magnolia lilliflora × stellata* **'Rosea'** was produced in the USA in the 1950s. ZONES 6–10.

Magnolia × soulangeana 'Lennei Alba' *(right)*

Magnolia sieboldii
(right)

OYAMA MAGNOLIA

This smallish tree or large shrub is one representative of a group of deciduous, summer-flowering species from China. Their pendent flowers distinguish them from the upright ones of the better known spring-flowering species. The white blooms are beautifully fragrant. **ZONES 7–10.**

Magnolia × soulangeana

SAUCER MAGNOLIA

This deciduous hybrid between *Magnolia denudata* and *M. liliiflora* first appeared in Europe in the 1820s. An erect tree to 25 ft (8 m) tall and 15 ft (4.5 m) wide, it is usually single trunked. The dark green leaves are tapered at the base and rounded at the tip, with a short point. Blooms in goblet, cup or saucer shapes and in white, pink or deep purple-pink appear from late winter to mid-spring, before and after the leaves emerge. '**Alexandrina**' flowers are pure white inside, flushed rose purple outside; and '**Brozzonii**' has large white flowers, purple at the base. Goblet-shaped cultivars include '**Lennei**', purplish pink outside, white to pale purple inside; '**Lennei**

Alba' with pure white flowers; and '**Rustica Rubra**', rose red outside and pink and white inside. **ZONES 5–10.**

Magnolia liliiflora '**Nigra**' *(right)*

Magnolia × soulangeana '**Alexandrina**' *(below)*

M

Magnolia ×
soulangeana *(left)*

Magnolia ×
soulangeana
'Brozzoni' *(right)*

M

Magnolia sprengeri

From central China, this deciduous, spreading
tree reaches a height of 70 ft (21 m) with a spread
of 30 ft (9 m). Closely related to *Magnolia
denudata*, it bears large, bowl-shaped, fragrant,
rose-pink flowers from early to mid-spring,
before the oval, dark green leaves appear. Popular
cultivars include **'Wakehurst'** and **'Diva'**.
ZONES 8–10.

Magnolia sprengeri
'Diva' *(left)*

Magnolia stellata
(left)

STAR MAGNOLIA

This many-branched,
compact, deciduous
shrub from Japan grows
10–15 ft (3–4.5 m) tall
and wide, with aro-
matic bark when
young, and narrow
dark green leaves.
Fragrant, star-like,
pure white flowers
open from silky buds in
late winter and early
spring, before the
leaves. It flowers when
quite young, and has
several cultivars in
shades of pink, includ-
ing **'Rosea'**. **'Waterlily'**, the most prolific
flowerer, has more
petals and slightly
larger white flowers.
ZONES 5–9.

M

Magnolia stellata
'Rosea' *(below)*

Magnolia virginiana *(left)*

SWEET BAY

From eastern America, this evergreen to semi-evergreen tree reaches a height of 20 ft (6 m) in gardens. In cooler climates it may become deciduous. Fragrant, creamy white, goblet-shaped flowers are produced in summer and are followed by red fruit 2 in (5 cm) long with scarlet seeds. The leaves of this species are smaller than those of most other magnolias. **ZONES 5–10.**

Magnolia wilsonii *(below)*

WILSON'S MAGNOLIA

From China, this spreading, deciduous shrub or small tree grows to 20 ft (6 m) high and wide. In late spring and early summer fragrant cup-shaped creamy white flowers with red or magenta stamens hang from arching branches among narrow, mid- to dark green leaves that are velvety beneath. Pink fruit follow, ripening to release shiny red seeds. It tolerates alkaline soil. **ZONES 7–10.**

M

MAHONIA

The 70 species of evergreen, low-growing to tall-flowering shrubs that make up this genus come from East Asia, and North and Central America. They have beautiful foliage, often fragrant yellow flowers, blue-black, dark red or purplish fruits that usually have a bloom of whitish or blue-gray wax on some taller species and cultivars, and interesting bark. The berries resemble miniature grapes and make an excellent jelly. They make useful hedges, wind-breaks and ground covers.

CULTIVATION

Cool-climate shrubs, they require a sunny aspect and well-drained, fertile soil with adequate water. In warmer climates they do better in shade or part-shade. They seldom need pruning, but old canes can be cut out at ground level. Propagate species from cuttings, basal suckers or seed; selected forms from cuttings or basal suckers.

Mahonia aquifolium (right)

OREGON GRAPE, HOLLY GRAPE

This dense, bushy species grows 6 ft (1.8 m) high and wide. Its 8 in (20 cm) long deep green pinnate leaves each consist of 5 to 9 holly-like leaflets; in the cooler months, these develop purple tones. Clustered heads of small, bright yellow flowers appear in spring, before the fruit. '**Compacta**' is a more compact form growing to about half the size of the species. ZONES 5–10.

Mahonia bealei (below)

LEATHERLEAF MAHONIA

This species is sometimes listed as a form of *Mahonia japonica* and differs mainly in its shorter, stiffer flower spikes and the fact that its leaflets often overlap and have a broader base. The leaf color is also deeper. *Mahonia bealei* is native to western China. ZONES 6–10.

M

Mahonia lomariifolia *(left)*

This is one of the tallest and most elegant mahonias, growing 10–15 ft (3–4.5 m) tall and 6–10 ft (1.8–3 m) wide. Its long, dark green leaves, borne mostly at the ends of the bamboo-like shoots, have narrow, holly-like spiny leaflets. Dense, upright racemes of fragrant, bright yellow flowers appear during late autumn and winter, before the purplish fruit. ZONES 7–10.

Mahonia repens

(left)

CREEPING MAHONIA

From western USA, this shrub grows to only 18 in (45 cm) or less in height. Its creeping habit makes it a useful ground cover, especially on uneven, rocky ground. The glaucous green leaves, with spiny leaflets, often turn a reddish shade in colder winters. Bunches of small, fragrant, yellow flowers are borne in spring, followed by the globular fruit. ZONES 6–9.

Mahonia × media *(left)*

This hybrid between *Mahonia japonica* and *M. lomariifolia* is one of several named cultivars of this cross that has been repeated several times in England to produce plants with the good foliage of the latter and the hardiness of the former. **'Charity'** has flowers in densely clustered racemes; **'Buckland'** bears its flowers in arching racemes. ZONES 6–10.

MALUS
APPLE, CRABAPPLE

This genus of 35 species of deciduous flowering and fruiting trees from the northern temperate zones contains the diverse crabapple as well as the many varieties of the long-cultivated edible apple, probably derived from crosses between several species and usually named *Malus* × *domestica* or *M. pumila*. The leaves are simple and toothed, sometimes lobed, and the flower clusters vary from white to deep rose pink or deep reddish purple. They are valued for their shapely form, moderate size and delicate spring blossom.

CULTIVATION
Very frost hardy, they prefer a cool, moist climate and full sun (but tolerate part-shade) and need fertile, well-drained, loamy soil with protection from strong winds. They grow in poorer soils if fertilized annually. Cut out dead wood in winter and prune for a balanced shape. Propagate by budding in summer or grafting in winter. Watch for aphids and fireblight.

Malus × *domestica*
'Jonathan' *(below)*

M

Malus × *domestica*
COMMON APPLE

This large hybrid group contains upright, spreading trees, usually with dark, gray-brown scaly bark and gray to reddish brown twigs. They can grow 30 ft (9 m) tall and 15 ft (4.5 m) wide. Their leaves are usually downy underneath and the white flowers are usually suffused with pink. The juicy, sweet fruit are green or yellow to red. These common orchard

Malus × *domestica*
cultivar *(left)*

trees are distinguished from the wild crab *(Malus sylvestris)* by their downy shoots, blunter leaves and juicy fruit that sweeten on ripening. Apples are not completely self-fertile and for fruit production a different cultivar growing nearby is needed. Advice on compatible pollinating cultivars should be obtained before buying apple plants. There are hundreds of cultivars; some of the best known are **'Crofton'**, **'Cox's Orange Pippin'**, **'Discovery'**, **'Delicious'**, **'Golden Delicious'**, **'Golden Harvest'**, **'Granny Smith'**, **'Gravenstein'**, **'James Grieve'**, **'Jonathan'**, **'McIntosh Rogers'** and **'Yvette'**. Many relatively new varieties are grown for their greater disease resistance. **'Gala'** is a small dessert fruit with excellent flavor and good storage qualities; **'Jonagold'** has large, yellow, red-striped fruit with good flavor and crisp texture; and **'Liberty'**, a highly productive and especially disease-resistant tree, bears striped dark red fruit with pale yellow, crisp flesh.

All the apples so far mentioned are generally accepted varieties that are grown commercially to supply year-round fruit. But there are many fine

M

Malus × *domestica*
'Granny Smith' *(left)*

Malus × *domestica*
'Golden Delicious' *(below)*

old apples worthwhile for home gardens and small orchards with special markets. **'Adam's Pearman'** is a quality dessert apple with golden yellow skin flushed bright red; **'Ashmead's Kernel'** is an upright spreading tree with light greenish yellow fruit and sweet white flesh; **'Blenheim Orange'** has yellow fruit with one half flushed dull orange red; **'Bramley's Seedling'** has large, late-ripening fruit best suited to cooking; and **'Ellison's Orange'** bears light greenish yellow fruit with soft juicy flesh and a rich flavor.

Some apple varieties have been bred as single-stemmed columnar forms, enabling the trees to be grown close together in a row without occupying a lot of ground. Named varieties include **'Starkspur Compact Mac'** and **'Starkspur Supreme Red Delicious'**. Some tall forms such as **'Jonamac'** can be trained over a path to make an arch. ZONES 3–9.

Malus × *domestica*
'Bramley's Seedling'
(above)

Malus × *domestica*
'Starkspur Supreme Red
Delicious' *(right)*

Malus × *domestica*
'Yvette' *(right)*

Malus florentina (left)
syn. × Malosorbus florentina

This species from northern Italy may be a natural hybrid between *Malus sylvestris* and *Sorbus torminalis*. It is a small round-headed tree with white flowers followed by small bright red berries. Its serrated gray-green foliage is similar to that of a hawthorn *(Crataegus)*. ZONES 6–9.

Malus hupehensis
(center)
syn. *Malus theifera*
HUPEH CRAB, TEA CRABAPPLE

From the Himalayas and China, where a tisane ('red tea') is made from the leaves, this vigorous, spreading crabapple grows 30 ft (9 m) tall and wide. The leaves are dark green, tinged purple when young. It bears large, fragrant white flowers, pink in bud, and small yellow and orange fruit that ripen to red. ZONES 4–10.

Malus floribunda
(left)
JAPANESE CRAB

This parent of many hybrids grows 25 ft (8 m) tall with a broad 30 ft (9 m) crown and arching branches. It bears profuse, pale pink flowers, red in bud, and tiny, pea-shaped, yellowish blushed red fruit. It is thought to have been introduced to Japan from China. ZONES 4–9.

M

Malus, ornamental crabapples

This group includes '**Beverly**', an upright spreading tree to 20 ft (6 m) high with white single flowers and small bright red fruit; '**Butterball**', up to 25 ft (8 m) tall with pink-tinged white flowers and bright orange-yellow fruit; '**Candied Apple**', a small, spreading tree with pink flowers and red fruit; '**Dolgo**', to 40 ft (12 m) with white flowers and purple-red fruit; '**John Downie**', conical when mature, with red-flushed orange fruit; '**Katherine**' with semi-double pink flowers and rich red fruit blushed yellow; '**Naragansett**', a good disease-resistant tree to 13 ft (4 m) high with showy red buds, white single flowers and pendulous clusters of cherry-red fruit; '**Pink Perfection**' with pale pink and white double flowers; '**Prince Georges**' with sterile, scented fully double pale pink flowers; '**Profusion**' with rich, dark wine red flowers and cherry-like, red-purple fruit; '**Radiant**', to 25 ft (8 m) high with deep red buds, deep pink single flowers and bright red fruit; '**Red Jade**', a weeping tree to 12 ft (3.5 m) with white- to pink-flushed flowers and glossy red fruit; and '**Strathmore**', a narrow upright tree to 9 ft (3 m) that bears fragrant dark pink flowers and purple fruit. ZONES 3–9.

Malus, ornamental crabapple, 'Pink Perfection' *(above right)*

Malus, ornamental crabapple, 'Butterball' *(right)*

Malus ioensis
(below right)

IOWA CRAB

Growing 20 ft (6 m) tall and 25 ft (8 m) wide, this leafy tree has a shrubby habit and good autumn color. Its heavy crop of large, fragrant, pale pink flowers is borne in late spring—it is one of the last crabapples to flower, and one of the finest. '**Plena**' has double flowers followed by green fruit; '**Prairiefire**' has glossy bark, red-purple single flowers and deep purple-red fruit. ZONES 2–9.

M

Malus pumila

This tree grows 12–15 ft (3.5–4.5 m) high and half as wide. It bears oval leaves with serrated margins, and pink and white flowers. The small, attractive fruit are ideal for stewing and have been used for generations for jellies and jams. **'Dartmouth'** is an open, spreading tree to 25 ft (8 m) with white flowers from pink buds and large crimson fruit. ZONES 3–9.

M

Malus sargentii *(below)*
SARGENT'S CRABAPPLE

A spreading shrub, this species reaches a height of 8–10 ft (2.4–3 m) and spread of 12–20 ft (3.5–6 m). It bears oval, dark green leaves with serrated margins, masses of white flowers and tiny, deep red fruit that last well into winter. Some branches may carry thorns. ZONES 4–9.

Malus pumila cultivar
(above)

Malus sieboldii
'Gorgeous' *(right)*

A cultivar whose breeder had no modesty, this green-leafed form has white blossoms from pink buds followed by good crops of green-red to deep red crabapples. This variety is considered a good one to harvest for jellies and preserves. **ZONES 5–10.**

Malus × purpurea
'Aldenhamensis' *(below)*

Malus × purpurea

These hybrid trees have very dark, sometimes glossy, bark and bronze or purple-red foliage. The flowers are large, red to purple-red, followed by small fruit of a similar color. Cultivars include **'Aldenhamensis'**, a spreading tree to 25 ft (8 m) with semi-double, wine-red flowers and purple-red fruit; and **'Eleyi'** with purple leaves, deep crimson flowers and purple-red fruit. **ZONES 4–9.**

Malus sylvestris *(above)*
WILD CRABAPPLE, COMMON CRABAPPLE

From Europe, this parent of orchard crabapples can grow 30 ft (9 m) tall and 10 ft (3 m) wide, and has a rounded crown and dark bark. It bears white flowers flushed with pink and its yellow, flushed orange-red fruit, although rather sour and bitter, make delicious conserves. The leaves have a partly red stalk and some branches may bear thorns. **ZONES 3–9.**

M

MANGIFERA

This is a genus of evergreen trees from India and Southeast Asia. Their dense, glossy leaves are drooping and tinged strongly with red when young; this feature of tropical trees is thought to protect them from sun and heavy rain. The fruits, which are drupes, consist of a big central stone usually containing 3 embryos: the first 2 result from pollination, the third arises entirely from the mother tree. If the first 2 are removed as the seed germinates, the third grows and replicates the parent fruit. Nonetheless, it is customary to graft selected varieties.

CULTIVATION

These trees tolerate subtropical conditions, but prefer tropical, monsoon climates. Rain at flowering time can rot the blossoms and ruin the crop. Plant in full sun in deep, rich soil; they need protection from strong winds. Prune when young to develop a single trunk. In addition to grafting, they can be propagated from ripe seed from summer to autumn. Check for fruit fly and fungal diseases.

Mangifera caesia (below)

This attractive tree can be planted as an ornamental in tropical parts of the world. It grows to about 120 ft (36 m) and its trunk at maturity can be attractively buttressed with fissured gray-brown bark. The fruit are elipsoid and 8 in (20 cm) long and 4 in (10 cm) wide, rough and yellow-brown. ZONES 11–12.

Mangifera indica (right)
MANGO

The mango can grow 80 ft (24 m) tall and wide, although grafted trees are normally smaller. The tiny, greenish spring flowers are borne in large sprays. The fruit resemble enormous peaches, though the skin is smooth, and ripens to orange or red. Seedling trees tend to have furry seeds, making juice extraction awkward, and their flavor is often marred by a bitter aftertaste. Selected cultivars have superior fruit, sweet to the last, with smooth pits; 'Alphonso' is universally regarded as the finest. ZONES 11–12.

MELALEUCA
PAPERBARK

The evergreen trees and shrubs that form this large genus are indigenous to Australia, except for a few species from Papua New Guinea, Indonesia and coastal Southeast Asia. Some species have beautiful papery bark which peels off in large sheets. They bear profuse, brush-like flowers with showy stamens, and their nectar provides food for birds and small mammals. The leathery leaves are small and cylindrical or flat.

CULTIVATION
Adaptable plants, they tolerate wet, even boggy conditions (but prefer well-drained soil), pollution, and salt-laden winds and soil. Although warm-climate plants, most species withstand light frosts if in full sun. Propagate from seed or cuttings taken just as growth begins. Prune shrubby species lightly straight after flowering. Melaleucas are remarkably pest- and disease-free.

Melaleuca armillaris (left)

BRACELET HONEY MYRTLE, DROOPING MELALEUCA

This 30 ft (9 m) tree has a spreading canopy of deep green needle-like leaves. The buds are usually pink or red, opening to white flowers in cylindrical spikes up to 2 in (5 cm) long in spring and summer. The gray, furrowed bark peels off in strips. Fast-growing, it adapts to a wide range of soil types. ZONES 9–11.

M

Melaleuca bracteata
'Revolution Green' *(left)*

Melaleuca bracteata

BLACK TEA-TREE, RIVER
TEA-TREE

This 30 ft (9 m) tree has dark gray, fissured bark and gray to deep green leaves scattered along branches. Creamy white flowers are held at the branch tips in summer. It adapts well to various soil and climatic conditions. Cultivars suitable for warm climates are **'Revolution Gold'**, with red stems and golden foliage that scorches in very hot weather; **'Revolution Green'**, 12 ft (3.5 m) tall with bright green foliage; and **'Golden Gem'**, 6 ft (1.8 m) tall. ZONES 9–11.

Melaleuca quinquenervia

(right)

BROAD-LEAFED PAPERBARK,
PUNK TREE

Best known of the broad-leaved melaleucas, this is a popular street and park tree in warm climates; it has become thoroughly naturalized in the Florida Everglades to the concern of environmentalists. Native to east-coastal Australia and New Caledonia, it usually grows in swamps, but adapts to quite dry soil in cultivation. The cream bark is very thick and papery, the leaves stiff and flat, and the white flowers appear in spring and sporadically at other times. It grows to 60 ft (18 m) or more tall. ZONES 10–12.

Melaleuca nesophila *(left)*

syn. *Melaleuca nesophylla*

WESTERN TEA MYRTLE, PINK
MELALEUCA

This bushy shrub, native to Western Australia, bears summer flowers that are brushes of mauve, gold-tipped stamens, fading to white, giving the plant a multicolored effect. Its leaves are oval, narrow, smooth and gray-green. It grows 10 ft (3 m) tall and 6 ft (1.8 m) wide. ZONES 9–11.

M

Melaleuca hypericifolia *(right)*

DOTTED MELALEUCA

This rounded shrub grows up to 15 ft (4.5 m) tall with oblong to elliptic leaves. Bottlebrush-like spikes, 3 in (8 cm) long, of pale red flowers appear in summer. ZONES 9–11.

Melaleuca thymifolia *(right)*

THYME HONEY MYRTLE

An upright or spreading shrub, this species grows to 3 ft (1 m). Its small, erect, blue-green leaves give off a spicy aroma when crushed. Pale to bright purple flowers with incurving stamens appear from late spring to autumn. It tolerates most soils, but thrives in a wet position in full sun. ZONES 9–11.

M

Melia azedarach (below)
syn. *Melia azedarach* var.
australasica

This is a fast-growing, spreading tree which grows to 30 ft (9 m) tall. The young leaves appear in late spring or early summer, with large sprays of small, delicately scented lilac flowers; these are followed by bunches of pale orange or cream berries, each containing a single woody seed, which persist after the leaves fall. They are poisonous to humans but much eaten by birds. **'Umbraculiformis'** has a curious yet attractive habit, like a blown-out umbrella. ZONES 8–12.

MELIA
PERSIAN LILAC, WHITE CEDAR, CHINABERRY, BEAD TREE, ROSARY TREE

This genus of only one very variable species of deciduous tree ranges across Asia from Iraq to Japan and south to Australia. *Melia azedarach* has many common names; 2 of them, bead tree and rosary tree, arise from the way the seeds have a hole through the middle, convenient for bead-making. The trees were formerly grown in southern Italy for making rosaries. *Melia* is Greek for 'ash' *(Fraxinus)*, although the only connection is that the pinnate or doubly pinnate leaves are vaguely similar.

CULTIVATION
A warm-climate plant, tolerating dry conditions and poor soil, it is a favorite street tree in arid climates. Propagate from seed in autumn.

MELIANTHUS

This small genus contains 6 species, all native to South Africa. Although they are shrubs, because of their often leggy growth, particularly the stunning *Melianthus major*, they are usually cut down to start again. Although grown for their foliage, the spikes of brownish red-bracted flowers are attractive, as well as drawing nectar-feeding birds; the flowers are followed by papery seed pods.

CULTIVATION

Grow in full sun or part-shade in moist but well-drained, fertile soil. They are only marginally frost hardy but a thick winter mulch will give added protection; they also need shelter from cold winds. Propagate from seed or cuttings in summer.

Melianthus major *(above)*
HONEY FLOWER, TOUCH-ME-NOT, HONEY BUSH

This sprawling bush grows to a height and spread of 6–10 ft (1.8–3 m). It is prized for its luxuriant foliage and for the brownish red, tubular flowers on terminal spikes that appear in spring and summer. The leaves have blue-gray, serrated leaflets. If pruned hard in early spring it will remain compact, but it will then flower less freely. The leaves have a strong, unpleasant smell when bruised, hence the common name touch-me-not. This species is slightly invasive in favored climates. ZONES 9–11.

MESPILUS

MEDLAR

Mespilus germanica (below)

In early summer, this species bears large, single, unperfumed white flowers, and its gnarled branches make it look ancient even when young. Its dark green leaves turn russet in autumn, particularly if the tree is grown in full sun. It spreads to 25 ft (8 m). ZONES 4–9.

Allied to the pears, the medlar, the single species in this genus from Europe and southwest Asia, has been cultivated for hundreds of years. A deciduous, sometimes thorny tree, it is grown primarily for its brown fruit, edible only after they are 'bletted' (almost rotten), which remain on the tree until well into autumn. Its large hairy leaves form a dense canopy.

CULTIVATION

Slow growing, the medlar resents being transplanted, but is easy to cultivate; it needs a temperate climate, well-drained soil and shelter from strong wind. It must not be allowed to dry out. Lightly prune for shape in early winter. Propagate from seed or by grafting.

M

METASEQUOIA
DAWN REDWOOD

Until shortly after World War II, *Metasequoia glyptostroboides,* the single species of the genus, was known only as a fossil conifer. Then a stand of living trees was discovered in western China; from these it has been propagated and widely planted in temperate-climate areas. It is notable for its gold and russet foliage in autumn—it is one of the few deciduous conifers. It grows very rapidly and, as the timber is durable and of fine quality, it is a very promising tree for cool-climate forestry.

CULTIVATION
It prefers full sun, deep fertile soil, good summer rainfall and shelter from strong winds. It is fully frost hardy. Propagate from seed or cuttings from side shoots in autumn.

Metasequoia glyptostroboides
(right)

Its gracefully conical outline and delicate foliage, light green in spring and summer, have made the dawn redwood a popular tree. It grows unusually fast in favorable conditions, and old trees may reach 200 ft (60 m) in height. As the tree matures, the rough-textured bark turns from reddish to dark brown to gray. It can be clipped to make a tall hedge.
ZONES 5–10.

M

Metrosideros excelsus
syn. *Metrosideros tomentosus*

POHUTUKAWA, NEW ZEALAND CHRISTMAS TREE

Reaching 40 ft (12 m) in height, this tree begins as a shrub with dense masses of spreading branches, then develops a stout main trunk and umbrella-shaped canopy. The oblong leaves are glossy deep green above and gray and felty underneath. The crimson stamens stand out from the flowers, borne from late spring to mid-summer in warm zones. The pohutukawa will survive in the most exposed seashore situations, as long as the soil is not saline. 'Variegata', with creamy yellow-edged leaves, is a popular cultivar. ZONES 10–11.

METROSIDEROS

The 50 or so species in this South Pacific genus are not all trees; some are shrubs or clinging vines. They are especially important in New Zealand where several species yield rata—the hard, dark red timber prized by the Maoris for sculpture—and where they range from the very edge of the sea to the high mountains. They have hard, leathery, evergreen leaves, often gray tinged, and red (sometimes bright yellow) summer flowers whose chief beauty, like those of the related *Eucalyptus* of Australia, comes from their long colored stamens.

CULTIVATION
Moderately frost hardy to frost tender, they do best in subtropical or warm-temperate climates, in full sun or light shade and fertile, well-drained soil. The shrubby species do very well as container plants. Propagate from seed in spring or cuttings in summer.

Metrosideros excelsus
'Variegata' *(left)*

Metrosideros carmineus *(left)*

AKAKURA

This New Zealand species is a self-clinging evergreen shrubby climber that, like ivy, starts as a juvenile non-flowering form while climbing. Later, as the branches grow out from it to support it, it starts to flower. If propagated from adult wood, it will make a small bush ideal for a rock garden. This species does best in moist semi-shade and is frost tender. ZONES 9–11.

Metrosideros kermadecensis

KERMADEC POHUTUKAWA

Though very similar to *Metrosideros excelsus,* the leaves of this species are slightly smaller and more oval, and the flowering season is usually longer. Much the same height as *M. excelsus,* it is more often seen in its variegated-leaf forms. '**Variegatus**' forms a neat shrub for many years, eventually making a tree of about 20 ft (6 m); the gray-green leaves are edged with an irregular creamy yellow margin. '**Sunninghill**' has the creamy yellow marking towards the middle of the leaf. ZONES 10–11.

Metrosideros excelsus
(right & below)

Metrosideros collina *(below right)*

One of the tropical species, this native of Samoa and southeast Polynesia ranges from being a 3 ft (1 m) high shrub to 65 ft (20 m) tree depending on the growing conditions and the particular form. Typically, it is a small, densely foliaged evergreen tree with lance-shaped leaves around 3 in (8 cm) long. Its flowers are orange-red to red and open in summer. ZONES 10–12.

M

*Metrosideros
kermadecensis
'Variegatus' (left)*

*Metrosideros
umbellatus (below)*
SOUTHERN RATA

Similar to the northern
rata, although not as
large, this species occurs
almost throughout New
Zealand and extends
into higher alpine
regions. It produces
masses of intensely
scarlet blooms from
late spring to autumn
and its flowering is a
feature of the bushlands
of the Southern Alps.
It grows very slowly.
ZONES 8–10.

M

*Metrosideros
robustus (right)*
NORTHERN RATA

This slow-growing
species from New
Zealand's North Island
and northern South
Island is a heavily
wooded tree 70 ft (21 m)
high. In the wild, it is
usually covered with
epiphytes and often
begins its own life as
an epiphyte, eventually
sending roots to
ground level. Masses
of brilliant orange-red
flowers open in sum-
mer. ZONES 9–11.

Michelia champaca *(left)*

CHAMPAK, CHAMPACA

From the lower Himalayas, this upright, conical tree reaches 100 ft (30 m) in its native habitat, but cultivated trees usually reach only a third of this height. Its long, slender, mid-green leaves droop from the somewhat horizontal branches. Cup-shaped creamy orange petals on a bed of recurved sepals are borne upright on the branch tips during late summer. The flowers are particularly fragrant. ZONES 10–11.

MICHELIA

Closely related to the magnolias, the 45 or so species of *Michelia* are found in tropical and subtropical Asia, with a few species in the cooler foothills of the Himalayas. They range from shrubs to substantial trees, mainly evergreen, and many bear intensely fragrant flowers. Some species are widely cultivated in India for their fragrant oil, which is extracted from the blooms for use in perfume and cosmetics.

CULTIVATION

They like frost-free climates and a position in full sun or part-shade in humus-rich, well-drained, neutral to acid soil; they resent being transplanted. Propagate from seed in autumn or spring, or from cuttings in summer.

Michelia yunnanensis *(below)*

In spring, this small, open-crowned 15 ft (4.5 m) tree produces furry brown buds which open to large, round, perfumed clusters of cream flowers with prominent yellow stamens. It is well suited to cool climates if protected from strong winds. Slow growing, it is a good tree for small gardens and for containers if consistently watered during its growing season. ZONES 9–11.

M

M

Michelia doltsopa
(left)

This 30 ft (9 m) tree
from the eastern Hima-
layas is slender while
young, developing a
broader crown with
age. The large, scented
white flowers, resem-
bling those of *Magnolia
denudata*, appear in the
axils of the glossy green
leaves in late winter and
early spring. **'Silver
Cloud'** was selected
due to its incredibly
abundant flower pro-
duction; otherwise it is
identical to the species.
ZONES 9–11.

Michelia figo
(below left)
syns *Magnolia fuscata,
Michelia fuscata*

PORT-WINE MAGNOLIA,
BANANA SHRUB

A slow-growing, com-
pact shrub from western
China, the port-wine
magnolia usually
grows as a dense 10 ft
(3 m)shrub. It bears
small, shiny, deep
green leaves and tiny,
spring-blooming, heav-
ily scented cream
flowers streaked with
purple. Pruning pro-
duces an abundance of
new flowering growth.
ZONES 9–11.

MICROBIOTA

There is just one species in this genus, a dwarf evergreen conifer that is excellent as a ground cover, as a specimen on its own, or grouped with other low-growing conifers or heathers. It also makes a good foil for other more colorful plants, such as bulbs.

CULTIVATION
Very frost hardy, it does best in free-draining soil with an open aspect, although it tolerates extremes of temperature and high altitudes. Prune only if absolutely necessary and then only into the new wood. Propagate from seed or from tip cuttings.

M

Microbiota
decussata (right)
RUSSIAN ARBORVITAE

This conifer from Siberia grows to only 18 in (45 cm) high with a spread of up to 10 ft (3 m). Its branches nod at the tips and bear flat sprays of scale-like, yellowish green leaves (bronze in winter). Its small, round cones are pale brown and contain one fertile seed each. ZONES 3–9.

M

MIMETES

This is a small genus of South African evergreen shrubs in the Protea family, about 11 in all. They are usually sparsely branched, and are well clothed with lance-shaped to ovate leaves. Those leaves towards the branch tips, between which the small flowers emerge, are often brightly colored. Most species grow on exposed heathland in phosphorus-poor soil. Like the related leucodendrons, these plants can be useful for floristry.

CULTIVATION

In Mediterranean climates with only light frosts, *Mimetes* will do well if given full sun, good drainage and a nutrient-deficient soil. The flowerheads can rot in prolonged wet conditions. Propagate from ripe seed. Seedlings should be potted individually without delay as they resent disturbance.

Mimetes cucullatus
(above)
ROOISTOMPIE

This handsome shrub from the southwestern and southern Cape area of South Africa reaches 5 ft (1.5 m) in height. Striking bright red and yellow and white inflorescences are produced from mid-winter to early summer. Plant in marshy, slightly acidic soil in full sun.
ZONES 9–10.

Mimulus
aurantiacus *(right)*
syns *Diplacus*
aurantiacus,
D. glutinosus,
Mimulus glutinosus
MONKEY MUSK

This marginally frost-hardy, evergreen shrub is native to North America. It bears crimson or yellow-orange flowers in spring and summer. The sticky, glossy, lance-shaped, rich green leaves have margins that roll slightly inwards. It grows 3 ft (1 m) tall and wide. ZONES 8–10.

MIMULUS
syn. *Diplacus*
MONKEY FLOWER, MUSK

The 180 or so species of annuals, perennials and shrubs of this genus are characterized by tubular flowers with flared mouths, often curiously spotted and mottled. They have been likened to grinning monkey faces, and come in a large range of colors, including brown, orange, yellow, red, pink and crimson. Mainly native to the cool Pacific coastal areas of Chile and the USA, most species are suited to bog gardens or other moist situations, although some are excellent rock garden plants.

CULTIVATION
Grow these plants in full sun or part-shade in wet or moist soil. Propagate by division in spring.

Mimulus longiflorus *(above)*
SALMON BUSH, MONKEY FLOWER

This shrubby species grows to about 3 ft (1 m) in height and spread, and has sticky 3 in (8 cm) long mid-green leaves. Its flowers, produced in spring and summer, can be from cream through yellow to orange and dark red. It is native to California and northwest Mexico. ZONES 9–11.

Morus nigra (left)
BLACK MULBERRY

Grown primarily for its fruit, this is the common mulberry of Britain and northern Europe, believed to have come from China or central Asia. It is similar to *Morus alba*, but has a thicker trunk, a more compact crown and darker leaves with velvety down underneath and blunt teeth. The fruit are dark red or almost black, sweet when ripe. **ZONES 6–10.**

Morus alba 'Pendula'
(below)

Morus alba
syn. *Morus bombycis*

WHITE MULBERRY, SILKWORM MULBERRY

This vigorous, low-branching tree has sustained the silk industry of China and Japan. It grows up to 40 ft (12 m) tall, with a broadly spreading crown and pendulous smaller branches. The almost hairless leaves are a fresh green-yellow in autumn, strongly veined and with sharp teeth. The rather rubbery fruit are cylindrical, sometimes lanceolate, and color varies from white through pink or red to purple-black. In east-coastal Australia a strain with purple-black fruit is regarded as the common mulberry. It prefers a climate with long, warm summers. 'Pendula' is a mushroom-shaped weeping form usually grafted onto standards to give initial height. **ZONES 5–10.**

MORUS
MULBERRY

There are about 10 species of deciduous shrubs and trees in this northern hemisphere genus. They bear broad, roughly heart-shaped leaves with closely toothed margins; the leaves on seedlings may be deeply lobed. Catkins of inconspicuous greenish flowers develop into tiny fruits, closely packed together to appear as a single fruit, the mulberry. Some species have been cultivated for centuries, for their edible fruit and for silk production: the silkworm larvae feed on the leaves.

CULTIVATION
They thrive under a wide range of conditions, but do best in fertile, well-drained soil in a sunny, sheltered position. Propagate from cuttings in winter, which can be quite large branches.

MURRAYA

Allied to *Citrus*, this small genus of evergreen trees and shrubs comes from India and Southeast Asia. They have aromatic foliage and attractive creamy white flowers, which resemble those of their relative, the orange, and are often strongly scented. The fruits are small, oval berries. They were named after John Andrew Murray, a pupil of Linnaeus.

CULTIVATION

Species of *Murraya* flourish in warm, frost-free climates in full sun or part-shade and humus-rich, moist but well-drained soil. When grown in borderline temperate situations, they need shelter. Early pruning ensures a shrub thickly branched from the ground up; clipping after the late flowering season will keep their shape. Gardeners in cooler areas should substitute it with the similar (though not so tall growing) *Choisya ternata*, from Mexico. Propagate from seed or cuttings.

Murraya koenigii (right)
CURRY LEAF TREE, KARAPINCHA

The leaves of this species are used in curries and other spicy dishes. From the Indian subcontinent, this aromatic shrub grows to about 10 ft (3 m). Loose sprays of small, fragrant, creamy white flowers stand out against the fresh green foliage in summer and are followed by small black fruit. ZONES 10–12.

Murraya paniculata (below)
syn. *Murraya exotica*
ORANGE JESSAMINE, MOCK ORANGE

Widely distributed in tropical Asia, this compact, rounded bush up to 10 ft (3 m) tall is densely covered with shiny, dark green leaflets. The small, creamy white, perfumed flowers are held in dense clusters at the branch tips in spring and at intervals thereafter. Red berries may appear after each flowering. ZONES 10–12.

M

MYRICA

Myrica is a genus of about 50 species of evergreen or deciduous shrubs and trees of worldwide distribution ranging in height from 5 ft (1.5 m) to 100 ft (30 m). Their fruits are clusters of bluish black berries enclosed in a white waxy crust. Tiny flowers appear in late spring; both sexes are borne on the one plant, the males in elongated catkins and the females in globular clusters.

CULTIVATION
Moderately frost hardy to frost tender, they thrive in part-shade, but will not grow in alkaline or chalky conditions, and must never be allowed to dry out. Propagate from seed or cuttings, or by layering in summer.

Myrica cerifera (below)
WAX MYRTLE

This evergreen shrub flourishes in southeastern North America, where it enjoys swampy conditions, peaty soil and the shade of taller trees. Reaching 30 ft (9 m) tall, *Myrica cerifera* bears narrow, glossy dark green leaves with unusual downy undersides. Its golden brown catkins are followed by the fruit, the wax on which is used in the manufacture of candles. ZONES 6–10.

Myrica californica (above right)
PACIFIC WAX MYRTLE

An evergreen shrub or small tree, this native of the west coast of the USA has dark green leaves and a decidedly upright habit, except where sheared by coastal winds. *Myrica californica* grows 25 ft (8 m) or more in height, less in spread. ZONES 7–10.

MYRTUS

MYRTLE

The Ancient Greeks and Romans knew these shrubs as *Myrtus*, from which 'myrtle' derives, via Old French. Contemporary botanists classify the southern hemisphere myrtles into several other genera, including *Lophomyrtus, Luma* and *Ugni*, leaving *Myrtus* with only 2 Mediterranean species. Myrtles are usually dense, evergreen shrubs with small, deep green, pointed leaves and starry white flowers in spring, sometimes followed by black-ish purple berries.

CULTIVATION

True myrtles prefer moist, well-drained soil and grow in sun or light shade. Trimming keeps them compact. They can be used for hedging or as container plants, clipped into a ball or pyramid. In cooler areas, container plants need protection during winter. Some foliage cultivars are available, but there is little variation in the flowers. Propagate from cuttings or from seed.

Myrtus communis
'Microphylla' *(below)*

Myrtus communis

TRUE MYRTLE

This erect shrub, to around 10 ft (3 m), has highly perfumed white flowers in spring, followed by edible berries ripening to blue-black with a delicate whitish, waxy bloom. The leaves, when crushed, are also very fragrant. Several cultivars exist including **'Compacta'**, a dwarf form with small-ish leaves; **'Flore Pleno'** with double white flowers; **'Microphylla'** with tiny leaves and flowers; **'Variegata'** with leaves edged white; and **'Tarentina'** with creamy white flowers and needle-like leaves. **ZONES 8–11.**

M

NANDINA

SACRED BAMBOO, HEAVENLY BAMBOO

This is a single-species genus from China and Japan. Despite its rather bamboo-like habit and the elegance of its leaves, it is actually related to the barberries. It grows as a clump of thin, upright stems, and bears sprays of white flowers in summer and red berries in autumn and winter. Plants are either male or female, and both are needed for the fruits to develop; hermaphrodite cultivars are available. The scientific name is a corruption of the Japanese name *nanten,* and the common name comes from the Oriental tradition of planting it in temple gardens; it is also popular in secular gardens.

CULTIVATION
This moderately frost-hardy species likes some shade, fertile soil and a warm-temperate or subtropical climate. In spring, prune straggly stems to the base on established plants. Propagate from seed or cuttings in summer.

Nandina domestica
'Nana' *(below)*

Nandina domestica

This shrub has strongly upright, cane-like stems and grows to 6 ft (1.8 m) high. The evergreen foliage is usually bipinnate and composed of many 1 in (25 mm), elliptical leaflets. These are red when young, becoming green and then developing intense yellow, orange and red tones when the cold weather arrives. The small white flowers appear in terminal panicles in summer. 'Nana' (syns 'Compacta', 'Pygmaea') makes a rounded, dwarf shrub of about 18 in (45 cm), often taking on deep scarlet and red tones in autumn and winter; 'Firepower' is similar in form, with bright pink or red winter foliage; 'Harbor Dwarf' is no more than 24 in (60 cm) high that spreads extensively by rhizomes to make a useful ground cover; 'Richmond' is an erect hermaphrodite that produces abundant dense clusters of fruit, without the need of a pollinating plant; 'Umpqua Chief' is a vigorous plant 5–6 ft (1.5–1.8 m) tall, with good winter color. ZONES 5–10.

Nandina domestica
(above)

Nandina domestica
'Richmond' *(right)*

NERIUM
ROSE LAUREL, OLEANDER

This small genus consists of 1 or 2 species of evergreen shrubs. They bear brightly colored, funnel-shaped flowers with 5 broad petals, followed by bean-like seed pods. The leaves are narrow, leathery and lance-shaped. *Nerium oleander* and its cultivars are the most common. All neriums are very poisonous and so very bitter that even goats will not eat them.

CULTIVATION
Plant these shrubs in full sun and in well-drained soil. If they get overgrown and leggy, they can be rejuvenated by severe pruning in spring. In frosty climates, they can be grown in containers and overwintered under glass. Propagate from seed in spring or from summer cuttings.

Nerium oleander

Depending on the cultivar selected, these plants can grow from 6–12 ft (1.8–3.5 m) tall. It is wise to keep the varying growth habits of the cultivars in mind if a uniform appearance or hedge is wanted. Some popular cultivars include: **'Album'** with single white flowers and a cream center; **'Little Red'** with single red flowers; **'Luteum Plenum'** with creamy yellow double flowers; **'Mrs Fred Roeding'** with salmon-pink double blooms and a relatively small growth habit; **'Petite Pink'** with single pale pink flowers and growing only 3–6 ft (1–1.8 m) tall; **'Punctatum'**, a vigorous plant with single pale pink blooms; **'Splendens Variegatum'**, with pink double flowers and variegated gold-green foliage borne at the expense of the profuse flowering habit of its parent **'Splendens'**; **'Algiers'** with its flowers of the darkest red; and **'Madonna Grandiflora'**, which has white double flowers. **'Casablanca'** (syn. **'Monica'**) has single, very pale pink, almost white flowers. **'Hawaii'** has apricot flowers edged with pink. ZONES 9–11.

Nerium oleander
'Petite Pink' *(left)*

Nerium oleander
'Hawaii' *(below)*

NEVIUSIA
SNOW-WREATH

This genus of only 2 species, is found on the cliffs above the Black Warrior River in Alabama, USA. A member of the rose family, it is a very frost-hardy plant, admired for its beautiful spring flowers.

CULTIVATION
This plant prefers reasonably fertile, well-drained soil but appreciates extra water in dry periods. After flowering, remove old wood by cutting back to the lowest outward-facing bud. Propagate by division or from cuttings or seed.

N

Neviusia alabamensis *(below)*
ALABAMA SNOW-WREATH

This deciduous shrub grows to around 5 ft (1.5 m) and has a stoloniferous root system. This means that it has a spreading, multi-stemmed habit, and needs ample room to develop. The spring-borne flowers, with distinctive spreading stamens, are pure white in their natural habitat, but usually creamy white in cultivation unless grown under glass. ZONES 5–10.

N

*Nothofagus
cunninghamii (above)*

TASMANIAN BEECH, MYRTLE
BEECH

This magnificent tree
attains a height of 150 ft
(45 m) or more when
grown in the cool,
mountainous regions
of its native southern
Australia. An ever-
green, it is one of the
faster growing species
in the genus, and is
valued for its reddish
timber. Its small,
triangular-toothed
leaves are held in fan-
shaped sprays and the
young foliage is a deep
bronze shade in spring.
Small catkin flowers
are borne in early
summer. **ZONES 8–9.**

NOTHOFAGUS
SOUTHERN BEECH

Wide ranging in the southern hemisphere from South America
to southeastern Australia, *Nothofagus* is a genus that contains
more than 25 species of evergreen and deciduous trees. They
are fast growing, and have dark green leaves often with toothed
margins. The foliage of several of the deciduous species displays
rich bronze hues before dropping in autumn. The small fruits
each contain 3 triangular seeds, which are commonly known
as beechnuts.

CULTIVATION

Southern beeches can be cultivated in a variety of climates provided they have protection from strong winds. They prefer acidic
soil deep enough to support their large root system and should
be planted out when small and never transplanted. Position in
full sun and water well when young. Propagate from cuttings in
summer or seed in autumn.

Nothofagus menziesii *(right)*

NEW ZEALAND SILVER BEECH

Famed for its beautiful
silver bark, this ever-
green species from
New Zealand bears a
mass of small, dense
leaves with coarsely
serrated margins.
Reaching a height of
70 ft (21 m), it needs
plenty of sun and pro-
tection from wind. The
flowers appear as small
catkins in summer.
ZONES 7–10.

Nothofagus obliqua *(right)*

ROBLE

Deriving its name from its characteristic, oblique
leaf base, the roble is a deciduous species from
Chile and Argentina. Growing to more than
150 ft (45 m), it has a broad spread of 20 ft (6 m)
and is suitable for cold regions. Its deeply toothed
leaves and attractive drooping habit make it one
of the most popular *Nothofagus* species in cultivation. Its leaves turn a deep reddish orange before
dropping. The roble is now grown as a plantation
crop for its fine timber and exceedingly rapid
growth. **ZONES 8–10.**

Nothofagus moorei
(left)

AUSTRALIAN BEECH, ANTARCTIC BEECH

This Australian ever-green tree prefers a part-shaded, frost-free position where its roots can stay moist during dry spells. It grows to a mature height of over 70 ft (21 m) with a broad head, and bears finely serrated, pointed ovate leaves up to 4 in (10 cm) long. Its mas-sive trunk is covered with brown, scaly bark. The tiny, insignificant flowers appear in early summer. **ZONES 9–11.**

Nothofagus gunnii
(opposite page)

TANGLEFOOT BEECH

This Tasmanian species is unusual among the southern beeches in that it is deciduous. That is in response to the harsh mountain environment in which it lives, as is its low-growing, often pros-trate growth habit. Tanglefoot refers to the twisted and contorted, sometimes foot-entan-gling, branch structure often displayed by weather-beaten plants in the wild; cultivated specimens, however, are neater and larger and can sometimes de-velop into small trees. The flowers are insig-nificant, but the small, rounded, crinkled leaves are attractive and often redden slightly before falling. **ZONES 8-9.**

Nothofagus fusca *(below)*

NEW ZEALAND RED BEECH

This attractive, erect evergreen has a dome-shaped crown and averages 20–40 ft (6–12 m) in height when cultivated and up to 120 ft (36 m) in the wild. The egg-shaped, roughly serrated foliage is up to 2 in (5 cm) long; immature leaves turn reddish bronze in cooler weather. Small, green flowers are followed by seed cups, each containing 3 angular seeds. **ZONES 7–10.**

N

Nothofagus gunnii
in winter *(right),*
in bud *(bottom right),*
in spring *(bottom left),*
in summer *(below)*

N

NOTOSPARTIUM

The 3 species of broom-like shrubs that comprise this genus are medium sized, reaching a maximum of 10 ft (3 m). They grow naturally in New Zealand, but have become popular in mild-winter climates elsewhere because of the profusion of charming, pea-shaped flowers that appear in mid-summer. The shrubs are leafless at maturity and attain their shape from graceful arching branches, which can spread to 6 ft (1.8 m).

CULTIVATION
They thrive in any well-drained soil, but must have full sun to flower. They may require staking. Propagate from seed in autumn or from cuttings taken in late summer.

N

Notospartium carmichaeliae *(left)*
NEW ZEALAND PINK BROOM

This deciduous shrub bears leaves only when the plant is young, and spends the rest of its life as a flat-stemmed, erect, slender bush. When in full spring flower, the shrub is smothered in lilac-pink blossoms which appear all along the branches. If protected from wind, flowering will continue for many weeks during warm weather.
ZONES 8–10.

Nuytsia floribunda
(right)

An evergreen species growing to 30 ft (9 m), *Nuytsia floribunda* has widely spreading branches and slender leaves about 3 in (8 cm) long. A magnificent display of honey-scented, orange-yellow flowers are borne in elongated clusters towards the end of the branches during the summer months. As the plants grow naturally in a moist position, cultivated specimens will need to be well watered, especially while young. ZONES 9–11.

NUYTSIA
WESTERN AUSTRALIAN CHRISTMAS TREE

This genus, consisting of a single species from Western Australia, was named after the Dutch navigator Pieter Nuyts. It is a terrestrial shrub or small tree that parasitizes the roots of grasses.

CULTIVATION
It seems that in cultivation this plant is not particular as to its host type—it germinates easily as long as a tuft of grass is added to the potting mix of young seedlings. Plant out when quite young in full sun, in combination with the initial host plant and in the vicinity of another likely companion. Propagate from seed or by root division.

NYSSA
TUPELO

Occurring naturally in southern Asia and North America, this genus is named after Nyssa, the water nymph, because the trees insist on adequate year-round water to survive. Fast growing and wind tolerant, they must be left undisturbed after planting and may reach a maximum height of 120 ft (36 m) with a broad-based, conical shape. Small clusters of greenish white flowers appear during summer, followed by vivid, dark purple berries up to 1 in (25 mm) long which provide an effective contrast to the stunning foliage. Few trees attract as much attention when they are clad in their spectacular red, crimson, yellow and orange autumn foliage.

CULTIVATION
They need fertile, moist but well-drained, neutral to acidic soil, sun or part-shade and a cool climate. Prune only to remove dead or crowded branches. Propagate from cuttings in summer or from seed in autumn.

Nyssa sylvatica
(above)

BLACK TUPELO, SOUR GUM, PEPPERIDGE

This elegant tree is one of the most decorative and useful of all deciduous plants, as it flourishes in swampy conditions. The glossy, 4 in (10 cm) long leaves, which are slightly wider towards the tip, are dark or yellowish green then turn brilliant red, often with shades of orange and yellow as well, before dropping. It grows to 70 ft (21 m) with a broad columnar conical habit and has an unusual trunk with brownish gray bark that breaks up into large pieces on mature specimens. ZONES 3–10.

N

Olea europaea
COMMON OLIVE

Olea europaea is a tree of wide distribution in Africa, Arabia and Himalayan Asia. The cultivated olive, *O. e.* subsp. *europaea*, is believed to have derived from smaller-fruited plants thousands of years ago. A slow grower to about 30 ft (9 m), it is very long lived, to compensate for its not coming into full bearing until it is at least 10 years old. Its picturesque habit, rough, gray bark and gray-green leaves, touched with silver on their undersides, make it a beautiful sight. *O. e.* subsp. *africana* has pea-sized black fruit and glossy dark green leaves, brown on the undersides. It makes a handsome small shade tree with a thick, gnarled trunk, but seeds itself so profusely as to become a problem weed in subtropical climates. ZONES 8–11.

OLEA
OLIVE

There are about 20 species in this genus, all long-lived, evergreen trees. They have leathery, narrow to broad leaves and tiny, off-white flowers that are followed by the fruit, known botanically as drupes. The most important species is the common olive *(Olea europaea)*, which has many cultivars and is the source of olive oil. Since ancient times it has been cultivated around the Mediterranean for its nourishing, oil-rich fruit. The fruit are too bitter to be eaten fresh: they must be treated with lye (sodium hydroxide) before being pickled or preserved in their own oil. The wood of the olive tree is prized for carving and turning.

CULTIVATION
Generally, these plants require a mild climate, but the winters need to be sufficiently cool to induce flowering, while the summers must be long and hot to ensure development and growth of the fruits. Although olives can survive on poor soils, better cropping will result if the trees are given a well-drained, fertile loam with ample moisture when the fruits are forming. Propagate from seed in autumn, from heel cuttings in winter or from suckers.

O

Olea europaea subsp. *europaea* (right)

OLEARIA
DAISY BUSH

Indigenous to Australia and New Zealand, this genus consists of 130 or more species of evergreen shrubs and small trees. The plants are characterized by daisy-like flowerheads, which can be white, cream, blue, lavender, purple or pink, that appear from spring to autumn.

CULTIVATION

Olearia species need full sun and fertile, well-drained soil; many species are tolerant of salt, wind and atmospheric pollution. Those species with dense foliage make excellent shrubs for hedging, particularly if pruned hard after flowering to encourage growth. Propagate from seed or cuttings in summer.

O

Olearia ilicifolia *(below)*
MOUNTAIN HOLLY, HAKEKE

This species earns both its botanical and common names from the resemblance of its leaves to those of the holly, *Ilex aquifolium*. It is a 10 ft (3 m) daisy bush with a rounded crown made up of stiff, dull, grayish green leaves with undulating margins. This is one of the few species in this genus whose white flowers are fragrant. From New Zealand, it prefers light soils and a protected position. ZONES 8–10.

Olearia paniculata *(above)*
AKIRAHO

Native to New Zealand, *Olearia paniculata* can grow to 20 ft (6 m), but is more usually seen as a shrub half that height. The bark is coarsely grooved and the pale yellow-green, wavy-edged leaves are grayish white on the undersides and up to 2½ in (6 cm) long. The clustered, creamy white flowerheads appear in autumn and, while lacking conspicuous ray florets, they are pleasantly scented. This species is tolerant of exposed coastal positions and can be planted as a windbreak or clipped hedge. ZONES 9–11.

Olearia macrodonta *(left)*

This New Zealand shrub has 2–4 in (5–10 cm) long, somewhat glossy, holly-like leaves. They are deep green above with grayish white hairs below. The flowerheads are white and yellow in the middle and the bush blooms heavily from early summer. It grows to about 6 ft (1.8 m) in cultivation; if necessary, trim to shape after flowering. **ZONES 8–10.**

Olearia × scilloniensis *(below)*

This dense, upright to rounded hybrid originated in Tresco in the Scilly Isles as a cross between the southeastern Australian species *Olearia lirata* and *O. phlogopappa*. Small white flowers are borne in spring. It grows to a height and spread of 6 ft (1.8 m). **ZONES 8–10.**

Olearia phlogopappa
(below right)
syn. *Olearia gunniana*
DUSTY DAISY BUSH

This 6–10 ft (1.8–3 m) high, erect shrub from southeastern Australia bears numerous white flowerheads up to 1 in (25 mm) across in late spring; in some selected forms they are mauve-blue or purplish. The oblong leaves are grayish green, under 2 in (5 cm) long with serrated margins. Its height makes it an effective screen or windbreak for seaside gardens or parks. Prune back hard or it can become very straggly. **ZONES 8–10.**

ORIGANUM
syn. *Marjorana*

MARJORAM, OREGANO

Native to the Mediterranean region and temperate Asia, these perennials and subshrubs in the mint family have aromatic leaves and stalked spikes or heads of small tubular flowers with crowded, overlapping bracts. Some species are grown as culinary herbs, while others are grown for their decorative pink flowerheads. With arching or prostrate stems arising from vigorously spreading rhizomes, they make useful plants for trailing over rocks, banks and walls.

CULTIVATION These plants like full sun and a moderately fertile, well-drained soil. Trim excess growth regularly and propagate from seed in spring or by root division in autumn or spring.

Origanum calcaratum (below)

This dense, shrubby perennial has heart-shaped to almost circular leaves densely clothed in white, woolly hairs. These help protect the plant from water loss during the hot, dry summers experienced on the islands of the Aegean Sea, where it occurs naturally. Small pink flowers are produced in summer, but this plant is more usually grown for its foliage. ZONES 9–11.

Origanum rotundifolium (right)

This deciduous species from Turkey and the Caucasus has small, rounded green leaves, and reaches a height and spread of about 12 in (30 cm), spreading by rhizomes. It bears nodding spikes of white or pale pink flowers with inflated pale green bracts in late summer and early autumn. ZONES 8–9.

OSMANTHUS
syn. *Siphonosmanthus*

Several of the 30 or so species of evergreen shrubs and trees in this genus are native to the Himalayas, China and Japan. Several are prized for the fragrance of their blooms, which some consider the sweetest and most attractive of all flowers, reminiscent of jasmine or gardenia. The Chinese use the flowers to enhance the scent of tea. The white or cream flowers of most species are rather inconspicuous. They are slow growing, with some eventually reaching 50 ft (15 m). The thick, rigid leaves may be edged with stout, even hooked, spiny teeth.

CULTIVATION
Plants should be clipped after flowering to maintain their compact shape. Plant in rich, well-drained soil in a sheltered position in either sun or part-shade. Propagate from seed or cuttings or by layering.

Osmanthus heterophyllus
syn. *Osmanthus ilicifolius*

HOLLY OSMANTHUS,
HOLLY TEA OLIVE

Native to Japan and Taiwan, this shrub produces leaves of rather variable shape, some toothed like holly leaves and others only toothed at the tip. It grows to a height and spread of some 15 ft (4.5 m), and is sometimes grown as a hedge.

Osmanthus heterophyllus 'Variegatus' *(above)*

It bears sparse, rather inconspicuous white flowers in early summer. **'Gulftide'** has very spiny leaves; **'Purpureus'** has very dark purple leaves; and **'Variegatus'** has leaves irregularly edged in white. ZONES 7–10.

Osmanthus delavayi *(below left)*
syn. *Siphonosmanthus delavayi*

DELAVAY OSMANTHUS

This species grows to a height and spread of around 6 ft (1.8 m). It has serrated, oval, dark green leaves, 1 in (25 mm) long, held on arching branches. The white flowers are tubular, about $^1/_2$ in (12 mm) long, and are borne profusely in the leaf axils and at ends of branches during summer. ZONES 7–9.

Osmanthus fragrans *(below)*

SWEET OSMANTHUS,
SWEET OLIVE

With a height of around 10 ft (3 m), this shrub can be trained as a small tree. Its broad, deep green leaves act as a foil to the clusters of very small, creamy white or yellow flowers, which are borne intermittently from spring to autumn. ZONES 7–11.

O

OSTEOSPERMUM

This genus of 70 or so species of evergreen shrubs, semi-woody perennials and annuals is mostly indigenous to South Africa. Allied to *Dimorphotheca*, they have irregularly toothed leaves and produce a profusion of large, daisy-like flowerheads in the white, pink, violet and purple range. Most of the commonly grown osteospermums are cultivars of uncertain origin, suspected to be hybrids. Tough plants, they are useful for rock gardens, dry embankments or the front rows of shrub borders, particularly as temporary filler plants.

CULTIVATION
Osteospermums are marginally to moderately frost hardy. They do best in open, well-drained soil of medium fertility. An open, sunny position is essential. Light pruning after flowering helps maintain shape and extends the ultimate lifespan. Propagation is from cuttings of non-flowering shoots or from seed in summer.

Osteospermum
ecklonis 'Starshine'
(below)

Osteospermum ecklonis
syn. *Dimorphotheca ecklonis*

BLUE-AND-WHITE DAISYBUSH, SAILOR BOY DAISY

Native to eastern Cape Province, this often shrubby plant is variable in growth habit. Some are erect forms to 5 ft (1.5 m) tall and other types are lower and more spreading, or even semi-prostrate. From late spring to autumn, it bears profuse, 3 in (8 cm) wide daisies, sparkling white with deep reddish violet centers and streaked bluish mauve on the undersides of petals. 'Starshine' is a more compact plant with white flowers. ZONES 8–10.

O

OSTRYA
HOP-HORNBEAM

There are 10 species of deciduous trees in this genus scattered through temperate regions of the northern hemisphere. Allied to the true hornbeams *(Carpinus)*, they have similar toothed leaves that are prominently veined and tapered to a point. In spring, the yellow male catkins look attractive against the bright green new leaves; these are followed in summer by the shorter fruiting catkins, each small nutlet enclosed in a bladder-like bract like those of hops *(Humulus)*, hence the common name. Hop-hornbeams may be rather slow growing in the early stages but are attractive small- to medium-sized trees, usually with a good autumn coloring.

CULTIVATION
To flourish, these frost-hardy trees need a sheltered position in full sun or part-shade and fertile, well-drained soil. Prune only to remove dead branches. Propagate from seed in spring.

Ostrya carpinifolia
(below)
HOP-HORNBEAM

Native to southern Europe and Turkey, the hop-hornbeam forms a compact tree of up to 60 ft (18 m) with a conical crown. Its toothed, dark green leaves turn a clear yellow before falling and look very attractive against the smooth gray bark of its trunk. The pendent fruiting catkins are cream to straw-colored, about 2 in (5 cm) long. ZONES 2–9.

O

OXYDENDRUM
SORREL TREE, SOURWOOD

The single deciduous tree species in this genus is a native of eastern USA and is grown for its autumn foliage and flowers. The leaves are alternate and finely toothed; the fragrant, small urn-shaped flowers are held in drooping terminal panicles. The genus takes its name from Greek words meaning 'sour tree', a reference to the sour-tasting foliage.

CULTIVATION
For the best autumn colors, it should be planted in an open position in sun or part-shade in moist soil. An occasional dressing of iron and/or ammonia after flowering may be required. Propagate from cuttings in summer or seed in autumn.

Oxydendrum arboreum (left)

Making a small, 20–40 ft (6–12 m) tree, this cool-climate species tolerates frost better than it does dry conditions. The trunk is slender and the crown pyramid-shaped. Streamers of small white lily-of-the-valley-like flowers appear in late summer sometimes prior to, sometimes coinciding with, the display of deep scarlet foliage. ZONES 3–9.

O

OZOTHAMNUS

This genus consists of about 50 species of evergreen shrubs from Australia and New Zealand, all of them until recently classified in the genus *Helichrysum*. Their foliage is aromatic, even quite resinous and sticky in some species; individual leaves are mostly small and whitish on the undersides or reduced to tiny scale-leaves in some species. Flowerheads are tiny, with white or yellowish papery bracts, but often massed into large flat or domed sprays.

CULTIVATION

Some of the smaller-growing species make attractive rock garden plants. They prefer freely draining soil and shelter from cold, drying winds. Most species will tolerate light frosts and some are moderately frost hardy. Prune leggy specimens before spring growth and propagate from cuttings in summer.

Ozothamnus ledifolius
(below)
syn. *Helichrysum ledifolium*
KEROSENE BUSH

From the mountains of Tasmania, this species bears small white flowerheads from reddish buds in early summer. The small blunt-tipped leaves, dark green above and yellow beneath, are crowded onto the yellowish twigs. It has a neat, rounded habit, with a height and spread of 3 ft (1 m). Plant in a sheltered situation to take full advantage of its sweetly aromatic foliage. Its common name comes from its highly resinous and hence inflammable foliage, used for kindling in Tasmania. ZONES 8–9.

O

PQ

PACHYSTACHYS
GOLDEN CANDLES

This genus of 12 species of evergreen perennials and small shrubs can reach 6 ft (1.8 m) and are grown for the splashes of bright yellow and red they add to gardens. In cool climates they are popular as indoor plants. They have large, bright green leaves and yellow floral bracts that almost hide the true flowers, which are small, white and tubular. The flowers themselves last only a few days, but the bracts are colorful over several weeks.

CULTIVATION
They require frost-free conditions in at least a warm-temperate climate, preferably subtropical, full sun and fertile, moist but well-drained soil. If used as indoor plants, they prefer warm, well-lit, humid conditions. Cold winter drafts will cause foliage loss. Propagate from seed or cuttings.

Pachystachys lutea
(below)

This small, shrubby plant forms a clump of upright stems with a 'candle' of bright golden yellow bracts at the tip of each stem. The creamy white flowers within do not reveal themselves until the bracts are fully developed. The leaves are a deep matt green, lance-shaped, up to 6 in (15 cm) long and have prominent veins. Widely grown as a house plant, it makes a cheerful display all summer, and can be treated as a bright summer annual in warm climates. ZONES 10–12.

PAEONIA
PEONY

There are 33 species in this genus of beautiful perennials and shrubs. The genus name goes back to classical Greek and arose from the supposed medicinal properties of some species. Peonies are all deciduous and have long-lived, rather woody rootstocks with swollen roots, and large compound leaves with the leaflets usually toothed or lobed. Each new stem in spring terminates in one to several large, rose-like flowers. Their centers are a mass of short stamens that almost conceal the 2 to 5 large ovaries, which develop into short pods containing large seeds. The flowers are mostly in shades of pink or red, but there are also white and yellow-flowered species. The great majority of peonies are herbaceous, dying back to the ground in autumn, but there is a small group of Chinese species, known as the 'tree peonies' that have woody stems, although no more than about 8 ft (2.4 m) in height, so strictly they are shrubs. Cultivars of this tree peony group produce the largest and most magnificent of all peony flowers, some approaching a diameter of 12 in (30 cm), mostly double and often beautifully frilled or ruffled.

CULTIVATION
Most peonies will only succeed in climates with a cold winter, allowing dormancy and the initiation of flower buds, but new foliage and flower buds can be damaged by late frosts. They appreciate a sheltered position in full or slightly filtered sunlight, but with soil kept cool and moist. Mulch and feed with well-rotted manure when leaf growth starts, but avoid disturbing roots. Pruning of the tree peonies should

Paeonia lutea (below)
YELLOW TREE PEONY

This shrub from western China was introduced to the West in the late nineteenth century. It grows to a height and spread of 5 ft (1.5 m) and from late spring to early summer bears single, clear yellow flowers about 6 in (15 cm) across. Leaves are dark green with saw-toothed margins. *Paeonia lutea* var. *ludlowii* grows to 8 ft (2.4 m) and produces bright yellow flowers in late spring. ZONES 6–9.

Paeonia suffruticosa (above)
TREE PEONY, MOUTAN

Native to China, this handsome deciduous shrub reaches a height and width of 3–6 ft (1–1.8 m) and produces very large single or double, cup-shaped flowers in spring. Depending on the variety, these are white, pink, red or yellow, and are set among attractive, large, mid-green leaves. *Paeonia suffruticosa* subsp. *rockii* has semi-double white flowers with a maroon blotch at the base of each petal. ZONES 4–9.

P

be minimal, consisting of trimming out weaker side shoots. Propagate from seed in autumn, or by division in the case of named cultivars. Tree peony cultivars are best propagated from basal suckers, but few are produced. Hence, plants on their own roots are very expensive. A faster and cheaper method is to graft them onto herbaceous rootstocks, but the resulting plants are often short lived.

Paeonia lactiflora Hybrids

These herbaceous Chinese peonies are derived mainly from *Paeonia lactiflora*. They have handsome foliage, which is maroon tinted when it first appears in spring, and usually scented flowers in a huge range of colors and forms. **'Bowl of Beauty'** grows to 3 ft (1 m) tall and between late spring and mid-summer bears dense clusters of slender, creamy white petaloids nesting in the center of broad, pink outer petals. **'Duchesse de Nemours'** is a fairly tall grower with fragrant, white to soft yellow flowers with frilled incurving petals. **'Félix Crousse'** bears deep pink double flowers with a red center. **'Festiva Maxima'** has large, fully double, scented flowers with frilled petals that are white with red flecks. **'Inspecteur Lavergne'** is late-flowering with fully double red flowers. **'Jan van Leeuwen'** is pure white. **'Monsieur Jules Elie'** has very deep cerise-pink single flowers. **'Sarah Bernhardt'** has scented, double, rose pink flowers with silvery margins. ZONES 6–9.

Paeonia lactiflora
'Duchesse de Nemours'
(left)

Paeonia lactiflora
'Festiva Maxima' *(left)*

PALIURUS

This genus is made up of 8 species of deciduous or evergreen
spiny shrubs or trees from the Mediterranean region. The trees
can reach 20 ft (6 m) or more in height. Because of their thorns,
the shrubs have long been used as hedging plants. The leaves are
oval and glossy green. The yellowish green star-shaped flowers
appear in summer; they are followed by small, winged fruits.

CULTIVATION
They require a position in full sun and well-drained, fertile soil.
Propagate from cuttings taken in late summer or from seed
in autumn.

Paliurus spina-christi (below)
CHRIST'S THORN

This is one of the plants thought to have been
used for Christ's crown of thorns. It can be grown
as a small tree, but is usually seen as a deciduous
tall shrub or hedge plant. Its branches, covered
with pairs of long thorns, form an excellent
barrier. Erect when young, these spiny branches
arch over as side branches appear. Tiny yellow
blooms are followed by decorative fruit. The
foliage turns a rich yellow before dropping in the
cooler months. ZONES 8–11.

P

Pandanus tectorius
(left)

HALA SCREW PINE, PANDANG

This species, found on seashores around the western Pacific, is often wider than its height of 25 ft (8 m), and the weight of its branches is supported by stout, buttress-like aerial roots. Male flowers are sweetly scented. The leaves, used for thatching and weaving, have long spines on their edges and on the undersides of their midribs. **ZONES 11–12.**

PANDANUS
SCREW PINE

This genus from East Africa, Malaysia, Australia and the Pacific contains about 600 species, a few of which make decorative trees for seaside gardens and swampy areas in frost-free climates. Palm-like evergreens, some grow 50 ft (15 m) or more tall, but they often lean at an angle. The sword-shaped, spiny-edged green leaves are arranged spirally at the ends of the branches. The white flowers are very small. The fruits, aggregations of reddish or yellow berries, up to 12 in (30 cm) in diameter, resemble a pineapple.

CULTIVATION
Pandanus require a tropical or subtropical climate, full sun or part-shade, and moist, well-drained soil. They can be treated as house plants when young if they are given ample water. Keep the plants tidy by removing dead or damaged leaves. Propagate from seed, soaked for 24 hours before planting, or by detaching rooted suckers.

Paraserianthes
lophantha (above)
syn. *Albizia lophantha*

CRESTED WATTLE, CAPE LEEUWIN WATTLE,
TREE-IN-A-HURRY

Occurring naturally in coastal south-western Australia and on some volcanic mountains of Indonesia, this tree grows quickly to about 25 ft (8 m). The yellowish green, brush-like flower spikes appear in late winter and spring. The feathery grayish green leaves have the unusual habit of folding up at night. In favorable conditions crested wattle may grow to 12 ft (3.5 m) in its first summer and often flowers within 12 months of germination; it self-sows freely and sometimes becomes a nuisance. ZONES 9–11.

PARASERIANTHES

This genus consists of 4 species of small to large evergreen trees that were formerly included in the genus *Albizia*. They occur wild in Australia and the islands to its north. All have feathery bipinnate leaves with small crowded leaflets, and mimosa-like flowers that are crowded into dense spikes in the upper leaf axils. The taller tropical species are grown in plantations for fuel and timber, having extraordinarily fast growth rates, while the smaller-growing *Paraserianthes lophantha* is used in gardens for instant effect and to provide shelter for slower-growing plants.

CULTIVATION
P. lophantha, the only species seen in gardens, grows in any soil and will thrive in full sun or part-shade. Marginally frost hardy, it may be grown as a greenhouse plant in cold climates. Propagate from seed in autumn. Held within flat pods, the seeds germinate faster if nicked or filed before planting.

PARROTIA
PERSIAN WITCH-HAZEL

Parrotia persica
(below)

This spreading, short-trunked, deciduous tree with flaking bark can reach 40 ft (12 m) in the wild, but rarely grows above 25 ft (7.5 m). The roughly diamond-shaped leaves turn magnificent shades of yellow, orange and crimson in autumn. ZONES 5–9.

This genus from Iran and the Caucasus was named after F. W. Parrot, a German botanist. It consists of one tree species grown for its rich autumn hues and unusual flowers. The petal-less flowers consist of upright, wiry, dark red stamens enclosed in brown bracts. They appear in early spring before the leaves, which are about 4 in (10 cm) long with undulating edges. The branches on older trees dip downwards.

CULTIVATION

A lime-tolerant tree, it is said to achieve its best colors when grown in slightly acid soil. It grows well in full sun, fertile soil and temperate climates. Propagate from softwood cuttings in summer or from seed in autumn—germination can take up to 18 months.

P

PAULOWNIA

Originating in eastern Asia, some of the 17 species of deciduous trees in this genus grow very fast, to 8 ft (2.4 m) in their first year, eventually growing to 50 ft (15 m). Their big, heart-shaped leaves and dense clusters of elegant flowers make them distinctive shade trees. Conspicuous, attractive buds appear in autumn, opening in spring to foxglove-like flower spikes; leaves and wing-seeded capsules follow. Some species are grown for timber in China and Japan.

CULTIVATION
Frost-hardy, they like well-drained, fertile soil, with ample moisture in summer and shelter from strong winds. Propagate from seed or root cuttings in late summer or winter.

Paulownia tomentosa (right & below)
syn. *Paulownia imperialis*
PRINCESS TREE, EMPRESS TREE

This tree, up to 40 ft (12 m) high and wide, is valued for its large, paired, heart-shaped leaves, up to 12 in (30 cm) wide, and erect, fragrant, pale violet flowers. Grown in both cool- and warm-temperate climates, it can suffer frost damage to the flower buds. If pruned almost to the ground each winter, the tree will develop branches about 10 ft (3 m) long with enormous leaves, but will not flower. ZONES 5–10.

P

PELARGONIUM

Pelargoniums are popularly known as 'geraniums', but should not be confused with members of the genus *Geranium* in the same plant family. The genus *Pelargonium* consists of perhaps 280 species, the vast majority endemic to South Africa and adjacent Namibia, with a sprinkling of species found elsewhere in the world including other parts of Africa, southwest Asia, Arabia, Australia, New Zealand and some Atlantic Ocean islands. Although pelargoniums are mostly soft-wooded shrubs and subshrubs, some are herbaceous perennials or even annuals. Only those considered shrubs and subshrubs are included in this book. The leaves of pelargoniums are often as broad as they are long and are variously toothed, scalloped, lobed or dissected; they are usually aromatic, containing a wide range of essential oils, and may secrete resin droplets which give the leaves a sticky feel. Flowers of the wild species have the 2 upper petals differently colored or marked from the 3 lower ones, a feature that distinguishes pelargoniums from true geraniums. Their seeds are plumed like thistledown, another distinguishing feature.

Only a few groups of hybrid pelargoniums are widely grown in gardens and as indoor plants, originating in the early nineteenth century from a small number of South African shrub species. The common garden and pot 'geraniums' are the **Zonal pelargoniums**, once known botanically as *Pelargonium* × *hortorum*. They have almost circular leaves with scalloped margins, often with horseshoe-shaped zones of brown, red or purple, and flower almost continuously. This group has the largest number of cultivars, and recent breeding has developed some very attractive subgroups. Somewhat similar are the **Ivy-leafed pelargoniums**, with their semi-scrambling habit and leaves that are fleshier with more pointed lobes; these are also the subject of intensive breeding, and are tending to merge with zonals in some of their characteristics. Another major group is the **Regal pelargoniums**, sometimes known as the **Martha Washington geraniums** or *Pelargonium* × *domesticum*; these have woody stems and sharply toothed and creased leaves, and the large flowers come in a range of gaudy colors and patterns. Then there is a large and varied group, grown primarily for their foliage, known as the **Scented-leafed pelargoniums**: these are mostly shrubby and usually have deeply lobed or dissected leaves that give off a quite remarkable range of odors when bruised or crushed, depending on the variety. They include both species and hybrids, and some also have quite pretty flowers. Some of these are grown commercially for 'geranium oil', used in perfumery.

CULTIVATION
These frost-tender plants are often treated as annuals for summer bedding in colder climates. In warmer climates with long hours of daylight they flower almost all the time, although they do not do well in extreme heat and humidity. Plant in pots or beds. The site should be sunny with light, well-drained, neutral soil. If grown in pots, fertilize regularly and cull dead heads. Avoid over-watering; Zonals in particular rot at the base if soil remains wet, although stems re-root higher up (but weaker plants result). Propagate from softwood cuttings from spring to autumn.

Pelargonium crispum

LEMON GERANIUM, FINGER-BOWL GERANIUM

A distinctive species from South Africa's south-west Cape Province, *Pelargonium crispum* is an erect, few-branched shrub to 3 ft (1 m) high, its straight stems regularly lined with small lobed leaves with crinkled margins, lemon-scented when bruised. The scattered pink flowers appear large in proportion, up to 1 in (25 mm) across with darker markings. **'Variegatum'** (syn. 'Prince Rupert Variegated') is a widely grown form with cream-edged leaves. **'Prince Rupert'** is a vigorous, larger-leafed form. ZONES 9–11.

Pelargonium crispum 'Variegatum' *(right)*

Pelargonium grandicalcaratum *(left)*

Only rarely seen in cultivation, this species comes from near-desert regions of South Africa's Cape Province and Namibia. An 18 in (45 cm) tall deciduous shrub, it has peppery scented leaves that are rather fleshy, 3-lobed and seldom over $\frac{1}{2}$ in (12 mm) long. The flowers have a $\frac{1}{2}$ in (12 mm) long tube-like base that, along with the calyx and stem, is red tinted. The small, mauve flowers with purple markings never open fully; the upper petals curl back, but the lower petals remain folded over one another. ZONES 9–11.

Pelargonium quercifolium *(right)*

OAK-LEAFED GERANIUM, ALMOND GERANIUM

This scented-leafed species is an erect shrub growing to around 5 ft (1.5 m) tall. It has deeply lobed and serrated-edged, dark green leaves that are perhaps, as the name suggests, slightly reminiscent of oak leaves. The leaves and stems are sticky and highly aromatic. The flowers are purple-pink with the 2 upper petals bearing darker markings. ZONES 9–11.

Pelargonium, Regal Hybrid,
'Morwenna' *(left)*

Pelargonium, Regal Hybrids

MARTHA WASHINGTON GERANIUMS, REGAL GERANIUMS,
REGAL PELARGONIUMS

The spectacular large blooms of these hybrids
make them suitable for exhibiting in flower shows
and conservatories, as well as for sale as flowering
pot plants. Originally derived from the South
African mauve-flowered *Pelargonium cucullatum,*
further breeding brought in red, purple and white
coloring from *P. fulgidum, P. angulosum* and
P. grandiflorum respectively. Sprawling shrubs,
about 24 in (60 cm) high, they have strong woody
stems and stiff, pleated, sharply toothed leaves. In
late spring and summer, they bear clusters of
large flowers, wide open and often blotched or
bicolored. Frost tender, they need a greenhouse in
cool areas. Cut back hard after blooming to keep
the bushes compact. **'Grand Slam'** is heavy
flowering and compact, its blooms deep pinkish
red suffused salmon pink with darker markings
and a small white center. **'Morwenna'** (syn.
'Morweena') has deep maroon flowers shading to
near black. **'Rembrandt'** has some of the largest
and most richly colored flowers—3 in (8 cm)
wide and deep purple edged with lavender, the
edges frilled. **'Rosmaroy'** is bright pink with reddish markings. **'Vicky Clare'** has multi-colored
blooms, deep purple-red on the upper petals,
pink veining on the lower and the whole edged in
white. **'White Glory'** is pure white. ZONES 9–11.

Pelargonium, Regal
Hybrid, 'Rembrandt'
(above left)

Pelargonium, Regal
Hybrid, 'Vicky Clare'
(left)

Pelargonium, Scented-leafed Hybrids

This varied group of hybrids derives from quite a few wild South African species. Many of them are primary hybrids whose origins go back to the early nineteenth century, although there are also a good number of more recent cultivars. Most are vigorous shrubs with dense branches and shallowly to deeply lobed or dissected leaves that in some are quite hairy. The range of essential oils in the leaves is very large, their scents ranging through peppermint, eucalyptus, lemon, cloves, aniseed, apple, rose and even coconut. Often a hot day will bring out the aroma, but it is released most strongly when the foliage is bruised or crushed. Some have quite showy flowers, in others they are small but still pretty. **'Fragrans'** (apple geranium) is a bushy, many-branched shrub reaching 12 in (30 cm) high and wide. A strong spicy smell like green apples comes off the small, roughly heart-shaped, lobed, gray-green leaves. Its flowers are small and white, sometimes with red veining on the upper petals. **'Mabel Grey'**, a vigorous cultivar, has lemon-scented leaves that are rough, serrated-edged and deeply lobed, and pale purple flowers with red markings. Considered to be the most strongly scented pelargonium, it grows to 15 in (38 cm) high. **ZONES 8–11.**

Pelargonium, Scented-leafed Hybrid, 'Fragrans' *(below)*

Pelargonium, Unique Hybrid, 'Scarlet Pet' *(above)*

Pelargonium, Unique Hybrids

This is a small group of hybrids that goes back to the early nineteenth century, with one of the parent species believed to be *Pelargonium fulgidum*. They have been the subject of renewed interest in recent years and a number of new cultivars have appeared. They are erect, shrubby plants, around 18 in (45 cm) tall, with sharply toothed leaves that have a strong musky smell, and heads of fairly large flowers with marked upper petals, a little like some Regal pelargoniums. **'Paton's Unique'** is typical, with fruity, verbena-scented leaves and rose-pink single flowers borne over a long season. **'Scarlet Pet'** has quite showy, 1 in (25 mm) wide red flowers, borne in bunches of 12 or so for most of the year. It grows to 15 in (38 cm) tall, sprawling rather wider, and makes a good knee-high ground cover in dry-summer climates. **ZONES 9–11.**

P

Pelargonium, Zonal Hybrids

ZONAL PELARGONIUM, BEDDING GERANIUM

This large group of hybrids, which have been known collectively as *Pelargonium* × *hortorum*, are derived principally from *P. inquinans*. They are compact plants, usually less than 24 in (60 cm) tall, with succulent green to pale bronze stems and almost circular to kidney-shaped, undulating leaves that have distinctive darker markings or 'zones'. The flowers, massed on long-stemmed heads, may be single or double, are usually brightly colored and appear over a long season. Although shrubs, Zonal pelargoniums may be treated as bedding annuals. There are a number of distinct subgroups that are recognized by enthusiasts. **Variegated** or **Fancy-leafed** zonals have foliage banded and dappled with red, purple, orange and yellow, sometimes with all these colors showing; **Miniature** and **Dwarf** varieties are very compact plants, the leaves sometimes quite small and often purple tinged; flowers vary, but include types with narrow petals—some of these are referred to as **Frutetorums**, reflecting the dominance of this parent species. **Stellars** (or 'Staphs') are an increasingly popular group with narrow, pointed, sometimes forked petals giving the flowers a very distinctive appearance; they come in both singles and doubles, in many colors. **Formosums** have very narrow petals and deeply lobed leaves. **Rosebuds** are a distinctive type of double with, as the name suggests, double flowers like a miniature rose bud. **Cactus-flowered** zonals have flowers with quilled petals like the cactus-flowered dahlias.

Another recent development has been the appearance of Zonal pelargoniums sold as seed, usually as mixed-color series. The following is just a selection of the thousands of zonal cultivars available. **'Caroline Schmidt'** (syn. 'Wilhelm Langguth') is a compact plant with white-edged, pale-centered, bright green leaves and bright red double flowers. **'Dolly Varden'** is a fancy-leafed cultivar with striking cream, bronze and green foliage and single red flowers. **'Flower of Spring'** is an upright grower with cream-edged leaves and vermilion, single flowers. **'Francis Parrett'** is a miniature with deep green leaves and tight clusters of double, fuchsia pink flowers. **'Frank Headley'** is a miniature with cream-edged leaves and soft pink, single flowers. **'Irene'**, which gives its name to a group of hybrids, has red semi-double flowers and clearly zonal, downy green leaves. **'Mr Henry Cox'** (syn. 'Mrs Henry Cox') is a fancy-leafed type with dark-zoned leaves edged in gold and shadowed with red; the flowers are dark-centered, bright pink singles. **'Mrs Parker'** has white-edged, gray-green leaves with darker markings, and deep pink double flowers in tight heads. **'Orange Ricard'** is a compact plant with tight heads of orange-red flowers. **'Apple Blossom Rosebud'** is one of the most popular rosebud zonals, the flowers are white and pink-flushed white, and the foliage bright green with little zonation. **'Gemini'** is a stellar cultivar with white-centered, pink flowers. **'The Boar'** is a miniature of the Frutetorum group with small salmon-pink flowers and toothed-edged, rounded leaves. ZONES 10–11.

Pelargonium, Zonal
Hybrid, 'Frank Headley'
(left)

Pelargonium, Zonal Hybrid, 'Mrs Parker' *(above)*

Pelargonium, Zonal Hybrid, 'Flower of Spring' *(above right)*

Pelargonium, Zonal Hybrid cultivar *(above)*

Pelargonium, Zonal Hybrid, 'Caroline Schmidt' *(right)*

P

PELTOPHORUM

At home in the tropics, these 15 species of evergreen, leguminous trees are grown primarily for the dense shade they cast. In the wild some species can reach 100 ft (30 m), but in cultivation 60 ft (18 m) is more usual. The fern-like leaves are deep glossy green, with individual leaflets up to 1 in (25 mm) long. Impressive spikes of perfumed yellow flowers, which are borne in summer, develop into long, brown seed pods.

CULTIVATION

These trees prefer fertile, moist but well-drained soil and a sheltered, part-shaded position, but they tolerate full sun if well watered. Propagate from pre-soaked or scarified seed, or cuttings taken in the wet season.

Peltophorum pterocarpum (above)
syns *Peltophorum ferrugineum*,
Peltophorum inerme

RUSTY-SHIELD TREE, YELLOW FLAME TREE, YELLOW POINCIANA

Growing to 60 ft (18 m) tall with a crown up to 25 ft (8 m) wide, this species is a good shade tree for tropical gardens. Clusters of heavily perfumed flowers with unusual crinkled petals open in early summer. The abundance of flattened seed pods that follow persist on the tree until the next flowering. ZONES 11–12.

PENSTEMON

Penstemon newberryi (below)

MOUNTAIN PRIDE

Native to California and Nevada, USA, this rather woody evergreen subshrub forms mats of foliage 6–12 in (15–30 cm) high. It leaves are elliptical, 1–1½ in (25–35 mm) long, with finely serrated edges. Its rose-red flowers are around 1 in (25 mm) long and open in late spring and summer. It is moderately frost hardy. ZONES 8–10.

This large genus consists of 250 species of deciduous, evergreen or semi-evergreen subshrubs and perennials, mostly native to Central and North America. The leaves appear in opposite pairs or whorls, while the flowers have 2 lobes on the upper lip and 3 on the lower. Hybrids are valued for their showy flower spikes in blues, reds, whites, and bicolors. Tall varieties suit sheltered borders, and dwarf strains brighten up bedding schemes. 'Bev Jensen' is red and 'Holly's White' is a favorite in the USA.

CULTIVATION

These marginally to very frost-hardy plants do best in fertile, well-drained soil and full sun. Cut plants back hard after flowering. They can be propagated from seed in spring or autumn, by division in spring, or from cuttings of non-flowering shoots in late summer (the only method for cultivars).

P

PEROVSKIA

Found in western Asia and the Himalayan region, the 7 species of deciduous subshrubs in this genus have gray-white stems and aromatic leaves that are covered with gray felt when young. As they mature, the deeply lobed, 2–3 in (5–8 cm) long leaves lose their felting and become gray-green. They form large clumps to 3–5 ft (1–1.5 m) tall and are topped in late summer with 12–18 in (30–45 cm) panicles of tiny purple-blue flowers.

CULTIVATION

They are very easily grown in any well-drained, rather dry soil in a sunny position. It is often best to contain their growth by planting them beside a path, wall or border edge. If allowed free rein, smaller, less vigorous plants may be smothered. They are very frost hardy and may be propagated from seed, or from cuttings of non-flowering stems.

Perovskia
abrotanoides (below)
Native to Afghanistan and the western Hima-layas, this 3 ft (1 m) tall species has 3 in (8 cm) long, deeply cut, oval, gray-green leaves. The small, tubular violet to pink flowers are borne in whorls of 4 to 6 blooms on 15 in (38 cm) panicles. It blooms in late summer. ZONES 5–9.

Persea americana *(below)*
syn. *Persea gratissima*
AVOCADO

This species can reach a height of 60 ft (18 m). On a usually erect stem, it bears glossy, dark green, leathery leaves and small, greenish flowers, held in the axils. Pear-shaped, nutritious, green or black fruit follow. The avocado is tender to both frost and dry conditions, but can be nurtured in mild climates outside of the tropics. There are many named cultivars, each with different growth patterns and requirements. ZONES 10–11.

PERSEA

This genus is made up of about 150 species of evergreen trees and shrubs mostly from tropical parts of Central and South America with a few from Asia and one, *Persea indica*, indigenous to the Azores and Canary Islands. The best known member of the genus is the avocado. They are large trees with deep green, elliptical leaves and inconspicuous unisexual flowers followed by the familiar large, rough-surfaced, pear-shaped fruits, which have a high fat content.

CULTIVATION

Frost tender and fast growing, they can be untidy trees as they drop leaves constantly. Although self-fertile, at least 2 trees are required for good crops. *Persea* demand rich soil, perfect drainage, ample moisture when fruiting and full sun; they are best sheltered from strong winds. Cuttings or grafted plants are superior to seedlings.

P

Phebalium squameum
'Illumination' *(left)*

PHEBALIUM

Primarily Australian, this genus contains around 40 species of evergreen shrubs and small trees that are members of the citrus family and, as might be expected, are aromatic. The foliage varies considerably with the species, though leaves are seldom large. The flowers are simple and starry, generally white or yellow, and may be showy or inconspicuous depending on the species; however, they are usually grown as foliage or hedging plants rather than for flowers.

CULTIVATION

Most species will tolerate light frosts only but are otherwise undemanding and thrive in any well-drained soil in sun or part-shade. They generally respond well to clipping for shape. Although not difficult to raise from seed, most plants are grown from semi-ripe cuttings.

Phebalium squameum
syn. *Phebalium billardieri*
SATINWOOD

This 10–20 ft (3–6 m) tall tree is favored for hedging and wind-breaks. A naturally narrow, upright plant, it really only needs close planting and topping at the desired height to make a hedge. It thrives in coastal conditions and is drought tolerant when established. The leaves are deep green, lance-shaped, 3–5 in (8–13 cm) long, with conspicuous oil glands on the underside. Its clusters of small white flowers open in late spring but are fairly inconspicuous. The yellow and green variegated cultivar 'Illumination' is just as popular as the green-leafed species. ZONES 9–11.

Phellodendron sachalinense *(right)*
syn. *Phellodendron amurense* var. *sachalinense*

SAKHALIN CORK TREE

This 25 ft (8 m) tall tree from northeast Asia has thin, dark brown bark that, despite its common name, is not corky like many *Phellodendron* species. The young growth is rusty red and the leaves are up to 12 in (30 cm) long with 7 to 11 leaflets. They are deep green above, blue-green below. ZONES 3–9.

Phellodendron amurense *(right)*
AMUR CORK TREE

Originally from China and Japan, this is the most common species of the genus in cultivation and earns its common name from its corky older branches. Growing to 40 ft (12 m) tall, it prefers humus-rich soil and summer moisture. Its bright green leaves with 5 to 11 leaflets have an unusual heart-shaped base and a pungent aroma. The 5-petalled flowers, male and female on separate trees, produce berries that are held above the foliage in dense bunches. ZONES 3–9.

PHELLODENDRON

Elegant, slender and requiring little maintenance, these 10 species of deciduous trees from East Asia grow to 50 ft (15 m) tall with a crown spreading to 12 ft (3.5 m). The shiny, light green pinnate leaves turn a rich shade of yellow in autumn. Small, yellowish green flowers appear in late spring or early summer, followed by blackberry-like fruits.

CULTIVATION

These trees are extremely hardy, tolerating both frost and harsh sun, although they prefer protection from wind. They grow best in full sun with fertile, well-drained soil. Seed may be germinated in spring, or propagate from cuttings or by grafting or layering in summer.

P

PHILADELPHUS
MOCK ORANGE, SYRINGA

Philadelphus coronarius (below)

From southern Europe and Asia Minor, this species grows to 6 ft (1.8 m) tall and has very fragrant 2 in (5 cm) wide white flowers. Its oval, bright green leaves are slightly hairy on the undersides. **'Aureus'** has bright yellow new growth and smaller flowers; **'Variegatus'** bears white flowers and has white-edged leaves. ZONES 2–9.

This genus of 60 species of deciduous shrubs comes from the temperate regions of the northern hemisphere, mainly from East Asia and North America. The cultivated species are all quite similar. They grow to a height and spread of 10 ft (3 m) and have light green, roughly elliptical leaves about 3 in (8 cm) long. They flower in late spring and early summer, bearing 4-petalled white or cream flowers in loose clusters. The flower scent strongly resembles that of orange blossom, hence the common name. *Philadelphus* 'Miniature Snowflake' is a dwarf cultivar of the popular 'Snowflake'. 'Natchez' is another cultivar often grown.

CULTIVATION
Moderately to very frost hardy, they are easily grown, preferring moist, well-drained soil and a position in sun or light shade. They may be pruned after flowering and can be used for informal hedging. Propagate from seed or from cuttings taken in summer.

P

Philadelphus
'Lemoinei' *(right)*
syn. *Philadelphus ×
lemoinei*

This hybrid between
Philadelphus coronarius
and *P. microphyllus* was
bred in the late 1880s
by the famous French
hybridist Lémoine,
who also raised many
hydrangeas and lilacs.
It grows to 6 ft (1.8 m)
and has arching
branches. The 1 in
(25 mm) flowers are
white, very fragrant
and are usually carried
in clusters of up to
7 blooms. **ZONES 3–9.**

*Philadelphus
coronarius* 'Aureus'
(left)

Philadelphus
'Virginal' *(right)*
Very frost hardy, this
vigorous, upright
shrub grows to a height
and spread of a little
under 10 ft (3 m).
From late spring to
early summer, it bears
large, fragrant, semi-
double flowers set
among dark green, oval
leaves. **ZONES 3–9.**

P

Philadelphus
'Belle Etoile' *(left)*

'Belle Etoile' is a relatively narrow, 6 ft (1.8 m) tall species with stems that arch at the top. Starry, $2^1/_2$ in (6 cm) wide white flowers with a small central red blotch are borne in late spring and early summer. **ZONES 5–9.**

Philadelphus pendulifolius *(below)*

Possibly a hybrid rather than a true species, this plant grows to about 8 ft (2.4 m) high and wide and bears racemes of cup-shaped white flowers. **ZONES 5–9.**

P

PHILLYREA
MOCK PRIVET

Closely related and very similar to *Osmanthus*, this genus of 4 evergreen shrubs or small trees is found in the Mediterranean region and the Middle East. They grow 10–30 ft (3–9 m) tall, depending on the species, and have small, leathery leaves, sometimes with toothed edges. Their flowers are very small but fragrant. They are white to greenish cream, clustered in the leaf axils and open in spring; the blooms are followed by small blue-black drupes.

CULTIVATION
Reasonably frost hardy, these plants are easily grown in moist, well-drained soil in full sun or part-shade. They will tolerate dry conditions once established and are tough, adaptable plants. Able to withstand frequent trimming, they are suitable for hedging. Propagate from cuttings.

Phillyrea angustifolia (below)
This species from dry hills around the Mediterranean has an olive-like appearance with narrow, lance-shaped leaves up to 3 in (8 cm) long and clusters of tiny greenish cream flowers in spring. It develops into a dense shrub up to 10 ft (3 m) tall.
ZONES 7–10.

P

PHILODENDRON

This genus of up to 500 species includes many well-known house plants as well as some shrubs and small trees. Native to tropical America and the West Indies, they are mainly epiphytic, evergreen vines and creepers with aerial roots, some dainty but others quite robust. They are known for their lush foliage; the leaves, which often have a dramatic outline or deep lobes, are mostly green but sometimes attractively marked with white, pink or red. The petal-less flowers are inconspicuous. All parts of the plant are poisonous.

CULTIVATION

All species need plenty of moisture and a tropical or subtropical climate to be cultivated outdoors. They need a sheltered, shady spot with well-drained, humus-rich soil. Water and fertilize house plants regularly, reducing watering during the cooler months. Propagate from cuttings taken in spring or from seed.

Philodendron bipinnatifidum (below)
syn. *Philodendron selloum*
TREE PHILODENDRON

This upright, robust species from Brazil grows to 10 ft (3 m) tall. It is noted for its shiny, oval, deep green leaves, 15–24 in (38–60 cm) long and many-lobed; in some hybrids, the leaves can be up to 3 times as large. The flowers are white or greenish. This species is variable in leaf outline; the common form with irregular lobing is sometimes known under the synonym. Other cultivars and hybrids include some of the most spectacular of all foliage plants. ZONES 10–12.

PHLOMIS

This genus consists of around 100 species of often downy-leaved perennials, subshrubs and shrubs found from the Mediterranean region to China. Although variable, in most cases their leaves are large, over 4 in (10 cm) long, and densely covered with hair-like felting. Like other members of the nettle family, the leaves occur in whorls on upright stems. The tubular flowers, borne on upright verticillasters, curl downwards and have 2 lips at the tip, the upper lip hooded over the lower. They occur in clusters of 2 to 40 blooms, depending on the species, and are usually in shades of cream, yellow, pink, mauve or purple.

CULTIVATION

Hardiness varies, though most will tolerate moderate frosts. Species with heavily felted foliage suffer in prolonged wet weather and are best grown in exposed positions where the foliage dries quickly after rain. Plant in moist, well-drained soil in full sun or part-shade. Propagate from seed, from small cuttings of non-flowering shoots, or by division where possible.

Phlomis fruticosa (above)
JERUSALEM SAGE

This evergreen shrub, a native of southern Europe, is grown for the strikingly beautiful yellow flowers it bears in whorls from early to mid-summer, among oval, wrinkled, felty green leaves. It tolerates coastal areas and grows to a height and spread of 30 in (75 cm). To keep its habit neat, prune to about half its size in autumn. ZONES 7–10.

Phlomis grandiflora (right)

This species is similar to the well-known *Phlomis fruticosa*, but the leaves are greener and less woolly and the yellow flowers are in tighter, more spherical heads. The plant has a rather sprawling habit. ZONES 8–10.

PHOTINIA

These 60 species of evergreen or deciduous
shrubs and small trees from the Himalayas
and East and Southeast Asia are mostly
fast growing. They are cultivated for their
brilliant young foliage and, if deciduous,
for their autumn color. The leaves are
alternate and the flowers, mostly white,
are followed by either red or dark blue
berries. The genus takes its name from a
Greek word meaning 'shining'; this is a
reference to the gleaming foliage.

CULTIVATION
Plant in sun or part-shade in fertile, well-
drained soil with protection from strong
winds. They make excellent hedges and
should be pruned to promote bushiness
and new growth. Propagate from seed or
cuttings in summer, or by grafting onto
hawthorn or quince stock.

Photinia davidsoniae (above right)

An evergreen shrub or tree to 40 ft (12 m) tall,
this species from central China has downy young
growth with small spines. Its leaves are 3–6 in
(8–15 cm) long, elliptical, dark glossy green above
with lighter undersides. The inflorescence is also
downy and opens in late spring. ZONES 9–11.

Photinia × *fraseri* (below)

The young growth of these evergreen shrubs
comes in shades of bright red, bronze-red and
purple-red, persisting in color over a long period.
The mature leaves are glossy and green. '**Red
Robin**' has brilliant red new growth and
'**Robusta**' (syn. *Photinia robusta*, *P. glabra*
'Robusta') bears eye-catching, coppery red
young leaves. The height of the shrub varies with
the cultivar, but most are around 10–12 ft
(3–3.5 m) tall. ZONES 8–10.

P

Photinia serratifolia *(right)*
syn. *Photinia serrulata*
CHINESE HAWTHORN, CHINESE PHOTINIA

From China, this evergreen shrub or small tree grows to a height of 20 ft (6 m) with a bushy crown, but can also be kept lower and clipped to form a hedge. The glossy oval leaves are large, serrated and bronze tinted in spring. The small, white spring flowers are followed by small, red berries. **ZONES 7–10.**

Prunus × *fraseri* 'Robusta' *(above)*

Prunus × *fraseri* 'Red Robin' *(right & below)*

P

PHYGELIUS

CAPE FUCHSIA

Related to *Penstemon* and *Antirrhinum* (the snapdragons) rather than *Fuchsia*, these 2 species of erect, evergreen shrubs or sub-shrubs—perennials in some winter conditions—are native to the Cape of Good Hope, South Africa. Good rock-garden plants, they grow to 3 ft (1 m) high and 18 in (45 cm) wide. They bear handsome, red flowers in summer, set among dark green, oval leaves.

CULTIVATION

They do best in sun or part-shade and like a fertile, well-drained soil that is not too dry. Propagate from cuttings in summer.

Phygelius aequalis

This species is a suckering shrub to 3 ft (1 m) tall with dark green leaves and pale pink flowers. **'Yellow Trumpet'** has leaves that are a paler green and creamy yellow flowers. ZONES 8–11.

Phygelius × *rectus* (right)

These hybrids of *Phygelius aequalis* and *P. capensis* tend to be fairly compact plants with large sprays of flowers. They are the best choice for most gardens as they combine the toughness of *P. capensis* with the heavy flowering of *P. aequalis* in compact, non-invasive plants. **'African Queen'** has almost straight-tubed, pendulous, light red flowers with orange-red lobes. **'Pink Elf'** is a dwarf form with red-lobed pale pink flowers; the inflorescences are rather sparse, but the plant flowers over a long season. ZONES 8–11.

P

Phygelius aequalis
'Yellow Trumpet' *(left)*

Phylica plumosa
(below)
syn. *Phylica pubescens*
FLANNEL FLOWER, FLANNEL BUSH

This 3–6 ft (1–1.8 m) tall
South African shrub is
covered in fine downy
hairs; even the flowerheads
are hairy. The leaves are
1 in (25 mm) long, nar-
row, deep green and have
rolled-back edges. Although
soft, they protrude straight
out from the branches,
giving a bristly appear-
ance. The flowers, or more
accurately the bracts, resemble hairy cream
daisies. They appear from
early winter and are good
cut flowers. ZONES 9–11.

PHYLICA
CAPE MYRTLE

This genus of around 150 species of evergreen shrubs is native
to South Africa, the nearby islands and the farther flung
Tristan da Cunha. They have bright green, narrow leaves and
tiny true flowers that are often largely hidden by the leafy
bracts or hairs that surround them. The stems, leaves and
bracts are all covered with fine silvery hairs. The flowerheads
are used dry or fresh in floral arrangements.

CULTIVATION
They thrive only in warm climates and need full sun and acid
soil. Although tolerant of high humidity, they suffer with
prolonged rain as it mats the foliage hairs and leads to rotting.
They do particularly well in coastal conditions. Little pruning
is required if the flowers are used, otherwise trim lightly
after flowering. Propagate from seed in spring or cuttings
in summer.

P

× Phylliopsis hillieri

Growing to a height of 12 in (30 cm), this shrub produces its small racemes of tiny, 5-lobed, red-purple flowers in spring. 'Coppelia' has relatively large, open lavender-pink flowers. 'Pinocchio' is a very compact cultivar with small glossy leaves and spikes of bright pink flowers. ZONES 3–9.

P

× PHYLLIOPSIS

This intergeneric hybrid genus results from crossing 2 small North American shrubs of the *Erica* family—*Phyllodoce breweri* and *Kalmiopsis leachiana*—a cross that produces dwarf, ever-green shrubs with dark brown bark and ½–1 in (12–25 mm) long glossy dark green, oblong leaves and bell-shaped flowers.

CULTIVATION

Plant in moist, humus-rich, well-drained soil in dappled shade. They are ideal for moist, shaded rockeries or pots in a cool alpine house, are very frost hardy and are easily propagated from small tip cuttings or by layering.

× Phylliopsis hillieri
'Pinocchio' (above)

PHYLLOCLADUS
CELERY PINE

Five species of evergreen conifers from the southern hemisphere make up this genus. The taller species grow to 70 ft (21 m), but there are some lower growing, shrubby plants—reaching a maximum of 6 ft (1.8 m)—that can be made into very attractive bonsai specimens. The stems are erect, with horizontal branches bearing brownish green flattened phylloclades (short stems that act as leaves) which sometimes darken in winter. Male cones are carried in terminal clusters, while the female cones appear on the base of the 'leaves'. The hard, close-grained timber is valued.

CULTIVATION
These conifers are tender in dry conditions. They perform best in well-composted, moist soil in sunny or part-shaded positions away from strong winds. Propagate from seed or cuttings.

Phyllocladus aspleniifolius (right)

From Tasmania in Australia, this slow-growing, 50 ft (15 m) tall conifer has an idiosyncratic foliage arrangement, producing striking diamond-shaped thick cladodes (modified branchlets) up to 3 in (8 cm) long. These are evergreen, but the true leaves, which appear as tiny scales, are deciduous. Its foliage bears some resemblance to that of celery. ZONES 8–9.

P

Phyllocladus trichomanoides (right)
TANEKAHA, NEW ZEALAND CELERY PINE

In the wild, this symmetrical conifer from New Zealand can reach 50–70 ft (15–21 m) in height, but in cultivation rarely exceeds 20 ft (6 m). Its stems, spreading to 12 ft (3.5 m), radiate in whorls from horizontal branches. The foliage resembles the fronds of maidenhair fern. It prefers cool, moist climates, and its slow growth rate makes it suitable for small gardens. ZONES 8–10.

PHYMOSIA

The 8 species of evergreen shrubs and small trees that make up this genus are native to Mexico, Guatemala and the Caribbean islands. They have 8–10 in (20–25 cm) wide, hand-shaped leaves with 5 to 7 lobes and serrated or toothed edges. Small clusters of abutilon-like flowers develop in the axils of the leaves near the stem tips. They are 1–3 in (2.5–8 cm) wide and usually pink or red, sometimes with white veining.

CULTIVATION

These are largely tropical plants and will not tolerate frost. They prefer moist, well-drained soil but will withstand dry conditions once established. Plant in full or half-day sun. Propagate from seed or cuttings.

Phymosia umbellata (below)

Up to 20 ft (6 m) tall with 8 in (20 cm) wide leaves, this Mexican species has 1½ in (35 mm) wide, deep pink flowers. It can be trimmed when young to form a multi-trunked shrub or trained as a single-trunked small tree. ZONES 10–12.

Physocarpus monogynus (below)

MOUNTAIN NINEBARK

This species from central USA grows to around 3–6 ft (1–1.8 m) tall with arching, spreading stems. The new stems are bright brown, sticky, often with fine hairs; the young leaves are light green. The 2 in (5 cm) wide leaves are 3- to 5-lobed with serrated edges. Flat 2 in (5 cm) wide heads of small white flowers open from late spring. **ZONES 5–10.**

PHYSOCARPUS

NINEBARK

The unusual inflated fruits of this genus of deciduous shrubs from Asia and North America are not edible—the 12 or so species are admired for their flowers and attractive foliage. In the wild, they reach a maximum height of 10 ft (3 m). The leaves are prominently veined, lobed and serrated, and change to a dull yellow in autumn. The 5-petalled white or pink flowers, appearing in spring or early summer, are small but are displayed in decorative clusters along the branches.

CULTIVATION

Physocarpus species require fertile, well-drained soil in a sunny position. They are easy to grow in temperate climates, but resent soil with a high lime content and dry roots. Thin out crowded plants by cutting back some of the arching canes after flowering. Propagate from seed or cuttings of semi-ripened wood in summer.

P

Physocarpus opulifolius (above right)

Native to eastern USA, this shrub has a height and spread of 5–10 ft (1.5–3m) and a graceful arching habit. The yellowish green, rounded, heart-shaped leaves complement the dense, pink-tipped white flowers, which are at their best in early summer. Reddish pods with yellow seeds contrast well with the bright autumn foliage and the dark brown bark that peels off in layers. **'Aureus'** has bright greenish yellow leaves and white flowers. **'Dart's Gold'**, to 4 ft (1.2 m) tall, has bright golden foliage and white flowers flushed pink. **ZONES 2–10.**

Physocarpus opulifolius 'Dart's Gold' (right)

Picea abies *(left & opposite page)*
syn. *Picea excelsa*
NORWAY SPRUCE, COMMON SPRUCE

Native to Scandinavia where it can grow to nearly 200 ft (60 m), but less in cultivation, this is the traditional Christmas tree in Europe. Its straight trunk is covered in orange-brown bark, maturing reddish, which it sheds in scales. The leaves are dark green and rectangular and the reddish cigar-shaped cones, erect at first, become pendulous and grow to 8 in (20 cm) long. Dwarf, shrubby cultivars have usually been propagated from witches' brooms, a tight clump of congested foliage that sometimes appears. Shallow rooted, this tree can be upended by strong winds. **'Conica'** is a low-growing cultivar, less than 15 ft (4.5 m) with a broad, conical crown. **'Maxwellii'**, the Maxwell spruce, is a low-growing, compact form ideal for rockeries and borders. **'Pumila Glauca'** is a semi-erect dwarf form with bluish green foliage. **'Pygmaea'** is a slow-growing dwarf form. **'Reflexa'** is a weeping cultivar distinguished by growing tips that point upwards when young; it makes a beautiful prostrate shrub. **'Inversa'** is a spreading bush with downward-trailing branches. **'Little Gem'** is a flat-topped dwarf shrub that grows very slowly. **'Nidiformis'**, the bird's nest spruce, is a dwarf form with outward- and upward-curving branches that form a nest-like bowl in the center of the plant. ZONES 2–9.

PICEA
SPRUCE

The 30 to 40 members of this genus of evergreen conifers originate in the cool-temperate regions of the northern hemisphere where there are deep pockets of moist, rich, acidic, freely draining soil. Sometimes reaching an impressive 220 ft (66 m) in height, they develop a stiff, narrow, conical, sometimes columnar growth habit with short, horizontal to upward-pointing branches. The leaves are arranged spirally on short pegs and their color varies from bright green to glaucous blue. Able to withstand strong winds, they bear large cones which hang downwards, distinguishing the genus from the superficially similar firs *(Abies)*. The slow growth and contorted habit of some cultivars make them ideal bonsai specimens; others are prostrate and make excellent ground covers. This genus produces valuable timber, plus pitch and turpentine.

CULTIVATION
Plant in full sun in deep, moist but well-drained, neutral to acid soil. Propagate from seed or cuttings in autumn or by grafting. They will not survive transplantation when large, nor grow well in heavily polluted environments. They may be prone to attack from aphids, red spider mites and, in warm, humid climates, fungal infections.

Picea abies 'Pumila Glauca' *(above right)*

Picea abies and *Betula pendula* under snow *(right)*

Picea abies 'Pygmaea' *(below right)*

Picea abies 'Maxwellii' *(below)*

P

Picea breweriana
(above)

WEEPING SPRUCE, BREWER'S
WEEPING SPRUCE

This North American conifer has branchlets of foliage, 3 ft (1 m) long, which hang in curtain-like streamers from its horizontally held branches. The needles are blue-green and flattened and the light brown cones grow to 4 in (10 cm) long. The tree forms a strong trunk, reaching a height of 100 ft (30 m) or more, with a broad conical shape that becomes narrow if the tree is grown in crowded conditions. **ZONES 2–9.**

Picea glauca var.
albertiana 'Conica'
(above)

Picea glauca

WHITE SPRUCE

From Canada and grown commercially for the paper industry, this slow-growing tree can reach 80 ft (24 m). Bright green shoots appear in spring, and the drooping branchlets carry aromatic, 4-angled needles up to ½ in (12 mm) long. The cones are small and narrow. **'Echiniformis'** is a dwarf, mounding form with a spiky, needle-studded surface. *Picea glauca* var. *albertiana* 'Conica', the dwarf Alberta spruce, is a very densely foliaged, bright green, conical tree that is usually seen as a 3 ft (1 m) shrub, though with great age it can reach 10 ft (3 m). **ZONES 1–8.**

Picea engelmannii
(below right)

ENGELMANN SPRUCE

Growing slowly to 150 ft (45 m) or more, this is one of the most cold-tolerant evergreen trees; it also grows well in poor soil. The densely textured, pyramid-shaped crown, spreading to 15 ft (4.5 m), is made up of sharply pointed, 4-angled, soft gray to steel-blue needles up to 1 in (25 mm) long. The cylindrical cones are green and tinged with purple. **ZONES 1–9.**

Picea omorika *(right)*

SERBIAN SPRUCE

From Serbia and Bosnia, this spruce reaches
100 ft (30 m) or more with pendulous branches
forming a narrow, spire-like crown. The bright
green, flattened needles have a square tip and a
grayish underside. The purplish cones mature to a
deep brown. Happy in a range of soils from acid
to limy and more tolerant of urban pollution than
most species, it is one of the best *Picea* for large,
temperate-climate gardens. *Picea omorika* ×
breweriana is a hybrid between the 2 popular,
award-winning species. **ZONES 4–9.**

Picea mariana 'Nana'

(below)

Picea mariana

AMERICAN BLACK SPRUCE

From the USA, this 60 ft (18 m) conifer has a
pyramidal crown, spreading to 15 ft (4.5 m),
composed of whorled branches bearing blunt,
bluish green needles. The $1\frac{1}{2}$ in (35 mm) long cones
are purplish brown and remain on the tree for up
to 30 years. This conifer prefers boggy soil and
must have an open, sunny position to thrive. **'Nana'**
is a slow-growing dwarf cultivar. **ZONES 1–8.**

Picea orientalis 'Aurea'
(right)

Picea orientalis

CAUCASIAN SPRUCE

Reaching 100 ft (30 m) in its native Turkey and
the Caucasus, this slow-growing spruce produces
abundant, pendent branches from ground level
up. The brilliant, glossy green foliage is short and
neat; spectacular brick-red male cones appear in
spring, and the purple female cones grow 3 in (8 cm)
long. This spruce prefers a sheltered site. **'Atrovirens'**
displays attractive, rich green foliage that flushes
to golden-yellow in early summer. **'Aurea'** has
golden-yellow juvenile foliage that greens as it
ages but retains a hint of gold. **ZONES 3–9.**

P

Picea pungens
COLORADO SPRUCE

This frost-hardy species from the west coast of the USA grows to 100 ft (30 m) or more in the wild, although less in gardens. It has a pyramid of bluish green foliage composed of stiff and sharply pointed needles; the bark is gray. Prune regularly as fresh growth will not bud from dead wood. The many cultivars include **'Aurea'** with golden leaves; **'Caerulea'** with bluish white leaves; **'Conica'** which grows into a cone-shaped cultivar; **'Glauca'**, the commonly grown Colorado blue spruce with striking, steel blue new foliage; **'Globosa'**, a rounded, dwarf form with attractive bluish leaves that takes a decade or more to reach 24 in (60 cm) high; **'Hoopsii'**, prized for its even bluer foliage; **'Iseli Fastigiate'** with upward-pointing branches and very sharp needles; **'Koster'** with foliage maturing from silvery deep blue to green, spiralled branches and tubular, scaled cones about 4 in (10 cm) long; **'Pendens'**, a prostrate, blue cultivar; **'Royal Blue'**, another striking blue cultivar; **'Moerheimii'**, with silvery blue foliage longer than other forms; and **'Viridis'** with very dark green foliage. ZONES 2–10.

Picea pungens 'Glauca'
(top left)

Picea pungens
'Royal Blue' *(left)*

Picea pungens cultivar
under snow *(below left)*

Picea sitchensis *(opposite page right & far right)*
SITKA SPRUCE

Fast growing to 150 ft (45 m), this is one of the few trees in the genus that can survive being transplanted when young. It also enjoys humid sites but needs good summer rainfall. Its trunk has pale bark. The pyramidal crown becomes broader as the tree matures and is composed of whorled branches; the leaves are flattened, stiff and bluish gray. The 4 in (10 cm) long cones are covered with thin papery scales and they release their winged seeds on warm spring days. The timber is not very strong. ZONES 4–9.

P

Picea pungens 'Pendens' *(left)*
Picea pungens 'Iseli Fastigiate'
(below left)

Picea smithiana *(below)*

MORINDA SPRUCE, WEST HIMALAYAN SPRUCE

This spruce, found from Nepal to Afghanistan, develops graceful branches that hang
in cascades. The dark green foliage is composed of fine, 4-angled needles up to 1½ in
(35 mm) long. Green cones maturing to
shiny brown grow to 8 in (20 cm) long,
often at the ends of the branches, accentu-
ating their pendulous effect. **ZONES 6–9.**

P

PIERIS

This genus consists of 7 species of evergreen shrubs and, more rarely, small trees. The shrubby species are valued for their neat, compact habit, attractive foliage and flowers. Their height rarely exceeds 12 ft (3.5 m). The flower buds are held throughout the winter, and in spring open into clusters of small, bell-shaped, waxy, usually white flowers.

CULTIVATION
These plants require a temperate climate and moist, peaty, acidic soil, in part-shade. They appreciate humidity. Propagate from seed in spring or from cuttings in summer, or by layering.

Pieris formosa

This dense, bushy shrub from China carries glossy, dark green leathery leaves and bears sprays of small white flowers in mid-spring. Frost resistant, it grows well in cool or mild climates but is not tolerant of dry conditions. It is one of the taller species, growing to 12 ft (3.5 m). The red-leaf pearl flower, **Pieris formosa var. forrestii** (syn. *P. forrestii*), is usually smaller, growing to a height and spread of 6 ft (1.8 m) with scarlet-bronze young growth, against which the flowers gleam in striking contrast. **P. f. var. forrestii 'Wakehurst'** is a tall shrub that can reach 15 ft (4.5 m), has large clusters of white flowers and red new growth that fades to pink before turning green. **ZONES 6–9.**

Pieris formosa var.
forestii (left)

Pieris formosa var.
forestii 'Wakehurst' *(left)*

Pieris japonica
(right)

LILY-OF-THE-VALLEY SHRUB

This Japanese shrub
can grow to 12 ft
(3.5 m) high, but usu-
ally reaches only 6 ft
(1.8 m) in cultivation.
Its pointed, elliptical,
deep green leaves, to
4 in (10 cm) long, are
reddish copper when
young. Panicles of
small, white, bell-
shaped flowers appear
from early spring. The
many cultivars include
'**Bert Chandler**' with
pink and cream new
growth; '**Christmas
Cheer**' with early, pale
pink flowers; '**Fla-
mingo**' with bright
pink flowers; '**Moun-
tain Fire**' with vivid
red new growth and
white flowers; '**Purity**'
with large, pure white
flowers; '**Red Mill**', a
vigorous, late-flower-
ing cultivar; '**Tickled
Pink**' with pale red
new growth and pink-
tinted to pale pink
flowers; and
'**Variegata**' with
cream-edged foliage.
ZONES 4–10.

Pieris japonica 'Bert
Chandler' *(top right)*

Pieris japonica
'Christmas Cheer'
(center)

Pieris japonica
'Flamingo' *(right)*

P

Pieris japonica
'Red Mill' *(above)*

Pieris japonica
'Tickled Pink' *(right)*

P

Pieris japonica
'Variegata' *(below)*

Pimelea ferruginea *(below)*

This species from Western Australia forms a compact, well-branched, rounded shrub with a height and spread of 3 ft (1 m). Tiny, recurved, oval leaves are crowded opposite each other along the stems. The leaves are smooth and light green on top and grayish green underneath. In spring, compact, rounded, rose pink flowerheads appear, up to 1½ in (35 mm) across. **'Magenta Mist'** has dusky mauve flowers. **ZONES 9–11.**

Pimelea spectabilis *(above)*

This Western Australian species is an upright shrub that grows to 4 ft (1.2 m) tall. Its stems are sticky when young and are clothed with 1½ in (35 mm) long narrow leaves with blue-green undersides. The flowers are relatively large, in shades of pink or yellow, and are massed in heads up to 3 in (8 cm) wide. It blooms in early summer. **ZONES 9–11.**

PIMELEA
RICE FLOWER

These 80 species of woody, evergreen shrubs, belonging to the same family as the daphnes, are native to Australasia and can grow to a height of 6 ft (1.8 m), though most species are smaller. Their great attraction is their terminal flowerheads in white, yellow, pink or purple, often surrounded by prominent colored bracts. Each flower is tubular and star-shaped.

CULTIVATION

They grow best in full sun in light, well-drained soil enriched with organic matter. Windy and seaside sites also suit them, but they dislike heavy frosts and lime soil. Lightly tip prune after flowering to keep them tidy. Propagate from seed in spring or cuttings in late summer. Attempts to transplant large specimens usually fail.

PINUS
PINE

Pines are arguably the most important genus of conifers. Consisting of around 120 species of needle-leafed evergreens, *Pinus* is represented in most parts of the northern hemisphere. The greatest concentration of species is in the Mexican highlands, southern USA and China—though the best-known species come from more northerly regions, for example, the Scots pine *(P. sylvestris)* of northern Eurasia. Most pines are medium to tall forest trees but a few are small and bushy. The characteristic feature of *Pinus* is the way the needles are grouped in bundles. The number per bundle, usually 2 to 7, is fairly constant for each species. Male (pollen) and female (seed) cones are borne on the same tree. *Pinus* species are divided into **white pines** (soft pines), with typically 5 needles and non-woody cone scales, and **black pines** (hard pines), with 2 to 4 needles and woody cone scales that take 2 years or more to mature their seeds. The white pines are typified by the North American *P. strobus* and include some of the tallest conifers; the black pines are typified by *P. sylvestris* or *P. radiata* and account for the majority of species, including nearly all those from the subtropics and tropics. Pines include many of the world's most important forest trees, especially in cool-temperate and subarctic regions, providing lumber for many everyday purposes including house construction, and paper pulp. In the past their aromatic resins (pitch) and turpentines had many uses but these have largely been replaced by petroleum products. The seeds of several species (pine nuts) are important foods in some cultures. In recent times the bark of pines has become widely used in horticultural growing mediums and as a mulch.

For smaller gardens, dwarf cultivars of species such as *P. sylvestris, P. thunbergii, P. strobus* and *P. mugo* can be grown as tub or rock-garden specimens. Many pines can also be used as bonsai subjects or Christmas trees.

CULTIVATION

Most pines grow in a wide range of conditions, though their tolerance of both cold and warmth varies and each species has its optimum climate. They are mostly very wind resistant and will thrive on soils of moderate to low fertility, but may need a symbiotic soil fungus to assist nutrient uptake on poorer soils—these fungi are likely to be already present in the pines' native regions, but a handful of decaying needles from a pine forest can be added if planting pines where none have grown before. The majority of pines require well-drained soil, and resent soil disturbance. Propagations is from seed; cultivars may be grafted.

Pinus aristata *(above)*

BRISTLE CONE PINE

Slow growing and long lived, this North American pine can reach 30 ft (9 m) or more in height. As a garden plant it forms a dense shrubby tree, making an effective informal windbreak. Its 2 in (5 cm) long, deep green needles flecked with resin press closely to the stem in groups of five. Its cones are glossy and 4 in (10 cm) long. ZONES 5–9.

Pinus canariensis *(below)*

CANARY ISLANDS PINE

This moderately fast-growing tree from the Canary Islands, though adaptable and tolerant of dry conditions, prefers an open, sunny spot where the soil is rich and moist yet well drained. It matures to a spreading tree, up to 80 ft (24 m) high. The upright trunk has reddish brown, fissured bark. The densely packed, shiny, grass-green needles are 12 in (30 cm) long and are carried in groups of three. The oval, brown cones are 8 in (20 cm) long. ZONES 8–11.

Pinus cembra *(opposite page left)*

AROLLA PINE, SWISS STONE PINE

Growing to 80 ft (24 m) in its native Alps, central Europe and Siberia, this pine is appreciated for its neat, conical shape, dense foliage and long-lived needles. It is tough and disease resistant, but must be kept moist. The 6 in (15 cm) long, dark green, glossy needles occur in groups of five. The 3 in (8 cm) cones mature from purple to deep bluish brown. The seeds are edible. ZONES 4–9.

Pinus coulteri
(right & far right)

BIG-CONE PINE, COULTER PINE

This tough pine from California withstands heat, wind and dry conditions and tolerates most soils, including heavy clay. Its spiny brown cones grow to a massive 15 in (38 cm) and weigh 5 lb (2.3 kg). It grows fast to a bushy tree up to 90 ft (30 m) high with attractive, stiff, bluish green needles up to 12 in (30 cm) long held in groups of three. **ZONES 8–10.**

Pinus contorta var. *latifolia (above)*

Pinus contorta

SHORE PINE, BEACH PINE

This species from the west coast of North America grows quickly to 30 ft (9 m) tall then develops horizontal branches and grows slowly to 70 ft (21 m). It has pairs of dark green, 2 in (5 cm) needles and small yellow-brown cones. It is easily trimmed to shape and does well as a garden specimen, but does not thrive in hot, dry areas. ***Pinus contorta* var. *latifolia*,** the lodgepole pine, is a straight-trunked, tapering tree to 80 ft (24 m) in its native Rocky Mountains, but is slow growing, low and bushy in cultivation. It has yellowish green, 2–3 in (5–8 cm) long needles in pairs and small, oval cones that release fine seeds carried by wind. **ZONES 7–9.**

Pinus jeffreyi *(left)*

JEFFREY PINE

From western North America, this slender, conical pine grows to 180 ft (55 m) but in harsh conditions is often naturally dwarf. It has 8 in (20 cm) long, thick, aromatic, bluish green needles and curved, often J-shaped cones up to 12 in (30 cm) long. Deep reddish brown, fissured bark flakes off to reveal bright new bark. It is susceptible to *Elytroderma deformans*, a disease that causes witches' brooms. **ZONES 6–9.**

P

Pinus densiflora *(below)*

JAPANESE RED PINE

Used as a timber tree in its native Japan, where it can reach 100 ft (30 m), in cultivation this distinctive pine with red bark and a twisted shape is slow growing and often multi-trunked. It can be pruned and makes a popular bonsai specimen. Ovoid, yellow-purplish cones stand out boldly from the bright green, 4 in (10 cm) long foliage. There are many popular cultivars including **'Tanyosho Nana'**. The dwarf cultivar **'Umbraculifera'** has an umbrella-like canopy and orange-red, flaky bark on its multiple trunks; an extremely slow grower, it eventually reaches 15 ft (4.5 m). **'Pendula'** is a strong-growing, semi-prostrate cultivar best grown near ponds or on banks where its weeping form can be most appreciated. **ZONES 4–9.**

Pinus densiflora
'Umbraculifera' *(left)*

Pinus densiflora
'Tanyosho Nana' *(top)*

P

Pinus halepensis

(left & below left)

ALEPPO PINE

From the eastern Mediterranean area, this pine is the most resistant to dry conditions, in fact tolerating most conditions except severe frost when young. Fast growing to 50 ft (15 m), it has a spreading crown and a distinctive rugged character. The young bark is ash gray, but ages to reddish brown. The soft, light green needles are 4 in (10 cm) long and are usually carried in pairs; the 3–4 in (8–10 cm) cones are reddish brown. **ZONES 7–10.**

Pinus montezumae *(below)*

MONTEZUMA PINE

Found in Mexico and Guatemala, this tree grows quickly to 100 ft (30 m). It has a columnar crown when young and eventually becomes a round-headed tree. Its bark is deep red-brown to near black and is deeply fissured. It has 6–12 in (15–30 cm), slightly blue-green, pendulous needles in groups of 5, and buff-colored cones up to 10 in (25 cm) long. **ZONES 9–11.**

Pinus monticola

(left)

WESTERN WHITE PINE

Native to western USA, this grows to 200 ft (60 m). The oldest recorded specimen is 500 years old. Upward-growing branches carry bluish green needles 4 in (10 cm) long in dense clumps of 5, and tapering, purplish cones up to 8 in (20 cm) long occur on the tips. It is prone to white pine blister rust in northwestern USA. **ZONES 5–9.**

Pinus mugo

MOUNTAIN PINE, SWISS
MOUNTAIN PINE

In the mountains of Europe this small tree grows slowly to 12 ft (3.5 m). Its windswept appearance reflects its habitat, making it an interesting bonsai and rock-garden specimen. Its pairs of 2 in (5 cm) long, bright green needles develop from resinous buds. The oval, dark brown cones are 1–2 in (2–5 cm) long. This species does not tolerate extreme heat or dry conditions. **'Aurea'** has golden foliage. **'Benjamin'** has rich green foliage. **'Gnom'**, a compact bush 6 ft (1.8 m) high with a similar spread, produces whitish new shoots against rich, black-green mature growth. **'Mops'** matures to 5 ft (1.5 m) over 10 years. *Pinus mugo* var. *pumilo*, the dwarf Swiss mountain pine, develops a compact bun shape, achieving 30 in (75 cm) in 10 years. **ZONES 2–9.**

Pinus nigra

(above & right)

AUSTRIAN BLACK PINE,
EUROPEAN BLACK PINE

From central and southern Europe, this pine grows to 120 ft (36 m) or more in the wild, though cultivated specimens rarely exceed 50 ft (15 m). It has an open, conical habit with a whitish brown trunk, whorled branches and a dense crown of dark green, 6 in (15 cm) long, paired needles; its cones are 3 in (8 cm) long. It grows in chalk and clay and tolerates coastal conditions. *Pinus nigra* var. *maritima*, the Corsican pine, forms a denser crown and is slower growing; its gray-green twisted needle pairs can exceed 6 in (15 cm) and it has cracking bark and a very straight trunk that is harvested for timber. **ZONES 4–9.**

Pinus mugo 'Benjamin'
(center)

Pinus mugo 'Mops'
(right)

Pinus parviflora
JAPANESE WHITE PINE

This pyramid-shaped pine usually grows to 40 ft (12 m) in cultivation but in its native Japan can reach 80 ft (24 m) tall with a similar spread. It has some of the shortest needles in the genus—1½ in (35 mm) long. Its dense, bluish green foliage and slow growth habit make it a popular bonsai or tub subject. **'Brevifolia'** is an upright, sparsely foliaged cultivar. The blue-foliaged **'Glauca'** takes many years to reach 5 ft (1.5 m); its needles have distinctive blue-white bands on their inner sides. **'Adcock's Dwarf'** is a bun-shaped cultivar that grows to only 30 in (75 cm). ZONES 3–9.

Pinus parviflora
'Brevifolia' *(left)*

Pinus palustris *(right)*
LONG-LEAF PINE

From eastern and central USA, this pine grows to 100 ft (30 m) with an open crown. It has blunt, bluish green needles up to 18 in (45 cm) long, arranged in groups of three. Its 6–10 in (15–25 cm) long, reddish brown cones have spines on the tips of their scales and are held on the tree for up to 20 years. This pine will not tolerate strong winds or dry conditions. ZONES 4–11.

Pinus patula *(left)*
MEXICAN WEEPING PINE,
SPREADING-LEAFED PINE

Long, slender, drooping needles and a spreading canopy make this a good shade tree. It is slow growing to 50 ft (15 m) with a 15 ft (4.5 m) spread. The 8 in (20 cm) long needles are soft, pale green to grayish green, and grouped in 3s; the oval cones are 4 in (10 cm) long. ZONES 9–11.

P

Pinus pinaster *(right)*
MARITIME PINE, CLUSTER PINE

From the Mediterranean region and growing quickly to 100 ft (30 m), this pine does not tolerate dry conditions or frost but enjoys coastal locations and is a good windbreak. Its bright reddish brown bark is deeply furrowed. The paired green needles, up to 10 in (25 cm) long, are stiff and shiny. Rich brown, oval cones 6 in (15 cm) or more long persist on the branches for years unopened. This pine is valued for timber and resin. **ZONES 7–10.**

Pinus pinea *(left)*
ROMAN PINE, STONE PINE, UMBRELLA PINE

From southern Europe and Turkey, this species can reach 80 ft (24 m) in the wild and has a flattened crown atop a straight, though often leaning trunk with furrowed, reddish gray bark. The rigid, paired needles, 4–8 in (10–20 cm) long, are bright green. The globe-shaped cones are shiny and brown; the edible seeds are known as pine nuts. Once established this pine copes with most conditions, including dryness and heat. **ZONES 8–10.**

P

Pinus ponderosa *(right)*
PONDEROSA PINE, WESTERN YELLOW PINE

Abundant in its native western North America, this pine has a deeply fissured bark with a mosaic of broad, smooth, yellowish brown, reddish brown and pinkish gray plates. An important timber tree, it can reach 200 ft (60 m) but in cultivation is usually smaller. It has dark brown cones on spire-like branches. Its dark green needles, in bundles of 3, are up to 10 in (25 cm) long. **ZONES 5–9.**

Pinus sylvestris
(left)

SCOTS PINE

This fast-growing species, found throughout northern Europe and western Asia and the only pine indigenous to the UK, is the most commonly grown pine in Europe and is often used in forestry. It reaches 100 ft (30 m) with a rounded head of foliage and orange-red bark. Twisted, bluish green needles grow in pairs and are 3 in (8 cm) long. This pine grows well in poor sandy soil but will not tolerate dry conditions. Dwarf cultivars make attractive tub specimens. **'Aurea'** has gold-tinted foliage, especially on new growth and in winter. **'Beuvronensis'** is a very densely foliaged dwarf cultivar with light blue-green needles that eventually reaches 6 ft (1.8 m) tall but is small for many years. **'Moseri'** is a small pyramidal cultivar with yellow foliage. **'Watereri'** only grows 2–3 in (5–8 cm) a year and can be thought of as a dwarf, blue-foliaged form of the Scots pine. It is ideal for rockeries or collections of dwarf conifers. ZONES 4–9.

Pinus radiata *(right)*
syn. *Pinus insignis*

MONTEREY PINE, RADIATA PINE, HIMALAYAN PINE

Fast growing to over 100 ft (30 m), this Californian pine is an important timber tree in other parts of the world, especially Australia and New Zealand. It grows best in well-drained soil but does not tolerate extreme dry conditions or heat and can be toppled by strong wind. It has a pyramidal shape when young, becoming more columnar with age. The deep green needles are 4–6 in (10–15 cm) long; the bark is grayish brown. The 4–6 in (10–15 cm) long cones are light brown. **'Aurea'**, a golden-foliaged cultivar, displays its best color in winter; smaller than the species, it is inclined to revert to green. ZONES 8–10.

Pinus radiata 'Aurea'
(left)

Pinus strobus
(center)

EASTERN WHITE PINE,
WEYMOUTH PINE

Occurring naturally in
eastern North America,
where it is valued for its
timber, this species
grows to 200 ft (60 m)
in the wild but to less
than 80 ft (24 m) in cul-
tivation. It is characterized by deeply fissured,
grayish brown bark and
whorled branches. The
conical crown becomes
flattish with age. Its
fine, 4 in (10 cm) long,
bluish green needles are
soft and are carried in
groups of five. The
pointed cones, clustered
at the branch ends, pro-
duce copious amounts
of white resin. This
species develops rapidly
if grown away from a
polluted environment
and, though cold hardy,
it is susceptible to dry
conditions and wind-
burn. **'Fastigiata'** has
vivid green growth on
upward-pointing
branches. **'Nana'** is a
rounded dwarf cultivar
with dense foliage that
completely obscures the
branches. **'Prostrata'** is
a very low-growing,
spreading cultivar that
eventually mounds to
around 18 in (45 cm)
high at the center. **'Radiata'** is a dwarf cultivar
that develops into a
slowly spreading hum-
mock of foliage up to
24 in (60 cm) high.
ZONES 3–9.

Pinus strobus 'Nana'
(above)

Pinus radiata
plantation *(below)*

P

Pinus torreyana

(above)

This southern Californian species grows quickly to 50 ft (15 m). It has an irregular, broad, open crown and 8–12 in (20–30 cm) long, gray-green needles in groups of five. The dark brown cones are 4–6 in (10–15 cm) long. It grows well in many situations but looks most attractive when shaped by coastal winds. **ZONES 8–10.**

Pinus thunbergii

(below right)

syn. *Pinus thunbergiana*

JAPANESE BLACK PINE

This pine has a rugged trunk, purplish black bark, pairs of thick needles, conspicuous white buds and an intricate framework of irregular, layered, horizontal branches. Widely grown in Japan as an ornamental, it has for centuries inspired artists and bonsai masters. It will stand any amount of pruning and trimming to shape; untrimmed it grows to 120 ft (36 m). It does very well in containers. **'Nishiki'** is a naturally dwarf, gnarled cultivar with corky bark very popular for bonsai. **ZONES 5–9.**

Pinus wallichiana *(above)*

BHUTAN PINE, BLUE PINE

This ornamental pine is an effective centerpiece for a large lawn, with its conical shape, broad base and graceful long branches bearing drooping, gray-green needles 6–8 in (15–20 cm) long. Its 12 in (30 cm) long cones are eyecatching. If grown in moist, deep soil it can reach 150 ft (45 m). It is cold and disease resistant but suffers in hot, dry conditions. **ZONES 5–9.**

PIPER
PEPPER

This genus of over 1,000 species of shrubs, climbers and trees is found throughout the tropics. As might be expected of such a large genus there is little to be said that applies to all of them. The source of pepper and kava, they are often aromatic plants and their leaves are smooth-edged, usually deep green and often heart- or lance-shaped. The flowers are minute, cream or green and are borne on short yellowish spikes that form in the leaf axils. Small green fruits that ripen to red follow the flowers.

CULTIVATION
All species are frost tender and need a warm climate with moist, humus-rich soil to grow well. They will grow in sun or shade and in the right conditions can be vigorous. Propagate from seed, cuttings, by division or layering.

Piper ornatum
(right)
CELEBES PEPPER

Native to the Indonesian island of Sulawesi (Celebes), this sprawling shrub has wiry stems that spread across the ground and climb into low vegetation. It can grow to about 15 ft (4.5 m) tall. The heart-shaped leaves are nearly as wide as they are long (4 in/10 cm). The upper leaf surfaces are a mottled pattern of green, pink and silver while the undersides are flushed purple-red. ZONES 11–12.

P

Pisonia umbellifera
BIRD-CATCHER TREE

Native to the western Pacific region, this erect, branching shrub or small tree grows to 15 ft (4.5 m) and 10 ft (3 m) wide. It has large, elliptical, glossy green leaves, insignificant flowers, and bears very sticky, purplish fruit all year round. Trees from temperate east Australia and New Zealand are now usually separated as *Pisonia brunoniana* (syn. *Heimerliodendron brunonianum*). 'Variegata' has oval leaves 12–15 in (30–38 cm) long and beautifully patterned in tones of pale to dark green and creamy white, and small, greenish flowers. ZONES 10–12.

Pinus umbellifera 'Variegata' *(below)*

PISONIA
syn. *Heimerliodendron*

These 35 species of fast-growing, evergreen shrubs, small trees and climbers occur naturally in tropical and subtropical areas, particularly in the Americas, northern Australia and the Malaysian region. They have large, oval leaves rather like those of the rubber tree *(Ficus elastica)*; cultivars with variegated foliage are often grown. The small greenish flowers, though borne in panicles, are not showy but are followed by the extremely sticky fruits for which the genus is best known. These often trap insects and even small birds, although why they do this is unknown.

CULTIVATION
These frost-tender plants require rich, well-drained soil in a sunny or part-shaded site. They will grow in containers and are sometimes used as house plants. The species may be raised from seed or cuttings; the variegated foliage forms are cutting grown.

Pistacia chinensis
(below right)
CHINESE PISTACHIO

Growing to 25 ft (8 m) in gardens, this deciduous species has glossy green leaves consisting of up to 10 pairs of leaflets that turn yellow, orange and scarlet in autumn. The inconspicuous flowers, borne in panicles, are followed in summer by small red spherical seed pods that turn blue in autumn and attract birds. An excellent street tree, it also makes a good canopy for shade-loving shrubs. It often forms a double trunk. ZONES 5–10.

Pistacia vera
(below right)
PISTACHIO NUT

This small deciduous tree reaching a height and spread of 30 ft (9 m) is native to western Asia and the Middle East, but is cultivated worldwide. The leaves consist of 1 to 5 pairs of oval leaflets and turn red-gold in autumn. Red male and white female flowers are borne on separate trees; at least one of each is needed for a crop of nuts. These are reddish, fleshy and oval with a green or yellow kernel. Hot, dry summers followed by mild to cold winters give the best yield. ZONES 8–10.

PISTACIA
PISTACHIO

This small genus consists of 9 species of deciduous and evergreen trees and shrubs occurring naturally in the warm-temperate regions of the northern hemisphere. It includes the familiar edible pistachio nuts as well as ornamental deciduous species that develop vivid foliage tones in autumn, and species grown for their resins and oils. The tallest species grow to 80 ft (24 m). The leaf arrangements are compound, usually composed of an even number of leaflets. The flowers are generally inconspicuous, male and female flowers occurring on separate plants. Female plants display clusters of small berries or fleshy fruits in autumn and early winter.

CULTIVATION
A well-drained soil in full sun is preferred. Propagate from seed sown in autumn and winter, or by budding or grafting.

P

Pittosporum crassifolium
KARO

Native to New Zealand, this moderately frost hardy species grows to 25 ft (8 m) tall with a spread of 10 ft (3 m). The single trunk bears low-growing branches and a domed canopy. The oblong to oval leaves are dark green and leathery, 3 in (8 cm) long with grayish white, felted undersides. Clusters of fragrant, star-shaped, reddish purple flowers are borne in spring and are followed by fleshy, greenish white, oval fruit up to 1 in (25 mm) long. Tolerant of dry conditions and suitable for seaside locations, it adapts to most soil types but needs an open, sunny aspect. 'Variegatum' has gray to bright green leaves with an irregular cream edge. ZONES 8–10.

Pittosporum crassifolium
'Variegatum' *(above left)*

Pittosporum tobira
'Variegatum' *(left)*

PITTOSPORUM

This genus consists of some 200 species of evergreen trees and shrubs from the tropical and subtropical regions of Australasia, Africa, Asia and the Pacific Islands. They make good specimen plants, screens and windbreaks or dense hedges in mild-winter climates. The leaves are arranged alternately along the stems or in whorls. Several species have striking foliage prized by flower arrangers. The fragrant flowers are followed by fruits with a hard outer capsule enclosing round seeds with a sticky covering.

CULTIVATION
Grow in fertile, well-drained soil and keep moist over summer to maintain the foliage at its best. They need full sun or part-shade, and a sheltered position in colder areas. Some species are frost tolerant and many are excellent for seaside gardens. Propagate from seed in autumn or spring, or from tip cuttings in summer.

Pittosporum tobira
JAPANESE MOCK ORANGE

From Japan and China, this shrubby species eventually reaches 8 ft (2.4 m). Its oval to oblong, shiny green leaves, 4 in (10 cm) long, occur in whorls along the stems. Star-shaped, cream flowers with an orange blossom scent appear in late spring and summer. It thrives in mild climates in an open, sunny position. It is a good hedge plant in coastal regions. 'Wheeler's Dwarf', a mound-like shrub, grows to 24 in (60 cm); 'Variegatum' has leaves with an irregular silvery white edge. ZONES 9–11.

P

Pittosporum eugenioides *(right)*

TARATA, LEMONWOOD

From New Zealand, this densely foliaged species is pyramidal when young and grows to 40 ft (12 m) tall with smooth, pale gray bark. The shiny, dark green, narrow, oval leaves have a wavy edge and a citrus-like aroma when crushed. The terminal clusters of small, star-shaped yellow flowers with a honey-like perfume appear in spring. Large clusters of green oval fruit follow, persisting through winter. Tolerant of both frost and dry conditions, it thrives in most soils if given an open, sunny spot. **'Variegatum'** has beautiful gray-green leaves blotched along the edge with white and grows 8–15 ft (2.4–4.5 m) tall. The species and its cultivars are suitable for clipped hedges. **ZONES 9–11.**

Pittosporum eugenioides 'Variegatum' *(above)*

Pittosporum rhombifolium *(below)*

QUEENSLAND LAUREL, AUSTRALIAN LAUREL

This rainforest tree from eastern Australia can reach 80 ft (24 m) tall. Springtime clusters of star-shaped, creamy white flowers are followed in autumn and winter by masses of round, bright orange fruit $^1\!/_2$ in (12 mm) across that split when ripe to reveal sticky black seeds. Upswept branches form a dense pyramidal crown; the 4 in (10 cm) long rhomboid leaves are toothed, leathery and shiny green. This tree prefers loamy to heavy soil and a frost-free climate. **ZONES 9–11.**

P

Pittosporum undulatum

SWEET PITTOSPORUM, AUSTRALIAN DAPHNE

This popular Australian species reaches 20–40 ft (6–12 m) tall with a wide dome. The dense green leaves are lance-shaped with scalloped edges. Profuse clusters of creamy white, bell-shaped flowers in spring are followed by yellow-brown fruit. Marginally frost hardy, it prefers moderate to warm climates. Watch for white scale and sooty mold. **'Sunburst'** is a popular cultivar. ZONES 9–11.

Pittosporum phillyraeoides *(above)*

syn. *Pittosporum phylliraeoides*

BERRIGAN, WEEPING PITTOSPORUM, WILLOW PITTOSPORUM

This species, which ranges across inland Australia, grows to 25 ft (8 m) tall with a graceful weeping habit and open canopy of shiny, dark green, lance-shaped leaves up to 4 in (10 cm) long. It bears creamy yellow flowers singly or in small clusters at the branch tips in spring and summer. Fleshy, oval, 1 in (25 mm) long fruit follow, ripening from yellow to reddish brown. They then split to reveal red seeds against a yellow interior. The seeds were used by Australian Aborigines to treat pain and cramps. ZONES 9–11.

Pittosporum tenuifolium

KOHUHU, TAWHIWHI

This New Zealand species can reach 30 ft (9 m); young plants are columnar, rounding as they mature. It has pale green oblong leaves, 3 in (8 cm) long, and black twigs and bark. Its small, dark brown flowers, borne in late spring, have an intense honey perfume at night. In late summer its round fruit ripen from green to almost black. It tolerates heavy pruning and prefers an open, sunny site. **'Silver Magic'** has small, silver-gray leaves that develop pink tints, especially in winter. **'Tom Thumb'** is a low-growing form usually under 3 ft (1 m) tall with deep purple-bronze leaves with wavy edges; **'Variegatum'** has olive-green leaves with cream margins. ZONES 9–11.

Pittosporum undulatum 'Sunburst' *(above)*

Pittosporum tenuifolium 'Tom Thumb' *(below)*

PLAGIANTHUS

This genus consists of *Plagianthus regius*, which is 40 ft (12 m) tall and one of the few deciduous trees native to New Zealand, and *P. divaricatus*, a shrub that eventually reaches 6 ft (1.8 m) in height and spread. They have light olive-green leaves with serrated edges and greenish white flowers in summer. They are very tough and adaptable plants.

CULTIVATION

Plant in moist, well-drained soil with light shade when young. Propagate from seed or grow selected male forms from cuttings.

Plagianthus regius (below)
syn. *Plagianthus betulinus*
RIBBONWOOD

When young this tree is a densely twiggy, spreading shrub and stays in this form for several years. The leaves are up to 4 in (10 cm) long. There are separate male and female plants, both producing panicles of yellowish or greenish white flowers; those of the male are slightly larger and more decorative. The name ribbonwood comes from the lacy inner bark. ZONES 7–9.

P

PLATANUS
PLANE, SYCAMORE

This genus consists of 6 species of large, vigorous, wide-crowned, deciduous trees from Eurasia, North America and Mexico. It contains some of the world's largest shade trees for dry-summer climates, many of which are widely used as street trees. They are called planes or plane trees in some countries, sycamores in others. The most conspicuous feature is the flaking, mottled bark, which is shed in winter. The 5-lobed leaves are large and maple-like, and the brown seed balls hang in clusters on the trees in winter. The flowers are insignificant.

CULTIVATION
They thrive in deep, rich, well-drained soil in a sunny site and can be transplanted. Propagate from seed or cuttings or by layering. Most tolerate severe pruning, air pollution and hard construction (such as paving) covering the roots.

Platanus × *acerifolia* *(above & opposite page top)* syns *Platanus* × *hispanica, P.* × *hybrida*
LONDON PLANE

A good street tree, this fast-growing hybrid grows to 120 ft (36 m). It withstands poor conditions and is resistant to leaf blight; however, the roots can lift paving and the large leaves can block small drains. Its straight, erect trunk is attractively blotched in gray, brown and white.
ZONES 3–10.

P

Platanus orientalis *(below)*
CHINAR, CHENNAR, ORIENTAL PLANE

Ranging from Turkey to the western Himalayas, this large tree grows about 100 ft (30 m) tall with spreading branches. Fully frost hardy, it has a relatively short, stout trunk and flaking gray to greenish white bark. Its deeply incised leaves form 5 to 7 narrow, pointed lobes, and 3 to 5 round, brown seed heads hang like beads on a thread. It is used as a street tree in Australia, southern Africa and southern Europe. The leaves of **'Digitata'** have elongated, narrow lobes that are more deeply cut. **ZONES 3–10.**

P

PLATYCLADUS
ORIENTAL ARBOR-VITAE

Platycladus is a genus from China and Korea that contains only a single species, an evergreen conifer featuring flat, fan-like sprays of aromatic foliage. You may also find it listed with the closely related *Thuja*. It is a slender, conical tree but the attraction for gardeners lies in the wide choice of selected small to dwarf cultivars. These offer a diversity of neat, conical or rounded bushes with changing foliage tones through the seasons. As all the branches are retained right down to the ground, they form excellent hedges and screens, rockery features or tub specimens. The leaves are tiny, scale-like needles that clasp the twigs. Female trees have small, erect, rather fleshy cones with overlapping scales that ripen from waxy blue to brown. The species prefers warmer climates than many conifers.

CULTIVATION
Choose a spot sheltered from strong winds, although preferably in full sun. A partly shaded position will also be suitable. Most moist, well-drained soils are appropriate. Prune *Platycladus* lightly in spring, if desired, to shape. Propagate from seed in spring, or from cuttings taken in the cooler months.

Platycladus orientalis
'Filiformus Erecta'
(below)

Platycladus orientalis
'Aurea Nana' *(above)*

P

Platycladus orientalis *(opposite page left)*
syns *Thuja orientalis, Biota orientalis*

This densely branched large shrub or small tree grows to 40 ft (12 m) tall. Young plants are coni-cal to columnar; older trees have a domed crown of upward-sweeping branches atop the short trunk. Some smaller varieties have very dense, crisp foliage and a symmetrical shape; others are more irregular. They can be recognized by the arrangement of their foliage which forms narrow, vertical planes. Some dwarf types keep their fuzzy, juvenile foliage. **'Aurea Nana'** is a golden-foliaged cultivar with a low, rounded growth habit seldom more than 3 ft (1 m) tall. **'Blue Cone'** is a dense, upright plant with a conical growth habit and blue-green foliage. **'Green Cone'** is similar, but with green foliage. **'Elegantissima'** is a neat, 8 ft (2.4 m) tall shrub with a broad columnar habit and yellow-tipped foliage sprays that develop golden tones in winter. **'Filiformis Erecta'** has thread-like foliage that droops slightly or lays flat along the stems and grows 5–6 ft (1.5–1.8 m) tall. **'Hillieri'** is another rounded dwarf cultivar. **'Raffles'** is a dense, low-growing, rounded cultivar with bright yellow foliage. **'Rosedalis'** looks prickly but feels soft and grows 3–5 ft (1–1.5 m) tall. ZONES 6–11.

Platycladus orientalis
'Hillieri' *(below)*

Platycladus orientalis
'Aurea Nana' *(right)*

P

Plectranthus saccatus *(below)*

From eastern South Africa, this species is a soft-stemmed 4 ft (1.2 m) tall shrub. The soft stems are tinged purple and its leaves are up to 3 in (8 cm) long, semi-succulent with just a few large teeth. Its flowers are pale violet, in clusters of 1 to 3, on 4 in (10 cm) spikes. ZONES 10–11.

Plectranthus ecklonii *(below)*

This attractive South African shrub grows to a height of 6 ft (1.8 m) under favorable conditions, preferring a sheltered position and tolerating moderate shade. It has an erect, bushy habit with large deep green leaves that taper into their stalks and are strongly veined on the upper side. The tubular violet flowers are borne in erect terminal panicles in autumn. Cutting the plant back hard in early spring induces a better show of flowers. ZONES 9–11.

PLECTRANTHUS

This genus contains more than 350 species of annuals, perennials and shrubs. Most are rather frost tender and several species are grown as house plants, others as garden ornamentals or herbs. They generally have succulent or semi-succulent stems. The leaves, too, are often fleshy and frequently oval to heart-shaped. The flowers are small and tubular, sometimes borne in showy spikes that extend above the foliage.

CULTIVATION
Plant in moist, well-drained soil in part-shade. Protect from frost and prolonged dry conditions. Propagate from seed or cuttings or by layering. Many species are spreading and will self-layer.

Plectranthus argentatus *(below)*

This Australian species is a spreading shrub up to 3 ft (1 m) high. Its branches and leaves are covered with short silver hairs. The leaves are 2–4 in (5–10 cm) long, oval with finely toothed edges. Its flowers are blue and white, in 9- to 11-flowered spikes, which are 12 in (30 cm) long. ZONES 10–11.

**Plumbago
auriculata** *(left)*
syn. *Plumbago
capensis*

BLUE PLUMBAGO, CAPE
PLUMBAGO

This fast-growing
species from South
Africa grows to 6 ft
(1.8 m) tall with a simi-
lar spread, and carries
its prolific pale blue
flowers through the
warmer months. The
pale green, oblong
leaves are 2 in (5 cm)
long. It suckers readily,
and grows higher on
supports or by climb-
ing on nearby shrubs.
It can be grown as an
informal hedge or as a
trimmed, formal
hedge. '**Alba**' has clear
white blooms. '**Royal
Cape**' has flowers of a
more intense blue and
is slightly more tolerant
of frost and dry condi-
tions. ZONES 9–11.

PLUMBAGO

LEADWORT

This genus of 10 to 15 species of annuals,
perennials, evergreen shrubs and scrambling climbers and semi-climbers is
found in warm-temperate to tropical
regions. The blue, white or red flowers
have 5 petals narrowing to a long slender
tube and are massed on short stems near
the tips of the arching branches. The
leaves are arranged alternately.

CULTIVATION
Plumbagos require well-drained soil,
perhaps enriched with some organic
matter. They grow best in warm climates;
in frost-prone areas they do well in a
mildly warmed greenhouse. Established
plants are tolerant of dry conditions, but
soil should be kept moist during summer
for a good flowering display. Prune in
late winter to tidy their vigorous stems,
and remove old wood to encourage new
growth and next season's flowers. Propagate from tip cuttings in summer or
semi-hardwood cuttings in autumn.

Plumbago indica
(below)
syn. *Plumbago rosea*
SCARLET LEADWORT

Although smaller and
less frost hardy than
Plumbago auriculata,
this species from India
is a first-rate pot plant
for a lightly shaded spot
in subtropical or warm-
temperate climates or
for mildly warmed
greenhouses in cool
climates. Its flowers are
a beautiful deep glow-
ing pink. ZONES 10–12.

P

PLUMERIA

FRANGIPANI, TEMPLE TREE

Plumeria commemorates Charles Plumier, a seventeenth-century French botanist who described several tropical species. The genus contains 8 species of mainly deciduous shrubs and trees, originally from Central America, known for their strongly fragrant flowers. The trees can reach 30 ft (9 m), though they are generally much smaller. Their fleshy branches contain a poisonous, milky sap. In the tropics, the terminally held flowers (generally white) appear before the leaves and continue to flower for most of the year. In subtropical climates the flowers appear in spring, after the leaves, and continue growing until the next winter. The fruits consist of 2 leathery follicles, although the trees rarely fruit in cultivation. Most plumerias in gardens are hybrids.

CULTIVATION
In colder climates, these trees and shrubs can be grown in a greenhouse. Outdoors, they prefer full sun and moderately fertile, well-drained soil. Propagate in early spring from cuttings that have been allowed to dry out for a couple of weeks.

Plumeria obtusa
(below)

WHITE FRANGIPANI, SINGAPORE PLUMERIA

This small tree grows to 25 ft (8 m) high and is best suited to a tropical climate where, unlike most frangipanis, it is reliably evergreen. It can be grown in frost-free, subtropical climates, but requires a sheltered site and a fairly constant water supply. The broad, blunt-ended leaves are 6 in (15 cm) or more long. The scented, creamy white flowers have a bright yellow center. With its elegant, rounded flowers and soft perfume, 'Singapore White' is one of the loveliest of all plumerias. ZONES 10–12.

P

Plumaria obtusa
'Singapore White' *(left)*

Plumaria rubra var.
acutifolia *(right)*

P

Plumeria rubra *(left)*

This popular, deciduous small tree, with its
broadly rounded canopy, grows to 25 ft (8 m) tall.
Distinguished by its pale pink to crimson flowers,
it is used extensively for decoration. *Plumeria
rubra* var. *acutifolia* features creamy white
flowers, sometimes flushed pink, with a deep
yellow center. **'Golden Kiss'** has large heads of
golden yellow flowers with a soft flush of apricot-
pink edging each petal. **ZONES 10–12.**

PODALYRIA

This is a genus of about 25 species of evergreen shrubs and small trees that occur naturally in the winter rainfall areas of southern Africa. They have oval leaves 1½ in (35 mm) long covered with very fine hairs that create a silvery effect. The flowering season varies, but usually starts in very early spring when fragrant clusters of mauve or white sweet-pea flowers open.

CULTIVATION

Plant in light, well-drained soil in full sun; these plants thrive in coastal conditions. Propagate from seed in spring or cuttings in summer, or by layering. A light trimming after flowering keeps the bushes compact.

Podalyria calyptrata *(above)*
SWEET PEA BUSH

This species grows to be a rather open, small tree about 12 ft (3.5 m) high and nearly as wide. The silver-gray foliage is as much a feature as the masses of pink spring flowers. This is an un-demanding and reliable plant in mild climates. ZONES 9–10.

PODOCARPUS
PLUM PINE

From the wet tropics and southern hemisphere continents extending also to Japan
and Mexico, the 100 or so species are all
moderately fast-growing evergreens, ranging from 3 ft (1 m) ground covers to 150 ft
(45 m) trees. They are grown for their
dense foliage and attractive habit. The flat,
generally narrow leaves are spirally
arranged. Male and female plants are
separate: males having catkin-like yellow
pollen cones; females having naked seeds
held on short stalks that develop into the
fleshy blue-black to red berry-like 'fruits'
that give them their common name. Some
species are harvested for softwood.

CULTIVATION
Although warm-temperate climates, free
from heavy frost, suit them best, they
grow in a range of soils and in full sun or
part-shade, depending on the species. In
cooler areas, they grow indoors. Leave
unpruned unless a hedge is desired.
Propagate from seed or cuttings.

Podocarpus macrophyllus (above)
KUSAMAKI, BUDDHIST PINE, YEW PINE

From mountainous Japan and China, where it
grows to 70 ft (21 m) tall with a spread of 12 ft
(3.5 m), this cold-tolerant species prefers moist,
rich soil. It has long, thick, dark green leaves up
to 6 in (15 cm) long and responds well to pruning, making a good thick hedge. Often grown
in Japanese temple gardens, it is suitable for
containers. Berries are small and black. **'Maki'**,
rarely bigger than a shrub, has an erect habit with
almost vertical branches. ZONES 7–11.

Podocarpus
macrophyllus 'Maki'
(right)

Podocarpus latifolius *(right)*
REAL YELLOWWOOD

In the forests of southern Africa, this erect species grows to 120 ft (36 m) or more in height; in culti-vation it seldom exceeds 50 ft (15 m). Fully grown trees have leaves grouped close to the tips of the branches, and longitudinally grooved bark that shreds in long strips. Male trees produce pinkish, 1½ in (35 mm) long cones. When mature, the fruit from female trees turn blue or purplish. It is slightly frost tender. ZONES 9–12.

Podocarpus totara *(right)*
TOTARA, MAHOGANY PINE

Slow growing to a height of 100 ft (30 m), this New Zealand tree is one of the tallest of the genus and can live for much more than 200 years. Its trunk grows to a diameter of 10 ft (3 m) and yields a valuable timber. Its dense, sharp-pointed leaves are stiff and bronze green; fresh reddish brown bark matures to grayish brown before peeling off in strips. Round crimson fruit, about ½ in (12 mm) in diameter, are carried on red stalks. ZONES 9–11.

Podocarpus elatus *(left)*
BROWN PINE

In its native eastern Australia, this species grows to 120 ft (36 m) with a spreading crown, but is smaller when cultivated as a shade tree or hedge. It has flaky, dark brown bark, and its shiny, dark green leaves, 4 in (10 cm) long, are oblong and sharply pointed. The purplish to black edible fruit are rounded and 1 in (25 mm) across. This species tolerates mild frosts, but needs water in dry periods. ZONES 9–12.

Podocarpus lawrencii *(left)*
syn. *Podocarpus alpinus*
MOUNTAIN PLUM PINE

This fairly slow-growing Australian shrub or small tree can withstand frost but requires a sunny position. It ranges in height from 24 in (60 cm) in mountain areas to 25 ft (8 m) in lower woodlands. The trunk is gnarled and twisted and the small, grayish green leaves contrast well with the red, fleshy berries. This species is suitable for container planting. ZONES 7–9.

POLYARRHENA

This South African genus is closely allied to the better known *Felicia* and consists of only 4 species of perennials and subshrubs, all restricted in the wild to southwestern Cape Province. They have smallish, toothed leaves and the daisy-like flowerheads are borne singly at branch ends; these have ray florets that are white or purple-flushed on the upper sides, but a dull reddish color beneath.

CULTIVATION

They require a warm, sunny position and well-drained soil that is not too rich. After flowering has finished, the plants can be cut back to improve shape, but not too hard. Propagate from seed or cuttings.

Polyarrhena reflexa *(below)*

This species is a rather untidy, straggling subshrub that grows to 3 ft (1 m) tall. Its leaves are lance-shaped and slightly curled. They have toothed edges. In summer it has small white, sometimes flushed pink, daisy flowers with red undersides. **ZONES 9–11.**

POLYGALA
MILKWORT, SENECA, SNAKEROOT

This genus consists of more than 500 species from warm areas all over the world. They include annuals, perennials and some shrubs, only a few of which are cultivated. Some species were used by the ancient Greeks to stimulate the secretion of milk in lactating mothers. The 2 biggest sepals of the pea-like flowers are rose purple, petal-like and known as wings. The keel terminates in a crown-like tuft that is characteristic of polygalas. The flowers are carried in racemes and are followed by a 2-chambered seed pod.

CULTIVATION
They need light, well-drained soil in a sunny to part-shaded spot. They are suitable for pot culture. To keep the growth dense, prune any straggly stems after the main flowering has finished. Propagate from seed in spring or early summer, or from cuttings in late summer.

Polygala ×
dalmaisiana (below)
syn. *Polygala
myrtifolia* var.
grandiflora of gardens
SWEET PEA SHRUB

A hybrid of 2 South African species, *Polygala myrtifolia* and *P. oppositifolia,* this shrub bears magenta-purple flowers almost non-stop in mild regions. It forms a mound 3–5 ft (1–1.5 m) tall and wide, and has slender, light green leaves. It may become bare at the base. It will tolerate shearing to encourage a dense habit. ZONES 9–11.

POMADERRIS

These woody evergreen shrubs and small trees are natives of Australia and New Zealand. Only a few of the 50 species have become garden subjects. They are most spectacular in late spring when large, feathery masses of small, cream, yellow or pale green flowers cover the plants. The foliage consists of alternate, hairy green leaves, and the twigs and branches are also hairy.

CULTIVATION
These plants require well-drained, even gravelly soil and shelter from strong winds. Trim to keep a compact shape. They cope with occasional light frosts if grown in a sheltered spot, but may need a greenhouse in colder areas. Propagate from seed or cuttings.

Pomaderris kumeraho (above)

KUMARAHOU, GOLDEN TAINUI, GUMDIGGER'S SOAP

This New Zealand shrub was used by the Maoris to treat asthma and other chest problems. It grows to 10 ft (3 m) tall and up to 6 ft (1.8 m) in spread. Its slender branches carry bluish green, wrinkled, oval leaves that are 4 in (10 cm) long and densely hairy underneath. In early spring, it bears masses of tiny yellow flowers in fluffy clusters up to 8 in (20 cm) across. **ZONES 8–10.**

Pomaderris aspera (above)

HAZEL POMADERRIS

Native to shady gullies in eastern Australia, this species grows into an open shrub 15 ft (4.5 m) tall with a spread of about half that. In spring, tiny greenish white flowers mass together into large plumes. The oval leaves have conspicuous veins and are about 4 in (10 cm) long. Keep moist as it does not tolerate dry conditions. **ZONES 8–10.**

P

PONCIRUS
TRIFOLIATE ORANGE, BITTER ORANGE

This genus, closely related to *Citrus,* consists of a single species—a small, fast-growing, deciduous tree originally from China and Korea that looks most attractive in winter without its leaves. Although mainly used as a rootstock for oranges and some other *Citrus* species, it is an attractive plant in flower. It also makes an impenetrably thorny hedge.

CULTIVATION
This very frost-hardy plant prefers full sun and fertile, well-drained soil. Shelter it from cold winds. Propagate from seed or cuttings in summer.

Poncirus trifoliata (above)

This species has flattened stems, long, stout spines and trifoliate leaves. It bears white, scented, 5-petalled flowers that open before or with the new growth in spring. These are followed by yellow fruit, which become quite fragrant when ripe, but are inedible. Prune in early summer when used in hedging. ZONES 5–11.

POPULUS

POPLAR, ASPEN, COTTONWOOD

This genus of some 35 species of fast-growing, deciduous trees is from temperate regions of the northern hemisphere. In autumn many blaze with yellow or gold. Cultivated in parks, large gardens and as avenue trees, windbreaks and screens, their soft white timber is used for making matches and packing cases. Male and female flowers, borne on separate trees, are hanging catkins and appear in late winter and early spring before the leaves, which are set on long, flexible stalks. The fruits are capsules containing seeds covered with cotton-like hairs. Most species live only 60 years or so.

CULTIVATION
Plant in deep, moist, well-drained, fertile soil in full sun; they dislike arid conditions. Many species have vigorous root systems that block drains and lift paving, and so are not suitable for small gardens; some species sucker freely from the roots. Propagate from cuttings in winter.

Populus deltoides
(below left)

EASTERN COTTONWOOD, EASTERN POPLAR

An upright, broad-headed tree from eastern North America growing to 100 ft (30 m), this species is less likely to sucker than other poplars. It is short lived and brittle in high winds. The triangular, glossy green leaves are up to 8 in (20 cm) long and are coarsely toothed; the bark is gray and deeply corrugated. The long catkins are yellow and red. The name cottonwood refers to the fluff that surrounds the seeds. This is a tough tree for extreme inland conditions. *Populus deltoides* var. *monilifera*, the northern cottonwood, bears slightly smaller leaves with the toothed margins more sharply delineated. ZONES 3–11.

P

Populus nigra *(left)*

BLACK POPLAR

At 100 ft (30 m), with a suckering habit, this tree is not for small gardens. It has dark, deeply furrowed bark. Its large, diamond-shaped leaves, bronze when young, become bright green, then yellow in autumn; held on thin stalks, they seem to 'dance' perpetually. Male trees produce black catkins in mid-winter. Best known of the many cultivars is '**Italica**' (syn. *Populus pyramidalis*), the Lombardy poplar, a male cultivar popular for its narrow, columnar shape and fast growth. **ZONES 6–10.**

Populus tremula *(right)*

COMMON ASPEN, EUROPEAN ASPEN

A vigorous, spreading tree from Europe suitable for cool climates, this species grows to about 50 ft (15 m). The rounded, toothed leaves are bronze-red when young, gray-green in maturity and turn a clear yellow in autumn. They are held on slim, flat stems and quiver and rustle in the slightest breeze. Long gray catkins are carried in late winter. In large gardens and parks constant mowing will control its suckering habit. **ZONES 1–9.**

P

POTENTILLA
CINQUEFOIL

This genus of approximately 500 perennials, annuals, biennials and deciduous
shrubs is indigenous mainly to the northern hemisphere, from temperate to arctic
regions. Most species have 5-parted leaves
(hence the common name cinquefoil), and
range from only 1 in (25 mm) or so tall to
about 18 in (45 cm). They bear clusters of
1 in (25 mm), rounded, bright flowers in
profusion through spring and summer.
Some *Potentilla* species are used medicinally: the root bark of one species is said
to stop nose bleeds and even internal
bleeding.

CULTIVATION
Plant all species in well-drained, fertile
soil. Lime does not upset them. Although
the species all thrive in full sun in temperate climates, the colors of pink, red and
orange cultivars will be brighter if protected from very strong sun. Perennials
are generally frost hardy. Propagate by
division in spring,
or from seed or by
division in autumn.
Shrubs can be
propagated from
seed in autumn or
from cuttings in
summer.

Potentilla fruticosa (below)
BUSH CINQUEFOIL

This dense, deciduous shrub, found in many parts
of the temperate northern hemisphere, grows to
over 3 ft (1 m) tall with a spread of 4 ft (1.2 m) or
more. From early summer to autumn garden
varieties bear 1 in (25 mm) wide flowers in shades
of white to yellow and orange, the orange ones
often fading to salmon pink in sunshine. The flat,
mid-green leaves comprise 5 or 7 narrow elliptical
leaflets arranged palmately. '**Tangerine**' has
golden orange flowers; '**Goldstar**' is an upright
shrub with large, deep yellow flowers; '**Maanleys**'
grows up to 4 ft (1.2 m) tall with blue-green
foliage and pale yellow flowers; and '**Red Ace**', a
low grower with small leaves and bright orange-
red flowers, is inclined to be untidy and short
lived. '**Abbotswood**' is a spreading, 24 in (60 cm)
tall shrub with white flowers; '**Beesii**' grows to
24 in (60 cm) tall with very silvery leaves and
bright yellow flowers; '**Daydawn**' is a 3 ft (1 m)
tall shrub with salmon-pink flowers; '**Elizabeth**'
is a dense, bushy, 3 ft (1 m) shrub with bright
yellow flowers; '**Goldfinger**' is a low grower with
narrow, bright green leaflets and very bright
yellow flowers; and '**Primrose Beauty**', up to 3 ft
(1 m) tall and 5 ft (1.5 m) wide, has primrose
yellow flowers very reminiscent of a small wild
rose. ZONES 2–9.

P

Potentilla fruticosa
'Goldfinger' *(left)*

Potentilla fruticosa
'Tangerine' *(left)*

P

Potentilla fruticosa
'Red Ace' *(right)*

Prostanthera cuneata *(right)*

ALPINE MINT BUSH

This compact shrub from southeastern Australia reaches 3 ft (1 m) in height but spreads over 5 ft (1.5 m). In summer it bears small, profuse clusters of white to mauve flowers with purple and yellow spots in the throat. The very aromatic, soft, dark green leaves, round and $^1/_2$ in (12 mm) across, form a dense crown. This plant thrives in medium to heavy soils if kept moist over summer. ZONES 8–9.

Prostanthera lasianthos *(left)*

VICTORIAN CHRISTMAS BUSH

Native to eastern Australia, this fast-growing, large shrub or small tree grows 15–30 ft (4.5–9 m) tall with an open canopy spreading out from a short trunk. From spring to midsummer it bears sprays of faintly perfumed, white flowers tinged with either pink or light blue, and marked with purple and orange spots in the throat. The lance-shaped leaves are up to 3 in (8 cm) long. It tolerates an occasional light frost. ZONES 8–10.

PROSTANTHERA

MINT BUSH

These 50 species of woody, evergreen shrubs grow naturally in Australia. Glands dotted over the leaves release a minty smell when crushed, hence the common name. The flowers, which appear during spring and summer, are trumpet-like with 2 lips. The upper lip is erect and hooded with 2 lobes; the broader, lower lip has 3 lobes. Flower colors include green, white, blue and purple, and even red and yellow. The fruits are small nuts.

CULTIVATION

A warm climate is essential. They prefer a sunny location sheltered from strong winds and very well-drained soil, which must be kept moist during the growing season. Even with the best of care, some species are notorious for their tendency to die suddenly. Prune after flowering. Propagate new plants from seed or cuttings taken in summer. Some of the more difficult species can be grafted.

Prostanthera ovalifolia *(above)*
PURPLE MINT BUSH

This spectacular but short-lived mint bush bears
large sprays of rich purple (occasionally mauve)
flowers in spring. It forms a large shrub or small
tree 6 ft (1.8 m) tall, either upright and dense or
more spreading. The small, oval leaves are dark
green above and grayish green underneath, and
are up to $^1/_2$ in (12 mm)long. Both the foliage and
stems are very aromatic. **ZONES 9–11.**

Prostanthera nivea var. *induta* *(right)*

The species is a bushy shrub to 10 ft (3 m) with
white flowers and bright green leaves.
Prostanthera nivea var. *induta* bears lilac flowers
in racemes in spring and summer and has silvery
green leaves. **ZONES 9–11.**

Prostanthera rotundifolia
ROUND-LEAFED MINT BUSH

This shrub features lilac or mauve but sometimes
whitish flowers, arranged in large, open or more
compact clusters. It has a bushy crown only 6 ft
(1.8 m) tall and 5 ft (1.5 m) wide. The dense, dark
green leaves are very aromatic, oval to round, and
$^1/_2$ in (12 mm) across with smooth edges. It
prefers part-shade. ***Prostanthera rotundifolia***
var. *rosea* has mauve-pink to deep pink flowers
and is usually a slightly more compact plant than
the species. **ZONES 9–10.**

*Prostanthera
rotundifolia* var. *rosea*
(left)

Protea cynaroides *(right)*

KING PROTEA, GIANT PROTEA

This species, South Africa's floral emblem, grows to 5 ft (1.5 m) tall with several sprawling stems. Each flowerhead is a huge, shallow bowl up to 12 in (30 cm) across. Widely spaced, pointed, downy pink bracts enclose a central dome of pink, snowy haired flowers, which are borne from mid-winter to spring. The oval, leathery leaves, 6 in (15 cm) long, are shiny green with a long red stalk. **ZONES 9–10.**

PROTEA

The 115 species in this outstanding genus of evergreen shrubs and small trees from Africa are prized for their flowerheads, especially by the cut flower industry. Most species grow 3–10 ft (1–3 m) tall. The characteristic cone-shaped flowerheads have a dense central mass of hairy flowers surrounded by brightly colored bracts. These range from yellow to red, crimson, pink, orange, silver or white, and flowering usually extends over several months. The leathery green leaves often have hairy or undulating margins.

CULTIVATION

Often difficult to grow, proteas prefer an open, sunny position with light, usually acidic, well-drained soil. They can cope with occasional light frosts, but young plants need protection during their first 2 winters. Mulch to suppress weeds. Prune after flowering to maintain shape and to promote new growth. Propagate from seed or cuttings in summer, or by grafting or budding.

Protea aristata
(above)

This slow-growing species forms a compact, round shrub 8 ft (2.4 m) tall and 10 ft (3 m) wide. The leaves, 3 in (8 cm) long, are fresh green with a black pointed tip. The blooms, 4–6 in (10–15 cm) long and 4 in (10 cm) across, are cup-shaped with a central cone of dark pink, hairy flowers surrounded by deep pink to red bracts. The flowers appear at the branch tips from early to mid-summer. **ZONES 9–10.**

P

Protea aurea (left)

Restricted in the wild to cool, moist hill slopes in southwest Cape Province, South Africa, this attractive species grows to 15 ft (4.5 m) tall, but often less than half that in gardens, with erect branches from a single trunk at the base. The broad leaves are heart-shaped at the base. The flowerheads are shuttlecock-shaped, with a funnel of creamy green to crimson bracts and a spreading tuft of long, straight styles extending well beyond the bracts but of the same color. Even more handsome is **Protea aurea** subsp. **potsbergensis** with broader, slightly silvery leaves and flowerheads of a pale silvery pink or greenish white. Found naturally on the coast, it is endangered in the wild. ZONES 9–10.

Protea compacta (right)

BOT RIVER PROTEA

This stiff, upright 10 ft (3 m) shrub has sparse, rangy branches arising from the single main stem. The cup-shaped flowerheads, borne from late autumn to early spring, are delicate and almost oblong—4–6 in (10–15 cm) long and 3–4 in (8–10 cm) across. Its velvety bracts are rich pinkish tones and are fringed with silver; the flowers are paler. The light green leaves are stemless, varying from oblong to broadly lance-shaped, and grow up to 6 in (15 cm) long. The new leaves are downy, mature leaves smooth. ZONES 9–10.

Protea eximia (left)

syn. *Protea latifolia*

RAY-FLOWERED PROTEA, DUCHESS PROTEA

This dense, upright shrub grows to 15 ft (5 m) tall with few branches. The leaves are broadly oval to heart-shaped and silvery to purplish green. The blooms are 4–6 in (10–15 cm) long and 3–4 in (8–10 cm) across. Their long, spoon-shaped, rose pink to crimson bracts surround a cone of pink, hairy flowers tipped with purple. These blooms are held well above the foliage. Flowering peaks in the spring months. **'Sylvia'** bears deep pink to red flowers profusely through summer. ZONES 9–10.

P

Protea repens *(right)*

SUGARBUSH, HONEY PROTEA

One of the easiest of the species to grow, this upright, multi-branched, rounded shrub reaches 10 ft (3 m) tall and wide. It features deep, V-shaped blooms with shiny, sticky bracts, creamish white to crimson or white with candy pink tips, surrounding an open cone of downy white flowers. The flowerheads are up to 4 in (10 cm) across, and bloom from early autumn through winter. The mid-green leaves, 2–6 in (5–15 cm) long, are tipped with a bluish tinge and are narrowly oblong to lance-shaped. **'Guerna'**, one of the first cultivars, bears large, upright, deep red flowers in summer. **ZONES 9–10.**

Protea neriifolia

(right)

BLUE SUGARBUSH, OLEANDER-
LEAFED PROTEA

This widely grown species has narrow, gray-green leaves up to 6 in (15 cm) long, covered with fine felting when young. From autumn to spring, upright, 4 in (10 cm) long, goblet-shaped flowerheads open at the tips of the branches. They have a felty central cone surrounded by overlapping, upward-facing, petal-like, deep reddish pink bracts tipped with a fringe of black hairs. There are forms with deeper or paler flowers, as well as a greenish white one. **ZONES 9–10.**

Protea longifolia

(above right)

SIR LOWRY'S PASS PROTEA

Restricted to the winter rainfall areas of southern Africa, this species makes a small spreading shrub up to 5 ft (1.5 m) tall. Blooms 3–6 in (8–15 cm) long and 2–4 in (5–10 cm) across are borne from autumn until late spring. They consist of pointed cream bracts, tinged with green or yellow, surrounding a mass of fluffy white flowers and a central peak of hairy black flowers. The leaves are long and narrow, point upwards, and are 6 in (15 cm) long. **ZONES 9–10.**

Protea 'Pink Ice' *(above)*

This evergreen shrub, a hybrid of *Protea susannae* and *P. neriifolia,* is the cultivar that is most important commercially as a cut flower. Its shiny pink flowerheads, appearing in autumn and winter, resemble those of *P. neriifolia* minus the soft, black hairs on the bracts. Marginally frost hardy, it grows to 10 ft (3 m) tall with a spread of 6 ft (1.8 m). **ZONES 9–10.**

P

PRUNUS

This large genus, mostly from the northern hemisphere, includes the edible stone fruits—cherries, plums, apricots, peaches, nectarines and almonds—but there are also ornamental species and cultivars with beautiful flowers. The genus includes several shrubby species, but most are trees growing on average to 15 ft (4.5 m), although some can reach 100 ft (30 m). Most of the familiar species are deciduous and bloom in spring (or late winter in mild climates) with scented, 5-petalled, pink or white flowers. The leaves are simple and often serrated, and all produce a fleshy fruit containing a single hard stone. Many have attractive autumn foliage, and others have interesting bark. Cherry and plum timber is sometimes used commercially. The 430 species in the genus are divided among 5 or 6 easily recognized subgenera. They are: *Prunus* in the narrow sense, which includes all the plums and sometimes (but not always) *Armeniaca,* the apricots; *Amygdalus,* which includes peaches, nectarines, almonds and a few ornamental species with similar stalkless blossoms and pitted stones; *Cerasus,* which includes all the cherries and flowering cherries with few-flowered umbels; *Padus,* which includes the bird cherries, mainly North American, with small flowers in long racemes; and finally, the evergreens in the subgenus *Laurocerasus,* also with flowers in racemes and including the well-known cherry laurel and its allies and a large group of tropical rainforest trees from Asia and the Americas.

CULTIVATION

Plant in moist, well-drained soil in full sun but with protection from strong wind for the spring blossom. Keep the base of trees free of weeds and long grass. Feed young trees with a high-nitrogen fertilizer. Many fruiting varieties respond well to espaliering. Propagate by grafting or from seed— named cultivars must be grafted or budded onto seedling stocks. Pests and diseases vary with locality.

P

Prunus avium *(below)*

SWEET CHERRY, GEAN, MAZZARD, WILD CHERRY

Native to Europe and western Asia, this species is the major parent of the cultivated sweet cherries. It can reach 60 ft (18 m) tall, with a rounded crown and a stout, straight trunk with banded reddish brown bark. The pointed, dark green leaves are up to 6 in (15 cm) long and turn red, crimson and yellow before they drop. Profuse white flowers appear in late spring before the leaves and are followed by black-red fruit. The cultivated cherries are rarely self-fertile, so trees of 2 or more different clones are often necessary for fruit production. Cherry wood is prone to fungus, so avoid pruning in winter or in wet weather. The ornamental cultivar **'Plena'** carries a mass of drooping, double white flowers. ZONES 3–9.

Prunus armeniaca

APRICOT

Now believed to have originated in northern China and Mongolia, the apricot was introduced to the Middle East more than 1000 years ago and thence to Europe. It grows to no more than about 25 ft (8 m) tall, the trunk becoming characteristically gnarled with age. White or pinkish blossoms are borne in early spring before the leaves appear. The twigs are reddish, and the smooth, heart-shaped leaves are about 3 in (8 cm) long. The yellow-orange fruit contains a smooth, flattened stone that separates easily from the sweet-tasting flesh. Prune moderately after flowering to encourage a good fruit crop. **'Story'** is a popular cultivar, fruiting mid-season. ZONES 5–10.

Prunus armeniaca 'Story' *(opposite page left)*

Prunus × blireana *(above)*

DOUBLE FLOWERING PLUM

This popular hybrid originated in the early twentieth century as a cross between the Japanese apricot *Prunus mume* and the purple-leaved plum *P. cerasifera* **'Pissardii'**. A rounded shrub or small tree, it grows to around 12 ft (3.5 m) high and has slender, arching branches and thin, red-purple leaves that change to golden brown in autumn. In early spring it bears fragrant pale rose pink, double flowers. ZONES 5–10.

Prunus avium 'Plena' *(above)*

P

Prunus cerasifera

CHERRY PLUM, MYROBALAN, PURPLE-LEAFED PLUM

Native to Turkey and the Caucasus region, this small-fruited, thornless plum has long been culti- vated in Europe. It grows to about 30 ft (9 m) and is tolerant of dry conditions, with an erect, bushy habit and smallish leaves that are slightly bronze tinted. Profuse, small white flowers appear before the leaves, in spring in cool climates and in late winter in milder ones, followed by edible red plums up to 1¼ in (30 mm) in diameter in sum- mer. This species has many ornamental cultivars, the most widely grown being those with deep purple foliage. **'Nigra'** has vibrant, deep purple leaves turning more blackish purple in late sum- mer; in spring it bears single, pale pink blossoms with a red calyx and stamens. The cherry-sized red fruit are edible but sour. **'Elvins'** is an Australian- raised cultivar grown for its white blossom, prettily flushed with flesh pink, which is densely massed on arching branches in mid-spring; it grows only to about 12 ft (3.5 m). ZONES 3–10.

Prunus cerasifera 'Nigra' *(above left)*
Prunus cerasifera 'Elvins' *(left)*

Prunus campanulata *(below)*

TAIWAN CHERRY, CARMINE CHERRY

This species from Taiwan, south China and the Ryukyu Islands is less frost tolerant than most deciduous *Prunus* species and likes warm- temperate climates. It can grow to 30 ft (9 m) but is mostly smaller in cultivation. Cherries bloom in mid- to late winter in a warm climate, or early spring in cooler climates. The bare branches are festooned with clusters of bell- shaped flowers, bright carmine red in the commonly grown form. The foliage turns bronze-red in autumn. Like most cherries, it responds poorly to pruning. ZONES 7–11.

Prunus × *domestica*

PLUM, EUROPEAN PLUM

The common plum of Europe is believed to be an
ancient hybrid, its probable ancestors thought to
include the blackthorn, *Prunus spinosa,* and the
cherry plum, *P. cerasifera.* It has numerous
cultivars, most grown for their sweet fruit but
some for their display of blossom. It is a vigorous
grower to a height of 30 ft (9 m) or even more,
with a tangle of strong branches spreading into a
broad, dense crown of foliage. Only the vigorous
new growths are sometimes spiny. Flowers are
white, borne in profuse small clusters in spring,
and the summer fruit are spherical to somewhat
elongated with a yellow, red or blue-black skin
and green or yellow flesh; they range in length
from 1¼–3 in (3–8 cm). Not as juicy as the red-
fleshed Japanese plums (*P. salicina),* the fruit of
most cultivars are best cooked or dried for
prunes; one of the best for eating is **'Coe's Golden
Drop'** a sweet, juicy, amber-yellow plum with red
spots. **'Stanley'** bears profuse purple-black fruit.
Another popular cultivar is **'President'.** *Prunus* ×
domestica subsp. *insititia,* the damson plum or
bullace, is a thornier tree that often succeeds in
districts too cold for large-fruited varieties; the
small purple-black fruit with tart acid flesh are
used for jams and jellies. ZONES 5–9.

Prunus × *domestica* 'President' *(above right)*
Prunus × *domestica* 'Stanley' *(right)*

Prunus 'Okame'

(right)

This attractive hybrid
cherry is a cross
between *Prunus
campanulata* and *P.
incisa.* In spring, before
the leaves appear, it
bears profuse blossoms
of a clear, bright pink
opening from more
reddish buds. It grows
to about 25 ft (8 m) tall
and has dark green foli-
age that turns brilliant
orange in autumn.
ZONES 7–10.

Prunus dulcis *(below right)*

syn. *Prunus amygdalus*

ALMOND

The almond is believed to come from the eastern Mediterranean region and requires a climate with hot dry summers and cool winters to bear well. It grows to over 20 ft (6 m) high, with a spreading habit. Stalkless pink blossoms are borne in clusters of 5 to 6 on the leafless branches in late winter or early spring. These are followed in summer by flattened, furry fruit; this dries and splits to release the weak-shelled stone, which contains the almond kernel. Almonds need a well-drained, salt-free soil and young trees are frost tender; they are not self-fertile and two varieties that blossom at the same time are needed to produce fruit. They are prone to shot-hole disease, which appears on the fruit as purple spots, spoiling the nut inside. Prune to an open vase shape encouraging 3 or 4 main branches. ZONES 6–9.

Prunus cerasus *(left)*

MORELLO CHERRY, SOUR CHERRY

The fruiting cherries of Europe and western Asia have been the subject of much confusion concerning their botanical identities. Many of the forms are placed under the name *Prunus cerasus*, characterized by a smaller, more bushy growth form than that of *P. avium*, suckering from the roots, and acid fruit. Its wild origin is unknown and botanists suspect it may have a common ancestry with *P. avium*. The plants are self-fertile, so an isolated tree is capable of setting fruit, but like the sweet cherry, it needs cold winters for successful growth. **P. c. var. austera**, the morello cherry, has pendulous branches and has blackish fruit with purple juice; the red amarelle cherries with clear juice belong to **P. c. var. caproniana**, while the famous maraschino cherries with very small blackish fruit are **P. c. var. marasca,** which grows in Dalmatia. ZONES 3–9.

Prunus maackii *(left)*

MANCHURIAN CHERRY, AMUR CHOKE-CHERRY

This cherry from Korea and nearby parts of China and eastern Siberia grows to around 50 ft (15 m) tall. The 3–4 in (8–10 cm) long leaves are downy when young and often color well in autumn. The small white flowers are carried in short dense spikes at the ends of the previous year's growth and are followed by tiny, dry, black fruit. Its background is uncertain, and it seems to show characteristics of both the bird cherries *(P. padus)* and the laurel cherries *(P. laurocerasus)*. ZONES 2–9.

Prunus glandulosa

DWARF FLOWERING ALMOND, ALMOND-CHERRY

This deciduous shrub from China and Japan
belongs to a group of dwarf *Prunus* species from
the cherry subgenus *(Cerasus)*, but shows some of
the characteristics of almonds and peaches. It
makes a showy, late spring-flowering shrub of up
to 5 ft (1.5 m) with thin, wiry branches, small
leaves, and profuse white to pale pink flowers,
borne along the stems. The dark red fruit, about
half the size of a cherry, are edible though rather
sour. It is common practice to cut the bushes
back almost to ground level as soon as flowering
finishes, producing a thicket of strong vertical
shoots that bloom very freely the next spring.
'Sinensis' (syn. 'Rosa Plena') bears double pink
flowers. **'Alba Plena'** has double white flowers.
ZONES 6–10.

Prunus glandulosa
'Sinensis' *(above)*

Prunus padus
'Watereri' *(below)*

Prunus padus *(above)*

BIRD CHERRY

This temperate Eurasian tree grows to around 50 ft
(15 m) tall, though usually considerably less in
gardens. It has 4 in (10 cm) long leaves with
serrated edges and fine hairs, often developing
orange tints in autumn. The flowers are white,
½ in (12 mm) wide, on racemes just over 4 in
(10 cm) long. Pea-sized black fruit, attractive to
birds, follow. **'Watereri'** is a shapely tree with
pendulous racemes up to 8 in (20 cm) long.
ZONES 3–9.

Prunus laurocerasus *(right)*
CHERRY LAUREL, LAUREL CHERRY

Both the botanical and common names of this handsome evergreen reflect the resemblance of its foliage to that of the true laurel *(Laurus nobilis)* and the 2 plants are sometimes confused. Native to the Balkans, Turkey and the Caspian region, it has been grown in western Europe since the sixteenth century. It is commonly grown as a hedge, but unclipped it can reach 50 ft (15 m) in height. The shiny, bright green leaves are 6 in (15 cm) or more long; in mid- to late spring it bears upright sprays of small, sweetly scented white flowers, followed by red berries that turn black in autumn. One of the toughest of evergreens, cherry laurel tolerates alkaline soils and will grow in shade. **'Otto Luyken'** is a free-flowering dwarf form growing to 3–4 ft m (1–1.2) in height and spreading to 5 ft (1.5 m). **'Zabeliana'** is a horizontally branched cultivar, usually under 3 ft (1 m) in height and 12 ft (3.5 m) or more in width, with narrow, willow-like leaves. ZONES 6–10.

Prunus mume
JAPANESE APRICOT

Closely related to the common apricot, this very early flowering species is a native of China but has been cultivated for many centuries in both China and Japan, where it has given rise to hundreds of named cultivars selected for both fruit and flower. It makes a round-headed tree of 15–30 ft (4.5–9 m) high with sharply pointed leaves up to 4 in (10 cm) long. The lightly scented, white to deep pink flowers, 1 in (25 mm) or more across, are carried in small clusters along the branches in late spring; yellowish, apricot-like fruit follow. Its blossoms feature in classical Chinese and Japanese paintings and it is also popular for bonsai work. Cultivars include **'Albo-plena'** with white double flowers; **'Beni-chidori'**, a later flowerer with fragrant pink double flowers; **'Pendula'** with a weeping habit; and **'Geisha'** with semi-double deep rose flowers. ZONES 6–9.

Prunus mume 'Geisha' *(above)*   *Prunus mume* 'Beni-chidori' *(right)*

P

Prunus persica
PEACH, FLOWERING PEACH, NECTARINE

Believed to have originated in China but introduced to the Mediterranean region over 1000 years ago, the peach grows 12 ft (3.5 m) or more tall. It bears an abundance of pinkish red flowers in early spring (or late winter in mild climates). The narrow, 6 in (15 cm) long, mid-green leaves appear after the blossoms. Its delicious mid-summer fruit, which vary from cream and pale pink to yellow or scarlet, are covered with a velvety down and contain a stone that is deeply pitted and grooved. Many cultivars include both fruiting and flowering types, the latter mostly with small, hard fruit that are of little use for eating; the fruiting cultivars, though, can also have showy flowers. Ornamental cultivars include the widely grown **'Alba Plena'**, with double white flowers; **'Klara Meyer'**, bearing double peach pink flowers with frilled petals; and **'Magnifica'**, noted for its double, deep crimson blooms that cover the branches. Other popular cultivars include **'Dixired'**, **'Kernechtor von Vorbebirge'**, **'Red Heaven'**, **'Rekord aus Alfter'** and **'Robert Blum'**. *P. persica* var. *nectarina*, the nectarine, is almost identical to the peach in habit and flowers, but its fruit are smooth skinned, mostly smaller and with a subtly different flavor. There are several named varieties and their seedlings often revert to the normal, downy-skinned peaches. ZONES 5–10.

Prunus persica 'Red Heaven' *(above)*

Prunus persica 'Rekord aus Alfter' *(below)*

Prunus persica var. *nectarina (below)*

Prunus persica 'Robert Blum' *(below right)*

Prunus sargentii *(left & below left)*
SARGENT CHERRY

This flowering cherry species, native to Japan, Korea and eastern Siberia, is one of the tallest of the Japanese flowering cherry group, growing to as much as 80 ft (24 m), with dark chestnut-colored bark. In mid-spring the branches are covered with pink flowers with deeper pink stamens, accompanied by the unfolding leaves, which are long-pointed and up to 5 in (12 cm) in length; in autumn they make a brilliant display of reddish bronze, turning orange and red. This species performs best away from polluted environments. **ZONES 4–9.**

Prunus persica 'Kernechter van Vorgebirge' *(above)*

Prunus persica 'Dixired' *(left)*

Prunus, Sato-zakura Group, 'Okumiyako' *(opposite page right)*

Prunus, Sato-zakura Group

These are the main group of Japanese flowering cherries, believed to be derived mainly from the species *Prunus serrulata* (under which name they are commonly found), but with probable hybrid influence of several closely related species. Mostly small to medium-sized trees, they can be recognized by their large leaves with fine, even teeth ending in bristle-like points, and their loose umbels of flowers that are mostly over $1\frac{1}{2}$ in (35 mm) in diameter; the bases of the umbels carry conspicuous, toothed bracts, like miniature leaves. They are among the most widely planted trees for spring blossom in cool climates but require good rainfall and a mild summer for the best display of blossom. The numerous cultivars are mostly of Japanese origin and there has been much confusion as to their names. Height and growth form vary with cultivar, as do the color, shape and size of the flowers and the color of the new leaves, which unfold with or just after the opening flowers. **'Amanogawa'** has a narrow habit, growing to 30 ft (9 m) high, and carries fragrant, semi-double white to shell-pink flowers. **'Sekiyama'** (syn. 'Kanzan'), a vigorous grower to 10 ft (3 m), bears double purple-pink flowers in mid-spring. **'Cheal's Weeping'** (syn. 'Kiku-shidare') flowers early, carrying double deep pink flowers on weeping branches. **'Shirotae'** (syn.

'Mount Fuji'), growing to 20 ft (6 m), has slightly drooping, spreading branches; green, lacy-edged leaves appear in early spring and turn orange-red in autumn; in mid-spring it carries a wealth of fragrant, single or semi-double white blossoms. **'Okumiyako'** (syn. 'Shimidsu sakura'), growing to 15 ft (4.5 m), has wide, spreading branches; pink-tinted buds appear in late spring and open to fringed, large, double white flowers, and the leaves turn orange and red in fall. **'Pink Perfection'** is a strong-growing cultivar with clusters of large, deep pink, double flowers that open from red buds. **'Shirofugen'**, strong growing to 20 ft (6 m), blooms late, and the purplish pink buds intermingle attractively with the young, copper leaves; clusters of double flowers open white and turn purplish pink. **'Shogetsu'** makes a 15 ft (4.5 m), spreading tree with arching branches and large clusters of semi-double to fully double, white-centered, pale pink flowers; it blooms late. **'Taihaku'**, known as the great white cherry, is a vigorous, spreading tree to 20 ft (6 m) or more; in mid-spring it bears large, pure white flowers and bronze-red, young leaves that mature to dark green. **'Takasago'**, the Naden cherry, with scented pink flowers, is thought by some to be a hybrid with *P.* × *yedoensis*. **'Ukon'**, an upright tree to 30 ft (9 m), bears large pink-tinged, greenish cream flowers in mid-spring. **ZONES 5–9.**

P

Prunus, Sato-zakura
Group, 'Takasago' *(above)*

Prunus, Sato-zakura
Group, 'Shirotae' *(right)*

Prunus, Sato-zakura
Group, 'Ukon' *(below)*

Prunus serotina *(opposite page bottom)*

BLACK CHERRY, RUM CHERRY

This fast-growing species of the bird cherry group
reaches heights of over 100 ft (30 m) in its native
eastern and central North America, where its
timber is highly prized for furniture-making; in
cultivation a tree of 50 ft (15 m) would be exceptional. It has dark brown bark and its pointed
leaves, up to 6 in (15 cm) long, are green above
with paler undersides and often have a downy
midrib. They turn yellow and pale scarlet before
falling. The small fragrant, white flowers are
borne in drooping spikes up to 6 in (15 cm) long
in late spring, followed by pea-sized black fruit in
summer; these are eaten by birds, which distribute the seeds widely. ZONES 3–9.

Prunus serrula *(right)*

TIBETAN CHERRY

Native to western China, this deciduous, neatly round-headed tree growing to 50 ft (15 m) is prized in gardens for its gleaming, mahogany red bark. Clusters of small white flowers appear in spring at the same time as the new leaves, which mature to dark green and turn yellow in autumn; the tiny round fruit are red to black. This species requires a cool climate. **ZONES 5–9.**

Prunus serrulata *(above)*

JAPANESE CHERRY, ORIENTAL CHERRY

This cherry from China is believed to be the main ancestor of the Japanese flowering cherries (*Prunus*, Sato-zakura Group). It has similar foliage, though the teeth on the leaves are not so noticeably bristle-tipped. It makes a spreading tree of about 30 ft (9 m) in height and bears pink-flushed white flowers before or with the leaves in mid- to late spring. **ZONES 5–9.**

P

Prunus spinosa *(right & below)*

SLOE, BLACKTHORN

A species of plum, this 12–15 ft (3.5–4.5 m) thorny shrub or small tree is found throughout temperate Eurasia and in North Africa. It has toothed 2 in (5 cm) long leaves and profuse small white flowers borne singly or occasionally in pairs on the leafless branches in early spring. The flowers are followed in summer by ½ in (12 mm) wide, prune-like fruit, which can be used to make a very tart jam or conserve. **ZONES 4–9.**

Prunus × subhirtella

HIGAN CHERRY, ROSEBUD CHERRY

This graceful cherry from Japan is now believed to be of hybrid origin. It grows to 30 ft (9 m) and produces a profusion of pale pink flowers in early spring. The leaves are dark green and pointed, and fade to shades of yellow before dropping. It thrives in cool climates but can be rather short-lived. '**Autumnalis**', growing to 15 ft (4.5 m), bears pink-budded white flowers intermittently from late autumn through winter and into early spring; '**Autumnalis Rosea**' is similar but has pale pink flowers. '**Pendula**' has slender, vertically pendulous branches like a weeping willow and is usually grafted onto a standard; it bears a profusion of small pale pink, 5-petalled flowers from late winter into spring, followed by little spherical brown-red fruit. The spring-blooming '**Pendula Rubra**' bears rich pink flowers. '**Accolade**' is a presumed hybrid between *Prunus × subhirtella* and *P. sargentii*: it makes a spreading tree to about 25 ft (8 m) with quite large pale pink semi-double flowers opening from deep pink buds in early spring. '**Hally Jolivette**' is the result of a backcross of the hybrid *P. × subhirtella × yedoensis* onto *P. × subhirtella*. It is a large shrub, growing to 8–15 ft (2.4–4.5 m) in height and spread. Of dense growth with many reddish, upright stems, it is covered for 2 to 3 weeks in spring with double white flowers opening from pink buds. **ZONES 5–9.**

Prunus × subhirtella 'Accolade' *(left)*

Prunus × subhirtella
'Pendula' *(left)*

Prunus × subhirtella
'Autumnalis Rosea'
(below)

Prunus × yedoensis

TOKYO CHERRY, YOSHINO CHERRY

This is another Japanese cherry that is now
regarded as a hybrid, the parents probably ***Prunus
speciosa*** and *P. × subhirtella*. It is a small tree,
growing quite rapidly to 30 ft (9 m) high and
wide. Massed fragrant white or pale pink flowers
usually open before the new foliage develops; the
deep green 4 in (10 cm) long leaves color well in
autumn. It makes a beautiful lawn specimen or
avenue tree and is the main flowering cherry
planted in Washington DC. **'Ivensii'** has an arching and weeping growth habit. **'Akebono'** has
pure pink flowers. **'Shidare Yoshino'** has a weeping habit and masses of pure white flowers.
ZONES 5–9.

Prunus × yedoensis
'Shidare Yoshino' *(above)*

PSEUDOLARIX

GOLDEN LARCH

This genus consists of a single species, a deciduous conifer from China. Slow growing to 120 ft (36 m), in cultivation it seldom exceeds 70 ft (21 m). It grows almost as wide as it does high. It differs from the larch *(Larix)* in that the cone scales taper to a point; the male cones are held in clusters, not singly, and the scales on the female cones spread and drop off.

CULTIVATION
Plant in moist, rich, deep, well-drained, acid soil. It requires shelter from strong winds and abundant light. Propagate from seed.

Pseudolarix amabilis *(below left)* syn. *Pseudolarix kaempferi*

The horizontal branches on this species form a broad conical crown, held on a trunk with reddish brown bark that is fissured and scaly. Its fine leaves are soft and pale green with bluish undersides and are arranged in rosettes along slender twigs. The foliage turns golden yellow in the cooler months before dropping. Its flowers appear as catkins, followed by green cones that mature to yellow and persist on the tree. It makes an excellent bonsai specimen. ZONES 3–9.

P

PSEUDOPANAX
syns *Neopanax, Nothopanax*

Members of this small genus of evergreen trees and shrubs are grown for their interesting fruits and foliage. Most of the 12 to 20 species are endemic to New Zealand with one each in Tasmania, New Caledonia and Chile. The leaves are simple when young, becoming compound as they mature. The 5-petalled, greenish summer flowers are inconspicuous. They are followed by clusters of berries. These plants make good tub specimens and attractive house plants.

CULTIVATION
Suited to warm-climate gardens, they need well-drained soil enriched with humus either in sun or part-shade. Propagate from seed or cuttings taken in summer.

Pseudopanax lessonii (below)
HOUPARA

This well-branched, slender shrub or small tree grows to 20 ft (6 m) and has rich green leathery leaves, each consisting of 3 to 5 oval to lance-shaped leaflets up to 4 in (10 cm) long. In warm-temperate areas the leaves may be tinged bronze to purple in winter. The houpara tolerates exposed windy conditions and also makes a good tub specimen. 'Cyril Watson' is a good cultivar. ZONES 9–10.

Pseudopanax crassifolius (left)
HOROEKA, LANCEWOOD

This small tree from New Zealand changes dramatically with age. Young plants have a single stem up to 8 ft (2.4 m) tall. The stiff, sword-like, narrow leaves, up to 3 ft (1 m) long, are dark shiny green above, purplish beneath, with sharply serrated edges and a reddish midrib. Older plants are branched, 30 ft (9 m) or so tall with a rounded canopy 10 ft (3 m) wide. The leaves then become compound, with leathery leaflets 12 in (30 cm) long and edges more deeply toothed. Small, black, ornamental fruit are produced by female plants. ZONES 9–11.

Pseudopanax laetus (below)

Ultimately up to 20 ft (6 m) tall, this species is widely grown as a tub plant when young. It has luxuriant hand-shaped leaves with 5 to 7 leaflets, each of which is up to 10 in (25 cm) long. New leaf buds are enclosed in a jelly and open from purplish young stems. The large heads of tiny green flowers are followed by small purple-red seed capsules. This is a great plant for adding a tropical touch to a temperate garden. ZONES 9–10.

PSEUDOTSUGA

Among the largest of all conifers, the 6 to 8 *Pseudotsuga* species are seldom seen at their maximum height outside their native North America, China, Taiwan, Japan and Mexico. They can reach 300 ft (90 m) with a cylindrical trunk supporting an attractive, broad pyramidal shape. The leaves are soft, green, flattened and tapered, with two bands of white on their undersides. The brown cones, 2 in (5 cm) long with pointed bracts, hang downwards; they take a year to mature.

CULTIVATION

These very frost-hardy trees prefer cold climates, cool, deep soil and sunny, open spaces. Propagate from seed or by grafting.

**Pseudotsuga
menziesii** *(right)*
syns *Pseudotsuga
douglasii, P. taxifolia*
DOUGLAS FIR, OREGON PINE

This fast-growing conifer can reach 300 ft (90 m). Very long lived, some specimens have reached the age of 400 years. Its timber has long been valued in North America. Its sturdy trunk is covered with dark, reddish brown, thick, corky bark. The branch tips curve upwards and have dense, soft, fragrant, bluish green, needle-like foliage. At each branch tip wine-red buds form in winter, opening as apple green rosettes of new growth in spring. Pendulous cones appear after the plant is 20 years old. ZONES 4–9.

P

Pseudowintera
colorata (left)
syn. *Drimys colorata*
ALPINE PEPPER TREE, HOROPITO

A spreading, bushy, evergreen shrub, this species grows to a height of 3–6 ft (1–1.8 m) with a spread of 5 ft (1.5 m). The yellow-green leaves, with scarlet markings and a silvery underside, are the main attraction, and these turn purple in the winter months. The greenish spring and summer blooms are insignificant but the black, olive-sized fruit that follow are quite conspicuous. ZONES 8–10.

PSEUDOWINTERA

This genus of 3 species of evergreen trees and shrubs is native to New Zealand. They are usually 3–8 ft (1.8–2.4 m) tall, though one species can become a small tree with great age. Their attraction lies in their multicolored, aromatic foliage. The rounded, leathery leaves are 2½ in (6 cm) long by 1½ in (35 mm) wide. They are basically a light greenish cream, but they can develop red, purple or orange markings and blotches and lighter silvery undersides. Although the small cream flowers are insignificant, they are followed by large black berries.

CULTIVATION

Plant in moist, well-drained soil in sun or light shade. They are moderately frost hardy and colorful throughout the year. They may be raised from seed, although particularly good forms should be perpetuated by cuttings.

Psidium guajava *(right)*

YELLOW GUAVA

Grown in all tropical and subtropical regions for its nutritious abundant fruit, this tree reaches 30 ft (9 m) with a dense, bushy canopy. It has scaly, greenish bark. The 6 in (15 cm) long leaves are leathery with prominent veins and downy undersides. Spring flowers bunched in the leaf axils are followed by round fruit, 3 in (8 cm) diameter, with pink flesh and yellow skins. ZONES 10–12.

Psidium cattleianum *(right)*

CHERRY GUAVA

This shrub, which grows to 20 ft (6 m), takes its common name from its deep red to purplish fruit about 1 in (25 mm) across. It has an upright trunk with smooth, beautifully mottled bark. The rounded, shiny green leaves, 3 in (8 cm) long, are leathery and form a canopy to 12 ft (3.5 m) across. Its single flowers are 1 in (25 mm) across. **Psidium cattleianum var. *littorale*** has yellow fruit; '**Lucidum**' has sweet purplish fruit. ZONES 9–11.

PSIDIUM

GUAVA

This genus has about 100 species of evergreen trees and shrubs, which can grow to 30 ft (9 m) tall. Native to Central and South America, they are grown for their fruits and foliage. Their simple leaves are arranged in opposite pairs. The clusters of usually large, 5-petalled white flowers are followed by decorative fruit. Each fruit is a globular to pear-shaped berry with red or yellow skin. They are used to make jellies, jams and juice, and are available fresh in subtropical areas.

CULTIVATION

Grow in a warm to hot climate, in a protected position with rich, moist but well-drained soil. Tip prune for compactness. Propagate from seed or cuttings, or by layering or grafting.

PTELEA

From the cooler parts of North America, this is a genus of 11 species of small, deciduous trees or large shrubs that grow slowly to an eventual height of 25 ft (8 m). The branching stems carry bushy foliage with leaves composed of 3 oblong leaflets. In common with the citrus family, to which they are related, the leaves have oily glands that release a scent when crushed. They turn a beautiful shade of gold in autumn. The small, greenish white flowers are fragrant and appear from late spring to early summer.

CULTIVATION
Plant in a shady site in free-draining soil and keep well watered. Propagate from seed in autumn or by layering and grafting in spring.

Ptelea trifoliata (above)
HOP TREE, WATER ASH, STINKING ASH

This tree can grow to 25 ft (8 m), given the shade of taller trees and plenty of mulch in the warmer months to conserve soil moisture. The bark is a rich brown, and the oval, dark green leaflets are up to 4 in (10 cm) long. The fruit resemble bunches of keys. This tree makes an attractive ornamental for cool-temperate gardens. **'Aurea'** has soft yellow leaves when young that mature to lime green. ZONES 2–9.

Pterocarya
carpinifolia (right)

The name of this species means 'with leaves like *Carpinus*' (the hornbeam genus). This presumably refers to the conspicuous, regular veining of the leaflets—though the hornbeams, of course, differ in having simple, not compound leaves. In other respects *Pterocarya carpinifolia* resembles *P. fraxinifolia*. ZONES 5–9.

PTEROCARYA
WING NUT

Ranging from the Caucasus to China, this genus consists of about 10 species of deciduous trees that are grown for their handsome leaves and pendent flowers. Reaching a height of 100 ft (30 m) or more, they have spreading crowns with abundant, pinnate, bright green leaves, each leaflet 4 in (10 cm) or more long. Members can be readily identified by the spring flowers, which appear as yellowish green catkins and grow to 18 in (45 cm) long. Winged nutlets, forming chains up to 18 in (45 cm) long, hang from the branches in ribbons and are an eye-catching feature.

CULTIVATION
These very frost-hardy trees prefer full sun and fertile, deep, moist but well-drained soil. Propagate from cuttings in summer or from suckers or seed in autumn.

Pterocarya fraxinifolia (right)
CAUCASIAN WING NUT

This large tree quickly reaches 100 ft (30 m) and has a wide crown adorned with numerous leaflets. Its flowers form long, pendulous, greenish golden catkins; these are followed by ribbons of winged fruit. This species needs a sheltered position and is an excellent shade tree for a large garden or park, especially near water. ZONES 5–9.

PTEROSTYRAX

This genus from Asia consists of 4 species of deciduous shrubs and trees that reach up to 50 ft (15 m) with a spread of 40 ft (12 m). The slender branches carry serrated leaves, which are 6 in (15 cm) or more long, bright green and oval. Creamy white, fluffy flowers are produced in pendulous sprays up to 10 in (25 cm) long. The fruits are bristly seed capsules.

CULTIVATION

Plant in deep, moist, well-drained soil in sun or part-shade. Propagate from seed in the cooler months, from cuttings in summer or by layering. These useful shade trees should be pruned only to control shape and size.

Pterostyrax hispida *(below)*
EPAULETTE TREE, FRAGRANT
EPAULETTE TREE

This species from China and Japan grows to 50 ft (15 m). Rich green, oval leaves with wedge-shaped bases and downy undersides form a dense crown. In summer it displays fragrant white flowers in drooping sprays. Gray, furry, 10-ribbed fruit appear in early autumn and stay on the bare branches during winter. ZONES 4–9.

PUNICA
POMEGRANATE

This genus, originating from the Mediterranean countries and southern Asia, consists of just 2 species of deciduous shrubs or trees. They have opposite, entire leaves and trumpet-shaped, bright red flowers. *Punica granatum*, the only species cultivated, has been valued for centuries for its edible fruit.

CULTIVATION
Pomegranates can be grown in a wide range of climates, from tropical to warm-temperate, but the red or orange fruit will ripen only where summers are hot and dry. Plant in deep, well-drained soil preferably in a sheltered, sunny position. Propagate from seed in spring, from cuttings in summer or by suckers. They can be pruned as a hedge and are also good in tubs.

Punica granatum *(left & below)*

This species, growing to 15 ft (4.5 m) tall and 10 ft (3 m) wide, has 3 in (8 cm) long, blunt-tipped, glossy leaves. Its large, 8-petalled, red-orange flowers appear at the branch tips in spring and summer. These are followed by the apple-like fruit, which have a thick rind and a mass of seeds in a reddish, sweet pulp. Many cultivars are available, the fruit varying from very sweet to acidic and the flowers from red to pink or white. **Punica granatum** var. **nana**, a dwarf cultivar to 3 ft (1 m) high, has single orange-red flowers and small fruit. The commercially grown **'Wonderful'** has double, orange-red flowers and large fruit. ZONES 9–11.

P

Pyracantha coccinea

SCARLET FIRETHORN

This species, originally from southern Europe, Turkey and the Caucasus, produces a spectacular display of fiery scarlet fruits that resemble tiny apples. Both fruits and foliage become darker if grown in cool climates. It grows to 15 ft (4.5 m) with arching branches spreading to 6 ft (1.8 m). Its narrow leaves are up to 1½ in (35 mm) long, held on slender stalks. Young leaves and twigs are finely downy. **'Kasan'** carries striking orange-red fruit. **'Lalandei'**, developed in France in the 1870s, is a vigorous plant with erect branches, displaying abundant fruit that ripen to bright orange-red. ZONES 5–9.

Pyracantha crenatoserrata (top)
syn. *Pyracantha fortuneana*

YUNNAN FIRETHORN

Native to central and western China, this species has dense, deep green foliage. The rather broad leaves are glossy and hairless on both sides. Its berries are orange, ripening to crimson red. It grows to a height and spread of 12 ft (3.5 m) and looks particularly effective if trained against a brick wall. **'Gold Rush'** bears orange-yellow berries. ZONES 6–10.

Pyracantha coccinea 'Lalandei' *(above)*

PYRACANTHA

FIRETHORN

These 7 species of large shrubs are grown for their evergreen foliage and abundant, bright red, orange or yellow berries in autumn and winter, which are much enjoyed by birds. Growing up to 20 ft (6 m), the branches are spiny and the foliage is usually glossy green. Clusters of small, white flowers are borne along the branches in spring.

CULTIVATION

Adapting to a wide range of soils, firethorns need a sunny position for the brightest berry display, and adequate moisture in dry weather. Propagate from seed or cuttings. Pruning is often necessary to control size, but bear in mind that fruits are produced on second-year wood. They can be espaliered and also make dense, informal hedges and screens. They tend to naturalize and become invasive in favorable conditions. Check for fireblight and scab.

Pyracantha 'Orange Glow' *(left)*

This upright cultivar, to 10 ft (3 m) in height, is well suited to espaliering. It has vivid orange berries that are very attractive to birds. ZONES 7–10.

Pyracantha 'Mohave' *(above)*

This bushy shrub grows to 12 ft (3.5 m) and has dark green leaves, small white flowers and long-lasting orange-red berries. ZONES 7–10.

Pyracantha 'Soleil d'Or' *(right)*

This spiny shrub grows 10–12 ft (3–3.5 m) tall with a spread of 8 ft (2.4 m). It has shiny, dark green leaves against which its abundant crops of golden-yellow berries contrast nicely. The berries begin to ripen in late summer and persist on the plant well into autumn. The small white flowers that produce them appear in late spring or early summer. ZONES 8–10.

PYRUS
PEAR

These 30 or so species from temperate Eurasia and North Africa are related to the apple (*Malus*). Slow-growing, deciduous and semi-evergreen trees, they can reach 80 ft (24 m) but are often smaller. Cultivated since antiquity for their grainy textured, sweet, juicy, yellowish green fruits, not all of which are pear-shaped, they are also valued for their attractive autumn foliage, which needs plenty of sun, and their clusters of fragrant, 5-petalled, white flowers, sometimes tinged pink, which appear with the leaves, or just before them, in spring. The glossy leaves vary from almost round to quite narrow.

CULTIVATION
Having modest moisture needs they suit coastal areas with heavy, sandy loams and good drainage in a sunny position. They are ideal for cool-temperate climates. Cross-pollinate for fruit. Prune to remove damaged branches and for shape in late winter or early spring. Propagate from seed or by grafting.

Pyrus communis 'Packam's Triumph' *(below)*

Pyrus communis 'Triumph von Vienne' *(above)*

Pyrus communis
COMMON PEAR

The parent of many garden cultivars, the wild pear is grown for its beautiful single, pinkish white flowers with red stamens. Long lived, it reaches 50 ft (15 m) but its short branches can look unappealing when not covered in flowers. The bark is dark gray or brown and cracks into small plates. The dark green, leathery leaves have serrated margins and long stalks. The greenish fruit, up to 2 in (5 cm) long, ripen to yellow and are usually gritty with a dull flavor—the fruit of the cultivars are sweeter and best when picked before fully ripe. '**Beurre Bosc**' is widely cultivated for its heavy crops of large, soft, sweet, brown-skinned pears that are good for baking. '**Bon Chrétien**' has been cultivated since medieval times, with medium-sized, succulent, musky-flavored fruit: it is the parent of the famous English **Williams** pear, known in North America, Australia and New Zealand as the Bartlett pear and grown for canning—the red-skinned cultivar is known as '**Red Bartlett**'. '**Packham's Triumph**' is an Australian cultivar with large, sweet, green-skinned fruit. '**Conference**', an early-flowering pear from Europe, produces the best quality fruit if cross-pollinated: its fruit start to ripen in mid-autumn and should be picked before fully ripe. Another popular cultivar is '**Triumph von Vienne**'. ZONES 2–9.

Pyrus calleryana
(right)

CALLERY PEAR

Grown as an ornamental, this shapely semi-evergreen tree from China reaches 60 ft (18 m) with a broad canopy. Clusters of white flowers appear in early spring, often followed by small, brown, inedible fruit. The 3 in (8 cm) long leaves stay on the tree until late autumn, when they turn shades of rich purplish claret, red, orange or yellow. Tolerating heat, dry conditions, wind and poor soil, it makes an ideal street tree. It is resistant to fireblight but is not very long lived. ZONES 5–9.

Pyrus salicifolia
(below left)

WILLOW-LEAFED PEAR, SILVER PEAR, WEEPING SILVER PEAR

This popular ornamental pear, to about 25 ft (8 m), comes from the Caucasus and Iran. Graceful, arching branches have long, silver-gray willow-like foliage covered with silky down when young. Small, creamy white flowers are often hidden by the foliage. The small, brown, pear-shaped fruit ripen in autumn. **'Pendula'** has a willowy habit and is more popular than the species itself; its foliage is smaller than that of its parent. Both are very frost hardy. ZONES 4–9.

Pyrus ussuriensis
(left)

MANCHURIAN PEAR, USSURI PEAR

This is the largest growing pear species and can reach 70 ft (21 m) or more. With a broad, pyramidal shape, it makes a neat, attractive street tree. In spring it is covered with a profusion of small, scented white flowers, which are followed by small, yellow-brown fruit. Its almost heart-shaped, dark shiny green leaves are up to 4 in (10 cm) wide and turn brilliant red and coral in autumn. ZONES 3–9.

QUERCUS

OAK

Most oaks are from temperate regions but some of the 600 or so evergreen, semi-evergreen and deciduous species are from tropical and subtropical regions of Mexico, Southeast Asia and New Guinea. Oaks range from shrubs 3 ft (1 m) high to trees of 120 ft (36 m), and are long lived; some species have been used for centuries for hardwood timber. Their leaves, mostly lobed and leathery, but in some species thin and lustrous, make good compost for acid-loving plants. The leaves of some deciduous oaks develop magnificent hues during the cooler months before they drop. Oaks divide into 'white oaks', with rounded leaf lobes and edible acorns that mature in one year, and 'red oaks', with pointed leaf lobes and acorns that mature in 2 years and are too bitter to eat. Female flowers are insignificant and greenish, but male flowers appear as yellow catkins in spring.

CULTIVATION

They thrive in deep, damp, well-drained soil. Some species like full sun; others prefer part-shade when young. They have extensive root systems and do not like to be transplanted. Prune only to remove damaged limbs. Oaks are susceptible to oak-leaf miner in humid climates, as well as oak root fungus and aphids. Propagate from fresh seed or by grafting in late winter just before new buds appear.

Quercus canariensis *(above)*
syns *Quercus lusitanica,* *Q. mirbeckii*
CANARY OAK, MIRBECK'S OAK

From North Africa and the Iberian Peninsula, this deciduous or semi-evergreen species keeps its 4 in (10 cm) long, coarsely toothed leaves until well into winter by which time they are a yellowish brown. It grows quickly to 40 ft (12 m) and its long acorns taper to a fine point. To a gardener, this is effectively a larger-leafed version of the English oak that can withstand drier conditions, though it is not suitable for really arid regions. In the wild it grows naturally in river valleys. ZONES 7–10.

Quercus cerris *(below)*

TURKEY OAK

Originating in central and southern Europe and Turkey, this deciduous oak is one of the grandest in the genus, reaching 120 ft (36 m) with a stout trunk. Its dark, rough bark is deeply fissured and its narrow leaves are gray-green and irregularly toothed, up to 4 in (10 cm) long. It can tolerate alkaline soils and seaside situations, though it rarely reaches its full size there. Its acorns are enclosed within shaggy cups and mature during their second year. **ZONES 7–10.**

Quercus acutissima *(above)*

syn. *Quercus serrata*

JAPANESE OAK, SAWTOOTH OAK

The 6 in (15 cm) long, narrow, glossy green leaves on this deciduous oak from China, Japan and Korea are similar to those of the chestnut and turn yellow in autumn. This slow-growing, lime-hating tree eventually reaches a height of 50 ft (15 m). The narrow foliage remains on the tree until well into winter and attractive long catkins appear in spring. The name sawtooth oak comes from the regular serration of the leaves, as was emphasized by the old name *Quercus serrata*. **ZONES 5–10.**

Quercus coccinea *(below)*

SCARLET OAK

This deciduous eastern North American oak has deeply lobed, glossy bright green leaves with bristly tips. The 6 in (15 cm) long leaves turn brilliant scarlet in a cool, dry autumn and stay on the tree for a long time. It reaches 80 ft (24 m) on a strong central trunk and is distinguished by its drooping branches. The bark is gray and darkens as it matures. *Quercus coccinea* can tolerate pollution and makes a good specimen for urban environments. **'Splendens'** has very deep red autumn foliage color. **ZONES 2–9.**

Quercus ilex *(below)*

HOLM OAK, HOLLY OAK

Native to southern Europe and North Africa, near the Mediterranean coast, this round-headed, dense evergreen grows to 90 ft (27 m). Its leaves may be toothed (similar to holly) or entire, and are silver-gray at first, becoming a lustrous dark green above, white and downy underneath with age. It grows well in an exposed position, particularly on the coast, and makes a good windbreak. **ZONES 7–10.**

Q

Quercus palustris (right)

PIN OAK

From the eastern and central USA, this species tolerates dry, sandy soil though it is at its best in deep alluvial soils with plenty of water in summer. Moderately fast growing, it matures to 80 ft (24 m)high. Its lustrous green leaves are 4 in (10 cm) long with deep, pointed lobes that turn crimson in autumn and persist on the tree well into winter. It has a shallow root system. **ZONES 3–10.**

Quercus petraea (left)

syn. Quercus sessiliflora

DURMAST OAK, SESSILE OAK

A deciduous tree from central and southeastern Europe and western Asia, this species grows to over 100 ft (30 m). Leaves are glossy green and leathery, and it often forms a broad crown. The bark is grayish and fissured and the trunk thick and stout, continuing to the crown of the tree, making it an important timber tree in Europe. The leaves have 5 to 8 rounded lobes. **ZONES 5–9.**

Quercus robur (right)

COMMON OAK, ENGLISH OAK, PEDUNCULATE OAK

Arguably the most famous of all the oaks and with a life span of 600 to 700 years, this species has spreading, densely leafed branches that provide good shade. Its 4 in (10 cm) long leaves are deciduous and remain dark green through autumn. It reaches a height of 120 ft (36 m) and trunks with a circumference of more than 70 ft (21 m) have been recorded. It is one of Europe's most valuable timber trees. **'Fastigiata'** is grown for its narrow, upright habit. **ZONES 3–10.**

Quercus virginiana (left)

syn. Quercus virens

LIVE OAK

This evergreen species is native to southeastern USA and Gulf States west to Mexico. It grows 40–80 ft (12–24 m) tall with a short trunk that supports horizontally spreading branches and a dense, broad-domed crown. The dark green leaves are white and downy underneath, oblong to rounded in shape and up to 4 in (10 cm) long. The acorns are small, arranged singly or in 2s or 3s and ripen to very dark brown within a year, which is unusual for a red oak. **ZONES 7–11.**

Quercus rubra *(above)*
syn. *Quercus borealis*

RED OAK, NORTHERN RED OAK

Originating in eastern USA and eastern Canada, this robust deciduous tree reaches up to 90 ft (27 m) with a broad canopy formed by strong, straight branches. The matt green leaves with pointed lobes are up to 8 in (20 cm) in length and display rich scarlet and red-brown autumn hues. The large acorn is held in a shallow cup. The red oak grows relatively quickly and does well in sun or part-shade. The young leaves of '**Aurea**' are bright yellow. ZONES 3–9.

Quercus rubra '**Aurea**' *(below)*

Quercus robur *(above)*

Quercus suber *(below)*

CORK OAK

The thick, furrowed, gray bark of *Quercus suber*, principally from Spain and Portugal and growing elsewhere around the Mediterranean, is the source of commercial cork. It reaches 60 ft (18 m) high with a broad, spreading canopy of 50 ft (15 m). The oval, evergreen leaves with a slightly toothed edge are up to 3 in (8 cm) long; they are a dark, shiny green on top and silvery beneath. Single or paired acorns mature to chocolate brown and are held loosely in a cup covering just over a third of the acorn. ZONES 8–10.

Q

R

RADERMACHERA

This genus contains about 15 species of evergreen trees and shrubs from tropical and subtropical areas of Asia. In sufficiently warm areas they are grown outdoors for their flamboyant blooms and attractive bipinnate foliage. The usually fragrant flowers are tubular- to trumpet-shaped, in tones of yellow, pink, orange and white; a number of species are night blooming. In cooler climates some species are grown in pots as foliage plants.

CULTIVATION
Plant in rich, well-drained soil in full sun or part-shade. Shelter them from wind, and water regularly during the growing season. Prune plants to maintain a neat habit. Propagate from seed or cuttings.

R

Radermachera sinica *(left)*

ASIAN BELL-FLOWER

This native of tropical southern China reaches 30 ft (9 m) tall. It has glossy, dark green bipinnate leaves to 3 ft (1 m) long, with leaflets to 2 in (5 cm) long. When mature it bears large panicles of trumpet-shaped white or yellow flowers at the branch tips or axils during spring and summer and slender, capsular fruit up to 15 in (38 cm) long. ZONES 10–12.

Rauvolfia caffra (above)
QUININE TREE

Growing wild in tropical and southern Africa, the quinine tree is the only species of this genus occurring naturally in South Africa. It has a wide, round crown and slightly drooping foliage. Fast growing, it can reach 40 ft (12 m) tall with a single, straight trunk up to 5 ft (1.5 m) in diameter. The bark, cream to gray or dark brown, may be cork-like or smooth and contains reserpine, which is used in tranquilizers. It has glossy, dark green leaves up to 8 in (20 cm) long and, in summer, bears fragrant white flowers followed by small, glossy black fruit. The fruit can be eaten by birds and monkeys but is poisonous to humans. ZONES 9–12.

RAUVOLFIA

There are over 50 species in this genus of trees and shrubs, which are found growing in the tropics of both hemispheres. Their large, glossy leaves are held in whorls of three or five. The flowers, held terminally, are either white or greenish and are followed by a berry containing 1 or 2 seeds. Different parts of the plants, including the watery or milky white poisonous sap, have been used as a tranquilizer, poison, purgative or sexual stimulant, or as a treatment for wounds, snakebite and malaria. The genus name commemorates the sixteenth-century German physician Leonhart Rauwolf, who travelled widely to collect medicinal plants.

CULTIVATION
Plant in rich, deep soil in a sunny position and water well. Propagate from seed or cuttings.

R

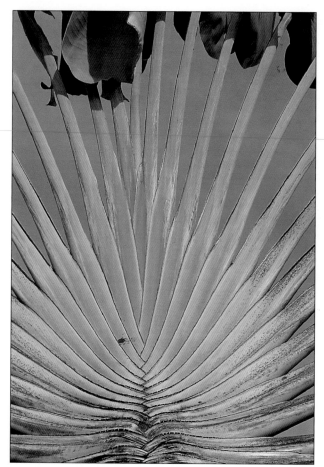

Ravenala madagascariensis
(left)

The leaves of this species grow up to 10 ft (3 m) long, form 2 opposite rows and are held on tightly overlapped long stalks. Its trunk terminates in the sheathing bases of the leaf stalks, which lap together. The tree grows 30 ft (9 m) tall, spreading out to form a wide, flat fan of foliage. Clusters of white flowers emerge from between the leaf bases in summer. **ZONES 11–12.**

R

RAVENALA
TRAVELLER'S PALM, TRAVELLER'S TREE

A member of a striking family, this genus, endemic to Madagascar, is now commonly grown throughout the tropics. It has only one species, an evergreen tree with huge, paddle-like leaves on long stalks similar to those of the banana *(Musa)*, but spreading fan-like from the base and looking exceptionally graceful although they tend to fray with age.

CULTIVATION
Ravenala needs rich, moist but well-drained soil and a sunny spot in a hot climate. Shelter from strong winds. Propagate from seed in spring or by division of suckers at any time.

Reinwardtia indica
(below)
syns *Reinwardtia
trigyna, Linum
trigynum* of gardens
YELLOW FLAX

This winter-flowering
shrub grows to about
3 ft (1 m) high and
bears sprays of 1 in
(25 mm) wide, golden
yellow flowers with
5 overlapping petals,
which form a wide-
flared funnel. Its leaves
are 3 in (8 cm) long,
bright green ovals.
ZONES 9–11.

REINWARDTIA

Funnel-shaped, 5-petalled flowers are produced on the single shrub species that
makes up this evergreen genus, which is
allied to flax *(Linum)* from mountains of
southern Asia. The alternate leaves are
either toothed or entire.

CULTIVATION
These marginally frost-hardy plants
should be grown in a greenhouse or conservatory in cold climates; outdoors, they
prefer full sun and fertile, moist but well-
drained soil. They can be watered freely
when in full growth, less so at other times.
Propagate from seed or cuttings.

R

RETAMA

This small genus of brooms is made up of about 4 species of graceful, deciduous shrubs from the Mediterranean region, the Canary
Islands and western Asia. They are a joy in spring when covered
with a mass of white or yellow pea-like flowers. These are followed
by the fruits: small pea-shaped pods that may be downy. The mid-
green leaves are small and last only a couple of days, and the plants
reach a height of 5 ft (1.5 m). This genus is related to *Genista*.

CULTIVATION
They are easy to grow providing they have moderately fertile, well-
drained soil and plenty of sun. They tolerate a range of climates
and dislike humidity. Prune lightly after flowering to keep them
bushy. Propagate from seed in spring or cuttings in summer.

R

*Retama
monosperma* *(left)*
syn. *Genista
monosperma*
WHITE BROOM

Like all brooms, this
shrub is popular for its
sweetly scented white
flowers borne profusely
on bare branchlets,
which have a weeping
habit from a short trunk
and are silvery green.
The plant blooms for a
long period if protected
from strong winds.
ZONES 8–10.

Rhabdothamnus solandri (above)

This species has small, birch-like leaves with coarsely serrated margins and a dark midrib and veins. The small flowers have a narrow corolla tube in shades of orange to orange-red with red veins and a purple throat. It grows to about 6 ft (1.8 m) high and wide. ZONES 10–11.

RHABDOTHAMNUS

MATATA, NEW ZEALAND GLOXINIA, WAIUATUA

This genus of the African violet family contains a single species from New Zealand, a slender, many branched evergreen shrub with rough, hairy leaves. The tubular flowers will bloom throughout the year in favored positions.

CULTIVATION

This marginally frost-hardy plant prefers a lightly shaded position and open, humus-rich soil. Prune frequently to produce a bushier plant. Propagate from seed or cuttings.

Rhamnus alaternus
'Argenteovariegatus' *(right)*

RHAMNUS
syn. *Frangula*
BUCKTHORN

This genus of 125 species of deciduous and evergreen shrubs and small trees occurs in a range of climates, mostly in the northern hemisphere. It tolerates dry conditions and salt-laden atmospheres. They are distinguished by smooth, dark bark and simple green leaves, often with serrated edges. The flowers, borne in clusters, are insignificant. The fruits are fleshy, pea-sized berries popular with birds. Some species are thorny, some produce dyes that are used commercially, and the bark of some species is the source of the purgative cascara sagrada.

CULTIVATION
These versatile plants require moderately fertile, well-drained soil and full sun or part-shade in hot areas. Propagate the deciduous species from seed and the evergreen species from cuttings in summer.

Rhamnus alaternus
ITALIAN BUCKTHORN, ALATERNUS

This large, evergreen, multi-stemmed shrub is valued for its tolerance of dry conditions and polluted environments. It grows quickly to 15 ft (4.5 m) and its thorny branches bear a mass of small, glossy dark green leaves. These hide the tiny greenish yellow flowers, which attract all kinds of insects. Its berries are purple-black. It can become invasive in certain areas. '**Argenteovariegatus**', which is more decorative than its parent but is less frost hardy, has leaves that are marbled with gray and edged with creamy white. ZONES 7–10.

Rhamnus californica *(left)*
syn. *Frangula californica*
COFFEEBERRY, CALIFORNIA BUCKTHORN

This evergreen or semi-evergreen shrub from western North America bears finely toothed oval leaves up to 2 in (5 cm) long with 12 pairs of veins. It grows to 12 ft (3.5 m) with a 10 ft (3 m) spread. Honey-bees are attracted to the greenish flowers. The fruit change from red to black as they ripen. '**Eve Case**', '**Sea View**' and '**Curly**' have full-flavored fruit. ZONES 7–10.

R

Rhaphiolepis indica (*above*)
INDIAN HAWTHORN

Despite its common name, this shrub comes from southern China. It grows 8 ft (2.4 m) high and wide, and in late winter and spring bears 3 in (8 cm) clusters of perfumed, star-shaped flowers. These are white with a pink blush and long, pink stamens. Its black berries have a bluish tinge. The shiny dark green, serrated leaves are lanceolate. ZONES 8–11.

Rhaphiolepis umbellata (*above*)
YEDDO HAWTHORN

This dense, rounded shrub normally 6 ft (1.8 m) tall, is a native of Japan and Korea. It has paddle-shaped, smooth-edged leaves that are covered with gray, downy hairs when young. Clusters of perfumed white flowers appear in summer; in warm climates they spot bloom for much of the year. The purplish berries ripen to blue-black and persist into winter. This species has adapted to seashore conditions. ZONES 8–11.

Rhaphiolepis × delacourii (*above*)

This rounded, evergreen shrub to a height and spread of 6 ft (1.8 m) is grown for its rose pink, early summer flowers. Blue-black berries follow in winter. Its oval, leathery leaves are toothed at the ends. '**Enchantress**' is a compact form with rose pink flowers. '**Springtime**' is a compact cultivar with pink and bronze new growth and large pink flowers. ZONES 8–11.

RHAPHIOLEPIS
syn. *Raphiolepis*

The 9 species in this genus are slow-growing, tough, evergreen shrubs native to sub-tropical Southeast and eastern Asia. Most spread wider than they are tall. Their leathery leaves, up to 3 in (8 cm) long and half as wide, are oblong and dark green, with pale undersides. New shoots are often coppery red. The fragrant, 5-petalled flowers, white or pink, are borne in loose terminal clusters, usually held rigidly away from the foliage. The fruits are blue-black berries.

CULTIVATION
Moderately frost hardy, these shrubs like plenty of sun, or semi-shade in hot climates. They do best in well-drained, sandy soil enriched with organic matter, and thrive in sheltered seaside gardens. Propagate from seed or cuttings, or by layering.

R

RHODODENDRON
syn. *Azalea*

The rhododendrons are a spectacular genus of around 800 evergreen, semi-deciduous and deciduous shrubs and trees. Although largely confined to the northern hemisphere with the majority of species native to southern China and the Himalayan region, many are found in North America, Japan and Southeast Asia, and the tropical branch of the genus extends the range to New Guinea and the far northeast of Australia. Rhododendrons are woody stemmed plants grown mainly for their massed display of flowers, which vary greatly in size from tiny thimbles to 8 in (20 cm) trumpets. They are usually clustered in inflorescences (trusses) at the branch tips and occur in every color except a true bright blue. The flowers may be self- or multi-colored, often with a contrasting throat blotch (flare) or spotting. Some species have scented flowers. Temperate-climate rhododendrons tend to bloom from late winter to early summer, but the tropical rhododendrons are far less seasonal and bloom throughout the year, usually reaching a peak in early autumn. Plant size ranges from near prostrate through to trees over 50 ft (15 m) tall. Yet despite this enormous variety of species, and the thousands of garden hybrids and cultivars, rhododendrons are all remarkably similar in general appearance and unlikely to be mistaken for any other plants. They are mainly broad leafed with roughly elliptical, usually deep green leaves and their 5-petalled (or more) flowers are flat, funnel-, bell- or trumpet-shaped. Rhododendrons also have beautiful foliage. The leaves of the evergreens are usually thick and leathery, often deep green and lustrous. The deciduous and semi-evergreen forms tend to have hairy leaves and their foliage may change color in autumn and winter. Leaf size varies enormously. Many of the alpines have tiny leaves under 1 in (25 mm) long, while the foliage of species from mild, high rainfall areas can exceed 24 in (60 cm) long. Rhododendrons are botanically divided by the presence (lepidote species) or absence (elepidote species) of scales on their leaves. While often barely noticeable, these scales sometimes take the form of felting (indumentum) on the foliage. This is usually confined to the leaf undersides and is a feature of many rhododendrons.

As far as gardeners are concerned there are 3 main categories of rhododendrons, namely: azaleas (deciduous and evergreen); tropical or Vireya rhododendrons; and the temperate climate plants we might call 'true' rhododendrons, which includes the small alpine or Arctic rhododendrons. All have been extensively developed and hybridized, so in addition to those 800-odd species there now are countless garden forms. With such a huge variety of plants from widely differing backgrounds, it is easy to become confused. Consequently, some of the main hybrid groups are subdivided into smaller blocks of plants with similar characteristics or parentage.

CULTIVATION
As would be expected of such a large group, rhododendrons vary considerably in their climatic preferences. However, they all share the same general cultivation

needs. This is because their roots lack the fine feeding hairs at the root tips that are found on most other plants; instead, the entire root ball is a mass of fine roots that serve the same function as root hairs. This lack of heavy, aggressive, spreading roots greatly influences the cultivation and uses of rhododendrons. A compact root ball and no tap roots make rhododendrons ideal for container cultivation and easy to transplant, but there are disadvantages. Fine roots dry out quickly in dry conditions, soon rot if kept waterlogged, suffer in compacted soils and cannot penetrate hard or rocky ground. Rhododendrons need loose, open, well-aerated, acidic soil with plenty of humus to retain moisture. They thrive with regular mulching that enables their predominantly surface roots to spread and develop. In wet areas or gardens with alkaline soil it is best to plant in raised beds filled with specially blended compost. Most rhododendrons are woodland plants that prefer dappled shade or at least protection from the hottest afternoon sun and strong winds. They require little maintenance apart from a light trim after flowering. They are not greatly troubled by pests and diseases but are prone to infestation by thrips, two-spotted mites and spider mites and powdery mildew or rust in humid areas. Evergreen azaleas are sometimes disfigured by azalea leaf gall. Taller varieties make good woodland or shrubbery plants, even hedges, while the dwarf forms are perfect for mass plantings or rock gardens. Azaleas are usually at their best planted *en masse*. Vireya rhododendrons are superb plants for tropical or subtropical gardens or as potted plants in conservatories. Rhodoendrons are propagated from seed or cuttings or by layering, the method and timing varying with the type of plant. Frost hardiness also varies greatly.

RHODODENDRON SPECIES

Although nearly all rhododendron species are worth cultivating, some are rather untidy, rangy growers that have little appeal for gardeners. The following are some of the more attractive, popular or influential species. Many more are available through specialist nurseries and rhododendron societies. The very rare species are often only available as seed. All are evergreen unless otherwise stated.

Rhododendron arboreum (below)

From northern India to southern China and over 100 ft (30 m) tall in the wild, this species reaches 40 ft (12 m) in cultivation with a narrow, cylindrical crown. Its leathery, bronze-green, 8 in (20 cm) long leaves have whitish or rust-colored undersides. Red, white or deep pink bell-shaped flowers in globular heads of 15 to 20 blooms open in very early spring. This species was an early introduction and is a parent of many cultivars. ZONES 7–11.

R

Rhododendron aurigeranum
(left)

Native to New Guinea and found in forest clearings, rocky areas or grassy slopes at moderate altitudes, this Vireya rhododendron grows to 8 ft (2.4 m) tall with orange to orange-yellow funnel-shaped flowers. It is popular with hybridizers of modern Vireya cultivars. **ZONES 10–12.**

Rhododendron brookeanum
(below)

Native to Malaysia and Indonesia, this Vireya may be epiphytic or terrestrial. At low altitudes it is found as an epiphyte on mangroves and other trees, and terrestrially on sandstone rocks at up to 4660 ft (1400 m). It reaches 6–15 ft (1.8–4.5 m) tall with fragrant funnel-shaped flowers that are orange, orange-pink or red, with white to golden yellow centers. **'Titan'** has flowers fading to light pink. **ZONES 10–12.**

Rhododendron augustinii *(above)*

This species has unusually small evergreen leaves that are dark green and tapered, with a prominent mid-vein. A medium-sized shrub reaching a height and width of 5 ft (1.5 m), *Rhododendron augustinii* is covered in late spring by a profusion of tubular blue or violet flowers, ranging from pale to deep hues—the deeper the color, the more tender the plant. The flowers occur in clusters of 3 or 5. It performs best in dappled shade. It is the parent of many blue-flowered hybrids. **ZONES 6–9.**

Rhododendron catawbiense
(below)

CATAWBA RHODODENDRON, MOUNTAIN ROSEBAY

This shrub from eastern USA is one of the most influential species in the development of frost-hardy hybrids. It grows to around 10 ft (3 m) tall and develops into a dense thicket of shiny, deep green foliage. Its cup-shaped flowers, which open from late spring, are pink, rosy pink, lilac-purple or white and carried in trusses of up to 20 blooms. '**Album**' is a heat-resistant form with white flowers that open from pink buds. ZONES 4–9.

Rhododendron calendulaceum *(left)*

FLAME AZALEA

This deciduous azalea, found from West Virginia to Georgia, USA develops into a spreading bush around 12 ft (3.5 m) tall and wide. Its orange to red (rarely yellow) funnel-shaped flowers open in late spring and are carried in trusses of 5 to 7 blooms. ZONES 5–9.

Rhododendron cinnabarinum subsp. *cinnabarinum* '**Mount Everest**' *(below)*

Rhododendron cinnabarinum

Native to the Himalayan region and northern Burma, this aromatic species is an upright shrub or small tree 5–20 ft (1.5–6 m) tall. Its peeling red-brown bark and narrowly oval deep green to blue-green leaves are very attractive, as are the 2 in (5 cm) long, pendulous, tubular flowers that open from mid-spring. Usually orange, the 3- to 5-flowered trusses may be red, salmon pink, pink, yellow, apricot or combinations of colors. *Rhododendron cinnabarinum* subsp. *cinnabarinum* '**Mount Everest**' has pale apricot flowers that are more widely open than usual. ZONES 6–9.

Rhododendron ciliatum *(right)*

Native to the Himalayan region, this species is a compact 4–6 ft (1.2–1.8 m) shrub. It has 2–3 in (5–8 cm) long, shiny deep green leaves with bluish undersides. The bark is red-brown and peeling. From early spring it produces white or white-flushed rose, bell-shaped flowers. It is an easily grown shrub that tolerates slightly alkaline soil. ZONES 7–9.

R

Rhododendron elliottii *(left)*

Native to moderate altitudes in northern India, this species grows to 6–25 ft (1.8–8 m) tall and has deep red flowers with very dark spotting and white-tipped anthers. The flowers open from mid-spring, are funnel- to bell-shaped, around 2 in (5 cm) long and in trusses of around 10 blooms. The leaves are glossy deep green and up to 4 in (10 cm) long. ZONES 9–10.

Rhododendron jasminiflorum
(below)

Native to the Malay Peninsula, this Vireya species can grow to 8 ft (2.4 m) tall. It has 2½ in (6 cm) long, bright green leaves in whorls of 3 to 5. Throughout the year it produces clusters of 1½–2 in (3.5–5 cm) long, scented, tubular pale pink flowers, fading to white. ZONES 10–12.

Rhododendron fastigiatum *(below)*

In the wild this alpine species from Yunnan Province, China, grows at altitudes of up to 15,000 ft (4500 m). It has ½ in (12 mm) long, blue-gray leaves and is a dense, wiry stemmed, 18–30 in (45–75 cm) tall shrub. It flowers in mid-spring when it is smothered in ½ in (12 mm) purple or lavender blooms, and is a superb plant for a rock garden or alpine house. ZONES 7–9.

Rhododendron hanceanum *(right)*

A 1½–6 ft (0.45–1.8 m) tall shrub from Sichuan, China, this species has upright, open growth and lance-shaped leaves up to 4 in (10 cm) long. Many-flowered trusses of cream to yellow, 1 in (25 mm) long, slightly scented, funnel-shaped flowers open from mid-spring. 'Nanum' is a compact plant with bright yellow flowers. ZONES 8–9.

R

Rhododendron johnstoneanum
(below right)

From northern India, this 8–15 ft (2.4–4.5 m) tall shrub, sometimes epiphytic in the wild, has bristly elliptical leaves up to 3 in (8 cm) long. Its flowers are scented, 3 in (8 cm) long, funnel-shaped, creamy white or pale yellow, sometimes with red or yellow spots, and open from early spring. **'Double Diamond'** has creamy yellow double flowers, often with darker markings. ZONES 7–9.

Rhododendron javanicum *(above)*

This 6–12 ft (1.8–3.5 m) tall epiphytic or terrestrial Vireya native to Malaysia and Indonesia has oval leaves up to 8 in (20 cm) long. The often fragrant, large-lobed, funnel-shaped flowers in loose trusses are 1½ in (35 mm) long and wide and are orange to orange-pink or red with cream or yellow centers. ZONES 10–12.

R

Rhododendron kiusianum *(above)*

Native to Kyushu, Japan, this dense, mounding evergreen azalea is usually less than 3 ft (1 m) tall. It has hairy, ½ in (12 mm) long, purple-green leaves that darken in winter. From mid-spring the foliage is hidden by tiny purple, pink or white flowers. It is an important parent of the Kurume azaleas, and there are many cultivated forms. **'Hinode'** is the brightest red-flowered selection. **'Komokulshan'** has white or pale pink flowers with darker petal tips. ZONES 6–10.

Rhododendron kaempferi *(center left)*

This 4–10 ft (1.2–3 m) tall evergreen azalea from Japan is fully frost hardy, though it loses much of its foliage in very cold conditions. The hairy, elliptical leaves are 1½ in (35 mm) long. Funnel-shaped flowers open from mid-spring and are red to orange-pink, occasionally white, sometimes with purple or red flecks. It is extensively used in hybridizing for frost hardiness. ZONES 5–9.

Rhododendron laetum *(left)*

From New Guinea, this Vireya is 5 ft (1.5 m) tall with 3 in (8 cm) long elliptical leaves. Its flowers are wide open, funnel-shaped and 2½ in (6 cm) long, usually deep yellow, sometimes suffused pink, orange or red and occasionally scented. ZONES 10–12.

Rhododendron
luteum *(right)*

This deciduous azalea
is found from eastern
Europe to the Cauca-
sus. It grows to 12 ft
(3.5 m) and has 2–4 in
(5–10 cm) long, bristly,
lance-shaped leaves.
Its flowers are bright
yellow and sweetly
scented. They are
around 1½ in (35 mm)
long, funnel-shaped
with a narrow tube in
trusses of up to 12
blooms. **ZONES 5–9.**

Rhododendron lochiae *(below)*

This Vireya species is found in northeast Queensland, and is the only rhododendron native to
Australia. It grows to 6 ft (1.8 m) tall with oval
leaves around 3 in (8 cm) long. It has large-lobed,
deep red, 1½ in (35 mm) long tubular flowers in
trusses of 2 to 7 blooms. **ZONES 10–11.**

R

Rhododendron molle

This deciduous azalea is found in eastern and central China. It grows 4–6 ft (1.2–1.8 m) tall and bears large, densely packed trusses of 2½ in (6 cm) long, funnel-shaped yellow or orange flowers from mid-spring. The flowers are sometimes fragrant. ***Rhododendron molle* subsp. *japonicum*** (syn. *R. japonicum*), from Japan, is a 3–10 ft (1–3 m) tall shrub with bright red, or-ange-red, pink or yellow flowers and brightly colored autumn foliage. This subspecies is the principal parent of the decidu-ous Mollis Azaleas. **ZONES 7–9.**

Rhododendron molle subsp. *japonicum (left)*

Rhododendron macabeanum *(below)*

This species from northern India is a tree up to 50 ft (15 m) tall. It has very dark green, heavily veined, leathery leaves up to 18 in (45 cm) long with white indumentum on the undersides. Pale yellow, bell-shaped, 2–3 in (5–8 cm) long flowers with a basal purple blotch are car-ried in rounded trusses of up to 20 blooms and open from early spring. **ZONES 8–9.**

R

Rhododendron nuttallii (right)

This species can grow to 25 ft (8 m) but usually makes a shrub 6 ft (1.8 m) high in gardens. The flowers are among the largest of any rhododendron, up to 5 in (12 cm) wide. Fragrant and funnel shaped, they form loose trusses of 3 to 9 blooms. They are white, tinted with yellow and pink. Leaves are metallic purple when young, becoming dark green and wrinkled as they mature. ZONES 9–10.

Rhododendron nakaharai (left)

This evergreen Taiwanese azalea is a near-prostrate shrub usually under 12 in (30 cm) tall. The pointed elliptical leaves are hairy and a little under 1 in (25 mm) long. The 1 in (25 mm) long orange-red, funnel-shaped flowers open in early summer. It is a good rockery, bonsai or ground cover plant. 'Mt Seven Star' is a densely foliaged, prostrate form with large deep orange-red flowers. ZONES 5–10.

Rhododendron occidentale (right)
WESTERN AZALEA

From western USA, this species is a 6–15 ft (1.8–4.5 m) tall deciduous azalea with slightly hairy, 4 in (10 cm) long elliptical leaves. The fragrant 3 in (8 cm) wide, funnel-shaped flowers are carried in trusses of up to 12 blooms, and are usually white or pale pink with a yellow, occasionally maroon, flare but may be red, yellow or orange-pink. The foliage turns red and copper in autumn. 'Leonard Frisbie' has large, frilled, fragrant flowers that are white suffused pink with a yellow flare. ZONES 6–9.

R

Rhododendron sinogrande *(below)*

This evergreen rhododendron is distinctive for its huge, glossy green leaves that reach 32 in (80 cm) in length and 12 in (30 cm) in width, and are silvery underneath. These are matched in spring by enormous trusses of bell-shaped, creamy white to yellow flowers with crimson blotches. Growing to a height of 40 ft (13 m), it needs a sheltered spot and a cool but mild climate. ZONES 8–10.

Rhododendron ponticum *(above)*

From Europe and the Middle East to Russia, this 6–20 ft (1.8–6 m) shrub has glossy deep green, oblong to lance-shaped leaves up to 8 in (20 cm) long. The 10- to 15-flowered trusses open in late spring and are 2 in (5 cm) long, funnel-shaped, purple, lavender, pink or rarely maroon or white-flushed pink, often with yellow, ochre or brown flecks. It is used in hybridizing. **'Variegatum'** has dark green leaves with cream edges and occasional stripes or flecks. ZONES 6–10.

Rhododendron simsii

The main parent of the Indica evergreen azaleas, this shrub found through much of northern Southeast Asia and southern China is 4–8 ft (1.2–2.4 m) tall with 1–3 in (2.5–3 cm) long elliptical leaves. The flowers are funnel-shaped, 2½ in (6 cm) wide, in shades of crimson and red and carried in trusses of 2 to 6 blooms. **'Arnagi Lack'** is pink with a paler center. ZONES 8–11.

Rhododendron simsii
'Arnagi Lack' *(above)*

Rhododendron yakushimanum *(below)*

Native to Yakushima Island, Japan, this dense, mounding, 3–8 ft (1–2.4 m) tall shrub has 3–4 in (8–10 cm) long, deep green leathery leaves with rolled edges and heavy fawn indumentum. The flowers appear quite early and are white or pale pink opening from deep pink buds and carried in rounded trusses of up to 10 blooms. **'Exbury Form'** makes a perfect dome of deep green, heavily indumented foliage with light pink flowers. **'Koichiro Wada'** is similar to 'Exbury Form' but has white flowers opening from deep pink buds. ZONES 5–9.

Rhododendron wardii var. *wardii (above)*

Rhododendron wardii

Named after collector and explorer Frank Kingdon Ward, this species from western China is variable and ranges from 3–25 ft (1–8 m) tall. It has deep green, oval, 4 in (10 cm) long leaves and saucer-shaped white to pale yellow, sometimes crimson-blotched flowers in trusses of 7 to 14 blooms from mid-spring. *Rhododendron wardii* var. *wardii* has bright yellow flowers, sometimes with a purple blotch, and is used extensively in hybridizing. ZONES 7–9.

Rhododendron williamsianum
(right)

This dense shrub grows 2–5 ft (0.6–1.5 m) tall and has rounded to heart-shaped, matt mid-green leaves up to 2 in (5 cm) long with bronze new growth. The mid-spring flowers are bell-shaped, 2 in (5 cm) long, pink to rose, sometimes with darker flecks and carried in loose clusters of 2 to 3 blooms. ZONES 7–9.

R

Rhododendron zoelleri *(left)*

Usually seen as a 4–6 ft (1.2–1.8 m) tall shrub, this Vireya from Indonesia, New Guinea and the Moluccas can reach 20 ft (6 m) tall. Its trumpet-shaped flowers are particularly bright shades of yellow and orange with orange-red lobes, which makes it popular with hybridizers. ZONES 10–12.

Rhododendron 'Alice' *(above)*

This is a *Rhododendron griffithianum* hybrid with 6 in (15 cm) long leaves that becomes large with age. Its large trusses of bright pink blooms with lighter centers appear mid-season. ZONES 6–9.

RHODODENDRON CULTIVARS

Unlike the azaleas, rhododendron cultivars are generally not divided into groups; they are most often simply referred to by their cultivar name. However, there are several recognizable styles. The alpine rhododendrons tend to be dense, twiggy plants with small leaves and masses of tiny flowers; those from high rainfall areas often have large leaves; and many of the fragrant cultivars are similar to one another. Knowledgeable gardeners often use alliance or grex names or refer to a hybrid by its dominant parent. Groups of similar rhododendrons are sometimes grouped as alliances *(maddenii* alliance, *ciliicalyx* alliance, etc.) and their offspring tend to be similar. A grex is a group of sister seedlings from the same cross. Grex names are rare among modern hybrids but are still found among popular old-timers such as Fabia, Naomi and Loderi. You may have heard such terms as *yakushimanum* or 'yak' hybrid, *williamsianum* hybrid or *griersonianum* hybrid. Hybrids of these and other species often closely resemble their parents in terms of foliage and general growth habit, although the flowers can vary markedly. Exact sizes are not given as rhododendrons are notoriously variable. Dwarf is under 18 in (45 cm), small is less than 4 ft (1.2 m), medium is 4–8 ft (1.2–2.4 m) and anything over 8 ft (2.4 m) is large. It is important to realize that rhododendrons are long lived and continue to grow throughout their lives. Very old specimens can be extremely large. The flowering season also varies considerably depending on the climate. Generally though, in mild temperate climates early is before the spring equinox, mid-season is from the equinox to 6 weeks later, and late is more than 6 weeks after the equinox.

R

Rhododendron 'Bibiani' *(right)*

This is a medium-sized *Rhododendron arboreum* hybrid raised in 1934 by the famous English breeder Lionel de Rothschild. It has 4–6 in (10–15 cm) long, dark green, heavy textured leaves and early, deep red, 2 in (5 cm) wide, bell-shaped flowers in trusses of 11 to 15 blooms. '**Gibraltar**' is a hybrid seedling of 'Bibiani' with similar blooms of very deep red. ZONES 7–10.

Rhododendron 'Blue Peter' *(above)*

Probably a *Rhododendron ponticum* hybrid, this medium-sized bush was introduced by the English company Waterer in 1933. It has glossy deep green leaves and frilled trusses of lavender-blue flowers with a prominent purple flare. It flowers mid-season. ZONES 6–9.

Rhododendron 'Brickdust' *(below)*

Typical of a *Rhododendron williamsianum* hybrid, this small plant forms a dense mound of 2 in (5 cm) long, rounded leaves with masses of loose trusses of bell-shaped flowers. The blooms are dusky pink and appear mid-season. ZONES 6–9.

R

Rhododendron 'Cilpinense' *(left)*

This Welsh hybrid between *R. ciliatum* and *R. moupinense* was raised in 1927 and is a small mounding plant with rather hairy, rounded deep green leaves. It becomes a mass of white-flushed-pink, bell-shaped flowers in early spring. The blooms are carried in loose drooping clusters. ZONES 7–10.

Rhododendron 'Countess of Haddington' *(right)*

Many fragrant rhododendrons are untidy bushes but this 1862 hybrid of unknown origin is a neat medium-sized bush with 4 in (10 cm) long, slightly glossy, bronze-green foliage. Its large bell-shaped flowers are white flushed pink, pleasantly scented and carried in heads of 3 to 5 blooms. ZONES 9–10.

Rhododendron 'Cherry Custard' *(left)*

This small Canadian hybrid shows its Fabia heritage in its flat 10- to 12-flowered trusses of yellow blooms that open from orange-red buds. It is a low, spreading plant with narrow, pointed elliptical leaves. ZONES 7–9.

Rhododendron 'Eldorado' *(above)*

This medium-sized, open-growing *Rhododendron johnstoneanum* hybrid has small, scaly, deep olive-green leaves and 2 in (5 cm) long, bright yellow, funnel-shaped flowers in clusters of 2 to 3 blooms. The flowers open early. **ZONES 8–10.**

Rhododendron 'Dido' *(above)*

Rhododendron 'Dido', raised in England in 1934, has had more influence as a parent plant than as a garden specimen. Used as one of the parents of 'Lem's Cameo', it has greatly influenced modern American rhododendron development. It grows to 4 ft (1.2 m) and has rounded, light green leaves and lax trusses of yellow-centered, orange-pink, trumpet-shaped flowers. **ZONES 7–9.**

Rhododendron 'Crest' *(above)*

Raised in England in 1953, this medium-sized shrub was one of the first hybrids to use *Rhododendron wardii* rather than *R. burmanicum* to produce yellow flowers with frost hardiness. It is an open grower with bronze-green foliage and flowers mid-season. **ZONES 6–9.**

R

Rhododendron Fabia
'Roman Pottery' *(left)*

Rhododendron Fabia

This collection of sister seedlings resulted from a 1934 *Rhododendron dichroanthum* and *R. griersonianum* cross by the Welsh breeder Aberconway. This grex has had enormous influence in the development of modern frost-hardy hybrids in yellow and orange shades. The plants grow to around 3 ft (1 m) tall and slightly wider with 3 in (8 cm) pointed elliptical leaves. The mid-season flowers are in soft orange tones, bell-shaped, and carried in open trusses of 3 to 7 blooms. **'Roman Pottery'** has unusual terracotta-colored flowers. ZONES 7–9.

Rhododendron 'Elisabeth Hobbie'
(right)

This is a small *Rhododendron forrestii* hybrid with rounded, 2 in (5 cm) long, deep green leaves. The petioles and new growth are red tinted. Bright to deep red, bell-shaped flowers in clusters of 5 to 7 blooms open mid-season. ZONES 6–10.

Rhododendron 'Elizabeth' *(left)*

This hybrid shows considerable *Rhododendron griersonianum* influence. It is a medium-sized, rather open bush with 3–4 in (8–10 cm) long, narrow pointed leaves and bright red 3 in (8 cm) wide, funnel-shaped flowers in lax 6- to 8-bloom trusses from early mid-season. ZONES 7–9.

Rhododendron 'Fastuosum Flore Pleno' *(above)*

Dating from before 1846 and still one of the few double-flowered 'true' rhododendrons, this large shrub has mid-green, 4–6 in (10–15 cm) long leaves. They open mid-season to late and are semi-double, deep lavender with greenish yellow throat markings in trusses of 7 to 15 blooms. **ZONES 5–8.**

Rhododendron
'Fragrantissimum'
(right)

This medium-sized, rather open-growing *Rhododendron edgeworthii* hybrid from before 1868 remains popular because of its large, funnel-shaped, white flushed pink flowers, which are fragrant. They are carried in loose trusses of 3 to 7 blooms and open mid-season. The foliage is bronze green, pointed and 3–4 in (8–10 cm) long. **ZONES 8–10.**

R

Rhododendron 'George's Delight'
(left)

This very distinctively colored small shrub is typical of the modern style of rhododendron hybrid. It has lustrous mid-green leaves and dense growth, and from mid-season it produces spectacular rounded trusses of soft yellow and cream flowers with pink margins. **ZONES 7–9.**

Rhododendron 'Furnivall's Daughter' *(right)*

This is a medium to large shrub with large bright green leaves and tall trusses of bright pink flowers with a darker blotch. It is a vigorous grower that flowers heavily from mid-season. **ZONES 6–9.**

R

Rhododendron
'Halopeanum' *(right)*
syn. *Rhododendron*
'White Pearl'

This is a fast-growing large shrub with deep green foliage and tall conical trusses of pale pink flowers that fade to white. Although largely superseded by better plants, it is still widely grown for its extreme vigor. It flowers mid-season. ZONES 7–9.

Rhododendron 'Golden Wit' *(below)*

This small shrub has a spreading habit and 2 in (5 cm) long, rounded, bright green leaves. Its bell-shaped flowers, which open mid-season, are soft golden yellow with red or red-brown markings and carried in loose clusters of up to 9 blooms. ZONES 7–9.

Rhododendron
'Grumpy' *(above)*

This is one of a group of *Rhododendron yakushimanum* hybrids known as The Seven Dwarfs bred by Water-er's in the 1970s. It is a small to medium-sized bush with deep green foliage and cream to pale yellow flowers flushed pink. The rounded trusses open mid-season. ZONES 6–9.

R

Rhododendron 'Impi' *(left)*

'Impi' combines dark green foliage with very deep purple-red flowers. It is a medium-sized bush that blooms from late mid-season. Its flowers are carried in small rounded trusses. ZONES 7–9.

Rhododendron 'Hydon Dawn' *(above)*

This is a *Rhododendron yakushimanum* hybrid of the same cross as the better known 'Hydon Hunter'. It is a small bush that develops into a mound of glossy, bright green foliage. The flowers, borne in small rounded trusses, open mid-season and are pink, lightening at the edges. ZONES 7–9.

R

Rhododendron 'Irene Stead' *(left)*

Of Loderi parentage and very similar to the plants of that grex, this New Zealand-raised hybrid is a large bush with mid-green leaves around 8 in (20 cm) long. Its mid-season, pale pink and white flowers are somewhat waxy and carried in large conical trusses. ZONES 6–9.

Rhododendron
'Jingle Bells' *(right)*

This Fabia hybrid is a neat, small bush with a dense covering of narrow deep green, 3–4 in (8–10 cm) long leaves. Orange bell-shaped flowers in lax trusses of 5 to 9 blooms open from orange-red buds and fade to yellow. They smother the plant in mid-season.
ZONES 7–9.

Rhododendron
'Kubla Khan'
(below right)

This medium-sized plant has bright green foliage and striking flowers with calyces so large they create a hose-in-hose effect. The color is pink with a large red flare on the upper lobes and calyx. It blooms from late mid-season and needs cool conditions for the flowers to last.
ZONES 6–9.

R

Rhododendron 'Lem's Aurora' *(left)*

This is a compact small to medium-sized bush with dark green, 4 in (10 cm) leaves and rounded trusses of crimson flowers with light golden-yellow centers and calyces. It blooms mid-season. **ZONES 6–9.**

Rhododendron 'Lemon Lodge'

(below)

Very distinctive foliage and soft pastel yellow flowers distinguish 'Lemon Lodge', a medium to large New Zealand-raised *Rhododendron wardii* hybrid. The leaves are a bright light to mid-green, oval, 3–4 in (8–10 cm) with a waxy texture. The flowers are in rather flat trusses that open mid-season. **ZONES 7–10.**

Rhododendron 'Lem's Cameo' *(above)*

This beautiful and very influential hybrid is a medium-sized mound of deep green, glossy 3–4 in (8–10 cm) long leaves with rich bronze new growth. The mid-season flowers, borne in trusses of up to 20 blooms, are delicate shades of apricot-pink and creamy yellow and funnel-shaped. **ZONES 7–9.**

R

Rhododendron
'Lem's Monarch' *(right)*

This impressive large
shrub is densely foliaged
with rounded, bright
mid-green leaves up to
8 in (20 cm) long. The
flowers, carried in large
conical trusses of 9 to 15
blooms, are funnel-
shaped and white to pale
pink flushed and edged
deep pink to crimson.
ZONES 6–9.

Rhododendron Loderi
'Pink Diamond' *(left)*

Rhododendron Loderi
'King George' *(below)*

Rhododendron Loderi

This grex consists of a large group of *Rhododendron griffithianum* × *R. fortunei* seedlings. They
are very similar to one another and have 6–8 in
(15–20 cm) long, mid-green to slightly glaucous
leaves and large trusses of white to mid-pink,
funnel-shaped, fragrant flowers. They are large,
tree-like shrubs that are very impressive in full
bloom. **'King George'** has white flowers opening from pink buds. **'Sir Edmond'** has very large
pale pink flowers. **'Sir Joseph Hooker'** has light
to mid-pink flowers. **'Pink Diamond'** has pink
flowers with a red mark inside. **ZONES 6–9.**

R

R

Rhododendron 'Moonstone' *(below)*

This *Rhododendron williamsianum* hybrid is a small to medium-sized shrub with 2–3 in (5–8 cm) long, rounded mid-green leaves. From early spring it is smothered in 3- to 5-flowered clusters of greenish white to pale cream, slightly pendulous, bell-shaped flowers. ZONES 6–9.

Rhododendron 'May Day' *(above)*

This vigorous small bush develops into a spreading mound of 3–4 in (8–10 cm) long, dark green leaves with light brown indumentum on the undersides. Lax trusses of 5 to 9 bright red to orange-red, bell-shaped flowers open from early mid-season. ZONES 7–9.

Rhododendron 'Mariloo' *(above)*

This is one of the best known hybrids from *Rhododendron lacteum*. It has heavy textured, rounded, 6 in (15 cm) long leaves with a blue-green to bronze bloom. New growth is very frost tender. Pale milky yellow, bell-shaped flowers, carried in large trusses, open early mid-season from yellow-green buds. ZONES 8–10.

Rhododendron 'Mrs Charles E. Pearson' *(right)*

An old hybrid still popular because of its frost hardiness, vigor and heavy flowering, this large bush becomes tree-like with age. The leaves are oval, deep green and 4–8 in (10–20 cm) long. The flowers, carried in trusses of 13 to 18 blooms, are funnel-shaped and light pink with darker markings. It is sun and heat tolerant. ZONES 6–9.

Rhododendron 'Mrs G. W. Leak' *(below)*

This medium to large bush is instantly recognizable when in bloom. Its light pink, funnel-shaped flowers have a beautiful red flare and spotting that stands out from a great distance. They are borne in upright trusses of 9 to 12 blooms from early mid-season. The leaves are mid-green, 4–6 in (10–15 cm) long and very sticky, especially when young. ZONES 6–9.

R

Rhododendron 'Olin O. Dobbs' *(left)*

Famed for its heavy, waxy flowers of intense red-purple, this medium-sized American hybrid also has lustrous deep green leaves up to 6 in (15 cm) long. The flowers are funnel-shaped and carried in conical trusses of 11 to 15 blooms that open from mid-season. **ZONES 5–9.**

Rhododendron 'Nancy Evans' *(below)*

With 'Hotei' and 'Lem's Cameo' as its parents, this should be something special and so it is. A compact small to medium-sized bush, it is worth growing for its 2–4 in (5–10 cm) long foliage alone. The leaves are deep bronze green with reddish new growth. Deep golden-yellow, bell-shaped flowers open from orange buds in trusses of 15 to 20 blooms. The large calyces create a hose-in-hose effect. **ZONES 7–9.**

Rhododendron Naomi

This Rothschild grex, while not greatly influential in hybridizing, nevertheless includes some beautiful plants. The best known form is a large, densely foliaged shrub with mid-green, slightly glaucous, 4–8 in (10–20 cm) long leaves. The flowers are waxy, in light biscuit and pink shades, and carried in large trusses. It blooms mid-season. **'Nautilus'** has excellent foliage and pink flowers flushed orange with a green throat. **'Pink Beauty'** has deep pink flowers. **ZONES 6–9.**

Rhododendron Naomi 'Pink Beauty' *(above)*

Rhododendron
'Percy Wiseman'
(below)

This beautiful *Rhodo-dendron yakushimanum* × 'Fabia Tangerine' hybrid combines the best characteristics of both its parents. It is a small to medium-sized bush with a dense covering of narrow, deep green, 2–4 in (5–10 cm) long leaves with a hint of indumentum when young. The trusses of 13 to 15 funnel-shaped blooms open mid-season and are pale pink with yellowish throats. **ZONES 6–9.**

Rhododendron
'Patty Bee' *(right)*

This pretty little dwarf hybrid develops into a mound of bright green elliptical leaves. From early mid-season it is smothered in 6-flowered clusters of soft yellow, funnel-shaped flowers up to 2 in (5 cm) wide. It is ideal for rock gardens or containers. **ZONES 6–10.**

R

Rhododendron 'Purple Splendour' *(left)*

Raised before 1900, this *Rhododendron ponticum* hybrid is still one of the best purple-flowered rhododendrons. It has narrow, slightly glossy, dark green leaves up to 6 in (15 cm) long. The flowers, which open late mid-season on trusses of 7 to 14 blooms, are purple with a near black blotch. ZONES 6–9.

Rhododendron 'Purple Heart' *(below)*

This large shrub is similar in shape and foliage to its parent 'Purple Splendour'. Its flowers are violet to purple with yellow-green throats. The upright, conical trusses hold 6 to 11 blooms and open mid-season. ZONES 6–9.

R

Rhododendron 'Queen Elizabeth II' *(above)*

This medium to large shrub has striking soft yellow, funnel-shaped flowers over 4 in (10 cm) across. They are carried in trusses of around 12 blooms and open mid-season. The leaves are deep green, up to 6 in (15 cm) long and relatively narrow. ZONES 7–9.

Rhododendron
'Ruby Hart' *(below)*

In the style of
'Elisabeth Hobbie' and
'Scarlet Wonder' but
taller, this small shrub
has 2 in (5 cm) long,
deep green rounded
leaves. The new growth
is red-tinted. 'Ruby
Hart' has widely funnel-
shaped flowers which
open early mid-season,
and are about 2 in
(5 cm) long. They are
deep rich red in color
and carried in trusses
of 5 to 7 blooms.
ZONES 6–9.

Rhododendron
'Rubicon' *(above)*

This densely foliaged,
medium-sized bush has
lush, somewhat puck-
ered, glossy green
leaves up to 4 in (10 cm)
long. 'Rubicon' has
funnel-shaped, attrac-
tive deep rich red
flowers that are carried
in trusses of 9 to 17
blooms. The flowers
open early to mid-
season. ZONES 7–9.

Rhododendron 'Sappho' *(left)*

Rhododendron 'Sappho' was raised before 1847 but it is still a very distinctive plant today. When not in flower this cultivar looks much like any other large rhododendron but in bloom it cannot be mistaken for any other. Its funnel-shaped flowers, carried in upright conical trusses of 5 to 11 blooms, are pure white in color with a large, sharply contrasting, blackish purple flare. **ZONES 5–8.**

Rhododendron 'Susan' *(right)*

Popular ever since its introduction around 1930, *Rhododendron* 'Susan' makes a medium to large shrub. It has superb glossy deep green leaves which are up to 6 in (15 cm) long with a light indumentum. The flowers, which open in the middle of the season, are lavender-blue in color with darker spots. They are funnel-shaped and are carried in trusses of between 5 and 11 blooms. **ZONES 6–9.**

R

Rhododendron 'Ted's Orchid Sunset' *(below left)*

A stunning hybrid in all respects, 'Ted's Orchid Sunset' makes a medium-sized bush with matt mid-green leaves up to 6 in (15 cm) long. The new growth is bronze-colored. The flowers, over 3 in (8 cm) wide and in trusses of 7 to 11 blooms, open mid-season and are funnel-shaped and a dazzling combination of deep lavender-pink shaded orange with orange-bronze throat markings. **ZONES 6–9.**

Rhododendron 'Too Bee' *(above)*

A development of 'Patty Bee', this dwarf shrub has small deep green leaves and masses of thimble-sized, funnel-shaped flowers that are deep pink on the out-side with apricot-pink interiors. It blooms from mid-season and is an irresistible plant for rock gardens or containers. ZONES 7–9.

Rhododendron 'Virginia Richards' *(below)*

This neat small to medium-sized bush has mid-green, 3–4 in (8–10 cm) long, pointed elliptical leaves. Its orange buds open in mid-spring to reveal funnel-shaped, red blotched, apricot-orange flowers with soft creamy orange centers. The compact trusses hold 9 to 13 blooms. ZONES 6–9.

R

Rhododendron 'Whitney's Orange' *(above)*

This medium-sized, rather open-growing bush has 4 in (10 cm) long, narrow, slightly rolled bright green leaves. Its flowers, which open late mid-season, are pinkish orange with yellow centers. They are funnel-shaped in lax trusses. ZONES 7–9.

R

Rhododendron 'Winsome' *(left)*

This small to medium-sized bush bears deep green, 3 in (8 cm) long pointed leaves with a pale buff indumentum. The new growth is bronze. From early mid-season the foliage disappears under 5- to 9-flowered clusters of deep pink, bell-shaped flowers. ZONES 7–9.

RHODODENDRON, VIREYAS

Also known as Malesian rhododendrons, Vireyas are mostly evergreen shrubs that can flower at any time of the year with clusters of wide open trumpet- or funnel-shaped flowers, ranging in color from yellow, orange, coral or pink to white. They thrive in humid, mild conditions, but few can survive even the lightest frost. Many hybrids have been developed, including **'Christo Ray'** with deep orange flowers; **'Gilded Sunrise'** with bright golden yellow flowers; **'Pink Ray'**; with delicate pink flowers; and **'Simbu Sunset'** with yellow flowers edged with orange. ZONES 10–11.

R

Rhododendron, Vireya Hybrid, 'Pink Ray' *(top)*

Rhododendron, Vireya Hybrid, 'Christo Ray' *(above)*

Rhododendron, Vireya Hybrid, 'Gilded Sunrise' *(right)*

RHODODENDRON, DECIDUOUS AZALEAS

Deciduous azaleas are really quite different from the other rhododendrons. They generally perform best in sunny locations; flower predominantly in yellow and orange shades, not pink, red or mauve; and, of course, they lose all their foliage in winter. Most are very frost hardy and many develop intense autumn foliage colors. Deciduous azalea hybrids are divided into groups based on their parentage. The main groups are as follows.

Rhododendron, Ghent Azaleas

In the early 1800s Ghent, Belgium, was the main center for azalea breeding. The earliest hybrids were raised from *Rhododendron calendulaceum*, *R. nudiflorum*, *R. luteum* and *R. viscosum*. Later, *R. molle* was crossed with *R. viscosum* to produce the **Viscosepalum hybrids**, which have now largely disappeared. Further developments include the double Ghent or **Rustica** strain. Introduced from the late 1850s, they were followed in 1890 by a similar group of double-flowered hybrids known as **Rustica Flore Pleno hybrids**. Ghent azaleas tend to be large, late-flowering plants with small flowers in large heads. They are often fragrant. At the height of their popularity over 500 Ghent cultivars were available. Today they have been largely superseded by later styles. **'Coccinea Speciosa'** has bright orange-pink flowers with a striking orange blotch. **'Daviesii'** is a tall, upright Viscosepalum hybrid with fragrant, white to pale yellow flowers late in the season. **'Nancy Waterer'** has large, bright yellow, scented flowers from late spring. **'Narcissiflora'** is a tall, upright hybrid with small, double, fragrant, pale yellow flowers from late spring. **'Norma'** is a Rustica Flore Pleno hybrid with small pink-edged orange-red, double flowers. **'Phebe'** (syn. 'Phoebe') is a Rustica Flore Pleno hybrid with yellow double flowers. **'Vulcan'** is an upright bush with deep red flowers that have an orange-yellow blotch. ZONES 5–9.

Rhododendron, Ghent Azalea cultivar *(top)*
Rhododendron, Ghent Azalea, 'Narcissiflora' *(left)*

Rhododendron, Mollis Azalea cultivar *(above)*

Rhododendron, Mollis Azaleas

The mollis azaleas were developed in Belgium and Holland from Ghent azaleas. They show a greater *Rhododendron molle* influence than the Ghents and some may actually be forms of *R. molle* var. *japonicum* rather than hybrids. They first appeared in the late 1860s and were further refined over the next 30 years. Mollis azaleas flower from mid-spring and are usually over 6 ft (1.8 m) tall. The flowers are larger than the Ghents, tend to be bright yellow, orange or red and they are all singles. Because mollis azaleas can be difficult to propagate from cuttings, this group includes seedling strains. These reproduce reasonably true to type, but plants are best chosen when in flower because any label description is likely to be an approximation only. **'Anthony Koster'** has bright yellow flowers with a vivid orange blotch. **'Dr M. Oosthoek'** (syn. 'Mevrouw van Krugten') has large, bright reddish orange flowers with a light orange blotch. **'Floradora'** has bright orange flowers with a red blotch. **'Hugo Hardijzer'** has orange flowers and grows to about 5 ft (1.5 m). **'Spek's Orange'** is a relatively small bush with very large orange-blotched red flowers in trusses of up to 9 blooms. **'Winston Churchill'** has orange-red flowers with a red blotch. ZONES 6–9.

Rhododendron, Mollis Azalea, 'Hugo Hardijzer' *(above)*

Rhododendron, Mollis Azalea, 'Anthony Koster' *(below)*

R

Rhododendron,
Occidentale Azalea,
'Exquisita' *(right)*

Rhododendron, Occidentale Azaleas

Rhododendron occidentale is a fragrant white- to pink-flowered deciduous azalea from the west coast of the USA. It was discovered in 1827 and entered cultivation in the 1850s. Occidentale hybrids are among the most fragrant azaleas and usually develop into large plants, although they are quite slow growing. They bloom from mid-spring and the flowers, up to 3 in (8 cm) in diameter, are white or pale pink, often with conspicuous golden throat markings. **'Delicatissima'** has scented creamy white flushed pink flowers with a yellow blotch. **'Exquisita'** has frilled, highly scented white flushed pink flowers with an orange-yellow blotch. **'Magnifica'** has purple-red flowers with a gold blotch. ZONES 6–9.

Rhododendron, Knap Hill, Exbury and Ilam Azaleas

The Knap Hill, Exbury and Ilam hybrids are the most widely grown deciduous azaleas. The original plants were developed from about 1870 at the Knap Hill, England nursery of Anthony Waterer. Starting with Ghent azaleas, he crossbred extensively and selected only the best of the resultant hybrids. Waterer named only one of his plants, **'Nancy Waterer'** (officially a Ghent hybrid), and it was not until the seedlings were acquired by Sunningdale Nurseries in 1924 that plants started to be made available to the public. Lionel de Rothschild of Exbury developed the Exbury strain from Knap Hill seedlings. The first of these, **'Hotspur'**, was introduced in 1934. The collection was almost lost during World War II and relatively few hybrids were introduced until the 1950s. Edgar Stead of Ilam, Christchurch, New Zealand, working with various species and Ghent and Knap Hill hybrids, further refined the strain. Stead's work was continued by Dr J. S. Yeates. Most are large bushes with vividly colored single flowers. Frost hardiness varies. **'Brazil'**, an Exbury hybrid, has bright orange red flowers. **'Carmen'** (syn. 'Ilam Carmen'), an early-flowering Ilam hybrid, has apricot flowers with a yellow-orange blotch. **'Chaffinch'**, a Knap Hill hybrid, has deep pink flowers and is often sold as a seedling as it is quite variable. **'Gibraltar'**, an Exbury hybrid, has bright orange-red flowers from mid-spring. **'Homebush'**, a Knap Hill hybrid, has semi-double purplish red flowers. **'Klondyke'**, an Exbury hybrid, has bright orange flowers with an orange-yellow blotch. **'Louie Williams'** (syn. 'Ilam Louis Williams'), an Ilam hybrid, has large, light pink and soft yellow flowers with an orange blotch. **'Ming'** (syn. 'Ilam Ming'), an Ilam hybrid, has large orange flowers with a yellow blotch and is among the first to flower. **'Red Rag'**, an Ilam hybrid, has slightly frilled, bright orange-red flowers. **'Yellow Giant'** (syn. 'Ilam Yellow Giant'), an Ilam hybrid, has very large bright yellow flowers. ZONES 5–9.

R

Rhododendron, Ilam
Azalea cultivar *(right)*

Rhododendron,
Knap Hill Azalea,
'Homebush' *(below)*

Rhododendron, Exbury Azalea,
'Klondyke' *(above)*

R

Rhododendron, Ilam Azalea,
'Louie Williams' *(right)*

Rhododendron, Belgian
Indica Azalea, 'Red Wings'
(left)

RHODODENDRON, EVERGREEN AZALEAS

Despite the name, evergreen azaleas are semi-deciduous. They have 2 types of leaf: the lighter textured, often larger spring leaves and the tougher, more leathery autumn growth. The spring foliage is shed in autumn but the summer leaves are largely retained over winter. Although with age many reach 6 ft (1.8 m) tall, they tend to be small to medium-sized shrubs. They occur naturally in Japan, China, Korea and through the cooler parts of Southeast Asia. Evergreen azaleas are divided into groups based on their parentage; the following is a very brief outline of the main groups.

1. *RHODODENDRON*, INDICA AZALEAS

The first Indica hybrids were developed in Belgium in the 1850s as house plants. Their main parent is *Rhododendron simsii*, a native of Southeast Asia, which often produces bicolor flowers and is easily forced into bloom in winter. Indicas are the fanciest azaleas with an enormous range of frilly doubles and multicolor flowers. Most Indicas will be badly damaged if regularly exposed to 20°F (–7°C), though if the climate is mild enough they are no more difficult than any other azalea. Most are around 24 in (60 cm) tall by 3 ft (1 m) wide, though some are stronger growing and can reach 5 ft (1.5 m) tall or more. There are several sub-groups, such as Kerrigan and Rutherford Indicas. Many are very similar to one another and simply represent various breeders' efforts along the same lines. **ZONES 8–11.**

R

1a. *Rhododendron,* Belgian Indica Azaleas

'**Anniversary Joy**', early to mid-season, has semi-double pale pink flowers with darker shading and edges, although the flowers show considerable variation. '**Centenary Heritage**', mid-season, has semi-double bright reddish pink flowers. '**Comptesse de Kerchove**', an early-flowering, low-growing, frost-hardy bush with light green foliage, has light apricot-pink double flowers with orange-pink shading. '**Elsa Kaerger**' has very vibrant, semi-double deep orange-red flowers from early mid-season. '**Goyet**', early spring, is capable of growing to 4 ft (1.2 m) tall and has very large, frilled, dark red double flowers. '**Inga**' is a compact, very early flowering plant with double, bright mid-pink flowers with a white border; it is very heavy flowering and needs shelter when young. '**Koli**', a neat compact plant that is popular for forcing, has semi-double purple-pink flowers from mid-season. '**Little Girl**', mid-season and a heavy flowering compact bush that is a little frost tender when young, has frilled, light pink, hose-in-hose flowers. '**Melodie**', mid-season, is a rather tall yet compact grower with single to semi-double pink flowers with a red blotch. '**Mrs Gerard Kint**' (syn. 'Mevrouw Gerard Kint'),

early to mid-season and frost hardy, is a very showy, compact bush with single to semi-double white to pale flowers with a broad red edge. '**Only One Earth**', frost hardy and named for the 1972 Stockholm Earth Summit, has semi-double, bright purplish pink flowers from mid-season. '**Pink Ice**' flowers early and is frost hardy; the flowers, which are at their best just before fully open, are semi-double and pale pink with occasional deep pink flecks and stripes. '**Red Wings**' is a frost-hardy, spreading bush with deep purple-red, hose-in-hose flowers from early spring; it is a strong grower when young. '**Rosa Belton**' is a heavy flowering bush that blooms early, is frost hardy and has single white flowers with a broad lavender edge and light green, hairy foliage. '**Rosina**' (syn. 'Nelly Kelly') is a vigorous grower with pale pink double flowers from early spring. '**Silver Anniversary**' is a large, upright bush with frilled, light pink hose-in-hose flowers with darker edges that is rather frost tender when young. '**Southern Aurora**' is a uniquely colored azalea with double white flowers, heavily flushed and edged orange-red. It is spectacular and never fails to attract attention. '**Stella Maris**' is a sport of 'Rosali', has semi-double white flowers with a purple-red blotch, blooms mid-season and is a neat compact grower but is quite frost tender when young. '**The Teacher**' has attractive white, double flowers flushed and edged reddish pink, blooms early but is rather frost tender until established. ZONES 9–11.

Rhododendron, Belgian Indica Azalea, 'Silver Anniversary' *(above)*

Rhododendron, Belgian Indica Azalea, 'Stella Maris' *(right)*

R

Rhododendron,
Southern Indica
Azalea, 'Fielders
White' *(left)*

1b. *Rhododendron,* Southern Indica Azaleas

Not long after the Belgian Indicas became popular in Europe they made their appearance in the USA. Most were too tender to be used as anything but house plants in the north, however, in the milder south they were immediately popular with many acres being planted by the plantation owners. With time the azaleas set seed, some of which germinated. Some of these seedlings were cultivated and sold as new varieties. These new plants were bred with the surviving cultivars to produce the Southern Indicas. The Southern Indicas of today are a mixed bag: old Belgian Indicas, chance seedlings perpetuated, and deliberately bred hybrids. As a group the Southern Indicas are usually hardier to both sun and frost than the Belgians and tend to be larger plants when mature. **'Alphonse Anderson'** (syn. 'George Lindley Taber') has large, single, white flushed with pink flowers with a deep pink throat blotch. It blooms mid-season and grows to 5–6 ft (1.5–1.8 m) tall. **'Fielder's White'** is a large shrub up to 8 ft (2.4 m) tall and widespreading that is used as a background or filler. It has narrow, light green leaves and slightly fragrant, single white flowers with a lemon-yellow throat from mid-spring. Remove any branches with mauve flowers as they may come to predominate. **'Mardi Gras'** is a low, shrubby plant growing to about 24 in (60 cm) tall by 3 ft (1 m) wide with semi-double, orange-pink flowers with a broad white edge. It blooms early to mid-season. ZONES 8–11.

Rhododendron,
Southern Indica Azalea,
'Alphonse Anderson'
(below)

R

1c. *Rhododendron,* Rutherford Indica Azaleas

These hybrids, developed in the USA in the 1920s, were bred for use as greenhouse forcing plants and as such they are very similar to the Belgian Indicas. The name Rutherford comes from the Bobbink and Atkins Nursery of East Rutherford, New Jersey where the hybrids were developed. **'Alaska'** has early, semi-double white flowers with a light green blotch. The flowers can be variable, with single to almost fully double blooms on the one plant. It grows 3 ft (1 m) tall by 4 ft (1.2 m) wide. **'Purity'** is an early to mid-season bloomer with double white flowers; it grows to 3 ft (1 m) tall and has deep green foliage. **'Rose Queen'** has semi-double, mid-pink flowers with darker markings from early spring; it is a low, spreading bush growing to around 24 in (60 cm) tall. **'White Gish'** (syn. 'Dorothy White Gish') has white hose-in-hose flowers. **ZONES 9–11.**

Rhododendron, Rutherford Indica Azalea, 'Rose Queen' (above)

Rhododendron, Rutherford Indica Azalea, 'White Gish' (below)

Rhododendron, Kerrigan Indica Azalea, 'Gay Paree' (above)

Rhododendron, Kerrigan Indica Azalea, 'Bride's Bouquet' (below)

1d. *Rhododendron,* Kerrigan Indica Azaleas

In effect these are just another form of the Belgian Indicas; they were bred in the USA from the 1950s onwards principally as greenhouse plants. Most are fairly frost tender when young but they do have showy flowers. **'Bride's Bouquet'** is a 3 ft (1 m) tall bush with beautiful formal, rosebud, double flowers that are white with greenish throat markings and open mid-season. The blooms need some shade if they are to last. **'Gay Paree'** has spectacular bicolor, semi-double, white flowers with deep pink edges. It blooms mid-season and grows to around 3 ft (1 m) tall. **'Ripples'** is an extremely heavy flowering plant with ruffled, double, deep purple-pink flowers that open from early spring. It is sun tolerant and grows to around 24 in (60 cm) tall by 3 ft (1 m) wide. **ZONES 8–11.**

R

Rhododendron, Mucronatum Azalea,
'Alba Magna' *(left)*

1e. *Rhododendron,* Indicum and Mucronatum Hybrid Azaleas

When *Rhododendron indicum* is crossed with
R. simsii the resultant plants are known as Indicum
hybrids. Mucronatum hybrids show the influence
of *R. ripense* as well as possible *R. indicum* parentage. The resulting plants usually have sticky, light
green leaves and scented white or mauve flowers.
'Alba Magna' is an Indicum hybrid with single,
white flowers with a green throat that open early
and are slightly fragrant. It is around 3 ft (1 m)
tall by 5 ft (1.5 m) wide. **'Alba Magnifica'** is a
Mucronatum hybrid with single white flowers with
yellowish markings; the flowers open mid-season
and are slightly fragrant. It grows to around 5 ft
(1.5 m) tall and wide. **'Magnifica Rosea'** (syn.
'Magnifica') is a Mucronatum hybrid with single,
mid-pink to mauve flowers that are slightly fragrant and open mid-season. It is around 5 ft
(1.5 m) tall and wide. ZONES 8–11.

Rhododendron,
Kurume Azalea, 'Venus'
(left)

Rhododendron,
Kurume Azalea,
'Osaraku' *(below)*

Rhododendron,
Kurume Azalea, 'Kirin'
(right)

2. RHODODENDRON, KURUME AZALEAS

Kurume, on Kyushu, the southernmost main island of Japan, has long been a major azalea growing area. In 1919 the famous plant collector Ernest Wilson visited Kurume and obtained examples of 50 cultivars, which he introduced to Western gardens as Wilson's Fifty. Since then many further hybrids have been raised and introduced. Kurume azaleas clearly show the influence of *Rhododendron kiusianum*, a species that grows wild on Mt Kirishima. They are dense, compact growers with small leaves and masses of small flowers early in the season. Many Kurume azaleas have hose-in-hose flowers in which the sepals become petal-like and create the effect of a second corolla. Most are best grown in full sun or very light shade; they respond well to trimming to shape after flowering. **'Christmas Cheer'** (syn. 'Ima Shojo') is a compact bush with small, rounded, bright green leaves that is smothered in tiny, vivid cerise, hose-in-hose flowers. It grows to about 3 ft (1 m) tall if trimmed, otherwise 6 ft (1.8 m) or more and is No. 36 of Wilson's Fifty. **'Iroha Yama'** (syn. 'Dainty') is a compact bush with small, bright green, rounded leaves and single white flowers that have deep apricot-pink edges. It grows to 4 ft (1.2 m) tall and is No. 8 of Wilson's Fifty. **'Kirin'** (syn. 'Coral Bells) is certainly one of the best of the Kurumes and probably the most popular azalea of all. It is a

dense, heavily foliaged bush with rounded bright green leaves that become bronze in winter. From very early spring it becomes a solid mass of soft pastel pink, hose-in-hose flowers and grows to 3 ft (1 m) if trimmed, otherwise 6 ft (1.8 m) or more. It is No. 22 of Wilson's Fifty. **'Kiritsubo'** (syn. 'Twilight') is a strong, upright bush with bright purplish single flowers. It grows to around 4 ft (1.2 m) tall if trimmed, otherwise over 6 ft (1.8 m) and is No. 24 of Wilson's Fifty. **'Osaraku'** (syn. 'Penelope') has single flowers with very delicate shadings of white suffused light purple. It is very dense and twiggy with tiny leaves, grows to 5 ft (1.5 m) tall and is No. 17 of Wilson's Fifty. **'Red Robin'** (syn 'Waka Kayede') is a relatively low, spreading bush that glows with single, bright orange-red flowers from mid-spring. It grows to 3 ft (1 m) tall by 5 ft (1.5 m) wide and is No. 38 of Wilson's Fifty. **'Sui Yohi'** (syn. 'Sprite') has delicately shaded and textured, single, white flushed pale pink flowers with pink petal tips. It is one of the more frost-tender Kurumes, grows to around 6 ft (1.8 m) tall and is No. 10 of Wilson's Fifty. **'Venus'** is one of an old group known as Sander and Forster azaleas; actually a Kurume/Indica cross, it is usually listed as a Kurume. It has small reddish flowers in abundance and grows to around 6 ft (1.8 m) tall. ZONES 7–10.

R

2a. *Rhododendron,* Amoenum Kurume Azaleas

These plants are very much in the Kurume style. The well-known **'Amoena'** is a form of the plant formerly known as *Rhododendron obtusum,* which is itself now regarded as a hybrid of *R. sataense, R. kiusianum* and *R. kaempferi.* Always a feature of early spring due to its tremendously prolific flower display, it has tiny, purple, hose-in-hose flowers and is not the most evergreen of azaleas but it becomes a solid block of color. It is extremely tough, makes a good hedge even in exposed positions and grows to 8 ft (2.4 m) tall unless trimmed. **'Princess Maude'** is a tall, twiggy bush with rather open growth and small, vivid deep pink flowers from early spring. It grows to 8 ft (2.4 m) tall and benefits from trimming when young. ZONES **6–10.**

Rhododendron, Amoenum Kurume Azalea, 'Amoena' *(above)*

3. *RHODODENDRON,* KAEMPFERI AZALEAS

Kaempferis are the frost hardiest of the evergreen azalea hybrids and are derived from *Rhododendron kaempferi* and *R. yedoense,* both of which will withstand –5°F (20°C). However, when exposed to very low temperatures they drop most of their foliage. Most Kaempferi hybrids originated from the USA and Holland. They have, until recently, been bred primarily for frost hardiness but many of the newer hybrids have quite fancy flowers. Kaempferis often develop red foliage tints in winter and tend to have simple, very brightly colored flowers. **'Double Beauty'** has hose-in-hose, pinkish flowers from early spring. It has light green foliage and a low, spreading habit and grows 30 in (75 cm) tall by 4 ft (1.2 m) wide. **'Johanna'** has deep red, single to semi-double flowers from mid-season. It is a vigorous grower with good bright purple-red autumn and winter foliage color and grows to 6 ft (1.8 m). **'John Cairns'** has upright, twiggy growth and small bright orange-red single flowers. It grows to around 6 ft (1.8 m) tall. ZONES **6–10.**

Rhododendron, Kaempferi Azalea, 'Double Beauty' *(left)*

R

3a. *Rhododendron,* Vuyk Hybrid Azaleas

These hybrids, which are very like the original Kaempferis, were developed from 1921 by Vuyk Van Nes Nursery of Boskoop, Holland. **'Palestrina'** has white to pale cream, single flowers with yellow-green spotting. It is a compact, free-flowering bush with bright green foliage that grows to 4 ft (1.2 m). **'Queen Wilhelmina'** is a large, spreading bush with long, narrow, lance-shaped leaves and large single, orange-red flowers with a black-red blotch. It grows to 6 ft (1.8 m) tall by 8 ft (2.4 m) wide and is late blooming. **'Vuyk's Rosy Red'** is very similar to 'Vuyk's Scarlet' except that the growth is not quite as compact and the flowers tend towards cerise rather than red. **'Vuyk's Scarlet'** has masses of large, single, bright red flowers from early spring. It is always impressive and reliably evergreen even under adverse conditions and grows to 3 ft (1 m) tall by 5 ft (1.5 m) wide. ZONES 6–10.

Rhododendron, Vuyk Hybrid Azalea, 'Palestrina' *(above)*

Rhododendron, Vuyk Hybrid Azalea, 'Vuyk's Scarlet' *(below)*

3b. *Rhododendron,* Gable Hybrid Azaleas

These hybrids, developed by Joseph Gable of Pennsylvania, were bred with frost hardiness as a prime objective; not only was this achieved but some quite showy double flowers were also raised. **'Lorna'** has very full double, bright mid-pink flowers from mid-season. It is a tough and colorful bush that grows to 5 ft (1.5 m) tall. **'Purple Splendor'** is a low, spreading bush with narrow leaves and frilled, light purple hose-in-hose flowers from mid-season; it grows to 3 ft (1 m) tall by 5 ft (1.5 m) wide. **'Rosebud'** is very like 'Lorna' but with deeper pink flowers and somewhat lower, more compact growth. ZONES 6–10.

Rhododendron, Gable Hybrid Azalea, 'Lorna' *(below)*

R

Rhododendron, Girard Hybrid Azalea, 'Girard's Chiara' *(left)*

3c. *Rhododendron,* Girard Hybrid Azaleas

Developed from the late 1940s onward by Peter Girard of Ohio, USA, these are good compact hybrids. **'Girard's Border Gem'** is a dwarf, small-leafed bush with deep pink single flowers from mid-season that grows 15 in (38 cm) tall by 24 in (60 cm) wide. **'Girard's Chiara'** has ruffled, deep cerise, hose-in-hose flowers with a reddish blotch. It blooms mid-season and grows 18 in (45 cm) tall and wide. **ZONES 6–10.**

Rhododendron, Satsuki Azalea, 'Issho No Haru' *(left)*

R

Rhododendron, Satsuki Azalea, 'Shugetsu' *(left)*

4. *Rhododendron*, Satsuki Azaleas

Most gardeners regard the Kurume as the traditional Japanese azalea, however, the Satsuki is more revered in Japan. The confusion probably arose because Kurumes have been cultivated in Western gardens for longer than the Satsukis, which have been widely grown only since the 1950s. 'Satsuki' means fifth month, and while not a direct reference to May in the northern hemisphere it does give an indication of the flowering time. Satsukis flower late and their blooms need protection from the summer sun to last. Satsukis have large, highly variable single flowers. One plant can display a wide range of color and pattern in its flowers. They are generally small, spreading plants and are hardy to around 10°F (12°C). **'Benigasa'** (syn 'Red Umbrella') has large, single, deep orange-red flowers from late spring and is intensely colored for a Satsuki. It has rounded deep green leaves and grows to 18 in (45 cm) tall by 3 ft (1 m) wide. **'Daishuhai'** (syn. 'Great Vermilion Cup') has single, white flowers with a clearly defined red tip to each petal and more open growth than most Satsukis though it is by no means rangy. It grows to 24 in (60 cm) tall by 3 ft (1 m) wide. **Gumpo** (a group of Phoenixes) is a group of dwarf bushes seldom exceeding 12 in (30 cm) tall by 24 in (60 cm) wide. They have single flowers from late mid-season, are among the most heavy flowering of azaleas and are ideally suited to rockeries or small gardens. Included in the Gumpo group is **Fancy** with mid-pink flowers with a white margin and pink markings; **Light Pink** with pale pink flowers with darker markings; **Salmon** with frilled bright salmon-pink flowers; and **White** with white, heavily frilled, extremely profuse flowers. **'Hitoya No Haru'** (syn. 'Glory of Spring') is among the last of the azaleas to bloom with large, single, bright lavender-pink flowers. It is an outstanding plant with glossy foliage year round and a superb flower display that grows 18 in (45 cm) tall by 3 ft (1 m) wide. **'Issho No Haru'** (syn. 'Spring of a Lifetime') has large, single, soft pastel pink flowers with occasional purple splashes; it blooms late spring and grows 15 in (38 cm) tall by 24 in (60 cm) wide. **'Shugetsu'** (syn. 'Autumn Moon') has large, single, white flowers edged bright purple, although many patterns can be seen on one bush. It blooms late mid-season and grows to 24 in (60 cm) tall by 3 ft (1 m) wide. ZONES 7–11.

Rhododendron, Satsuki Azalea, 'Daishuhai' *(below)*

R

5a. *Rhododendron*, Glenn Dale Hybrid Azaleas

In 1935 B. Y. Morrison of the US Department of Agriculture Plant Introduction Section at Glenn Dale, Maryland, USA started breeding azaleas in an attempt to produce frost-hardy plants in a good color range and to fill a then existing mid-season gap in flowering. Thousands of clones were trialled over a ten-year period with the majority of the selected types being released in 1947–49 with the remainder following in 1952. Four hundred and forty clones were released, though many are no longer common. **'Ben Morrison'** has striking single, deep rusty red flowers with darker markings and a broad white border. It blooms mid-season and grows to 5 ft (1.5 m) tall by 6 ft (1.8 m) wide. This hybrid was raised by Morrison but not released by him; it was introduced after his death to commemorate his work. **'Festive'** has single, white flowers flecked and striped with purple. It flowers early and grows to 6 ft (1.8 m). **'Glacier'** has single, white flowers tinted light green. It blooms from early mid-season and has a vigorous upright growth habit to 6 ft (1.8 m) tall. **'Martha Hitchcock'** is a very tough and vigorous bush that has large, single white flowers with a broad purplish pink edge. It flowers from mid-season and grows to 4 ft (1.2 m) tall by 6 ft (1.8 m) wide. **'Vespers'** has single to semi-double white flowers with green markings and occasional pink splashes. It is a very vigorous, early-flowering bush that grows to 5 ft (1.5 m) tall. **ZONES 7–10.**

5. *RHODODENDRON*, INTER-GROUP AZALEAS

This catch-all collection of sub-groups includes the hybrids produced by breeding between the other groups and also includes those raised from newly introduced species.

Rhododendron, Glenn Dale Hybrid Azalea, 'Ben Morrison' *(above)*

Rhododendron, Glenn Dale Hybrid Azalea, 'Martha Hitchcock' *(below right)*

Rhododendron, Glenn Dale Hybrid Azalea, 'Festive' *(below)*

5b. *Rhododendron,* Back Acres Hybrid Azaleas

Morrison produced these compact hybrids after his retirement from the US Department of Agriculture. '**Debonaire**' has bright pink, single flowers with darker edges and a light center. It blooms mid-season and grows to 3 ft (1 m) tall and wide. '**Fire Magic**' has apricot-red, double flowers with bright red spotting. It flowers mid-season and grows to 4 ft (1.2 m). '**Hearthglow**' has double, mid-pink, camellia-like flowers flushed reddish orange that open from late mid-season. It grows to 4 ft (1.2 m) tall. '**Miss Jane**' has white flowers flushed pink. It is a compact, late-flowering bush that requires shade for the display to last and grows to 24 in (60 cm) tall by 3 ft (1 m) wide. **ZONES 7–10.**

Rhododendron, August Kehr Hybrid Azalea, 'Anne Kehr' *(below)*

Rhododendron, Back Acres Hybrid Azalea, 'Miss Jane' *(above right)*

5c. *Rhododendron,* Greenwood Hybrid Azaleas

Developed in Oregon, USA, by using Kurume, Glenn Dale and Gable hybrids, these are frost-hardy hybrids noted for doing well in cool climates. Most are very compact bushes. '**Greenwood Orange**' has masses of small orange-red, double flowers from mid-season and a rather open growth habit that benefits from trimming to shape when young. It grows to 3 ft (1 m). '**Royal Robe**' is a compact, mound-forming bush with light purple hose-in-hose flowers from mid-season. It is excellent for rockeries and grows to 15 in (38 cm) tall by 24 in (60 cm) wide. '**Tenino**' has hose-in-hose, deep pinkish purple flowers from mid-season. It grows to 15 in (38 cm) tall by 3 ft (1 m) wide. **ZONES 6–10.**

5d. *Rhododendron,* August Kehr Hybrid Azaleas

Developed by another US Department of Agriculture employee, Dr August Kehr, these hybrids represent a lifetime's work. From the many clones that he bred he released only a handful of the frost hardiest and most beautiful plants. Of all the evergreen azaleas, they probably best combine showy double flowers and frost hardiness. '**Anna Kehr**' has full double, deep pink flowers from mid-season. It often takes time to settle down to serious blooming and requires shaping when young but is well worth the effort, growing to 30 in (75 cm) tall by 24 in (60 cm) wide. '**White Rosebud**' has full double, white flowers with green throats. It blooms mid-season, is sun tolerant for a white and grows 3 ft (1 m) tall and wide. **ZONES 6–10.**

Rhododendron, Greenwood Hybrid Azalea, 'Royal Robe' *(above)*

R

5f. *Rhododendron,* Harris Hybrid Azaleas

Developed by James Harris from 1970 onwards, these cultivars are very compact and heavy flowering. They are frost hardy once established. **'Fascination'** has large single flowers with a broad deep red border and a white or pale pink center, very much in the Satsuki style. It grows to 3 ft (1 m) tall. **'Frosted Orange'** is a twiggy, spreading bush with white flowers that have striking, broad orange-toned borders. It is spectacular but blooms late and needs shade for the display to last, and grows 30 in (75 cm) tall by 4 ft (1.2 m) wide. **'Gloria Still'** is a compact, slowly spreading plant that grows to 30 in (75 cm) tall by 4 ft (1.2 m) wide. It has variegated pink and white flowers in large clusters. **'Miss Suzie'** is a compact, low-growing bush with bright red hose-in-hose flowers from midseason. It grows to 24 in (60 cm) tall. ZONES 6–10.

Rhododendron, Harris Hybrid Azalea, 'Frosted Orange' *(above)*

Rhododendron, Harris Hybrid Azalea, 'Miss Suzie' *(left)*

Rhododendron, Nuccio Hybrid Azalea, 'Happy Days' *(below)*

5e. *Rhododendron,* Nuccio Hybrid Azaleas

The Nuccios of California, perhaps better known for their camellias, also breed azaleas. They have used a wide range of the material and as a result Nuccio hybrids cover the whole spectrum of flower type, size and frost hardiness. **'Bit of Sunshine'** is a Kurume-style cultivar with masses of vivid pinkish red, hose-in-hose flowers from early spring. It grows 3 ft (1 m) tall by 4 ft (1.2 m) wide. **'Happy Days'** is an Indica-style cultivar with bright midpurple, rosebud, double flowers from early spring; the flowers last well over a long season. It grows to 30 in (75 cm) and is fairly frost tender when young. **'Purple Glitters'**, a large, upright bush around 5 ft (1.5 m) tall, is a Kurume-style cultivar that is smothered in vivid purplish pink single flowers from early spring. **'Rose Glitters'** is a deep cerise form. ZONES 6–11.

R

5g. *Rhododendron,* Robin Hill Hybrid Azaleas

These hybrids were bred from 1937 to 1981 by Robert Gartrell of Wyckoff, New Jersey, USA. From 20,000 seedlings trialled he eventually released 69 cultivars. Most are medium-sized, relatively frost-hardy shrubs. **'Betty Ann Voss'** is a vigorous, low, spreading cultivar with late, semi-double to hose-in-hose, bright mid-pink flowers. It grows 18 in (45 cm) tall by 3 ft (1 m) wide with glossy foliage. **'Early Beni'** is a mounding, 24–30 in (60–75 cm) tall bush with semi-double, deep orange-red flowers from early spring. It is sun tolerant. **'Lady Louise'** has mid-season, semi-double to double, deep apricot-pink flowers with reddish markings on a spreading, 30 in (75 cm) tall bush; winter foliage is bronze. **'Nancy of Robin Hill'** is a bushy cultivar to 24 in (60 cm) tall with semi-double, light pink flowers with darker markings. It blooms from mid-spring. **'Watchet'** is a dwarf cultivar to about 15 in (38 cm) tall by 24 in (60 cm) wide. It has single, mid-pink flowers with white throats and blooms from just after mid-spring. **'White Moon'** is a Satsuki-like, 15 in (38 cm) tall spreading cultivar. It produces its large, single, white flowers in late spring. The flowers are occasionally splashed with pink and need shade to prevent them burning. ZONES 6–10.

Rhododendron, Robin Hill Hybrid Azalea, **'Nancy of Robin Hill'** *(above)*

Rhododendron, Robin Hill Hybrid Azalea, **'Betty Ann Voss'** *(below)*

R

RHODOLEIA

These small evergreen trees native to Southeast Asia have alternate and leathery leaves, waxy, underneath. Spring flowers hang clustered from the leaf axils, each rose red flower surrounded by colored bracts. Fruits are capsules, in clusters. The genus is usually regarded as comprising a single variable species from South China to Java, but up to 7 species have been recognized.

CULTIVATION
Frost-tender, grow in full sun or part-shade with shelter from wind. They need light, slightly acid, well-drained soil enriched with organic matter. Propagate from seed in spring or from cuttings in winter.

Rhodoleia championii (below)
SILK ROSE, HONG KONG ROSE

This tree can grow at least 20 ft (6 m) tall. Thick, obtuse, dark green leaves 6 in (15 cm) long crowd together at the branch tips and have a cream midrib and pink stalks. It bears drooping clusters of 5 to 10 rose red, bell-shaped flower-heads, each with a whorl of pink to crimson bracts 2 in (5 cm) across. ZONES 9–11.

R

RHODOTYPOS

This genus, closely allied to *Kerria,* contains one species, a 15 ft (4.5 m) deciduous shrub native to China and Japan with soft mid-green leaves and simple, 2 in (5 cm) diameter white flowers. The calyces remain after the flowers fall and enclose ¼–½ in (6–12 mm) glossy black berries. As the sepals dry they fold back to reveal the pea-shaped fruit, which appear to be unattractive to birds and lasts well into winter.

CULTIVATION
This plant grows happily in any well-drained soil in sun or light shade. It is fully frost hardy and may be propagated from cuttings or seed or by layering.

Rhodotypos scandens (above)

This upright or slightly arching shrub bears its shallowly cupped, single, 4-petalled flowers in late spring and early summer. The sharply toothed leaves are most appealing when young.
ZONES 5–9.

R

Rhus chinensis 'September Beauty' *(left)*

Rhus chinensis

CHINESE SUMAC, NUTGALL TREE

This small, broad-headed, deciduous shrub or small tree, found in Japan as well as China, reaches 20 ft (6 m) or more and is grown for its spectacular autumn hues. Its compound leaves are coarsely toothed and arranged on winged stalks. Clusters of whitish flowers are borne in late summer and are followed by red, downy berries. **'September Beauty'** is grown for its striking blaze of autumn color. ZONES 8–11.

RHUS

Rhus is a large, diverse genus consisting of 200 species of deciduous and evergreen shrubs, trees and scrambling vines. One group of species, now separated into a new genus, *Toxicodendron*, contains trees and shrubs notorious for causing allergies. Some deciduous species turn brilliant shades of red, purple, orange, yellow and bronze in autumn; others bear reddish or brownish velvety fruit. Many produce male and female flowers on different trees. Some of the numerous evergreen species are moderately frost tolerant. Many species tolerate pollution.

CULTIVATION

They like a sunny position in moderately fertile, moist but well-drained soil with protection from wind. Propagate from seed or cuttings, or by dividing root suckers.

Rhus typhina *(below)*

syn. *Rhus hirta*

STAG'S HORN SUMAC

This deciduous shrub or small tree from temperate eastern North America makes a brilliant autumn display. It grows a slender erect trunk or thicket of stems up to 15 ft (4.5 m) high and spreads to 12 ft (3.5 m). It bears pinnate leaves with toothed, 6 in (15 cm) leaflets, yellowish green flower clusters and striking 'candles' of velvety red fruits. **'Dissecta'** (syns *Rhus typhina* 'Laciniata', *R. hirta* 'Laciniata') carries its dark fruit well into winter and has deeply dissected, fern-like foliage. ZONES 3–9.

Rhus aromatica 'Gro-Low' *(below)*

Rhus aromatica

FRAGRANT SUMAC

This sprawling, deciduous species from eastern USA reaches 3 ft (1 m) tall and 5 ft (1.5 m) wide. Tiny yellow flowers, borne in spikes on bare stems, are followed by downy, deep green, coarsely toothed and aromatic foliage maturing to spectacular shades of orange and purple in autumn. Small red berries appear in mid-summer. **'Gro-Low'** is an very low-growing form with fragrant flowers that are a deeper yellow than those of the species. ZONES 2–9.

R

RIBES
CURRENT

This genus, from cool-temperate, northern hemisphere regions, contains some 150 species of evergreen and deciduous, ornamental and fruiting shrubs. The white, scarlet, purple, green or black berries are usually edible. They can grow to 10 ft (3 m) and have long, arching stems. Some species have reddish brown branches, and some produce prickles on the stems or fruit, or on both. The lobed, mid-green leaves, sometimes with downy or felted undersides and toothed edges, may turn red and orange before dropping. Masses of yellow, red or pink blossoms, which are sometimes fragrant, appear in late winter or early spring.

CULTIVATION
These unisexual plants must be planted in groups to ensure vigorous fruiting. They are fully frost hardy and need to be grown in moist, rich soil with a site in full sun or semi-shade. In the USA, some species are host to white pine blister rust. The best method of propagation is from seed or cuttings.

Ribes alpinum (left)
MOUNTAIN CURRANT, ALPINE CURRANT

This dense, twiggy, deciduous shrub from northern Europe to Russia grows 6 ft (1.8 m) tall and wide. Reddish purple, smooth stems bear 3- to 5-lobed rounded, serrated leaves. The pale, greenish yellow flower clusters carry 7 to 15 blossoms. These are followed by large bunches of scarlet berries, provided both male and female plants are grown. *Ribes alpinum* is a neat and versatile shrub that tolerates heavy shade. ZONES 5–9.

Ribes odoratum (above)
syn. *Ribes aureum* of gardens

CLOVE CURRANT, BUFFALO CURRANT

A spreading 8 ft (2.4 m) shrub with prickle-free stems, this species is native to the prairies and high plains of midwestern USA. The shiny, 3-lobed leaves color well in autumn. The large, downturned flowerheads are greenish yellow, deepening with age and followed by black berries. The plant is grown mainly for the spicy, clove-like fragrance of its leaves. ZONES 6–9.

R

Ribes silvestre *(left)*
syns *Ribes rubrum, R. sativum*

REDCURRANT, WHITE CURRANT

Native to western Europe, this deciduous, prickle-free species is an
erect 6 ft (1.8 m) shrub with 2½ in
(6 cm) long, lobed leaves that have
silvery undersides. Racemes of small
flowers open in spring, followed by
clusters of small, very juicy, round
red or pale amber (white) fruit. They
are rather tart and are excellent fresh
or cooked. Cultivars of note include
'Viking'; **'Jonkheer van Tets'**, a vigorous, open redcurrant that flowers
and fruits very early; **'Red Lake'**,
vigorous, densely branched and disease-resistant with an early crop of
dark red, rather small fruit; and
'White Grape' with large clusters of
pale pinkish yellow fruit. ZONES 6–9.

Ribes sanguineum
'Tydeman's White' *(left)*

Ribes sanguineum *(below left)*
RED FLOWERING CURRANT, WINTER CURRANT, FLOWERING CURRANT

This prickle-free, deciduous shrub grows to 12 ft
(3.5 m) high. It has aromatic, lobed leaves. The deep
pink or red flowers, appearing in late spring, are
borne on erect to drooping spikes. Bluish black berries follow in summer. **'King Edward VII'** bears
carmine flowers; **'Brocklebankii'** has golden leaves
and pink flowers; **'Tydeman's White'** has white
flowers; **'White Icicle'** has pure white flower clusters; and **'Pulborough Scarlet'** carries a mass of
deep red flowers. *Ribes sanguineum* var.
glutinosum has hanging clusters of pink flowers
and leaves more sparsely pubescent than *R.
sanguineum*. **'Barrie Coate'** was found on Fremont
Peak in California growing in full sun and has deep
rose-colored, pendent flower clusters. **'Spring
Showers'** is a bushy, vase-shaped shrub with
downy bright green leaves and hanging clusters of
pink flowers. ZONES 6–10.

R

Ribes uva-crispa
(right)
syn. *Ribes grossularia*

GOOSEBERRY, EUROPEAN
GOOSEBERRY

This stiff, spiny, deciduous shrub is native to central Europe and North America. It grows about 3 ft (1 m) tall, with upright canes and small green leaves held at stiff angles from the stems. Pinkish green flowers are followed by greenish fruit covered with soft bristles. This species rarely fruits well in frost-free climates. There are many cultivars in a variety of sizes and shapes, bearing green, russet green or yellow green fruit. **'Careless'** is a spreading bush with few thorns, the fruit being yellow, elongated and bland; **'Invicta'** (syn. 'Malling Invicta') is an early ripener with a heavy crop of large yellow fruit; **'Leveller'** has well-flavored fruit and is fairly vigorous; and **'Whinham's Industry'** is a slow-growing bush with a good crop of tasty, round, yellow berries with purple red bristles. *Ribes uva-crispa* var. *reclinatum* has bristly, round to slightly elongated fruit that may be yellow or red when ripe. **ZONES 5–9.**

Ribes speciosum
(below)
FUCHSIA FLOWERING GOOSEBERRY

This deciduous, spiny, bushy shrub from California in the USA reaches 6 ft (1.8 m) in height and spread. Fully frost hardy, it has red juvenile shoots and oval, 3- to 5-lobed glossy green leaves. Its slender, drooping red flowers, which open in late winter, have long red stamens; they are followed by spherical red fruit. **ZONES 7–10.**

R

Richea dracophylla
(left)

Richea dracophylla is
an erect, sparsely
branched species from
Tasmania. It has nar-
row leaves to 8 in
(20 cm) long in a
tapering, zigzag form
that crowd at the ends
of the stems. Reaching
to as much as 15 ft
(4.5 m) in height, it
bears its terminal
spikes of white or pink
flowers with purplish
bracts in summer.
ZONES 8–9.

RICHEA

All but 2 of these beautiful but rarely cultivated Australian evergreens of the epacris family are endemic to Tasmania. Most of
the 12 species are bushy shrubs, but some can grow as tall as
50 ft (15 m). The strap-like leaves can vary from ½ in (12 mm)
to over 3 ft (1 m) long. Dense flower clusters appear in summer
and are pink, white, yellow or cream, thrust above the foliage on
upright spikes. These plants do well in containers.

CULTIVATION
They must have humus-rich, moist but well-drained, preferably
acid soil and shelter from full sun and wind to produce the best
blooms. Plants benefit from an annual mulch of organic matter.
Prune spent flowerheads in early autumn. Propagate from seed
in autumn or from cuttings in summer.

RICINUS

This genus from northeastern Africa and southwestern Asia contains a single species, a fast-growing, tree-like shrub grown for its foliage. The spikes of small, cup-shaped flowers appear in summer. All parts of the plant, especially the seeds, are extremely poisonous and can cause death in children; however, the seed oil is used medicinally after heat treatment and purification.

CULTIVATION

This marginally frost-hardy plant prefers full sun and fertile, humus-rich, well-drained soil. It may need staking. Propagate from seed.

Ricinus communis
'Carmencita' *(below)*

Ricinus communis

CASTOR OIL PLANT

The purgative of universal renown comes from the seeds of this species, which is mostly grown as an annual. Rounded, prickly seed pods follow the summer display of felty clusters of red and greenish flowers. The plant's leaves are large, glossy and divided deeply into elliptical lobes. *Ricinus communis* grows rapidly, reaching 12 ft (3.5 m) in height and in warm climates it often becomes a weed. **'Carmencita'** is a tall form that grows to 10 ft (3 m) with bronze-red foliage and red female flowers. ZONES 9–11.

R

ROBINIA
BLACK LOCUST

These 20 species of leguminous deciduous shrubs and trees from the USA are fast growing and tolerate pollution. Some grow 80 ft (24 m) tall but many are shrublike, reaching only 6 ft (1.8 m). Most spread by suckers and self-seed. The pinnate leaves, usually with a pair of spines at each base, have small oval leaflets, sometimes turning buttery yellow in autumn. They bear pendulous sprays of pink, purple or white, fragrant pea-blossoms in spring. Fruits are flat pods less than 4 in (10 cm). Cultivars have been grafted to produce a mop-like head of foliage.

CULTIVATION
Robinias prefer poor but moist soil in a sunny position sheltered from strong winds. Propagate from scarified seed, cuttings or suckers or by division. Cultivars must be grafted.

Robinia pseudoacacia
'Frisia' *(above)*

Robinia hispida
(left)
ROSE ACACIA

Robinia hispida is a deciduous shrub from the dry woods and scrub of southeastern USA. It has pinnate leaves that are fresh green, long and fern-like; the erect stems and branches are clothed in brown bristles. In summer, rose-pink pea-flowers are followed by bristly seed pods up to 3 in (8 cm) long. In favorable conditions the plant quickly reaches 6 ft (1.8 m). This species is sometimes grafted on to stems of *R. pseudoacacia* to produce a small, mop-headed tree. On *Robinia hispida* var. *kelseyi* (syn. *R. kelseyi*) only the flower stalks and raceme axes have bristles; it bears glossy rose-pink flowers. ZONES 5–10.

Robinia pseudoacacia
FALSE ACACIA, BLACK LOCUST

This fast-growing 80 ft (24 m) tree has dark, deeply grooved bark and prickly branches. The pinnate, fern-like leaves, with about 23 leaflets, turn yellow in autumn. Scented white pea-flowers appear in late spring or summer, followed by reddish brown pods with black, kidney-shaped seeds. The cultivar 'Frisia' carries golden foliage deepening in autumn. 'Rozynskiana' is a small tree with drooping branches and leaves. 'Tortuosa' has short, twisted branches. 'Umbraculifera', the mop-head acacia, is also thornless and rarely flowers. These cultivars rarely exceed 30 ft (9 m). ZONES 3–10.

R

Robinia × *slavinii* 'Hillieri' *(above)*

Robinia × *slavinii* 'Hillieri' is a small tree
with a compact, rounded head of foliage.
Its fragrant flowers are lavender-pink and
open from early summer. It is ideal in
large containers or as a feature plant for
small gardens. **ZONES 5–10.**

Robinia pseudoacacia 'Tortuosa' *(right)*

Robinia pseudoacacia 'Umbraculifera'
(below)

R

ROLDANA

This genus of 48 species of large annuals, perennials and subshrubs is from Mexico and central America. They have slender stems and alternate leaves, and flowers bearing 5 to 45 yellow florets.

CULTIVATION
These frost-tender plants prefer moderately fertile, moist but well-drained soil and full sun. Propagate from seed or cuttings, or by division.

Roldana petasitis
(above)
syn. *Senecio petasitis*

This weak-stemmed subshrub is found from Mexico to Nicaragua. Growing to around 6 ft (1.8 m) tall, it has large leaves with 7 or more broad, blunt lobes. The daisy-like yellow flowerheads are borne in leafy panicles; each has about 6 ray petals.
ZONES 9–11.

RONDELETIA

These striking evergreen trees and shrubs are native to tropical America and the West Indies. Only 3 of the 125 to 150 species are commonly cultivated; they grow to 10 ft (3 m) in warm climates. The tough foliage is distinctly veined and remains attractive all year. The red, yellow, pink or white tubular flowers appear in terminal or axillary clusters in spring and summer; being rich in nectar, they attract birds. The fruits are small capsules containing many seeds.

CULTIVATION
Grow in sun or part-shade in well-drained, slightly acid soil enriched with organic matter. If kept in pots, they should be well watered during growth. Cut back the flowered stems each year in early spring. Propagate from seed in spring or from cuttings.

Rondeletia strigosa
(right)

This native of Guatemala is an evergreen shrub of about 4 ft (1.2 m) in height, with arching cane branches springing from the base. The leaves are small, broad at the base and drawn out into a point at the tip, and are mostly arranged in whorls of three. The flowers are rather striking, ¾ in (18 mm) across, and deep crimson with a golden 'eye' surrounded by a raised circular rim, borne in groups of 3 to 5 at the branch ends. It blooms through summer and autumn, or for much of the year in a sufficiently warm climate.
ZONES 10–12.

R

ROSA
ROSE

The 150 species of roses and their countless hybrid derivatives, valued for their beauty and perfume and sometimes for their bright fruits, have been at the forefront of garden design and plant hybridization. In centuries past roses had medicinal uses too, yet even in the Middle Ages when most plants had to have practical uses to justify their cultivation, a few roses were grown for their beauty alone. Found over most of the northern hemisphere, though primarily in the temperate regions, roses are woody stemmed shrubs or scrambling climbers. Almost all are deciduous, and even those regarded as evergreen or semi-evergreen often shed much of their foliage in cold winters. They range from small shrubs under 24 in (60 cm) tall through to the huge spreading climbers such as *Rosa gigantea*, which can have a spread of over 100 ft (30 m). Roses have trifoliate or pinnate leaves with finely toothed leaflets. The foliage may be bright green, very deep lustrous, almost black-green or distinctly blue-tinted. Most species have arching, thorny stems, and both the young stems and new foliage are often tinted red. The thorns of cultivated roses are usually broad based and recurved to a fine point, but many wild species, especially the briars, have a dense covering of prickles rather than thorns. Garden roses often have semi-double to very full double flowers, but that is the result of extensive hybridizing. The species and the less highly developed cultivars most often have single flowers, usually 5-petalled. Flower color among the modern hybrids now covers everything except a true natural blue. The species, too, cover a wide color range but without the flamboyant combinations seen in the hybrids. Clusters of brilliant red or orange fruits known as hips (more rarely heps or haws) sometimes follow the flowers, particularly those of the species or single-flowered hybrids. These add interest in late summer and autumn and can be almost as much a feature as the flowers.

CULTIVATION

Roses are generally frost-hardy, vigorous plants with a great zest for life. However, they do have some climatic and soil preferences, and though prone to a few pests and diseases these problems are lessened or prevented with the right planning and cultivation. Roses prefer a temperate climate and most do best with at least 2 months of winter chilling. They do not actually need exposure to frost, just enough prolonged cold to induce dormancy and proper bud formation. However, light to moderate frosts are useful for killing off any overwintering pests. Roses are adaptable: they can be planted in beds of roses alone or blended into the overall garden design, and a few can even be left to run wild. The miniatures and smaller types mix well with shrubs, perennials and annuals and make marvellous informal hedges along pathways or edging larger beds. Use ground cover roses to carpet sloping ground or for cascading over retaining walls. Climbers can be used on fences, for covering unsightly sheds or old trees and for growing over archways or entrances to provide a fragrant greeting for visitors. Small shrub roses, miniature climbers and trailers grow well in containers provided they are regularly fed and do not dry out.

Siting and planting: Roses require at least

half-day sun, good ventilation without being exposed to strong winds; slightly acid, moisture-retentive yet well-drained soil; and limited competition from large shrubs and trees. Shade leads to poor flowering, rank growth and fungal problems. Strong winds damage the foliage and flowers and may break the branches, while poor ventilation is sure to encourage the spread of fungal diseases. Prepare the site well in advance, beginning by planning their layout: large bushes need more width than small, climbers need something to climb and large growers should not overshadow smaller plants. Allow easy access for pruning and spraying. As a rule a bush rose will spread to at least two-thirds its height. Before planting, trim any damaged stems or roots. Examine the main stem near the bud union for a color change that indicates the level at which it was planted in the field, then plant the bush at the same level in the garden. Dig a hole large enough to ensure there is a good depth and spread of loosened soil so the root system can quickly develop. Position the plant, spread its roots, add a light dusting of mild fertilizer and check the depth, then back fill by gently firming the soil into place. Stake standards and tall bushes to prevent damage from wind; position the stake before refilling the hole so that roots are not inadvertently damaged by driving the stake through them. After planting, water and mulch around the new rose.

Pruning: Prune to encourage new growth, rejuvenate plants, improve their shape and to enable light to penetrate to the center of the bush to promote even growth. Hard pruning tends to promote strong stems with fewer but better blooms, while leaving longer stems promotes dense bushy growth with many but smaller blooms. Despite the tradition of pruning to an outward facing bud to create an open vase-shaped bush, recent research suggests that roses will thrive with a far more casual approach to pruning. Just removing the old or damaged wood and trimming to shape should be sufficient. Roses are normally pruned when dormant in winter, although there is no reason why they should not be trimmed and thinned in summer, this in fact being the best option for small roses with masses of fine twiggy stems where careful trimming is impractical.

Pests and diseases: Good ventilation, avoiding overcrowding and providing the right growing conditions will all help to prevent problems with pests and diseases. Should problems occur, the key is early control. Pests such as aphids, thrips and mites can be controlled by systemic insecticides, however it is fungal diseases that are more likely to cause lasting damage. Mildews and black spot lead to premature foliage drop and general debilitation. Rust spreads rapidly, can cause almost total defoliation if allowed to take hold, and may be carried over to the following season. Even with the best of care, mild cases of these diseases will occur and spraying may be unavoidable.

Propagation: Most hybrid roses are budded onto vigorous, disease-resistant, non-suckering rootstocks. Although roses can also be grown from cuttings, some modern varieties do not grow well on their own roots and suckering varieties become nuisances. Propagation from seed is generally restricted to species or raising new hybrids. The seed germinates well but it must be stratified for 8 to 12 weeks before sowing.

R

ROSA, SPECIES AND THEIR CULTIVATED FORMS (WILD ROSES)

Roses have been in existence for at least 35 million years and, although they have only been cultivated for about the last 2,700 of those years, their development from untamed shrubs to the plants we know is a long and complicated story beginning with the wild species. Rose species are divided into 4 main groups: Hulthemia, Hesperhodos, Platyrhodon and Eurosa. The first 3 groups include only 5 species; the rest belong to the Eurosa group, which is itself divided into 10 sections. Plants from almost all those groups and sections have been used for breeding, but relatively few have had a major influence. Most garden roses are hybrids, but some species are cultivated. Species roses are often quite different from modern hybrids, tending to be rather untidy, scrambling bushes, while many smaller growers are covered in thorns, spines or prickles. The flowers are generally rather small, very simple and only appear for a short time in late spring. Yet the species are usually tough and adaptable, able to shrug off pests and diseases, and many produce a marvellous display of rose hips from late summer.

Rosa banksiae var.
banksiae *(above)*

Rosa banksiae var.
normalis 'Lutea' *(right)*

Rosa banksiae

DOUBLE WHITE BANKSIAN ROSE

This climbing species has thornless stems to 40 ft (12 m) in height and half that in spread. The double, rosette-shaped white flowers appear in clusters in spring. *Rosa banksiae* var. *banksiae* (syn. *R. b.* 'Alba Plena'), the Lady Banks rose, has long, arching, thornless canes and slender, pointed, dark green, smooth and leathery leaflets, 3 or 5 per leaf; the foliage is evergreen and disease free. The sweetly scented, double white flowers appear in spring in clusters of 3 to 7 flowers. The hips, borne rarely, are small and dull red. *R. b.* var. *normalis* 'Lutea', from central and western China, has long, arching, thornless canes and grows to 12 ft (3.5 m) in height and spread. There are 3 to 7 evergreen, slender, dark green, leathery leaflets per leaf. The yellow spring flowers, with prominent stamens, are sweetly scented and grow in clusters of 3 to 7 flowers. The hips are small and dull red. **ZONES 7–10.**

Rosa chinensis 'Viridiflora' *(below)*

GREEN ROSE, MONSTOSA

Reported to have been in cultivation in England as early as 1743, this climber has mid-green, smooth foliage and somewhat twiggy, prickly growth. Clusters of 3 to 7 small oval buds of soft blue-green open to flowers with 35 long thin bracts, light green streaked reddish brown bracts, and hairy reddish brown centers. ZONES 7–10.

Rosa bracteata *(above)*

syns 'Chicksaw Rose', 'Macartney Rose'

A dense shrub or wall plant to 10 ft (3 m), *R. bracteata* has long, grayish brown stems that are well armed with hooked thorns, often arranged in pairs. There is a plentiful covering of dark green, roundish and glossy leaves that have tomentose undersides. There are nine leaflets. The white flowers, with pronounced stamens, sometimes have a hint of cream showing through. They are borne singly on the end of stubby laterals throughout summer, and are followed by plumply rounded, orange hips. Although it is not suitable for cold climates, it makes an excellent shrub in temperate zones; it has, in fact become naturalized in the southern states of the USA. 'Mermaid' is a famous offspring of this species and is much hardier. ZONES 4–11.

Rosa foetida *(right)*

syn. *Rosa lutea*

AUSTRIAN BRIAR, AUSTRIAN YELLOW

This shrub grows to 8 ft (2.4 m) tall with smooth young growth and numerous slender, straight thorns on reddish brown older wood that ages silvery gray. The foliage is dull, with light to grayish green leaves. The rich golden yellow flowers, with prominent stamens, appear singly in spring. It has quite an overpowering fragrance, and is prone to black spot. '**Bicolor**' (syn. *Rosa lutea punicea*), the Austrian copper, has single flowers with a golden yellow reverse, the yellow showing through the thin petal texture of the intense nasturtium red of the flower face. '**Persiana**', the Persian yellow, has very double, cupped, paler yellow flowers than the species that open flat. ZONES 4–9.

R

Rosa glauca *(left)*
syn. *R. rubrifolia*

This rose makes an open dense shrub of around 6 ft (1.8 m) tall. The arching, reddish purple, thornless shoots are well furnished with broadly oval, heavily serrated, grayish purple leaves that are made up of five to nine leaflets. Borne in small clusters, the flowers are little more than 1 in (25 mm) wide, single, star-like in formation and soft lilac-pink in color with soft creamy yellow stamens. They appear in early sum-mer, and have no scent. The hips are at first red, then turn to burnished coppery purple in autumn. **ZONES 4–10.**

Rosa gigantea *(right)*
syn. *R. × odorata gigantea*

A medium to tall climber up to 20 ft (6 m), taller in its natural habitat, *R. gigantea* has long, arching branches of purplish green that are randomly armed with hooked thorns. The leaves are made up of seven prominently veined, long and nar-row leaflets. The flowers are white, very large—up to 4 in (10 cm) in diameter at their best—sweetly scented and are produced in early summer. Yellowy orange, pear-shaped hips about 1 in (25 mm) long appear after the blooms. This tender species is unsuitable for cold climates. It is an ancestor of the early Tea Roses. **ZONES 4–11.**

Rosa gallica *(below left)*
syns 'French Rose', 'Rose of Provins'

Growing to 3 ft (1 m), this free-suckering rose's dark green stems are almost thornless, and the foliage is light green, of medium to small size, somewhat rounded in shape and each leaf is made up of just five leaflets. The single flowers are only slightly scented and are produced in early summer. They are about 2½ in (6 cm) in diameter, clear mid-pink in color and have pro-nounced yellow stamens. The hips are a dull reddish color when ripe, held upright and are roundly urn shaped. *R. gallica* was important in the early development of the cultivated rose. **ZONES 5–11.**

R

Rosa moyesii *(below)*

A sturdy and angular shrub to 10 ft (3 m) tall, this species has strong, reddish brown stems with numerous sharp, stout thorns often arranged in pairs. Each leaf has 7 to 11, mid-green to grayish green, serrated and oval leaflets. The flowers, which appear in early summer, are arranged in small groups and are dark glowing red in color and have very prominent golden colored stamens; the petals are often dusted with their profuse pollen. The hips appear in late summer and are drooping, flagon shaped and bright orange-red in color. ZONES 4–10.

Rosa moschata *(above)*
syn. 'The Musk Rose'

A tall shrub or small climber to 10 ft (3 m) tall with firm, grayish green wood, *R. moschata* is sparsely populated with brown, hooked thorns. The gray-green leaves are soft to touch, downy on the undersides, especially on its prominent veins, inclined to droop and are made up of 5 to 7 leaflets. The flowers are fragrant and creamy white, with well-spaced single petals; on hot days they reflex backwards. Each flower is about 1½ in (4 cm) across and loosely arranged in large corymbs that first appear in late summer, and repeat well into autumn. ZONES 4–10.

Rosa laevigata *(right)*
syn. 'The Cherokee Rose'

This evergreen climber grows up to 15 ft (5 m) tall in warm climates. It needs protection or a sheltered warm position in cold areas. The mid-green stems have well-spaced, broad-hooked, reddish thorns and glossy dark green leaves that are made up of just 3 leaflets. The scented flowers, which appear in late spring for a short season only, are large, single, creamy white in color and have prominent yellow stamens. Very bristly, oval to pear-shaped, orange hips follow the flowers, but quickly change to brown with age. ZONES 4–10.

R

Rosa rugosa *(left)*

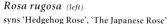

syns 'Hedgehog Rose', 'The Japanese Rose'

This rose makes a dense, free-branching shrub to a height of 8 ft (2.5 m). Its fawny brown stems are heavily endowed with sharp, similar colored thorns. The leaves usually have 7 to 9 leaflets that are dark green and semi-glossy, broadly oval and serrated, often appearing wrinkled. They change to shades of rich yellow in the autumn. The single, scented flowers, produced solitarily or several together, open to 2½ in (6.5 cm) across and are bright deep pink in color with soft yellow stamens. They continue to appear from early summer through to autumn. The hips are large, globose, bright red and held on short stalks and are a major ornamental feature of this species and of its many forms and hybrids. **ZONES 3–10.**

Rosa sericea subsp. **omeiensis** f. **pteracantha** *(right)*

syn. *Rosa omeiensis* f. *pteracantha*

MALTESE CROSS ROSE

This upright shrub grows to 10 ft (3 m) in height with strong arching canes that are adorned with an almost continuous array of large red-winged thorns, popular in flower arrangements. The new wood is gray-green with a reddish hue and is often covered with fine hairs, while the foliage has a fern-like appearance. The 4-petalled white flowers are borne singly at the nodes. The hips are oval and red. **ZONES 6–10.**

R

Rosa spinosissima *(left)*

syn. *Rosa pimpinellifolia*

SCOTCH BRIAR, BURNET ROSE,
SCOTS ROSE

This species forms a low, suckering thicket up to 3 ft (1 m) tall with bristles and prickles the full length of the stems. The smooth leaflets are small and fern-like with good autumn coloring. The prolific, single, spring to early summer flowers are creamy white often shaded pink, and have golden-yellow stamens. The round hips are purple to shiny black and make almost as good a display as the flowers. **ZONES 4–9.**

Rosa willmottiae
(right)

Wider than tall, this shrub will attain a height of about 10 ft (3 m) in good soil. It produces long thin shoots that are purplish red in color and often covered in grayish bloom that is armed with tiny bristles and sharp prickles. The leaves are made up of 3 to 9, small and grayish, heavily serrated, oval leaflets. The flowers, which are borne all along the branches, are single, purplish pink and slightly scented, first appearing in early summer. Small, orange-red, pear-shaped hips follow. ZONES 3–11.

ROSA, HYBRIDS

Rose hybrids cover a range of classifications within both the Old Garden Roses and the Modern Garden Roses. The majority of the hybrids featured here fall into the classifications of the Large-flowered/Hybrid Teas and the Cluster-flowered/Floribundas, although there are numerous other rose types featured as well.

Rosa 'Abraham Darby' *(below)*
syns 'Abraham', 'Country Darby', AUScot

The cup-formed, very large flowers of 'Abraham Darby' appear in small clusters; they are a peachy pink/apricot blend and have a strong, pronounced fragrance. A Modern Shrub Rose, it has dark green foliage and bushy growth that spreads slightly but is well shaped and tall. It enjoys moderate resistance to disease but can be susceptible to rust. Popular in a shrub border, it is repeat-flowering and was named after one of the founders of the Industrial Revolution. It was introduced by Austin, UK, in 1985. ZONES 4–9.

R

Rosa 'Albéric Barbier' *(left)*

This very popular once-blooming Rambler has many uses—as a climber, as a tree and even as a ground cover. It has been used effectively as a weeping standard. Its creamy white flowers, rather large for a Rambler, have a yellow center, and the pliable, glossy branches are dotted with flower clusters outlined against the dark foliage. The vigorous, thin canes can be easily trained, while no real pruning is needed. The apple fragrance in early summer is strong, and blooms appear on lateral shoots as well as new ones. 'Albéric Barbier' does well in the shade and can grow to 20 ft (6 m) in a year. It was raised by the Barbier nursery in Orléans and dates from 1900. ZONES 4–10.

Rosa 'Alba Maxima' *(left)*

syns *Rosa alba maxima,* 'Great Double White', 'Maxima', 'The Jacobite Rose', 'Cheshire Rose'

This is the creamiest of all the Albas. A popular rose for centuries, dating from pre-1500, it grows to a large bush, reaching 8 ft (2.4 m) with a sparse habit. The white flowers are 3–4 in (8–10 cm) in diameter, opening flat with a faint buff edge and a lovely fragrance. Pale, gray-green foliage covers the canes, which have a few large prickles. 'Alba Maxima' flowers in summer, is disease resistant and needs little pruning. ZONES 3–9.

Rosa 'Albertine' *(left)*

'Albertine' has been popular since it was introduced by Barbier, France, in 1921. A very vigorous Large-flowered Climber with striking deep green, almost purple stems and foliage, it has semi-lax stems that require continuous securing as the plant grows. It does well on pergolas, while a position on a wall in full sun can encourage a magnificent plant. The heavily scented flowers are deep pink to salmon with hints of copper, but sadly they flower only for about 3 weeks in mid-summer. The cupped blooms are medium sized and appear in clusters. The foliage is prone to mildew but not to its detriment. ZONES 4–9.

R

Rosa 'America' *(right)*
syn. JACclam

This Large-flowered Climber flowers very freely in summer, with a reasonably good repeat bloom. The medium to large-sized blooms are full and prettily formed with overlapping petals, opening cupped from high-centered buds, and well scented. They appear in open clusters in a warm shade of coral-salmon, and pale as they age. The growth is vigorous and free branching, while the leaves are of medium size, semi-glossy and reasonably healthy. It makes an excellent climber of lower than average height so is suitable for walls, fences and pillars, and it does not resent being pruned to form a big shrub. It was introduced by the US breeder Warriner in 1976. ZONES 4–9.

Rosa 'Amadis' *(below)*
syns 'Crimson Boursault', 'Elegans'

Of the 50 Boursaults listed 200 years ago, there are only a few left. However, 'Amadis' has survived, surely because of its elegant, upright posture and large, cupped, semi-double flowers. They are deep crimson and purple and are borne in large, long-lasting clusters. The young wood is whitish green; the old wood is red-brown, and there are no prickles. Although it has neither perfume nor fruits, its deeply serrated leaves of brilliant green add to its winning traits. It blooms early in the season on old growth, and partial shade brings out the subtle colors. It was introduced by Laffay, France, in 1829. ZONES 5–10.

Rosa 'Alchymist' *(above)*
syns 'Alchemist', 'Alchymiste'

'Alchymist' is an extremely vigorous, upright Modern Shrub Rose with glossy bronze foliage that is very healthy. Its round buds produce very large, cupped flowers that are extremely fragrant; they are a yellow shaded orange color that is officially described as an apricot blend. It makes a good shrub or a short climber. It was introduced by Kordes, Germany, in 1956. ZONES 3–9.

Rosa 'Archiduc Joseph' *(left)*

The buds of 'Archiduc Joseph' are dark pink, open-ing lighter and then turning copper, with strong pink overtones as well. Thin canes with glossy foli-age are sometimes not strong enough to hold the quartered blooms upright. Colors vary depending on the weather and the location: the petals become purple-orange in humid climates but rose and pink in dry, hot weather. The canes are brownish red with dark, ashy green leaves. This is one of the heaviest blooming Tea Roses and is repeat-flowering. It was introduced by Nabonnand, France, in 1892. **ZONES 7–8.**

Rosa 'Auckland Metro' *(below)*
syns 'Métro', 'Precious Michelle', MACbucpal

The flowers of this Large-flowered/Hybrid Tea are made up of many overlapping petals, giving them a camellia-like appearance. They are creamy blush to white, well scented, and often produced in large trusses with the individual stems long enough to cut, a purpose for which the rose is well suited because the flowers are at their most beautiful when fully open. It is repeat-flowering. The plant is sturdy and bushy, below average height and well furnished with glossy dark leaves, and good for bedding. It does best in warmer climates and is popular in New Zealand and Australia. It was introduced by McGredy, New Zealand, in 1988. **ZONES 5–9.**

Rosa 'Arthur Bell' *(below)*

This most satisfying Cluster-flowered/Floribunda Rose has flowers that are clear yellow, bright in bud, opening paler and finishing almost primrose and transforming from pointed buds to pretty cups along the way. The 20 or so petals are firm and well able to withstand wet weather, which must have been needful on the Ulster breeder's nursery. The flower clusters are held above the foliage on up-right, stiff stems, and the vigorous bush is clothed with shiny bright green leaves. The sweetly scented flowers repeat their bloom through summer and autumn, making this an excellent choice for a bed or group. They are also used for cutting and exhi-bition, as they last well. It was introduced by McGredy, UK, in 1965. **ZONES 4–9.**

R

Rosa 'Bantry Bay' (right)

Through summer and autumn this Large-flowered Climber always seems to have something to show. The loosely double cupped flowers are deepish rose pink, a warm and kindly shade, showing their stamens as they open; they have a light fragrance. They are borne in clusters and appear at different levels on the plant, which clothes itself effectively in dark green foliage. This vigorous, free-branching rose is an excellent garden performer of restrained growth, with a good health record and suitable for all purposes. It was introduced by McGredy, UK, in 1967. **ZONES 4–9.**

Rosa 'Autumn Damask' (below)

syns 'Quatre Saisons', 'Four Seasons Rose', 'Rose of Castile', *Rosa damascena semperflorens*

The shapely pink buds open to a crumpled bed of blowzy petals, darker pink in the center. The yellowish green serrated leaves cover a sparse and open plant. If it is happy, the rose will be covered with strongly perfumed blooms. It flowers in early summer and again in autumn and does not like any shade. This Damask Rose makes an attractive container plant and contributes a good share of perfume to potpourri. It dates from pre-1633. **ZONES 4–10.**

Rosa 'Autumn Delight' (above)

The buds are pointed and apricot-yellow in color, opening to near single flowers of very soft creamy yellow with beautiful stamens. The flowers fade quickly to white in hot weather, but are particularly beautiful in autumn when huge heads of 30–50 blooms appear on strong shoots. These are quite long lasting and retain their color well. It forms a large shrub with dark green, leathery, disease-resistant foliage and very few thorns and is useful for beds, borders, hedges and for planting in groups among perennials. It was introduced by Bentall, UK, in 1933. **ZONES 3–9.**

R

Rosa 'Blue Moon' *(left)*
syns 'Blue Monday', 'Mainzer Fastnacht', 'Sissi', TANnacht

This Large-flowered/Hybrid Tea Rose is deservedly the most commercially successful of the 'blue' roses, being very close to the blue side of lavender. The flowers are large and full-petalled, with high centers and good symmetry of form, and they last well, finally opening cupped to show the stamens. Usually there is one flower on the long stems, which makes them excellent for cutting. They are sweetly fragrant, and are produced through summer and autumn. The plant grows vigorously but it is somewhat splayed and reluctant to make new wood, and has a rather sparse cover of deep green foliage. Generally the plant is healthy and can overcome occasional mildew and black spot, but it is liable to die back in hard winters. It was introduced by Tantau, Germany, in 1965. ZONES 4–9.

Rosa 'Buff Beauty' *(below)*

This is a Modern Shrub Rose for the enthusiast, a desirable garden item even when not in bloom, thanks to its gracefully rounded plant habit and ample covering of handsome dark shiny leaves. In summer and again in autumn it produces trusses of pale apricot blooms that show up tellingly against this dark background. The flowers have many petals that open out in the shape of powder puffs, showing charming muddled centers. They carry hints of buff yellow as well as apricot, have a pleasing fragrance and withstand bad weather well. It grows to average height or more, is excellent in borders or to plant against a low wall, and has a good health record. It was introduced by Bentall, UK, in 1939. ZONES 4–9.

Rosa 'Botanica' *(above)*
syn. TOMboy

'Botanica' has beautiful pink flowers with just a touch of lilac. These are borne in large clusters and have a delicious fruity perfume. What sets this glorious rose apart from the other Cluster-flowered Roses is its ability to produce blooms in profusion. The foliage is healthy, matt and medium green on an extremely vigorous, disease-resistant bush with a slightly spreading habit. It is repeat-flowering. It can reach between 3–4 ft (1–1.2 m) high and about 3 ft (1 m) wide. It was bred by George Thomson of Mount Barker in South Australia, and named for the successful plant book *Botanica* which was published in 1997. ZONES 5–9.

R

Rosa 'Capitaine John Ingram' *(right)*

This Moss Rose has one of the richest colors in good weather. The pine-scented buds are well covered with reddish, sticky, dark greeny brown moss. They open to pompon, flat blooms that change color from dark purple to velvety crimson to reddish purple. There may be recurring bloom in late summer. The recurving blossoms have a button eye. Attaining about 5 ft (1.5 m) in good soils, this is a vigorous, dense shrub with many small prickles on its stems and lots of dark brownish red bristles. With its numerous dark green leaves of medium size, it makes an effective hedge. It was introduced by Laffay, France, in 1854. ZONES 4–9.

Rosa 'Cécile Brünner' *(left)*

syns 'Mme Cécile Brünner', 'Mlle Cécile Brünner', 'Mignon', 'Sweetheart Rose', 'Maltese Rose'

This long-lived Polyantha, which is classed as a China Rose by some authorities, patently has its origins in Asia, although authorities are divided between *Rosa multiflora* and *R. chinensis*. Almost thornless, it repeatedly produces large clusters of very small, perfectly shaped pink blooms. The long, pointed bud opens to pale, silvery pink blossoms. The perfectly formed, miniature blooms are double and rise above light red peduncles. The scent is sweet and slightly spicy. It is a small bush with sparse, dull green foliage of 3–5 leaflets, but it is very healthy. The shrub is low growing, which makes it ideal for small gardens or small beds. It was introduced by Ducher, France, in 1881. ZONES 4–9.

Rosa 'Casino' *(right)*

syn. 'Gerbe d'Or', MACca

This Large-flowered Climber really is one of the best yellow-flowered climbing roses around; it is good to grow on a warm wall, and its floriferousness is quite remarkable. The soft yellow, double, quartered blooms are well formed, very full and fragrant; they hold their large, old-fashioned shape well and usually repeat superbly: up to 5 times per year. The hips, if deadheading is not completed, are large, round and attractive. 'Casino' also makes a good cut flower. The foliage is dark green and healthy. Growers in regions with hard winters may be discouraged from growing this rose because it likes warm climates. It has not received the attention that it deserves. It was introduced by McGredy, New Zealand, in 1963. ZONES 5–9.

R

Rosa 'Charles de Mills' *(left)*
syns 'Charles Mills', 'Charles Wills', 'Bizarre Triomphant'

Often seen in photographs as the 'perfect Old Garden Rose,' this Gallica is the largest of its family. The flowers, which are made up of a multitude of petals, are quite large, and at their best often exceed 3 in (8 cm) in diameter. They emerge in mid-summer from flat-topped buds, at first cupped and then flatly saucer shaped; their color is rich glowing purple with subtle crimson highlights. The petals, which have the feel of textured velvet, are only slightly scented. The arching canes reach 6 ft (1.8 m) on an erect bush with very few prickles and dark green leaves. It was first grown in The Netherlands, and dates back to pre-1700. ZONES 4–9.

Rosa 'Champion of the World' *(below)*
syns 'Mrs DeGraw', 'Mrs de Graw'

This Hybrid Perpetual Rose, which needs plenty of time to establish itself, is a vigorous repeat-flowering shrub that likes to sprawl. The rose pink blooms are double, large and fragrant. The light green foliage is small, and the prickles are light brown. It grows to 4 ft (1.2 m) and makes a good pot plant. It was introduced by Woodhouse, UK, in 1894. ZONES 5–9.

R

Rosa 'Cabbage Rose' *(above)*
syn. *Rosa × centifolia*, 'Centifolia'

This Centifolia Rose can attain a height of some 6 ft (1.8 m) in good soil, producing long strong shoots with numerous reddish thorns and prickles. Its leaves are coarse, both in appearance and to touch, and are grayish green in color. The flowers, which appear in early to mid-summer, are arranged in small clusters and emerge from tight feathery buds. They are flattish, very double and very fragrant, and are a deep glowing pink in color. It was introduced pre-1596. ZONES 4–9.

Rosa 'Commandant Beaurepaire' *(right)*
syn. 'Panachée d'Angers'

This is an elegant plant in any situation, and is often proclaimed the best of striped roses. The rose pink blooms are streaked with purple-violet and marble white. They are cupped and upright and offer a strong fragrance. The foliage is light green with long, pointed leaves and the plant has prickly canes that need to be thinned after blooming has finished. 'Commandant Beaurepaire' does well in cool weather in the shade where it can reach 5 ft (1.5 m) high, which makes it a good candidate for a hedge. A Bourbon Rose, it was introduced by Moreau and Robert, France, in 1879. **ZONES 5–9.**

Rosa 'Complicata'
(bottom)
syn. 'Ariana d'Algier'

This is a broad, dense, vigorous Gallica attaining a height of 6 ft (1.8 m) or even more if given something to scramble on or into, such as a small tree. It has strong, gray-green, partially thorned stems that are abundantly clothed in large, durable foliage. The flowers appear in early summer only and are up to 4 in (10 cm) in diameter at their best. Very bright, clear pink and single, they are moderately fragrant and are considerably enhanced with a lovely boss of bright creamy yellow stamens. It is very healthy, tolerant of impoverished soils and very hardy. **ZONES 5–9.**

Rosa 'Compassion' *(left)*
syn. 'Belle de Londres'

This is the most popular climbing rose in England. Throughout summer and autumn, 'Compassion' is completely repeat-flowering. It bears large salmon-pink, apricot-shaded blooms that are filled with about 36 petals. They are borne either singly or in clusters of 3 amid the large, dark green, leathery foliage. The plant itself is an extremely healthy Large-flowered Climber with reasonably vigorous growth and a bushy, branching habit that can be propagated by budding. It was introduced by Harkness, UK, in 1973. **ZONES 4–9.**

R

Rosa 'Constance Spry'

(bottom)

syn. 'Constanze Spry'

For anyone who wishes to grow roses, 'Constance Spry' would be a premier choice for every garden that has the room for this exceptional, lax-growing, rampant plant with large, soft luminous pink, cup-shaped, double flowers. Being a cross between a Modern Cluster-flowered Rose and an Old Garden Gallica Rose, it is not repeat-flowering, but this is not really a drawback because the single summer blooms are long lasting, spectacular and have a delicious fragrance of myrrh, a feature that has been passed on to many of its progeny. The growth is covered with large, dark green foliage that is very winter hardy and has a good health record. It is useful in groups at the back of a mixed border, but because it can be quite sprawling it is better trained as a climber on walls to attain its best. It was introduced by Austin, UK, in 1961. ZONES 4–9.

Rosa 'Deep Secret'

(left)

syn. 'Mildred Scheel'

The very deep crimson flowers of this Large-flowered/Hybrid Tea are double with 40 petals, large and very fragrant; they appear continuously throughout summer and autumn. It has upright growth to medium height and glossy dark green foliage, and is a good subject for a bedding scheme. It was introduced by Tantau, Germany, in 1977. ZONES 4–9.

Rosa 'Comte de Chambord' *(center)*

This is a sturdy Portland Rose to 4 ft (1.2 m) with strong, grayish green stems well populated with reddish prickles and thorns. The light gray-green foliage is serrated and slightly downy. The flowers are borne in small clusters or singly, and in great profusion from early summer to autumn. In the late stage of bud they are beautifully high centered and scrolled, then later densely packed with petals; they go through a cupped stage to become fully flat, often quartered and up to 3 in (8 cm) across when fully open. These powerfully perfumed flowers are dense rich pink, with hints of lilac and lavender. 'Comte de Chambord' is ideal for group planting; it also makes a good hedge and is excellent as a container plant. It was introduced by Robert and Moreau, France, in 1863. Some think this rose is actually 'Mme Boll' (Boll, France, 1859). ZONES 5–9.

Rosa 'Dublin Bay' *(right)*
syn. MACdub

One of the best red Large-flowered Climbers available today, 'Dublin Bay' has oval buds and well-shaped, intensely bright red, fragrant flowers produced singly and in clusters. The repeat-flowering is outstanding: no sooner has one crop of flowers finished than another is on the way. It has dark green glossy foliage and good disease resistance. It is one of the most popular Climbers in New Zealand, also gaining great acclaim in Australia. It was introduced by McGredy, New Zealand, in 1975. ZONES 4–11.

Rosa 'Echo' *(above)*
syn. 'Baby Tausendschön'

This offspring of a very popular China Rose does best in partial shade. It has prolific, large, semi-double blooms that are cupped, and change from white to deep pink. The outer curved petals shape the rose like a bowl. The large trusses of blooms cover the strong, erect stems, which can reach 3 ft (1 m) on a compact bush with glossy foliage. It is prone to mildew where there is no air circulation. There are no prickles. The shrub needs deadheading during its flowering from summer until autumn. It is an ideal subject for a container or the border, and it also makes a long-lasting cut flower. It was introduced by Lambert, Germany, in 1914. ZONES 4–9.

Rosa 'Double Delight' *(below)*
syn. ANDeli

This very bushy Large-flowered/Hybrid Tea has large and double, high-centered blooms that are unique and immensely popular. They are creamy white turning to strawberry red, have a considerable spicy scent and appear from spring to autumn. It is a fine bedding rose although its disease resistance is suspect. It has an upright and spreading growth habit. It was introduced by Swim and Ellis, USA, in 1977. **'Climbing Double Delight'** (AROclidd; syn. 'Grimpant Double Delight'; Christensen, USA, 1982) has precisely the same coloring as the bush variety. Summer flowering, it grows well on walls. ZONES 4–9.

R

Rosa 'Elina' *(left)*
syn. 'Peaudouce', DICjana

This Large-flowered/Hybrid Tea is a strong, vigorous, repeat-flowering bush with excellent dense, glossy dark green, disease-resistant foliage that acts as a foil to the huge, magnificently formed deep cream blooms. The flowers, which are often 6 in (15 cm) across and have 35 petals, last particularly well when picked and are beautiful at all stages of development from bud to full bloom, forming perfect exhibition subjects. The first flush is a little later than most varieties, a bonus that extends the spring flowering season, and flower production is excellent. The flowers have a slight fragrance. It was introduced by Dickson, UK, in 1983. **ZONES 4–9.**

Rosa 'Evelyn Fison' *(right)*
syn. 'Irish Wonder', MACev

'Evelyn Fison' is a compact, robust, repeat-flowering Cluster-flowered/Floribunda with plentiful glossy dark green, disease-resistant foliage. The slightly fragrant blooms are large, to 3 in (8 cm) across, and are produced singly and in well-spaced clusters of up to 20. The buds are well shaped and open to long-lasting, semi-double flowers of excellent substance, the scarlet color of which does not fade in heat or cold. The growth is rather thorny, but this variety well deserved its gold medal and is still widely grown today in spite of stiff opposition from more modern varieties. It was introduced by McGredy, UK, in 1962. **ZONES 4–9.**

Rosa 'Eyepaint' *(left)*
syns 'Eye Paint', 'Tapis Persan', MACeye

This Cluster-flowered/Floribunda can be classed as hand painted since the bright red, single flowers with 5–6 petals and a white eye and golden stamens have streaks of white through them. It is repeat-flowering and the medium-sized flowers come in large and small clusters. Strong in growth and having disease-free, plentiful glossy foliage, it makes a good border or hedge, can be used in groups plantings and even as a short pillar rose. It was introduced by McGredy, New Zealand, in 1975. **ZONES 4–9.**

Rosa 'Ferdinand Pichard' *(right)*

One of the last Hybrid Perpetuals put on the market, this striped, cupped rose has stayed on the bestseller list since its birth. The 25 scarlet, streaked, clear pink petals change to a blush purple as they age. The tight clusters are cupped and may reach 4 in (10 cm) across. It likes the sun, but very hot weather may crisp the blooms. It is a vigorous, tall, up-right, repeat-flowering bush that is suitable for a small garden; how-ever, if it is pegged down it will produce twice the amount of blooms. The foliage is smooth and light green. This rose makes an ef-fective hedge as long as it is deadheaded and fed well. It was introduced by Tanne, France, in 1921. ZONES 4–9.

Rosa 'Félicité Parmentier' *(below right)*

The fat buds of this Alba Rose have a trace of yellow before opening to reveal soft, flesh pink blossoms that are white at the edges, fading to almost white in hot climates. A magnificent cut flower, the petals appear to swirl in circles. After opening flat the dou-ble, sweetly scented blooms reflex during the late spring–early summer flowering. A compact, sturdy if slightly sprawling rose, it grows to 4 ft (1.2 m) with stout, moderately thorny stems and profuse light grayish green foliage. It is ideal for a small garden or to grow in containers, and is happiest in partial shade; it will do well in poor soil. The strong per-fume and its disease resistance make it a great land-scaping plant. It dates from pre-1834. ZONES 4–9.

Rosa 'Fantin-Latour' *(left)*

The sumptuous powdery pink blooms of this Centifolia Rose appear in mid-summer, and can be 3 in (8 cm) across when fully open. At first they are cupped; later the outer petals reflex to expose a central button of tightly packed smaller petals. The scent is in-toxicating and there are few prickles. The shrub usually reaches about 4 ft (1.2 m); if not pruned it can climb to 10 ft (3 m). Pruning after flowering in-creases the number of blooms for the following year. It is not bothered by hot, dry weather but doesn't get as big as it does when cooler, and it is prone to some mildew. ZONES 4–9.

R

Rosa 'Flower Carpet' *(left)*

syns 'Blooming Carpet', 'Emera', 'Emera Pavement', 'Heidetraum', 'Pink Flower Carpet', NOAtraum

This Modern Shrub makes a very good ground cover rose with deep pink globular flowers with 15 petals of good substance, borne in sprays of 10–25. There is a slight scent. The globular fruit are small and do not seem to inhibit any flowering if spent blooms are not removed, while the spring flowering is particularly profuse. If it gets too woody a hard winter prune every few years will bring back vigor without much loss of flower production. Black spot can occur in moist climates. It was introduced by Noack, Germany, in 1989. **ZONES 4–9.**

Rosa 'Francis E. Lester' *(right)*

'Francis E. Lester' is a very vigorous climbing Modern Shrub Rose growing to 13–16 ft (4–5 m) that has thorny stems and pliable canes. The blooms, which appear rather late in spring in large panicles of up to 60 blooms, are white flushed with pale pink, single, 2 in (5 cm) across and look like huge heads of apple blossom. The huge hips that follow the flowers also appear in big clusters and last right through winter as birds do not seem to like them. Some growers get repeat bloom, but this is not common. It is an excellent rose for growing into trees, where it can cascade downwards and show its huge sprays of flowers and hips to perfection. It was introduced by Lester Rose Gardens, USA, in 1946. **ZONES 4–9.**

Rosa 'Frau Dagmar Hartopp' *(left)*

syn. 'Fru Dagmar Hastrup'

This is an excellent Modern Shrub Rose that produces large single flowers of a very clear silvery pink continuously from spring until winter that show up very well against the healthy rich green wrinkled foliage. A short, stocky grower, it produces a large crop of bright red, round hips, the first lot ripening for Christmas and able to be used for Christmas decorations in lieu of holly, which of course is not in fruit in summer in the Southern Hemisphere. 'Frau Dagmar Hartopp' suckers and forms a small thicket if the bud union is planted below ground level. It makes a lovely low hedge when the flowers and fruit are on the bush at the one time, and it can also be planted in the woodland or shrub border as a foreground to large-growing species roses. It was introduced by Hastrup, Denmark, in 1914. **ZONES 3–9.**

R

Rosa 'Fritz Nobis' *(right)*

This rose produces arching branches and covers them with an abundance of leathery grayish green leaves, then produces a show of flower in summer that creates as lovely a shrub as you could find in any species. The blooms are like small-scale Large-flowered Roses in the young flower then open cupped. They are double, of medium size, are borne in clusters of up to 20 and are chiefly light rose and salmon-pink in color, though cream and yellow hints are also present. There is a pleasing fragrance, but, unfortunately, no extension of the flowering period beyond the first wonderful flush. For a shrubbery or mixed border this is a splendid rose to grow. It needs room, being about twice the size of an average shrub rose, and is remarkably healthy and hardy. It was introduced by Kordes, Germany, in 1940. **ZONES 4–9.**

Rosa 'Gertrude Jekyll' *(right)*
syn. AUSbord

The large full-petalled flowers of 'Gertrude Jekyll' open in the random fashion associated with Old Garden Roses, and the comparison is enhanced by their sweet scent and rich deep pink color. The flowering period extends right through summer and autumn. It is splendid in a mixed bed or border. In cool climates the plant grows vigorously to average height with a somewhat uneven and lanky habit, but in warm conditions it makes much taller growth and is best treated as a climber. It is well furnished with grayish green leaves. Classed a Modern Shrub Rose, it was introduced by Austin, UK, in 1986. **ZONES 4–9.**

Rosa 'Gold Fever' *(left)*
syn. MORfever

This repeat-flowering Miniature Rose has elegant, pointed buds that finally open to medium yellow blooms that age to a much lighter pale yellow. The cupped florets have 40–50 petals and a spicy fragrance. The blooms are usually borne one to a stem, but in early spring clusters can develop. They hold their color well in the heat. The foliage is of medium size, semi-glossy and has slender prickles, and the plant has a vigorous, compact, upright habit. It is ideal as a container-grown plant. It was introduced by Moore, USA, in 1990. **ZONES 4–11.**

R

Rosa 'Graham Thomas' (above)

syns 'English Yellow', 'Graham Stuart Thomas', AUSmas

'Graham Thomas' is a clear yellow, deeper in the heart of its cupped blooms, which are borne with remarkable freedom considering their size and full petallage. They are carried on long arching stems, which often bow over under their weight. There is a pleasant fragrance, and flowering continues through summer and autumn, making this a good garden shrub for a border; it can also make a fine standard. In cool climates it usually grows to average height, but in warmer countries it extends much further and can be treated as a climber on a wall, fence or tall pillar. It is classified as an English Rose and was introduced by Austin, UK, in 1983. **ZONES 4–9.**

Rosa 'Golden Showers' (below)

The virtues of 'Golden Showers' are its cheerful blooms, elegant in the young bud; the sweet scent of its wide opening semi-double flowers and the way they drop cleanly when they are done; its continuance in bloom almost without pause from summer to late autumn; its pleasing glossy foliage; its compliance in growing as far as gardeners wish it to, and not sulking however badly it is pruned; and its comparative smoothness, which makes it an easy rose to handle. Against the assets must be weighed the snags—the fleeting nature of the flowers, their loss of color as they age, and a tinge of seasonal mildew. However, this all-purpose Large-flowered Climber must be considered still a front rank rose. It was introduced by Lammerts, USA, in 1956. **ZONES 4–9.**

Rosa 'Golden Wings' (above)

Roy Shepherd was an eminent rose historian who died in 1962, and it is fitting that his inspiration lives on in this remarkable repeat-flowering Modern Shrub Rose. It produces large, pale yellow flowers with only a few petals that open like saucers, showing dark stamens. They look frail but in fact withstand wind and rain very well. Deadheading will help bring on more blooms. There is a light and pleasing scent, and for a mixed border this is an excellent healthy garden plant. The bush is vigorous and prickly, with many twiggy stems and light green leaves, and it grows to average height or more. It was introduced by Shepherd, USA, in 1956. **ZONES 4–9.**

R

Rosa 'Great Maiden's Blush' *(right)*

The blush pink flowers of this large, arching
Alba Rose are finely perfumed, the color aptly
described in the name. The foliage is grayish in
the Alba fashion. There is also a 'Small Maiden's
Blush', which was recorded and perhaps raised at
Kew Gardens in 1797. These roses are inclined to
sport variations, and there is a deeper-flowered
version named 'Cuisse de Nymphe Emué'. Thrips
and wet weather can damage this rose considerably. It dates from around 1400. ZONES 5–9.

Rosa 'Green Ice' *(above)*

This repeat-flowering Miniature Rose has white pointed
buds that open to white to
soft green flowers. These
small, double blooms are
complemented by equally
small, attractive, glossy foliage. The flower form is
decorative with the fully
open blooms reminiscent of
Old Garden Roses. Large
trusses of flowers start off
white with just a hint of pink
and as the blooms mature,
they gradually acquire an
attractive light green hue.
The plant has a sprawling
and spreading habit, which
makes it an excellent choice
for a hanging basket. It was
introduced by Moore, USA,
in 1971. ZONES 5–11.

Rosa 'Hannah Gordon' *(below)*
syn. 'Raspberry Ice', KORweiso

The flowers of this Cluster-flowered/Floribunda
Rose are a delightful combination of blush and
cherry-pink, the petals being mostly blush with a
generous decoration of the deeper color along
their rims. They are well proportioned, and develop from plump buds into double, cupped
blooms that are quite large when fully open and
yield a pleasant light fragrance. Flowering continues through summer and autumn. This is a useful
rose for a bed or border, and the flowers last well
if cut. This is a vigorous plant with a rather open
habit, growing to less than average height, and has
large, dark green leaves. It was introduced by
Kordes, Germany, in 1983. ZONES 4–9.

R

Rosa 'Henri Martin'
(left)

syn. 'Red Moss'

The double flowers of this Moss Rose, which are loosely arranged in large clusters, open flat and are up to 3 in (8 cm) across. They are rich claret red to crimson and pale slightly to a softer red before going over. They are very fragrant. It is a vigorous, wide-growing shrub to 6 ft (1.8 m) with few thorns but many soft bristles on gracefully arching stems. The foliage is rich green, as is the moss on the flower buds and calyces; the moss is aromatic and smells like balsam. 'Henri Martin' does not mind poor soil, but needs space to develop as it can get considerably broad. It needs support of some kind, such as a tripod or trellis, to give its best. It was introduced by Laffay, France, in 1863. ZONES 4–9.

Rosa 'Helmut Schmidt'
(below right)

syns 'Goldsmith', 'Simba', KORbelma

The large, pointed buds of this Large-flowered/Hybrid Tea Rose give promise of big flowers to come, and they are beauties. The urn-shaped, young blooms develop high centers around which the outer petals are arranged with wonderful symmetry. They usually appear one per stem, making the variety an excellent cutting rose, especially as the blooms hold their shape and last well. It is a good rose for general garden use, flowering through summer and autumn though tending to produce a flush of bloom followed by a pause. The plant grows neat and upright to below average height, with matt green foliage. It was introduced by Kordes, Germany, in 1979. ZONES 4–9.

Rosa 'Ipsilanté' *(right)*
syn. 'Ypsilante'

A popular Gallica, this rose offers a strong, rich
perfume in addition to its attractive mauve-pink
flowers. Round, fat buds open in mid-summer to
large, cupped, double blooms with crinkled petals that twist in different directions. The outer
petals fade with age. This sprawling, vigorous
shrub will reach 5 ft (1.5 m) and has dense,
rough, dark green foliage and red prickles. It
does well on poor soil and is disease resistant.
This variety was named for the Greek patriot and
general Prince Alexandr Ypsilante who lived
from 1792–1828. It was introduced by Vibert,
France, in 1821. **ZONES 4–9.**

Rosa 'Irish Rich Marbled' *(left)*

This Scots Rose has soft, rounded, pink buds that
are followed by deep pink flowers with a lilac-
pink reverse. Three rows of petals outline a yellow
center around the stamens, and the outer petals
reflex. As they age, the blooms fade towards the
center. There is a musky scent. It is a very prickly
shrub to 3 ft (1 m) high with small, dark, ferny
leaves and round, black hips. It suckers freely and
should be planted either in a container or where it
will not interfere with other plants. **ZONES 4–9.**

Rosa 'Iceberg' *(right)*
syns 'Fée des Neiges',
'Schneewittchen', KORbin

The flowers are semi-double and
well formed and pure white. The
blooms are produced in clusters
of up to 15 per spray and they
have a moderate but not overpowering rose fragrance. This repeat-
flowering Cluster-flowered/
Floribunda can be used as a bedding plant for massed display; it is
almost entirely resistant to mildew
and suffers only mildly from black
spot. All in all it is one of the best
roses produced this century.
It was introduced by Kordes,
Germany, in 1958. **ZONES 4–9.**

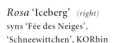

Rosa 'Ispahan' *(below)*
syn. 'Pompon des Princes', 'Rose d'Isfahan'

The flowers of this Damask Rose appear in clusters in early summer and continue through to late summer. They are full and almost modern looking, at first being high centered and shapely and later becoming loosely double and muddled when fully open, but always with the most delicate texture. The fragrant blooms are up to 2½ in (6.5 cm) across and are consistently bright clear pink. The bush can reach about 5 ft (1.5 m) with an erect and fairly dense habit. The stems are grayish green and there are few thorns. The foliage is smooth, semi-glossy and mid-green with hints of gray. It is seldom afflicted by any disease other than an occasional touch of mildew. ZONES 4–9.

Rosa 'Jacqueline du Pré' *(above)*
syn. HARwanna

This Modern Shrub Rose, which keeps flowering for the whole season until the weather stops it, has clusters of loose blooms that appear freely. Cupped and semi-double, they show golden yellow stamens well when fully open and are a creamy white with a blushing of pink in cooler weather that is more pronounced in the bud than in the full-blown flower. They have a pronounced musk scent. The moderately disease-resistant bush is average height and has a good covering of glossy green leaves. It was introduced by Harkness, UK, in 1988. ZONES 4–10.

Rosa 'Jeanne LaJoie' *(below left)*

This popular, repeat-flowering Climbing Miniature Rose has long pointed buds which open to medium pink, exhibition type blooms. The flowers are double with 40 or more petals, and have just a hint of fragrance. The foliage is small, glossy, dark green and embossed. The tall canes can be easily trained to assume the lateral horizontal position to optimize bloom production along the cane. Trained on a fence or trellis, the bloom production is staggering! The non-fading florets have good form and substance making it one of the best climbers around. It has a vigorous nature and is an excellent choice when a huge display of color against a wall is desired. It was introduced by Sima, USA, in 1975. ZONES 5–11.

Rosa 'Just Joey' *(right)*

This is an ever-popular variety that will still be so for many years to come. It has big, loose, double flowers that are an orange blend. and they are usually found in small clusters. They are well recommended both for cutting or for garden display. The bush is sprawling and grows to medium height, while the leaves are dark green. It is hard to compare 'Just Joey' with other Large-flowered Roses, as the richness of the flower and the looseness of the form make it so exciting and unusual. It was introduced by Cant, UK, in 1972. **ZONES 5–10.**

Rosa 'Lady Hillingdon'
(right)

Popular around the world, this Tea Rose offers a wide range of colors during its extended blooming period. The long, pointed buds open to flat, deep apricot-yellow blooms that fade in the sun. The large, thin petals are semi-double and hang down in a blowzy fashion. There are attractive stamens, a few prickles and a strong, tea fragrance. Red-bronze when young, the somewhat sparse, attractive foliage lines the thin canes. It is one of the healthiest of roses and is a lovely cut flower. It was introduced by Lowe and Shawyer, UK, in 1910. **ZONES 5–10.**

R

Rosa 'Loving Memory' *(left)*
syns 'Burgund 81', 'Red Cedar',
KORgund 81

This Large-flowered/Hybrid Tea Rose is one of the best red garden and exhibition roses available. The tall plant produces long stems carrying large abundant, semi-glossy, rich green foliage. The well-formed buds open slowly to huge full blooms with 40 symmetrically arranged petals that are high centered with excellent exhibition form. There is a slight fragrance and disease resistance is particularly good. The bush is rather too tall for bedding but is excellent for the back of a rose border; it can also be used as a very tall hedge. It was introduced by Kordes, Germany, in 1981. **ZONES 5–10.**

Rosa 'Leander' *(below)*
syn. AUSlea

An English Rose, 'Leander' has pink to apricot flowers, more intense in the center depths. They are darker in bud. In terms of growth it is very large, especially in warm climates, where it can reach half as tall again as an average shrub rose or be supported and grown as a sizeable climber on a wall, fence or pillar. It therefore needs careful placement so that it has enough room. The blooms are scented, are borne in wide sprays on slim stems and give of their best in summer, for the production of later flowers is limited. It has a somewhat open growth habit and smooth, mid-green foliage. It was introduced by Austin, UK, in 1982. **ZONES 4–9.**

Rosa 'Lamarque' *(above)*
syns 'General Lamarque', 'The Marshal'

An amateur hybridizer raised this valuable, repeat-flowering Noisette Rose in a window box in Angers, France, little knowing that it would become one of the most popular ramblers in rose history. The high-centered buds are followed by pure white, double blooms with a lemon-yellow center. The large, full, loose flowers have muddled centers and are pendulous. The violet fragrance is very strong, especially in the sun. Once established, this hardy climber will grow 20 ft (6 m) in a single season. The long, trailing canes are covered with smooth, gray-green foliage and there are small, hooked, red prickles. It is quite lovely on a trellis or large arch. It was introduced by Maréchal, France, in 1830. **ZONES 4–10.**

Rosa 'Loving Touch' *(right)*

This Miniature Rose has double, fragrant flowers
with 25 petals, which are a wonderful deep apricot in cool climates and a lighter apricot in hot
climates. The large flowers are high centered and
are borne one to a stem or in small clusters of
3–5. It has attractive foliage on a well-rounded,
healthy, disease-resistant bush. The repeat-
flowering is very fast on a vigorous and easy to
maintain plant. It was introduced by Jolly, USA,
in 1983. **ZONES 5–11.**

Rosa 'Maigold' *(center)*
syn. 'Maygold'

This Modern Shrub can be used as a shrub or as a
climbing rose. The flowers appear very early. The
semi-double blooms are a rich orange-bronze, and
have only 14 petals. They are large, 4 in (10 cm)
across, cupped and very fragrant. The upright
growth is very thorny, and there are next to no
flowers after the initial burst. The glossy foliage can
be susceptible to black spot. This rose holds its color
best in cool climates; it is fleeting but lovely in warm
areas and heralds the rose season. It was introduced
by Kordes, Germany, in 1953. **ZONES 4–11.**

Rosa 'Margaret Merril'
(below right)
syn. HARkuly

This is a remarkable rose, as its many
awards testify. The double, high-
centered, white flowers have a faint
blush tint in the center. There are
28 petals. It is large for a Cluster-
flowered Rose, being up to 4 in
(10 cm) across. The petals have very
heavy substance and are very fragrant.
The abundant foliage is big and
glossy and the leaves come very
close to the flower, giving a high-
shouldered effect that shows the
crisp flowers to perfection. At its
best in cooler climates, it will tolerate a wide range of climates, and is a
superb bedding rose with no disease
problems. Flower production is
very high on short to medium-
length stems and repeat bloom is
quite remarkable. It was introduced
by Harkness, UK, in 1978. **ZONES 5–11.**

R

Rosa 'Mister Lincoln' *(left)*

This splendid repeat-flowering Large-flowered/Hybrid Tea Rose has urn-shaped buds that open to dark red flowers with superb petal substance. The buds can open rather quickly in summer. The full blooms are at first cupped and then flat, and there are 35 huge petals that are very fragrant. The foliage is leathery, matt and dark. Growth is extremely vigorous, making 'Mister Lincoln' unsuitable for bedding but superb for the back row of a rose bed. This is a very popular rose in Mediterranean-type climates. It was introduced by Swim and Weeks, USA, in 1964. ZONES 5–11.

Rosa 'Mermaid' *(right)*

The fragrant flowers of this rose are soft creamy yellow and are 5–6 in (12–15 cm) across. It comes into flower later than most varieties, but the display continues through summer and autumn and into winter. In warm areas it is gigantic—to 30 ft (9 m) or more across and 20 ft (6 m) high if given sufficient support. The dark foliage is glossy and the plant has large, red, hooked thorns. It needs no pruning but can be cut back when it gets out of control, which makes it a great rose for covering unsightly sheds and old trees. It should not be planted near paths because of the vicious thorns. The growth is much less vigorous in cold climates. It was introduced by Paul, UK, in 1918. ZONES 4–11.

R

Rosa 'Mme Caroline Testout'
(right)
syn. 'City of Portland'

This Large-flowered/Hybrid Tea
Rose was named after a Parisian
couturière and, although well over
a century old, it is still grown in
gardens throughout the world. The
buds are large and globular, and
the large flowers are bright rose with
a darker center tinted carmine. They
are very double and very fragrant.
The petals are inclined to turn inwards at the center, giving a globular look. It is a tough and hardy,
repeat-flowering bush but the
flowers are perhaps a little lacking
in substance, a trifle papery in texture
and they can ball in wet weather. It
was introduced by Pernet-Ducher,
France, in 1890. ZONES 5–11.

Rosa 'Mme Alfred Carrière' *(below)*

Known for its reliable health, this rampant Noisette Rose produces a continuous display of pale, pinkish white blooms over a
long period. There is yellow at the base below the curly central
petals. The large, full, globular blooms have a Tea-like fragrance.
The light, pale green foliage has well-serrated edges, and the flexible canes make it easy to train on a fence, wall, or pergola. It
doesn't mind shade and can be propagated easily from cuttings. It
was introduced by Schwartz, France, in 1879. ZONES 4–10.

Rosa 'Mutabilis' *(above)*
syns *Rosa chinensis mutabilis*,
'Tipo Idéale'

This China Rose was first probably
introduced to horticulture in 1934
by Swiss botanist Henri Correvon
of Geneva, who obtained it from
Prince Ghilberto Borromeo's garden at Isola Bella. It normally makes
a large, spreading bush but can go
up to the eaves on a house wall in
time. The flowers are butterfly-like
and are borne in masses. They
open yellow, turn to pink and then
crimson and have a long flowering
period. 'Masquerade' seems to be
derived from this rose. ZONES 5–10.

R

Rosa 'New Zealand' *(left)*
syn. 'Aotearoa', MACgenev

This Large-flowered/Hybrid Tea has large, soft warm pink blooms with excellent shape and form that are borne one to a stem on strong straight stems. The double florets have 30–35 petals with a strong honeysuckle fragrance. The foliage is glossy, dark green and very disease resistant on a vigorous, upright bush with good overall shape and architecture. It is repeat-flowering and prefers consistent temperatures on the warm side to show off its best characteristics. The real winner among its many attributes is the great fragrance. The plant takes a year to establish in the garden and then it performs beautifully. It was introduced by McGredy, New Zealand, in 1991. ZONES 4–10.

Rosa 'Nevada' *(below)*

This Modern Shrub Rose has pink to apricot ovoid buds that open to large white flowers that are 4 in (10 cm) in diameter with a reverse that is sometimes splashed carmine. The weatherproof, single-petalled blooms are borne in clusters on short stems and cover the bush. The foliage is medium green and usually disease resistant; in some wet climates black spot will develop if the plant is not protected by spraying. It is a tall, vigorous plant growing to 7 ft (2 m) in most climates. It was introduced by Dot, Spain, in 1927. ZONES 4–10.

Rosa 'New Dawn' *(above)*
syns 'Everblooming Dr W. Van Fleet', 'The New Dawn'

This Large-flowered Climber has no faults and some great attributes that make it an all-time favorite of many rose growers. Large, double, fragrant, cameo pink flowers fading to a flesh-toned white are the hallmarks of this rose. The foliage is glossy, dark green and disease resistant on a bush that climbs to about 20 ft (6 m). It is winter hardy and blooms all year long with an exceptional crop of flowers, both in small clusters and one bloom per stem whatever the climate zone. The sweet scent of the blooms is another plus. The canes and stems are pliable enough to accommodate any garden design. It was introduced by Dreer, USA, in 1930. ZONES 4–10.

R

Rosa 'Old Port' *(below)*
syn. MACkati

The flowers of this Cluster-flowered/Floribunda are a wonderful blend of red and mauve rather than purple. The double florets have 26–40 petals and an interesting flower form—old-fashioned quartered. The blooms are very fragrant. In hot climates the color can fade to a grayish blend and most rose growers plant this in partial shade to help sustain the beautiful color. It is repeat-flowering. The foliage is matt medium green on a bushy plant. In some cool climates vigor has been reported as poor; it does much better in temperate zones. Spraying to protect the plant from black spot is recommended. It was introduced by McGredy, New Zealand, in 1990. **ZONES 5–10.**

Rosa 'Old Master' *(above)*
syn. MACesp

The flowers of this Cluster-flowered/Floribunda are a striking combination of carmine with a silver eye and reverse. The florets have only 15 petals but what a color display—this is one of the first hand-painted creations from pioneer Sam McGredy. The fragrant blooms are large, reaching about 4–5 in (10–12 cm) in diameter and are borne in medium-sized sprays. The foliage is semi-glossy, medium green on a vigorous bushy plant with good disease-resistant characteristics. It is repeat-flowering, winter hardy and will tolerate most soil types and climates. It was introduced by McGredy, New Zealand, in 1974. **ZONES 4–10.**

R

Rosa 'Parkdirektor Riggers' *(left)*

The long, pointed buds of this Modern Shrub Rose open to reveal velvety crimson flowers with a small center of yellow stamens and a little white and purple at the base of the petals. The color is non-fading even in warm climates. The fragrant, semi-double blooms are borne in large clusters of up to 50 blooms on a plant that can reach up to 12 ft (3.5 m) high by 6 ft (1.8 m) wide. The foliage is glossy dark green on a vigorous, climbing, spreading plant that is very disease resistant. It was introduced by Kordes, Germany, in 1957. ZONES 4–10.

Rosa 'Paul Shirville' *(below)*
syns 'Heart Throb', 'Saxo', HARqueterwife

This Large-flowered/Hybrid Tea is rosy salmon-pink, lighter in tone on the petal reverse. The flowers on the first blooming are especially good, being large, high centered and well formed. They are double, borne either singly or in 3s, and have a sweet, enduring fragrance. Blooming continues through summer and autumn, but mid-season flowers are usually smaller. The variety makes a fine bed, hedge or standard rose. The semi-glossy leaves are large, purplish when young, maturing dark green, and are sometimes touched by seasonal mildew; they furnish a plant of vigorous, slightly spreading growth that reaches average height or less. It was introduced by Harkness, UK, in 1983. ZONES 4–9.

R

Rosa 'Paul Transon' *(above)*

This Large-flowered Climber has medium-sized double blooms that open flat to show a charming formation, with the center petals infolded in a random, confused fashion while the outer ones slowly reflex. They are bright coppery pink, paling as they age, and there is a pleasant apple scent. After a prolific first flush a few flowers are likely to appear intermittently through summer and autumn, especially in warmer climates. This variety has the lax and arching stems of a rambler, which means it lends itself to being trained up arches, tall pillars, pergolas and similar structures. The shiny, dark green foliage is plentiful and attractive. It was introduced by Barbier, France, in 1900. ZONES 4–9.

Rosa 'Perdita' *(right)*
syn. AUSperd

The medium to large-sized flowers of this Modern Shrub Rose are full-petalled and open cupped, becoming flat as the petals reflex. They are a pretty shade of creamy blush with touches of apricot. After the initial blooming more flowers are produced through summer and autumn, when the color tends to be pinker. This makes a welcome addition to the flower border, thanks to its excellent fragrance. It grows shorter than the average size expected of a shrub rose, with plentiful dark green foliage. It was introduced by Austin, UK, in 1983. ZONES 4–9.

Rosa 'Petite de Hollande' *(left)*
syns 'Petite Junon de Hollande', 'Pompon des Dames', *Rosa centifolia minor*

This short-growing and rather relaxed Centifolia Rose to 4 ft (1.2 m) bears grayish green branches covered with reddish thorns and small, well-serrated, soft grayish green leaves. The small flowers are slightly cupped at first, then open flat to show a full set of layered petals often with a button eye. There is a fine scent, but blooms appear in early summer only. It makes a useful shrub or low hedge and is excellent in tubs or urns. It originates from an unknown breeder in The Netherlands, pre-1838. ZONES 5–9.

Rosa 'Peace' *(right)*
syns 'Béke', 'Fredsrosen', 'Gioia', 'Gloria Dei', 'Mme A. Meilland', 'Mme Antoine Meilland'

The blooms are yellow flushed pink, full-petalled and rounded in form, with the ability to open slowly and look delightful at every stage. They have a pleasant scent, and maintain a good succession of bloom, seeming impervious to weather conditions and succeeding in a wide range of climates, though the yellow turns pale in hot conditions while the pink flushes become more pronounced. This is a splendid variety for beds, borders, hedges and for cutting, and it is one of the best roses to grow in standard form. The vigorous, shrub-like plants grow larger than average for a bush rose, and have glossy, rich green leaves. It was introduced by Meilland, France, in 1942. ZONES 4–9.

R

Rosa 'Playboy' (below)
syn. 'Cheerio'

Originating in northern Scotland, this Cluster-flowered/Floribunda Rose has proved a real sun lover, for it is most popular in warm climates where the bright orange-yellow flowers with scarlet shading attain a size and intensity of color not so evident at home. The blooms are almost single, and open from clusters of pointed buds to display their flamboyant tones and reveal attractive golden stamens. There is only a light scent. It is excellent for beds, borders and hedges and serviceable as a cut flower. The plant is vigorous with a bushy, free-branching habit, growing a little below average height and with an ample covering of dark glossy foliage. It was introduced by Cocker, UK, in 1976. **ZONES 4–9.**

Rosa 'Popcorn' (above)

The ovoid buds of this Miniature Rose open to pure white flowers with golden yellow stamens and look just like freshly burst popcorn. The florets have only 13–15 petals and display an informal decorative form that is at its best when fully open. They have a fragrance that improves in warmer climates. The blooms are borne in clusters on a vigorous, completely disease-resistant plant that is furnished with fern-like foliage. It has an upright habit and is self-cleaning—there is no need to deadhead spent blooms as the blooms fall off and the next cycle starts immediately. Its sport, **'Gourmet Popcorn'**, is an even more vigorous plant with larger clusters and a better overall shape. It was introduced by Morey, USA, in 1973. **ZONES 4–11.**

Rosa 'Precious Platinum' *(above)*
syns 'Opa Pötschke', 'Red Star'

This Large-flowered/Hybrid Tea Rose has cardinal red double blooms that are full and high centered and have thick-textured petals. Slightly fragrant, they are produced in quantity from spring to autumn on long stems and make excellent cut flowers. This vigorous variety has glossy green foliage that is highly resistant to fungal disease. It can be planted singly or massed, or it can be used as a standard. It was introduced by Dickson, UK, in 1974. **ZONES 4–9.**

Rosa 'Radox Bouquet' *(above)*
syn. 'Rosika', HARmusky

The very fragrant blooms of this Cluster-flowered/Floribunda Rose are produced in small clusters, with 1–3 soft pink blooms per cluster. The medium-sized, cupped flowers have 30 petals each. The foliage is large, glossy and mid-green on an upright plant that is useful for bedding and for grouping in borders. It is repeat-flowering and has large dark prickles. It was introduced by Harkness, UK, in 1981. **ZONES 4–9.**

R

Rosa 'Prince Charles' *(right)*

This medium to tall Bourbon is not unlike the more well-known 'Bourbon Queen'. The stems are almost thornless and the large leaves are deep green on a vigorous bush. The well-scented, loose, semi-double flowers are crimson or bright cherry in color. There may also be some purple and some veining in the flowers, leading to the American Rose Society color attribution. There are few flowers after mid-summer. It was introduced by Hardy, France, in 1842. **ZONES 5–9.**

Rosa 'Remember Me' *(right)*
syn. 'Remember',
COCdestin

This rose, which can justifiably be described as probably the deepest copper variety presently available, has in addition a subtle blend of yellow. Repeat-flowering, it has single or small clusters of double, large, cupped flowers with 20 petals and has little fragrance. The raisers are undetermined as to its type, but Large-flowered is probably closer than Cluster-flowered. The foliage, which is dark and glossy, is small for the type, but the spreading plant is bushy and makes for a good bedding variety and a marvelous standard. It was introduced by Cocker, UK, in 1984. **ZONES 4–9.**

Rosa 'Ripples'
(center)

The semi-double flowers with 18 wavy petals on this Cluster-flowered/Floribunda Rose are large and slightly fragrant. They are a lovely lilac-lavender color and appear in clusters, adding novelty to the flower border. The foliage is small and matt green, and is relatively disease resistant. It is repeat-flowering and was introduced by LeGrice, UK, in 1971. **ZONES 4–9.**

Rosa 'Robusta'
(below left)

The well-scented, rosette-style flowers of this Bourbon are large, flat and quartered. They are fiery crimson in color, fading to purple, and are borne in clusters. It is an upright, open bush with large foliage and repeat-flowering. There are two other roses with the name 'Robusta'—a Climbing Tea, possibly extinct, and a modern Hybrid Rugosa from Kordes in 1979. It was introduced by Soupert et Notting, Luxembourg, in 1877. **ZONES 5–9.**

Rosa 'Sander's White Rambler' (right)

This *wichuraiana*-type Rambler has small, white, rosette-style flowers that are borne in large clusters. The blooms have a fruity fragrance. The foliage is bright green and glossy. Although it is a little late in flowering, it is very reliable and is one of the better Ramblers. It can also be grown as an extended ground cover. Like the majority of the Ramblers, it flowers only once in the season. It was introduced by Sander, UK, in 1912. **ZONES 5–9.**

Rosa 'Rosa Mundi' (right)

syns *Rosa gallica rosa mundi* 'Weston', *R. gallica variegata* 'Thory', *R. gallica versicolor* 'Linnaeus', *R. mundi*

This striped form of *Rosa gallica* is pale pink splashed with crimson. It is sometimes confused with the Damask 'York and Lancaster' (also called 'Versicolor'), which is inferior. The branches in these roses tend to flop over under the weight of the flowers, and definitely need support. This can be solved by pruning halfway in early spring, giving a better effect. 'Rose Mundi' can grow to a medium to tall height and is suitable for low hedging. It dates from 1581. **ZONES 4–9.**

R

Rosa 'Roseraie de l'Haÿ' (left)

Probably the most widely grown and certainly the most popular of all the Rugosa family, this rose is a typical Hybrid Rugosa with vigorous, very thorny stems that is very healthy and is repeat-flowering. The big open flowers in small clusters are an intense crimson-purple with cream stamens and the scent is memorable, a rich concentration of cloves and honey. 'Roseraie de l'Haÿ' is probably the finest in its class and is useful in many situations, but it is most excellent as a hedge plant; a group of specimen plants in a wild garden will add color and scent. An unusual feature for this type of rose is that it does not have any hips. It was introduced by Cochet-Cochet, France, in 1901. **ZONES 4–9.**

Rosa 'Savoy Hotel' *(left)*
syns 'Integrity', 'Vercors', 'Violette Niestlé', HARvintage

The large, light pink flowers of this Large-flowered/Hybrid Tea have deeper undersides. The high-centered blooms have a slight fragrance. This is a repeat-flowering rose with medium-sized, bushy growth and dark green, semi-glossy, healthy foliage. In temperate climates it is a first-class bedding rose, and a good choice for grouping in mixed borders. It was introduced by Harkness, UK, in 1989. **ZONES 4–9.**

Rosa 'Si' *(below)*

This repeat-flowering rose has the smallest flowers of any known Miniature and qualifies as the first member of the micro-miniature class. The tiny pink buds are no larger than a grain of wheat and open to tiny semi-double, light pink flowers. It has a dwarf habit and is disease resistant, and is best planted in a container as its unbelievable beauty and charm are a delightful novelty. The tiny florets are a favorite with floral arrangers and add petiteness and delicacy to a design. 'Si' is still grown extensively throughout the world although it is now over 40 years old. It was introduced by Dot, Spain, in 1957. **ZONES 5–10.**

Rosa 'Sexy Rexy' *(above)*
syn. 'Heckenzauber', MACrexy

'Sexy Rexy' has medium to light pink flowers that are borne on very strong straight stems in large clusters. The fragrant, double blooms have 40 petals, and the flower form is more like that of a camellia, opening flat with a nice colorful finish. The trusses last for weeks and the repeat cycle is fast, although for continuous blooming the plant requires some dead-heading to stimulate the next bloom cycle. The foliage is small and mid-green on a compact, healthy, disease-resistant bush. This is a great contribution to the development of colorfast, productive and easily maintained Cluster-flowered Roses. It was introduced by McGredy, New Zealand, in 1984. **ZONES 5–11.**

Rosa 'Souvenir d'un Ami' *(right)*

The cupped, double and intensely fragrant flowers of this Tea Rose are pale rose tinted with salmon. The bush is vigorous and tall and repeat-flowering. This was one of the best-loved roses of Victorian England, because of its hardiness and ease of cultivation. The name means 'in remembrance of a friend', which sounds romantic, but it has been said that the friend was only the person who negotiated the deal between the amateur raiser and the distributor. It was introduced by Belot-Defougère, France, in 1846. **ZONES 7–9.**

Rosa 'Snow Carpet' *(left)*
syn. 'Blanche Neige', MACcarpe

The small, pompon-style, snow white flowers on this repeat-flowering Miniature variety have just a hint of cream in cooler climates. The blooms have 55 petals and a light fragrance. This rose was a major breakthrough in the development of Miniature ground covers with a sprawling, vigorous habit and dainty foliage. It generally forms giant mounds of informal flowers against a background of small, mid-green foliage. When it is first transplanted it may sulk for a while, but it will establish itself within months. It has also been used as a weeping tree rose. It was introduced by McGredy, New Zealand, in 1980. **ZONES 5–10.**

Rosa 'Souvenir de St Anne's' *(below)*

This sport of 'Souvenir de la Malmaison' was discovered in the garden of St Anne's: a property of Lady Ardilaun near Dublin. Graham Thomas recounts that it was preserved for many years by Lady Moore of Rathfarnham in Dublin. A Bourbon Rose, it has fewer petals than its parent and stands up better to rain, but it is less spectacular. However, it is more fragrant, the scent residing, according to Thomas, in the many stamens. It makes a very bushy, quite tall shrub and is repeat-flowering. It was introduced by Hilling, UK, in 1950. **ZONES 5–9.**

R

Rosa 'Tequila Sunrise' *(left)*
syn. 'Beaulieu', DICobey

An asset of this Large-flowered/Hybrid Tea is its ability to keep on flowering. The flowers are of medium size, rounded in form, and are made up of broad, bright yellow petals that are randomly tipped and margined with red. They are carried sometimes singly and quite often in wide, candelabra-type sprays, which afford plenty of blooms for flower arranging. They open slowly, taking on a cupped form; they should be deadheaded because the old petals discolor. For beds, borders and hedges, this is a popular rose. It grows vigorously with a bushy, free-branching habit to average height, and is furnished with glossy dark green leaves. It was introduced by Dickson, UK, in 1989. ZONES 4–9.

Rosa 'Sparrieshoop' *(right)*

Named for the village where the Kordes' organization have their famous nursery, this Modern Shrub Rose has long, pointed buds that open to almost single, perfumed flowers that are borne in large trusses of apple blossom pink. They are large and sweetly fragrant with many golden yellow stamens. The bush tends to cover itself with flowers all season long. The vigorous growth habit permits the long canes, which are bronze when young, to be trained as either a short climber or a big spreading shrub. The glossy dark foliage is subject to mildew if not protected. It was introduced by Kordes, Germany, in 1953. ZONES 4–11.

Rosa 'Sunsprite' *(left)*
syns 'Friesia', 'Korresia', KOResia

This rose is one of the best deep yellow Cluster-flowered/Floribunda Roses. The attractive, oval buds open to flat, double flowers with 28 very symmetrically arranged petals. These large blooms are intense rich yellow, extremely fragrant and are produced in great quantities; the repeat-blooming is extremely fast. The foliage is abundant, dark green and very glossy on a plant with a short to medium, stocky habit. The open blooms shatter rather quickly, which makes them unsuitable for cutting, although deadheading keeps the bush neat and tidy. This is one of the best of all bedding roses, and makes a very colorful low hedge as well as a standard. It was introduced by Kordes, Germany, in 1977. ZONES 5–11.

R

Rosa 'The Fairy' *(below)*
syns 'Fairy', 'Féerie'

This Polyantha Rose provides a prolific show for weeks on end. The rosette-shaped flowers are made up of scores of tiny petals, and are carried in dainty sprays all over the bush in an even tone of light rose pink. Even during rare intervals through summer and autumn when not in flower the plant remains attractive, forming hummocks of small, bright, pointed leaves. 'The Fairy' has all manner of uses: as a low hedge, to front a border, trail over a low wall, occupy a small space or planted in a container. Its only failing is a lack of fragrance. If kept pruned it will stay quite dwarf, or it can achieve the stature of a small shrub by being allowed to grow unchecked; it is also excellent as a weeping standard. It was introduced by Bentall, UK, in 1932. **ZONES 4–9.**

Rosa 'Trigintipetala' *(above)*
syns *Rosa damascena trigintipetala*, 'Kazanlik'

This Damask Rose is extensively grown in Kazanlik, Bulgaria, because it is one of the varieties used to make the famous 'attar of roses'. The flowers, which are arranged in loose clusters on short thin stalks and appear in early to mid-summer, are soft pink in color and a bit more than semi-double when fully open; each is about 2 in (5 cm) across and exposes many creamy colored stamens. They are deliciously fragrant. 'Trigintipetala' is an angular shrub to some 6 ft (1.8 m) high and almost as wide, with a twiggy growth habit and moderately thorny, brownish green wood. The light gray-green, serrated leaves are soft to touch. It dates from pre-1700. **ZONES 5–11.**

Rosa 'The World' *(right)*
syn. 'Die Welt', DIEkor

Large, perfectly formed flowers that are slightly fragrant and are a blend of orange, red and yellow appear through summer and autumn on this Large-flowered/Hybrid Tea. They are double, with 25 petals, and high centered, which makes 'The World' a very popular exhibition rose. It is a very tall plant with glossy foliage that can sometimes be prone to mildew in autumn. It was introduced by Kordes, Germany, in 1976. **ZONES 4–9.**

R

Rosa 'Variegata di Bologna' *(left)*

This Bourbon is a sport of 'Victor Emmanuel'. The fragrant flowers are white, striped purplish red; they are double and globular and are borne in clusters. There are few repeat flowers after the main summer flush. The plant is tall and lax and needs good cultivation, without which it is susceptible to black spot. It will occasionally sport back to the parent. The foliage is somewhat coarse and sparse. It can be grown as a short climber or pruned to a bush. It was introduced by Bonfiglioli & Son, Italy, in 1909. **ZONES 5–9.**

Rosa 'Tropicana'
(left)
syn. 'Super Star', TANorstar

The flowers are substantial and well formed, borne sometimes singly and sometimes in wide-spaced candelabra heads. There is a light scent. As a cut flower and for exhibition, it is very useful and continues to produce flowers very satisfactorily through summer and autumn, the mid-season ones often appearing with ragged edges to the petals. 'Tropicana' is used in beds and borders, though its growth habit tends to be uneven and it is liable to mildew readily wherever the circulation of air is limited. The plant grows vigorously with a lanky habit to average height or above, and has rather small matt leaves. It was introduced by Tantau, Germany, in 1960. **ZONES 4–9.**

R

Rosa 'Winchester Cathedral' *(right)*
syn. 'Winchester', AUScat

This Modern Shrub is identical to its parent 'Mary Rose' in every way except color. The white blooms are bright and free, but sometimes revert on the bush to pink, like its parent, or both pink and white. This is either an endearing habit or a nuisance, depending on the individual taste of the grower. The frequency of the repeat-flowering and the wonderful loose blooms make this plant ideal for any garden; it is untroubled by disease right through the year. 'Winchester Cathedral' has a habit like that of an Old Garden Rose, which makes it easy to prune and grow. It is also classified as an English Rose. It was introduced by Austin, UK, in 1988. ZONES 5–9.

Rosa 'Veilchenblau' *(right)*
syns 'Blue Rambler', 'Blue Rosalie', 'Violet Blue'

This is a very popular Rambler in the *Rosa multiflora* style—it is vigorous, semi-rigid and almost thornless; it has fresh green leaves. The fragrant flowers, taking after the 'male' parent, are violet streaked with white, fading to gray. They are small, semi-double and incurved, and show prominent yellow stamens. This is the best known of the three similar violet-purple ramblers, the others being 'Rose-Marie Viaud' and 'Violette'. It flowers early in the season. It was introduced by Schmidt, Germany, in 1909. ZONES 5–9.

Rosa 'Wedding Day' *(left)*
syn. 'English Wedding Day'

Rosa sinowilsonii was discovered in China in 1904; it is a single, white, vigorous rose. 'Wedding Day' is an improved version with rampant growth and clear green foliage. The flowers are larger and are white with pronounced orange stamens. They come in big trusses and have a citrus scent. It is classed as a Rambler. It was introduced by Stern, UK, in 1950. ZONES 7–9.

R

Rosa 'Zéphirine Drouhin' *(above)*
syns 'Belle Dijonnaise',
'Charles Bonnet',
'Ingegnoli Prediletta',
'Mme Gustave Bonnet'

This thornless Bourbon Rose can be grown as a pillar rose, over an arch, or as a moderate to large, open shrub. The fragrant, medium-sized flowers are semi-double and loose petalled. They are cerise-pink with a white base. This vigorous plant is easy to cultivate. **'Kathleen Harrop'** is a pink sport of this rose. Both make good hedge roses but should be kept away from walls for fear of black spot. It was introduced by Bizot, France, in 1868. **ZONES 5–10.**

Rosa 'York and Lancaster' *(left)*
syns *Rosa damascena versicolor,* 'Versicolor',
'York et Lancastre'

A lanky, lax-growing Damask of branching habit, 'York and Lancaster' has grayish green wood armed with hooked, sharp thorns. The many leaves are also grayish green and have a soft texture. The blooms are carried on long stalks in nodding, loose clusters, each raggedly semi-double and about $2\frac{1}{2}$ in (6.5 cm) across. Their color is variable, some consisting of soft mid-pink and others consistently white; both shades may even be present in the same flower. The variety is very fragrant, but a little shy in its yield of flowers. Historically it is very interesting, but it is not a rose to overly enhance the average garden. It dates from pre-1629. **ZONES 5–10.**

Rothmannia globosa *(right)*
TREE GARDENIA

This shrub or small tree from South Africa bears masses of creamy white spring flowers, sometimes with yellowish throats, and with a gardenia-like perfume; they occur in the leaf axils or at the branch tips. It reaches 12 ft (3.5 m) in height and has dark-colored bark. Its fruits, 1 in (25 mm) in diameter, are brownish black when ripe. ZONES 10–11.

ROTHMANNIA

There are about 30 species in this genus of evergreen shrubs or small trees native to tropical and southern Africa. They were once classified with *Gardenia,* which they resemble somewhat. Growing to 15 ft (4.5 m) high, they sometimes form several stems. Their lanceolate or oval, opposite leaves, up to 6 in (15 cm) long, are a glossy green. Stalkless, bell-shaped flowers with a strong fragrance appear from spring to summer, and are followed by fleshy, rounded fruits.

CULTIVATION
Grow these frost-tender plants in a sheltered, sunny or semi-shaded spot. A well-drained soil enriched with organic matter is ideal, preferably with a neutral to slightly acid pH. Propagate from seed in spring or from cuttings in summer.

Rothmannia capensis *(right)*
CAPE GARDENIA

In cultivation, this fast-growing species from South Africa reaches 15 ft (4.5 m). Its leathery, 4 in (10 cm) leaves have slightly wavy edges, while the gray-brown bark conceals pink underbark. Its cream to yellow 3 in (8 cm) flowers have reddish spots in the throat. The sap of the green fruit was once used to heal wounds. ZONES 10–11.

R

RUBUS

This large genus of 250 or more species of deciduous and evergreen shrubs and scrambling climbers occurs in most parts of the world. The plants range from the tiny cloudberry *(Rubus chamaemorus)* through to viciously armed, 12 ft (3.5 m) high thickets and high forest climbers. Their cane-like stems bear flowers and fruits in their second year. The leaves, usually felted underneath, are mostly compound with 3 to 7 leaflets arranged pinnately or palmately. The summer flowers are white, pink or purple, resembling those of a small single rose, for example, *Rubus* 'Navajo'. They are followed by the sweet, juicy fruits, a mass of tiny, usually red or black drupes.

CULTIVATION

These moderately to fully frost-hardy plants prefer moist, well-drained, moderately fertile soil in a sunny position. Some forms naturalize freely and become a menace. After fruiting, cut the canes back to ground level. Propagate by root division in winter, or from seeds, cuttings or suckers.

Rubus cockburnianus
(above)

This deciduous shrub from China grows to 8 ft (2.4 m) in height and spread. The black fruit, while edible, are unpalatable; they follow the racemes of purple flowers, which appear in summer. The ovate leaves are deep green above and felty white beneath. ZONES 6–10.

Rubus 'Benenden'
(left)

This deciduous, arching, thornless shrub has peeling bark and lobed, deep green leaves. Reaching 10 ft (3 m) in height and spread, it bears its large, pure white flowers in late spring and early summer. ZONES 5–9.

Rubus deliciosus
(right)

ROCKY MOUNTAIN RASPBERRY

This 10 ft (3 m) decidu-
ous shrub is found in
western USA, especially
the Rocky Mountains. Its
leaves are rounded or
kidney-shaped, 3- to 5-
lobed and slightly less
than 3 in (8 cm) wide.
The stems are thornless
with peeling bark. Spring-
borne, 2 in (5 cm) wide
white flowers are fol-
lowed by purple-red
fruit. ZONES 5–9.

Rubus fruticosus *(right)*

BLACKBERRY, BRAMBLE

This widespread, northern European bramble
grows wild in woods and hedgerows. It is an ag-
gregate, consisting of over 2,000 micro-species, all
differing in small details. The cultivated blackberry's prickly, arching stems grow to 10 ft (3 m)
with a similar spread. They bear deep green leaves
with 3 to 5 leaflets, white or pink flowers 1 in
(25 mm) across, and delicious blackberries with
purple juice. **'Himalayan Giant'** (syn. 'Himalaya')
is very vigorous with very dark medium-sized
berries which are produced over a long season;
'Loch Ness' has spineless semi-erect canes.
ZONES 5–10.

Rubus idaeus *(left)*

RASPBERRY, RED RASPBERRY

The northern hemisphere raspberry is a cool-climate, deciduous, perennial shrub 5 ft (1.5 m) tall
and wide. It has smooth, reddish brown stems
bearing many or few prickles and serrated leaflets
6 in (15 cm) long. The small, 5-petalled white
flowers appear on the side shoots of the branches
produced over the previous summer. The succulent, aromatic berries are usually red, but can occasionally be white or yellowish in color. There are
many cultivars. **'Autumn Bliss'** is an easily grown,
repeat-fruiting cultivar with medium-sized red
fruit; **'Taylor'** has large strong canes with late season bright red, medium-sized fruit; and **'Killarney'**
and **'Glen May'** produce full-flavored fruit in early
summer. ZONES 4–9.

R

Rubus occidentalis
(left)

BLACK RASPBERRY

A parent of many cultivars of black raspberries, this erect shrub from North America reaches 8 ft (2.4 m) in height. Its prickly canes arch and root from their tips. The 3-lobed leaves are serrated and whitish underneath. Its small white flowers are held in dense clusters, and the berries are usually black, with some occasionally golden. **'Black Hawk'** and **'Jewel'** are hardy, high-yielding cultivars. **ZONES 3–9.**

Rubus thibetanus

This deciduous, arching shrub from western China has white-bloomed, brownish purple young shoots in winter and fern-like, glossy deep green foliage that is white beneath. Growing to 8 ft (2.4 m) in height and spread, *Rubus thibetanus* bears its small pink flowers from mid- to late summer; the flowers are followed by the black fruit. **'Silver Fern'** is a popular cultivar. **ZONES 6–10.**

Rubus thibetanus
'Silver Fern' *(left)*

R

Ruellia macrantha
(above)

CHRISTMAS PRIDE

This Brazilian species' common name refers to its large, deep pink, trumpet flowers that are in full bloom during the southern hemisphere Christmas; they are 3 in (8 cm) long with darker veins and appear from autumn to winter. It reaches 6 ft (1.8 m) in height and 18 in (45 cm) in spread. ZONES 10–12.

RUELLIA
syns *Stephanophysum, Arrhostoxylum*

This genus from tropical and subtropical America with a few species in temperate North America contains about 150 species of evergreen perennials, shrubs and subshrubs. The funnel-shaped flowers, usually red, pink or blue, occur in densely packed terminal panicles and axillary clusters. They have smooth-edged, oblong to lance-shaped leaves up to 6 in (15 cm) long and look good in informal borders.

CULTIVATION

The plants are fairly tolerant of dry conditions and like sun or semi-shade, so they do well in dry places at the feet of trees. In cooler climates they are grown indoors or in greenhouses. Plant in humus-rich, fertile, moist soil. Propagate from seed in spring, or cuttings in spring or early summer.

R

RUSCUS
BROOM

This genus consists of 6 species of evergreen, clump-forming subshrubs grown
for their foliage and fruits. The leaves are
actually flattened shoots (cladophylls), on
which flowers and fruits are borne. The
flowers are tiny, star-shaped and green to
greenish white, and the fruits, for which
both male and female plants are required,
are red and showy.

CULTIVATION
These plants will tolerate anything from
full sun to part-shade and any soil as long
as it is not waterlogged. Propagate from
seed or by division.

Ruscus aculeatus (left)
BUTCHER'S BROOM,
BOX HOLLY

A tough, erect, branching,
evergreen subshrub, *Ruscus
aculeatus* is native to northern Africa. Its spring flowers
are followed by bright red
berries. The flowers and
fruits are borne in the center
of the cladophylls, which
end in spines. Moderately
frost hardy, it grows to a
height of 30 in (75 cm) and
a spread of 3 ft (1 m).
Butcher's broom is so called
because butchers once used
the brush of the spiky stems
to brush down their chop-
ping blocks. ZONES 7–10.

R

Russelia
equisetiformis *(left)*
syn. *Russelia juncea*
CORAL PLANT, CORAL FOUNTAIN

This erect, slender
subshrub with wiry,
near-leafless green
stems is a native of
Mexico. It is grown for
the clusters of hand-
some red flowers it
bears all year round, set
among tiny, green
leaves. Fast growing, it
is well suited to spilling
over a wall, or as a sea-
side specimen. It grows
to a height and spread
of just under 3 ft (1 m).
ZONES 9–12.

R

RUSSELIA

Consisting of around 50 species of evergreen and deciduous
subshrubs and shrubs, this genus ranges from Mexico and
Cuba to Colombia. They have showy tubular flowers, which are
red, pink or white. The scale-like leaves appear on pendent
stems.

CULTIVATION
These frost-tender plants prefer full sun and humus-rich, light,
well-drained soil. Propagate from cuttings or by dividing
rooted layers.

S

SALIX
WILLOW, OSIER, SALLOW

This genus includes about 300 species of deciduous trees, shrubs and subshrubs mainly from cold and temperate regions in the northern hemisphere. The fast-growing but relatively short-lived trees are the most widely grown, mainly for their timber, their twigs which are used in basket-making and their strong suckering habit, which aids soil retention. Willow bark was the original source of aspirin. The leaves are usually bright green, lance-shaped and narrow. The flowers, which are borne in fluffy cat-kins, are conspicuous in some species, appearing before or with the new leaves; male and female catkins are usually borne on separate trees.

CULTIVATION
These frost-hardy plants do best in areas with clearly defined seasons and prefer cool, moist soil with sun or part-shade. Propagation is from seed or cuttings in either winter or summer, or by layering. They are vulnerable to attack by caterpillars, aphids and gall mites as well as canker-causing fungal diseases.

Salix alba
WHITE WILLOW

A very adaptable tree from Europe, northern Africa and central Asia, this species grows to about 80 ft (24 m) high. Its erect branches weep somewhat at the tips and are clothed with 3 in (8 cm) long, narrow leaves that are bright green above with flattened silky hairs on the undersides. The white willow makes a good windbreak tree, but has invasive roots. 'Britzensis' (syn. 'Chermesina') has bright red stems; 'Chrysostela' has yellow shoots tipped with orange; *Salix alba* var. *caerulea* has blue-green leaves and is the willow from which cricket bats are made; *S. a.* var. *sericea* has silvery foliage; and 'Vitellina', the golden willow, has young growth of a brilliant clear yellow. ZONES 2–10.

Salix alba 'Britzensis'
(left)

Salix alba var. sericea
(below left

Salix alba 'Vitellina'
(below)

S

Salix babylonica in spring *(right)* and in winter *(below right)*

Salix babylonica

WEEPING WILLOW, BABYLON
WEEPING WILLOW

Probably the most widely grown and easily recognized willow, this Chinese species grows to about 50 ft (15 m) high and wide. Narrow, bright green leaves, 3–6 in (8–15 cm) long, densely cover the flexible, arching branches, which often droop right down to ground level. The catkins are insignificant. **'Crispa'** has twisted leaves and a narrower growth habit. *Salix babylonica* var. *pekinensis* 'Tortuosa' has bright green lance-shaped, serrated leaves that turn yellow in autumn. *Salix matsudana* is hardly distinguishable from *S. babylonica* but is smaller growing. *S. m.* 'Tortuosa' (corkscrew willow) is a popular cultivar. **ZONES 4–10.**

Salix caprea *(right)*

PUSSY WILLOW, GOAT WILLOW, GREAT WILLOW, FLORIST'S WILLOW

Native to Europe and northeast Asia, this dense shrub or tree grows 10–30 ft (3–9 m) tall. The oval mid-green leaves are 2–4 in (5–10 cm) long with fleecy gray undersides. The male plant has large yellow catkins called 'palm', the female has silvery catkins known as 'pussy willow', both appearing in spring before the foliage. This species grows well in brackish marshlands but its very strong suckering habit can cause problems in smaller gardens. **'Kilmarnock'** is a stiffly pendulous weeping tree, usually grafted at 6 ft (1.8 m), with a dense head of yellow and brown shoots. **ZONES 5–10.**

S

Salix gracilistyla
ROSE-GOLD PUSSY WILLOW

This vigorous shrub, to 10 ft (3 m) tall, has gray downy leaves and young shoots. The oblong leaves, up to 4 in (10 cm) long, are silky at first, the upper surface becoming smooth. The silky gray male catkins can be up to 2 in (5 cm) long, appearing in spring before the leaves. It is found naturally in eastern Asia. **'Melanostachys'** has black bracts over the catkins, so that the whole catkin appears black. ZONES 6–10.

Salix gracilistyla 'Melanostachys' *(top)*

Salix fragilis *(above)*
CRACK WILLOW, BRITTLE WILLOW

This fast-growing, erect species from Europe and northwestern Asia can reach 50 ft (15 m) tall, its many branches forming a broad crown. The toothed leaves, to 6 in (15 cm) long, turn yellow in autumn. Its wood has been used to produce high-quality charcoal. This tree grows easily and can naturalize and become a problem, spreading along the banks of streams. Several cultivars are known. The common name brittle willow comes from the tree's brittle twigs; old trees rot easily and break apart in storms. ZONES 5–10.

S

Salix lanata *(right)*

WOOLLY WILLOW

This small shrub from northern Europe grows to 3 ft (1 m) tall and is of slow spreading habit, becoming gnarled with age. The silvery gray, rounded leaves, up to 2 in (5 cm) long, mature to a dull green on top and become slightly wavy. Erect, felty yellow-gray catkins appear in spring after the leaves. **ZONES 2–9.**

Salix purpurea

PURPLE OSIER, PURPLE WILLOW, BASKET WILLOW

This species from Europe, northern Africa to central Asia and Japan grows to about 15 ft (4.5 m) high. In its darkest forms, the catkins are an intense reddish purple. The leaves are silver gray, often with a hint of purple on the undersides, and the stems are tinted purple. **'Nana'** is a compact form to 3 ft (1 m) with slender shoots and gray-green leaves. **ZONES 5–10.**

Salix purpurea 'Nana'
(above)

S

SALVIA
SAGE

The largest genus of the mint family, *Salvia* consists of as many as 900 species of annuals, perennials and soft-wooded shrubs, distributed through most parts of the world except very cold regions and tropical rainforests. Their tubular, 2-lipped flowers are very distinctive. The lower lip is flat but the upper lip helmet- or boat-shaped; the calyx is also 2-lipped and may be colored. The flowers come in a wide range of colors, including some of the brightest blues and scarlets of any plants, though yellows are rare. Many beautiful sage species are grown as garden plants, including some with aromatic leaves grown primarily as culinary herbs, but even these can be grown for their ornamental value alone. The genus name goes back to Roman times and derives from the Latin *salvus*, 'safe' or 'well', referring to the supposed healing properties of *Salvia officinalis*.

CULTIVATION
Most of the shrubby Mexican and South American species will tolerate only light frosts, but some of the perennials are more frost-hardy. Sages generally do best planted in full sun in well drained, light-textured soil with adequate watering in summer. Propagate from seed in spring, cuttings in early summer, or division of rhizomatous species at almost any time. Foliage of many species is attacked by snails, slugs and caterpillars.

Salvia africana-lutea (*below left*)
syn. *Salvia aurea*
BEACH SALVIA, BROWN SALVIA

Native to coastal areas of South Africa's Cape Province, this is one of the longest-lived and woodiest sages, and is also remarkable for its flower color. It makes a spreading tangle of branches about 6 ft (1.8 m) tall with gray and densely woolly foliage. Through spring and summer. It produces an abundant succession of $1^1/_2$ in (35 mm) long flowers shaped like parrots' beaks. They open creamy yellow but soon turn a rich rust brown, with a shriveled, papery appearance as though they were dead. As well as tolerating coastal conditions, it attracts birds. ZONES 9–10.

S

Salvia clevelandii *(right)*

CLEVELAND SAGE

This shrubby sage is a characteristic plant of the dry chaparral and scrublands of California, where its aromatic foliage and flowers add a distinct fragrance to the air. A gray-green mound reaching 3–5 ft (1–1.5 m) tall and wide, its soft lavender-blue flowers are produced on stems rising 12–24 in (30–60 cm) above the foliage. 'Winifred Gilman' is more compact, with deeper blue flowers. ZONES 8–10.

Salvia leucantha

(right)

MEXICAN BUSH SAGE

This tropical Mexican and Central American native is a woody subshrub grown for its seemingly endless display of downy purple and white flowers on long, arching spikes. The soft, gray-green foliage is attractive all year round. It will reach 3–4 ft (1–1.2 m) in height and spread, making it suitable for the middle of the border; it is often used as a flowering hedge in mild-winter regions. Sun, good drainage and occasional water suit this dependable sage. ZONES 8–10.

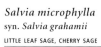

Salvia microphylla var. *neurepia (right)*

Salvia microphylla

syn. *Salvia grahamii*

LITTLE LEAF SAGE, CHERRY SAGE

This small-leafed, rounded shrub bears masses of scarlet flowers from late spring to early winter and rounded leaves. *Salvia microphylla* var. *neurepia* has larger leaves, and deeper cherry-red flowers over a shorter period. Many different color forms are available including some excellent *S. microphylla* × *S. greggii* hybrids. ZONES 9–11.

S

SAMBUCUS

ELDERBERRY, ELDER

This genus includes about 25 species of perennials, deciduous shrubs and soft-wooded trees. Although most are rarely cultivated because of their tendency to become weedy and invasive, some species are useful for their edible flowers and berries, and are attractive in foliage and flower. Most have pinnate leaves and, in late spring and early summer, bear large radiating sprays of tiny white or creamy flowers followed by clusters of usually purple-black, blue or red berries.

CULTIVATION
Usually undemanding, *Sambucus* thrive in any reasonably well-drained, fertile soil in sun or shade. Prune out old shoots and cut young shoots by half. Propagate from seed in autumn, or cuttings in summer or winter.

S

Sambucus canadensis *(left)*

AMERICAN ELDER, SWEET ELDER

An upright, deciduous shrub from cold-climate regions in the northeast of North America, this fast-growing species reaches about 10 ft (3 m) tall with a similar spread and has soft pithy stems. The compound leaves have 5 to 11 leaflets. The tiny, white, starry flowers are borne in large sprays about 8 in (20 cm) across in spring; they are followed by purple-black berries. '**Aurea**' features golden-yellow foliage and red berries. '**York**' was raised in New York State in 1964 and is considered one of the best cultivars; it is a large bush with large fruit and requires cross-pollination by another cultivar to produce its best crops.
ZONES 2–10.

Sambucus nigra
'Aurea' *(right)*

Sambucus nigra *(above)*

EUROPEAN ELDER, BLACK ELDER, COMMON ELDER

This species, sometimes regarded as a weed, is
cultivated for its large, spring-borne sprays of tiny
white flowers and the clusters of purple-black
berries that follow. Originally from Europe,
northern Africa and western Asia, it is a deciduous shrub or small tree to 20 ft (6 m) high with
pinnate leaves made up of 5 to 9 deep green,
serrated leaflets. The berries are used in pies, the
flowers and fruit to make wine or liqueurs.
'Aurea' has creamy white, star-shaped, fragrant
flowers and yellow leaves; **'Laciniata'** has irregularly, finely cut leaves. ZONES 4–10.

SANTOLINA

Small, aromatic, frost-hardy evergreens from the Mediterranean region, the 18 shrub species in this genus are grown for their scented, usually silvery gray foliage and dainty, button-like yellow flowerheads. They are useful for covering banks and as a ground cover.

CULTIVATION

They require well-drained soil and a sunny situation. Cut back old wood immediately after flowering to encourage new growth from the base, and remove dead flowerheads and stems in autumn. Propagate from cuttings in summer.

Santolina chamaecyparissus *(right)*

COTTON LAVENDER, LAVENDER COTTON

This low-spreading, aromatic shrub, native to mild, coastal areas of the Mediterranean, grows to a height of 18 in (45 cm) and spread of 3 ft (1 m). It bears bright yellow, rounded flowerheads on long stalks in summer, set among oblong, grayish green leaves divided into tiny segments. **'Lemon Queen'** is a compact form—to 24 in (60 cm)—with lemon yellow flowerheads. ZONES 7–10.

Santolina rosmarinifolia *(right)*
syn. *Santolina virens*

HOLY FLAX

Native to Spain, Portugal and southern France, this species has green, thread-like, 1½ in (35 mm) long leaves and bears heads of bright yellow flowers in mid-summer. It has a dense bushy habit, reaching a height of 24 in (60 cm) with a spread of 3 ft (1 m). **'Morning Mist'** has golden-yellow flowers; **'Primrose Gem'** has paler yellow flowers. ZONES 7–10.

S

SARCOCOCCA
SWEET BOX, CHRISTMAS BOX

This is a genus of 11 species of wiry stemmed, evergreen shrubs from India, China and Southeast Asia with glossy, deep green, elliptical leaves. They produce small, white to pink flowers that are not very showy but are sweetly scented. The flowers are followed by conspicuous berries.

CULTIVATION
While often grown in difficult, dry, shady areas, sweet boxes look better with a little care and attention. They prefer a relatively cool, moist climate with well-drained soil. Propagate from seed in autumn, from cuttings in summer or by layering. They are largely trouble free.

S

Sarcococca confusa *(above)*

This dense species with multiple basal green branches slowly grows 6 ft (1.8 m) tall and has smooth, shiny dark green leaves 1½–2 in (3.5–5 cm) long. The small white flowers are borne in clusters along the stems during late autumn and winter. Shiny black berries follow. The origin of this species remains unknown; it could be from China but it has not been found in the wild. It may be a natural hybrid. ZONES 5–10.

Sarcococca hookeriana

Indigenous to the Himalayan region, this rhizomatous species develops into a dense clump of upright, somewhat arching stems. Its cream flowers, borne in winter, have reddish pink anthers. The berries are black. **Sarcococca hookeriana** var. **digyna** has male flowers with cream anthers and slender leaves. **S. h. var. humilis** (syn. *S. humilis*) is a low, spreading, evergreen shrub, superb for deep shade, with tiny white flowers that have a honey-like fragrance. ZONES 8–10.

Sarcococca hookeriana var. *digyna* (below left)

Sarcococca hookeriana var. *humilis* (below)

Sarcococca ruscifolia (right)

The most commonly grown species, this plant is native to central China. It has an upright, arching habit, reaching a height and spread of 3 ft (1 m). The milky white flowers appear in winter, and are followed by brilliant, scarlet berries. The leaves are oval, deep lustrous green above and paler beneath. **Sarcococca ruscifolia** var. *chinensis* has lance-shaped to ovate leaves. ZONES 8–10.

SCHEFFLERA
syns *Brassaia, Dizygotheca, Heptapleurum*

This vast genus of small trees, shrubs and scrambling climbers, includes over 700 species from most of the wetter tropical and subtropical regions of the world. Leaves consist of similar-sized leaflets arranged like a cartwheel at the ends of long stalks. Small flowers are in branching, usually radiating spikes. Fruits are small, fleshy berries. In their native rainforests many scheffleras grow as epiphytes on other trees or rocks. Several are popular house plants in cool and cold climates; a few species are grown for their luxuriant foliage.

CULTIVATION
In warm to hot climates plant in a spot sheltered from wind in the sun or part-shade. Young plants make excellent tub specimens. Grow in well-drained, preferably enriched soil; keep moist over summer. Propagate from fresh seed in late summer, cuttings in summer or by air-layering in spring.

Schefflera actinophylla (above)
syn. *Brassaia actinophylla*

QUEENSLAND UMBRELLA TREE, AUSTRALIAN IVY PALM, OCTOPUS TREE

Each leaf of this plant resembles an umbrella and consists of 7 to 15 light green, glossy leaflets up to 15 in (38 cm) long. From rainforests of northern Australia and New Guinea, this species grows to 40 ft (12 m) in cultivation, with multiple erect trunks and a dense canopy 20 ft (6 m) wide. Numerous clusters of flowers are arranged in spectacular radiating spikes on red stems; these appear near the top of the plant from late summer to early spring. Each ruby red flower has contrasting cream stamens and is rich in nectar. Reddish fleshy berries follow. **ZONES 10–12.**

Schefflera arboricola (above)
HAWAIIAN ELF SCHEFFLERA

Endemic to Taiwan, this species makes a shrub 6–15 ft (1.8–4.5 m) tall with a similar spread. It produces many branches near the ground and can be pruned to a rounded shape, which makes it a popular pot plant for indoors and out. The leaves consist of 5 to 10 leaflets radiating from a leaf stalk; each is shiny green and up to 6 in (15 cm) long. Greenish yellow flowers in sprays appear near the branch tips in spring and summer, followed by orange fruit that ripen to purple. **'Renate'** has variegated leaves, as does **'Samoa Snow'. ZONES 10–12.**

S

SCHINUS

The 30 species of evergreen shrubs and trees from this genus, indigenous to Central and South America, are grown for their graceful habit and resistance to very dry conditions. Leaves usually consist of many leaflets but are sometimes simple. The flowers are tiny and arranged in clusters, male and female flowers on the same or separate trees. Female trees feature attractive round berries. They make excellent shade and street trees.

CULTIVATION
Plant these marginally frost-hardy to frost-tender plants in a site in full sun in well-drained, coarse soil; they grow best in warm to hot climates. Propagate from fresh seed in spring or cuttings in summer.

Schinus molle var. *areira* (left)
syn. *Schinus areira*
PEPPER TREE, PEPPERCORN

This fast-growing tree with graceful, drooping leaves and branchlets develops an attractive, gnarled trunk as it ages to 30–50 ft (9–15 m) tall. The dark green, shiny leaves are 6 in (15 cm) long, composed of 10 to 18 pairs of small pointed leaflets; they are resinous and aromatic when crushed. Pendulous clusters of tiny cream flowers appear from late spring to early summer. Decorative sprays of tiny rose pink berries follow; these have a peppery taste and have been used like pepper, but are somewhat toxic. In hot dry climates it naturalizes readily and may become a weed. ZONES 9–11.

Schinus terebinthifolius (left)
BRAZILIAN PEPPER TREE

A round-headed tree up to 30 ft (9 m) high, this species has bronze-green pinnate leaves usually composed of 7 leaflets. The drooping panicles of tiny cream flowers borne in summer are followed by small green berries that redden as they ripen in winter. When trimmed, it makes an excellent shade tree. In some warm, wet climates, such as in Hawaii, it has become a serious weed. ZONES 10–12.

S

SCIADOPITYS
JAPANESE UMBRELLA PINE

This genus consists of just one species, a very distinctive and handsome conifer from Japan. It is very slow growing, eventually forming an upright, single-trunked, conical tree to over 100 ft (30 m) tall. It can be kept in a container for long periods and is often used as a bonsai subject.

CULTIVATION
Sciadopitys prefers a cool maritime climate with cool, moist, humus-rich soil and light shade when young. Propagate from seed.

Sciadopitys verticillata *(right)*

The distinctive foliage of this species is composed of deep green, flattened needles, up to 6 in (15 cm) long, carried in stiff whorls of 20 to 30 and facing upwards, like the ribs of an umbrella. Interestingly, the needles are not true leaves at all but they do photosynthesize; the true 'leaves' are the tiny scales that lie almost flat along the stems. The small oval cones take 2 years to mature. **ZONES 5–10.**

S

SENNA

This large genus consists of 260 species of fast-growing, mostly evergreen shrubs as well as some herbaceous perennials and small trees. It includes several species grown for medicinal use. Formerly classified under *Cassia*, they occur in most warm parts of the world, with most species in the Americas, Africa and Australia. They are grown for their clusters of buttercup-like flowers, mostly golden yellow but sometimes pink. The compound leaves consist of paired leaflets. The fruits are long pods, either flattened or rounded.

CULTIVATION

Most species thrive in light, well-drained soil with full sun and shelter from wind. Prune plants lightly after flowering to maintain dense foliage. Propagate from seed (first soaked in warm water for 24 hours) or from cuttings.

Senna artemisioides (left)
syn. *Cassia artemisioides*

SILVER CASSIA, PUNTY, FEATHERY CASSIA

This dense, rounded, evergreen shrub reaches 6 ft (1.8 m) tall and is endemic to dry parts of southern Australia. The foliage is silver gray and silky due to a covering of minute hairs. The leaves are up to 2 in (5 cm) long, made up of 3 to 8 pairs of narrow leaflets. The flowers are a rich yellow with contrasting brown anthers, arranged in clusters of 10 to 12; flowering extends from winter to early summer. The fruits are flattened pods that mature dark brown. ZONES 9–11.

Senna didymobotrya (right)
syn. *Cassia didymobotrya*

Indigenous to tropical Africa, this evergreen shrub grows to 10 ft (3 m) and has a rounded canopy on a short trunk. Fine downy hairs cover both the leaves and shoots. The foliage has an unpleasant smell when crushed; the leaves may be 12–18 in (30–45 cm) long. From summer to winter, yellow flowers are carried near the shoot tips in erect spikes up to 12 in (30 cm) long, bursting from bud scales. The fruits are long, flattened pods. ZONES 10–12.

Senna multiglandulosa *(right)*
syn. *Cassia tomentosa*

This is a widespread and variable leafy shrub or
small tree from Central and South America, southern USA, eastern Australia, India and South Africa.
It grows 3–20 ft (1–6 m) high. The new branches
of this species are downy, but become dark
brownish gray with age. The leaves are up to 8 in
(20 cm) long and are composed of about 8 paired
leaflets with sharp tips. The yellow flowers, up to
$\frac{3}{4}$ in (18 mm) across, are borne in heads of up to
20 blooms. The 6 in (15 cm) seed pods are black,
softly hairy and hang vertically down. ZONES 8–12.

Senna multijuga
(right)
syn. *Cassia multijuga*

This species from Cen-
tral and South America
is a fast-growing ever-
green tree that reaches
25 ft (8 m) in height.
It forms a rounded
crown with attractive,
pinnate leaves with 10
to 15 pairs of leaflets.
Golden-yellow flowers
are borne in large,
terminal panicles in
late summer, followed
by long seed pods.
ZONES 10–12.

S

SEQUOIA
CALIFORNIA REDWOOD, COAST REDWOOD

This genus, containing a single species, boasts the world's tallest tree, at about 360 ft (110 m). The redwood is extremely long lived, with some specimens estimated to be about 3500 years old. An evergreen conifer, it is indigenous to the west coast of the USA from Monterey, California north to southern Oregon. It is valued for its timber, and it has been necessary to provide statutory protection for the most notable groves in national parks and elsewhere to save it from exploitation.

CULTIVATION
This tree will survive in a wide range of climates; extremely cold weather may affect the foliage but not the plant itself. It grows quickly when young and needs plenty of water, full sun or part-shade and deep, well-drained soil. Suckers should be removed immediately and general pruning is tolerated. Propagate from seed or heeled cuttings; this is one of the few conifers that will sprout from the cut stump.

Sequoia sempervirens *(below left)*

This single-trunked, conical tree has bright green, flattened, leaf-like needles up to 1 in (25 mm) long. The foliage is held horizontally on small side branches, with the main branches drooping slightly. The whole tree has a resinous aroma like pine wood, especially the red-brown, fibrous bark which is very thick and deeply fissured in parallel lines running straight up the trunk. **'Adpressa'** is very dwarf, remaining about 3 ft (1 m) high and 6 ft (1.8 m) wide for many years, maturing to 20 ft (6 m) high; **'Aptos Blue'** has blue-green foliage and slightly pendulous branch tips; **'Los Altos'** has deep green, heavy-textured foliage on arching branches; and **'Santa Cruz'** has pale green, soft-textured, slightly drooping foliage. ZONES 8–10.

Sequoia sempervirens 'Adpressa' *(below)*

SEQUOIADENDRON
GIANT SEQUOIA, BIG TREE

From the Sierra Nevada area of California, the only species in this genus is a true giant of a tree. While not quite as tall as the California redwood *(Sequoia sempervirens)*, it is more heavily built and contains the largest timber volume of any tree. It is also very long lived, and is an impressive tree for large parks and gardens. Its huge trunk is covered in rough, deeply fissured, reddish brown bark.

CULTIVATION

Trees of this size need a solid base, so plant in deep, well-drained soil in an open, sunny position and water well when young; it is frost resistant but dislikes dry conditions. Propagate from seed or cuttings.

Sequoiadendron giganteum
(right & below)
syns *Sequoia gigantea,*
Wellingtonia gigantea

This conifer can grow to 300 ft (90 m) tall, with a trunk up to 40 ft (12 m) in diameter at the base. It is an upright, single-trunked, conical tree with sprays of deep green, slightly prickly, cypress-like foliage. A specimen of this species in the Sequoia National Park in California is said to be 3800 years old. '**Pendulum**' has pendent side branches. ZONES 7–10.

S

SERRURIA

Members of the protea family, *Serruria* includes about 55 species of evergreen shrubs that are endemic to the southwestern Cape area of South Africa. Each flowerhead consists of a central tuft of flowers surrounded by leafy bracts, often the dominant feature of the bloom. The flowerheads may be solitary at the branch ends or borne in clusters. Some are given a very feathery appearance by the mass of central stamens. *Serruria* range from prostrate shrubs to plants 5 ft (1.5 m) tall. The leaves are fern-like, divided into many fine segments. The fruits are small hard nuts covered with hairs.

CULTIVATION
These plants thrive only in sandy, perfectly drained soil and with a warm climate; plant in an open, sunny spot. They grow faster than most other proteas and are best propagated from seed or cuttings.

S

Serruria florida
(left)
BLUSHING BRIDE

This species forms a slender shrub to 4 ft (1.2 m) tall. It is rare in the wild, but is popular due to its long-lasting, 2 in (5 cm) wide, dainty flowerheads. These consist of showy, broad, papery, creamy white bracts, flushed pink or rarely green, which surround a central tuft of feathery, silvery white to pinkish flowers and appear in clusters of 3 to 5 from winter to spring. The leaves are delicate and divided into needle-like segments. **'Sugar 'n' Spice'** has white bracts flushed deep rose pink, surrounding the central mass of pale pink flowers. ZONES 9–11.

SKIMMIA

This genus includes 4 species of evergreen shrubs and trees. They have glossy deep green, oval leaves about 4–6 in (10–15 cm) long and about half as wide. The small starry flowers, which open from late winter, are white or cream and densely packed in conical clusters. They are followed by red or black berries, depending on the species. Most species require male and female plants to be present for pollination.

CULTIVATION

Skimmias are plants for shade or part-shade and grow very well with rhododendrons, azaleas and camellias. Like them they prefer moist, humus-rich, well-drained soil. They can be raised from seed in autumn or from cuttings in late summer.

Skimmia japonica
(right)

JAPANESE SKIMMIA

This fully frost-hardy shrub grows to about 20 ft (6 m) high and wide. It has 4 in (10 cm) long, glossy, deep green, leathery, oval leaves. In spring, terminal clusters of slightly fragrant, creamy white flowers are borne, followed by ½ in (12 mm) round, bright red berries. Both male and female plants are required to obtain berries. **'Rubella'** has red-margined leaves and dark red flower buds. ***Skimmia japonica* subsp.** *reevesiana* **'Robert Fortune'** is a hermaphrodite with pale green leaves margined in dark green. ZONES 7–10.

S

SOLANUM
syn. *Lycianthes*

There are over 1400 species in this genus including trees, shrubs, annuals, biennials, perennials and climbers from a range of habitats worldwide. Some are evergreen, others semi-evergreen or deciduous. The genus includes important food plants like the potato and eggplant (aubergine), though many species are dangerously poisonous. Ornamental species are grown for their flowers and fruits. The leaves are arranged alternately, while the showy flowers are solitary or borne in clusters and are star-shaped to bell-shaped, ranging in color from white and yellow to blue and purple. The fruits are berries that contain many seeds.

CULTIVATION
These warm-climate plants have a wide range of requirements; most prefer full sun and rich, well-drained soil. They are commonly grown from seed in spring or cuttings in summer. They are prone to attack by spider mite, white fly and aphids.

Solanum aviculare *(right)*
KANGAROO APPLE, PORO PORO

Indigenous to Australia and New Zealand, this evergreen shrub is fast growing but short lived. Reaching 10–12 ft (3–3.5 m) tall, its single upright stem has spreading branches forming a wide crown. The large, dark green to bluish green leaves are oval to lance-shaped, often with deeply lobed edges. In spring and summer, the purple flowers, 1¹/₂ in (35 mm) across, appear in large clusters at the branch tips. The fruits of *Solanum aviculare*, oval berries about 1 in (25 mm) long, hang from thin stalks and ripen from green to yellow to red. ZONES 9–11.

Solanum rantonnetii *(right)*
syn. *Lycianthes rantonnetii*
PARAGUAY NIGHTSHADE, BLUE POTATO BUSH

This South American relative of the potato is a valuable long-blooming shrub or scrambling vine for warm-climate gardens. Simple green leaves cover the branches and provide a good foil for the summer-long profusion of deep violet-blue flowers. It can be used as a 6–8 ft (1.8–2.4 m) tall background shrub, or trained on a trellis or arbor, where it may reach 12 ft (3.5 m) or more. **'Royal Robe'** has deeper purple flowers and nearly year-round bloom in mild-winter areas. ZONES 9–11.

S

SOPHORA

This legume genus of some 50 species of deciduous and ever-green trees, shrubs and perennials is scattered widely through warmer parts of the world. All have pinnate leaves and short racemes of clusters of pea-flowers, mostly in shades of yellow, cream, grayish blue or lilac. The seed pods are constricted between the seeds and are often slow to split open; the very hard, waxy seeds are long lived and resistant to water penetration. An interesting group of closely related species, which some botanists believe should be treated as a separate genus, *Edwardsia*, are widely scattered around the southern oceans on small islands such as Easter Island, Gough Island and Mauritius as well as larger landmasses such as New Zealand, Hawaii, and the south-ern tip of South America; typified by the New Zealand *Sophora tetraptera*, they have large yellow flowers and pods with 4 slightly translucent wings. Their seeds are resistant to saltwater, and are believed to have floated around the southern oceans, with lim-ited evolution taking place after establishing in new lands.

Sophora japonica
(below & below right)

JAPANESE PAGODA TREE,
PAGODA TREE

Despite its name, this deciduous tree origi-nates from central China and Korea. It grows to about 100 ft (30 m) high. The light green pinnate leaves are 8 in (20 cm)long, and the cream or occa-sionally pale pink flowers are borne in long panicles. The pods that follow are like bead necklaces. **'Pendula'** is often grafted onto 8 ft (2.4 m) standards to produce a small weep-ing tree. ZONES 4–10.

CULTIVATION

Sophoras thrive under a wide range of conditions. They can be grown in small groves, or used as shade trees or lawn specimens. Most prefer moist, well-drained soil in sun or part-shade. Propa-gate from seed or cuttings. In Australia and New Zealand cater-pillars of the kowhai moth can defoliate plants in summer.

S

Sophora microphylla *(right)*
WEEPING KOWHAI

This New Zealand evergreen species grows 12–20 ft (3.5–6 m) tall and its weeping, interlocking, wiry branches form a wide, rounded crown. Leaves are fernlike; many are shed in late winter before the flowers appear. The deep yellow, sometimes lemon to deep orange blooms, up to $1^1/_2$ in (35 mm) long, are borne in dense clusters from late winter to early summer. Fruits are pods about 6 in (15 cm) long. **Sophora microphylla** var. **longicarinata** has lemon flowers and smaller, more numerous leaflets. **'Golden Shower'** forms a symmetrical tree with strongly weeping outer branches and golden yellow flowers. ZONES 8–10.

Sophora prostrata

This New Zealand native is prized for the clusters of pale yellow flowers it bears in summer amid small, oval leaflets. Frost hardy, it is a many-branched, prostrate or bushy semi-evergreen shrub with a maximum height and spread of 6 ft (1.8 m). **'Little Baby'** has very angular twiggy growth, very fine leaves and yellow flowers in early spring. ZONES 8–10.

Sophora prostrata 'Little Baby' *(center left)*

Sophora tetraptera *(center right)*
KOWHAI

This free-flowering, usually evergreen tree from the North Island is New Zealand's national flower. It may grow to 30 ft (9 m) tall but usually less. Mature specimens develop a semi-pendulous habit, with interlocking branches. Leaves consist of 20 to 30 pairs of small, gray-green leaflets. The abundant spring pea-flowers are about $1^1/_2$ in (35 mm) long; pale to golden yellow, they are borne in showy pendulous clusters. Fruit are narrow pods that ripen to dark gray. ZONES 8–10.

Sophora tomentosa *(above)*
SILVERBUSH

This species is a tropical member of a predominantly temperate-zone genus. It is a large, sprawling shrub or small tree to 10 ft (3 m), fairly common on tropical seashores and worth growing in the garden for its unusual color scheme—the leaves are silver-gray, the flowers lime yellow. ZONES 10–12.

SORBARIA

The 10 shrub species of this genus originate from the cool to cold mountain regions of Asia. All are deciduous and have pinnate leaves with serrated leaflets. The small, starry white flowers, usually in large terminal panicles, have a cup-shaped calyx, 5 reflexed petals and many prominent stamens. The fruits are berries.

CULTIVATION
Most species sucker freely; they thrive in full sun in rich, moist soil and prefer cool climates. Prune in winter to restrict size; remove some older canes if necessary. Propagate from seed or cuttings in late winter or summer, or by division in autumn.

Sorbaria kirilowii
(right)
syns *Sorbaria arborea,*
Spiraea arborea
FALSE SPIRAEA

This large, spreading shrub from China and Tibet grows to 20 ft (6 m) tall with cane-like stems and com-pound leaves consisting of up to 17 long, nar-row leaflets. The flowers are held in upright fluffy panicles, 12 in (30 cm) long. The young growth is often covered in masses of hair. ZONES 4–10.

S

SORBUS
ROWAN, SERVICE TREE, MOUNTAIN ASH

This genus is made up of 100 species of deciduous trees and shrubs from cool climates of the northern hemisphere, grown for their foliage, timber and decorative fruits. Most species have pinnate leaves and terminal clusters of small, creamy white flowers in spring. The flowers, often rather unpleasantly scented, are followed by showy berries. A few species have attractive autumn foliage.

CULTIVATION
Rowans are easily grown in sun or part-shade in any well-drained, fertile soil and are most at home in areas with distinct winters. The species may be raised from stratified seed; selected forms are usually grafted. They are susceptible to fireblight.

Sorbus aria
(below right)
WHITEBEAM

This European species grows to 30 ft (9 m) tall. Its coarsely toothed, simple leaves, 4 in (10 cm) long, have white felting on the undersides and develop orange and yellow autumn tones. The ½ in (12 mm) berries are red. This species is very tough, tolerating chalky soil, salt winds and air pollution. **'Aurea'** has light yellowish green leaves; **'Chrysophylla'** has yellow leaves; **'Lutescens'** has young foliage covered with fine silvery hairs; **'Majestica'** has leaves and berries larger than those of the species; and **'Theophrasta'** has orange berries and glossy green foliage. ZONES 2–9.

Sorbus americana
(left)
AMERICAN MOUNTAIN ASH

This is a vigorous tree to 30 ft (9 m) with ascending reddish branches and red sticky buds. The pinnate leaves are bright green, turning bright golden yellow in autumn. Large dense bunches of small red berries follow. It comes from eastern North America. ZONES 3–9.

Sorbus aucuparia in winter *(above)* and in summer *(right)*

Sorbus aucuparia

ROWAN, MOUNTAIN ASH, EUROPEAN MOUNTAIN ASH

The most commonly grown species, this tree grows to about 50 ft (15 m) high in gardens, much taller in its native European and Asian forests. The 11 to 15 small, toothed leaflets turn rich gold in autumn. The white spring flowers are followed by scarlet berries. **'Asplenifolia'** has very finely cut leaves; **'Edulis'** is a large-berried form used for jams and preserves; **'Fructu Luteo'** has orange-yellow berries; **'Pendula'** has wide-spreading growth and a weeping habit; **'Sheerwater Seedling'** is narrowly upright; and **'Xanthocarpa'** has yellow berries. ZONES 2–9.

Sorbus cashmiriana *(right)*

KASHMIR MOUNTAIN ASH

Indigenous to the western Himalayas, this spreading tree can attain a height of 25 ft (8 m), although it is often smaller. Its mid-green leaves are made up of 17 to 19 elliptical leaflets, which are gray-green underneath. The pendent clusters of white to pale pink flowers appear in early summer, followed by $^1/_2$ in (12 mm) wide globular white fruit that endure into winter. ZONES 5–9.

S

Sorbus domestica
(left)

SERVICE TREE

This 70 ft (21 m) high, spreading tree, indigenous to southern and eastern Europe and northern Africa, has deeply fissured bark. The leaves are made up of 13 to 21 toothed leaflets. The 1 in (25 mm) long fruit, brownish green with a rosy tint, are somewhat pear-shaped and edible when fully ripe. ZONES 3–9.

Sorbus hupehensis
(left)

HUBEI ROWAN

Indigenous to Hubei province in central China, this tall, vigorous tree has blue-green pinnate leaves of 9 to 17 leaflets, which develop orange, red and purple autumn tones. White berries, tinged pink, are carried on red stems. ZONES 5–9.

Sorbus 'Joseph Rock' *(left)*

This vigorous upright tree of unknown East Asian origin grows to about 30 ft (9 m) high. Its leaves are made up of 15 to 21 sharply toothed leaflets, which develop rich red, orange and purple tones in autumn. It produces large clusters of bright yellow berries. ZONES 4–9.

Sorbus pohuashanensis *(right)*

Indigenous to mountainous regions of northern China where it reaches 70 ft (21 m) tall, this species is closely related to the European rowan *(Sorbus aucuparia)*. The pinnate leaves are up to 8 in (20 cm) long, green above but hairy and blue-green beneath; young shoots and flower buds are also covered in hair. The flat-topped clusters of flowers are held above the foliage, as are the shiny red fruit. The cultivar **'Pagoda Red'** has a fine display of fruit. ZONES 4–9.

Sorbus reducta *(right)*

This small shrub to 5 ft (1.5 m) forms a thicket by suckering. The elliptical leaflets become bronze and purplish in autumn. The flowers are white but sparse, and white or ruby fruit follow. It comes from western China. **'Gnome'** is a smaller, tighter form. ZONES 6–9.

Sorbus terminalis *(left)*

WILD SERVICE TREE

This species from the Mediterranean grows to 50 ft (15 m) or more with a rounded crown. The twigs are felted when young, the leaves maple-shaped, dark green and glossy but white and downy beneath, becoming bronzed yellow in autumn. Reddish brown fruit follow the white flowers. ZONES 6–9.

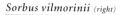

Sorbus vilmorinii *(right)*

This shrub or small tree to 20 ft (6 m) tall spreads to 13–16 ft (4–5 m). The buds and shoots are downy and reddish brown. The many leaflets are grayish underneath, becoming red and purple in the autumn. The white flowers are followed by drooping clusters of rosy berries that fade to pinkish white. It is native to China. ZONES 6–9.

SPARRMANNIA

The 3 to 7 species of evergreen trees and shrubs in this small genus from Madagascar and parts of Africa bear stems and leaves that are covered with soft hairs. The large, soft leaves have a toothed edge and may be lobed. Its attractive flowers, on long stalks, are arranged in clusters near the shoot tips, or arise from the leaf axils. The fruits are spiny capsules.

CULTIVATION

These plants need a sunny position with shelter from wind and frost, and well-drained soil enriched with organic matter. Keep the soil moist during the active growth period. These are plants for warm climates, often grown in greenhouses in cooler areas. Propagate from cuttings in late spring.

Sparrmannia africana (right)

AFRICAN HEMP, WILD HOLLY-HOCK, AFRICAN LINDEN

This fast-growing shrub or small tree reaches 20 ft (6 m) and bears clusters of striking white flowers with prominent purple and gold stamens. Flowering peaks in winter to early spring, but the species blooms sporadically throughout most of the year. The large leaves may be oval to heart-shaped with a pointed tip, or have several finger-like lobes. The stems are erect and woody with many spreading branches. The fruits are rounded. **'Flore Plena'** has double flowers. ZONES 9–11.

Sparrmania africana 'Flore Plena' *(below)*

SPARTIUM
SPANISH BROOM

This genus includes just one species: a deciduous, almost leafless shrub that is indigenous to the Mediterranean region. A yellow dye is derived from the flowers.

CULTIVATION
This adaptable plant thrives in well-drained soil enriched with a little organic matter. Full sun is best. It is a shrub for warm to coolish climates. Pruning after flowering will maintain compact, well-shaped bushes. Propagate from seed or cuttings.

S

Spartium junceum (above)

This shrub bears masses of large, golden yellow, fragrant pea-flowers carried in loose, 18 in (45 cm) long spikes at the shoot tips. It flowers profusely through spring into early summer. The leaves are narrow, bluish green and less than 1 in (25 mm) long; they are shed from the new growth soon after they appear. Spanish broom makes a bushy shrub 6–10 ft (1.8–3 m) tall; on older specimens the stems arch downwards. The fruits are flat, silvery pods, maturing to brown. ZONES 6–11.

SPIRAEA

This genus consists of 80 species of deciduous or semi-evergreen shrubs valued for their spring and summer flower display and autumn foliage color. Spiraeas form clumps of wiry stems that shoot up from the base and are densely covered with narrow, toothed leaves. They belong to the rose family, and under a magnifying glass the flowers do resemble tiny roses but are so small that the individual flower is lost among the mass of blooms carried on each flower cluster.

CULTIVATION

Spiraeas are adaptable plants that thrive under most garden conditions in temperate climates, though they prefer a warm summer. They thrive in moist, well-drained soil and a position sheltered from the hottest sun, especially in warm summer areas where the foliage may burn. Most should be pruned after flowering. Propagate from cuttings in summer.

Spiraea cantoniensis *(right)*
REEVES' SPIRAEA

This deciduous or semi-evergreen shrub is very showy when in flower in spring, with rounded, 2 in (5 cm) clusters of small, white, 5-petalled flowers densely clothing the reddish, gracefully arching branches. The narrow leaves are dark green above and blue-green below. This 3–6 ft (1–1.8 m) tall species originated in China. It can be used for hedging, and is the best spiraea for warm-temperate regions. The double-flowered form is the most popular in gardens. ZONES 5–11.

Spiraea japonica
(below left)
JAPANESE SPIRAEA

This low, mounding, deciduous shrub bears rose pink to red flowers from late spring to mid-summer. It grows to a height and spread of about 6 ft (1.8 m). The cream and pink variegated new leaves turn green as they mature. It has the best foliage of any plants in the genus. There are many varieties and cultivars, including: 'Little Princess' to 3 ft (1 m) tall; 'Anthony Waterer', the most commonly cultivated selection; 'Goldflame', popular for its bronze new growth that turns golden as it matures; 'Nyewoods' with small leaves and dark pink flowers; 'Shirobana' with both dark pink and white flowers on one plant; and 'Nana' (syn. 'Alpina'), more compact at only 18 in (45 cm). ZONES 3–10.

Spiraea japonica 'Anthony Waterer' *(below)*

S

Spiraea nipponica *(above)*

From Japan, this upright to spreading deciduous
shrub reaches 6 ft (1.8 m) high and wide. Its
rounded leaves are finely serrated and in early
summer it bears pure white flowers in neat, round
heads crowded along the branches. **'Snowmound'**
is a particularly vigorous cultivar. ZONES 5–10.

Spiraea nipponica
'Snowmound' *(right)*

Spiraea prunifolia
'Plena' *(right)*

Spiraea prunifolia

This deciduous shrub from China, Taiwan and
Japan grows to 6 ft (1.8 m) tall. Snowy white,
5-petalled flowers with greenish centers appear in
early spring. They are arranged in small clusters
of 3 to 6 all along the pendulous branches before
the leaves appear. The leaves turn red in autumn.
The double-flowered **'Plena'** is the only form
commonly grown. ZONES 4–10.

STACHYURUS

This genus includes some 6 species of deciduous or semi-evergreen shrubs and trees from the Himalayas and eastern Asia. Although reminiscent of the witch hazels and *Corylopsis,* they belong in a different family. They are generally not spectacular plants, though one species, *Stachyurus praecox,* is fairly widely grown. They bloom in late winter or early spring before or just as the leaves are developing, and produce small, cream to pale yellow flowers in drooping racemes at every leaf bud. They also have broadly lance-shaped leaves.

CULTIVATION
These plants prefer humus-rich, well-drained, acidic soil in sun or light shade and are usually propagated from seed or cuttings in summer.

Stachyurus praecox *(above)*

This 6 ft (1.8 m) high and wide deciduous shrub, indigenous to Japan, is noted for its early flowering. Gracefully drooping, 3 in (8 cm) long racemes of buds appear in autumn, opening as small pale yellow-green flowers and persisting on bare branches through to early spring. The leaves are up to 6 in (15 cm) long and are carried on somewhat tiered, reddish brown stems. ZONES 5–10.

S

STENOCARPUS

A genus of 22 species of evergreen shrubs and trees belonging to the protea family and indigenous to Australia, Malaysia and New Caledonia, these plants bear umbels of tubular, cream to red flowers with knob-shaped stigmas protruding through splits in the tubes. The leaves are alternate and simple.

CULTIVATION

They need full sun and fertile, well-drained soil. Water generously in summer, less in winter. Propagate from seed in spring or cuttings in summer.

Stenocarpus sinuatus *(above)*

FIREWHEEL TREE

This handsome but slow-growing tree endemic to rainforests of Australia's warm east coast can reach 30–70 ft (9–21 m) tall; it has an upright, thick trunk with dark brown bark topped by a dense crown of foliage. The leaves are shiny and dark green and up to 12 in (30 cm) long. The interesting skittle-shaped buds, opening to contorted flowers, about 3 in (8 cm) across, are orange to red and are arranged in a cluster like spokes on a wheel. The woody, boat-shaped fruit are 2–4 in (5–10 cm) long. ZONES 9–12.

S

STEPHANANDRA

This genus is made up of 4 species of deciduous shrubs related to *Spiraea*. From the eastern Asian region, they tolerate low temperatures. The toothed and lobed mid-green leaves, which turn orange and gold in autumn, are very ornamental, as are the sepia-tinted bare stems in winter. Tiny, star-shaped, white or greenish flowers appear in summer in soft panicles; each has many stamens.

CULTIVATION

Species of *Stephanandra* grow well in sun or part-shade, preferring rich, moist, loamy soil. They can be pruned to shape in winter. Propagate from cuttings or by division in autumn.

Stephanandra incisa (left)
LACE SHRUB, CUTLEAF STEPHANANDRA

Occurring naturally in Japan, Taiwan and Korea, this shrub grows to about 6 ft (1.8 m) tall with a similar spread. The lace shrub has graceful arching branches with diamond-shaped, deeply toothed leaves. The tiny greenish white flowers appear in summer. This shrub tolerates neglect. **'Crispa'** is a dwarf-growing cultivar with slightly curled leaves. ZONES 4–10.

Stephanandra tanakae (left)

Valued for its decorative, arching growth habit and attractive leaves, this shrub from Japan grows to about 10 ft (3 m) tall with a similar spread. The plant's leaves are 2–4 in (5–10 cm) long with shallowly toothed lobes with long points. The new foliage is pinkish brown. The tiny white flowers are borne through summer. ZONES 4–10.

S

Stewartia pseudocamellia *(below right)*

syn. *Stuartia pseudocamellia*

FALSE CAMELLIA, JAPANESE STEWARTIA

Indigenous to Japan (not Hokkaido) and Korea, this species can grow to 70 ft (21 m) high in the wild, but is more commonly about 20 ft (6 m) in cultivation. It blooms from late spring to early summer and the white flowers are followed by small, spherical, nut-like seed capsules, which are a prominent feature from mid-summer. It has attractive peeling bark and yellow, orange and red autumn foliage. **Stewartia pseudocamellia var. koreana** (syn. *S. koreana*) hardly differs from the typical Japanese species; its distinguishing features are flowers with spreading, not cupped, petals and leaves that are broader and less silky when young. ZONES 6–10.

STEWARTIA
syn. *Stuartia*

This eastern Asian and North American genus consists of 15 to 20 species of deciduous or evergreen small trees or shrubs closely allied to the camellias. The flowers are usually white with prominent golden stamens, about 3 in (8 cm) across, and resemble single camellia blooms. The leaves are elliptical, 2–6 in (5–15 cm) long, and often develop bright orange and red autumn tones.

CULTIVATION

Best grown in moist, humus-rich, well-drained, slightly acidic soil in sun or part-shade. Propagate from seed in autumn or cuttings in summer.

S

Stewartia sinensis *(right)*

syn. *Stuartia sinensis*

A 30 ft (9 m) tall tree indigenous to China, this species blooms in late spring and summer with small, fragrant, rose-like, white flowers about 2 in (5 cm) across. The color of the flaking bark is a warm reddish brown to purple and the autumn foliage is crimson. ZONES 6–10.

STREPTOSOLEN
MARMALADE BUSH

This genus consists of only one species: a loosely scrambling shrub with alternate, simple leaves. It occurs in parts of the northern Andes and is cultivated mainly for its clusters of brightly colored, long-tubed, funnel-shaped flowers.

CULTIVATION

In the garden it does best in full sun with shelter from strong winds. A light, well-drained soil is ideal, preferably enriched with organic matter, and it needs adequate moisture during warmer months. Light pruning after flowering will keep it compact. Propagate from cuttings in summer.

Streptosolen jamesonii (left) syn. *Browallia jamesonii*

This fast-growing, evergreen shrub reaches 6 ft (1.8 m) high, with long flexible stems that arch slightly under the weight of the flowerheads. Flowering peaks in spring to summer, but continues for much of the year. Individual, bright orange flowers are borne on thin stalks, and strangely twisted; they form large dense clusters at the branch tips. The leaves are neat, oval and shiny dark green above, paler underneath. Both foliage and flowers have fine hairs. The fruits are small capsules. ZONES 9–11.

S

STYRAX
SNOWBELL

This genus consists of about 100 species of deciduous and ever-green shrubs and small trees occurring naturally over a wide area of the Americas and eastern Asia, with one species native to Europe. Several cool-temperate, deciduous species are cultivated for their neat growth habit and attractive spring display of slightly drooping sprays of small, bell-shaped, white flowers, which appear on the previous year's wood.

CULTIVATION
They prefer cool, moist, well-drained soil and cool, moist, summer climates. Usually raised from stratified seed in autumn, they can also be grown from cuttings in summer.

Styrax japonicus (right)

JAPANESE SNOWBELL, JAPANESE SNOWDROP TREE

This species is a native of Japan, Korea and China. It grows to about 25 ft (8 m) high and flowers from mid-spring. Its branches, which are clothed with rather narrow, 3 in (8 cm) long, deep green shiny leaves, tend to be held horizontally which creates a somewhat tiered effect. This species does best shaded from the hottest sun. ZONES 6–9.

Styrax obassia (right)

FRAGRANT SNOWBELL

Indigenous to Japan, Korea and northern China, this species grows to 30 ft (9 m) high. Its flowers, less pendulous than those of other species, are slightly fragrant. Large deep green, paddle-shaped leaves, up to 8 in (20 cm) long have whitish down on the undersides. It is worth growing for the foliage alone. ZONES 6–9.

SUTERA
syn. *Bacopa*

There are 130 species in this genus, comprising annuals, perennials and small shrubs from South Africa. The leaves are opposite or clustered and simple or lobed. The flowers are borne in the leaf axils or are terminal or both, and are white, pink, lilac or purple. These compact plants are suitable for the garden in mild climates.

CULTIVATION
Frost tender, these plants prefer full sun and well-drained, fertile soil. Propagation is from cuttings in summer, from seed or by division.

Sutera cordata *(above)*

This 24 in (60 cm) woody shrub has opposite, elongated heart-shaped leaves and terminal white flowers borne over a long period in summer and autumn. It is usually sold as *Bacopa* 'Snow Flake'.
ZONES 9–11.

SYMPHORICARPOS
SNOWBERRY

This genus is made up of about 17 species of deciduous shrubs allied to *Lonicera* and from North America, with one rare and obscure species from China. They have elliptical to nearly round leaves and bear very small, bell-shaped, pink or white flowers in spring. They are mostly grown for their large crops of distinctive berries, which stand out clearly in winter when the branches are bare.

CULTIVATION
They are easily grown in any moist, well-drained soil in sun or shade, and are usually propagated from open-ground winter hardwood cuttings. As they are resistant to shade, poor soil and pollution, they are very suitable for city gardens.

Symphoricarpos × *chenaultii* (right)

A hybrid between *Symphoricarpos microphyllus* and *S. orbiculatus*, this is an upright shrub that grows to around 8 ft (2.5 m) high. Its young stems are downy, as often are the undersides of its small, rounded, dark green leaves. Like most species, its flowers are pink, but the fruit is rather unusual. Most commonly it is red and white spotted in an attractive mottled pattern, but occasionally it will be pure white with an increasing amount of red on the exposed sunny side, creating a distinct two-tone effect. ZONES 4–9.

Symphoricarpos microphyllus (right)

This upright 6 ft (1.8 m) tall shrub has felted shoots. The oval leaves are 1¼ in (30 mm) long. The white flowers appear in summer and are followed by small pink-tinged white fruit. It comes from Mexico. ZONES 9–10.

Symphoricarpos orbiculatus (right)
INDIAN CURRANT, CORAL BERRY

This tough, adaptable shrub from the USA and Mexico grows to about 6 ft (1.8 m) high and wide. It is very dense and twiggy, with oval leaves around 1½ in (35 mm) long. The fruits are small, under ¼ in (6 mm) in diameter, but abundant and a conspicuous bright pink. The berries last long after the leaves have fallen. A hot summer will yield a heavier crop of berries. ZONES 3–9.

S

SYRINGA

LILAC

Lilacs are prized for their upright to arching panicles of small, highly fragrant flowers, which are massed in loose heads. They appear from mid-spring and range in color from white and pale yellow to all shades of pink, mauve and purple. Most of the common garden varieties of *Syringa vulgaris* were raised in France in the late 1800s to early 1900s, though new forms appear from time to time; not all cultivars are fragrant. The genus contains about 20 species, all deciduous shrubs and trees from Europe and northeastern Asia. Most reach about 8 ft (2.4 m) high and 6 ft (1.8 m) wide, with opposite leaves that sometimes color well in autumn.

CULTIVATION

Lilacs prefer moist, humus-rich, well-drained soil in sun or light shade. They do best where winters are cold because they require a few frosts in order to flower well. Any pruning is best done immediately after flowering. Species may be raised from seed or cuttings. Named cultivars are usually grafted, but can sometimes be struck from hardwood or semi-ripe cuttings. Established plants produce suckers that can be used for propagation.

Syringa josikaea
(right)

HUNGARIAN LILAC

This is an erect shrub to 12 ft (3.5 m) with rigid warty branches. The leaves are glossy on top and gray underneath with felted veins. The richly colored flowers are held upright in loose heads in summer.
ZONES 5–9.

Syringa meyeri 'Palibin'
(right)

Syringa meyeri

From China, this small spreading shrub grows to about 6 ft (1.8 m) tall and wide. The leaves are elliptical, and the deep purplish mauve flowers appear in spring in dense heads. **'Palibin'** is a slow-growing dwarf cultivar with violet to rose pink flowers in small dense clusters. **'Superba'** has dark pink flowers that fade as they mature; it is a long-flowering form with some flowers produced from mid-spring to mid-summer. All forms of *Syringa meyeri* may have a lesser flowering in autumn. ZONES 4–9.

Syringa × *persica*
'Alba' *(above)*

Syringa × persica

PERSIAN LILAC

This is thought to be a hybrid of *Syringa laciniata* and *S. afghanica* or else a stable juvenile form of *S. laciniata*. Probably native to Afghanistan, it is a deciduous, bushy, compact shrub. In spring it bears profuse heads of small, delightfully fragrant flowers set amid narrow, pointed, dark green leaves. It grows to a height and spread of just under 6 ft (1.8 m) and will grow in warmer winter climates than most lilacs. **'Alba'** has dainty, sweetly scented white flowers. **ZONES 5–9.**

Syringa pubescens subsp. patula

'Miss Kim' *(above)*

syn. *Syringa patula* 'Miss Kim'

MISS KIM LILAC

Syringa pubescens subsp. *patula* 'Miss Kim' is a compact selection of an excellent lilac notable for its late-season flowering. It has relatively large leaves and fragrant flowers, which are pale lilac pink. This plant will reach a height of 6–8 ft (1.8–2.4 m) with a similar spread, but is slow growing and will remain only 3–4 ft (1–1.2 m) tall for many years. **ZONES 4–9.**

Syringa reticulata

(right)

JAPANESE TREE LILAC

This Japanese lilac has comparatively small flowers, but they produce a wonderful spring display of creamy white flower-heads at the ends of the branches. Sweetly fragrant, they stand out against the dark green foliage and make excellent cut flowers. Although the Japanese tree lilac can grow to 30 ft (9 m), forming a squat, wide-crowned tree it is usually seen as a large shrub. **ZONES 3–9.**

Syringa vulgaris *(below)*
COMMON LILAC

This is the species from which most garden
cultivars derive. It is native to southeastern
Europe and grows to about 20 ft (6 m) high with
pointed, oval or heart-shaped leaves up to 4 in
(10 cm) long. The flowers are borne in dense pyramidal heads and are strongly fragrant, white or
pale mauve. **'Andenken an Ludwig Späth'** (syn.
'Souvenir de Louis Spaeth') has single, deep
purple flowers in large heads in mid-season;
'Aurea' has yellowish green leaves and darker lilac
flowers; **'Charles Joly'** is a double deep reddish
purple lilac with very fragrant flowers and
strongly upright growth; **'Congo'** has single rich
dark purple flowers; **'Edith Cavell'** is white;
'Firmament' is light blue; **'Katherine
Havemeyer'** has fully double, large-flowered
heads of lavender-purple buds opening to a soft
mauve-pink; **'Lavender Lady'** is mid-mauve;
'Marechal Foch' is purplish pink; **'Miss Ellen
Willmott'** has double white flowers with buds
tinged green; **'Mme Antoine Buchner'** is pale
mauve-pink; **'Mme F. Morel'** is purplish pink;
'Mme Lemoine' is a double white with medium-
sized tight flowerheads on a free-flowering and
compact shrub; **'Mrs Edward Harding'** has
double reddish purple flowers in large heads;
'President Lincoln' is light blue; **'Président
Poincaré'**, introduced by Lemoine in 1913, has
double flowers of a rich claret-mauve in large
heads; **'Primrose'** has early soft single lemon
flowers on a compact shrub; **'Souvenir d'Alice
Harding'** has small heads of white flowers in
summer; **'Vestale'** is pure white; **'Volcan'** bears
single ruby purple flowers; and **'William Robin-
son'** bears single royal purple flowers. ZONES 5–9.

Syringa vulgaris 'Andenken an Ludwig Späth' *(top)*
Syringa vulgaris 'Katherine Havemeyer' *(center)*
Syringa vulgaris 'Mme Lemoine' *(above)*

Syzygium jambos
(top)
syn. *Eugenia jambos*
ROSE APPLE

Indigenous to Southeast Asia, this tree reaches a height of 30–40 ft (9–12 m) with a rounded crown. The leaves are dark green and glossy and the fluffy, greenish white flowers are borne in large rounded clusters. The edible, creamy pink to yellow, fragrant fruit taste of rose water. ZONES 10–12.

Syzygium luehmannii (center)
syn. *Eugenia luehmannii*

SMALL-LEAFED LILLYPILLY, RIBERRY

This is a large tree with a buttressed trunk endemic to eastern Australian rainforests. When cultivated it reaches only 20 ft (6 m) or so with low spreading branches and a domed crown. A good shade and specimen tree for warm to hot climates, it is also grown as a formal hedge. Leaves are very shiny and oval to lance-shaped with a prominent midrib. New growth is pink to red. Creamy white summer flowers in small clusters are followed by coral red, pear-shaped fruit. ZONES 10–12.

SYZYGIUM
LILLYPILLY, BRUSH CHERRY

These 400 to 500 species of evergreen trees and shrubs, once part of the genus *Eugenia*, are from tropical and subtropical rainforests of Southeast Asia, Australia and Africa. They have attractive foliage, flowers and berries. The white, pink, magenta or purple, edible berries ripen in late summer to autumn. The plants have a dense canopy of shiny green leaves with contrasting red, pink or copper spring growth. Spring and summer flowers are mostly small with protruding white to mauve or crimson stamens giving a fluffy appearance.

CULTIVATION
The plants prefer full sun to part-shade and deep, moist, well-drained, humus-rich soil; they do best in warm climates with only occasional light frosts. Prune to shape if necessary. Propagate from fresh seed in spring or cuttings in summer.

Syzygium paniculatum (bottom)
syn. *Eugenia paniculata*

MAGENTA BRUSH CHERRY, AUSTRALIAN BRUSH CHERRY

This small to medium Australian tree grows to 50–60 ft (15–18 m) with an irregular rounded and densely foliaged crown. Leaves are shiny green, variable in shape from oval to rounded, coppery brown when young and held on reddish stalks. Fragrant creamy white flowers are ½ in (12 mm) wide and borne in dense clusters, mainly in late spring. The large, decorative fruit are rose purple, oval to rounded and up to 1 in (25 mm) long. This species is used as a hedge in southeastern and southwestern USA. ZONES 9–12.

S

TU

TABEBUIA
TRUMPET TREE

The 100 or so shrubs and trees of this genus occur naturally in tropical America and the West Indies, where some are valued for their durable timber. With spectacular flowers and attractive foliage, they make good shade trees. Many are briefly deciduous during the tropical dry season, but some are almost evergreen. Flowers are trumpet- to bell-shaped in shades of white, yellow, pink, red or purple, and are clustered at the branch tips, usually when the leaves have fallen in late winter to spring. Fruits are bean-like capsules. Leaves may be simple or palmately compound, with 3 to 7 leaflets, their edges often toothed.

CULTIVATION
Trumpet trees need a hot to warm frost-free climate and deep, humus-rich soil with good drainage. A sunny position is best, with shelter from wind to protect the flowers. Propagate from seed or by layering in spring or from cuttings in summer; selected types are grafted.

Tabebuia chrysantha (above)

This small deciduous tree from Venezuela grows to 20 ft (6 m) and forms an open crown of slender branches. Its leaves are composed of 5 hairy, finger-like leaflets. It bears a profusion of mustard yellow, trumpet-shaped flowers about 3 in (8 cm) long. These are grouped in large heads at the ends of leafless branches from late winter to spring. Fruit are slightly hairy. ZONES 11–12.

T

Tabebuia chrysotricha (right)
GOLDEN TRUMPET TREE

Native to Central America, this deciduous tree reaches 30–50 ft (9–15 m) and spreads to 25 ft (8 m) with an open canopy. Brownish hairs cover the branches, flowers and leaf stalks, lower leaf surfaces and fruit. Dark green leaves, of mostly 3 to 5 oval to oblong leaflets, are held on long stalks. Flower clusters smother the crown in late winter or early spring; each bloom is trumpet-shaped, about 2 in (5 cm) across, with bright yellow ruffled petals. Brownish lines and golden brown hairs highlight the throat. The fruit is golden brown. ZONES 9–11.

Tabebuia impetiginosa (right)
syns *Tabebuia ipe, T. avellanedae, T. heptaphylla*

PINK TRUMPET TREE, ARGENTINE FLAME TREE, PAU D'ARCO

This handsome deciduous tree grows to 50 ft (15 m). Its rounded crown is formed by a network of branching stems, sparsely clad with slender palmate leaves with oval leaflets; the leaves are shed briefly in spring. Spectacular clusters of rose pink or purple-pink trumpet-shaped flowers are borne on bare branches in spring. **'Pink Cloud'** is one of a number of attractive cultivars. ZONES 9–11.

T

TAMARIX
TAMARISK

The 50 or so species of tough shrubs and small trees in this genus occur naturally in southern Europe, North Africa and temperate Asia in dry riverbeds, often in saline soils. Most *Tamarix* species are deciduous, but a few are evergreen. They develop a short trunk and a graceful, dense canopy of drooping branchlets. The leaves are minute and scale-like, and have salt-secreting glands. The flowers are small and white or pink, occurring in abundant, slender spikes; the fruits are capsules.

CULTIVATION
Grown for ornament and as windbreaks, these trees adapt to a wide range of soils and climates, and can cope with salt spray and very dry conditions. Very to moderately frost hardy, they do best in deep, sandy soil with good drainage, and can be pruned after flowering. Propagate from ripe seed or from hardwood cuttings in winter, and semi-ripe cuttings in late spring or autumn. They are prone to attack by stem borers in poorly drained soil.

T

Tamarix aphylla (left)
syn. *Tamarix articulata*
ATHEL TREE

This vigorous, evergreen tree grows to 30 ft (9 m) in height with a spread of 25 ft (8 m). It is frost hardy and has dense, weeping branches. A spreading crown tops the short, single, grayish trunk. It has slender, grayish twigs and gray-green linear leaves. In summer and autumn, tiny white to pale pink flowers appear, arranged in spikes. This species helps stabilize sandy soil, but its rapid spread along watercourses is causing much concern in warm, arid regions of the USA and Australia. ZONES 8–11.

Tamarix parviflora *(right)*
syn. *Tamarix tetrandra var. purpurea*

EARLY TAMARISK

This species grows well in mild climates; it is frost hardy but drought sensitive. A deciduous, spreading shrub or small tree, up to 15 ft (4.5 m) in height, it is a pretty sight when smothered in spring with a haze of tiny, pale pink flowers, which are carried in small spikes along the previous year's growth. The toothed, mid-green leaves are small and narrow, and turn orange-red in autumn. This tree is often confused with the similar *Tamarix gallica*. **ZONES 5–10.**

Tamarix ramosissima *(right)*
syn. *Tamarix pentandra*

LATE TAMARISK

Perhaps the most widely grown *Tamarix* species, this elegant, deciduous shrub grows to about 15 ft (4.5 m) with a spread of about 10 ft (3 m). Occurring from eastern Europe to central Asia, it is very frost hardy and has tiny blue-green leaves. The branches and twigs are a dark red-brown. Clusters up to 6 in (15 cm) long of profuse, small pink flowers are borne in plumes during late summer and early autumn. **'Pink Cascade'** is a vigorous cultivar that bears rich rose pink flowers. **ZONES 2–10.**

Tamarix tetrandra
(right)

This species grows to 10 ft (3 m) with arching purplish brown shoots and needle-like leaves. In spring, it bears lateral racemes of 4-petalled, pink flowers on the previous year's growth. **ZONES 6–10.**

T

TAXODIUM

This small genus of deciduous or semi-evergreen conifers consists of 3 species, which occur naturally on the edges of rivers and lakes in eastern North America and parts of Mexico. The genus name comes from the supposed similarity of their foliage to that of the yews *(Taxus)*. *Taxodium* species develop large, spreading branches and shed their leaves in autumn, still attached to the small branchlets. These are feather-like and turn coppery brown. The male (pollen) cones are tiny; the female ones are globular, up to 1 in (25 mm) in diameter. The wood of *Taxodium* species is strong, tough and termite resistant.

CULTIVATION
These trees thrive in boggy soils in full sun and will even grow in shallow water. However, they will grow equally well in a normal well-drained soil that is sufficiently deep and moist. Propagate from seed or cuttings.

Taxodium ascendens (left)
POND CYPRESS

Occurring mainly in the coastal sandy 'pine barrens' of eastern USA, this species grows in shallow pools in the wild. A narrowly conical tree, it reaches a height of 60 ft (18 m) in cultivation and has spirally arranged leaves on erect branchlets. The new spring growth is erect and fresh green, becoming rich brown in autumn. The small cones hang from the branch tips. As its common name suggests, this tree makes an excellent feature beside rivers, ponds and lakes. **'Nutans'** has shoots that are erect at first, becoming nodding as they mature. ZONES 7–10.

T

Taxodium distichum (left)
BALD CYPRESS, SWAMP CYPRESS

Found in the swamp regions of southeastern USA, this fast-growing tree reaches a height of 120 ft (36 m) in the wild, but only about 80 ft (24 m) in cultivation. It is distinguished by its deeply fissured, fibrous, reddish brown bark and knobbly 'knees'. These special structures are vertical woody growths sent up from the roots when the plant is standing in water and are thought to allow the tree to breathe with its root system submerged. It has tiny, light green, slender, pointed leaves which, as they mature, turn rusty red in autumn then golden brown before falling. It has resinous, round, purple cones, 1 in (25 mm) across. ZONES 6–10.

Taxus baccata (top)
ENGLISH YEW, COMMON YEW

TAXUS
YEW

Indigenous to western Asia, North Africa and Europe, this dense, dark tree has had legendary and religious associations for centuries. The wood of this tree was once used for making longbows. It grows best in a moist alkaline soil in an open position. The dark-colored trunk is erect and very thick in maturity; the leaves are dark green. The male tree bears scaly cones, while the female tree bears cup-shaped, scarlet berries which encase a poisonous seed. Old trees may reach 50 ft (15 m), but cultivars rarely achieve this height. '**Aurea**' has golden yellow foliage when young, turning green in the second year. '**Dovastoniana**', known as the Westfelton Yew because the original tree was planted in 1777 at Westfelton in Shropshire, England, is a distinct form with tiers of wide-spreading, horizontal branches; it normally is found only in the female form. '**Dovastoniana Aurea**' is similar in habit but the leaves are edged bright yellow. '**Fastigiata**', the Irish yew, is columnar, while '**Repandens**' has a spreading habit. '**Semperaurea**' is a

The evergreen conifers of this small genus, from cool-climate regions of the northern hemisphere, are slow growing but very long lived. Young trees are conical in shape, but as they age—over the centuries—they develop a domed crown and a massive, thick trunk clothed in reddish brown or grayish brown bark which peels off in thin scales. The flat green leaves are shortish, needle-like and sharply pointed; male and female flowers are borne on separate trees in spring. The single, small brown seed of the female plant is enclosed in a vivid red, fleshy cup; this cup is the only part of the plant that is not poisonous to humans and animals. Yews make excellent dense hedges and are often used for topiary.

CULTIVATION

These frost-hardy trees tolerate a wide range of conditions, including heavy shade and chalky soil. However, they do not enjoy warm winters or hot, dry summers. Propagate from seed or cuttings or by grafting.

slow-growing male bush with ascending branches and gold leaves that fade with age to a russet yellow. ZONES 5–10.

Taxus baccata '*Fastigiata*' (below)

Taxus baccata '*Repandens*' (below right)

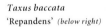

Taxus × media
'Everlow' *(left)*

Taxus cuspidata
(left)

JAPANESE YEW

Faster growing than *Taxus baccata*, this conifer is popular in cold climates and is tolerant of very dry and shady conditions. It forms a large shrub or small tree to 15 ft (4.5 m) or more in height and spread, with an erect trunk which is covered in grayish brown bark. The dense foliage is composed of small, narrow leaves arranged in V-shaped rows on the stems. The leaves are dull green above and lighter below. Tolerant of pollution, it is one of the few conifers that performs well in difficult urban environments. **'Aurescens'** is a low-growing compact form with deep yellow young leaves that turn green in the second year. Equally compact is the dwarf cultivar **'Densiformis'**, which forms a dense mound about 3 ft (1 m) high. **ZONES 4–9.**

Taxus × media

These hybrids between the English and Japanese yews offer a range of sizes and shapes for the garden. **'Brownii'**, a male form, and **'Everlow'** are low and rounded, eventually reaching 8 ft (2.4 m) tall and wide; they are easily kept smaller by pruning. **'Hatfield'** is the broad, upright male form, while **'Hicksii'** is narrow, upright and female; both are good for hedging. **ZONES 5–9.**

TELOPEA
WARATAH

These sturdy evergreen shrubs and small trees are indigenous to the open forests of southeastern Australia, including Tasmania; only 4 species exist, but there are also some attractive hybrids such as 'Starburst' and 'Sunflower'. They bear spectacular flowerheads in spring, each distinctive bloom a dense head of tubular flowers surrounded by showy red bracts. Flowers develop at the shoot tips. The leathery green leaves are alternate along the woody stems and have long stalks. The fruits are leathery pods.

CULTIVATION
Waratahs can be difficult to grow successfully, needing well-drained, sandy soil with low fertility and an acid pH; they are prone to fungal root and stem rot. Moderately frost hardy, they prefer full sun to part-shade, and need shelter from the wind. Regular pruning after flowering will keep them bushy. Waratahs are best propagated from seed or cuttings in spring, and can also be grafted.

Telopea oreades
(right)

GIPPSLAND WARATAH,
VICTORIAN WARATAH

Occurring naturally in cool hill forests, this waratah has a slender, upright, well-branched habit and forms an open crown, reaching a height of 20–25 ft (6–8 m). In cultivation it can be treated as a tall shrub, of around 10 ft (3 m). It bears crimson flowers from spring to early summer. These are arranged in broad, loose, spidery heads, up to 3 in (8 cm) across, and have pale reddish to green, oval to oblong bracts at the base. There is also a rare white-flowered form. The fruits are boat-shaped pods. **ZONES 9–10.**

Telopea speciosissima (left)

WARATAH

The waratah is the floral emblem of New South Wales, Australia. The leaves vary from oblong to wedge-shaped, often having a serrated edge and are sometimes slightly lobed. Magnificent scarlet to crimson flowers are borne in large, domed heads 4–6 in (10–15 cm) across in spring and early summer. These are surrounded by bright red bracts of variable size and prominence. This sturdy, vigorous shrub grows to 10 ft (3 m) tall with a spread of 6 ft (1.8 m). The fruits are brown. **'Sunflare'** has particularly large, showy bracts and flat-topped flowers. **'Wirrimbirra White'** features creamy white flowers and cream to greenish bracts. **ZONES 9–11.**

Telopea speciosissima
'Wirrimbirra White'
(left)

TEUCRIUM

GERMANDER

This genus of around 100 species in the mint family was named after King Teucer of Troy, who reputedly used the plants medicinally. Evergreen or deciduous shrubs, subshrubs and perennials, they have 2-lipped flowers and slightly aromatic foliage. These plants are able to withstand hot, dry conditions and poor soils. They can be used as hedges and will grow in sheltered maritime conditions.

CULTIVATION

Mostly fairly frost hardy, they prefer light, well-drained soil and sun. Low-growing species do best in poor soils. Propagate from cuttings in summer.

Teucrium chamaedrys (above)

WALL GERMANDER

This hardy, evergreen, alpine subshrub is native to Europe and southwestern Asia. It grows 1–2 ft (30–60 cm) tall with a spread of 2–3 ft (60–90 cm). The toothed, ovate leaves are glossy deep green above and gray beneath. It is suitable for walls, steep banks and edging, and has long been used as a medicinal herb. Spikes of pale to deep rosy purple flowers are produced in summer and autumn. **'Prostratum'** is, as its name suggests, a prostrate form. ZONES 5–10.

Teucrium cossonii (above)

This species is a low spreader with rounded heads of deep pink flowers. Its narrow, gray-green leaves are reminiscent of some *Lavandula* species. ZONES 8–11.

Teucrium polium
'Aureum' (left)

Teucrium polium

This deciduous subshrub with procumbent stems forms low hummocks 1–2 in (2.5–5 cm) in height. Its narrow, gray, felted leaves have scalloped margins and white to yellow or pinkish purple flowers in terminal heads are produced in summer. It is moderately frost hardy. **'Aureum'** has leaves edged with creamy yellow. ZONES 7–10.

T

THEVETIA

All 8 species of this genus of evergreen trees and shrubs have a poisonous milky sap; in fact, all parts of the plants are very poisonous. Relatives of the oleander *(Nerium)*, they are indigenous to tropical America. They feature clusters of showy, mostly yellow, funnel-shaped flowers at the shoot tips; flowering peaks in summer. The fruits are berry-like. The leaves are arranged spirally on the branchlets.

CULTIVATION

These frost-tender plants grow best in a sandy, well-drained soil enriched with organic matter. They need plenty of water while in flower. The ideal location provides shelter from wind, plus full sun to part-shade. Prune the plants after flowering to maintain their dense growth. Propagate from seed in spring or from cuttings in summer.

Thevetia peruviana
(below left)
syn. *Thevetia neriifolia*
YELLOW OLEANDER, LUCKY NUT

This domed tree can grow to 25 ft (8 m) tall, but in gardens is usually seen as a shrub of 6.5–13 ft (2–4 m). The long, shiny, rich green leaves are hard and strap-like to narrowly lance-shaped, with barely any stalk. The yellow to soft orange, slightly perfumed flowers, each 2 in (5 cm) across, are held on long stalks. They bloom on and off for most of the year in their native habitat; in cooler climates, they bloom only in summer. The fruits are oddly shaped, fleshy drupes, rounded and with prominent ridges. They ripen from green through red to black and are regarded by some as a lucky charm, even though dangerously poisonous. ZONES 10–12.

Thevetia
thevetioides
(below right)

LARGE-FLOWERED YELLOW OLEANDER, BE-STILL TREE, GIANT THEVETIA

This species grows to 15 ft (4.5 m) tall. Its erect but rather weak stems form an untidy crown. The leaves are narrowly lance-shaped, 4 in (10 cm) long and ½ in (12 mm) wide, with a pointed tip and prominent veins. The flowers, about 3 in (8 cm) across, are orange or pale to strong yellow, and more open than those of *Thevetia peruviana.* The fruits are green drupes. ZONES 10–12.

THRYPTOMENE

This Australian genus is made up of about 40 species of wiry-stemmed, woody evergreen shrubs, only a few of which are in cultivation. They grow up to 5 ft (1.5 m) high with a similar spread, and have tiny, heath-like, green leaves that are aromatic when crushed. An abundance of small, starry flowers appear all along the branches.

CULTIVATION

Thryptomenes make good cut flowers and, as they need regular trimming to keep them compact, cutting for flowers is a good way to prune. They prefer light, lime-free, well-drained soil in full sun or part-shade, and a mild climate, frost free or almost so. They are usually propagated from cuttings.

Thryptomene calycina *(right)*
GRAMPIANS THRYPTOMENE

This species from a limited area of western Victoria, Australia—in particular, the rugged sandstone Grampians mountains—has slightly pointed leaves and white flowers with dark centers, which are carried in great profusion through winter and spring. It is widely cultivated for cut flowers. A distinctive characteristic of *Thryptomene calycina* is that the 5 sepals are identical in shape, size and color to the 5 petals. There are several cultivars. **ZONES 9–11.**

Thryptomene saxicola *(right)*
syn. *Thryptomene* 'Paynei'

This open, slightly pendulous species has somewhat rounded leaves, and light pink or white flowers that occur mainly in winter and spring. It is a neat, compact plant that seldom exceeds 4 ft (1.2 m) high with a spread of 5 ft (1.5 m), and only requires light trimming after flowering. **ZONES 9–11.**

THUJA
ARBOR-VITAE

This small genus contains 5 evergreen conifers from high-rainfall, cool-temperate regions of northeastern Asia and North America. All are valuable timber trees and several are widely cultivated on a commercial basis. They feature erect, straight trunks covered in deeply fissured, fibrous bark and are columnar to pyramidal in habit. The aromatic foliage consists of sprays of scale-like leaves, often flattened. The egg-shaped cones are covered with overlapping scales and are green, maturing to brown; they are notably small for such large trees, mostly less than ½ in (12 mm) long. Dwarf cultivars, some no more than 15 in (38 cm) high, make excellent rockery or container specimens; most are juvenile forms.

CULTIVATION
These plants tolerate cold and are not fussy about soil as long as it is well drained; most species prefer full sun and dislike dry conditions. Propagation is from seed or cuttings in winter.

Thuja occidentalis *(left)*
AMERICAN ARBOR-VITAE, WHITE CEDAR

Growing to 50 ft (15 m) in height with a pyramidal crown, this species has attractive, reddish brown, peeling bark. Its dense foliage is composed of yellow-green glandular leaves with bluish undersides held on flat, spreading branchlets. The leaves turn bronze in autumn, and tiny, yellow-green cones are produced, which ripen to brown. This species has given rise to more than 140 cultivars, which range from dwarf shrubs to large trees. **'Ericoides'** is a small dense bush to 18 in (45 cm) tall and has soft, loose, bronze juvenile foliage, becoming brownish green as it matures. **'Lutea'** grows to 8 ft (2.4 m) in 10 years; its leaves become rich golden bronze in winter. **'Lutea Nana'** is a small conical bush, very dense, with golden yellow foliage in winter. **'Micky'** is a bun-shaped, green-foliaged cultivar. Slow-growing **'Rheingold'** forms a spreading, semi-prostrate dome 30 in (75 cm) high and 5 ft (1.5 m) wide; its leaves turn rich golden brown in winter. **'Smaragd'**, with a compact pyramidal habit, has bright green foliage all year round and forms a dense hedge 6 ft (1.8 m) high. ZONES 4–10.

T

Thuja occidentalis
'Ericoides' *(above)*

Thuja occidentalis
'Rheingold' *(above right)*

Thuja occidentalis
'Lutea Nana' *(right)*

Thuja occidentalis
'Smaragd' *(right)*

T

Thuja plicata (left)
WESTERN RED CEDAR

This fast-growing conifer reaches about 80 ft (24 m) in cultivation, but is much taller in its natural habitat. It has long been harvested for its durable and versatile softwood timber. Of conical habit, it becomes columnar in maturity, with branches sweeping the ground. When the rich, coppery green foliage is crushed, it exudes a sweet, tangy aroma. The dwarf cultivar **'Rogersii'** forms a round bun shape 18 in (45 cm) across. Compact **'Zebrina'**, growing to 20 ft (6 m) high and 5 ft (1.5 m) wide, has glossy bright green foliage striped with yellow. **'Aurea'** has rich, old gold foliage. **'Stoneham Gold'** is slow growing, but eventually makes a large bush with dense foliage and a narrowly conical form; the foliage is bright gold topped with copper bronze. Similar to 'Stoneham Gold', and also slow growing, **'Collyer's Gold'** has brighter yellow foliage. **'Atrovirens'** is a compact shrub ideal for hedging. ZONES 5–10.

Thuja plicata 'Zebrina'
(left)

T

Thujopsis dolabrata *(below)*

This evergreen conifer is variable in growth habit, from upright and pyramidal to spreading and bushy. It reaches a height of 20–50 ft (6–15 m) with a spread of 25–30 ft (8–9 m). Its foliage is composed of flattened, scale-like leaves which are dark green above with frosted white undersides. Its small cones are bluish gray, round and scaly. The dwarf cultivar **'Nana'** forms a spreading, bun shape 24 in (60 cm) high by 5 ft (1.5 m) wide, with fresh green foliage, sometimes tinged bronze. The slow-growing **'Variegata'** matures to a broad pyramid 10 ft (3 m)high and 5 ft (1.5 m) wide; its vivid green, shiny foliage is splashed with white. ZONES 5–10.

THUJOPSIS
MOCK THUJA, HIBA, FALSE ARBORVITAE

This genus from Japan contains only a single species, *Thujopsis dolabrata*. It resembles *Thuja*, but is distinguished by several important features, namely round, woody cones, winged seeds and larger leaves. It is the parent of several cultivars, which vary in habit and foliage color.

CULTIVATION
Tolerant of cold, this plant thrives in moist, well-drained, acidic or alkaline soil and an open, sunny position. Propagation is from seed, or cuttings for selected forms.

Thujopsis dolabrata 'Nana' *(above)*

Thujopsis dolabrata 'Variegata' *(below)*

T

THUNBERGIA

This genus of 90 to 100 species of mainly twining climbers and evergreen, clump-forming shrubs, was named after the eighteenth-century Swedish botanist Dr Carl Peter Thunberg, who collected plants in Africa and Japan. Native to Africa, Asia and Madagascar, their leaves are entire or lobed, and the mostly trumpet-shaped blooms are borne individually from the leaf axils or in trusses.

CULTIVATION

The species range from marginally frost hardy to frost tender, and prefer temperatures above 50°F (10°C). They will grow in any reasonably rich soil with adequate drainage. Full sun is preferred, except during the summer months, when part-shade and liberal water should be provided. Support the stems and prune densely packed foliage during early spring. Propagate from seed in spring and cuttings in summer.

Thunbergia natalensis *(left)*

This very attractive species from South Africa is not a climber but a soft-wooded shrub that reaches 3 ft (1 m) in height. It bears its soft blue flowers throughout summer and dies down completely in winter. Subtropical and warm-temperate climates suit it best. **ZONES 10–11.**

T

Thunbergia togoensis *(left)*

This semi-climbing African shrub produces hairy buds, opening into dark blue flowers with yellow centers. **ZONES 10–12.**

THYMUS
THYME

This genus consists of over 300 evergreen species of herbaceous perennials and subshrubs, ranging from prostrate to 8 in (20 cm) high. Chosen for their aromatic leaves, these natives of southern Europe and Asia are frequently featured in rockeries, between stepping stones or used for a display on banks. Some species are also used in cooking. The flowers are often tubular and vary from white through pink to mauve. Historically, thyme has been associated with courage, strength, happiness and well-being.

Thymus serpyllum 'Coccineus Minor' *(below)*

Thymus × citriodorus 'Argenteus' *(below right)*

CULTIVATION
These plants are mostly frost hardy. For thick, dense plants, the flowerheads should be removed after flowering. Plant out from early autumn through to early spring in a sunny site with moist, well-drained soil. Propagate from cuttings in summer or by division.

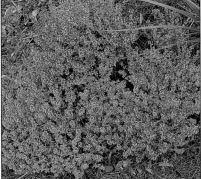

Thymus serpyllum
WILD THYME, CREEPING THYME, MOTHER OF THYME

This subshrub grows to 10 in (25 cm) with a spread of 18 in (45 cm), forming a useful ground cover. Its creeping stem is woody and branching, and the scented, bright green leaves are elliptical to lanceolate. The bluish purple flowers are small and tubular with 2 lips, and are borne in spring and summer in dense terminal whorls. It is very frost hardy and will take moderate foot traffic. **'Annie Hall'** has rounded leaves and mauve flowers; **'Coccineus Minor'**, has crimson-pink flowers; and **'Pink Ripple'**, has bronze-pink flowers. ZONES 3–9.

Thymus × citriodorus
syn. *Thymus serpyllum* var. *citriodorus*
LEMON-SCENTED THYME

This delightful rounded, frost-hardy shrub grows 12 in (30 cm) high and has tiny oval lemon-scented leaves and pale lilac flowers. The leaves are used fresh or dry in poultry stuffings or to add lemon flavor to fish, meat and vegetables. **'Anderson's Gold'** is a yellow-foliaged spreader that is inclined to revert to green; **'Argenteus'** has silver edges to the leaves; **'Aureus'** has golden variegated leaves; **'Doone Valley'** is prostrate with gold variegated leaves that develop red tints in winter; and **'Silver Queen'** has silvery white foliage. ZONES 7–10.

T

TIBOUCHINA
LASIANDRA, GLORY BUSH

There are more than 300 species in this genus of evergreen perennials, shrubs, small trees and scrambling climbers from South
America. The flowers are large and vivid, commonly purple, pink
or white, with 5 satiny petals. They are borne either singly or in
clusters at the shoot tips, and sometimes the whole plant is
smothered with blooms over several months, usually from late
summer to early winter. The flower buds are rounded and fat,
while the leaves are simple and hairy, deeply marked with
3 to 7 veins. New growth is often a contrasting reddish bronze.
The stems are square and the fruits are capsules.

CULTIVATION
They prefer full sun and do best in light soil with added organic
matter and a slightly acidic to neutral pH. Keep plants moist
during the growing season. Prune after flowering. They have
brittle stems and need shelter from wind; they do not like frost.
Propagate from cuttings in late spring or summer.

Tibouchina granulosa *(left)*

Indigenous to Brazil, this fast-growing
species is usually a large shrub 12–15 ft
(3.5–4.5 m) in height and spread. It
sometimes becomes tree-like, reaching a
height of 30–40 ft (9–12 m). The flower
clusters are 12 in (30 cm) long and may
completely hide the foliage in autumn;
each bloom is rose purple to violet or
pink and 2 in (5 cm) across. The branching stems are thick and woody. The
leaves are lance-shaped to oblong and
6–8 in (15–20 cm) long. They are dark
green and shiny on top, bright green and
hairy underneath, and hairy along the
edges. ZONES 10–12.

T

Tibouchina 'Jules'
(right)

This is like a miniature
version of *Tibouchina
urvilleana*. Its rich
purple flowers and
velvety leaves are half
the size of *T. urvilleana,*
and the bush grows to
only about 3 ft (1 m)
tall. It flowers in late
summer. **ZONES 10–11.**

Tibouchina lepidota *(right)*

Native to Ecuador and Colombia, this leafy shrub
usually has a short trunk to 12 ft (3.5 m) high.
However, it can become tree-like, growing to
40 ft (12 m) tall with a neat round canopy. The
leaves are dark green and shiny, oblong to lance-
shaped, with 5 main veins and 2 outer minor
ones; they are paler and hairy underneath. Its
violet to purple flowers are borne in clusters; the
buds are enclosed by pink, silky bracts and the
stems have reddish hairs. **'Alstonville'** has particularly vibrant flowers. **ZONES 10–12.**

Tibouchina urvilleana *(right)*
syns *Lasiandra semidecandra, Tibouchina
semidecandra*
PRINCESS FLOWER, GLORY BUSH

This slender-branched species develops a short
trunk topped by a bushy rounded crown and
reaches 15 ft (4.5 m) in height. The young stems
are reddish and slightly hairy, turning brown later.
The oval to slightly oblong leaves are 2–4 in
(5–10 cm) long, shiny dark green above and
slightly hairy below. The rich purple to violet,
satiny flowers, 3 in (8 cm) wide with purple
stamens, are borne singly or in small groups.
The flower buds are large, reddish and hairy.
ZONES 9–12.

T

TILIA
LIME TREE, LINDEN

From temperate regions of Asia, Europe and North America, this genus consists of 45 species of tall, handsome, deciduous trees, often planted in avenues and streets because they are fast growing and withstand regular heavy pruning and atmospheric pollution. They are generally upright, with thick, buttressed trunks, and have a tendency to sucker. Rounded to heart-shaped leaves, held on thin stalks, briefly turn yellow in autumn. The small, fragrant, cup-shaped cream flowers are borne in clusters in summer; each cluster has a whitish bract which persists and helps to disperse the fruits on the wind. Both flowers and bracts are dried to make linden tea. The fruits are small, round, hard, green berries. Several species are valued for their pale, strong but lightweight wood.

CULTIVATION
Very frost hardy, they do best in cool climates and prefer full sun, neutral, well-drained soil and plenty of water in dry periods. Even quite large trees can be readily transplanted during their winter dormancy. Propagate from seed in autumn, from cuttings or by layering; selected forms and hybrids can be grafted in late summer.

T

Tilia americana (left)
BASSWOOD, AMERICAN LINDEN

This attractive, sturdy tree from eastern-central USA and Canada grows to 120 ft (36 m) tall. It has an erect trunk with smooth gray bark which becomes fissured with age. Its young branches are green and form a compact, narrow crown. The heart-shaped, dull green leaves are up to 6 in (15 cm) long and have toothed edges. Yellowish white, fragrant flowers in pendent clusters appear in summer, followed by small, hairy fruit. **'Redmond'**, a selected form raised in Nebraska in about 1926, has a dense conical habit. ZONES 3–9.

Tilia cordata *(right)*
syn. *Tilia parvifolia*
SMALL-LEAFED LINDEN, LITTLE-LEAF LINDEN

An inhabitant of European woodlands, this species grows to 100 ft (30 m) tall with a dome-shaped crown. Its leathery leaves, 2 in (5 cm) across, are bright green on top with pale undersides. Its small flowers are pale yellow and sweetly scented; the fruit are gray. This long-lived species can make a handsome specimen for parks and formal gardens where it has plenty of space. The soft whitish timber is often used for wood carving and musical instruments. '**Greenspire**' is a fast-growing American selection with an upright habit and oval-shaped crown. '**June Bride**' is heavy-flowering with conical growth and glossy leaves. **ZONES 2–9.**

Tilia × europaea *(center)*
syn. *Tilia × vulgaris*
EUROPEAN LINDEN, COMMON LIME TREE

Widely grown in Europe, this handsome, vigorous hybrid between *Tilia cordata* and *T. platyphyllos* grows to 100 ft (30 m) tall. It is characterized by a dense, shapely crown held on a stout trunk which has a strong tendency to sucker. Shoots should be removed from the burl at the base from time to time. The smooth green shoots grow in a distinct zigzag pattern and the bright green, rounded to heart-shaped leaves have toothed edges. Its pale yellow flowers appear among the leaves in early summer; they are sometimes infused and drunk as a tea. The rounded fruit are faintly ribbed. The foliage of '**Wratislaviensis**' is golden yellow when young, maturing to a dark green. **ZONES 3–9.**

Tilia 'Petiolaris' *(right)*
syn. *Tilia petiolaris*
WEEPING SILVER LINDEN, PENDENT SILVER LIME, WEEPING LIME

Possibly no more than a form of *Tilia tomentosa*, this weeping tree reaches 60–80 ft (18–24 m) in height. It has a spreading, conical form which expands with age. The pointed, cordate leaves are 2–4 in (5–10 cm) long, deep green on top and silver-felted underneath. Creamy yellow flowers bloom in terminal clusters and are followed by bumpy, nut-like seed pods. **ZONES 5–9.**

T

Tilia platyphyllos
(left)

BROAD-LEAFED LINDEN, BIG-LEAF LINDEN

Reaching a height of 80 ft (24 m), this vigorous European species has a straight, rough, gray trunk and a rounded crown spreading to a broad shape. The young shoots are reddish brown and downy; the large, dark green leaves are heart-shaped, bluish underneath. Pale yellow flowers in groups of 13 are followed by hard, pear-shaped, ribbed fruit. In **'Rubra'**, the bark of the young twigs is a vivid red. **ZONES 5–9.**

Tilia tomentosa *(left)*

SILVER LINDEN, SILVER LIME

This graceful tree native to eastern Europe and Turkey is distinguished by its young shoots, which are pale gray and felted. Growing to 90 ft (27 m) tall, its ascending branches are often pendulous at the tips. Large round leaves, with serrated edges and whitish undersides, seem to shimmer in the wind. The highly fragrant, lime-green flowers, which are borne in summer and are toxic to bees, are followed by rough, oval fruit. This species is tolerant of dry conditions and smog-laden atmospheres. **ZONES 5–9.**

Torreya californica
(below right)

CALIFORNIA NUTMEG

This neat, erect tree grows to a height of 70 ft (21 m); conical in habit, its horizontal branches sweep the ground in maturity. The dark green, needle-like leaves, about 2½ in (6 cm) long, are yellowish green beneath. Male and female organs are borne on separate trees; woody, olive-like fruit, similar to the nutmeg of commerce, follow on female trees. It is moderately frost hardy. **ZONES 7–10.**

TORREYA

The yew-like, evergreen coniferous trees and shrubs of this small genus of 6 or so species occur naturally in eastern Asia and North America. The spiny pointed leaves are spirally arranged on twisted shoots and are often paler on the undersides. The fruits are oval drupes which contain a single seed.

CULTIVATION:

These plants adapt to a wide variety of soils, from chalk to heavy clay and poor sand, and are reasonably cold tolerant provided they are planted in a sheltered position. All demand adequate water during dry spells. Propagate from seed or by grafting.

T

Torreya nucifera *(right)*

NAYA

Native to Japan, this attractive, symmetrical conifer reaches about 70 ft (21 m) in height. Its stiff, spiky, yew-like foliage is dark gray-green and pleasantly pungent when crushed. The bark is a smooth reddish brown. The fruit are edible green drupes which ripen to purple with a white bloom; they contain a rich oil. **ZONES 7–10.**

TRISTANIOPSIS

This genus of 30 species of evergreen trees or shrubs is closely related to *Tristania* and used to be included in that once larger genus. Species have obscurely veined leaves and 5-petalled yellow to white flowers. The seeds are usually winged. The genus contains several species indigenous to the high-rainfall coastal forests of eastern Australia and others from Southeast Asia, Papua New Guinea and New Caledonia. These plants make excellent screen or hedge plants.

CULTIVATION

Marginally frost hardy, they adapt to a range of situations, but grow best in deep, well-drained, moist soil in shade or part-shade. Water freely during the warmer months and prune to size as necessary. Propagate from seed in late summer.

Tristaniopsis laurina
(below left & bottom)
syn. *Tristania laurina*
WATER GUM, KANUKA

A conical tree, 30–50 ft (9–15 m) high, the water gum has a smooth, creamy brown trunk attractively streaked with gray. The branches start low to the ground and form a dense canopy. The leaves are oblong to lance-shaped and 4 in (10 cm) long. Their upper surfaces are dark green and the undersides paler; in colder areas, they turn red. New leaves are pinkish. Clusters of small, deep yellow flowers appear in summer, each blossom rich with nectar. The fruit are round capsules. **ZONES 10–12.**

T

TSUGA
HEMLOCK

The 10 or so species of elegant evergreen conifers from cool-temperate areas of North America and East Asia that make up this genus are widely grown as ornamentals in cool climates. They range from tall trees to (in the case of dwarf cultivars) small shrubs good for hedging and rockeries. Conical to pyramidal in habit, the spreading branches droop gracefully. Both male and female cones are small, the latter with thin scales and containing winged seeds. Despite the name the trees are not poisonous.

CULTIVATION

These frost-hardy trees are tolerant of shade and thrive in slightly acid, deep, well-drained soil with plenty of organic matter. They dislike being transplanted and urban or very exposed sites. Propagate from seed in spring or cuttings in autumn.

Tsuga canadensis 'Pendula' *(right)*

Tsuga canadensis *(right)*
EASTERN HEMLOCK, CANADIAN HEMLOCK

From the cool northeast of North America, this slow-growing tree reaches a height of 80 ft (24 m), with a trunk that is often forked at the base. It forms a broad pyramidal crown, the thin branches with pendulous tips. The short, oblong needles, arranged in 2 rows, are grayish brown and hairy when young, maturing to dark green with 2 grayish bands on the undersides. Oval cones, 1 in (25 mm) long and borne at the branchlet ends, disperse their seeds in autumn. 'Pendula', a semi-prostrate mound to 6 ft (1.8 m) tall and wide, has lime green juvenile foliage that ages to grayish green.
ZONES 2–9.

T

Tsuga chinensis (above)
CHINESE HEMLOCK

This conifer reaches a height of 70 ft (21 m) in the wild, less in cultivation. It has been in cultivation for thousands of years and is often a feature of formal Japanese gardens. It forms a narrow crown with a spread of around 12 ft (3.5 m) and is one of the neatest members of the genus. Its yellowish young shoots precede glossy green needles that are distinctly notched at the tips. ZONES 6–10.

Tsuga heterophylla (left)
WESTERN HEMLOCK

From northwestern North America, this large, fast-growing tree can reach nearly 200 ft (60 m) in the wild (generally less in cultivation) and is harvested commercially for its pale yellow timber and tannin-rich bark. As with *Sequoia*, the harvest comes almost entirely from natural forests, to the great concern of environmentalists. As a specimen in parks and large gardens it is particularly elegant, with a spire-like habit, weeping branchlets and a rusty brown, fissured trunk. New young shoots are grayish, and the flat needles are deep green. ZONES 6–10.

UGNI

This small genus of evergreen shrubs to 10 ft (3 m) tall is closely related to *Myrtus* and was formerly included in that genus. Indigenous to areas of South and Central America and Mexico, the species most commonly found in cultivation is *Ugni molinae*, which is grown for its attractive, edible fruit and glossy, deep green leaves.

CULTIVATION
Species need well-drained, moist, lime-free soil and prefer partial to full sun. Prune in winter to keep the plants compact and bushy. Propagate from seed or cuttings in summer.

Ugni molinae *(above)*
syn. *Myrtus ugni*
CHILEAN GUAVA, CHILEAN CRANBERRY

Indigenous to Chile and Bolivia, this species bears fragrant, purplish red, berry-like fruit. These are edible, though tart, and are often made into jam or conserves. The abundant small, bell-shaped flowers are pink or white with prominent stamens, and are borne in the leaf axils. Its dense growth and height of 6 ft (1.8 m) or more makes *Ugni molinae* suitable for hedges; it needs partial shade in hot climates. ZONES 8–10.

ULEX
GORSE

This genus consists of about 20 species of leafless or almost leafless, densely spiny shrubs from western Europe and North Africa. It belongs to the broom tribe of legumes along with *Cytisus, Genista* and *Spartium.* Young plants have small, compound leaves with 3 leaflets, but on mature plants the leaves are reduced to sharp spines, as are the branch tips. The flowers are profuse, mostly golden yellow and fragrant, borne singly or in small clusters. Small, hairy pods release their seeds explosively in mid-summer. Gorses are valued for their ability to thrive on sites too exposed or infertile for most other shrubs. Common gorse (*Ulex europaeus*) is apt to become a nuisance, however, especially in regions other than its native Europe.

CULTIVATION
Fully frost hardy, gorses thrive under most conditions (though not in the tropics or subtropics) as long as they receive full sun. They are tolerant of very poor, sandy soils and exposure to salt-laden winds. In more sheltered positions, they may need pruning to keep a compact form. Propagate from seed in autumn or spring, or from cuttings in summer.

U

Ulex europaeus
(left)
COMMON GORSE, FURZE

This species is a broad, mound-like shrub which reaches about 6 ft (1.8 m) in height. When it blooms in spring, it is completely covered in pea-flowers borne in groups of 2s or 3s; their fragrance resembles coconut. The double-flowered form, **'Flore Pleno'**, has rather distorted blooms, but is more compact; it is also preferred for cultivation because it cannot form seeds and is thus not invasive. ZONES 6–9.

ULMUS
ELM

The 30 or so species in this genus of trees occur naturally in temperate regions of the northern hemisphere. In Europe and North America elm trees have been devastated by Dutch elm disease, caused by the fungus *Ophiostoma ulmi*, which is transmitted by the elm bark beetle. All but a few east Asian species are deciduous, turning yellow in autumn. The leaves, usually one-sided at the base, have prominent, parallel lateral veins and regularly toothed margins; the small, disc-like fruits have a membranous wing and are carried in clusters. Most elms are large limbed with furrowed gray bark and high, domed crowns.

CULTIVATION
Mostly very frost hardy, they require cool to cold winters and prefer full sun and deep, moist, fertile soil. Propagate from semi-ripe cuttings in summer, from suckers or by grafting or budding in autumn. Propagation from seed in autumn yields low germination rates.

Ulmus americana *(right)*
AMERICAN ELM, WHITE ELM

The largest North American elm, this species occurs naturally over eastern and central USA, and southern Canada. It can reach a height of 120 ft (36 m) in the wild—about half that in cultivation—and has high-arching limbs. Mature trees develop a broad crown and may become strongly buttressed at the base; the ash-gray bark is deeply fissured. The leaves, 4–6 in (10–15 cm) long, have smooth upper sides with slightly downy undersides, and unforked lateral veins. **'Delaware'** is broadly vase-shaped, fast growing and claimed to be resistant to Dutch elm disease. **'Princeton'** is also vase-shaped, and vigorous with some resistance to elm leaf beetle. **'Washington'** is thought to be a hybrid of *Ulmus americana* and an unknown species. ZONES 3–9.

U

Ulmus glabra
'Camperdownii' *(left)*

Ulmus glabra *(far left)*
syns *Ulmus montana, U. scabra*
SCOTCH ELM, WYCH ELM

This major European elm can grow to more than 100 ft (30 m) high with a wide, spreading crown, and does not sucker from the roots. Its dull, dark green leaves, up to 6 in (15 cm) long and broadest near the apex, have a rough raspy upper surface. **'Camperdownii'** forms a dome-like mound of weeping branches when grafted onto a standard; **'Lutescens'**, the common golden elm, has spring and summer foliage colored lime green and tipped with pale yellow. ZONES 3–9.

Ulmus × *hollandica* *(left)*
DUTCH ELM, HYBRID ELM

This hybrid name covers several clones believed to be crosses of *Ulmus glabra* and *U. minor*. Their glossy dark green leaves, yellowing in autumn, are mostly smaller and less raspy than *U. glabra* leaves, and broader and shorter stalked than those of *U. minor*. The original, **'Hollandica'**, has broad, rounded leaves. **'Jacqueline Hillier'** is a small bushy shrub to 8 ft (2.4 m). **'Purpurascens'**, a vigorous, open tree, has purplish green new growth. **'Vegeta'**, the Huntingdon elm (an old clone), bears pale yellowish green leaves in flattened sprays. ZONES 4–9.

U

Ulmus minor
syn. *Ulmus carpinifolia*
FIELD ELM, SMOOTH-LEAFED ELM

Widespread throughout Europe, western Asia and North Africa, this deciduous species is usually smaller than the other European elms and the crown is pointed. It grows to 100 ft (30 m) with a spread of up to 70 ft (21 m) in the wild. The leaves are also smaller, tapering at both ends, with smooth upper sides and a slender stalk. Due to its suckering habit, a single tree may form a

small, dense grove. **'Variegata'**, with white-streaked leaves, is just as vigorous, but less inclined to sucker. **Ulmus minor 'Cornubiensis'** (syn. *U. angustifolia* var. *cornubiensis*) is a tall, slender tree growing 60–70 ft (18–21 m) tall and 20 ft (6 m) wide. Commonly known as Cornish elm, it forms a dense conical head of ascending branches, later becoming more open and loose. The leaves are smooth and glossy above and conspicuously tufted beneath. It thrives in coastal situations. **ZONES 4–9.**

Ulmus minor in spring *(right)* and in winter *(far right)*

Ulmus parvifolia *(right)*
CHINESE ELM, LACEBARK ELM

Native to China and Japan, this elm grows to 60 ft (18 m) tall and has a spreading, sinuous habit and bark mottled with dark gray, reddish brown and cream. It is semi-evergreen in mild climates. The small, leathery, dark green leaves, smooth and shiny on top, have small, blunt teeth. The fruit mature in autumn, much later than those of most other elms. It is relatively resistant to Dutch elm disease. **'Frosty'** is a shrubby, slow-growing form with small, neatly arranged leaves bearing white teeth. **ZONES 5–10.**

Ulmus procera *(right)*
ENGLISH ELM

This elm, which can reach 150 ft (45 m) in height, has a high-branched, billowing crown and straight or slightly sinuous trunk. In the UK, few have survived Dutch elm disease. Cultivated in the southern hemisphere, it produces a compact, rounded crown up to 80 ft (24 m) high. Its smallish, rounded leaves have a rough surface. Seldom setting fertile seed, it is usually propagated from suckers. The rare cultivar **'Louis van Houtte'** has golden-green leaves. **ZONES 4–9.**

U

VWXYZ

VACCINIUM

This is a large and varied genus of about 450 species of deciduous and evergreen shrubs and occasionally small trees and vines. The species seen in gardens are shrubs valued for either their edible berries or their notable autumn color. The berries, known according to the species as bilberry, blueberry, cranberry, huckleberry or whortleberry, are red or blue-black and are often covered with a bloom when ripe. They are grown commercially for fresh fruit, as well as for juicing and canning. Vacciniums are indigenous mainly to the northern hemisphere in a wide range of habitats, stretching from the Arctic to the tropics. The leaves are bright green, often leathery and sometimes coppery red when young; their edges can be toothed or smooth. Small bell-shaped flowers, pale pink, white, purple or red, appear in late spring or early summer.

CULTIVATION

Vaccinium species are generally frost hardy and shade loving; many form dense, thicket-like shrubs. The plants need acidic, well-drained soil with plenty of humus and regular water; some, indeed, prefer boggy ground. Propagate by division or from cuttings in autumn.

Vaccinium cylindraceum (above)

Native to the Azores, this deciduous or semi-evergreen, medium-sized shrub has dark green, glossy, finely toothed leaves and produces flowers in short dense racemes on the previous year's shoots. The flowers are cylindrical and about $\frac{1}{2}$ in (12 mm) long. Red when in bud, they open to pale yellow-green and are produced in summer and autumn. They are followed by cylindrical, blue-black berries covered with a bloom. ZONES 10–11.

Vaccinium corymbosum
BLUEBERRY, HIGHBUSH BLUEBERRY

This deciduous species from New England, USA, has a preference for boggy soils. It is grown mainly for its edible, blue-black berries. It also displays fine scarlet autumn foliage. Forming a dense thicket of upright stems with a height and spread of 6 ft (1.8 m), its new leaves are bright green. The clusters of pendulous flowers are pale pink. **'Blue Ray'** has delicious, sweet, juicy fruit. **'Earliblue'** is tall and vigorous with very large berries. For heavier cropping, grow 2 cultivars together. ZONES 2–9.

Vaccinium corymbosum
'Earliblue' *(left)*

Vaccinium ovatum
(above)

EVERGREEN HUCKLEBERRY

Occurring naturally from Oregon through to southern California, this is a dense, compact shrub. Its dark green, glossy foliage is much in demand by florists as it lasts well in water; in fact, this demand has driven the wild plants very nearly to extinction. The plant forms a spreading clump 3 ft (1 m) high and 5 ft (1.5 m) wide and can reach 8–10 ft (2.4–3 m) in shady spots. The white or pink flowers appear in early summer. Its tangy, edible berries are red when young, maturing to blue-black. **ZONES 7–10.**

Vaccinium macrocarpon *(below)*
syn. *Oxycoccus macrocarpon*

AMERICAN CRANBERRY

Native to eastern North America, this evergreen is commercially grown there and several cultivars are known. Prostrate in habit, it forms mats of interlacing wiry stems with alternate leaves spreading to around 3 ft (1 m) when fully mature. Pink, nodding flowers are produced in summer, followed by relatively large, tart red fruit. **ZONES 2–9.**

V

VELLA

The name of this genus from the western Mediterranean region is derived from the Celtic *veller*, meaning cress, and the genus is related to the cabbage family. It consists of 4 species of deciduous or evergreen low shrubs which are much branched. The yellow flowers, occasionally veined with violet, have 4 petals and are borne in racemes.

CULTIVATION

These are plants suitable for a rock garden in a sunny, rather dry position, but they are liable to be damaged or killed by severe winters. Prune only to remove dead wood after flowering. Propagate from cuttings taken in autumn and plant out in spring.

Vella spinosa (above)

Native to the limestone mountains in Spain, this small, rounded, deciduous shrub grows 12 in (30 cm) tall with the upper branches of the stems tipped with spines. The leaves are gray-green, fleshy and dull; the creamy summer flowers are veined with violet. ZONES 8–10.

VESTIA

Like its relative the potato, the evergreen shrub that is the only member of this genus comes from temperate areas of South America. The leaves have an unpleasant smell when crushed. The flowers are pendent and borne singly or in clusters.

CULTIVATION

This shrub appreciates shelter from strong winds and does best in rich, well-drained soil with plenty of water in warmer months. Full sun or light shade suit it best. In warm-temperate or even subtropical climates, it can be cut back hard in winter and will shoot from the base in spring. Propagate from seed in autumn or spring or cuttings in summer.

Vestia foetida (right)
syn. *Vestia lycioides*

Indigenous to Chile, this fast-growing shrub reaches 6 ft (1.8 m) in height with many erect stems. Its shiny green leaves are thin and narrow, crowding down the stems. Dainty, lemon-yellow, tubular flowers with prominent stamens are produced through spring and summer, followed by small, inedible, blue berries. The sap has a most unpleasant smell, hence the specific name 'foetida' meaning stinking. ZONES 9–11.

V

VIBURNUM

This important genus is made up of some 150 species of evergreen, semi-evergreen and deciduous, cool-climate shrubs or small trees primarily of Asian origin with fewer species from North America, Europe and northern Africa. Many of the cultivated species and forms are noted for their fragrant, showy flowers, and may also produce colorful berries or bright autumn foliage. In several species, flowers are arranged in a similar way to those of the lacecap hydrangeas, with small fertile flowers and large sterile ones on the same plant; these have all given rise to cultivars with all-sterile flowerheads known as 'snowball viburnums'. The evergreen species are often used for hedging.

Viburnum × bodnantense
(above)

A hybrid between *Viburnum farreri* and *V. grandiflorum,* this deciduous shrub reaches 10 ft (3 m) in height. It has slightly glossy, deep green, oval leaves that are pale green on the undersides. Before they drop in autumn, they develop intense orange, red and purple tones. The heavily scented flowers, which bloom from autumn to early spring depending on the climate, are bright pink in the bud, open pale pink and fade to white. **'Dawn'** has slightly darker blooms, especially those that open in spring; and **'Deben'** has light pink to white, somewhat tubular flowers. ZONES 7–10.

CULTIVATION

Fully to moderately frost hardy, most species are remarkably trouble-free plants, growing in any well-drained soil in sun or light shade. They can be trimmed heavily after flowering, although this will prevent fruits forming. They are usually propagated from cuttings in summer or from seed in autumn.

Viburnum × bodnantense 'Dawn'
(below)

V

Viburnum carlesii
'Aurora' *(right)*

Viburnum carlesii *(left)*

KOREAN VIBURNUM, KOREAN SPICE VIBURNUM

Indigenous to Korea and Tsushima Island, this densely foliaged deciduous shrub grows to about 5 ft (1.5 m) tall with a similar spread. It has pointed oval leaves 2–3 in (5–8 cm) long with finely serrated edges. The starry flowers open from mid- to late spring; they are pale pink ageing to white, around $\frac{1}{2}$ in (12 mm)across and sweetly scented. The flowers are carried in rounded clusters up to 3 in (8 cm) in diameter. The fruits ripen to black. Several cultivars are available, including **'Aurora'**, with deep pink buds; **'Cayuga'**, which has very fragrant white flowers and a heavy crop of black berries; **'Charis'**, bearing white flowers; and **'Diana'**, with deep pink buds. ZONES 9–10.

Viburnum × *burkwoodii* *(right)*

BURKWOOD VIBURNUM

A hybrid between *Viburnum carlesii* and *V. utile*, this 8–10 ft (2.4–3 m) high, semi-evergreen shrub has glossy, deep green, pointed oval leaves to about 3 in (8 cm) long. They are pale sage green on the undersides, and those that drop in autumn develop bright yellow and red tones. From early to late spring, ball-shaped clusters of small, starry, fragrant flowers open; they are pink in the bud, opening white. **'Anne Russell'**, the result of a backcross with *V. carlesii*, has clusters of fragrant flowers. **'Park Farm'** has a more spreading habit and larger flowers. **'Mohawk'** has dark glossy leaves that turn to orange in autumn, and fragrant, red-blotched white flowers that open from red buds. ZONES 5–10.

V

Viburnum lantana *(above)*
WAYFARING TREE

Often used as hedging, this deciduous species is tolerant of cold climates. It forms a tall, branching shrub 15 ft (4.5 m) high, and is distinguished by its new shoots, which are unusually furry for a viburnum. The oval leaves have hairy undersides and turn burgundy red in autumn. In early summer, small, creamy white flowers are profusely borne in flat clusters. The oblong red fruits ripen to black. **'Rugosum'** has larger and more wrinkled leaves, and larger flower clusters. ZONES 3–9.

Viburnum dilatatum
'Iroquois' *(above)*

Viburnum dilatatum
LINDEN VIBURNUM

From Japan and China, this 10 ft (3 m) tall deciduous shrub has coarsely toothed, hairy oval leaves. Its flowers are white and abundant and carried in heads 4–6 in (10–15 cm) wide; bright red fruit follow. **'Iroquois'** is slightly smaller and bushier than the species with flowers more of a creamy white. ZONES 5–10.

Viburnum farreri
syn. *Viburnum fragrans*

Discovered in mountain regions of western China at the beginning of the twentieth century by Reginald Farrer, this deciduous shrub grows to about 8–10 ft (2.4–3 m) tall. Its lightly arching branches are clad in oval, deeply toothed leaves with prominent veins; bronze when young, they mature to rich green and turn red before falling. The pink buds open to white, sweetly smelling flowers clustered at the branch tips in early spring before the leaves appear. Glossy red fruit are produced only occasionally. **'Candidissimum'** has pure white flowers and buds bright green leaves. ZONES 6–10.

Viburnum farreri 'Candidissimum' *(below)*

Viburnum davidii *(below)*
DAVID VIBURNUM

This evergreen species from Sichuan, China, grows 3–5 ft (1–1.5 m) tall and spreads slowly to form a densely foliaged shrub up to 6 ft (1.8 m) across. If massed, it makes an excellent, large-scale ground cover. The pointed oval leaves are bright glossy green and up to 6 in (15 cm) long; leaf petioles and new wood are reddish brown. The spring-borne clusters of white flowers are not spectacular, but are followed by turquoise-blue berries. **'Femina'** is a reliable, heavy-fruiting cultivar. ZONES 7–10.

Viburnum opulus *(top)*

GUELDER ROSE, EUROPEAN CRANBERRY BUSH

This deciduous shrub from Europe and northern Africa produces clusters of snowy white, lacy flowers in summer. It has attractive fruits and autumn color, and can be grown in wet or boggy situations. This large shrub grows to 12 ft (3.5 m) tall, has gray bark and a spreading habit with long, pale green shoots. Its leaves turn crimson in autumn. Generous bunches of shiny, translucent, red fruit remain on the bush until well into winter. **'Aureum'** has bronze-colored shoots turning yellow then green, and yellowish leaves that may burn in the sun; **'Compactum'** is a dense, compact shrub bearing large quantities of flowers and fruits; **'Nanum'** has small leaves and seldom produces flowers or fruits; **'Roseum'** (syn. *Viburnum opulus* 'Sterile'), the snowball bush, has snowball-like heads of pale green to white, sterile flowers, which are so large they weigh the branches down; **'Pink Sensation'** is similar to 'Roseum' except the flowers have a pinkish hue; and **'Xanthocarpum'** has clear yellow fruits that are quite translucent when ripe. ZONES 2–10.

Viburnum opulus
'Roseum' *(above)*

Viburnum opulus
'Compactum' *(below)*

Viburnum opulus
'Xanthocarpum' *(above)*

Viburnum macrocephalum *(left)*

CHINESE SNOWBALL TREE

The distinctive characteristic of this species native to China is the presence of small, fertile flowers and large sterile ones, but the cultivar **'Sterile'** has all-sterile flowers. Huge, rounded trusses of white flowers, up to 6 in (15 cm) across, give a spectacular display in early summer on this upright shrub. The dark green, leathery leaves are oval, 4 in (10 cm) long and tinted red and yellow in autumn; normally deciduous, this species may be semi-evergreen in milder climates. It grows to 6–10 ft (1.8–3 m) tall. ZONES 6–10.

V

Viburnum plicatum *(left)*
syn. *Viburnum tomentosum*

This deciduous shrub from Japan and China grows to about 15 ft (4.5 m) tall with a similar spread. It has hazel-like, 3 in (8 cm) long, mid-green, pointed oval leaves with serrated edges and a somewhat tiered growth habit, a feature emphasized in the cultivar **'Mariesii'**. The large, creamy white flower clusters have a mass of tiny fertile flowers in the center, surrounded by large sterile flowers. They open in spring and are followed by small berries that are red at first, ripening to black. **'Lanarth'** is a fine cultivar, with branches less arching than the species; **'Pink Beauty'** has a pale pink tinge to the flowers; and **'Sterile'** (syn. *Viburnum plicatum* var. *plicatum*) is a sterile form. **'Rosace'** has overlapping horizontal branches and foliage that colors well in autumn; it has sterile heads of mixed white and pink flowers, and bronze spring foliage. **ZONES 4–9.**

Viburnum plicatum
'Pink Beauty' *(left)*

Viburnum plicatum
'Rosace' *(above)*

Viburnum plicatum
'Mariesii' *(left)*

Viburnum sargentii

SARGENT VIBURNUM

From northeastern Asia, this 10–15 ft (3–4.5 m) deciduous shrub has 4 in (10 cm) wide, 3-lobed leaves, yellow-green when young, ageing to dark brown. The large, individual flowers are carried on heads up to 4 in (10 cm) wide. The berries are red. **'Onondaga'** has maroon young growth that becomes purple-red in autumn. ZONES 4–9.

Viburnum sargentii 'Onondaga' *(above)*

Viburnum rhytidophyllum *(above)*

LEATHERLEAF VIBURNUM

This fast-growing, evergreen shrub has distinctive, handsome foliage. Its long leaves are corrugated, deeply veined and dark glossy green with gray felted undersides. Growing to 10–15 ft (3–4.5 m) tall and almost as wide, it tolerates alkaline soil. Small, creamy white spring flowers appear in large, flat clusters followed by oval berries, red turning to black. Plant in groups to ensure fruiting. ZONES 6–10.

Viburnum tinus *(right)*

LAURUSTINUS

This densely foliaged evergreen shrub from the Mediterranean region may eventually grow to 15 ft (4.5 m) tall and 20 ft (6 m) wide, although it is usually kept smaller through trimming. The dark green, pointed elliptical leaves are up to 4 in (10 cm) long and develop purplish tones in cold weather. Cream and yellow variegated foliage forms are available. Clusters of white flowers open from pink buds from late winter, followed by blue-black berries. **'Compactum'** (syn. 'Spring Bouquet') is a smaller form with dense compact growth; **'Eve Price'** has smaller leaves, carmine buds and pink-tinged flowers; **'Gwenllian'** has pink buds that open into pinkish white flowers followed by clusters of blackish seeds; and **'Pink Prelude'** has white flowers becoming deep pink. ZONES 7–10.

V

Viburnum tinus
'Gwenllian' *(left)*

Viburnum tinus
(above)

Viburnum trilobum *(left)*
syns *Viburnum americanum, V. opulus* var. *americanum*

HIGHBUSH CRANBERRY, AMERICAN CRANBERRY BUSH

The North American equivalent of *Viburnum opulus*, this species has showy flowers, fruit and autumn foliage. A tall shrub growing 8–12 ft (2.4–3.5 m) tall and wide, it is useful as a hedge or screening plant. The white flowers appear in spring in flat-topped clusters. The bright red fruit appear in autumn and last through winter. **'Wentworth'** has a very heavy crop of fruit. ZONES 3–9.

Virgilia oroboides
(right)

syn. *Virgilia capensis*

CAPE LILAC, TREE-IN-A-HURRY

This species features masses of mauve-pink, fragrant flowers in clusters scattered through the crown from early summer to autumn. It is called tree-in-a-hurry because of its speedy growth habit—up to 15 ft (4.5 m) in 2 years. However, it is often short lived and older trees become quite straggly, so it is mainly useful for new gardens or as a nursery plant. It makes a rounded shrub to small tree 20–30 ft (6–9 m) tall. Leaves are dark green, up to 8 in (20 cm) long, with 13 to 21 oblong, leathery leaflets. Pods are 2–3 in (5–8 cm) long. ZONES 9–11.

VIRGILIA

Only 2 species belong to this genus, both evergreen trees and both indigenous to South Africa. They are notable for their fast growth and have a tendency to fall over as they age. Over the warmer months, they make a great display of showy pea-flowers. The fruits are flat pods, while the leaves are fern-like with an odd number of leaflets.

CULTIVATION

Very adaptable, they grow best in an open, sunny position and well-drained soil. They cope well with wind and suit warm climates, as they are frost tender, particularly when young. Propagate in spring from seed pre-soaked in warm water for 24 hours.

Virgilia divaricata
(right)

SPRING-FLOWERED VIRGILIA

This small evergreen tree grows rapidly to a mature height of about 20 ft (6 m) with relatively horizontal branches. It bears clusters of pea-shaped pink flowers in spring followed by flat pods. The fern-like leaves are divided into many leaflets. It comes true to type when grown from seed. ZONES 9–11.

V

Vitex lucens *(below)*
PURIRI, NEW ZEALAND CHASTE TREE

This fine evergreen tree from New Zealand reaches a height of 30–60 ft (9–18 m) and features a rounded crown and a smooth pale trunk. Sprays of bright red or pink flowers are a winter bonus, each flower 1 in (25 mm) long. The large, bright red drupes mature in spring. The leaves consist of 3 to 5 large, oval to round leaflets, which are smooth and shiny rich green with a wavy edge. It is moderately frost hardy. ZONES 9–11.

Vitex negundo *(below)*

This useful shrub or small tree, native to warm-climate areas from southern and eastern Asia, is grown for its pleasantly aromatic foliage and fragrant flowers. It grows to 25 ft (8 m) tall and produces long leaves composed of deeply cut leaflets which are dark green above with pale, furry undersides. The fragrant flowers are mauve and appear in loose sprays in spring. ZONES 8–11.

VITEX

This genus is made up of about 250 mainly tropical and subtropical trees and shrubs—some evergreen, some deciduous. The leaves are compound with 3 to 7 leaflets radiating from the stalk—less commonly, the leaves are simple. Highlights are the sprays of tubular flowers in shades of white, yellow, red, blue or purple; the fleshy drupes are usually not a feature. In some species, both the leaves and the flowers are aromatic.

CULTIVATION
Moderately to marginally frost hardy, *Vitex* adapt to most soils, but do best in fertile soil with good drainage and with plenty of summer moisture. A sheltered spot in full sun is ideal. Propagate from seed in autumn or spring or from cuttings in summer.

Vitex agnus-castus *(below)*
CHASTE TREE

This moderately frost-hardy shrub, indigenous to southern Europe and western Asia, has aromatic leaves; these are 6–8 in (15–20 cm) long with 5 to 7 lance-shaped to rounded leaflets, deep green on top and felty gray underneath. The chaste tree is a deciduous, rounded shrub or small tree, 10–20 ft (3–6 m) tall with an upright, branching, woody stem. From early summer to autumn it bears dense, erect sprays of faintly perfumed, lavender flowers up to 12 in (30 cm) long. Small purple fruit follow. White-flowered and variegated-leaf forms are also available. ***Vitex agnus-castus* var. *latifolia*** has shorter, broader leaves. ZONES 7–10.

V

Weigela floribunda *(right)*
syn. *Diervilla floribunda*

From Japan, this deciduous shrub
reaches about 10 ft (3 m) in height and
has slender, pointed leaves which are
hairy on both sides. Young shoots are
also hairy, as are the outsides of the
flowers. These are deep crimson,
crowded on short lateral branchlets,
tubular in form with the style projecting
out from the opened petals. ZONES 6–10.

WEIGELA

This genus includes about 12 species of arching, deciduous shrubs. Most grow 6–10 ft
(1.8–3 m) high and wide, and have pointed,
elliptical, deep green leaves about 4 in (10 cm)
long. The foliage often develops orange, red
and purple tones in au-
tumn. In spring, masses
of white, pink or crim-
son, sometimes yellow-
ish, bell- or trumpet-
shaped flowers appear,
1½ in (35 mm) long.

CULTIVATION
Fully frost hardy, most
species prefer full sun
or light shade in moist,
fertile, well-drained
soil. Prune out older
branches after flowering
to maintain vigor. Prop-
agate from summer
cuttings.

Weigela 'Bristol Ruby' *(below)*

This erect hybrid, bred from *Weigela florida*
and *W. coraeensis*, is grown for the profusion
of crimson flowers which adorn the shrub from
late spring to early summer. It grows to 6 ft
(1.8 m) tall, with slender, arching branches and
dark green oval leaves. ZONES 4–10.

W

Weigela florida
'Foliis Purpureis'
(left)

Weigela florida *(below)*

This arching, deciduous shrub from Japan, Korea and northeastern China, grows up to 10 ft (3 m) or so. It is cultivated for its lavish spring display of rose pink, trumpet-shaped flowers. **'Appleblossom'**, with variegated leaves, has flowers that open white and age to pink. **'Aureovariegata'** has bright green, cream-edged leaves, and wide, bright pink, trumpet-shaped flowers to 1½ in (35 mm) wide. **'Eva Rathke'** bears crimson flowers developing from purplish red buds. Fully frost hardy, it grows 5 ft (1.5 m) tall and wide with a dense, erect habit. **'Foliis Purpureis'** has purplish green leaves; the flowers are deep pink, paler inside the tube and appear from late spring to early summer and sometimes again in autumn. **ZONES 4–10.**

Weigela florida
'Aureovariegata' *(above)*

W

Westringia fruticosa 'Morning Light' *(above)*

Westringia fruticosa *(below)*
syn. *Westringia rosmariniformis*

COAST ROSEMARY, AUSTRALIAN ROSEMARY

This species has rosemary-like foliage, and makes a compact, rounded shrub to 6 ft (1.8 m) high and about as wide, with rather stiffly spreading branches. The narrow leaves, arranged in 4s, are pale to dark green on top and white-felted underneath. The small flowers, white with purple blotches in the throat, appear most of the year. Coast rosemary will tolerate salt-laden winds and can be grown as a hedge in seaside gardens. '**Morning Light**' is a smaller, variegated form to 3 ft (1 m) high. The green leaves are surrounded by a cream band. ZONES 9–11.

WESTRINGIA

These 25 or so species of evergreen shrubs are indigenous to Australia. The square, woody stems are clothed in small stiff leaves arranged in whorls of 3 or 4. The tubular flowers are 2-lipped, the upper lip with 2 lobes, the lower with 3; they appear for many months in the leaf axils, peaking in spring. The fruits are tiny and nut like.

CULTIVATION

Westringias grow best in mild-winter climates. Many grow naturally near the sea and thrive on coastal conditions. They prefer an open, sunny site and adapt to most well-drained soils; some species benefit from the addition of organic matter. All species thrive if adequately watered over summer. Clip them annually to keep them compact. Propagate from seed in spring or from cuttings in late summer.

W

XANTHOCERAS
YELLOW HORN

Native to China, this genus consists of only one species. Although related to *Koelreuteria*, it is very different in general appearance. Except for its vulnerability to occasional injury by late spring frosts, this deciduous shrub or small tree is easily grown. The fragrant, erect flower spikes recall those of the horse chestnut.

CULTIVATION
While it tolerates low winter temperatures, the yellow horn should be protected from late frosts and needs long hot summers to flower well. It prefers well-drained, good loamy soil and will tolerate mild alkalinity. It requires plenty of sunshine but does well in cooler areas if sited in a warm sheltered position. Propagate from stratified seed in spring or root cuttings or suckers in late winter; prune lightly to maintain shape. It is susceptible to coral spot fungus.

Xanthoceras sorbifolium (above)

This deciduous upright shrub or small tree to about 15 ft (4.5 m) is native to China. The bright green leaves are composed of many sharply toothed leaflets. The white flowers are borne in erect sprays from the leaf axils in late spring and summer; each flower has a carmine red blotch at the base of the petals. The common name refers to the horn-like growths between the petals. The large fruiting capsules are pear-shaped and contain small seeds like chestnuts. It has thick, fleshy yellow roots. ZONES 6–10.

X

XANTHORRHOEA
GRASS TREE

This is a small genus of evergreen plants with grass-like foliage, all indigenous to Australia; they are very slow growing but long lived. Mature plants are stemless or develop a thick, sometimes branching trunk topped by a dense crown of long, arching, rather rigid leaves. Long, spear-like flower spikes are produced spasmodically, usually in spring or in response to burning. The spikes, up to 5 ft (1.5 m) long, consist of many densely packed, small white flowers, held on woody stalks up to 6 ft (1.8 m) long. The fruits are leathery capsules, packed along the spikes and surrounded by the blackened floral bracts. The glassy resin that exudes from the trunks was formerly used in varnishes and other products. The grass trees have, in the past, been variously classified with the rushes and the lilies, but are now placed in their own unique family.

CULTIVATION
Marginally frost hardy, grass trees need an open, sunny spot and well-drained soil as they are susceptible to root rot. They can also be grown in containers. Propagate from seed in autumn or spring.

Xanthorrhoea australis
(right)

This species is confined to the rocky hills of southeastern Australia. A dense tuft of narrow, arching, grassy leaves 3 ft (1 m) long sprout from a trunk made up of a mass of old leaf bases held together by natural resin. It takes 30 years or more for the leaf tuft to rise above the trunk. Spears of small white or cream flowers, smelling of honey, appear after 10 to 15 years, but only erratically; often it will bloom after a bushfire. ZONES 9–11.

X

Xanthorrhoea malacophylla
(below)

This grass tree, one of the tallest species, has a trunk as much as 20 ft (6 m) high and often branched when older, each branch terminating in a luxuriant rosette of long, bright green leaves that are rather soft and drooping. Each rosette may send up a flower spike to 5 ft (1.5 m) long on top of a stout stalk to 6 ft (1.8 m) long. The numerous small white flowers open from late autumn to mid-spring. The species is confined to wet coastal ranges of northeastern New South Wales, Australia. **ZONES 10–11.**

Xanthorrhoea preissii *(above)*

This species has an upright or slightly twisted trunk, often black and scorched. It can reach 20 ft (6 m) when mature, with a crown of long, arching, grass-like leaves. The small, creamy yellow flowers are densely packed at the top of a long spike that stands high above the crown. Brownish capsular fruit follow. **ZONES 10–11.**

X

Xylomelum occidentale *(below)*
WESTERN WOODY PEAR

This Western Australian tree reaches 25 ft (8 m) tall, with a spreading crown and dark brown, flaky bark. The large, deep green leaves resemble those of some oaks and have prickly edges. Sprays of creamy flowers appear in summer; these are followed by the showy, pear-shaped fruit, up to 4 in (10 cm) long. They ripen to reddish brown and persist on the plant after they have split open to release their seeds. They can be used in arrangements of dried flowers. ZONES 9–11.

XYLOMELUM
WOODY PEAR

This small Australian genus consists of 5 species of evergreen small trees with leathery leaves and short spikes of flowers resembling those of grevilleas and hakeas, which are members of the same family. Occurring in warmer temperate and tropical regions, these unusual plants have unique woody, pear-shaped large seed capsules, hence their common name.

CULTIVATION

Marginally frost hardy, they need fertile, well-drained, sandy soil and full sun. Young plants need to be given ample water and protection from frosts. Prune when young to encourage a compact shape. Propagate from seed in winter.

X

YUCCA

The 40 or so species of unusual evergreen perennials, shrubs and trees in this genus are found in drier regions of North America. Often slow growing, they form rosettes of stiff, sword-like leaves usually tipped with a sharp spine; as the plants mature, some species develop an upright woody trunk, often branched. Yuccas bear showy, tall panicles of drooping, white or cream, bell- to cup-shaped flowers. The fruits are either fleshy or dry capsules, but in most species are rarely seen away from the plants' native lands as the flowers must be pollinated by the yucca moth.

CULTIVATION

Yuccas do best in areas of low humidity; they prefer full sun and sandy soil with good drainage. Depending on the species, they are frost hardy to frost tender. Propagate from seed (if available), cuttings or suckers in spring.

Yucca aloifolia 'Marginata' *(left)*

Yucca aloifolia
SPANISH BAYONET, SPANISH DAGGER

This species gets its common name from its very sharp, sword-like, grayish green leaves, each 24 in (60 cm) long and 1–2 in (2.5–5 cm) wide with smooth edges. It develops a branched trunk up to 25 ft (8 m) high, but in cultivation is often much smaller. The flowers are carried in an upright spike up to 24 in (60 cm) long, mainly in summer but sometimes continuing into autumn. Each bell-shaped flower is white flushed with purple and about 2 in (5 cm) across. The fruits are fleshy. There are several cultivars with variegated leaves: **'Marginata'** has yellow-edged leaves; **'Tricolor'** has white or yellow in the center of the leaf; and **'Variegata'** has leaves that are edged with creamy white. ZONES 8–11.

Y

Yucca brevifolia *(right)*

JOSHUA TREE

Of striking if somewhat misshapen appearance, this well-known tree reaches 40 ft (12 m) tall in its natural habitat. The short leaves are narrow and sharply pointed, with minute teeth along the edges. Its greenish white flowers about $2\frac{1}{2}$ in (6 cm) long, arranged on a long erect spike, are followed by dry capsules. Extremely slow growing, it can be difficult to cultivate, even in its native regions of southern USA and northern Mexico. Flowering is irregular and dependent on rain in the wild; in cultivation, late spring is the usual flowering season. **ZONES 7–10.**

Yucca elephantipes *(left)*

syn. *Yucca gigantea*

SPINELESS YUCCA, GIANT YUCCA

This yucca occurs naturally in southern Mexico and Central America. It develops a rough, thick trunk that often branches and reaches a height of 30 ft (9 m); in cultivation it is usually smaller. The leaves are 4 ft (1.2 m) long and 3 in (8 cm) wide, shiny dark green with finely serrated edges. White, often somewhat drooping, bell-shaped flowers are clustered in large panicles from summer to autumn. **ZONES 10–12.**

Yucca australis *(right)*

TREE YUCCA, ST PETER'S PALM

The epithet *australis* means simply 'of the south' and is found in the names of many plant species. In this case it refers to the south of Mexico, where this yucca species is native. *Yucca australis* is one of the larger species and in cultivation has achieved impressive size—there is an old specimen in Valencia, Spain, that has a trunk 30 ft (9 m) in girth, and about 25 ft (7.5 m) tall overall; it branches into numerous heads of foliage with narrow, sword-shaped leaves and erect panicles of white flowers. This yucca has been used medicinally in Mexico, as a purgative or laxative. **ZONES 9–12.**

Y

Yucca gloriosa *(left)*

SPANISH DAGGER, MOUND LILY

The stiff, sword-like leaves of this species start out with a grayish cast, maturing to a deeper green. White, bell-shaped flowers, tinged flesh pink on the outside, appear in erect panicles to 8 ft (2.4 m) tall from summer to autumn. Native to southeastern USA, it is usually seen as a stemless clump of leaves, but with age can develop trunks to 6 ft (1.8 m) or more tall. ZONES 7–10.

Yucca filamentosa *(right)*

ADAM'S NEEDLE-AND-THREAD

The leaves on this plant form basal rosettes and are edged with white threads. Up to 3 ft (1 m) long, they are thin-textured and a slightly bluish gray-green. The nodding, white flowers are 2 in (5 cm) long, borne on erect panicles to 6 ft (1.8 m) tall in summer. It is native to eastern USA and is the most frost hardy of the yuccas. ZONES 4–10.

Yucca filifera

Normally seen as a low clump of foliage, this Mexican species may eventually become tree-like, reaching up to 30 ft (9 m) in height and eventually much branched. When young it resembles *Yucca filamentosa*, but the leaves are shorter and thinner, with the margins sparsely threaded. The flowers on the tall summer panicles are creamy white and pendulous. 'Golden Sword' has yellow leaf margins; 'Ivory' has creamy white flowers tinged green. ZONES 7–10.

Yucca filifera 'Golden Sword' *(left)*

Zelkova carpinifolia *(right)*
ELM ZELKOVA

From the Caucasus and Asia Minor, this slow-growing tree can live to a great age, reaching 100 ft (30 m) high and 50 ft(15 m) wide. It has a dense, rounded head, slender upright branches and weeping branchlets. The mid-green, pointed leaves have serrated edges; their upper sides are rough to the touch. Fragrant but insignificant flowers appear in spring. ZONES 4–10.

Zelkova serrata
(right)
JAPANESE ZELKOVA

This ornamental tree from Japan, Korea and Taiwan grows to a height of 80 ft (24 m) or more with a wide, spreading crown. It has smooth bark dappled gray and brown and new shoots are tinged purple. The pointed, oblong, sharply serrated leaves are dull green and slightly hairy above, with shiny undersides. The foliage turns golden yellow to rusty brown in autumn. Cultivars include **'Village Green'**, and **'Green Vase'**, growing to 40 ft (12 m) tall in a graceful vase shape. ZONES 3–10.

ZELKOVA

Occurring naturally from Asia Minor across cool-climate areas of western Asia to China and Japan, these deciduous trees are cultivated for their attractive habit and handsome foliage. They are important timber trees in China and Japan. The leaves resemble those of the English or American elms, but are smaller, giving an effect of airy elegance. Although related to the elms, they are not plagued by the same diseases and are becoming popular as elm substitutes. The small, greenish flowers, borne in spring, may be perfumed; both these and the fruits are insignificant.

CULTIVATION

Although frost hardy, they prefer some shelter. They need full sun and deep, fertile, well-drained soil and plenty of water during summer. Propagate from seed or root cuttings in autumn, or by grafting.

Z

ZIZIPHUS

This genus of about 80 or so species of deciduous or evergreen trees and shrubs occurs naturally in warm- to hot-climate areas of both the northern and southern hemispheres. Some have spiny branches. Their leaves are usually marked with 3 veins and there are spines at the base of each leaf stalk. The insignificant flowers are small, greenish, whitish or yellow, arranged in clusters in the leaf axils. The small, fleshy fruits of some species are edible. *Ziziphus macronata* is widespread in riverine areas.

CULTIVATION
Frost tender, grow ziziphus species in open, loamy, well-drained soil in full sun, and provide plenty of water. Tip prune to maintain compact growth. Propagate from seed or root cuttings in late winter, or by grafting.

Ziziphus jujuba
(below)
CHINESE DATE, JUJUBE

This deciduous tree is distributed from western Asia to China and grows to 40 ft (12 m) tall. It bears oval to lance-shaped leaves that are 1–2 in (2.5–5 cm) long and green in color, with 2 spines at the base of the leaf stalk, one of which is usually bent backwards. Small greenish flowers are borne in spring. The dark red, oblong to rounded fruit are up to 1 in (25 mm) long: they ripen from autumn to winter on the bare branches and are apple-like in taste. They may be stewed, dried or used in confections. ZONES 7–10.

Z

Reference Table

This table will help you choose trees and shrubs for your garden. Information on plant type, climate zones, height at maturity, whether evergreen or deciduous and chief attractions will help you find the trees and shrubs best suited to your purposes.

Plant Type

The reference table uses the following symbols for plant type:

- S for shrub;
- T for tree; and
- S(T) for shrubs that can grow large enough for people to think of them as trees.

Climate Zones

These match the climate zones given in the main text for each plant. An explanation of climate zones can be found on pages 31–33.

Deciduous or Evergreen

The reference table uses the following to describe whether plants are deciduous or evergreen:

- D for deciduous plants;
- E for evergreen plants;
- Semi for plants that are semi-deciduous

NAME	TYPE	ZONE	HEIGHT at MATURITY	DECIDUOUS or EVERGREEN	CHIEF ATTRACTIONS
Abelia floribunda	S	9–11	6–8 ft (1.8–2.4 m)	E	Flowers (rosy red, early summer)
Abelia × grandiflora	S	7–10	6–8 ft (1.8–2.4 m)	E	Flowers (white & mauve, spring–autumn); graceful habit.
Abelia × grandiflora 'Francis Mason'	S	7–10	6–8 ft (1.8–2.4 m)	E	As for A. grandiflora but with golden-bronze foliage.
Abeliophyllum distichum	S	5–9	6 ft (1.8 m)	D	Flowers (white, spring)
Abies alba	T	6–9	100 ft (30 m)	E	Foliage; symmetrical form
Abies amabilis	T	5–9	100 ft (30 m)	E	Foliage; symmetrical form
Abies balsamea	T	3–8	50 ft (15 m)	E	Foliage
Abies balsamea 'Hudsonia'	S	3–8	24 in (60 cm)	E	Dwarf size & neat habit
Abies bracteata	T	7–10	80 ft (24 m)	E	Foliage; symmetrical form
Abies cephalonica	T	6–9	75 ft (22 m)	E	Foliage; symmetrical form
Abies concolor	T	7–10	100 ft (30 m)	E	Aromatic foliage; symmetrical form
Abies concolor 'Glauca'	T	5–9	30 ft (9 m)	E	Foliage color & compact growth
Abies concolor var. *lowiana*	T	7–10	75 ft (22 m)	E	Aromatic foliage & color
Abies firma	T	6–9	80 ft (24 m)	E	Foliage
Abies grandis	T	6–9	150 ft (45 m)	E	Foliage; symmetrical form fast growth
Abies homolepis	T	5–9	60 ft (18 m)	E	Foliage; purple young cones
Abies koreana	T	5–9	20–30 ft (6–9 m)	E	Foliage; decorative cones at early age
Abies lasiocarpa	T	4–9	60 ft (18 m)	E	Foliage; symmetrical form
Abies nordmanniana	T	4–9	100 ft (30 m)	E	Foliage
Abies numidica	T	6–9	50 ft (15 m)	E	Foliage; symmetrical form
Abies pinsapo	T	5–9	60 ft (18 m)	E	Foliage; purple pollen cones
Abies pinsapo 'Glauca'	T	5–9	60 ft (18 m)	E	Foliage color
Abies procera	T	4–9	100 ft (30 m)	E	Foliage; symmetrical form
Abies procera 'Glauca'	T	4–9	75 ft (22 m)	E	Foliage color; symmetrical form & cones
Abutilon × hybridum	S	9–11	8 ft (2.4 m)	E	Flowers (yellow, red, pink, orange, summer–autumn)
Abutilon × hybridum 'Kentish Belle'	S	9–11	8 ft (2.4 m)	E	Flowers (brilliant orange, summer–autumn)
Abutilon × hybridum 'Orange King'	S	9–11	8 ft (2.4 m)	E	Flowers (orange, summer–autumn)
Abutilon megapotamicum	S	9–11	8 ft (2.4 m)	E	Flowers (yellow & red, most of year)
Abutilon megapotamicum 'Variegatum'	S	9–11	8 ft (2.4 m)	E	Flowers (yellow & red, most of year); low growth & yellow-variegated foliage
Abutilon × suntense	S	8–9	12 ft (3.5 m)	E	Flowers (purple, mauve, spring–early summer)
Abutilon vitifolium	S	8–9	12 ft (3.5 m)	E	Flowers (mauve, white, spring–early summer)
Acacia baileyana	T	8–10	20 ft (6 m)	E	Profuse flowers (yellow, late winter)
Acacia cultriformis	S	8–11	6–12 ft (1.8–3.5 m)	E	Flowers (yellow, spring) foliage
Acacia decurrens	T	9–10	30–50 ft (9–15 m)	E	Flowers (yellow, late-winter–early spring), foliage
Acacia greggii	S	7–11	6–8 ft (1.8–2.4 m)	D	Flowers (yellow, late spring) & hedging
Acacia iteaphylla	S(T)	8–10	15 ft (4.5)	E	Flowers (pale yellow, autumn)
Acacia karroo	T	9–11	25 ft (8 m)	E	Flowers (yellow, spring)
Acacia longifolia	S	9–11	15 ft (4.5 m)	E	Flowers (yellow, late winter–early spring)
Acacia melanoxylon	T	8–11	50–90 ft (15–27 m)	E	Flowers (cream, spring); foliage
Acacia neriifolia	S(T)	9–11	15–25 ft (4.5–8 m)	E	Flowers (yellow, late winter–spring); graceful habit

NAME	TYPE	ZONE	HEIGHT at MATURITY	DECIDUOUS or EVERGREEN	CHIEF ATTRACTIONS
Acacia pendula	T	9–11	20 ft (6 m)	E	Foliage
Acacia podalyriifolia	T	9–11	20 ft (6 m)	E	Flowers (yellow, winter–early spring) & foliage
Acacia pravissima	S(T)	8–10	12–20 ft (3.5–6 m)	E	Flowers (yellow, late winter–early spring)
Acacia pycnantha	S(T)	9–11	20 ft (6 m)	E	Flowers (yellow, spring)
Acacia verticillata	S	8–10	10 ft (3 m)	E	Flowers (yellow, spring–summer), foliage
Acalypha hispida	S	11–12	6 ft (1.8 m)	E	Flowers (red, summer)
Acalypha wilkesiana	S	10–11	10 ft (3 m)	E	Coloured foliage
Acalypha wilkesiana 'Macrophylla'	S	10–11	10 ft (3 m)	E	Coloured foliage
Acalypha wilkesiana 'Obovata'	S	10–11	10 ft (3 m)	E	Coloured foliage
Acer buergerianum	T	6–10	25 ft (8 m)	D	Autumn foliage; bark
Acer campestre	T	4–9	15–20 ft (4.5–6 m)	D	Autumn foliage
Acer cappadocicum	T	5–9	30–50 ft (9–15 m)	D	Autumn foliage
Acer cappadocicum 'Rubrum'	T	5–9	30–50 ft (9–15 m)	D	Spring & autumn foliage
Acer cissifolium	T	5–9	20–30 ft (6–9 m)	D	Autumn foliage
Acer davidii	T	6–9	20–25 ft (6–8 m)	D	Bark & autumn foliage
Acer × *freemanii*	T	5–9	50 ft (15 m)	D	Growth habit & autumn color
Acer × *freemanii* 'Autumn Blaze'	T	5–9	50 ft (15 m)	D	Growth habit & autumn color
Acer griseum	T	5–9	20–30 ft (6–9 m)	D	Striking cinnamon bark, peeling in large flakes
Acer japonicum	T	5–9	20 ft (6 m)	D	Foliage texture; autumn tones
Acer japonicum 'Aconitifolium'	T	5–9	20 ft (6 m)	D	Foliage shape & autumn color
Acer monspessulanum	T	5–10	30 ft (9 m)	D	Toughness & some autumn color
Acer negundo	T	4–10	30–50 ft (9–15 m)	D	Fast early growth; delicate flowers on leafless twigs
Acer negundo 'Variegatum'	T	4–10	30 ft (9)	D	As *A. negundo* with broader yellow-margined variegated foliage
Acer negundo 'Violaceum'	T	4–10	30 ft (9)	D	As *A. negundo* with violet flower tassels
Acer palmatum and cultivars	T	5–10	20–25 ft (6–8 m)	D	Foliage, shapes & textures; compact size, autumn color
Acer pensylvanicum	T	5–9	30 ft (9 m)	D	Striped bark; autumn foliage
Acer pentaphyllum	T	6–9	25 ft (8 m)	D	Bark, foliage & growth habit
Acer platanoides	T	4–9	50 ft (15 m)	D	Shade; autumn foliage
Acer platanoides 'Crimson King'	T	4–9	30 ft (9 m)	D	Deep red-purple foliage
Acer platanoides 'Drummondii'	T	4–9	30 ft (9 m)	D	Variegated cream-edged leaves
Acer pseudoplatanus	T	4–10	40–60 ft (12–18 m)	D	Fast growth; shade
Acer pseudoplatanus 'Brilliantissimum'	T	4–10	20 ft (6 m)	D	Spring foliage; compact growth
Acer pseudoplatanus 'Erythrocarpum'	T	4–10	40 ft (12 m)	D	Foliage or samara (fruit) color
Acer rubrum 'October Glory'	T	4–9	50–60 ft (15–18 m)	D	Autumn color; shade
Acer rufinerve	T	5–9	20–30 ft (6–9 m)	D	Bark, striped & autumn color
Acer saccharinum	T	4–9	60–80 ft (18–24 m)	D	Autumn foliage; fast early growth
Acer saccharum	T	5–9	60–80 ft (18–24 m)	D	Autumn foliage
Acer saccharum ssp. *nigrum*	T	5–9	60–80 ft (18–24 m)	D	Bark, summer foliage & autumn color
Acer saccharum 'Globosum'	T	5–9	20–30 ft (6–9 m)	D	Compact habit; autumn color
Acer tataricum and ssp. *ginnala*	T	4–9	30 ft (9 m)	D	Compact habit; flowers; red fruit (samara) in summer

NAME	TYPE	ZONE	HEIGHT at MATURITY	DECIDUOUS or EVERGREEN	CHIEF ATTRACTIONS
Acmena smithii	T	9–11	30–50 ft (9–15 m)	E	Display of pale violet to mauve fruit, autumn–spring
Adansonia digitata	T	11–12	30–50 ft (9–15 m)	D	Swollen trunk; flowers, cream in summer
Adansonia gregorii	T	11–12	30–50 ft (9–15 m)	D	Swollen trunk; flowers, cream in summer
Adenandra uniflora	S	8–10	24 in (60 cm)	E	Flowers (white, spring–autumn)
Adenium obesum	S	11–12	12 ft (3.5 m)	E	Flowers (red, pink or white, midwinter–spring)
Aeschynanthus speciosus	S	11–12	12–24 in (30–60 cm)	E	Flowers (yellow-green marked red)
Aesculus × carnea	T	6–9	30 ft (9 m)	D	Flowers (red, late spring)
Aesculus × carnea 'Briotii'	T	6–9	30 ft (9 m)	D	Flowers (red, late spring)
Aesculus flava	T	4–9	50 ft (15)	D	Flowers (yellowish, late spring–early summer)
Aesculus hippocastanum	T	6–9	50 ft (15 m)	D	Flowers (white, late spring–early summer); autumn foliage & fruit
Aesculus indica	T	6–9	50 ft (15 m)	D	Flowers (white, early to midsummer)
Aesculus parviflora	S	7–10	6–10 ft (1.8–3 m)	D	Flowers (white & pink, summer)
Aesculus pavia	T	7–10	20 ft (6 m)	D	Flowers (crimson, early summer); autumn foliage
Aesculus turbinata	T	6–9	30 ft (9 m)	D	Flowers (cream, early summer); autumn foliage
Agapetes incurvata	S	10–11	3 ft (1 m)	E	Flowers (flesh pink with darker bars), pendulous
Agapetes incurvata 'Scarlet Elf'	S	10–11	3 ft (1 m)	E	Flowers (red)
Agapetes serpens	S	9–10	3 ft 91 m)	E	Flowers (red, late winter–midsummer)
Agathis australis	T	9–10	100 ft (30 m)	E	Foliage; compact shape
Agathis robusta	T	9–12	100 ft (30 m)	E	Foliage; straight, narrow habit
Agonis flexuosa	T	9–10	30 ft (9 m)	E	Weeping foliage; flowers (white, late spring)
Agonis juniperina	T	9–10	15–25 ft (4.5–8 m)	E	Flowers (white, most of year)
Ailanthus altissima	T	6–10	30–50 ft (9–15 m)	D	Dense foliage & decorative fruit
Alberta magna	S(T)	10–11	10–20 ft (3–6 m)	E	Flowers (red, summer–autumn); decorative fruit
Albizia julibrissin and varieties	T	8–10	15–20 ft (4.5–6 m)	D	Flowers (pink & white, late spring–autumn)
Allamanda schottii	S	11–12	6 ft (1.8 m)	E	Flowers (yellow, summer–autumn)
Allocasuarina decaisneana	T	9–11	30 ft (9 m)	E	Dense needle-like drooping foliage
Allocasuarina littoralis	T	9–11	20–30 ft (6–9 m)	E	Fine needle-like foliage; massed male flowers (red-brown in winter)
Allocasuarina torulosa	T	8–11	30–40 ft (9–12 m)	E	Drooping needle-like foliage (purplish in winter)
Alloxylon flammeum	T	9–11	30 ft (9 m)	E	Flowers (orange-red, late spring–early summer)
Alloxylon pinnatum	T	9–11	30–40 ft (9–12 m)	E	Flowers (crimson, midsummer); bird-attracting
Alnus firma	T	5–9	15–20 ft (4.5–6 m)	D	Foliage
Alnus glutinosa	T	4–9	30–40 ft (9–12 m)	D	Foliage & moisture tolerance
Alnus glutinosa 'Imperialis'	T	4–9	30–40 ft (9–12 m)	D	Finely cut foliage
Alnus rubra	T	6–9	30–40 ft (9–12 m)	D	Foliage; male catkins (yellow, early spring)
Aloysia triphylla	S	8–11	10 ft (3 m)	E	Flowers (pale lavender, summer–autumn); aromatic foliage
Alyogyne huegelii	S	10–11	8 ft (2.4m)	Semi	Flowers (lilac or mauve, spring–summer)
Amelanchier arborea	T	4–9	20 ft (6 m)	D	Flowers (white in spring); decorative fruit; autumn color
Amelanchier lamarckii	T	6–9	20–30 ft (6–9 m)	D	Flowers (white, late spring); autumn foliage
Anacardium occidentale	T	11–12	15–20 ft (4.5–6 m)	E	Edible nut & fruit stalk
Andromeda polifolia	S	2–9	24 in (60 cm)	E	Flowers (pink or white, spring)

NAME	TYPE	ZONE	HEIGHT at MATURITY	DECIDUOUS or EVERGREEN	CHIEF ATTRACTIONS
Angophora costata	T	9–11	50 ft (15 m)	E	Smooth pinkish bark; contorted limbs; flowers (white, spring–summer)
Anisodontea 'African Queen'	S	9–11	6 ft (1.8 m)	E	Flowers (soft pink)
Anisodontea capensis	S	9–11	6 ft (1.8 m)	E	Flowers (pink, most of the year)
Anisodontea × hypomadarum	S	9–11	6 ft (1.8 m)	E	Flowers (pink with darker veins, spring–autumn)
Annona muricata	T	10–12	15-20 ft (4.5–6 m)	Semi	Edible fruit (soursop)
Annona squamosa	T	10–12	15 ft (4.5 m)	Semi	Edible fruit (soursop)
Anopterus glandulosus	S	8–9	6–8 ft (1.8–2.4 m)	E	Flowers (white in spring)
Aphelandra squarrosa	S	11–12	3–4 ft (1–1.2 m)	E	Foliage & long flower spikes (bright yellow)
Aphelandra squarrosa 'Dania'	S	11–12	3–4 ft (1–1.2 m)	E	Variegated foliage
Aphelandra squarrosa 'Louisae'	S	11–12	3–4 ft (1–1.2 m)	E	Foliage and flowers (yellow)
Aralia chinensis	S(T)	7–10	10–20 ft (3–6 m)	D	Foliage; flowers (cream in autumn)
Aralia elata	S(T)	5–9	10–20 ft (3–6 m)	D	Flowers (white, late summer–early autumn); autumn foliage
Aralia elata 'Variegata'	S(T)	5–9	10–20 ft (3–6 m)	D	Variegated foliage; flowers (white, late summer–autumn)
Araucaria araucana	T	8–9	50–60 ft (15–18 m)	E	Symmetrical branching habit
Araucaria cunninghamii	T	9–12	60–80 ft (18–24 m)	E	Distinctive branching habit; shiny brown bark
Araucaria heterophylla	T	10–11	40–50 ft (12–15 m)	E	Symmetrical form; foliage
Arbutus canariensis	S(T)	8–10	4.5m (15ft)	E	Attractive bark; flowers (pink, late summer–early autumn)
Arbutus menziesii	T	7–9	40–50 ft (12–15 m)	E	Bark; flowers (white); decorative fruit
Arbutus unedo	T	7–10	15–20 ft (4.5–6 m)	E	Flowers (white or pink, autumn); decorative fruit
Arctostaphylos manzanita	S	8–10	6–8 ft (1.8–2.4 m)	E	Attractive bark; flowers (pink or white)
Arctostaphylos uva-ursi	S	4–9	4–8 in (10–20 cm)	E	Foliage; flowers (white or pink, late spring); decorative/edible fruit
Ardisia crenata	S	8–11	3 ft (1 m)	E	Fruit (bright red)
Argyranthemum frutescens and cultivars	S	8–11	3 ft (1 m)	E	Flowers (white, pink or yellow tones); coastal tolerance
Argyranthemum maderense	S	9–11	2 ft (60 cm)	E	Flowers (yellow)
Argyrocytisus battandieri	S	8–10	8–12 ft (2.4–3.5 m)	E	Flowers (yellow, early summer); silvery foliage
Aronia arbutifolia	S	4–9	6 ft (1.8 m)	D	Decorative fruit; autumn foliage
Aronia melanocarpa	S	5–9	6 ft (1.8 m)	D	Decorative fruit; autumn foliage
Artemisia absinthium	S	4–10	3 ft (1 m)	E	Foliage
Artemisia absinthium 'Lambrook Silver'	S	4–10	3 ft (1 m)	E	Bright silver-gray foliage
Artemisia ludoviciana	S	4–10	4 ft (1.2 m)	Semi	Foliage
Artemisia ludoviciana 'Valerie Finnis'	S	4–10	4 ft (1.2 m)	Semi	Bright silver-gray foliage
Artemisia 'Powis Castle'	S	6–10	24–36 in (60–90 cm)	E	Silver-gray foliage; compact habit
Artemisia vulgaris	S	4–10	5–6 ft (1.5–1.8 m)	Semi	Foliage
Artemisia vulgaris 'Variegata'	S	4–10	5–6 ft (1.5–1.8 m)	Semi	Variegated foliage
Artocarpus altilis	T	11–12	20–25 ft (6–8 m)	E	Edible fruit; foliage
Artocarpus heterophyllus	T	11–12	30 ft (9 m)	E	Edible fruit; foliage
Asclepias curassavica	S	9–12	3 ft (1 m)	E	Flowers (bright orange-red)
Asimina triloba	T	5–10	25–30 ft (8–9 m)	D	Edible fruit; flowers (purple, early summer); autumn foliage

NAME	TYPE	ZONE	HEIGHT at MATURITY	DECIDUOUS or EVERGREEN	CHIEF ATTRACTIONS
Astartea 'Winter Pink'	S	9–11	3–5 ft (1–1.5 m)	E	Flowers (pink, late winter–spring)
Atherosperma moschatum	T	8–9	30–50 ft (9–15 m)	E	Symmetrical habit; flowers (white in spring)
Athrotaxis selaginoides	T	8–9	50–60 ft (15–18 m)	E	Foliage texture; symmetrical shape
Atriplex cinerea	S	9–10	36 in (90 cm)	E	Coastal tolerance; silver-gray foliage
Aucuba japonica	S	7–10	6 ft (1.8 m)	E	Foliage; decorative fruit
Aucuba japonica 'Variegata'	S	7–10	6 ft (1.8 m)	E	Yellow-spotted foliage; decorative fruit
Aurinia saxatilis	S	4–9	8–10 in (20–25 cm)	E	Flowers (yellow, spring–early summer)
Aurinia saxatilis 'Citrina'	S	4–9	8–10 in (20–25 cm)	E	Flowers (lemon-yellow, spring–early summer)
Austrocedrus chilensis	T	7–9	50–60 ft (15–18 m)	E	Foliage texture
Averrhoa carambola	T	11–12	20 ft (6 m)	E	Edible fruit
Avicennia marina	T	10–11	15 ft (4.5 m)	E	Foliage; coastal tolerance
Azadirachta indica	T	10–12	30–40 ft (9–12 m)	E	Flowers (white, late spring); decorative fruit; herbal uses
Azara lanceolata	S(T)	8–9	12–20 ft (3.5–6 m)	E	Foliage; flowers (yellow, fragrant, in spring)
Azara microphylla	T	7–9	20 ft (6 m)	E	Foliage; flowers (yellow, fragrant, late winter)
Azara serrata	S(T)	8–10	10–15 ft (3–4.5 m)	E	Flowers (yellow, late spring–early summer)
Baccharis pilularis	S	7–10	24–36 in (60–90 cm)	E	Growth habit & general hardiness
Baccharis pilularis 'Twin Peaks'	S	7–10	24 in (60 cm)	E	Compact growth habit
Banksia coccinea	S	9–10	6–12 ft (1.8–3.5 m)	E	Flowers (scarlet, winter–summer)
Banksia ericifolia	S	8–11	6–12 ft (1.8–3.5 m)	E	Flowers (golden-orange, autumn–winter)
Banksia 'Giant Candles'	S	9–11	12 ft (3.5 m)	E	Flowers (bronze-yellow, long spikes, autumn–winter)
Banksia integrifolia	T	9–11	20–30 ft (6–9 m)	E	Flowers (greenish-yellow, autumn–winter, foliage)
Banksia marginata	S(T)	8–11	8–15 ft (2.4–4.5 m)	E	Flowers (greenish yellow, autumn–winter)
Banksia prionotes	T	10–11	20 ft (6 m)	E	Flowers (orange-yellow, autumn–winter, foliage)
Banksia serrata	S(T)	9–11	10–20 ft (3–6 m)	E	Flowers (greenish-white, summer–autumn, decorative fruit)
Barleria cristata	S	10–12	3 ft (1 m)	E	Flowers (blue, mauve or white, most of the year)
Bauera rubioides	S	8–10	3 ft (1 m)	E	Flowers (deep pink to white, winter–midsummer)
Bauera sessiliflora	S	9–10	4–6 ft (1.2–1.8 m)	E	Flowers (rose-magenta, spring–early summer)
Bauhinia × blakeana	T	10–12	20 ft (6 m)	E	Flowers (crimson, spring)
Bauhinia monandra	T	11–12	20 ft (6 m)	Semi	Flowers (cream to pink, late spring–summer)
Bauhinia variegata	T	9–12	15–25 ft (4.5–8 m)	Semi	Flowers (pink to white, spring–summer)
Berberis darwinii	S	7–10	6 ft (1.8 m)	E	Flowers (orange, late winter–spring)
Berberis julianae	S	5–10	10–12 ft (3–3.5 m)	E	Foliage, flowers & fruit
Berberis × ottawensis	S	3–10	6 ft (1.8 m)	D	Foliage
Berberis × ottawensis 'Superba'	S	3–10	6 ft (1.8 m)	D	Foliage & fruit
Berberis × stenophylla	S	6–9	8 ft (2.4 m)	E	Flowers (yellow, in spring); fruit
Berberis × s. 'Corallina Compacta'	S	6–9	12 in (30 cm)	E	Compact growth; flowers (yellow, in spring); fruit
Berberis thunbergii	S	4–10	5 ft (1.5 m)	D	Colored foliage
Berberis thunbergii 'Atropurpurea'	S	4–10	5 ft (1.5 m)	D	Purple-bronze foliage
Berberis thunbergii 'Atropurpurea Nana'	S	4–10	12–18 in (30–45 cm)	D	Compact habit; purple foliage
Berberis thunbergii 'Rose Glow'	S	4–10	5 ft (1.5 m)	D	Purple-bronze & pink foliage
Berberis verruculosa	S	5–9	5 ft (1.5 m)	E	Flowers (yellow, late spring); fruit

NAME	TYPE	ZONE	HEIGHT at MATURITY	DECIDUOUS or EVERGREEN	CHIEF ATTRACTIONS
Berberis wilsoniae	S	5–10	5 ft (1.5 m)	D	Foliage; decorative fruit
Berzelia languinosa	S	9–11	6 ft (1.8 m)	E	Foliage; flowers (white, spring–summer)
Betula albosinensis	T	6–9	30–40 ft (9–12 m)	D	Bark; winter twigs
Betula nana	S	1–7	2–4 ft (0.6–1.2 m)	D	Foliage; extreme hardiness
Betula nigra	T	4–9	10–20 ft (3–6 m)	D	Attractive bark; winter twigs
Betula papyrifera	T	2–9	30–40 ft (9–12 m)	D	Attractive bark
Betula papyrifera var. *kenaica*	T	2–9	30–40 ft (9–12 m)	D	Attractive bark
Betula pendula	T	2–9	30–40 ft (9–12 m)	D	Attractive bark; graceful habit; autumn foliage
Betula pendula 'Tristis'	T	2–9	20–30 ft (6–9 m)	D	Weeping growth habit; bark & autumn color
Betula pendula 'Youngii'	T	2–9	15–25 ft (4.5–8 m)	D	Weeping growth; bark & autumn foliage color
Betula platyphylla	T	4–9	30–40 ft (9–12 m)	D	Attractive bark
Betula pubescens	T	2–9	30–40 ft (9–12 m)	D	Bark & autumn color
Betula utilis	T	7–9	30–40 ft (9–12 m)	D	Attractive bark
Betula utilis var. *jacquemontii*	T	7–9	30–40 ft (9–12 m)	D	Attractive bright white bark
Bixa orellana	S(T)	10–12	10–20 ft (3–6 m)	E	Flowers (pink in summer); decorative fruit
Boronia 'Carousel'	S	9–11	5 ft (1.5 m)	E	Flowers (pink to red, early spring–summer)
Boronia heterophylla	S	9–10	5 ft (1.5 m)	E	Flowers (red, late winter–early spring)
Boronia megastigma	S	9–10	3 ft (1 m)	E	Fragrant flowers (brown & yellow, late winter–spring)
Boronia megastigma 'Harlequin'	S	9–10	3 ft (1 m)	E	Fragrant flowers (brownish pink & white, late winter–spring)
Boronia molloyae	S	9–11	5 ft (1.5 m)	E	Flowers (scarlet, spring)
Boronia pinnata	S	9–11	5 ft (1.5 m)	E	Flowers (pink, in spring)
Bouvardia longiflora	S	10–11	3 ft (1 m)	E	Fragrant flowers (white, autumn–winter)
Bouvardia ternifolia	S	9–11	6 ft (1.8 m)	E	Flowers (red)
Brachychiton acerifolius	T	9–12	30–40 ft (9–12 m)	D	Flowers (scarlet, spring–early summer)
Brachychiton discolor	T	10–12	40–50 ft (12–15 m)	E	Flowers (pink, early summer)
Brachychiton populneus	T	8–11	40–50 ft (12–15 m)	E	Foliage; flowers (cream, in summer)
Brachyglottis greyi	S	7–9	5–6 ft (1.5–1.8 m)	E	Foliage; flowers (yellow, summer–autumn)
Brachyglottis repanda	S	9–11	15–20 ft (4.5–6 m)	E	Foliage; flowers (greenish silver, late winter–early spring)
Brachyglottis repanda 'Purpurea'	T	9–11	15 ft (4.5 m)	E	Purple-bronze foliage; flowers (greenish silver, late winter–early spring)
Brachyglottis 'Sunshine'	S	7–10	5–6 ft (1.5–1.8 m)	E	Foliage (flowers, yellow, summer–autumn)
Browallia speciosa	S	9–11	30 in (75 cm)	E	Flowers (purple-blue to deep purple or white)
Brugmansia × *candida*	T	10–12	10–15 ft (3–4.5 m)	E	Flowers (white, fragrant, summer–autumn)
Brugmansia × *candida* 'Grand Marnier'	T	10–12	10–15 ft (3–4.5 m)	E	Flowers (soft apricot, fragrant, summer–autumn)
Brugmansia 'Charles Grimaldi'	S	10–12	6 ft (1.8 m)	E	Flowers (pale orange-yellow, fragrant, autumn–spring)
Brugmansia sanguinea	S	9–11	8–10 ft (2.4–3 m)	E	Flowers (orange-red, late spring–summer)
Brugmansia suaveolens	S(T)	10–12	10–15 ft (3–4.5 m)	E	Flowers (white, summer–autumn)
Brunfelsia australis	S	9–12	8 ft (2.4 m)	E	Flowers (violet-blue to white, spring)
Brunfelsia pauciflora	S	10–12	5 ft (1.5 m)	Semi	Flowers (purple-mauve to white, spring–early summer)
Buddleja alternifolia	S	6–9	15–20 ft (4.5–6 m)	D	Flowers, mauve to pink, fragrant, late spring–early summer
Buddleja davidii	S	5–10	8–12 ft (2.4–3.5 m)	Semi	Flowers (purple, red, pink, white, late summer–early autumn)

NAME	TYPE	ZONE	HEIGHT at MATURITY	DECIDUOUS or EVERGREEN	CHIEF ATTRACTIONS
Buddleja davidii 'Cardinal'	S	5–10	8–12 ft (2.4–3.5 m)	Semi	Flowers, purple-pink, summer–early autumn
Buddleja davidii 'Pink Delight'	S	5–10	8–12 ft (2.4–3.5 m)	Semi	Flowers (pink, long spikes, late summer–early autumn)
Buddleja davidii 'Royal Red'	S	5–10	8–12 ft (2.4–3.5 m)	Semi	Flowers (magenta, summer–early autumn)
Buddleja davidii 'White Profusion'	S	5–10	8–12 ft (2.4–3.5 m)	Semi	Flowers (white & yellow, late summer–early autumn)
Buddleja fallowiana	S	8–9	12–15 ft (3.5–4.5 m)	D	Flowers (fragrant, lavender, summer)
Buddleja fallowiana 'Lochinch'	S	8–9	12–15 ft (3.5–4.5 m)	D	Flowers (fragrant, violet-blue with orange, summer)
Buddleja globosa	S	7–10	10–15 ft (3–4.5 m)	Semi	Flowers (orange, late spring–summer)
Buddleja × *weyeriana*	S	7–10	8–12 ft (2.4–3.5 m)	Semi	Flowers (cream to orange-yellow)
Buddleja × *weyeriana* 'Wattle Bird'	S	7–10	8–12 ft (2.4–3.5 m)	Semi	Flowers (yellow, long spikes)
Bupleurum fruticosum	S	7–10	4–8 ft (1.2–2.4 m)	E	Foliage; flowers (yellow-green, mid summer)
Buxus balearica	S(T)	8–10	10–20 ft (3–6 m)	E	Foliage texture
Buxus microphylla	S	6–10	3–6 ft (1–1.8 m)	E	Foliage texture
Buxus microphylla var. *japonica*	S	6–10	6–10 ft (1.8–3 m)	E	Foliage texture
Buxus sempervirens	S	5–10	3–6 ft (1–1.8 m)	E	Foliage texture
Buxus sempervirens 'Suffruticosa'	S	5–10	12–18 in (30–45 cm)	E	Dwarf habit & foliage texture
Caesalpinia gilliesii	S(T)	9–11	8–12 ft (2.4–3.5 m)	Semi	Flowers (yellow & scarlet, in summer)
Caesalpinia pulcherrima	S(T)	11–12	8–15 ft (2.4–4.5 m)	E	Flowers (scarlet & gold, spring–autumn)
Calceolaria integrifolia	S	8–10	4–6 ft (1.2–1.8 m)	E	Flowers (yellow, late spring–early autumn)
Calliandra californica	S	10–12	4 ft (1.2 m)	E	Flowers (deep red to purple-red)
Calliandra haematocephala	S	10–12	10–12 ft (3–3.5 m)	E	Flowers (red, most of the year)
Calliandra tweedii	S	9–11	6–8 ft (1.8–2.4 m)	E	Flowers (crimson, spring–summer)
Callicarpa americana	S	7–10	3–6 ft (1–1.8 m)	D	Flowers (purple, summer); decorative fruit
Callicarpa bodinieri	S	6–9	6–10 ft (1.8–3 m)	D	Flowers (lilac, summer); decorative fruit
Callicarpa b. var. *giraldii* 'Profusion'	S	6–9	6–10 ft (1.8–3 m)	D	Flowers (lilac, summer); decorative fruit
Callistemon citrinus	S	8–11	8–10 ft (2.4–3 m)	E	Flowers (scarlet to crimson, late spring-summer)
Callistemon citrinus 'Burgundy'	S	8–11	8–10 ft (2.4–3 m)	E	Flowers (wine red, late spring-summer)
Callistemon citrinus 'Splendens'	S	8–11	8–10 ft (2.4–3 m)	E	Flowers (scarlet, late spring-summer); compact habit
Callistemon citrinus 'White Anzac'	S	8–11	8–10 ft (2.4–3 m)	E	Flowers (white, late spring-summer)
Callistemon phoeniceus	S	9–11	10 ft (3 m)	E	Flowers (red, spring–early summer)
Callistemon salignus	T	9–11	15–30 ft (4.5–9 m)	E	Flowers (greenish-yellow or red, spring–summer); pink new growth
Callistemon viminalis	T	9–12	15–25 ft (4.5–8 m)	E	Flowers (scarlet, spring)
Callistemon viminalis 'Hannah Ray'	S	9–12	10 ft (3 m)	E	Flowers (scarlet, spring); compact habit
Callitris columellaris	T	9–11	40–50 ft (12–15 m)	E	Foliage; symmetrical form
Callitris rhomboidea	T	8–11	30 ft (9 m)	E	Foliage; symmetrical form
Calluna vulgaris	S	4–9	12–36 in (30–90 cm)	E	Flowers (pink to purplish, summer to autumn)
Calluna vulgaris 'Allegretto'	S	4–9	12 in (30 cm)	E	Flowers (cerise)
Calluna vulgaris 'Dark Beauty'	S	4–9	12–24 in (30–60 cm)	E	Flowers (pinkish-red)
Calluna vulgaris 'Heidesinfonia'	S	4–9	24–36 in (60–90 cm)	E	Flowers (mauve pink, long spikes)
Calluna vulgaris 'Multicolor'	S	4–9	8–12 in (20–30 cm)	E	Flowers (mauve); foliage (orange-red)
Calluna vulgaris 'Orange Queen'	S	4–9	12 in (30 cm)	E	Flowers (pink); foliage (golden-yellow in summer, orange in winter)

NAME	TYPE	ZONE	HEIGHT at MATURITY	DECIDUOUS or EVERGREEN	CHIEF ATTRACTIONS
Calluna vulgaris 'Robert Chapman'	S	4–9	12 in (30 cm)	E	Flowers (lavender); foliage (golden-yellow in summer, bronze in winter)
Calluna vulgaris 'Velvet Dome'	S	4–9	4–8 in (10–20 cm)	E	Foliage (dense, deep green)
Calocedrus decurrens	T	5–9	40 ft (12 m)	E	Foliage; symmetrical form
Calodendrum capense	T	9–11	30–50 ft (9–15 m)	E	Flowers (pink, late spring–early summer)
Calothamnus quadrifidus	S	8–11	6–8 ft (1.8–2.4 m)	E	Flowers (red, late spring–early summer); foliage
Calothamnus rupestris	S	9–11	10 ft (3 m)	E	Flowers (reddish-pink, spring)
Calpurnia aurea	T	9–12	15–20 ft (4.5–6 m)	E	Flowers (yellow, summer), pendulous
Calycanthus floridus	S	6–10	6–9 ft (1.8–2.7 m)	D	Flowers (brownish-red, late spring–summer)
Calycanthus occidentalis	S	7–10	10–12 ft (3–3.5 m)	D	Flowers (brownish-red, late spring–summer)
Calytrix tetragona	S	9–11	2–6 ft (0.6–1.8 m)	E	Flowers (pink to white, late winter–early summer)
Camellia cuspidata	S	7–10	10 ft (3 m)	E	Flowers (white); foliage (copper new growth)
Camellia cuspidata 'Spring Festival'	S	7–10	10 ft (3 m)	E	Flowers (mid pink); narrow growth habit
Camellia, garden hybrids	S	8–10	12–20 ft (3.5–6 m)	E	Flowers (white, pink, red, winter–spring); hundreds of hybrids available
Camellia × *grijsii*	S	8–10	3–10 ft (1–3 m)	E	Flowers (white, sometimes fragrant, late winter–spring)
Camellia hiemalis	S	8–10	10–15 ft (3–4.5 m)	E	Flowers (white or pink, winter–spring)
Camellia hiemalis 'Somerset'	S	8–10	10–15 ft (3–4.5 m)	E	Flowers (reddish pink, semi-double)
Camellia japonica and cultivars	S	8–11	4–5m (3.5–4.5 m)	E	Flowers (white, pink, red, winter–early spring); thousands of cultivars available
Camellia oleifera	S(T)	7–10	10–15 ft (3–4.5 m)	E	Flowers (white, fragrant, early autumn–early winter)
Camellia pitardii and cultivars	S(T)	7–10	20 ft (6 m)	E	Flowers (red, pink, white, mid-winter– early spring)
Camellia reticulata and cultivars	S	8–10	15 ft (5 m)	E	Flowers (red, pink, white, mid-winter–early spring); cultivars include the largest-flowered of all camellias
Camellia sasanqua and cultivars	S	8–11	12–20 ft (3–6 m)	E	Flowers (pink & white, early autumn–early winter); informal habit; many cultivars available
Camellia sinensis	S	8–11	8 ft (2.5 m)	E	Foliage; flowers (white in spring & autumn)
Camellia sinensis var. *assamica*	S	9–11	8 ft (2.5 m)	E	Flowers (white in spring & autumn); large leaves
Camellia × *vernalis* and cultivars	S	8–10	6–10 ft (1.8–3 m)	E	Flowers (pink & white, mid winter–mid spring)
Camellia × *williamsii*	S	7–10	10–15 ft (3–4.5 m)	E	Flowers (pink, winter–spring)
Camellia × *williamsii* cultivars	S	7–10	10–15 ft (3–4.5 m)	E	Flowers (white, pink, red, winter–spring)
Camptotheca acuminata	T	10–11	30–40 ft (9–12 m)	D	Foliage; flower (white in summer); decorative fruit
Cananga odorata	T	11–12	40–50 ft (12–15 m)	E	Flowers (greenish-yellow in summer)
Cantua buxifolia	S	8–9	6–10 ft (1.8–3 m)	E	Flowers (purple to pink, late spring)
Caragana arborescens	S(T)	3–9	12–20 ft (3.5–6 m)	D	Flowers (yellow, late spring–early summer)
Caragana arborescens 'Lorbergii'	S(T)	3–9	12–20 ft (3.5–6 m)	D	Flowers (yellow, late spring–early summer); foliage
Carissa macrocarpa	S	9–11	6–10 ft (1.8–3 m)	E	Edible fruit; flowers (white, spring–summer)
Carissa macrocarpa 'Horizontalis'	S	9–11	8–12 in (20–30 cm)	E	Edible fruit; flowers (white, spring–summer); low, spreading growth habit
Carmichaelia odorata	S	9–10	6 ft (1.8 m)	E	Flowers (white & purple, fragrant, late spring–summer)
Carpenteria californica	S	7–9	10–20 ft (3–6 m)	E	Flowers (white, early summer)
Carpinus betulus	T	6–9	30–50 ft (9–15 m)	D	Autumn foliage; decorative fruit; bark
Carpinus betulus 'Columnaris'	T	6–9	30 ft (9 m)	D	Autumn foliage; decorative fruit; bark, upright growth habit
Carpinus japonica	T	5–9	30–40 ft (9–12 m)	D	Autumn foliage; decorative fruit; bark

NAME	TYPE	ZONE	HEIGHT at MATURITY	DECIDUOUS or EVERGREEN	CHIEF ATTRACTIONS
Carpodetus serratus	T	8–10	30 ft (9 m)	E	Bark; young foliage; flowers (white, late spring–early autumn); fruit
Carya cordiformis	T	4–9	50–60 ft (15–18 m)	D	Autumn foliage; winter twigs
Carya illinoinensis	T	6–11	50–60 ft (15–18 m)	D	Edible nuts (pecans)
Carya ovata	T	4–9	50–60 ft (15–18 m)	D	Edible nuts; autumn foliage; striking bark
Caryopteris × *clandonensis*	S	5–9	3 ft (1 m)	D	Flowers (purple-blue, late summer–autumn)
Caryopteris × *clandonensis* 'Ferndown'	S	5–9	3 ft (1 m)	D	Flowers (dark violet-blue, late summer–autumn)
Cassia fistula	T	10–12	25–30 ft (8–9 m)	Semi	Flowers (pale yellow, late spring–summer)
Cassia javanica	T	11–12	30–40 ft (9–12 m)	D	Flowers (pink, late spring–summer)
Cassinia aculeata	S	8–11	5 ft (1.5 m)	E	Flowers (white to pink, summer)
Cassiope 'Edinburgh'	S	4–8	12 in (30 cm)	E	Dwarf habit; flowers (white, spring)
Castanea sativa	T	5–9	40–50 ft (12–15 m)	D	Edible nuts (chestnuts); autumn foliage
Castanospermum australe	T	10–12	40 ft (12 m)	E	Flowers (orange & yellow, early summer); curious fruit
Casuarina cunninghamiana	T	8–12	50–60 ft (15–18 m)	E	Foliage; pine-like growth form; vigorous growth
Casuarina equisetifolia	T	10–12	40–60 ft (12–18 m)	E	Foliage; pine-like growth form; coastal tolerance
Catalpa bignonioides	T	5–10	30–40 ft (9–12 m)	D	Flowers (white in summer); foliage
Catalpa speciosa	T	4–10	50–60 ft (15–18 m)	D	Flowers (white in summer); foliage
Cavendishia acuminata	S	9–10	3–6 ft (1–1.8 m)	E	Flowers (scarlet to crimson, autumn)
Ceanothus arboreus	T	8–10	20–30 ft (6–9 m)	E	Flowers (pale to deep blue, spring–early summer)
Ceanothus arboreus 'Mist'	T	8–10	20–30 ft (6–9 m)	E	Flowers (long spikes, pale gray-blue, spring–early summer)
Ceanothus 'Blue Cushion'	S	8–10	3 ft (1 m)	E	Flowers (soft lilac-blue, spring)
Ceanothus × *delilianus*	S	7–9	12 ft (3.5 m)	D	Flowers (sky blue, summer–early autumn)
Ceanothus × *delilianus* 'Gloire de Versailles'	S	7–9	12 ft (3.5 m)	D	Flowers (sky blue, fragrant, summer–early autumn)
Ceanothus griseus	S	8–10	8 ft (2.4 m)	E	Flowers (pale blue, spring)
Ceanothus impressus	S	8–10	6–10 ft (1.8–3 m)	E	Flowers (deep blue, spring)
Ceanothus papillosus	S	8–10	10–12 ft (3–3.5 m)	E	Flowers (deep blue, spring)
Ceanothus thyrsiflorus	S(T)	7–9	15–20 ft (4.5–6 m)	E	Flowers (pale blue, late spring–early summer)
Cecropia palmata	T	11–12	30–40 ft (9–12 m)	E	Foliage
Cedrela mexicana	T	10–12	60–80 ft (18–24 m)	E	Foliage
Cedrus atlantica	T	6–9	50–80 ft (15–24 m)	E	Foliage; symmetrical form
Cedrus atlantica 'Glauca'	T	6–9	50–80 ft (15–24 m)	E	Foliage (silver-blue); symmetrical form
Cedrus deodara	T	7–10	100 ft (30 m)	E	Foliage; symmetrical form
Cedrus deodara 'Aurea'	T	7–10	100 ft (30 m)	E	Foliage (yellow-tipped); symmetrical form
Cedrus libani	T	6–9	50–70 ft (15–21 m)	E	Foliage; majestic form
Ceiba pentandra	T	12	100 ft (30 m)	D	Foliage; flowers (white, yellow, pink, winter); massive trunk
Celtis occidentalis	T	3–10	40–60 ft (12–18 m)	D	Autumn foliage
Cephalotaxus harringtonia	S	6–10	6–10 ft (1.8–3 m)	E	Foliage; compact form
Cephalotaxus harringtonia 'Fastigiata'	S	6–10	6 ft (1.8 m)	E	Foliage; Narrow upright growth habit
Ceratonia siliqua	T	9–11	20–25 ft (6–8 m)	E	Foliage; edible pulp around seeds (carob)
Ceratopetalum gummiferum	S(T)	9–11	12–20 ft (3.5–6 m)	E	Flowers (white, late spring); decorative fruit (red, early summer)

NAME	TYPE	ZONE	HEIGHT at MATURITY	DECIDUOUS or EVERGREEN	CHIEF ATTRACTIONS
Ceratostigma willmottianum	S	6–10	2–4 ft (0.6–1.2 m)	D	Flowers (blue, late summer–autumn)
Cercidiphyllum japonicum	T	6–9	40 ft (12 m)	D	Autumn foliage
Cercidium floridum	T	8–11	25–30 ft (8–9 m)	D	Flowers (yellow, spring); extreme drought tolerance
Cercis canadensis	T	5–9	12–20 ft (3.5–6 m)	D	Flowers (pink, spring–early summer)
Cercis canadensis 'Forest Pansy'	T	5–9	12–20 ft (3.5–6 m)	D	Flowers (pink, spring–early summer); foliage (purple)
Cercis siliquastrum	T	7–9	20–25 ft (6–8 m)	D	Flowers (deep pink, late spring)
Cercis siliquastrum 'Alba'	T	7–9	20–25 ft (6–8 m)	D	Flowers (white, late spring)
Cestrum fasciculatum	S	9–11	10 ft (3 m)	E	Flowers (red, summer)
Cestrum 'Newellii'	S	9–11	6 ft (1.8 m)	E	Flowers (crimson, most of the year)
Cestrum nocturnum	S	10–12	10–12 ft (3–3.5 m)	E	Flowers (pale green, very fragrant, late summer); decorative fruit
Cestrum parqui	S	9–11	10 ft (3 m)	E	Flowers (yellow-green, very fragrant, late summer); decorative fruit
Chaenomeles japonica	S	4–9	3–4 ft (1–1.2 m)	D	Flowers (orange-red to scarlet, spring–summer); aromatic decorative fruit
Chaenomeles speciosa	S	6–10	5–10 ft (1.5–3 m)	D	Flowers (scarlet to crimson); edible/decorative fruit
Chaenomeles speciosa 'Apple Blossom'	S	6–10	5–10 ft (1.5–3 m)	D	Flowers (white flushed pink); edible/decorative fruit
Chaenomeles speciosa 'Moerloosii'	S	6–10	5–10 ft (1.5–3 m)	D	Flowers (white, flushed & blotched pink & carmine); edible/decorative fruit
Chaenomeles speciosa 'Nivalis'	S	6–10	5–10 ft (1.5–3 m)	D	Flowers (white); edible/decorative fruit
Chaenomeles × superba	S	6–10	4–6 ft (1.2–1.8 m)	D	Flowers (white, pink, orange-red, scarlet, spring–summer)
Chamaecyparis funebris	T	9–10	30 ft (9 m)	E	Foliage; weeping habit
Chamaecyparis lawsoniana	T	6–9	40–50 ft (12–15 m)	E	Foliage; symmetrical form
Chamaecyparis l. 'Argentea Compacta'	T	6–9	10–15 ft (3–4.5 m)	E	Foliage (green, variegated cream); compact habit
Chamaecyparis l. 'Alumii'	S(T)	6–9	10–15 ft (3–4.5 m)	E	Foliage (blue-gray)
Chamaecyparis l. 'Erecta'	T	6–9	30 ft (9 m)	E	Foliage; narrow upright growth habit
Chamaecyparis l. 'Fraseri',	S(T)	6–9	10 ft (3 m)	E	Foliage; erect upright habit
Chamaecyparis l. 'Golden Wonder'	T	6–9	10–15 ft (3–4.5 m)	E	Foliage (pale yellow)
Chamaecyparis l. 'Green Globe'	S	6–9	18 in (45 cm)	E	Foliage; dwarf growth habit
Chamaecyparis l. 'Lane'	S(T)	6–9	10–15 ft (3–4.5 m)	E	Foliage (lemon yellow in summer, bronze gold in winter)
Chamaecyparis l. 'Pembury Blue'	S	6–9	10 ft (3 m)	E	Foliage (silver-blue)
Chamaecyparis l. 'Winston Churchill'	S	6–9	10 ft (3 m)	E	Foliage (golden yellow); conical growth habit
Chamaecyparis nootkatensis	T	4–9	30 ft (9 m)	E	Foliage; symmetrical shape
Chamaecyparis nootkatensis 'Pendula'	T	4–9	30 ft (9 m)	E	Foliage (weeping sprays)
Chamaecyparis obtusa	T	5–10	25–30 ft (8–9 m)	E	Foliage; symmetrical form
Chamaecyparis obtusa 'Crippsii'	S	5–10	10–15 ft (3–4.5 m)	E	Foliage (golden); symmetrical form
Chamaecyparis obtusa 'Kosteri'	S	5–10	30 in (80 cm)	E	Foliage (bright green); compact habit
Chamaecyparis obtusa 'Minima'	S	5–10	4–6 in (10–15 cm)	E	Very dwarf growth habit
Chamaecyparis obtusa 'Nana Gracilis'	S	5–10	12–24 in (30–60 cm)	E	Foliage texture
Chamaecyparis pisifera	T	5–10	25–30 ft (8–9 m)	E	Foliage; symmetrical form
Chamaecyparis p. 'Boulevard'	S(T)	5–10	12–15 ft (3.5–4.5 m)	E	Foliage (silver-blue); symmetrical form

NAME	TYPE	ZONE	HEIGHT at MATURITY	DECIDUOUS or EVERGREEN	CHIEF ATTRACTIONS
Chamaecyparis pisifera 'Filifera Aurea'	S	5–10	10 ft (3 m)	E	Foliage (golden-green); spreading habit
Chamaecyparis p. 'Plumosa'	S(T)	5–10	10–20 ft (3–6 m)	E	Foliage; symmetrical form
Chamaecyparis pisifera 'Plumosa Aurea'	S(T)	5–10	10–20 ft (3–6 m)	E	Foliage (yellow-green); symmetrical form
Chamaecyparis p. 'Squarrosa'	T	5–10	30 ft (9 m)	E	Foliage (silver-blue in summer, purple in winter); symmetrical form
Chamaecyparis thyoides	T	4–9	30 ft (9 m)	E	Foliage
Chamaecyparis thyoides 'Red Star'	S	4–9	6 ft (1.8 m)	E	Foliage (silver-green, purple in winter)
Chamaecytisus purpureus	S	6–9	18 in (45 cm)	D	Flowers (yellow & pale pink to light purple, spring–early summer)
Chamelaucium uncinatum	S	10–11	10 ft (3 m)	E	Flowers (mauve, pink, white, late winter–spring); aromatic foliage
Chilopsis linearis	S(T)	7–10	10–20 ft (3–6 m)	E	Flowers (pink, late spring–summer); drought tolerance
Chimonanthus praecox	S	6–10	10–15 ft (3–4.5 m)	E	Flowers (pale yellow, very fragrant, late autumn–winter)
Chionanthus retusus	T	6–10	30 ft (9 m)	D	Flowers (white, late spring–early summer)
Chionanthus virginicus	T	5–9	10–20 ft (3–6 m)	D	Flowers (white, late spring)
Choisya 'Aztec Pearl'	S	8–11	6 ft (1.8 m)	E	Flowers (white, fragrant, spring); foliage
Choisya ternata	S	7–11	6 ft (1.8 m)	E	Flowers (white, fragrant, spring)
Choisya ternata 'Sundance'	S	7–11	6 ft (1.8 m)	E	Flowers (white, fragrant, spring); foliage (bright yellow)
Chorisia speciosa	T	9–11	50 ft (15 m)	D	Flowers (pink, autumn); interesting trunk form
Chorizema cordatum	S	9–11	3–5 ft (1–1.5 m)	E	Flowers (yellow to orange-red & pink, spring)
Chrysanthemoides monilifera	S	9–11	4–6 ft (1.2–1.8 m)	E	Flowers (yellow, most of the year), drought & coastal tolerance
Cinnamomum camphora	T	9–11	50–60 ft (15–18 m)	E	Foliage; flowers (cream in spring), pink new growth
Cistus albidus	S	7–9	4 ft (1.2 m)	E	Flowers (lilac pink in spring); aromatic foliage
Cistus ladanifer	S	8–10	5–6 ft (1.5–1.8 m)	E	Flowers (white & chocolate, mid spring–early summer)
Cistus ladinifer 'Albiflorus'	S	8–10	5–6 ft (1.5–1.8 m)	E	Flowers (white, mid spring–early summer)
Cistus laurifolius	S	7–9	5–6 ft (1.5–1.8 m)	E	Flowers (white, summer)
Cistus × lusitanicus	S	8–9	24 in (60 cm)	E	Flowers (white, spring–early summer)
Cistus × pulverulentus	S	8–10	24 in (60 cm)	E	Flowers (rose pink, summer)
Cistus × pulverulentus 'Sunset'	S	8–10	24 in (60 cm)	E	Flowers (deep rose pink, summer)
Cistus × purpureus	S	7–9	3 ft (1 m)	E	Flowers (rose pink, summer)
Cistus × purpureus 'Brilliancy'	S	7–9	3 ft (1 m)	E	Flowers (bright rose pink, summer)
Cistus salviifolius	S	8–10	24–36 in (60–90 cm)	E	Flowers (white, late winter–early summer)
Cistus 'Snow Mound'	S	8–10	60cm (24in)	E	Flowers (white, late spring–summer)
Citrus aurantifolia	T	10–12	12 ft (3.5 m)	E	Edible fruits; flowers (white, fragrant, spring–early summer)
Citrus aurantium	T	9–12	30 ft (10 m)	E	Edible fruits; flowers (white, fragrant, spring–early summer)
Citrus limon	T	9–11	12–15 ft (3.5–4.5 m)	E	Edible fruits; flowers (white, fragrant, most of the year)
Citrus limon 'Meyer'	T	9–11	8–12 ft (2.4–3.5 m)	E	Edible fruits; flowers (white, fragrant, most of the year)
Citrus × paradisi	T	10–12	15 ft (4.5 m)	E	Edible fruits
Citrus sinensis	T	10–11	12–15 ft (3.5–4.5 m)	E	Edible fruits; flowers (white, fragrant, spring –summer)
Citrus × tangelo	T	9–11	20–30 ft (6–9 m)	E	Edible fruits
Cladrastis lutea	T	6–10	30 ft (9 m)	D	Flowers (white, early summer)

NAME	TYPE	ZONE	HEIGHT at MATURITY	DECIDUOUS or EVERGREEN	CHIEF ATTRACTIONS
Clerodendrum bungei	S	7–10	6 ft (1.8 m)	E	Flowers (rose-red to purple, fragrant, summer)
Clerodendrum trichotomum	S(T)	7–10	12–15 ft (3.5–4.5 m)	D	Flowers (white to mauve, fragrant, late summer); decorative fruit
Clerodendrum ugandense	S	10–11	10 ft (3 m)	E	Flowers (blue, summer–autumn)
Clethra arborea	T	9–10	20–25 ft (6–8 m)	E	Flowers (white, summer)
Clethra barbinervis	S(T)	6–9	8–15 ft (2.5–4.5 m)	D	Flowers (white, late summer–early autumn); foliage
Clianthus puniceus	S	8–10	5–8 ft (1.5–2.4 m)	E	Flowers (red, spring–early summer)
Clianthus puniceus 'Roseus'	S	8–10	5–8 ft (1.5–2.4 m)	E	Flowers (deep pink, spring–early summer)
Clusia rosea	T	11–12	30 ft (9 m)	E	Flowers (pale pink, summer–early autumn); foliage
Codiaeum variegatum and cultivars	S	11–12	6–8 ft (1.8–2.4 m)	E	Colored foliage
Coffea arabica	S	10–12	12–15 ft (3.5–4.5 m)	E	Fruit (coffee berries); flowers (white & fragrant in spring); foliage
Coleonema album	S	9–10	5 ft (1.5 m)	E	Flowers (white in spring); aromatic foliage
Coleonema pulchellum	S	9–10	5 ft (1.5 m)	E	Flowers (pink, spring–summer); aromatic foliage
Coleonema pulchellum 'Sunset Gold'	S	9–10	5 ft (1.5 m)	E	Flowers (pink, spring–summer); aromatic foliage (yellow-gold)
Colquhounia coccinea	S	8–10	10 ft (3 m)	E	Flowers (pink to reddish-orange, late summer–autumn); foliage (large, felted)
Columnea gloriosa	S	11–12	18 in (45 cm)	E	Flowers (red & yellow, most of the year)
Columnea gloriosa 'Purpurea'	S	11–12	18 in (45 cm)	E	Flowers (red & yellow, most of the year); foliage (purple)
Combretum erythrophyllum	T	9–11	30 ft (9 m)	D	Autumn color
Coprosma 'Kiwi Silver'	S	9–11	12 in (30 cm)	E	Foliage (variegated)
Coprosma lucida	S(T)	8–10	10–20 ft (3–6 m)	E	Foliage
Coprosma repens	S	9–11	5–8 ft (1.5–2.4 m)	E	Foliage; coastal tolerance
Coprosma repens 'Golden Splash'	S	9–11	5–8 ft (1.5–2.4 m)	E	Foliage (yellow variegated); coastal tolerance
Cordia sebestena	S(T)	10–12	15–20 ft (4.5–6 m)	E	Flowers (orange-red, most of the year)
Cordia wallichii	S(T)	10–12	12–20 ft (3.5–6 m)	E	Flowers
Cordyline australis	T	8–11	15–25 ft (4.5–8 m)	E	Flowers (cream, fragrant, summer); upright growth habit
Cordyline australis 'Albertii'	S(T)	9–11	8–15 ft (2.4–4.5 m)	E	Flowers (cream, fragrant, summer); foliage (cream & pink variegated)
Cordyline banksii	S	9–11	10 ft (3 m)	E	Foliage; flowers (white, late spring–summer)
Cordyline fruticosa	S(T)	10–12	8–15 ft (2.4–4.5 m)	E	Foliage
Coriaria japonica	S	8–10	4–6 ft (1.2–1.8 m)	D	Autumn foliage; fruit (red)
Cornus alba	S	4–9	6–10 ft (1.8–3 m)	D	Winter twigs; flowers (cream, late spring to summer)
Cornus alba 'Elegantissima'	S	4–9	6–10 ft (1.8–3 m)	D	Variegated foliage; winter twigs; flowers (cream, late spring to summer)
Cornus capitata	T	8–10	20–25 ft (6–8 m)	E	Flowers (creamy yellow, late spring–early summer); decorative fruit
Cornus controversa	T	6–9	30 ft (9 m)	D	Autumn foliage; flowers (white, early summer)
Cornus controversa 'Variegata'	T	6–9	30 ft (9 m)	D	Variegated summer foliage; autumn foliage; flowers (white, early summer)
Cornus florida	T	5–9	20 ft (6 m)	D	Flowers (pink or white, spring); autumn foliage; decorative fruit.
Cornus florida 'Rubra'	T	5–9	20 ft (6 m)	D	Flowers (deep pink, spring); autumn foliage; decorative fruit.
Cornus kousa	S(T)	6–9	12–20 ft (3.5–6 m)	D	Flowers (white, early summer), autumn foliage; decorative fruit

NAME	TYPE	ZONE	HEIGHT at MATURITY	DECIDUOUS or EVERGREEN	CHIEF ATTRACTIONS
Cornus kousa var. chinensis	S(T)	6–9	12–20 ft (3.5–6 m)	D	Flowers (white, early summer), autumn foliage; decorative fruit; vigorous
Cornus mas	T	6–9	25 ft (8 m)	D	Flowers (yellow, late winter–early spring)
Cornus nuttallii	S(T)	7–9	12–20 ft (3.5–6 m)	D	Flowers (white, mid-spring–early summer)
Cornus stolonifera	S	2–10	6–10 ft (1.8–3 m)	D	Bark, flowers (white, spring); decorative fruit
Cornus stolonifera 'Flaviramea'	S	2–10	6–10 ft (1.8–3 m)	D	Bark, flowers (white, spring); decorative fruit
Cornus stolonifera 'Kelsey Gold'	S	2–10	6–10 ft (1.8–3 m)	D	Foliage (yellow-green); bark, flowers (white, spring); decorative fruit
Corokia buddlejoides	S	8–10	10 ft (3 m)	E	Foliage; flowers (yellow, spring)
Corokia × virgata	S	8–10	10 ft (3 m)	E	Foliage; flowers (yellow, spring–early summer); decorative fruit
Coronilla emerus	S	6–9	3 ft (1 m)	D	Flowers (yellow, spring–autumn)
Coronilla valentina	S	9–10	3–5 ft (1–1.5 m)	E	Flowers (yellow, fragrant, spring & autumn)
Correa backhousiana	S	8–10	4 ft (1.2 m)	E	Flowers (cream to pale green, winter); coastal tolerance
Correa 'Dusky Bells'	S	9–10	24 in (60 cm)	E	Flowers (dusky pink, autumn–spring)
Correa pulchella	S	9–10	3 ft (1 m)	E	Flowers (orange-pink, winter–spring)
Correa reflexa	S	9–10	2–4 ft (0.6–1.2 m)	E	Flowers (red, green tipped, spring)
Correa reflexa 'Fat Fred'	S	9–10	2–4 ft (0.6–1.2 m)	E	Flowers (large, red, green tipped, spring)
Corylopsis glabrescens	S	6–9	15 ft (4.5 m)	D	Flowers (lemon yellow, mid spring)
Corylopsis spicata	S	6–9	6–8 ft (1.8–2.4 m)	D	Flowers (greenish-yellow, early spring)
Corylus avellana	S(T)	4–9	12–20 ft (3.5–6 m)	D	Edible nuts (hazels); male flowers (yellow, late winter–early spring)
Corylus avellana 'Contorta'	S	4–9	6–10 ft (1.8–3 m)	D	Branch structure
Corylus maxima	S(T)	4–9	12–20 ft (3.5–6 m)	D	Edible nuts; foliage
Corylus maxima 'Purpurea'	S(T)	4–9	12–20 ft (3.5–6 m)	D	Edible nuts; foliage (purple-bronze)
Corymbia aparrerinja	T	10–12	50 ft (15 m)	E	Bark; flowers (white)
Corymbia calophylla	T	9–10	30 ft (9 m)	E	Flowers (cream or pink, summer–autumn)
Corymbia citriodora	T	10–11	40–50 ft (12–15 m)	E	Bark; elegant form
Corymbia ficifolia	T	9–10	20–25 ft (6–8 m)	E	Flowers (orange or scarlet, late spring–summer); curious fruit
Corymbia maculata	T	9–10	40–60 (12–18 m)	E	Bark; flowers (white, winter)
Corynocarpus laevigata	T	9–11	20–30 ft (6–9 m)	E	Foliage; decorative fruit
Cotinus coggygria	S(T)	6–10	10–15 ft (3–4.5 m)	D	Foliage; flowers stalks (pinkish, early summer)
Cotinus coggygria 'Royal Purple'	S(T)	6–10	10–15 ft (3–4.5 m)	D	Foliage (purple); flowers stalks (purple-pink, early summer)
Cotinus coggygria 'Velvet Cloak'	S(T)	6–10	10–15 ft (3–4.5 m)	D	Foliage (deep purple-bronze); flowers stalks (purple-pink, early summer)
Cotinus obovatus	S(T)	5–10	15–30 ft (3–9 m)	D	Foliage; autumn color
Cotoneaster dammeri	S	5–10	6–12 in (15–30 cm)	E	Foliage; decorative fruit
Cotoneaster dammeri 'Coral Beauty'	S	5–10	6–12 in (15–30 cm)	E	Foliage; decorative fruit (orange)
Cotoneaster franchetii	S	6–10	10 ft (3 m)	E	Decorative fruit
Cotoneaster horizontalis	S	5–10	2–3 ft (0.6–1 m)	D	Autumn/winter foliage; decorative fruit
Cotoneaster 'Hybridus Pendulus'	S	6–9	3 ft (1 m)	Semi	Pendulous habit; decorative fruit
Cotoneaster lacteus	S	7–11	10–12ft	E	Decorative fruit
Cotoneaster microphyllus	S	5–10	12in–4 ft (0.3–1.2 m)	E	Foliage; decorative fruit

NAME	TYPE	ZONE	HEIGHT at MATURITY	DECIDUOUS or EVERGREEN	CHIEF ATTRACTIONS
Cotoneaster salicifolius	S	6–10	10–15 ft (3–4.5 m)	E	Autumn/winter foliage; decorative fruit
Cotoneaster splendens	S	5–9	5–10 ft (1.5–3 m)	D	Decorative fruit; autumn foliage
Couroupita guianensis	T	11–12	30–40 ft (10–12 m)	E	Flowers (red & orange, fragrant, most of the year); curious fruit
Crataegus diffusa	T	4–9	30 ft (10 m)	D	Flowers (white, spring); decorative fruit
Crataegus flava	T	4–9	15–20 ft (4.5–6 m)	D	Flowers (white, early summer)
Crataegus laevigata	T	4–9	25 ft (8 m)	D	Flowers (white, late spring); decorative fruit
Crataegus laevigata 'Paul's Scarlet'	T	4–9	25 ft (8 m)	D	Flowers (red, late spring); decorative fruit
Crataegus l. 'Punicea Flore Pleno'	T	4–9	25 ft (8 m)	D	Flowers (pink, double, late spring); decorative fruit
Crataegus × *lavallei*	T	6–10	15–20 ft (4.5–6 m)	D	Flowers (white, early summer); decorative fruit
Crataegus monogyna	T	4–9	20–30 ft (6–9 m)	D	Flowers (white, late spring–early summer); decorative fruit
Crataegus phaenopyrum	T	4–10	20–30 ft (6–9 m)	D	Flowers (white, midsummer); decorative fruit
Crataegus punctata	T	5–9	30 ft (9 m)	D	Flowers (white, early summer); decorative fruit
Crataegus viridis	T	4–9	20–30 ft (6–9 m)	D	Flowers (white, summer); decorative fruit
Crataegus viridis 'Winter King'	T	4–9	20–30 ft (6–9 m)	D	Flowers (white, summer); decorative fruit; autumn color
Crowea exalata	S	8–10	24 in (60 cm)	E	Flowers (pink, most of the year)
Crowea exalata 'Bindelong Compact'	S	8–10	18 in (45 cm)	E	Compact growth; flowers (pink, most of the year)
Cryptomeria japonica and var. *sinensis*	T	7–10	30–40 ft (9–12 m)	E	Foliage; winter color
Cryptomeria japonica 'Elegans'	T	7–10	30 ft (9 m)	E	Growth habit; foliage; winter color
Cryptomeria japonica 'Globosa Nana'	S	7–10	10 ft (3 m)	E	Growth habit; foliage
Cunonia capensis	S(T)	9–10	10–20 ft (3–6 m)	E	Foliage; flowers (white, autumn)
Cuphea hyssopifolia	S	10–12	24 in (60 cm)	E	Flowers (mauve or white, summer–autumn)
Cuphea ignea	S	10–12	24 in (60 cm)	E	Flowers (orange, summer–autumn)
Cuphea micropetala	S	9–11	24–36 in (60–90 cm)	E	Flowers (orange-yellow, summer–early winter)
× *Cupressocyparis leylandii*	T	5–10	50 ft (15 m)	E	Foliage; vigorous growth
× *Cupressocyparis l.* 'Haggerston Gray'	T	5–10	50 ft (15 m)	E	Foliage (gray-green); vigorous open growth
Cupressus arizonica	T	7–10	50 ft (15 m)	E	Foliage (gray-blue)
Cupressus cashmeriana	T	9–11	30 ft (9 m)	E	Foliage; weeping habit
Cupressus lusitanica	T	8–10	40 ft (12 m)	E	Foliage; vigorous growth
Cupressus macrocarpa	T	7–10	50 ft (15 m)	E	Foliage; vigorous growth
Cupressus m. 'Greenstead Magnificent'	T	7–10	2 ft (60 cm)	E	Foliage; vigorous ground covering growth
Cupressus macrocarpa 'Aurea'	T	7–10	50 ft (15 m)	E	Foliage (gold tipped); vigorous growth
Cupressus sempervirens	T	8–10	30 ft (9 m)	E	Foliage; columnar shape
Cupressus sempervirens 'Stricta'	T	8–10	30 ft (9 m)	E	Foliage; narrow columnar shape
Cupressus sempervirens. 'Swane's Golden'	T	8–10	30 ft (9 m)	E	Foliage (golden yellow); narrow columnar shape
Cupressus torulosa	T	8–10	40 ft (12 m)	E	Foliage; conical shape
Cussonia spicata	S(T)	8–11	10–20 ft (3–6 m)	E	Foliage; flowers (greenish white, spring–summer)
Cydonia oblonga	T	6–9	12–15m (3.5–4.5 m)	E	Edible fruit; flowers (pale pink, late spring)

NAME	TYPE	ZONE	HEIGHT at MATURITY	DECIDUOUS or EVERGREEN	CHIEF ATTRACTIONS
Cyphomandra betacea	S	9–11	10 ft (3 m)	E	Edible fruit; flowers (white, summer)
Cyrilla racemiflora	S	6–11	5 ft 91.5 m)	D/E	Flowers (white, fragrant, summer)
Cytisus × praecox	S	5–9	3–4 ft (1–1.2 m)	E	Flowers (yellow, white, fragrant, mid to late spring)
Cytisus × praecox 'Allgold'	S	5–9	3 ft (1–1.2 m)	E	Cascading growth habit; flowers (golden yellow, fragrant, mid to late spring)
Cytisus scoparius	S	5–9	6–8 ft (1.8–2.4 m)	D	Flowers (yellow, late spring–early summer)
Cytisus scoparius 'Pendulus'	S	5–9	6–8 ft (1.8–2.4 m)	D	Weeping growth habit; flowers (yellow, late spring–early summer)
Daboecia cantabrica	S	7–9	24 in (60 cm)	E	Flowers (purple, summer–autumn)
Daboecia cantabrica 'Alba'	S	7–9	24 in (60 cm)	E	Flowers (white, summer–autumn)
Dacrycarpus dacrydioides	T	8–10	70–100 ft (21–30 m)	E	Foliage; moisture tolerance
Dacrydium cupressinum	T	8–9	30–50 ft (9–15 m)	E	Foliage; weeping habit
Dais cotinifolia	S(T)	9–11	10 ft (3 m)	D/E	Flowers (pink, late spring–early summer)
Danäe racemosa	S	7–10	3 ft (1 m)	E	Foliage; fruit
Daphne bholua	S	6–9	6–10 ft (1.8–3 m)	E	Flowers (pale pink, fragrant, winter)
Daphne bholua 'Ghurka'	S	6–9	6–10 ft (1.8–3 m)	D	Flowers (pale pink, fragrant, winter)
Daphne bholua 'Jacqueline Postill'	S	6–9	6–10 ft (1.8–3 m)	E	Flowers (pale pink, fragrant, winter)
Daphne × burkwoodii	S	5–9	3 ft (1 m)	Semi	Flowers (pink, spring)
Daphne × burkwoodii 'Somerset'	S	5–9	3 ft (1 m)	Semi	Flowers (deep pink, spring); vigorous
Daphne cneorum	S	6–9	1 ft (30 cm)	E	Flowers (rose pink in spring, fragrant)
Daphne mezereum	S	5–9	5 ft (1.5 m)	D	Flowers (pink, fragrant, late winter–early spring); decorative fruit
Daphne odora	S	8–10	3–4 ft (1–1.2 m)	E	Flowers (deep pink & white, fragrant, late autumn–spring)
Daphne pontica	S	5–9	5 ft (1.5 m)	E	Flowers (green, night-scented, spring); decorative fruit
Daphne retusa	S	6–9	30 in (75 cm)	E	Flowers (pale pink, fragrant, spring–early summer)
Davidia involucrata	T	8–9	25–30 ft (8–9 m)	D	Flowers (white, late spring)
Delonix regia	T	11–12	25–30 ft (8–9 m)	D	Flowers (scarlet, late spring–early summer)
Dendromecon rigida	S	8–10	10 ft (3 m)	E	Flowers (golden yellow, spring–autumn)
Desfontainea spinosa	S	8–9	6 ft (1.8)	E	Flowers (orange, late summer)
Deutzia crenata var. nakaiana 'Nikko'	S	5–9	24 in (60 cm)	D	Flowers (white, summer); compact habit
Deutzia × elegantissima	S	7–9	6 ft (1.8 m)	D	Flowers (pink, late spring–early summer)
Deutzia purpurascens	S	5–9	5 ft (1.5 m)	D	Flowers (white & purple, late spring–early summer)
Deutzia × rosea	S	7–9	3 ft (1 m)	D	Flowers (pink, late spring–early summer)
Deutzia × rosea 'Carminea'	S	7–9	3 ft (1 m)	D	Flowers (bright pink, late spring–early summer)
Deutzia scabra	S	6–10	10 ft (3 m)	D	Flowers (white, mid-spring–early summer)
Deutzia scabra 'Pride of Rochester'	S	6–10	10 ft (3 m)	D	Flowers (white tinted mauve, double, mid-spring–early summer)
Diospyros kaki	T	8–9	15–20 ft (4.5–6 m)	D	Edible fruit; autumn foliage
Diospyros virginiana	T	5–9	25 ft (8 m)	D	Autumn foliage; edible fruit
Dipelta floribunda	S	6–9	10 ft (3 m)	D	Flowers (pink, fragrant, late spring–early summer)
Disanthus cercidifolius	S	7–9	8 ft (2.4 m)	D	Autumn foliage; flowers (purple-red, autumn)
Dodonaea boroniifolia	S	9–11	5 ft (1.5 m)	E	Foliage; decorative fruit
Dodonaea viscosa	S(T)	8–11	12–20 ft (3.5–6 m)	E	Foliage; decorative fruit

NAME	TYPE	ZONE	HEIGHT at MATURITY	DECIDUOUS or EVERGREEN	CHIEF ATTRACTIONS
Dodonaea viscosa 'Purpurea'	S(T)	8–11	12–20 ft (3.5–6 m)	E	Foliage (purple-bronze); decorative fruit
Dombeya × cayeuxii	S	10–11	15 ft (4.5 m)	E	Flowers (pink, summer–autumn)
Dombeya tiliacea	T	9–11	20 ft (6 m)	E	Flowers (white, autumn–early spring)
Dovyalis caffra	S	9–11	12 ft (3.5 m)	E	Edible fruit
Dovyalis hebecarpa	T	10–11	20 ft (6 m)	E	Edible fruit
Dracaena draco	T	10–11	8–12 ft (2.4–3.5 m)	E	Foliage; symmetrical form
Dracaena fragrans	T	10–12	20–30 ft (6–9 m)	E	Flowers (cream, fragrant, summer); decorative fruit
Dracaena marginata	T	10–12	10 ft (3 m)	E	Foliage
Dracaena marginata 'Tricolor'	T	10–12	10 ft (3 m)	E	Foliage (striped cream & edged red)
Dracaena reflexa	S(T)	11–12	10–15 ft (3–4.5 m)	E	Flowers (green & white); formal habit
Dracaena reflexa 'Song of India'	S(T)	11–12	10–15 ft (3–4.5 m)	E	Foliage (white variegated); flowers (green & white); formal habit
Dracophyllum traversii	S(T)	7–9	15–30 ft (4.5–9 m)	E	Flowers (cream, summer); graceful habit
Durio zibethinus	T	11–12	20–30 ft (6–9 m)	E	Edible fruit
Echium candicans	S	9–10	6 ft (1.8 m)	E	Flowers (violet-blue, late spring–summer)
Edgeworthia chrysantha	S	7–9	6 ft (1.8 m)	D	Flowers (yellow & silvery white, spring)
Elaeagnus angustifolia	T	7–9	20 ft (6 m)	D	Flowers (yellow, fragrant, late spring–early summer); edible fruit
Elaeagnus pungens	S	7–10	8 ft (2.4 m)	E	Foliage; flowers (white, fragrant, autumn)
Elaeagnus pungens 'Variegata'					
Enkianthus campanulatus	S	6–9	6–10 ft (1.8–3 m)	D	Flowers (cream & red, spring); autumn foliage
Enkianthus perulatus	S	6–9	6 ft (1.8 m)	D	Flowers (white, early spring); autumn foliage
Ephedra americana var. andina	S	6–9	8 ft (2.4 m)	E	Decorative fruit
Ephedra gerardiana	S	7–10	8–12 in (10–30 cm)	E	Decorative fruit, ground-covering habit
Erica arborea	S	8–10	8 ft (2.4 m)	E	Flowers (white, spring)
Erica arborea 'Alpina'	S	8–10	6 ft (1.8 m)	E	Flowers (white, spring)
Erica australis	S	9–10	6 ft (1.8 m)	E	Flowers (magenta-pink, spring)
Erica bauera	S	8–9	3 ft (1 m)	E	Flowers (white or pink, spring–autumn)
Erica bauera 'Alba'	S	8–9	3 ft (1 m)	E	Flowers (white, spring–autumn)
Erica carnea	S	5–9	12 in (30 cm)	E	Flowers (purple-pink, winter–spring)
Erica carnea 'March Seedling'	S	5–9	12 in (30 cm)	E	Flowers (purple-pink over a long season)
Erica carnea 'Myretoun Ruby'	S	5–9	12 in (30 cm)	E	Flowers (rose pink, winter–spring); dark foliage
Erica carnea 'Springwood White'	S	5–9	12 in (30 cm)	E	Flowers (rose pink, winter–spring); vigorous spreader
Erica cerinthoides	S	8–10	3 ft (1 m)	E	Flowers (orange, scarlet, pink, winter–spring)
Erica cinerea	S	5–9	12 in (30 cm)	E	Flowers (pink, summer–early autumn)
Erica cinerea 'Crimson King'	S	5–9	12 in (30 cm)	E	Flowers (crimson, summer–early autumn)
Erica × darleyensis	S	6–9	24 in (60 cm)	E	Flowers (pink, late autumn-spring)
Erica × darleyensis 'Darley Dale'	S	6–9	24 in (60 cm)	E	Flowers (pink, late autumn-spring)
Erica × darleyensis 'Silberschmelze'	S	6–9	24 in (60 cm)	E	Flowers (white, late autumn-spring)
Erica erigena	S	7–9	24 in (60 cm)	E	Flowers (pink, winter–spring)
Erica erigena 'Alba Compacta'	S	7–9	24 in (60 cm)	E	Flowers (white, winter–spring); compact habit
Erica erigena 'Hibernica'	S	7–9	24 in (60 cm)	E	Flowers (shell pink, winter–spring)

NAME	TYPE	ZONE	HEIGHT at MATURITY	DECIDUOUS or EVERGREEN	CHIEF ATTRACTIONS
Erica erigena 'W. T. Rackliff'	S	7–9	24 in (60 cm)	E	Flowers (white, winter–spring); compact habit
Erica linnaeoides	S	9–10	3 ft (1 m)	E	Flowers (pink & white, spring)
Erica lusitanica	S	9–10	6 ft (1.8 m)	E	Flowers (pink & white, winter–spring)
Erica mackaiana	S	6–9	18 in (45 cm)	E	Flowers (pink, summer–early autumn)
Erica mackaiana 'Galicia'	S	6–9	8 in (20 cm)	E	Flowers (mauve-pink, summer–early autumn)
Erica melanthera	S	8–10	3 ft (1 m)	E	Flowers (purple, pink, late autumn–winter)
Erica regia	S	9–10	24 in (60 cm)	E	Flowers (white & red, spring)
Erica sessiliflora	S	9–11	3–4 ft (1–1.2 m)	E	Flowers (green, autumn–spring)
Erica × *stuartii* 'Irish Lemon'	S	6–9	18 in (45 cm)	E	Flowers (mauve, late spring–autumn); yellow spring foliage
Erica vagans	S	5–9	24 in (60 cm)	E	Flowers (pink or white, summer–autumn)
Erica vagans 'St Keverne'	S	5–9	24 in (60 cm)	E	Flowers (pink, summer–autumn)
Erica × *veitchii*	S	8–9	6 ft (1.8 m)	E	Flowers (white, late winter–spring)
Erica × *veitchii* 'Exeter'	S	8–9	6 ft (1.8 m)	E	Flowers (white, fragrant, spring)
Eriobotrya japonica	T	9–10	20 ft (6 m)	E	Edible fruit; flowers (white, late autumn)
Eriogonum arborescens	S	9–10	5 ft (1.5 m)	D	Flowers (pink to rose, early summer–autumn)
Eriogonum umbellatum	S	6–9	12–24 (30–60 cm)	D	Flowers (creamy yellow, summer)
Erysimum bicolor	S	9–10	3 ft (1 m)	E	Flowers (white to pale yellow ageing lilac, fragrant, most of the year)
Erysimum 'Bowles' Mauve'	S	6–11	3 ft (1 m)	E	Flowers (deep rosy purple, fragrant, most of the year)
Erysimum 'Harpur Crewe'	S	8–10	12 in (30 cm)	E	Flowers (yellow, double, fragrant, most of the year)
Erythrina caffra	T	9–11	20–30 ft (6–9 m)	D	Flowers (scarlet, late spring–early summer)
Erythrina crista-galli	S(T)	9–11	12–15 ft (3.5–4.5 m)	D	Flowers (red, spring–summer)
Erythrina fusca	T	10–12	20 ft (6 m)	D	Flowers (orange-red)
Erythrina humeana	S	9–11	12 ft (3.5 m)	D	Flowers (scarlet, summer–early autumn)
Erythrina × *sykesii*	T	9–10	25 ft (8 m)	D	Flowers (red, winter & spring)
Escallonia 'Donard Star'	S	8–10	6 ft (1.8 m)	E	Flowers (rose pink, late spring–autumn)
Escallonia × *exoniensis*	S	8–10	12–20 ft (3.5–6 m)	E	Flowers (pale pink, late spring–autumn)
Escallonia rubra	S	8–10	10 ft (3 m)	E	Flowers (pink, spring–early autumn)
Eucalyptus camaldulensis	T	9–10	50 ft (15 m)	E	Foliage; bark; massive stature
Eucalyptus dalrympleana	T	8–9	50–70 ft (15–21 m)	E	Flowers (white, summer); bark
Eucalyptus erythrocorys	T	9–10	20–30 ft (6–9 m)	E	Flowers (yellow & red, early summer)
Eucalyptus globulus	T	8–10	60 ft (18 m)	E	Bark; vigorous growth; foliage
Eucalyptus leucoxylon	T	9–10	40 ft (12 m)	E	Flowers (cream, pink, crimson, autumn–spring)
Eucalyptus nicholii	T	8–9	40 ft (12 m)	E	Foliage; bark
Eucalyptus pauciflora	T	7–9	30–40 ft (9–12 m)	E	Bark; twisted trunk
Eucalyptus p. subsp. *niphophila*	T	7–9	15–30 ft (4.5–9 m)	E	Bark; twisted trunk
Eucalyptus regnans	T	8–9	60 ft (18 m)	E	Stately form
Eucalyptus rubida	T	8–9	40 ft (12 m)	E	Bark
Eucalyptus salmonophloia	T	9–10	30 ft (9 m)	E	Bark
Eucalyptus sideroxylon	T	9–11	40 ft (12 m)	E	Bark; foliage, flowers (white to crimson, autumn–spring)
Eucalyptus torquata	T	9–11	20 ft (6 m)	E	Flowers (orange & yellow, spring–autumn); curious fruit
Eucalyptus viminalis	T	9–10	60–80 ft (18–24 m)	E	Flowers (white, summer); peeling strips of bark

NAME	TYPE	ZONE	HEIGHT at MATURITY	DECIDUOUS or EVERGREEN	CHIEF ATTRACTIONS
Eucryphia cordifolia	T	8–9	30 ft (9 m)	E	Flowers (white, late summer); foliage
Eucryphia × intermedia	T	8–9	20 ft (6 m)	D	Flowers (white, late summer)
Eucryphia × intermedia 'Rostrevor'	T	8–9	20 ft (6 m)	D	Flowers (white, late summer)
Eucryphia lucida	T	8–9	20 ft (6 m)	E	Flowers (white, fragrant, early summer)
Eucryphia lucida 'Leatherwood Cream'	T	8–9	20 ft (6 m)	E	Variegated foliage; flowers (white, fragrant, early summer)
Eucryphia moorei	T	8–9	25 ft (8 m)	E	Flowers (white, midsummer–early autumn)
Eucryphia × nymansensis	T	7–9	20 ft (6 m)	D	Flowers (white, late summer)
Euonymus alatus	S	5–9	6–10 ft (1.8–3 m)	D	Autumn foliage; decorative fruit
Euonymus alatus 'Compactus'	S	5–9	6 ft (1.8 m)	D	Autumn foliage; decorative fruit
Euonymus europaeus	S(T)	6–9	12–15 ft (3.5–4.5 m)	D	Autumn foliage; decorative fruit
Euonymus fortunei	S	5–9	12–15 ft (3.5–4.5 m)	E	Flowers (greenish-white, early–midsummer)
Euonymus fortunei 'Emerald Gaiety'	S	5–9	3 ft (1 m)	E	Variegated foliage; flowers (greenish-white, early–midsummer)
Euonymus fortunei 'Emerald 'n' Gold'	S	5–9	12–18 in (30–45 cm)	E	Variegated foliage; flowers (greenish-white, early–midsummer)
Euonymus fortunei 'Silver Queen'	S	5–9	6 ft (1.8 m)	E	Variegated foliage; flowers (greenish-white, early–midsummer)
Euonymus japonicus	S	8–10	8 ft (2.4 m)	E	Foliage
Euonymus japonicus 'Ovatus Aureus'	S	8–10	8 ft (2.4 m)	E	Variegated foliage
Eupatorium megalophyllum	S	10–11	5 ft (1.5 m)	D	Flowers (lilac, spring)
Eupatorium purpureum	S	4–9	5–8 ft (1.5–2.4 m)	D	Flowers (purple-pink, autumn)
Euphorbia mellifera	S	8–10	6 ft (1.8 m)	E	Flowers (green & brown, fragrant, spring)
Euphorbia milii	S	10–12	3–4 ft (1–1.2 m)	D	Flowers (yellow with red bracts, variable)
Euphorbia pulcherrima	S	10–11	8–12 ft (2.4–3.5 m)	D	Flowers (red bracts, late autumn–spring)
Euryops pectinatus	S	9–11	3–4 ft (1–1.2 m)	E	Flowers (yellow, winter–spring); foliage
Euryops virgineus	S	9–11	4 ft (1.2 m)	E	Flowers (yellow, late winter–spring)
Euscaphis japonica	T	6–9	20 ft (6 m)	D	Foliage; decorative fruit; bark
Exochorda × macrantha	S	6–9	8–10 ft (2.4–3 m)	D	Flowers (mid- to late spring)
Exochorda × macrantha 'The Bride'	S	6–9	6 ft (1.8 m)	D	Flowers (mid- to late spring); weeping growth habit
Exochorda racemosa	S	6–10	8 ft (2.4 m)	D	Flowers (white, late spring)
Fagus orientalis	T	6–9	30 ft (9 m)	D	Foliage; elegant form
Fagus sylvatica	T	5–9	30–50 ft (9–15 m)	D	Foliage; elegant form
Fagus sylvatica f. purpurea	T	5–9	30–50 ft (9–15 m)	D	Foliage (purple-bronze); elegant form
Fallugia paradoxa	S	7–9	8 ft (2.4 m)	D	Flowers (white, summer); decorative fruit
× Fatshedera lizei	S	7–11	4–8 ft (1.2–2.4 m)	E	Foliage
Fatsia japonica	S	8–11	6–8 ft (1.8–2.4)	E	Foliage; flowers (white, autumn); decorative fruit
Feijoa sellowana	S	9–11	12 ft (3.5 m)	E	Edible fruit; flowers (white & red, late spring–early summer)
Felicia aethiopica	S	9–11	24 in (60 cm)	E	Flowers (blue, summer)
Felicia echinata	S	9–11	24 in (60 cm)	E	Flowers (lilac to white, summer)
Ficus benghalensis	T	11–12	30 ft (9 m)	E	Aerial roots forming multiple trunks; foliage
Ficus benjamina	T	10–12	30 ft (9 m)	E	Foliage

NAME	TYPE	ZONE	HEIGHT at MATURITY	DECIDUOUS or EVERGREEN	CHIEF ATTRACTIONS
Ficus carica	T	8–10	15 ft (4.5 m)	D	Edible fruit
Ficus dammaropsis	T	10–11	20 ft (6 m)	E	Foliage
Ficus elastica	T	10–12	30 ft (9 m)	E	Foliage
Ficus elastica 'Decora'	T	10–12	30 ft (9 m)	E	Foliage (bronze new growth)
Ficus elastica 'Doescheri'	T	10–12	30 ft (9 m)	E	Multi-colored variegated foliage
Ficus lyrata	T	10–12	20 ft (6 m)	E	Foliage
Ficus macrophylla	T	9–11	30–50 ft (9–15 m)	E	Foliage; massive trunk
Ficus microcarpa	T	9–12	30 ft (9 m)	E	Foliage; smooth bark
Ficus microcarpa var. *nitida*	T	9–12	30 ft (9 m)	E	Foliage; smooth bark, upright growth habit
Ficus religiosa	T	11–12	20–30 ft (6–9 m)	Semi	Foliage; graceful habit
Ficus rubiginosa	T	10–11	30–50 ft (9–15 m)	E	Foliage; decorative fruit
Ficus rubiginosa 'Variegata'	T	10–11	30–50 ft (9–15 m)	E	Variegated foliage; decorative fruit
Forsythia × *intermedia*	S	5–9	8 ft (2.4 m)	D	Flowers (yellow, mid-spring)
Forsythia × *intermedia* 'Arnold Giant'	S	5–9	8 ft (2.4 m)	D	Flowers (yellow, large, mid-spring)
Forsythia suspensa	S	4–9	12 ft (3.5 m)	D	Flowers (yellow, early–mid-spring)
Fortunella japonica	S	9–11	8 ft (2.4 m)	E	Edible decorative fruit
Fothergilla gardenii	S	5–9	3 ft (1 m)	D	Flowers (white, fragrant, early spring); autumn foliage
Fothergilla major	S	5–9	6–10 ft (1.8–3 m)	D	Flowers (white, fragrant, spring & autumn); autumn foliage
Franklinia alatamaha	T	7–9	15 ft (4.5 m)	D	Flowers (white, late summer–autumn); autumn foliage
Fraxinus americana	T	4–10	40 ft (12 m)	D	Autumn foliage
Fraxinus americana 'Autumn Purple'	T	4–10	40 ft (12 m)	D	Purple autumn foliage
Fraxinus angustifolia	T	7–10	30 ft (9 m)	D	Autumn foliage
Fraxinus angustifolia subsp. *oxycarpa*	T	7–10	30 ft (9 m)	D	Foliage; autumn color
Fraxinus angustifolia 'Raywood'	T	7–10	30 ft (9 m)	D	Purple autumn foliage
Fraxinus excelsior	T	4–9	30 ft (9 m)	D	Autumn foliage
Fraxinus excelsior 'Aurea'	T	4–9	30 ft (9 m)	D	Golden autumn foliage
Fraxinus ornus	T	6–9	25 ft (8 m)	D	Flowers (white, late spring); autumn foliage
Fraxinus pennsylvanica	T	3–10	30–40 ft (9–12 m)	D	Autumn foliage
Fremontodendron californicum	S	8–10	15 ft (4.5 m)	E	Flowers (yellow, mid- to late spring)
Fremontodendron 'San Gabriel'	S	8–10	12–15 ft (3.5–4.5 m)	E	Flowers (yellow, summer)
Fuchsia arborescens	S	9–10	10 ft (3 m)	E	Flowers (purple, autumn–spring)
Fuchsia boliviana	S	10–11	12 ft (3.5 m)	E	Flowers (scarlet, summer–autumn)
Fuchsia denticulata	S	9–10	8 ft (2.4 m)	E	Flowers (red & green, spring–summer)
Fuchsia hybrids	S	8–11	2–5 ft (0.6–1.5 m)	E/D	Flowers (huge range of cultivars & colors)
Fuchsia magellanica	S	7–10	8 ft (2.4 m)	E/D	Flowers (red & purple, summer–autumn)
Fuchsia magellanica 'Versicolor'	S	7–10	8 ft (2.4 m)	E/D	Variegated foliage; flowers (red, summer–autumn)
Fuchsia paniculata	S	9–10	12 ft (3.5 m)	E	Flowers (pink, spring); decorative fruit
Fuchsia triphylla and cultivars	S	10–11	3–5 ft (1–1.5 m)	E	Flowers (orange to scarlet, summer–autumn)
Gardenia augusta	S	9–11	6 ft (1.8 m)	E	Fragrant flowers (white, spring–autumn)
Gardenia thunbergia	S	10–11	8 ft (2.4 m)	E	Fragrant flowers (white, early summer)

NAME	TYPE	ZONE	HEIGHT at MATURITY	DECIDUOUS or EVERGREEN	CHIEF ATTRACTIONS
Garrya elliptica	S	8–9	12 ft (3.5 m)	E	Flowers (pale green, midwinter–early spring)
Gaultheria fragrantissima	S	8–10	8 ft (2.4 m)	E	Flowers (white or pink, fragrant, spring); decorative fruit
Gaultheria mucronata	S	7–9	5 ft (1.5 m)	E	Flowers (white, spring); decorative fruit
Gaultheria shallon	S	5–9	4 ft (1.2 m)	E	Flowers (white, spring); decorative fruit
Gaultheria × wisleyensis	S	7–9	4 ft (1.2 m)	E	Flowers (white, spring); decorative fruit
Genista hispanica	S	4–9	24 in (60 cm)	D	Flowers (yellow, spring–early summer)
Genista lydia	S	5–9	24 in (60 cm)	D	Flowers (yellow, spring–early summer)
Genista pilosa	S	5–9	12–24 in (30–60 cm)	D	Flowers (yellow, early summer)
Genista pilosa 'Vancouver Gold'	S	5–9	12–24 in (30–60 cm)	D	Flowers (golden yellow, early summer); mounding habit
Genista sagittalis	S	4–9	6–12 in (15–30 cm)	D	Flowers (yellow, early summer)
Genista × spachiana	S	6–9	8 ft (2.4 m)	E	Flowers (yellow, winter–spring)
Genista × spachiana 'Nana'	S	6–9	3 ft (1 m)	E	Flowers (yellow, winter–spring)
Genista tinctoria	S	3–9	3 ft (1 m)	D	Flowers (yellow, summer)
Genista 'Yellow Imp'	S	8–10	5–6 ft (1.5–1.8 m)	E	Flowers (yellow, late spring)
Ginkgo biloba	T	3–10	25–30 ft (8–9 m)	D	Autumn foliage
Ginkgo biloba 'Fastigiata'	T	3–10	25–30 ft (8–9 m)	D	Autumn foliage; columnar habit
Gleditsia triacanthos	T	3–10	40 ft (12 m)	D	Autumn foliage; large pods with edible pulp
Gleditsia triacanthos 'Shademaster'	T	3–10	40 ft (12 m)	D	Foliage; large pods with edible pulp
Gleditsia triacanthos 'Skyline'	T	3–10	40 ft (12 m)	D	Summer & autumn foliage; large pods with edible pulp
Gleditsia triacanthos 'Sunburst'	T	3–10	40 ft (12 m)	D	Spring & autumn foliage; large pods with edible pulp
Gordonia axillaris	S(T)	9–10	15 ft (4.5 m)	E	Flowers (white, autumn–spring)
Gossypium sturtianum	S	9–11	6–8 ft (1.8–2.4 m)	E	Flowers (mauve)
Grevillea banksii	S	9–11	12 ft (3.5 m)	E	Flowers (red or cream, most of the year)
Grevillea baueri	S	8–10	3 ft (1 m)	E	Flowers (deep pink & cream, winter–spring)
Grevillea 'Bonnie Prince Charlie'	S	9–10	3 ft (1 m)	E	Flowers (red & yellow, late winter–summer)
Grevillea 'Canberra Gem'	S	8–10	8 ft (2.4 m)	E	Flowers (pink & red, winter–late summer)
Grevillea 'Clearview David'	S	8–10	10 ft (3 m)	E	Flowers (red, winter–spring)
Grevillea 'Honey Gem'	S	10–12	12 ft (3.5 m)	E	Flowers (orange, most of the year)
Grevillea juniperina	S	9–10	6 ft (1.8 m)	E	Flowers (scarlet, orange, yellow, summer)
Grevillea lanigera	S	8–10	3 ft (1 m)	E	Flowers (red & cream, late winter–spring); foliage contrast
Grevillea lanigera 'Mt Tamboritha'	S	8–10	6–8 in (15–20 cm)	E	Flowers (red & cream, late winter–spring); foliage contrast; low, spreading habit
Grevillea robusta	T	9–11	40 ft (12 m)	E	Flowers (orange-yellow, late spring)
Grevillea 'Robyn Gordon'	S	9–11	3–4 ft (1–1.2 m)	E	Flowers (soft red, most of the year); foliage
Grevillea rosmarinifolia	S(T)	8–10	8–12 ft (2.4–3.5 m)	E	Flowers (red, spring)
Grevillea victoriae	S	8–10	6 ft (1.8 m)	E	Flowers (rusty red, spring & autumn)
Greyia sutherlandii	S	9–11	10 ft (3 m)	D	Flowers (scarlet, late winter–early spring)
Griselinia littoralis	S	8–11	10–20 ft (3–6 m)	E	Foliage; decorative fruit
Griselinia lucida	S	8–11	12 ft (3.5 m)	E	Foliage
Griselinia lucida 'Variegata'	S	8–11	12 ft (3.5 m)	E	Cream & green variegated foliage
Gymnocladus dioica	T	3–10	25 ft (8 m)	D	Foliage; flowers (white, fragrant, late spring–early summer)

NAME	TYPE	ZONE	HEIGHT at MATURITY	DECIDUOUS or EVERGREEN	CHIEF ATTRACTIONS
Hakea laurina	S	9–11	12 ft (3.5 m)	E	Flowers (crimson & cream, winter–spring)
Hakea microcarpa	S	8–10	5 ft (1.5 m)	E	Flowers (white, late winter–summer)
Hakea victoria	S	9–10	10 ft (3 m)	E	Colored foliage
Halesia carolina	T	3–9	20 ft (6 m)	D	Flowers (white, spring); curious fruit; autumn foliage
Halimium lasianthum	S	8–9	3 ft (1 m)	E	Flowers (yellow blotched crimson, spring–summer
Hamamelis × intermedia	S	4–9	12 ft (3.5 m)	D	Flowers (yellow to orange, fragrant, winter); autumn foliage
Hamamelis × intermedia 'Diane'	S	4–9	12 ft (3.5 m)	D	Flowers (deep red, fragrant, winter); autumn foliage
Hamamelis × intermedia 'Ruby Glow'	S	4–9	12 ft (3.5 m)	D	Flowers (copper red, fragrant, winter); autumn foliage
Hamamelis japonica	S	4–9	12 ft (3.5 m)	D	Flowers (yellow, fragrant, mid- to late winter); autumn foliage
Hamamelis mollis	S	4–9	12 ft (3.5 m)	D	Flowers (golden, midwinter–early spring); autumn foliage
Hamamelis virginiana	S	2–9	12 ft (3.5 m)	D	Flowers (yellow, fragrant, autumn); autumn foliage
Hebe albicans	S	8–9	24 in (60 cm)	E	Flowers (white, early summer)
Hebe 'Alicia Amherst'	S	9–10	4 ft (1.2 m)	E	Flowers (violet-purple, late summer–autumn)
Hebe cupressoides	S	8–10	3–6 ft (1–1.8 m)	E	Foliage & dense growth
Hebe diosmifolia	S	8–10	4 ft (1.2 m)	E	Flowers (pale mauve, spring–autumn)
Hebe × franciscana 'Blue Gem'	S	8–10	24–30 in (60–75 cm)	E	Flowers (violet-pink, summer–early winter)
Hebe 'Hagley Park'	S	8–10	12–18 in (30–45 cm)	E	Flowers (soft pink, summer)
Hebe 'Hartii'	S	8–10	4 in (10 cm)	E	Flowers (pale mauve, summer); prostrate spreading habit
Hebe 'La Séduisante'	S	8–10	3–6 ft (1–1.8 m)	E	Flowers (violet-purple, summer–autumn)
Hebe × lindsayi	S	9–11	24 in (60 cm)	E	Flowers (rose pink, late spring–summer)
Hebe 'Pamela Joy'	S	8–10	24–30 in (60–75 cm)	E	Flowers (violet-purple, summer)
Hebe pinguifolia	S	7–10	24–36 in (60–90 cm)	E	Foliage; flowers (white, summer)
Hebe ochracea	S	8–9	3 ft (1 m)	E	Foliage
Hebe speciosa	S	8–10	3–4 ft (1–1.2 m)	E	Flowers (red to purple, summer-autumn)
Hebe 'Wiri Joy'	S	8–10	3 ft (1 m)	E	Flowers (purple-pink, summer)
Hebe 'Wiri Mist'	S	8–10	18–24 in (45–60 cm)	E	Flowers (white, late spring–summer)
Helianthemum 'Fire King'	S	6–10	12–18 in (30–45 cm)	E	Flowers (bright orange-red, late spring–summer)
Helichrysum petiolare	S	9–10	24 in (60 cm)	E	Foliage; spreading habit
Helichrysum splendidum	S	7–10	5 ft 91.5 m)	E	Flowers (golden yellow, summer–autumn)
Heteromeles arbutifolia	S(T)	9–10	12–20 ft (3.5–6 m)	E	Flowers (white, summer); decorative fruit
Hibiscus arnottianus	T	10–11	20 ft (6 m)	E	Flowers (white, summer–autumn)
Hibiscus coccineus	S	7–11	8–10 ft (2.4–3 m)	D	Flowers (red, summer)
Hibiscus mutabilis	S	9–12	12 ft (3.5 m)	E	Flowers (white ageing pink, autumn)
Hibiscus rosa-sinensis cultivars & hybrids	S	10–12	12 ft (3.5 m)	E	Flowers (various colours, summer–early winter)
Hibiscus schizopetalus	S	10–12	10 ft (3 m)	E	Flowers (scarlet, summer–autumn)
Hibiscus syriacus	S	6–10	12 ft (3.5 m)	D	Flowers (white, pink, lilac, red, late summer–autumn)
Hibiscus syriacus 'Blue Bird'	S	6–10	12 ft (3.5 m)	D	Flowers (violet-blue centered red, late summer–autumn)
Hibiscus syriacus 'Diana'	S	6–10	12 ft (3.5 m)	D	Flowers (white, late summer–autumn)
Hibiscus syriacus 'Woodbridge'	S	6–10	12 ft (3.5 m)	D	Flowers (pink, late summer–autumn)
Hippophaë rhamnoides	S	2–9	10 ft (3 m)	D	Silvery foliage; decorative fruit

NAME	TYPE	ZONE	HEIGHT at MATURITY	DECIDUOUS or EVERGREEN	CHIEF ATTRACTIONS
Hoheria lyallii	T	8–9	15–20 ft (4.5–6 m)	D	Flowers (white, fragrant, late summer)
Hoheria populnea	T	9–10	20–25 ft (6–8 m)	E	Flowers (late summer–early autumn)
Hoheria sexstylosa	T	8–10	20 ft (6 m)	E	Flowers (white, fragrant, late summer–autumn)
Hovenia dulcis	T	8–10	25 ft (8 m)	D	Edible fruit stalks; autumn foliage
Hydrangea arborescens	S	6–9	6–8 ft (1.8–2.4 m)	D	Flowers (white ageing green, late spring–summer)
Hydrangea arborescens 'Grandiflora'	S	6–9	6–8 ft (1.8–2.4 m)	D	Flowers (white ageing green, late spring–summer)
Hydrangea aspera	S	7–9	8 ft (2.4 m)	D	Flowers (mauve & blue, summer)
Hydrangea heteromalla	S	6–9	10 ft (3 m)	D	Flowers (white & pink, summer)
Hydrangea heteromalla 'Bretscheideri'	S	6–9	10 ft (3 m)	D	Flowers (white & pink, summer); bark
Hydrangea macrophylla	S	6–10	6–8 ft (1.8–2.4 m)	D	Flowers (pink or blue, summer)
Hydrangea macrophylla 'Altona'	S	6–10	6–8 ft (1.8–2.4 m)	D	Flowers (deep pink to purplish blue, summer)
Hydrangea m. 'Geoffrey Chadbund'	S	6–10	6–8 ft (1.8–2.4 m)	D	Flowers (bright red, summer)
Hydrangea macrophylla 'Libelle'	S	6–10	6–8 ft (1.8–2.4 m)	D	Flowers (white, summer)
Hydrangea macrophylla 'Taube'	S	6–10	6–8 ft (1.8–2.4 m)	D	Flowers (pinkish scarlet, summer)
Hydrangea macrophylla 'Veitchii'	S	6–10	6–8 ft (1.8–2.4 m)	D	Flowers (white ageing pink, summer)
Hydrangea paniculata	S	4–9	8 ft (2.4 m)	D	Flowers (cream, midsummer)
Hydrangea paniculata 'Grandiflora'	S	4–9	8 ft (2.4 m)	D	Flowers (large heads, cream, midsummer)
Hydrangea quercifolia	S	5–10	6 ft (1.8 m)	D	Autumn foliage; flowers (cream, midsummer–mid-autumn)
Hydrangea serrata	S	6–10	5 ft (1.5 m)	D	Flowers (mauve-blue, summer)
Hymenosporum flavum	T	9–11	25 ft (8 m)	E	Flowers (cream ageing gold, fragrant, spring)
Hypericum beanii	S	5–9	6 ft (1.8 m)	E	Flowers (yellow, summer)
Hypericum beanii 'Gold Cup'	S	5–9	6 ft (1.8 m)	E	Flowers (yellow, large, summer)
Hypericum frondosum	S	5–10	4 ft (1.2 m)	D	Flowers (bright yellow, summer)
Hypericum 'Hidcote'	S	7–10	4 ft (1.2 m)	E	Flowers (yellow, midsummer–autumn)
Hypericum monogynum	S	7–10	3 ft (1 m)	E	Flowers (yellow, summer)
Hypericum × *moserianum*	S	7–10	24–36 in (60–90 cm)	E	Flowers (yellow, summer)
Hypericum × *moserianum* 'Tricolor'	S	7–10	24–36 in (60–90 cm)	E	Variegated foliage; flowers (yellow, summer)
Hypericum 'Rowallane'	S	8–10	5 ft (1.5 m)	Semi	Flowers (golden yellow, midsummer–auutmn)
Iberis gibraltarica	S	7–11	12 in (30 cm)	E	Flowers (white tinged pink or red, summer)
Idesia polycarpa	T	8–10	30 ft (9 m)	D	Foliage; decorative fruit
Ilex × *altaclerensis*	T	5–10	25 ft (8 m)	E	Foliage; decorative fruit
Ilex aquifolium	T	5–10	20 ft (6 m)	E	Foliage; decorative fruit
Ilex aquifolium 'Amber'	T	5–10	20 ft (6 m)	E	Foliage; decorative fruit (yellow)
Ilex aquifolium 'Ferox Argentea'	T	5–10	20 ft (6 m)	E	Very spiny variegated foliage
Ilex aquifolium 'Golden Queen'	T	5–10	20 ft (6 m)	E	Variegated foliage
Ilex aquifolium 'Pyramidalis'	T	5–10	20 ft (6 m)	E	Foliage; decorative fruit; conical habit
Ilex aquifolium 'Silver Milkmaid'	T	5–10	20 ft (6 m)	E	Variegated foliage; decorative fruit (red)
Ilex aquifolium 'Silver Queen'	T	5–10	20 ft (6 m)	E	Variegated foliage; pink young growth
Ilex × *aquipernyi*	T	6–10	20 ft (6 m)	E	Foliage; decorative fruit
Ilex cornuta	S	4–10	12 ft (3.5 m)	E	Foliage; decorative fruit

NAME	TYPE	ZONE	HEIGHT at MATURITY	DECIDUOUS or EVERGREEN	CHIEF ATTRACTIONS
Ilex crenata	S	4–9	8 ft (2.4 m)	E	Foliage; decorative fruit
Ilex crenata 'Convexa'	S	4–9	8 ft (2.4 m)	E	Foliage; purple stems
Ilex crenata 'Golden Gem'	S	4–9	8 ft (2.4 m)	E	Yellow foliage
Ilex crenata 'Microphylla'	S	4–9	8 ft (2.4 m)	E	Foliage
Ilex glabra	T	3–9	10 ft (3 m)	E	Foliage; decorative fruit
Ilex glabra 'Compacta'	T	3–9	10 ft (3 m)	E	Foliage; decorative fruit; dense growth
Ilex × *meserveae*	S	5–9	6–10 ft (1.8–3 m)	E	Foliage; decorative fruit
Ilex × *meserveae* 'Blue Angel'	S	5–9	6–10 ft (1.8–3 m)	E	Foliage; decorative fruit
Ilex × *meserveae* 'Blue Prince'	S	5–9	10 ft (3 m)	E	Foliage; decorative fruit
Ilex opaca	T	4–9	20 ft (6 m)	E	Decorative fruit
Ilex pernyi	T	4–9	15 ft (4.5 m)	E	Foliage; decorative fruit
Ilex verticillata	S	4–9	10 ft (3 m)	D	Decorative fruit, spring & autumn foliage
Illicium anisatum	S	8–10	15 ft (4.5 m)	E	Flowers (white, fragrant, spring)
Indigofera australis	S	9–11	6 ft (1.8 m)	E	Flowers (mauve-pink, winter–summer)
Indigofera decora	S	8–10	24 in (60 cm)	D	Flowers (mauve-pink, spring–autumn)
Iochroma cyaneum	S	10–11	8 ft (2.4 m)	E	Flowers (violet, summer–autumn)
Iochroma grandiflorum	S	9–11	12 ft (3.5 m)	E	Flowers (purple, late summer–autumn)
Isoplexis canariensis	S	9–11	5 ft (1.5 m)	E	Flowers (orange-yellow to rusty red, summer)
Isopogon anemonifolius	S	9–11	6 ft (1.8 m)	E	Flowers (cream, spring)
Isopogon dawsonii	S	9–11	10 ft (3 m)	E	Flowers (pale yellow tinged pink, spring)
Itea ilicifolia	S	7–10	10 ft (3 m)	E	Flowers (pale green to cream, summer–early autumn
Itea virginica	S	3–9	6 ft (1.8 m)	D	Flowers (white, fragrant, summer); autumn foliage
Jacaranda mimosifolia	T	10–11	30 ft (9 m)	D	Flowers (mauve-blue, late spring)
Jasminum humile	S	8–11	12 ft (3.5 m)	E	Flowers (yellow, spring–autumn)
Jasminum humile 'Revolutum'	S	8–11	12 ft (3.5 m)	E	Flowers (yellow, fragrant, spring–autumn)
Jasminum mesnyi	S	6–10	8 ft (2.4 m)	E	Flowers (yellow, late winter–early spring)
Jasminum nudiflorum	S	6–9	6–10 ft (1.8–3 m)	D	Flowers (yellow, winter–early spring)
Jasminum officinale	S	6–10	5–10 (1.5–3 m)	D	Flowers (white, fragrant, summer–autumn)
Juglans regia	T	4–9	25–30 ft (8–9 m)	D	Edible nuts
Juniperus chinensis	T	4–10	25–30 ft (8–9 m)	E	Foliage
Juniperus chinensis 'Aurea'	T	4–10	25 ft (8 m)	E	Golden yellow foliage
Juniperus chinensis 'Kaizuka'	T	4–10	20 ft (8 m)	E	Foliage
Juniperus communis	T	2–9	15 ft (4.5 m)	E	Foliage
Juniperus communis 'Depressa Aurea'	T	2–9	24 in (60 cm)	E	Foliage; low spreading habit
Juniperus communis 'Hibernica'	T	2–9	10–15 ft (3–4.5 m)	E	Foliage; columnar growth habit
Juniperus horizontalis	S	4–9	24 in (60 cm)	E	Foliage; low, spreading habit
Juniperus horizontalis 'Wiltonii'	S	4–9	24 in (60 cm)	E	Blue-green foliage; low, spreading habit
Juniperus × *media*	S(T)	4–10	10–15 ft (3–4.5 m)	E	Foliage
Juniperus × *media* 'Pfitzeriana'	S(T)	4–10	10 ft (3–4.5 m)	E	Foliage; weeping branch tips
Juniperus × *media* 'Plumosa Aurea'	S(T)	4–10	3 ft (1 m)	E	Yellow–green foliage; spreading growth habit
Juniperus recurva	T	7–9	20 ft (6 m)	E	Weeping foliage; decorative fruit

NAME	TYPE	ZONE	HEIGHT at MATURITY	DECIDUOUS or EVERGREEN	CHIEF ATTRACTIONS
Juniperus recurva var. coxii	T	7–9	20 ft (6 m)	E	Weeping foliage; decorative fruit
Juniperus rigida	T	4–9	15 ft (4.5 m)	E	Weeping foliage; decorative fruit
Juniperus sabina	S	3–10	6 ft (1.8 m)	E	Foliage
Juniperus squamata	S	4–9	10–15 ft (3–4.5 m)	E	Foliage
Juniperus virginiana	T	2–10	25 ft (8 m)	E	Foliage, symmetrical shape; decorative fruit
Juniperus virginiana 'Glauca'	T	2–10	25 ft (8 m)	E	Blue-green foliage, symmetrical shape; decorative fruit
Justicia brandegeana	S	9–11	3 ft (1 m)	E	Flowers (reddish pink, white & yellow, summer)
Justicia carnea	S	10–12	5 ft (1.5 m)	E	Flowers (white, pink, purple, summer–autumn); foliage
Kalmia angustifolia	S	2–9	3–4 ft (1–1.2 m)	E	Flowers (pink, late spring–early summer)
Kalmia latifolia	S	3–9	5–6 ft (1.5–1.8 m)	E	Flowers (pink, mid spring–early summer)
Kalmia latifolia 'Ostbo Red'	S	3–9	5–6 ft (1.5–1.8 m)	E	Flowers (deep pinkish red, mid spring–early summer)
Kerria japonica	S	5–10	6–8 ft (1.8–2.4 m)	D	Flowers (yellow, spring)
Kerria japonica 'Pleniflora'	S	5–10	6–8 ft (1.8–2.4 m)	D	Flowers (yellow, double, spring)
Kigelia africana	T	10–12	25 ft (8 m)	Semi	Flowers (dark red, most of the year); curious fruit.
Kingia australis	S	9–10	3 ft (1 m)	E	Grassy foliage: symmetrical form
Koelreuteria bipinnata	T	8–10	30 ft (9 m)	D	Flowers (yellow, summer); decorative fruit
Koelreuteria paniculata	T	4–9	25 ft (8 m)	D	Flowers (yellow, summer); decorative fruit; autumn foliage
Kolkwitzia amabilis	S	4–9	8 ft (2.4 m)	D	Flowers (pink, spring)
Kunzea ericoides	S(T)	8–11	10–15 ft (3–4.5 m)	E	Flowers (white, spring–early summer)
Kunzea parvifolia	S	8–10	5 ft (1.5 m)	E	Flowers (mauve, late spring–early summer)
Laburnum anagyroides	T	3–9	15 ft (4.5 m)	D	Flowers (yellow, late spring–early summer)
Laburnum × watereri	T	3–9	20 ft (6 m)	D	Flowers (yellow, late spring–early summer)
Lagerstroemia indica	T	6–11	20 ft (6 m)	D	Flowers (white to dark red, summer–autumn); bark
Lagerstroemia speciosa	T	11–12	30 ft (9 m)	Semi	Flowers (pink to purple, summer–autumn)
Lantana camara	S	9–12	2–6 ft (0.6–1.8 m)	E	Flowers (white yellow, orange, pink, red, spring–autumn)
Lantana camara 'Chelsea Gem'	S	9–12	2–6 ft (0.6–1.8 m)	E	Flowers (orange & red, spring–autumn)
Lantana camara 'Radiation'	S	9–12	2–6 ft (0.6–1.8 m)	E	Flowers (red, spring–autumn)
Larix decidua	T	2–9	40 ft (12 m)	D	Weeping foliage; autumn color
Larix kaempferi	T	4–9	40 ft (12 m)	D	Foliage; vigorous growth
Laurus azorica	T	8–10	25 ft (8 m)	E	Foliage; flowers (yellow–green, spring)
Laurus nobilis	T	8–10	20 ft (6 m)	E	Aromatic foliage; flowers (yellow, fragrant, spring)
Lavandula angustifolia	S	6–10	3 ft (1 m)	E	Flowers (purple, spring–autumn); aromatic foliage
Lavandula angustifolia 'Alba'	S	6–10	5 ft (1.5 m)	E	Flowers (white, spring–autumn); aromatic foliage
Lavandula angustifolia 'Hidcote'	S	6–10	24 in (60 cm)	E	Flowers (purple, spring–autumn); aromatic foliage
Lavandula angustifolia 'Munstead'	S	6–10	12 in (30 cm)	E	Flowers (purple, spring–autumn); aromatic foliage
Lavandula dentata	S	7–10	3 ft (1 m)	E	Flowers (mauve-blue, spring–early summer); aromatic foliage
Lavandula × intermedia	S	6–10	3 ft (1 m)	E	Flowers (mauve to purple, spring–early summer); aromatic foliage
Lavandula × intermedia 'Provence'	S	6–10	3 ft (1 m)	E	Flowers (mauve-pink, spring–early summer); aromatic foliage
Lavandula stoechas	S	8–10	24–36 in (60–90 cm)	E	Flowers (purple, spring–early summer)
Lavandula stoechas 'Marshwood'	S	8–10	24–36 in (60–90 cm)	E	Flowers (pinkish purple, spring–early summer)

NAME	TYPE	ZONE	HEIGHT at MATURITY	DECIDUOUS or EVERGREEN	CHIEF ATTRACTIONS
Lavatera thuringiaca	S	6–10	5–6 ft (1.5–1.8 m)	Semi	Flowers (mid pink, summer)
Lavatera thuringiaca 'Barnsley'	S	6–10	5–6 ft (1.5–1.8 m)	Semi	Flowers (pale pink, summer)
Ledum groenlandicum	S	2–8	3 ft (1.8 m)	E	Flowers (white, late spring–summer), herbal uses
Leonotis leonurus	S	9–11	6 ft (1.8 m)	Semi	Flowers (tawny orange, late summer–autumn)
Leptospermum laevigatum	S(T)	9–11	15–20 ft (3.5–4.5 m)	E	Flowers (white, spring–early summer)
Leptospermum macrocarpum	S	8–11	2–6 ft (0.6–1.8 m)	E	Flowers (cream & pink, spring–early summer)
Leptospermum petersonii	T	9–11	15 ft (4.5 m)	E	Aromatic foliage; flowers (white, spring–early summer)
Leptospermum scoparium	S	8–11	8–10 ft (2.4–3 m)	E	Flowers (white, pink, red, late winter–summer)
Leptospermum scoparium 'Kiwi'	S	8–11	12–18 in (30–45 cm)	E	Flowers (crimson, spring–summer)
Leptospermum scoparium 'Pink Cascade'	S	8–11	24 in (60 cm)	E	Flowers (pink, late winter–summer); trailing habit
Leptospermum s. 'Red Damask'	S	8–11	8–10 ft (2.4–3 m)	E	Flowers (red, double, late winter–summer)
Leptospermum scoparium 'Ruby Glow'	S	8–11	8–10 ft (2.4–3 m)	E	Flowers (red, double, winter–spring)
Leschenaultia biloba	S	10–11	24 in (60 cm)	E	Flowers (blue, late winter–late spring)
Leschenaultia formosa	S	9–11	12 in (30 cm)	E	Flowers (scarlet, orange, yellow, late winter–early summer)
Leucadendron argenteum	T	9–10	20 ft (6 m)	E	Foliage
Leucadendron eucalyptifolium	S	9–10	12 ft (3.5 m)	E	Flower bracts (yellow, winter–spring)
Leucadendron laureolum	S	9–11	6 ft (1.8 m)	E	Flower bracts (greenish-yellow, winter–spring)
Leucadendron 'Safari Sunset'	S	9–11	5–6 ft (1.5–1.8 m)	E	Flower bracts (red, autumn–spring)
Leucadendron salignum	S	9–10	3–5 ft (1–1.5 m)	E	Flowers bracts (yellow, autumn–spring)
Leucadendron 'Silvan Red'	S	9–11	5–6 ft (1.5–1.8 m)	E	Flower bracts (red, autumn–spring)
Leucadendron strobilinum	S	9–11	6 ft (1.8 m)	E	Flower bracts (creamy yellow, winter–spring)
Leucadendron strobilinum 'Waterlily'	S	9–11	6 ft (1.8 m)	E	Flower bracts (creamy yellow edged red, winter–spring)
Leucadendron tinctum	S	9–10	3 ft (1 m)	E	Flower bracts (pink, red, winter)
Leucophyta brownii	S	9–11	3 ft (1 m)	E	Foliage; flowers (creamy white, summer)
Leucospermum cordifolium	S	9–10	6 ft (1.8 m)	E	Flowers (yellow, orange, red, late spring–early summer)
Leucospermum c. 'Flame Spike'	S	9–10	6 ft (1.8 m)	E	Flowers (deep orange-red, late spring–early summer)
Leucospermum grandiflorum	S	9–11	5 ft (1.5 m)	E	Flowers (yellow, midwinter–summer)
Leucospermum reflexum	S	9–10	10 ft (3 m)	E	Flowers (red & yellow, spring–summer)
Leucospermum reflexum var. luteum	S	9–10	10–12 ft (3.5 m)	E	Flowers (light yellow, spring–summer)
Leucospermum reflexum 'Chittick Red'	S	9–10	10 ft (3 m)	E	Flowers (red, spring–summer)
Leucospermum tottum	S	9–10	5 ft (1.5 m)	E	Flowers (scarlet & cream, spring–summer)
Leucospermum tottum 'Scarlet Ribbon'	S	9–10	5 ft (1.5 m)	E	Flowers (pink & yellow, spring–summer)
Leucothoe davisiae	S	5–10	3 ft (1 m)	E	Flowers (white, summer)
Leucothoë fontanesiana	S	6–10	5 ft 91.5 m)	E	Flowers (white or pink, spring)
Ligustrum japonicum	S	6–10	10 ft (3 m)	E	Foliage; flowers (white, midsummer–early autumn); decorative fruit
Ligustrum japonicum	S	6–10	6 ft (1.8 m)	E	Foliage; flowers (white, midsummer–early autumn); decorative fruit
Ligustrum lucidum	T	6–11	30 ft (9 m)	E	Flowers (white, late summer–early autumn); decorative fruit

NAME	TYPE	ZONE	HEIGHT at MATURITY	DECIDUOUS or EVERGREEN	CHIEF ATTRACTIONS
Ligustrum lucidum 'Tricolor'	T	6–11	30 ft (9 m)	E	Variegated young foliage; Flowers (white, late summer–early autumn); decorative fruit
Ligustrum obtusifolium	S	3–10	10 ft (3 m)	D	Flowers (white, summer); decorative fruit
Ligustrum vulgare	S	3–9	10 ft (3 m)	D	Flowers (white, fragrant, summer); decorative fruit
Liquidambar orientalis	T	5–10	30 ft (9 m)	D	Autumn foliage; dense spreading habit
Liquidambar styraciflua	T	5–10	30–50 ft (9–15 m)	D	Autumn foliage
Liquidambar styraciflua	T	5–10	30–50 ft (9–15 m)	D	Purple to orange autumn foliage
Liriodendron chinense	T	4–10	40 ft (12 m)	D	Autumn foliage; flowers (green & orange, midsummer)
Liriodendron tulipifera	T	3–10	40–50 ft (12–15 m)	D	Autumn foliage; flowers (yellow-green blotched orange, late spring–early summer)
Litchi chinensis	T	10–11	20 ft (6 m)	E	Edible fruit
Lobelia gibberoa	S	9–10	10–20 ft (3–6 m)	E	Impressively tall flower spike
Lobelia laxiflora	S	9–11	3 ft (1 m)	E	Flowers (red & yellow, summer)
Lomatia ferruginea	T	8–9	20 ft (6 m)	E	Foliage; flowers (red & yellow, late winter–spring)
Lomatia silaifolia	S	9–11	5 ft (1.5 m)	E	Foliage; flowers (white, summer)
Lonicera fragrantissima	S	4–10	10 ft (3 m)	D	Flowers (cream, fragrant, winter–early spring)
Lonicera nitida	S	6–10	5 ft (1.5 m)	E	Foliage
Lonicera nitida 'Baggesen's Gold'	S	6–10	5 ft (1.5 m)	E	Yellow foliage
Lonicera × purpusii	S	6–10	6 ft (1.8 m)	Semi	Flowers (cream, winter–early spring); decorative fruit
Lonicera tatarica	S	2–9	8 ft (2.4 m)	D	Flowers (white–pink, late spring–early summer); decorative fruit
Lophomyrtus bullata	S(T)	9–10	8–12 ft (2.4–3.5 m)	E	Foliage; flowers (cream, summer); decorative fruit
Lophomyrtus bullata 'Variegatum'	S(T)	9–10	8–12 ft (2.4–3.5 m)	E	Variegated foliage; flowers (cream, summer); decorative fruit
Lophomyrtus obcordata	S	8–10	6 ft (1.8 m)	E	Foliage; flowers (white, summer); decorative fruit
Lophomyrtus × ralphii	S	8–10	6 ft (1.8 m)	E	Foliage; bark
Lophomyrtus × ralphii 'Lilliput'	S	8–10	12–18 in (30–45 cm)	E	Foliage; dwarf growth habit
Lophostemon confertus	T	10–11	40 ft (12 m)	E	Foliage; flowers (white, late spring–early summer); bark
Luculia gratissima	S	9–11	5 ft (1.5 m)	E	Flowers (pink, fragrant, autumn–winter)
Luculia intermedia	S	9–11	12 ft (3.5 m)	E	Flowers (pale pink, fragrant, winter–early spring)
Luma apiculata	S	8–9	15 ft (4.5 m)	E	Flowers (white, summer); decorative fruit; bark
Macadamia tetraphylla	T	10–11	25 ft (8 m)	E	Edible nuts; flowers (white or pink, spring)
Mackaya bella	S	10–11	8 ft (2.4 m)	E	Flowers (pale lilac, spring–summer)
Magnolia acuminata	T	4–9	25–30 ft (8–9 m)	D	Flowers (greenish-yellow, fragrant, early–mid-summer)
Magnolia campbellii	T	7–9	20–30 ft (6–9 m)	D	Flowers (pink, white, purple, late winter–mid-spring)
Magnolia campbellii 'Charles Raffill'	T	7–9	20–30 ft (6–9 m)	D	Flowers (white & rose-purple, late winter–mid-spring)
Magnolia campbellii 'Lanarth'	T	7–9	20–30 ft (6–9 m)	D	Flowers (deep purple-pink, late winter–mid-spring)
Magnolia grandiflora	T	6–11	25 ft (8 m)	E	Flowers (white, summer); foliage
Magnolia liliiflora	S	5–10	10 ft (3 m)	D	Flowers (purple, pink, mid-spring–summer)
Magnolia liliiflora 'Nigra'	S	5–10	10 ft (3 m)	D	Flowers (dark purple centered pale purple, mid-spring–summer)
Magnolia sieboldii	S(T)	7–10	12–15 ft (3.5–4.5 m)	D	Flowers (white, fragrant, spring)
Magnolia × soulangeana	T	4–9	20 ft (6 m)	D	Flowers (white to pink or purple, late winter–mid-spring)

NAME	TYPE	ZONE	HEIGHT at MATURITY	DECIDUOUS or EVERGREEN	CHIEF ATTRACTIONS
Magnolia × soulangeana 'Alexandrina'	T	4–9	20 ft (6 m)	D	Flowers (white flushed purple-pink, late winter–mid-spring
Magnolia × soulangeana 'Brozzoni'	T	4–9	20 ft (6 m)	D	Flowers (white with purple base, late winter–mid-spring)
Magnolia × soulangeana 'Lennei Alba'	T	4–9	20 ft (6 m)	D	Flowers (white, late winter–mid-spring)
Magnolia sprengeri	T	5–9	25 ft (8 m)	D	Flowers (pink, early–mid-spring)
Magnolia sprengeri 'Diva'	T	5–9	25 ft (8 m)	D	Flowers (deep reddish pink, early–mid-spring)
Magnolia stellata	S	5–10	8 ft (2.4 m)	D	Flowers (white, fragrant, late winter–early spring)
Magnolia stellata 'Rosea'	S	5–10	8 ft (2.4 m)	D	Flowers (light pink, fragrant, late winter–early spring)
Magnolia virginiana	T	3–9	15–20 ft (4.5–6 m)	E	Flowers (cream, fragrant, summer)
Magnolia wilsonii	T	5–9	15 ft (4.5 m)	D	Flowers (white, fragrant, late spring–early summer)
Mahonia aquifolium	S	3–9	6 ft (1.8 m)	E	Foliage; flowers (yellow, spring); decorative fruit
Mahonia bealei	S	6–10	6 ft (1.8 m)	E	Flowers (yellow, autumn–spring); decorative fruit
Mahonia lomariifolia	S	7–10	12 ft (3.5 m)	E	Foliage; flowers (yellow, fragrant, late autumn–winter); decorative fruit
Mahonia repens	S	3–9	24 in (60 cm)	E	Foliage; flowers (yellow, spring); decorative fruit
Malus × domestica and cultivars	T	3–9	20 ft (6 m)	D	Edible fruit (apples); flowers (white & pink, spring)
Malus florentina	T	6–9	15 ft (4.5 m)	D	Flowers (white, spring); decorative fruit
Malus floribunda	T	3–9	20 ft (6 m)	D	Flowers (pink, early spring); decorative fruit
Malus hupehensis	T	4–10	30 ft (9 m)	D	Foliage; flowers (white, spring); decorative fruit
Malus ioensis	T	4–9	15 ft (4.5 m)	D	Flowers (pink, fragrant, late spring); autumn foliage
Malus, Orn. Crab-Apple, 'Butterball'	T	3–9	25 ft (8 m)	D	Flowers (pink-tinged white, spring); decorative fruit (orange-yellow)
Malus, Orn. Crab-Apple, 'Butterball'	T	3–9	25 ft (8 m)	D	Flowers (pink & white, double, spring)
Malus pumila	T	3–9	12–15 ft (3.5–4.5 m)	D	Flowers (pink & white, spring); edible fruit
Malus × purpurea	S(T)	4–9	12–15 ft (3.5–4.5 m)	D	Foliage; flowers (purple-red, spring); decorative fruit
Malus × purpurea 'Aldenhamensis'	T	4–9	25 ft (8 m)	D	Foliage; flowers (purple-red, semi-double, spring); decorative fruit
Malus sargentii	S	3–9	8 ft (2.4 m)	D	Flowers (white, spring); decorative fruit
Malus sieboldii 'Gorgeous'	S	5–10	10–12 ft (3–4.5 m)	D	Flowers (pink & white, spring); decorative fruit
Malus sylvestris	T	3–9	25 ft (8 m)	D	Flowers (white & pink, spring); decorative edible fruit
Mangifera caesia	T	11–12	50–70 ft (15–21 m)	E	Bark; fruit
Mangifera indica	T	11–12	30–50 ft (9–15 m)	E	Edible fruit (mango)
Melaleuca armillaris	T	9–11	25 ft (8 m)	E	Flowers (white, spring–summer); dense foliage
Melaleuca bracteata	T	9–11	20 ft (6 m)	E	Flowers (white, summer); foliage
Melaleuca bracteata 'Revolution Green'	T	9–11	15 ft (4.5 m)	E	Flowers (white, summer); golden foliage; red stems
Melaleuca hypericifolia	S(T)	9–11	12–15 ft (3.5–4.5 m)	E	Flowers (light red, summer)
Melaleuca nesophila	S	9–11	10 ft (3 m)	E	Flowers (mauve, ageing white, summer)
Melaleuca quinquenervia	T	10–11	40 ft (12 m)	E	Bark; flowers (white, mainly spring)
Melaleuca thymifolia	S	9–11	3 ft (1 m)	E	Flowers (purple, spring–autumn)
Melia azedarach	T	8–12	30 ft (9 m)	D	Foliage; flowers (lilac, late spring–early summer); decorative fruit
Melianthus major	S	9–11	6–10 ft (1.8–3 m)	Semi	Foliage; flowers (brownish red, summer)

NAME	TYPE	ZONE	HEIGHT at MATURITY	DECIDUOUS or EVERGREEN	CHIEF ATTRACTIONS
Mespilus germanica	T	3–9	15 ft (4.5 m)	D	Edible fruit; flowers (white, early summer)
Metasequoia glyptostroboides	T	5–10	40 ft (12 m)	D	Autumn foliage
Metrosideros carmineus	S	9–11	12–15 ft (3.5–4.5 m)	E	Flowers (red, summer); vigorous shrubby climber
Metrosideros collina	S(T)	10–12	6–25 ft (1.8–8 m)	E	Flowers (orange-red to scarlet, summer)
Metrosideros excelsa	T	10–11	20 ft (6 m)	E	Flowers (crimson, late spring–summer); dense foliage
Metrosideros excelsa 'Variegata'	T	10–11	15 ft (6 m)	E	Variegated foliage; flowers (crimson, late spring–summer); dense foliage
Metrosideros kermadecensis	T	10–11	15 ft (4.5 m)	E	Flowers (crimson, spring–summer); foliage
Metrosideros k. 'Variegatus'	T	10–11	10–12 ft (3–3.5 m)	E	Variegated foliage; flowers (crimson, spring–summer); foliage
Metrosideros robustus	T	9–10	20 ft (6 m)	E	Flowers (orange-red, summer)
Metrosideros umbellatus	T	8–10	10–15 ft (3–4.5 m)	E	Flowers (scarlet, late spring–summer)
Michelia champaca	T	10–11	30 ft (9 m)	E	Flowers (pale orange, very fragrant, late summer)
Michelia doltsopa	T	9–10	20 ft (6 m)	E	Flowers (white, fragrant, late winter–early spring)
Michelia figo	S	9–11	10–12 ft (3–3.5 m)	E	Flowers (purple & cream, very fragrant, spring–summer)
Michelia yunnanensis	T	9–11	12–15 ft (3.5–4.5 m)	E	Flowers (green, fragrant, spring)
Microbiota decussata	S	3–9	24 in (60 cm)	E	Foliage
Mimetes cucullatus	S	9–10	5 ft (1.5 m)	E	Flowers (red, yellow & white, mid-winter–early summer)
Mimulus aurantiacus	S	8–10	3 ft (1 m)	E	Flowers (red or orange, spring–summer)
Mimulus longiflorus	S	9–11	3 ft (1 m)	E	Flowers (cream, yellow, orange, red, spring–summer)
Morus alba	T	7–10	25 ft (8 m)	D	Edible fruit; foliage
Morus alba 'Pendula'	T	7–10	6–8 ft (1.8–2.4 m)	D	Arching & weeping stems
Morus nigra	T	6–9	15–20 ft (4.5–6 m)	D	Edible fruit; foliage
Murraya koenigii	S	10–12	10 ft (3 m)	E	Aromatic foliage; flowers (white, fragrant, summer)
Murraya paniculata	S	10–12	10 ft (3 m)	E	Flowers (white, fragrant, mainly summer–autumn); foliage
Myrica californica	S(T)	7–10	15–25 ft (4.5–8 m)	E	Foliage; decorative fruit
Myrica cerifera	S	4–9	10 ft (3 m)	E	Foliage; decorative fruit
Myrtus communis	S	8–10	8 ft (2.4 m)	E	Flowers (white, spring); decorative fruit
Myrtus communis 'Microphylla'	S	8–10	8 ft (2.4 m)	E	Flowers (white, small, spring); tiny leaves
Nandina domestica	S	5–10	6–8 ft (1.8–2.4 m)	E	Foliage; decorative fruit; flowers (white, summer)
Nandina domestica 'Nana'	S	5–10	12–18 in (30–45 cm)	E	Foliage; autumn color
Nandina domestica 'Richmond'	S	5–10	6–8 ft (1.8–2.4 m)	E	Foliage; decorative fruit; flowers (white, summer)
Nerium oleander and cultivars	S	9–11	10 ft (3 m)	E	Flowers (white, cream, pink, red, late spring–autumn)
Neviusia alabamensis	S	5–10	5 ft (1.5 m)	D	Flowers (white to creamy yellow, spring)
Nothofagus cunninghamii	T	8–9	30 ft (9 m)	E	Foliage
Nothofagus fusca	T	7–10	30–40 ft (9–12 m)	E	Foliage
Nothofagus gunnii	S	8–9	2–6 ft (0.6–1.8 m)	E	Foliage; spreading, mounding habit
Nothofagus menziesii	T	8–9	25–40 ft (8–12 m)	E	Bark; foliage
Nothofagus moorei	T	8–9	40 ft (12 m)	E	Foliage
Nothofagus obliqua	T	7–9	50 ft (15 m)	D	Autumn foliage; drooping habit
Notospartium carmichaeliae	S	8–9	10 ft (3 m)	D	Flowers (pink, late spring–midsummer)
Nuytsia floribunda	T	9–10	15 ft (4.5 m)	E	Flowers (orange, summer)

NAME	TYPE	ZONE	HEIGHT at MATURITY	DECIDUOUS or EVERGREEN	CHIEF ATTRACTIONS
Nyssa sylvatica	T	3–10	30 ft (9 m)	D	Autumn foliage
Olea europaea	T	8–10	25 ft (8 m)	E	Edible fruit; gnarled trunk
Olearia ilicifolia	S	9–10	10 ft (3 m)	E	Flowers (white, fragrant, summer)
Olearia macrodonta	S	7–9	6–8 ft (1.8–2.4 m)	E	Flowers (white, late spring–summer)
Olearia paniculata	S	9–10	12 ft (3.5 m)	E	Foliage; flowers (cream, fragrant, autumn)
Olearia phlogopappa	S	7–9	6 ft (1.8 m)	E	Flowers (white to purple, late spring–early autumn)
Olearia × *scilloniensis*	S	8–9	6 ft (1.8 m)	E	Flowers (white, spring)
Origanum calcaratum	S	9–11	20–30cm (8–12in)	E	Foliage; flowers (pink, summer)
Origanum rotundifolium	S	8–9	20–30cm (8–12in)	E	Foliage; flowers (white to pink, late summer–autumn)
Osmanthus delavayi	S	7–9	6 ft (1.8 m)	E	Flowers (white, fragrant, summer)
Osmanthus fragrans	S	7–10	10 ft (3 m)	E	Very fragrant flowers (white to pale orange, spring–autumn)
Osmanthus heterophyllus	S	7–10	8 ft (2.4 m)	E	Foliage; flowers (white, fragrant, early summer)
Osmanthus heterophyllus 'Variegatus'	S	7–10	8 ft (2.4 m)	E	Variegated foliage; flowers (white, fragrant, early summer)
Osteospermum ecklonis	S	8–10	5 ft (1.5 m)	E	Flowers (white tinted purple-red, late spring–autumn)
Osteospermum ecklonis	S	8–10	3 ft (1 m)	E	Flowers (white, late spring–autumn)
Ostrya carpinifolia	T	2–9	30 ft (9 m)	D	Autumn foliage; decorative fruit clusters; bark
Oxydendrum arboreum	T	3–9	25–30 ft (8–9 m)	D	Autumn foliage; flowers (white, fragrant, late summer)
Ozothamnus ledifolius	S	8–9	3 ft (1 m)	E	Flowers (white, summer); foliage
Pachystachys lutea	S	10–12	6 ft (1.8 m)	E	Flowers (white with yellow bracts, summer); foliage
Paeonia lactiflora Hybrids	S	6–9	3–4 ft (1–1.2 m)	D	Flowers (white, pink, apricot, mauve, red, spring–early summer)
Paeonia lutea	S	4–9	6 ft (1.8 m)	D	Flowers (yellow, late spring–early summer)
Paeonia suffruticosa	S	4–9	4 ft (1.2m)	D	Flowers (white, pink or red, late spring)
Paliurus spina-christi	S	6–10	10 ft (3 m)	D	Decorative fruit; flowers (yellow, summer); autumn foliage
Pandanus tectorius	T	11–12	15–20 ft (4.5–6 m)	E	Symmetrical habit; foliage; decorative fruit
Paraserianthes lophantha	T	9–11	25 ft (8 m)	E	Foliage; flowers (yellowish-green, winter–spring)
Parrotia persica	T	3–9	20 ft (6 m)	D	Autumn foliage; flowers (red, late winter–spring); bark
Paulownia tomentosa	T	4–9	30 ft (9 m)	D	Flowers (violet, spring); foliage
Pelargonium crispum	S	9–11	3 ft (1 m)	E	Aromatic foliage; flowers (pink, summer)
Pelargonium crispum 'Variegatum'	S	9–11	3 ft (1 m)	E	Variegated aromatic foliage
Pelargonium grandicalcaratum	S	9–11	18 in (45 cm)	E	Aromatic foliage; flowers (mauve & purple, summer)
Pelargonium quercifolium	S	9–11	5 ft (1.5 m)	E	Aromatic foliage; flowers (purple-pink, summer)
Pelargonium, Regal Hybrids	S	9–11	2–4 ft (0.6–1.2 m)	E	Flowers (all colors except blue or yellow, spring–autumn)
Pelargonium, Scented-leafed Hybrids	S	8–11	12–36 in (30–90 cm)	E	Aromatic foliage
Pelargonium, Unique Hybrids	S	9–11	18 in (45 cm)	E	Aromatic foliage; flowers (pink or red, summer)
Pelargonium, Zonal Hybrids	S	10–11	12–24 in (30–60 cm)	E	Foliage; flowers (white, pink, red, late spring–early autumn)
Peltophorum pterocarpum	T	11–12	40 ft (12 m)	E	Flowers (yellow, fragrant, early summer)
Penstemon newberryi	S	8–10	6–12 in (15–30 cm)	E	Flowers (rose-red, late spring–summer)
Perovskia abrotanoides	S	5–9	3 ft (1 m)	E	Foliage; flowers (violet to pink, summer)

NAME	TYPE	ZONE	HEIGHT at MATURITY	DECIDUOUS or EVERGREEN	CHIEF ATTRACTIONS
Persea americana	T	10–11	30 ft (9 m)	E	Edible fruit (avocado); foliage
Phebalium squameum	S(T)	9–11	15–20 ft (4.5–6 m)	E	Aromatic foliage; columnar habit; flowers (white, spring)
Phebalium squameum 'Illumination'	S(T)	9–11	15–20 ft (4.5–6 m)	E	Aromatic variegated foliage; columnar habit; flowers (white, spring)
Phellodendron amurense	T	5–9	25 ft (8 m)	D	Autumn foliage; decorative fruit; bark
Phellodendron sachalinense	T	3–9	25–30 ft (8–9 m)	D	Bark; red new growth
Philadelphus 'Belle Etoile'	S	5–9	6 ft (1.8 m)	D	Flowers (white, spring–early summer)
Philadelphus coronarius	S	2–10	6 ft (1.8 m)	D	Flowers (white, fragrant, mid to late spring)
Philadelphus coronarius 'Aureus'	S	2–10	6 ft (1.8 m)	D	Flowers (white, fragrant, mid to late spring); yellow new growth
Philadelphus 'Lemoinei'	S	3–9	6 ft 91.8 m)	D	Flowers (white, fragrant, spring)
Philadelphus pendulifolius	S	5–9	8 ft (2.4 m)	D	Flowers (white, spring)
Philadelphus 'Virginal'	S	3–9	6–8 ft (1.8–2.4)	D	Flowers (white, semi-double, fragrant, late spring–early summer)
Phillyrea angustifolia	S	7–10	10 ft (3 m)	E	Flowers (greenish-cream, spring)
Philodendron bipinnatifidum	S	10–12	10 ft (3 m)	E	Foliage
Phlomis fruticosa	S	7–10	30 in (75 cm)	Semi	Flowers (yellow, summer)
Phlomis grandiflora	S	8–10	5 ft (1.5 m)	Semi	Foliage; flowers (yellow, summer)
Photinia davidsoniae	S(T)	9–11	15–30 ft (4.5–9 m)	E	Foliage
Photinia × fraseri	S	8–10	10 ft (3 m)	E	Foliage, new growth red
Photinia × fraseri 'Red Robin'	S	8–10	10 ft (3 m)	E	Foliage, new growth red
Photinia × fraseri 'Robusta'	S	8–10	10–12 ft (3–3.5 m)	E	Foliage, new growth red
Photinia serratifolia	T	7–10	15 ft (4.5 m)	E	Flowers (white, spring); decorative fruit
Phygelius aequalis	S	8–11	3 ft (1 m)	Semi	Flowers (orange-pink, summer)
Phygelius aequalis 'Yellow Trumpet'	S	8–11	3 ft (1 m)	Semi	Flowers (pale yellow, summer)
Phygelius × rectus	S	8–11	4–6 ft (1.2–1.8 m)	Semi	Flowers (orange, summer)
Phylica plumosa	S	9–10	6 ft (1.8 m)	E	Flowers (cream bracts, winter–spring); foliage
× Phylliopsis hillieri	S	3–9	12 in (30 cm)	E	Flowers (red-purple, spring)
× Phylliopsis hillieri 'Pinocchio'	S	3–9	8 in (20 cm)	E	Flowers (pink, spring)
Phyllocladus aspleniifolius	T	8–9	12–20 ft (3.5–6 m)	E	Foliage
Phyllocladus trichomanoides	T	9–10	15–25 ft (4.5–8 m)	E	Foliage
Phymosia umbellata	S(T)	10–12	15–20 (4.5–6 m)	E	Flowers (pink, summer)
Physocarpus monogynus	S	5–10	3–6 ft (1–1.8 m)	D	Flowers (white, late spring); foliage
Physocarpus opulifolius	S	2–9	5 ft (1.5 m)	D	Flowers (white, early summer); autumn foliage
Physocarpus opulifolius 'Dart's Gold'	S	2–9	4 ft (1.5 m)	D	Flowers (white, early summer); golden-yellow foliage
Picea abies	T	2–9	30 ft (9 m)	E	Symmetrical form; foliage
Picea abies 'Maxwellii'	T	2–9	30 in (75 cm)	E	Dwarf habit
Picea abies 'Pumila Glauca'	T	2–9	3 ft (90 cm)	E	Dense foliage; dwarf habit
Picea abies 'Pygmaea'	T	2–9	12 in (30 cm)	E	Symmetrical form; foliage
Picea breweriana	T	2–9	25–30 ft (8–9 m)	E	Symmetrical form; weeping branches
Picea engelmannii	T	1–8	25–30 ft (8–9 m)	E	Symmetrical form
Picea glauca	T	1–8	25–30 ft (8–9 m)	E	Symmetrical form

NAME	TYPE	ZONE	HEIGHT at MATURITY	DECIDUOUS or EVERGREEN	CHIEF ATTRACTIONS
Picea glauca var. *albertiana* 'Conica'	T	1–8	3 ft (1 m)	E	Compact conical form
Picea mariana	T	1–8	20–25 ft (6–8 m)	E	Symmetrical form
Picea mariana 'Nana'	T	1–8	3 ft (1 m)	E	Compact growth
Picea omorika	T	4–9	30–40 ft (9–12 m)	E	Symmetrical form, pendulous foliage
Picea orientalis	T	3–9	20–25 ft (6–8 m)	E	Symmetrical form; foliage; red male cones
Picea orientalis 'Aurea'	T	3–9	20–25 ft (6–8 m)	E	Symmetrical form; yellow young foliage; red male cones
Picea pungens	T	2–10	25–30 ft (8–9 m)	E	Symmetrical form; stiff blue foliage
Picea pungens 'Glauca'	T	2–10	25–30 ft (8–9 m)	E	Symmetrical form; stiff silvery blue foliage
Picea pungens 'Iseli Fastigiate'	T	2–10	25–30 ft (8–9 m)	E	Upward pointing branches
Picea pungens 'Pendens'	T	2–10	2–3 ft (0.6–1 m)	E	Low, spreading habit
Picea pungens 'Royal Blue'	T	2–10	25–30 ft (8–9 m)	E	Symmetrical form; bright silver-blue foliage
Picea sitchensis	T	4–9	40 ft (12 m)	E	Symmetrical form; vigorous growth
Picea smithiana	T	6–9	40 ft (12 m)	E	Symmetrical form; vigorous growth; weeping foliage
Pieris formosa	S	6–9	10 ft (3 m)	E	Flowers (white, mid-spring); red new growth
Pieris formosa var. *forestii*	S	6–9	6 ft (1.8 m)	E	Flowers (white, mid-spring); red new growth
Pieris formosa var. *forestii* 'Wakehurst'	S	6–9	10–15 ft (3–4.5 m)	E	Flowers (white, mid-spring); red new growth
Pieris japonica	S	4–10	6–8 ft (1.8–2.4 m)	E	Flowers (white or pink, late winter–spring); pink or red new growth
Pieris japonica 'Bert Chandler'	S	4–10	6–8 ft (1.8–2.4 m)	E	Flowers (white or pink, late winter–spring); pink & cream new growth
Pieris japonica 'Christmas Cheer'	S	4–10	6–8 ft (1.8–2.4 m)	E	Flowers (pale pink, late winter); pink or red new growth
Pieris japonica 'Flamingo'	S	4–10	6–8 ft (1.8–2.4 m)	E	Flowers (bright pink, late winter–spring)
Pieris japonica 'Red Mill'	S	4–10	6–8 ft (1.8–2.4 m)	E	Flowers (white spring); red new growth
Pieris japonica 'Tickled Pink'	S	4–10	6–8 ft (1.8–2.4 m)	E	Flowers (pale pink, late winter–spring); pale red new growth
Pieris japonica 'Variegata'	S	4–10	5 ft (1.5 m)	E	Flowers (white late winter–spring); variegated foliage
Pimelea ferruginea	S	9–10	3 ft (1 m)	E	Flowers (rose pink, spring)
Pimelea spectabilis	S	9–11	4 ft (1.2 m)	E	Flowers (pink or yellow, early summer)
Pinus aristata	T	5–9	15–20 ft (4.5–6 m)	E	Foliage
Pinus canariensis	T	8–10	40 ft (12 m)	E	Foliage; symmetrical form; bark
Pinus cembra	T	3–9	20 ft (6 m)	E	Foliage; neat form
Pinus contorta	T	7–9	40–50 ft (12–15 m)	E	Foliage
Pinus contorta var. *latifolia*	T	5–9	30 ft (9 m)	E	Straight trunk; symmetrical form
Pinus coulteri	T	8–9	25–40 ft (8–12 m)	E	Foliage; spreading crown; very large cones
Pinus densiflora	T	4–9	25 ft (8 m)	E	Foliage; bark; twisted limbs
Pinus densiflora 'Tanyosho Nana'	S	4–9	8 ft (2.4 m)	E	Foliage; bark; multiple trunks
Pinus densiflora 'Umbraculifera'	S	4–9	15 ft (4.5 m)	E	Foliage; bark; multiple trunks
Pinus halepensis	T	7–10	30 ft (9 m)	E	Vigorous growth; dense foliage
Pinus jeffreyi	T	6–9	30–40 ft (9–12 m)	E	Symmetrical form; bark; foliage
Pinus montezumae	T	9–11	50 ft (15 m)	E	Long blue-green needles; bark
Pinus monticola	T	5–9	40 ft (12 m)	E	Smooth, straight trunk; foliage
Pinus mugo	S	2–9	15 ft (4.5 m)	E	Dense foliage; bushy habit

NAME	TYPE	ZONE	HEIGHT at MATURITY	DECIDUOUS or EVERGREEN	CHIEF ATTRACTIONS
Pinus mugo 'Mops'	S	2–9	5 ft (1.5 m)	E	Dense foliage; bushy habit
Pinus nigra	T	4–9	30 ft (9 m)	E	Symmetrical form
Pinus palustris	T	4–10	30–40 ft (9–12 m)	E	Foliage; straight trunk
Pinus parviflora	T	3–9	20–25 ft (6–8 m)	E	Foliage; crooked habit
Pinus parviflora 'Brevifolia'	T	3–9	20 ft (6 m)	E	Sparse blue-green foliage; crooked habit
Pinus patula	T	9–11	40 ft (12 m)	E	Weeping needles; symmetrical form
Pinus pinaster	T	7–10	40 ft (12 m)	E	Foliage; bark
Pinus pinea	T	8–10	25 ft (8 m)	E	Umbrella-shaped crown; bark
Pinus ponderosa	T	5–9	30–40 ft (9–12 m)	E	Symmetrical form; foliage; bark
Pinus radiata	T	8–10	50 ft (15 m)	E	Vigorous growth
Pinus radiata 'Aurea'	T	8–10	50 ft (15 m)	E	Yellow new foliage; vigorous growth
Pinus strobus	T	3–9	40 ft (12 m)	E	Foliage; symmetrical form
Pinus strobus 'Nana'	T	3–9	4 ft (1.2 m)	E	Foliage; compact habit
Pinus sylvestris	T	4–9	30 ft (9 m)	E	Slender form; bark
Pinus thunbergii	T	5–9	30 ft (9 m)	E	Open form; bark
Pinus torreyana	T	8–10	50 ft (15 m)	E	Rugged form; bark
Pinus wallichiana	T	5–9	40 ft (12 m)	E	Broad symmetrical form; foliage; interesting cones
Piper ornatum	S	11–12	15 ft (4.5 m)	E	Colored foliage
Pisonia umbellifera	S	10–12	15 ft (4.5 m)	E	Foliage
Pisonia umbellifera 'Variegata'	S	10–12	12 ft (3.5 m)	E	Variegated foliage
Pistacia chinensis	T	5–10	20–25 ft (6–8 m)	D	Autumn foliage; decorative fruit
Pistacia vera	T	8–10	25 ft (8 m)	D	Edible nuts
Pittosporum crassifolium	T	9–10	20 ft (6 m)	E	Bushy habit; flowers (reddish purple, spring); decorative fruit
Pittosporum crassifolium 'Variegatum'	T	9–10	15 ft (4.5 m)	E	Variegated foliage; bushy habit; flowers (reddish purple, spring); decorative fruit
Pittosporum eugenioides	T	9–10	25 ft (8 m)	E	Bushy habit; foliage; decorative fruit
Pittosporum eugenioides 'Variegatum'	T	9–10	25 ft (8 m)	E	Variegated foliage; bushy habit; foliage; decorative fruit
Pittosporum phillyraeoides	T	9–11	20 ft (6 m)	E	Weeping habit; decorative fruit
Pittosporum rhombifolium	T	9–11	25 ft (8 m)	E	Dense symmetrical form; decorative fruit; flowers (cream, spring)
Pittosporum tenuifolium	T	9–11	20 ft (6 m)	E	Dense foliage; flowers (chocolate, fragrant, late spring)
Pittosporum tenuifolium 'Tom Thumb'	T	9–11	24 in (60 cm)	E	Purple-bronze foliage
Pittosporum tobira	S	9–11	8 ft (2.4 m)	E	Flowers (cream, fragrant, late spring–summer)
Pittosporum tobira 'Variegatum'	S	9–11	8 ft (2.4 m)	E	Variegated foliage; flowers (cream, fragrant, late spring–summer)
Pittosporum undulatum	T	9–11	30 ft (9 m)	E	Flowers (cream, spring); decorative fruit
Pittosporum undulatum 'Sunburst'	T	9–11	30 ft (9 m)	E	Yellowish new growth; flowers (cream, spring); decorative fruit
Plagianthus regius	S	7–9	30 ft (9 m)	Semi	Flowers (white to greenish white, summer)
Platanus × acerifolia	T	3–10	30–40 ft (9–12 m)	D	Stately habit; bark; autumn foliage
Platanus orientalis	T	6–10	30–40 ft (9–12 m)	D	Vigorous growth; foliage
Platycladus orientalis	T	6–11	20 ft (6 m)	E	Foliage

NAME	TYPE	ZONE	HEIGHT at MATURITY	DECIDUOUS or EVERGREEN	CHIEF ATTRACTIONS
Platycladus orientalis 'Aurea Nana'	S	6–11	24–30 in (60–75 cm)	E	Golden foliage; dwarf habit
Platycladus orientalis 'Filiformus Erecta'	S	6–11	5–6 ft (1.5–1.8 m)	E	Drooping thread-like foliage
Platycladus orientalis 'Hillieri'	S	6–11	24–30 in (60–75 cm)	E	Compact habit
Plectranthus argentatus	S	10–11	3 ft (1 m)	E	Flowers (blue & white, late spring)
Plectranthus ecklonii	S	9–11	4–6 ft (1.2–1.8 m)	E	Flowers (violet, autumn)
Plectranthus saccatus	S	10–11	4 ft (1.2 m)	E	Flowers (pale blue, spring)
Plumbago auriculata	S	9–11	6–8 ft (1.8–2.4 m)	E	Flowers (pale blue, late spring–early winter)
Plumbago indica	S	10–12	4 ft (1.2 m)	E	Flowers (orange-pink, most of the year)
Plumeria obtusa	T	10–12	15 ft (4.5 m)	E	Flowers (white & yellow, fragrant, spring–autumn)
Plumeria obtusa 'Singapore White'	T	10–12	15 ft (4.5 m)	E	Flowers (white, fragrant, spring–autumn)
Plumeria rubra	T	10–12	15–20 ft (4.5–6 m)	D	Flowers (pink, crimson, yellow or white, fragrant, late spring–late autumn)
Plumaria rubra var. acutifolia	T	10–12	15–20 ft (4.5–6 m)	D	Flowers (creamy white & yellow, fragrant, late spring–late autumn)
Podalyria calyptrata	S	9–10	12 ft (3.5 m)	E	Flowers (pink, spring); foliage
Podocarpus elatus	T	9–11	30–40 ft (9–12 m)	E	Foliage; bark; edible/decorative fruit
Podocarpus latifolius	T	9–11	30 ft (9 m)	E	Foliage
Podocarpus lawrenceii	S	8–9	5 ft (1.5 m)	E	Foliage; decorative fruit
Podocarpus macrophyllus	T	7–11	15 ft (4.5 m)	E	Foliage
Podocarpus macrophyllus 'Maki'	T	7–11	8 ft (2.4 m)	E	Erect growth habit
Podocarpus totara	T	9–10	30–40 ft (9–12 m)	E	Foliage; bark; decorative fruit
Polyarrhena reflexa	S	9–11	3 ft (1 m)	E	Flowers (white to pink, summer)
Polygala × dalmaisiana	S	9–11	8 ft (2.4 m)	E	Flowers (purple & green, most of the year)
Pomaderris aspera	S	8–10	15 ft (4.5 m)	E	Flowers (white, spring); foliage
Pomaderris kumeraho	S	8–10	10 ft (3 m)	E	Flowers (yellow, spring); foliage
Poncirus trifoliata	S	5–10	12 ft (3.5 m)	D	Decorative fruit; flowers (white, fragrant, spring)
Populus deltoides	T	3–11	60 ft (18 m)	D	Stately habit; autumn foliage
Populus nigra	T	6–10	50 ft (15 m)	D	Stately habit; autumn foliage
Populus tremula	T	1–9	40 ft (12 m)	D	Autumn foliage; bark
Potentilla fruticosa	S	2–9	3 ft (1 m)	D	Flowers (white to yellow & orange, early summer–autumn)
Potentilla fruticosa 'Goldfinger'	S	2–9	18–24 in (45–60 cm)	D	Flowers (bright yellow, early summer–autumn)
Potentilla fruticosa 'Red Ace'	S	2–9	18–24 in (45–60 cm)	D	Flowers (orange-red, early summer–autumn)
Potentilla fruticosa 'Tangerine'	S	2–9	18–24 in (45–60 cm)	D	Flowers (golden orange, early summer–autumn)
Prostanthera cuneata	S	8–9	3 ft (1 m)	E	Flowers (white to pale mauve, summer)
Prostanthera lasianthos	T	8–10	20 ft (6 m)	E	Flowers (white, late spring–midsummer)
Prostanthera nivea var. induta	S	9–11	10 ft (3 m)	E	Flowers (lilac, spring–summer)
Prostanthera ovalifolia	S	9–11	8 ft (2.4 m)	E	Flowers (violet-purple, spring); aromatic foliage
Prostanthera rotundifolia	S	9–10	6 ft (1.8 m)	E	Flowers (mauve, spring)
Prostanthera r. var. rosea	S	9–10	6 ft (1.8 m)	E	Flowers (pink, spring)
Protea aristata	S	9–10	8 ft (2.4 m)	E	Flowers (deep pink, summer); foliage
Protea aurea	S	9–10	10–15 ft (3–4.5)	E	Flowers (creamy green to crimson, spring–summer)

NAME	TYPE	ZONE	HEIGHT at MATURITY	DECIDUOUS or EVERGREEN	CHIEF ATTRACTIONS
Protea compacta	S	9–10	10 ft (3 m)	E	Flowers (pink, late autumn–early spring)
Protea cynaroides	S	9–10	5 ft (1.5 m)	E	Flowers (pink, mid-winter–spring)
Protea eximia	S	9–10	12 ft (3.5 m)	E	Flowers (pink to crimson, winter–spring)
Protea longifolia	S	9–10	5 ft (1.5 m)	E	Flowers (cream, green & black, autumn–spring)
Protea neriifolia	S	9–10	8 ft (2.4 m)	E	Flowers (deep pink & black, autumn–spring)
Protea 'Pink Ice'	S	9–10	6–10 ft (1.8–3 m)	E	Flowers (pink, autumn–winter)
Protea repens	S	9–10	10 ft (3 m)	E	Flowers (white to crimson, autumn–winter)
Prunus armeniaca	T	5–10	20 ft (6 m)	D	Edible fruit (apricot); flowers (white or pink, early spring)
Prunus avium	T	3–9	30 ft (9 m)	D	Edible fruit; flowers (white, spring); autumn color
Prunus avium 'Plena'	T	3–9	30 ft (9 m)	D	Flowers (white, double, spring); autumn color
Prunus × blireana	S	5–10	12 ft (3.5 m)	D	Flowers (rose pink, double, fragrant, spring); autumn foliage
Prunus campanulata	T	8–10	30 ft (9 m)	D	Flowers (carmine pink, late winter–early spring)
Prunus cerasifera	T	3–10	25 ft (8 m)	D	Flowers (white, late winter–spring); decorative/edible fruit; foliage
Prunus cerasifera 'Elvins'	T	3–10	12 ft (3.5 m)	D	Flowers (white flushed pink, late winter–spring); decorative/edible fruit; foliage
Prunus cerasifera 'Nigra'	T	3–10	20 ft (6 m)	D	Foliage (purple-red); flowers (pale pink, late spring); decorative/edible fruit
Prunus cerasus	T	3–9	20 ft (6 m)	D	Edible fruit; flowers (white, spring)
Prunus × domestica and cultivars	T	2–10	20 ft (6 m)	D	Edible fruit (plums); flowers (white, spring)
Prunus dulcis	T	6–9	20–30 ft (6–9 m)	D	Flowers (pink, late winter–early spring); edible fruit (almonds)
Prunus glandulosa	S	7–10	5 ft (1.5 m)	D	Flowers (white to pink, late spring)
Prunus glandulosa 'Sinensis'	S	7–10	5 ft (1.5 m)	D	Flowers (pink, double, late spring)
Prunus laurocerasus	T	5–9	25 ft (8 m)	E	Foliage; flowers (white, spring); decorative fruit
Prunus maackii	T	2–9	30 ft (9 m)	D	Flowers (white, spring); decorative fruit
Prunus mume	T	5–9	15–20 ft (4.5–6 m)	D	Flowers (white to deep pink, late winter–spring); edible fruit
Prunus mume 'Beni-chidori'	T	5–9	15–20 ft (4.5–6 m)	D	Flowers (pink, double, fragrant, spring)
Prunus mume 'Geisha'	T	5–9	15–20 ft (4.5–6 m)	D	Flowers (pink, semi-double, late winter)
Prunus 'Okame'	T	7–10	20–25 ft (6–8 m)	D	Flowers (pink, spring); autumn foliage
Prunus padus	T	3–9	30 ft (9 m)	D	Flowers (white, spring); decorative fruit; autumn foliage
Prunus padus 'Watereri'	T	3–9	30 ft (9 m)	D	Flowers (long racemes, white, spring); decorative fruit; autumn foliage
Prunus persica and cultivars	T	5–10	12–20 ft (3.5–6 m)	D	Edible fruit (peaches) ; flowers (white, pink, red, late winter–early spring)
Prunus persica var. nectarina	T	5–10	12–20 ft (3.5–6 m)	D	Edible fruit (nectarines) ; flowers (white, pink, red, late winter–early spring)
Prunus sargentii	T	4–9	25 ft (8 m)	D	Flowers (pink, spring); autumn foliage
Prunus, Sato-zakura Group	T	5–9	15–30 ft (4.5–9 m)	D	Flowers (white, pink, apricot, single or double, spring); autumn foliage
Prunus serotina	T	2–9	30 ft (9 m)	D	Autumn foliage; flowers (white, fragrant, spring); decorative fruit
Prunus serrula	T	6–9	25 ft (8 m)	D	Bark; flowers (white, spring); autumn foliage
Prunus serrulata	T	4–9	30 ft (9 m)	D	Flowers (white & pink, mid-spring); autumn foliage
Prunus spinosa	S(T)	4–9	12–15 ft (3.5–4.5 m)	D	Flowers (white, spring); edible/decorative fruit

NAME	TYPE	ZONE	HEIGHT at MATURITY	DECIDUOUS or EVERGREEN	CHIEF ATTRACTIONS
Prunus × *subhirtella* and cultivars	T	4–9	20 ft (6 m)	D	Flowers (pale pink, late winter–early spring); autumn foliage
Prunus × *yedoensis*	T	3–9	25 ft (8 m)	D	Flowers (white or pale pink, spring); autumn foliage
Prunus × *yedoensis* 'Shidare Yoshino'	T	3–9	25 ft (8 m)	D	Flowers (white, spring); weeping branches; autumn foliage
Pseudolarix amabilis	T	3–9	20–30 ft (6–9 m)	D	Autumn foliage
Pseudopanax crassifolius	T	9–10	20 ft (6 m)	E	Foliage
Pseudopanax laetus	S(T)	9–10	15–20 ft (4.5–6 m)	E	Foliage; decorative fruit
Pseudopanax lessonii	T	9–10	20 ft (6 m)	E	Foliage
Pseudotsuga menziesii	T	4–9	30–50 ft (9–15 m)	E	Foliage; symmetrical form
Pseudowintera colorata	S	8–10	5–6 ft (1.5–1.8 m)	E	Foliage; decorative fruit
Psidium cattleianum	S	9–12	15 ft (4.5 m)	E	Edible fruit; bark; foliage
Psidium guajava	S	10–12	20 ft (6 m)	E	Edible fruit; bark
Ptelea trifoliata	T	2–9	20 ft (6 m)	D	Autumn foliage; decorative fruit
Pterocarya carpinifolia	T	5–9	40 ft (12 m)	D	Foliage; flowers (greenish-yellow, spring); curious fruit
Pterocarya fraxinifolia	T	5–9	50–60 ft (15–18 m)	D	Foliage; flowers (greenish-yellow, spring); curious fruit
Pterostyrax hispida	T	4–9	25 ft (8 m)	D	Flowers (white, fragrant, summer); decorative fruit
Punica granatum	S	8–11	15 ft (4.5 m)	E	Edible/decorative fruit; flowers (orange-red, spring–summer)
Pyracantha coccinea	S	5–9	10 ft (3 m)	E	Decorative fruit
Pyracantha coccinea 'Lalandei'	S	5–9	10 ft (3 m)	E	Decorative fruit
Pyracantha crenatoserrata	S	6–10	12 ft (3.5 m)	E	Upright habit; decorative fruit (orange-red)
Pyracantha 'Mohave'	S	7–10	12 ft (3.5 m)	E	Flowers (white, late spring); decorative fruit (bright orange-red)
Pyracantha 'Orange Glow'	S	7–10	10 ft (3.5 m)	E	Flowers (white, late spring); decorative fruit (bright orange)
Pyracantha 'Soleil d'Or'	S	8–10	12 ft (3.5 m)	E	Flowers (white, late spring); decorative fruit (bright golden yellow)
Pyrus calleryana	T	5–10	30 ft (9 m)	D	Flowers (white, early spring); autumn foliage
Pyrus communis & cultivars	T	2–9	25 ft (8 m)	D	Edible fruit (pears); flowers (white, spring)
Pyrus salicifolia	T	4–9	20 ft (6 m)	D	Silvery foliage; flowers (white, spring)
Pyrus ussuriensis	T	4–9	40 ft (12 m)	D	Autumn foliage; flowers (white, spring)
Quercus acutissima	T	5–10	30–40 ft (9–12 m)	D	Autumn foliage; bark
Quercus canariensis	T	5–10	30–40 ft (9–12 m)	D	Foliage; symmetrical form
Quercus cerris	T	7–10	30–40 ft (9–12 m)	D	Autumn foliage
Quercus coccinea	T	2–9	40 ft (12 m)	D	Autumn foliage
Quercus ilex	T	6–10	30–40 ft (9–12 m)	E	Dense foliage; rounded shape
Quercus palustris	T	3–10	40 ft (12 m)	D	Autumn foliage
Quercus petraea	T	5–9	40–50 ft (12–15 m)	D	Foliage; broad canopy; bark
Quercus robur	T	3–10	30–40 ft (9–12 m)	D	Foliage; broad canopy
Quercus rubra	T	3–9	40 ft (12 m)	D	Autumn foliage
Quercus rubra 'Aurea'	T	3–9	40 ft (12 m)	D	Bright yellow new growth; autumn foliage
Quercus suber	T	6–10	25–30 ft (8–9 m)	E	Bark; gnarled trunk
Quercus virginiana	T	7–11	30–40 ft (9–12 m)	E	Foliage; dense canopy
Radermachera sinica	T	10–12	30 ft (9 m)	E	Foliage; flowers (white, summer)

NAME	TYPE	ZONE	HEIGHT at MATURITY	DECIDUOUS or EVERGREEN	CHIEF ATTRACTIONS
Rauvolfia caffra	T	9–11	30 ft (9 m)	E	Flowers (white, fragrant, summer); decorative fruit
Ravenala madagascariensis	T	11–12	20 ft (6 m)	E	Foliage; symmetrical form
Reinwardtia indica	S	9–11	3 ft (1 m)	E	Flowers (yellow, winter)
Retama monosperma	S	7–10	5 ft (1.5 m)	E	Flowers (white, fragrant, spring); weeping foliage
Rhabdothamnus solandri	S	10–11	5–6 ft (1.5–1.8 m)	E	Flowers (orange-red, most of the year); foliage
Rhamnus alaternus	S	6–10	12 ft (3.5 m)	E	Foliage; flowers (greenish-yellow, late winter–early spring)
Rhamnus californica	S	6–10	6 ft (1.8 m)	E	Decorative fruit; foliage
Rhaphiolepis × delacourii	S	7–10	6 ft (1.8 m)	E	Flowers (pale to deep pink, late winter–spring); decorative fruit
Rhaphiolepis indica	S	8–11	8 ft (2.4 m)	E	Flowers (white & pink, late winter–spring); decorative fruit
Rhaphiolepis umbellata	S	7–11	6 ft (1.8 m)	E	Foliage; flowers (white, spring–early summer); decorative fruit

Rhododendron, species

NAME	TYPE	ZONE	HEIGHT at MATURITY	DECIDUOUS or EVERGREEN	CHIEF ATTRACTIONS
Rhododendron arboreum	T	6–9	12–20 ft (3.5–6 m)	E	Flowers (red, white or pink, spring)
Rhododendron augustinii	S	6–9	5 ft (1.5 m)	E	Flowers (mauve-blue, spring)
Rhododendron aurigeranum	S	10–12	8 ft (2.4 m)	E	Flowers (orange-yellow, mainly late summer)
Rhododendron brookeanum	S	10–12	6–15 ft (1.8–4.5 m)	E	Flowers (orange, orange-pink or red, mainly late summer)
Rhododendron calendulaceum	S	4–9	8 ft (2.4 m)	D	Flowers (scarlet, orange or yellow, spring); autumn foliage
Rhododendron catawbiense	S	3–9	8–12 ft (2.4–3.5 m)	E	Flowers (lilac, purple or white, early summer)
Rhododendron ciliatum	S	7–9	4–6 ft (1.2–1.8 m)	E	Flowers (white or white flushed rose, early spring)
Rhododendron cinnabarinum	S	8–9	6–8 ft (1.8–2.4 m)	E	Flowers (orange-red, early summer)
Rhododendron elliottii	S(T)	9–10	6–25 ft (1.8 m)	E	Flowers (deep red with white spots, mid-spring)
Rhododendron fastigiatum	S	7–9	18–30 in (45–70 cm)	E	Flowers (purple or lavender, mid-spring); compact habit
Rhododendron hanceanum	S	8–9	3–6 ft (1–1.8 m)	E	Flowers, cream to yellow, scented, mid-spring)
Rhododendron jasminiflorum	S	10–12	8 ft (2.4 m)	E	Flowers (white, fragrant, most of the year)
Rhododendron javanicum	S	10–12	6–12 ft (1.8–3.5 m)	E	Flowers (orange, orange-pink or red, scented, mainly late summer)
Rhododendron johnstoneanum	S	7–9	8–15 ft (2.4–4.5 m)	E	Flowers (cream to pale yellow, scented, early spring)
Rhododendron kaempferi	S	5–9	4–8 ft (1.2–2.4 m)	E	Flowers (red to orange-pink, spring)
Rhododendron kiusianum	S	8–10	3 ft (1 m)	E	Flowers (purple-pink, spring); autumn–winter foliage
Rhododendron laetum	S	10–12	5 ft (1.5 m)	E	Flowers (golden yellow, mainly late summer)
Rhododendron lochiae	S	9–11	5 ft (1.5 m)	E	Flowers (red, spring–summer)
Rhododendron luteum	S	5–9	8–10 ft (2.4–3 m)	D	Flowers (bright yellow, fragrant, spring)
Rhododendron macabeanum	T	8–9	20–25 ft (6–8 m)	E	Flowers (pale yellow, early spring); large leaves
Rhododendron molle	S	7–9	4–6 ft (1.2–1.8 m)	D	Flowers (yellow or orange, mid-spring); autumn foliage
Rhododendron molle ssp. *japonicum*	S	7–9	3–10 ft (1–3 m)	D	Flowers (red, orange-red, pink, yellow, mid-spring); autumn foliage
Rhododendron nakaharai	S	5–10	6–12 in (15–30 cm)	E	Flowers (orange-red, early summer); low, spreading habit
Rhododendron nuttallii	S	9–10	8–10 ft (2.4–3 m)	E	Flowers (white, pale yellow & pink, fragrant, spring); bark; foliage

NAME	TYPE	ZONE	HEIGHT at MATURITY	DECIDUOUS or EVERGREEN	CHIEF ATTRACTIONS
Rhododendron occidentale	S	5–9	6–8 ft (1.8–2.4 m)	D	Flowers (white to pink & yellow, fragrant, late spring–early summer); autumn foliage
Rhododendron ponticum	S	5–9	12–15 ft (3.5–4.5 m)	E	Flowers (mauve, late spring–early summer)
Rhododendron simsii and cultivars	S	9–11	5 ft (1.5 m)	E	Flowers (deep pink or red, winter–spring)
Rhododendron sinogrande	T	8–10	10–20 ft (3–6 m)	E	Huge leaves; flowers (cream to yellow, spring)
Rhododendron wardii	S	7–9	6–15 ft (1.8–4.5 m)	E	Flowers (white to pale yellow, mid-spring)
Rhododendron wardii var. *wardii*	S	7–9	6–15 ft (1.8–4.5 m)	E	Flowers (bright yellow with a purple blotch, mid-spring)
Rhododendron williamsianum rounded leaves	S	7–9	2–5 ft (0.6–1.5 m)	E	Flowers (white-tinted-pink to rose pink; mid-spring);
Rhododendron yakushimanum	S	5–9	3–6 ft (1–1.8 m)	E	Flowers (white to mid pink, spring); heavily felted foliage
Rhododendron zoelleri	S	10–12	4–6 ft (1.2–1.8 m)	E	Flowers (orange & yellow, mainly late summer)

Rhododendron, garden hybrids

Dwarf or alpine	S	4–9	8–24 in (20–60 cm)	E	Flowers (most colours, early to mid spring); compact habit
Shrub	S	5–10	2–10 ft (0.6–3 m)	E	Flowers (most colours, late winter–early summer)
Tall shrub or tree	S(T)	5–10	10–25 ft (3–8 m)	E	Flowers (most colours, late winter–early summer); foliage

Rhododendron, Vireyas

Rhododendron, Vireyas	S	9–11	2–6 ft (0.6–1.8 m)	E	Flowers (white, yellow, pink, orange, red, most of the year)

Rhododendron, Deciduous Azaleas

Ghent Azaleas	S	6–9	6–8 ft (1.8–2.4 m)	D	Flowers (white, yellow, orange, red, fragrant, late spring); autumn foliage
Knap Hill, Exbury & Ilam Azaleas	S	5–9	5–8 ft (1.5–2.4 m)	D	Flowers (yellow, orange, red, spring); autumn foliage
Mollis Azaleas	S	5–9	5–8 ft (1.5–2.4 m)	D	Flowers (yellow, orange, red, spring); autumn foliage
Occidentale Azaleas	S	6–9	6–10 ft (1.8–3 m)	D	Flowers (white or pale pink with yellow, fragrant, mid-spring); autumn foliage

Rhododendron, Evergreen Azaleas

1. Indica Azaleas

Belgian Indica Azaleas	S	9–11	2–6 ft (0.6–1.8 m)	E	Flowers (white, pink, red, purple, winter–spring)
Indicum & Mucronatum Azaleas	S	8–11	2–8 ft (0.6–2.4 m)	E	Flowers (white, pink, mauve, fragrant, early spring)
Kerrigan Indica Azaleas	S	8–11	2–4 ft (0.6–1.2 m)	E	Flowers (white, pink, red, purple, winter–spring)
Rutherford Indica Azaleas	S	9–11	2–4 ft (0.6–1.2 m)	E	Flowers (white, pink, red, purple, winter–spring)
Southern Indica Azaleas	S	8–11	2–8 ft (0.6–2.4 m)	E	Flowers (white, pink, red, purple, early spring)

2. Kurume Azaleas

Amoenum Kurume Azaleas	S	6–10	6–8 ft (1.8–2.4 m)	E	Flowers (purple-pink, spring)
Kurume Azaleas	S	8–10	2–6 ft (0.6–1.8 m)	E	Flowers (white, pink, red, purple, spring)

3. Kaempferi Azaleas

Gable Hybrid Azaleas	S	6–10	4–6 ft (1.2–1.8 m)	E	Flowers (white, pink, apricot, red, purple, early to mid-spring)
Girard Hybrid Azaleas	S	6–10	1–4 ft (0.3–1.2 m)	E	Flowers (white, pink, apricot, red, purple, mid-spring)
Kaempferi Azaleas	S	6–10	2–6 ft (0.6–1.8 m)	E	Flowers (white, pink, apricot, red, purple, early to mid-spring)

NAME	TYPE	ZONE	HEIGHT at MATURITY	DECIDUOUS or EVERGREEN	CHIEF ATTRACTIONS
Shammarello Hybrid Azaleas	S	6–10	3–6 ft (1–1.8 m)	E	Flowers (white, mauve, pink, red, purple, mid-spring)
Vuyk Hybrid Azaleas	S	6–10	4–6 ft (1.2–1.8 m)	E	Flowers (white, pink, apricot, red, purple, early to mid-spring)
4. Satsuki Azaleas	S	8–10	12–24 in (30–60 cm)	E	Flowers (white, pink, orange, red, late spring–early summer)
5. Inter-Group Azaleas					
August Kehr Hybrid Azaleas	S	6–10	2–4 ft (1–1.2 m)	E	Flowers (white, mauve, pink, red, purple, mid-spring)
Back Acres Hybrid Azaleas	S	7–10	2–4 ft (1–1.2 m)	E	Flowers (white, mauve, pink, red, purple, mid-spring)
Glenn Dale Hybrid Azaleas	S	7–10	4–8 ft (1.2–2.4 m)	E	Flowers (white, mauve, pink, red, purple, mid-spring)
Greenwood Hybrid Azaleas	S	6–10	1–4 ft (0.3–1.2 m)	E	Flowers (white, mauve, pink, red, purple, mid-spring)
Harris Hybrid Azaleas	S	6–10	1–3 ft (0.3–1 m)	E	Flowers (white, mauve, pink, red, orange-red, purple, mid to late spring)
North Tisbury Hybrid Azaleas	S	6–10	12–24 in (30–60 cm)	E	Flowers (white, pink, red, late spring–early summer); low, spreading habit
Nuccio Hybrid Azaleas	S	8–11	2–5 ft (0.6–1.5 m)	E	Flowers (white, mauve, pink, red, orange-red, purple, mid to late spring)
Robin Hill Hybrid Azaleas	S	6–10	1–3 ft (0.3–1 m)	E	Flowers (white, mauve, pink, red, orange-red, purple, mid to late spring)
Rhodoleia championii	T	9–11	15–20 ft (4.5–6 m)	E	Flowers (red, winter–early spring)
Rhodotypos scandens	S	5–9	12–15 ft (3.5–4.5 m)	D	Flowers (white, late spring–summer)
Rhus aromatica	S	2–9	3 ft (1 m)	D	Autumn foliage
Rhus aromatica 'Gro-Low'	S	2–9	24 in (60 cm)	D	Autumn foliage
Rhus chinensis	S(T)	3–9	12–15 ft (3.5–4.5 m)	D	Autumn foliage; flowers (white, late summer)
Rhus chinensis 'September Beauty'	S(T)	3–9	12–15 ft (3.5–4.5 m)	D	Vivid autumn foliage; flowers (white, late summer)
Rhus typhina	S(T)	3–9	12–15 ft (3.5–4.5 m)	D	Autumn foliage; decorative fruit
Ribes alpinum	S	5–9	6 ft (1.8 m)	D	Decorative fruit; foliage
Ribes odoratum	S	6–9	8–10 ft (2.4 m)	D	Flowers (yellow, fragrant, spring); decorative fruit
Ribes sanguineum	S	6–9	8–10 ft (2.4–3 m)	D	Flowers (pink to red, late spring)
Ribes sanguineum 'Tydeman's White'	S	6–9	8–10 ft (2.4–3 m)	D	Flowers (white, late spring)
Ribes silvestre	S	6–9	6 ft (1.8 m)	D	Edible fruit (currants)
Ribes speciosum	S	7–10	6 ft (1.8 m)	D	Flowers (red, late winter–spring); decorative fruit, red young stems
Ribes uva-crispa	S	6–9	3 ft (1 m)	D	Edible fruit (gooseberry)
Richea dracophylla	S	8–9	12–15 ft (3.5–4.5 m)	E	Foliage; flowers (white or pink, summer)
Ricinus communis	S	9–11	12 ft (3.5 m)	E	Foliage; flowers (red & green, summer); ornamental seed pods
Ricinus communis 'Carmencita'	S	9–11	10 ft (3 m)	E	Bronze-red foliage; flowers (red & green, summer); ornamental seed pods
Robinia hispida	T	3–9	10–15 ft (3–4.5 m)	D	Flowers (pink, summer); decorative fruit
Robinia pseudoacacia	T	3–10	30 ft (9 m)	D	Autumn foliage; flowers (white, fragrant, late spring–summer)
Robinia pseudoacacia 'Frisia'	T	3–10	30 ft (9 m)	D	Yellow foliage; thornless stems
Robinia pseudoacacia 'Tortuosa'	S(T)	3–10	10–15 ft (3–4.5 m)	D	Twisted stems; autumn foliage; flowers (white, fragrant, late spring–summer)

NAME	TYPE	ZONE	HEIGHT at MATURITY	DECIDUOUS or EVERGREEN	CHIEF ATTRACTIONS
Robinia pseudoacacia 'Umbraculifera'	S(T)	3–10	10–15 ft (3–4.5 m)	D	Autumn foliage; flowers (white, fragrant, late spring–summer); compact growth
Robinia × *slavinii* 'Hillieri'	S(T)	5–10	10–12 ft (3–3.5 m)	D	Flowers (lavender-pink, fragrant, early summer); compact rounded head
Roldana petasitis	S	9–11	6 ft (1.8 m)	E	Foliage; flowers (yellow, summer–autumn)
Rondeletia strigosa	S	10–12	4 ft (1.2 m)	E	Flowers (deep crimson, summer–autumn)

Rosa, Modern Garden Rose Hybrids

NAME	TYPE	ZONE	HEIGHT at MATURITY	DECIDUOUS or EVERGREEN	CHIEF ATTRACTIONS
Cluster-flowered (Floribunda) Roses	S	6–10	3–6 ft (1–1.8 m)	D	Flowers (most colors, often fragrant, late spring to autumn)
Cluster-flowered (Floribunda) Climbing Roses	S	6–10	8–15 ft (2.4–4.5 m)	D	Flowers (most colors, often fragrant, late spring to autumn)
English Roses	S	6–10	3–8 ft (1–2.4 m)	D	Flowers (most colors, usually pastel, often fragrant); spring–autumn
Ground-cover Roses	S	4–10	12–24 in (30–60 cm)	D	Flowers (most colors, spring–autumn); low, spreading growth
Hybrid Musk Roses	S	5–10	5–10 ft (1.5–3 m)	D	Flowers (white, or pastel pink, lavender or yellow shades, fragrant, spring–summer)
Hybrid Rugosa Roses	S	3–10	4–6 ft (1.2–1.8 m)	D	Flowers (white, pink, purple-red, red, spring–autumn); decorative fruit
Large-flowered (Hybrid Tea) Roses	S	7–11	3–6 ft (1–1.8 m)	D	Flowers (most colors, often fragrant, late spring to autumn)
Large-flowered (Hybrid Tea) Climbing Roses	S	7–11	8–15 ft (2.4–4.5 m)	D	Flowers (most colors, often fragrant, late spring to autumn)
Miniature Roses	S	5–10	1–5 ft (0.3–1.5 m)	D	Flowers (most colors, spring–autumn)
Polyantha Roses	S	6–10	3–5 ft (1–1.5 m)	D	Flowers (white or pink shades, spring–autumn); compact habit

Rosa, Old Garden Rose Hybrids

NAME	TYPE	ZONE	HEIGHT at MATURITY	DECIDUOUS or EVERGREEN	CHIEF ATTRACTIONS
Alba Roses	S	4–9	5–12 ft (1.5–3.5 m)	D	Flowers (white or pink shades, fragrant, late spring–early summer)
Bourbon Roses	S	5–10	5–8 ft (1.5–2.4 m)	D	Flowers (white, pink, purple-red, red, fragrant, late spring–early autumn)
Boursault Roses	S	6–10	8–15 ft (2.4–4.5 m)	D	Flowers (white, pink, purple-red, red, summer)
Centifolia or Provence Roses	S	5–9	3–4 ft (1–1.2 m)	D	Flowers (white or pink shades, fragrant, late spring–early summer)
China Roses	S	7–11	5–8 ft (1.5–2.4 m)	D	Flowers (white, pink & soft yellow shades, scented, late spring–early summer)
Climbing Roses	S	5–11	6–15 ft (1.8–4.5 m)	D	Flowers (white, pink, purple-red, red, soft yellow to apricot, late spring–early summer)
Damask Roses	S	5–10	4–6 ft (1.2–1.8 m)	D	Flowers (white, pink to purple-red shades, fragrant, late spring–early summer)
Gallica Roses	S	5–10	3–5 ft (1–1.5 m)	D	Flowers (white, pink, purple-red, red, fragrant, late spring–early summer)
Hybrid Perpetual Roses	S	5–10	4–6 ft (1.2–1.8 m)	D	Flowers (white, pink, purple-red, red, fragrant, late spring–early autumn)
Moss Roses	S	5–9	3–4 ft (1–1.2 m)	D	Flowers (white, pink to purplish shades, fragrant, late spring–early summer)
Noisette Roses	S	6–10	5–15 ft (1.5–4.5 m)	D	Flowers (white, cream, soft yellow or pale pink shades, summer), shrubs or climbers
Portland Roses	S	5–10	4–6 ft (1.2–1.8 m)	D	Flowers (white or pink shades, fragrant, late spring–early autumn)
Rambling Roses	S	5–10	8–20 ft (2.4–6 m)	D	Flowers (white, pink, purple-red, red, soft yellow to apricot, late spring–early summer)

NAME	TYPE	ZONE	HEIGHT at MATURITY	DECIDUOUS or EVERGREEN	CHIEF ATTRACTIONS
Scotch, Burnet or Pimpinellifolia Roses	S	4–9	3–5 ft (1–1.5 m)	D	Flowers (white, cream or pink shade, mid-spring–early summer)
Tea Roses	S	7–11	5–12 ft (1.5–3.5 m)	D	Flowers (white, pink, soft yellow to apricot shades, fragrant, late spring–early summer)

Rosa, species and their cultivated forms (Wild Roses)

NAME	TYPE	ZONE	HEIGHT at MATURITY	DECIDUOUS or EVERGREEN	CHIEF ATTRACTIONS
Rosa banksiae	S	7–10	12–20 ft (3.5–6 m)	Semi	Vigorous climber; flowers (white, scented, spring)
Rosa banksiae var. banksiae	S	7–10	12 ft (3.5 m)	Semi	Vigorous climber; flowers (white, double, scented, spring)
Rosa b. var. normalis 'Lutea'	S	7–10	12 ft (3.5 m)	Semi	Vigorous climber; flowers (soft yellow, double, scented, spring)
Rosa bracteata	S	7–10	12–20 ft (3.5–6 m)	D	Flowers (white, late spring–autumn); decorative fruit; vigorous climber
Rosa chinensis 'Viridiflora'	S	7–10	3–5 ft (1–1.5 m)	D	Unusual flowers (green, streaked red, late spring)
Rosa foetida	S	4–9	10 ft (3 m)	D	Flowers (yellow, late spring)
Rosa gallica	S	3–9	4–5 ft (1.2–1.5 m)	D	Flowers (pink, fragrant, spring–early summer)
Rosa gigantea	S	9–11	20–40 ft (6–12 m)	Semi	Extremely vigorous climber; flowers (cream, fragrant, late spring)
Rosa glauca	S	2–9	6 ft (1.8 m)	D	Flowers (pink, summer); foliage; decorative fruit
Rosa laevigata	S	7–11	12–20 ft (3.5–6 m)	D	Flowers (white, early spring); vigorous climber
Rosa moschata	S	6–10	12–15 ft (3.5–4.5 m)	D	Flowers (creamy white, summer); decorative fruit, shrub or climber
Rosa moyesii	S	3–9	6 ft (1.8 m)	D	Flowers (crimson, summer); decorative fruit
Rosa pimpinellifolia (syn. R. spinosissima)	S	4–9	3–4 ft (1–1.2 m)	D	Flowers (white to pink, spring–early summer); decorative fruit; autumn colour
Rosa rugosa	S	2–10	5–6 ft (1.5–1.8 m)	D	Flowers (white, pink, crimson, spring–autumn); foliage; decorative fruit
Rosa sericea subsp. omeiensis f. pteracantha	S	6–9	6 ft (1.8 m)	D	Decorative thorns; flowers (white, late spring)
Rosa willmottiae	S	6–10	10 ft (3 m)	D	Flowers (lilac-pink, fragrant, spring); decorative fruit
Rothmannia capensis	T	10–11	15 ft (4.5 m)	E	Flowers (cream to yellow, summer)
Rothmannia globosa	T	10–11	12–15 ft (3.5–4.5 m)	E	Flowers (cream, fragrant, spring–summer)
Rubus 'Benenden'	S	5–9	10 ft (3 m)	D	Flowers (white, late spring–early summer)
Rubus cockburnianus	S	6–10	8 ft (2.4 m)	D	Flowers (purple-pink, summer); decorative fruit
Rubus deliciosus	S	5–9	10 ft (3 m)	D	Edible fruit
Rubus fruticosus	S	5–10	10 ft (3 m)	D	Edible fruit
Rubus idaeus	S	4–9	5 ft (1.5 m)	D	Edible fruit (raspberry)
Rubus occidentalis	S	2–9	5 ft (1.5 m)	D	Edible fruit (black raspberry)
Rubus thibetanus	S	6–10	8 ft (2.4 m)	D	Flowers (pink, summer); decorative fruit
Rubus thibetanus 'Silver Fern'	S	6–10	8 ft (2.4 m)	D	Foliage; flowers (pink, summer); decorative fruit
Ruellia macrantha	S	10–12	4–6 ft (1.2–1.8)	E	Flowers (pink, summer)
Ruscus aculeatus	S	7–10	2–3 ft (0.6–1 m)	E	Flowers (white, spring); decorative fruit
Russelia equisetiformis	S	9–12	3–5 ft (1–1.5 m)	E	Flowers (red, most of the year)
Salix alba	T	2–10	30–40 ft (9–12 m)	D	Foliage; vigorous growth
Salix alba 'Britzensis'	T	2–10	30–40 ft (9–12 m)	D	Foliage; vigorous growth; red new growth
Salix alba var. sericea	T	2–10	30–40 ft (9–12 m)	D	Silvery foliage; vigorous growth

NAME	TYPE	ZONE	HEIGHT at MATURITY	DECIDUOUS or EVERGREEN	CHIEF ATTRACTIONS
Salix alba 'Vitellina'	T	2–10	30–40 ft (9–12 m)	D	Yellow young foliage; vigorous growth
Salix babylonica	T	4–10	40 ft (12 m)	D	Weeping habit, autumn foliage; moisture tolerance
Salix caprea	S(T)	5–10	10–30 ft (3–9 m)	D	Fluffy spring catkins
Salix fragilis	T	2–9	40 ft (12 m)	D	Vigorous growth; autumn foliage
Salix gracilistyla	S	6–10	10 ft (3 m)	D	Fluffy spring catkins
Salix lanata	S	2–9	3 ft (1 m)	D	Foliage, velvety spring catkins
Salix purpurea	S	2–9	12 ft (3.5 m)	D	Foliage; catkins (red-purple, spring)
Salix purpurea 'Nana'	S	2–9	3 ft (1 m)	D	Foliage; catkins (red-purple, spring)
Salvia africana-lutea	S	9–11	6 ft (1.8 m)	E	Flowers (yellow to brown, spring–early summer)
Salvia clevelandii	S	8–10	3–5 ft (1–1.5 m)	E	Flowers (lavender-blue, summer)
Salvia leucantha	S	8–10	3–4 ft (1–1.2 m)	E	Flowers (purple-blue, most of the year)
Salvia microphylla	S	9–11	3–4 ft (1–1.2)	E	Flowers (scarlet, late spring–early winter)
Salvia microphylla var. neurepia	S	9–11	3–4 ft (1–1.2)	E	Flowers (cherry red, late spring–autumn)
Sambucus canadensis	S	2–10	10 ft (3 m)	D	Flowers (white, spring), decorative fruit; foliage
Sambucus nigra	S	2–10	15 ft (4.5 m)	D	Flowers (white, spring), decorative/edible fruit; foliage
Sambucus nigra 'Aurea'	S	2–10	10–12 ft (3–3.5 m)	D	Flowers (white, spring), decorative/edible fruit; golden-yellow foliage
Santolina chamaecyparissus	S	7–10	18–24 in (45–60 cm)	E	Silver-gray foliage; flowers (yellow, summer)
Santolina rosmarinifolia	S	7–10	24 in (60 cm)	E	Flowers (yellow, summer)
Sarcococca confusa	S	5–10	6 ft (1.8 m)	E	Flowers (white, autumn–winter); decorative fruit
Sarcococca hookeriana	S	6–10	5 ft (1.5 m)	E	Foliage; flowers (cream, fragrant, late winter–spring); decorative fruit
Sarcococca hookeriana var. digyna	S	6–10	1–3 ft (0.3–1 m)	E	Foliage; flowers (cream, fragrant, late winter–spring); decorative fruit
Sarcococca hookeriana var. humilis	S	6–10	8–18 in (20–45 cm)	E	Foliage; flowers (cream, fragrant, winter); decorative fruit
Sarcococca ruscifolia decorative fruit	S	6–9	5 ft (1.5 m)	E	Foliage; flowers (cream, fragrant, late winter–spring);
Schefflera actinophylla	T	10–12	25 ft (8 m)	E	Foliage; flowers (red, late summer–early spring); decorative fruit
Schefflera arboricola	S	10–11	12 ft (3.5 m)	E	Foliage; decorative fruit
Schinus molle var. areira	T	9–11	25–30 ft (8–9 m)	E	Foliage; weeping habit; gnarled trunk; decorative fruit
Schinus terebinthifolius	T	10–12	25 ft (8 m)	E	Foliage; decorative fruit
Sciadopitys verticillata	T	5–9	15–25 ft (4.5–8 m)	E	Foliage; symmetrical form
Senna artemisioides	S	8–11	3 ft (1 m)	E	Flowers (yellow, winter–early summer); foliage
Senna didymobotrya	S	10–11	8–10 ft (2.4–3 m)	E	Flowers (yellow, summer–winter)
Senna multiglandulosa	S	8–12	3–15 ft (1–4.5 m)	E	Flowers (yellow, autumn–spring)
Senna multijuga	T	10–12	20 ft (6 m)	E	Flowers (yellow, late summer)
Sequoia sempervirens	T	7–10	60–80 ft (18–24 m)	E	Foliage; stately habit; bark
Sequoia sempervirens 'Adpressa'	T	7–10	3–8 ft (1–2.4 m)	E	Foliage; compact habit
Sequoiadendron giganteum	T	6–9	80–100 ft (24–30 m)	E	Foliage; stately habit; bark
Serruria florida	S	9–10	4 ft (1.2 m)	E	Flowers (white to pale pink, winter–spring); foliage
Skimmia japonica	S	7–9	4–5 ft (1.2–1.5 m)	E	Foliage; decorative fruit; flowers (white, spring)
Solanum aviculare	S	9–11	8 ft (2.4 m)	E	Flowers (purple, spring–summer); decorative fruit; foliage
Solanum rantonnetii	S	9–10	6 ft (1.8 m)	E	Flowers (violet-blue, spring–summer); decorative fruit

NAME	TYPE	ZONE	HEIGHT at MATURITY	DECIDUOUS or EVERGREEN	CHIEF ATTRACTIONS
Sophora japonica	T	4–10	25 ft (8 m)	D	Autumn foliage; flowers (cream, summer)
Sophora microphylla	T	7–10	15 ft (4.5 m)	D	Flowers (yellow, late winter–early summer); foliage
Sophora prostrata	S	8–10	18in–6 ft (45cm–1.8 m)	D	Twisted branches; flowers (pale yellow, summer)
Sophora prostrata 'Little Baby'	S	8–10	18–24 in (45–60 cm)	D	Twisted branches; flowers (pale yellow, summer)
Sophora tetraptera	T	8–10	15–20 ft (4.5–6 m)	D	Flowers (golden yellow, spring); foliage
Sophora tomentosa	S(T)	10–12	6–10 ft (1.8–3 m)	D	Foliage; flowers (lime-yellow, summer)
Sorbaria kirilowii	S	4–10	20 ft (6 m)	D	Flowers (white, summer)
Sorbus americana	T	3–9	30 ft (9 m)	D	Autumn foliage; decorative fruit
Sorbus aria	T	2–9	12–20 ft (3.5–6 m)	D	Autumn foliage; flowers (white, late spring); decorative fruit
Sorbus aucuparia	T	2–9	20 ft (6 m)	D	Decorative fruit; autumn foliage; flowers (white, spring)
Sorbus cashmiriana	T	5–9	25 ft (8 m)	D	Flowers (pale pink); decorative fruit
Sorbus domestica	T	3–8	25 ft (8 m)	D	Edible/decorative fruit
Sorbus hupehensis	T	5–9	20–25 ft (6–8 m)	D	Autumn foliage; decorative fruit
Sorbus 'Joseph Rock'	T	4–9	20 ft (6 m)	D	Decorative fruit; autumn foliage
Sorbus pohuashanensis	T	4–9	20 ft (6 m)	D	Decorative fruit; flowers (white, late spring)
Sorbus reducta	S	6–9	3–5 ft (1–1.5 m)	D	Autumn foliage; flowers (white, spring); decorative fruit
Sorbus terminalis	T	6–9	30–40 ft (9–12 m)	D	Flowers (white, spring); decorative fruit; autumn foliage
Sorbus vilmorinii	T	6–9	20 ft (6 m)	D	Flowers (white, spring); decorative fruit; autumn foliage
Sparrmannia africana	T	10–11	15 ft (5 m)	E	Flowers (white, winter–spring); foliage
Spartium junceum	S	6–10	8–10 ft (2.4–3 m)	E	Flowers (yellow, fragrant, spring–early summer)
Spiraea cantoniensis	S	5–10	6 ft (1.8 m)	D	Flowers (white, spring)
Spiraea japonica	S	4–9	5 ft (1.5 m)	D	Flowers (pink, summer)
Spiraea japonica 'Anthony Waterer'	S	4–9	5 ft (1.5 m)	D	Flowers (pink, summer)
Spiraea nipponica	S	5–9	6 ft (1.8 m)	D	Flowers (white, early summer)
Spiraea nipponica 'Snowmound'	S	5–9	6 ft (1.8 m)	D	Flowers (white, early summer); upright habit
Spiraea prunifolia	S	4–9	5–6 ft (1.5–1.8 m)	D	Flowers (white, early spring); autumn foliage
Stachyurus praecox	S	5–10	8 ft (2.4 m)	D	Flowers (pale yellow, winter–early spring); autumn foliage
Stenocarpus sinuatus	T	10–11	20–30 ft (6–9 m)	E	Flowers (scarlet, autumn); foliage
Stephanandra incisa	S	4–9	6 ft (1.8 m)	D	Autumn foliage
Stephanandra tanakae	S	4–9	5 ft (1.5 m)	D	Autumn foliage; flowers (white, summer)
Stewartia pseudocamellia	T	6–9	15–20 ft (4.5–6 m)	D	Flowers (white, late spring–early summer); autumn foliage; decorative fruit
Stewartia sinensis	T	6–9	15–20 ft (4.5–6 m)	D	Flowers (white, late spring–summer); autumn foliage; bark
Streptosolen jamesonii	S	9–11	6 ft (2 m)	E	Flowers (orange, most of the year)
Styrax japonicus	T	7–9	20 ft (6 m)	D	Flowers (white, late spring–early summer)
Styrax obassia	T	6–9	20 ft (6 m)	D	Flowers (white, late spring–early summer); bark; autumn foliage
Sutera cordata	S	9–11	24 in (60 cm)	E	Flowers (white, summer–autumn); low, spreading habit
Symphoricarpos × *chenaultii*	S	5–9	3–6 ft (1–1.8)	D	Flowers (pink, spring); decorative fruit
Symphoricarpos microphyllus	S	9–10	6 ft (1.8 m)	D	Flowers (white, summer); decorative fruit
Symphoricarpos orbiculatus	S	4–9	6 ft (1.8 m)	D	Decorative fruit

NAME	TYPE	ZONE	HEIGHT at MATURITY	DECIDUOUS or EVERGREEN	CHIEF ATTRACTIONS
Syringa josikaea	S	5–9	10–12 ft (3–3.5 m)	D	Flowers (violet, summer)
Syringa meyeri	S	4–9	3–6 ft (1–1.8 m)	D	Flowers (purple-red, spring)
Syringa meyeri 'Palibin'	S	4–9	3 ft (1 m)	D	Flowers (violet to rose pink, spring)
Syringa × persica	S	5–9	6 ft (1.8 m)	D	Flowers (lilac, fragrant, late spring)
Syringa × persica 'Alba'	S	5–9	6 ft (1.8 m)	D	Flowers (white to pale pink, fragrant, late spring)
Syringa pubescens ssp. *patula* 'Miss Kim'	S	4–9	6–8 ft (1.8–2.4)	D	Flowers (pale lilac-pink, fragrant, summer)
Syringa reticulata	S	3–9	15–20 ft (4.5–6 m)	D	Flowers (white, fragrant, spring)
Syringa vulgaris and cultivars	S	2–9	8–10 ft (2.4–3 m)	D	Flowers (mauve to purple shades or white, fragrant, late spring–early summer)
Syzygium jambos	T	10–12	25–30 ft (8–9 m)	E	Flowers (greenish-white, spring–autumn); edible fruit
Syzygium luehmannii	T	10–11	25–30 ft (8–9 m)	E	Decorative fruit; pink new growth; flowers (white, summer)
Syzygium paniculatum	T	10–11	30–40 ft (9–12 m)	E	Decorative fruit; flowers (white, late spring)
Tabebuia chrysantha	T	11–12	20 ft (6 m)	Semi	Flowers (golden yellow, spring)
Tabebuia chrysotricha	T	10–11	20 ft (6 m)	Semi	Flowers (golden yellow, spring)
Tabebuia impetiginosa	T	9–11	30–40 ft (9–12 m)	D	Flowers (rose to purple-pink, spring)
Tamarix aphylla	T	8–11	30 ft (9 m)	E	Foliage; dense canopy
Tamarix parviflora	S	4–10	12 ft (4.5 m)	D	Flowers (pink, spring)
Tamarix ramosissima	S	3–10	12 ft (4.5 m)	D	Flowers (pink, late summer)
Tamarix tetrandra	S(T)	6–10	10 ft (3 m)	D	Flowers (pink, spring)
Taxodium ascendens	T	4–10	30–40 ft (9–12 m)	D	Autumn foliage; moisture tolerance
Taxodium distichum	T	4–10	30–40 ft (9–12 m)	D	Autumn foliage; stately habit; moisture tolerance
Taxus baccata	T	5–9	15 ft (4.5 m)	E	Foliage; decorative fruit
Taxus baccata 'Fastigiata'	T	5–9	15 ft (4.5 m)	E	Narrow upright growth; decorative fruit
Taxus baccata 'Repandens'	T	5–9	4 ft (4.5 m)	E	Low, spreading habit; decorative fruit
Taxus cuspidata	T	3–9	20 ft (6 m)	E	Foliage; decorative fruit
Taxus × media	T	5–9	8–15 ft (2.4–4.5 m)	E	Foliage
Taxus × media 'Everlow'	T	5–9	4–8 ft (1.2–2.4 m)	E	Foliage
Telopea oreades	T	9–10	15 ft (4.5 m)	E	Flowers (red, spring)
Telopea speciosissima	S	9–10	10–15 ft (3–4.5 m)	E	Flowers (red, spring)
Telopea s. 'Wirrimbirra White'	S	9–10	10–15 ft (3–4.5 m)	E	Flowers (white, spring)
Teucrium chamaedrys	S	5–10	12–24 in (30–60 cm)	E	Flowers (pale to deep purple, summer–autumn)
Teucrium cossonii	S	8–11	8–12 in (20–30 cm)	E	Flowers (deep pink, summer); low, spreading habit
Teucrium polium	S	7–10	2–10 in (5–25 cm)	D	Flowers (white, yellow, pink or purple, summer)
Thevetia peruviana	S	10–12	12 ft (3.5 m)	E	Flowers (pale yellow or orange, most of the year)
Thevetia thevetioides	S	10–12	12 ft (3.5 m)	E	Flowers (yellow, winter–summer)
Thryptomene calycina	S	9–10	4 ft (1.2 m)	E	Flowers (white, winter–spring)
Thryptomene saxicola	S	9–10	4 ft (1.2 m)	E	Flowers (pale pink, winter–spring)
Thuja occidentalis	T	4–9	20 ft (6 m)	E	Foliage; symmetrical form; winter coloring
Thuja occidentalis 'Ericoides'	S	4–9	18 in (45 cm)	E	Foliage; compact habit
Thuja occidentalis 'Lutea Nana'	T	4–9	24–36 in (60–90 cm)	E	Yellow-gold foliage; compact habit
Thuja occidentalis 'Rheingold'	T	4–9	30 in (75 cm)	E	Foliage; symmetrical form; winter coloring

NAME	TYPE	ZONE	HEIGHT at MATURITY	DECIDUOUS or EVERGREEN	CHIEF ATTRACTIONS
Thuja occidentalis 'Smaragd'	T	4–9	6 ft (1.8 m)	E	Foliage; symmetrical form
Thuja plicata	T	5–10	25 ft (8 m)	E	Foliage; vigorous growth, symmetrical form
Thuja plicata 'Zebrina'	T	5–10	20 ft (6 m)	E	Yellow variegated foliage
Thujopsis dolabrata	T	4–9	15–20 ft (4.5–6 m)	E	Foliage
Thujopsis dolabrata 'Nana'	T	4–9	24 in (60 cm)	E	Foliage
Thujopsis dolabrata 'Variegata'	T	4–9	10 ft (3 m)	E	Variegated foliage
Thunbergia natalensis	S	10–11	3 ft (1 m)	D	Flowers (blue, summer)
Thunbergia togoensis	S	10–12	2–3 ft (60–90 cm)	E	Flowers (blue & yellow, summer)
Thymus × citriodorus	S	7–10	12 in (30 cm)	E	Flowers (lilac, summer); aromatic foliage
Thymus serpyllum	S	3–9	10 in (25 cm)	E	Flowers (bluish-purple, spring–summer); aromatic foliage
Thymus serpyllum 'Coccineus Minor'	S	3–9	10 in (25 cm)	E	Flowers (crimson-pink, spring–summer); aromatic foliage
Tibouchina granulosa	S(T)	9–11	15 ft (4.5 m)	E	Flowers (rose-purple or pink, autumn)
Tibouchina 'Jules'	S	10–11	3 ft (1 m)	E	Flowers (purple, summer)
Tibouchina lepidota	S(T)	9–11	15 ft (5 m)	E	Flowers (purple, late summer–early winter)
Tibouchina urvilleana	S(T)	9–11	10–12 ft (3–3.5 m)	E	Flowers (purple, summer–autumn)
Tilia americana	T	2–9	30–40 ft (9–12 m)	D	Foliage; flowers (cream, summer); bark
Tilia cordata	T	2–9	30 ft (9 m)	D	Foliage; flowers (cream, summer); bark
Tilia × europaea	T	3–9	30 ft (9 m)	D	Foliage; flowers (pale yellow, fragrant, early summer)
Tilia 'Petiolaris'	T	5–9	50 ft (15 m)	D	Weeping foliage; flowers (cream, summer)
Tilia platyphyllos	T	3–9	30–40 ft (9–12 m)	D	Foliage; flowers (pale yellow, summer)
Tilia tomentosa	T	4–9	30 ft (9 m)	D	Foliage; flowers (pale green, summer)
Torreya californica	T	6–10	15–20 ft (4.5–6 m)	E	Foliage
Torreya nucifera	T	4–10	15–20 ft (4.5–6 m)	E	Foliage; edible seeds; bark
Tristaniopsis laurina	T	9–11	25 ft (8 m)	E	Bark; flowers (yellow, summer)
Tsuga canadensis	T	2–9	20–25 ft (6–8 m)	E	Foliage; dense canopy
Tsuga canadensis 'Pendula'	S	2–9	6 ft (1.8 m)	E	Foliage; weeping, spreading habit
Tsuga chinensis	T	6–9	20–25 ft (6–8 m)	E	Foliage; symmetrical form
Tsuga heterophylla	T	4–9	25–30 ft (8–9 m)	E	Foliage; symmetrical form
Ugni molinae	S	8–10	8–12 ft (2.4–3.5 m)	E	Flowers (white, spring); decorative/edible fruit
Ulex europaeus	S	6–9	6–8 ft (1.8–2.4 m)	E	Flowers (yellow, late winter–spring)
Ulmus americana	T	3–9	25–40 ft (8–12 m)	D	Autumn foliage; bark; stately form
Ulmus glabra	T	3–10	30 ft (9 m)	D	Autumn foliage; stately form
Ulmus glabra 'Camperdownii'	T	3–10	30 ft (9 m)	D	Widespreading dome-like habit; autumn foliage
Ulmus × hollandica	T	3–10	40 ft (12 m)	D	Autumn foliage; stately form
Ulmus minor	T	4–10	40 ft (12 m)	D	Autumn foliage; vigorous growth
Ulmus parvifolia	T	5–10	25–30 ft (8–9 m)	D	Bark; foliage
Ulmus procera	T	4–9	30 ft (9 m)	D	Autumn foliage; stately form
Vaccinium corymbosum	S	2–9	6 ft (1.8 m)	D	Edible fruit; flowers (white or pink, late spring); autumn foliage
Vaccinium corymbosum 'Earliblue'	S	2–9	6–8 ft (1.8–2.4 m)	D	Edible fruit; flowers (white, late spring); autumn foliage
Vaccinium cylindraceum	S	10–11	6–8 ft (1.8–2.4 m)	Semi	Flowers (yellow-green, summer–autumn); decorative fruit

NAME	TYPE	ZONE	HEIGHT at MATURITY	DECIDUOUS or EVERGREEN	CHIEF ATTRACTIONS
Vaccinium macrocarpon	S	2–9	24–30 in (60–75 cm)	E	Flowers (pink, summer); decorative/edible fruit
Vaccinium ovatum	S	4–9	3 ft (1 m)	E	Edible fruit; flowers (white or pink, late spring); foliage
Vella spinosa	S	8–10	12 in (30 cm)	D	Flowers (cream veined violet, summer)
Vestia foetida	S	9–11	5–6 ft (1.5–1.8 m)	E	Flowers (yellow, spring–summer)
Viburnum × bodnantense	S	6–9	10–12 ft (3–3.5 m)	D	Flowers (pink & white, fragrant, autumn–early spring); autumn foliage
Viburnum × bodnantense 'Dawn'	S	6–9	10–12 ft (3–3.5 m)	D	Flowers (pink, fragrant, autumn–early spring); autumn foliage
Viburnum × burkwoodii	S	6–9	8–12 ft (2.4–3.5 m)	Semi	Flowers (white, fragrant, spring); autumn/winter foliage
Viburnum carlesii	S	3–9	5 ft (1.5 m)	D	Flowers (pale pink, fragrant, spring); decorative fruit
Viburnum carlesii 'Aurora'	S	3–9	5 ft (1.5 m)	D	Flowers (pale pink form deep pink buds, fragrant, spring); decorative fruit
Viburnum davidii	S	6–10	2–3 ft (0.6–1 m)	E	Foliage; flowers (white, spring); decorative fruit
Viburnum dilatatum	S	5–10	10 ft (3 m)	D	Flowers (white, late spring–summer); decorative fruit
Viburnum farreri	S	5–9	8 ft (2.5 m)	D	Flowers (white to pale pink, fragrant, winter–early spring); autumn foliage
Viburnum farreri 'Candidissimum'	S	5–9	8 ft (2.5 m)	D	Flowers (white, fragrant, winter–early spring); autumn foliage
Viburnum lantana	S	3–9	8–12 (2.4–3.5 m)	D	Flowers (white, summer); decorative fruit; autumn foliage
Viburnum macrocephalum	S	5–10	6–10 ft (1.8–3 m)	D	Flowers (green & white, mid spring–early summer)
Viburnum opulus	S	2–10	10–12 ft (3–3.5 m)	D	Flowers (white, late spring–summer); decorative fruit, autumn foliage
Viburnum opulus 'Compactum'	S	2–10	5 ft (1.5 m)	D	Flowers (white, late spring–summer); decorative fruit, autumn foliage
Viburnum opulus 'Roseum'	S	2–10	10–12 ft (3–3.5 m)	D	Flowers (white–green, late spring–summer); autumn foliage
Viburnum opulus 'Xanthocarpum'	S	2–10	10–12 ft (3–3.5 m)	D	Flowers (white, late spring–summer); decorative fruit, autumn foliage
Viburnum plicatum	S	5–10	8–12 ft (2.4–3.5 m)	D	Flowers (white, spring), decorative fruit; foliage
Viburnum plicatum 'Mariesii'	S	5–10	8–12 ft (2.4–3.5 m)	D	Flowers (white, spring), decorative fruit; tiered growth habit
Viburnum plicatum 'Pink Beauty'	S	5–10	8–12 ft (2.4–3.5 m)	D	Flowers (white tinted pink, spring), decorative fruit; foliage
Viburnum plicatum 'Rosace'	S	5–10	8–12 ft (2.4–3.5 m)	D	Flowers (white & pink, spring), autumn foliage; tiered growth habit
Viburnum sargentii	S	4–9	10–15 ft (3–4.5 m)	D	Flowers (white to cream, spring–summer); decorative fruit
Viburnum sargentii 'Onondaga'	S	4–9	10–15 ft (3–4.5 m)	D	Flowers (white to cream, spring–summer); decorative fruit; colored foliage
Viburnum rhytidophyllum	S	4–10	6–10 (1.8–3 m)	E	Foliage; flowers (white, spring); decorative fruit
Viburnum tinus	S	6–10	10–12 ft (3–3.5 m)	E	Flowers (white, late winter–spring); decorative fruit
Viburnum tinus 'Gwenllian'	S	6–10	10–12 ft (3–3.5 m)	E	Flowers (pinkish white, late winter–spring); decorative fruit
Viburnum trilobum	S	3–9	8–12 ft (2.4–3.5 m)	D	Flowers (white, spring–early summer); decorative fruit; autumn foliage
Virgilia divaricata	T	9–11	20 ft (6 m)	E	Flowers (mauve-purple, spring–summer)
Virgilia oroboides	T	9–11	20–25 ft (6–8 m)	E	Flowers (mauve-pink, early summer–autumn); vigorous growth
Vitex agnus-castus	S	7–10	12–15 ft (3.5–4.5 m)	D	Aromatic foliage; flowers (lavender, summer–autumn)
Vitex lucens	T	9–11	25 ft (8 m)	E	Foliage, flowers (red or pink, winter); decorative fruit

NAME	TYPE	ZONE	HEIGHT at MATURITY	DECIDUOUS or EVERGREEN	CHIEF ATTRACTIONS
Vitex negundo	S	6–11	20 ft (6 m)	E	Aromatic foliage; flowers (mauve, fragrant, spring)
Weigela 'Bristol Ruby'	S	4–10	6 ft (1.8 m)	D	Flowers (crimson, spring)
Weigela floribunda	S	6–10	10 ft (3 m)	D	Flowers (deep crimson, spring–early summer)
Weigela florida	S	4–10	8–10 ft (2.4–3 m)	D	Flowers (white, pink crimson, spring)
Weigela florida 'Aureovariegata'	S	4–10	8–10 ft (2.4–3 m)	D	Cream variegated foliage; flowers (light pink, spring)
Weigela florida 'Foliis Purpureis'	S	4–10	8–10 ft (2.4–3 m)	D	Purple-red foliage; flowers (deep pink, spring)
Westringia fruticosa	S	9–11	4–6 ft (1.2–1.8 m)	E	Foliage; flowers (white, most of the year)
Westringia fruticosa 'Morning Light'	S	9–11	3 ft (1 m)	E	Variegated foliage; flowers (white, most of the year)
Xanthoceras sorbifolium	S(T)	6–10	20 ft (6 m)	D	Flowers (yellow, spring–summer)
Xanthorrhoea australis	S	9–11	3 ft (1 m)	E	Foliage; symmetrical form
Xanthorrhoea malacophylla	S(T)	10–11	6 ft (1.8 m)	E	Foliage; symmetrical form
Xanthorrhoea preissii	S(T)	10–11	6 ft (1.8 m)	E	Foliage; symmetrical form
Xylomelum occidentale	T	9–11	20–25 ft (6–8 m)	E	Decorative fruit, bark, foliage; flowers (cream, summer)
Yucca aloifolia	S	9–12	4–8 ft (1.2–2.4 m)	E	Foliage; symmetrical form; flowers (white, summer)
Yucca aloifolia 'Variegata'	S	9–12	4–8 ft (1.2–2.4 m)	E	Variegated foliage; symmetrical form; flowers (white, summer)
Yucca australis	T	9–12	25 ft (8 m)	E	Flowers (white, summer); symmetrical form
Yucca brevifolia	T	7–10	30 ft (9 m)	E	Flowers (greenish-white, late spring)
Yucca elephantipes	T	9–12	12 ft (3.5 m)	E	Foliage; symmetrical form; flowers (white, summer)
Yucca filamentosa	S	4–10	3 ft (1 m)	E	Flowers (white, late summer)
Yucca filifera	S(T)	7–10	3–20 ft (1–6 m)	E	Flowers (creamy white, pendulous, summer)
Yucca filifera 'Golden Sword'	S(T)	7–10	3–20 ft (1–6 m)	E	Variegated foliage; flowers (creamy white, pendulous, summer)
Yucca gloriosa	S	7–10	8 ft (2.4)	E	Flowers (white tinged pink, summer–autumn); symmetrical form
Zelkova carpinifolia	T	4–10	20–30 ft (6–9 m)	D	Autumn foliage
Zelkova serrata	T	3–10	25–30 ft (8–9 m)	D	Autumn foliage; bark
Zizyphus jujuba	T	9–11	15 ft (5 m)	D	Edible fruit

Index to Common Names and Synonyms